MORRISON'S MIRACLE

THE 2019 AUSTRALIAN FEDERAL ELECTION

MORRISON'S MIRACLE

THE 2019 AUSTRALIAN FEDERAL ELECTION

EDITED BY ANIKA GAUJA,
MARIAN SAWER
AND MARIAN SIMMS

Australian
National
University

PRESS

In memory of Dr John Beaton FASSA, Executive Director of the
Academy of the Social Sciences in Australia from 2001 to 2018
and an avid supporter of this series of election analyses

ANU
PRESS

Published by ANU Press
The Australian National University
Acton ACT 2601, Australia
Email: anupress@anu.edu.au

Available to download for free at press.anu.edu.au

ISBN (print): 9781760463618
ISBN (online): 9781760463625

WorldCat (print): 1157333181
WorldCat (online): 1157332115

DOI: 10.22459/MM.2020

Cover design and layout by ANU Press

Cover photograph: Scott Morrison Campaign Day 11. Photo by Mick Tsikas, AAP.

CONTENTS

FIGURES

PLATES

TABLES

ABBREVIATIONS

AA	Advance Australia
ABC	Australian Broadcasting Corporation
ABCC	Australian Building and Construction Commission
ABS	Australian Bureau of Statistics
ACCC	Australian Competition and Consumer Commission
ACCI	Australian Chamber of Commerce and Industry
ACT	Australian Capital Territory
ACTU	Australian Council of Trade Unions
AEC	Australian Electoral Commission
AES	Australian Election Study
AFR	*Australian Financial Review*
Ai Group	Australian Industry Group
ALP	Australian Labor Party
AMA	Australian Medical Association
AMEP	Australian Motoring Enthusiasts Party
ANMF	Australian Nursing and Midwifery Federation
ANU	The Australian National University
ASIC	Australian Securities and Investments Commission
ASSA	Academy of the Social Sciences in Australia
AWU	Australian Workers' Union
BCA	Business Council of Australia
CA	Centre Alliance
CEO	chief executive officer

CFMMEU	Construction, Forestry, Maritime, Mining and Energy Union
CLP	Country Liberal Party
CLT	Central Limit Theorem
C|T	Crosby Textor Group
DVC	direct voter contact
ERC	Expenditure Review Committee
GST	goods and services tax
GVT	group voting ticket
HIA	Housing Industry Association
IPA	Institute of Public Affairs
IVR	interactive voice response
JLN	Jacqui Lambie Network
JSCEM	Joint Standing Committee on Electoral Matters
KAP	Katter's Australian Party
LGBTQI	lesbian, gay, bisexual, transgender, queer and intersex
List-PR	list proportional representation
LNP	Liberal National Party
LP	Liberal Party of Australia
MBA	Master Builders Australia
MCA	Minerals Council of Australia
MDB	Murray–Darling Basin
MDBA	Murray–Darling Basin Authority
MOP(S) Act	*Members of Parliament (Staff) Act 1984*
MP	Member of Parliament
MYEFO	Mid-Year Economic and Fiscal Outlook
NDIS	National Disability Insurance Scheme
NEG	National Energy Guarantee
NFF	National Farmers' Federation
NGO	non-governmental organisation
NRA	National Rifle Association (US)
NSW	New South Wales

NT	Northern Territory
NXT	Nick Xenophon Team
OECD	Organisation for Economic Co-operation and Development
PBR Act	*Parliamentary Business Resources Act 2017*
PCA	Property Council of Australia
PGA	Pharmaceutical Guild of Australia
PHON	Pauline Hanson's One Nation
PR-STV	proportional representation by single transferable vote
PUP	Palmer United Party
Qld	Queensland
RACGP	Royal Australian College of General Practitioners
REIA	Real Estate Institute of Australia
ROG	Registered Organisations Commission
SA	South Australia
SBS	Special Broadcasting Service
SFFP	Shooters, Fishers and Farmers Party
STEMM	science, technology, engineering, mathematics and medicine
TAFE	Technical and Further Education
Tas.	Tasmania
TPP	two-party preferred
UAP	United Australia Party
UK	United Kingdom
US	United States
Vic.	Victoria
VOW	Voices of Warringah
WA	Western Australia

ACKNOWLEDGEMENTS

The Australian federal election books are always a demanding enterprise and the editors have many people to thank.

First, and foremost, the Academy of the Social Sciences in Australia (ASSA) has been unwavering in its continuing support for this series. We acknowledge the role of long-time director John Beaton (1944–2018). ASSA's generous funding for the 2019 election workshop enabled it to be held at the Museum of Australian Democracy, Old Parliament House, in Canberra. This was facilitated by Mark Evans, Director of Democracy 2025, which is a joint initiative of the Museum of Australian Democracy and the University of Canberra.

The ASSA funding was matched by the School of Politics and International Relations at The Australian National University (ANU) and by the Institute for Governance and Policy Analysis at the University of Canberra. Liliana Oyarzun Silva, Nilima Mathai and Hannah Mills played an invaluable role in the organising of the workshop.

Both authors and discussants at the election workshop contributed to lively discussion of the draft chapters. They helped to identify the key themes emerging from the election and to place them in comparative context.

The discussants included:

- Frank Bongiorno (The Australian National University)
- Patrick Dumont (The Australian National University, smartvote Australia)
- Mark Evans (University of Canberra, Democracy 2025)
- Michelle Grattan (University of Canberra, *The Conversation*)
- Andrew Hughes (The Australian National University)
- Michael Jensen (University of Canberra)

- Mark Kenny (The Australian National University)
- Damon Muller (Parliamentary Library)
- Rod Tiffen (University of Sydney)

Thanks also to the anonymous reviewers of the manuscript for their thoughtful suggestions, to Jan Borrie for her meticulous copyediting and the ANU Publication Subsidy Committee for their support. Members of the Social Sciences Editorial Board of ANU Press and staff of the press, particularly Emily Tinker, also made valuable contributions. In addition, we would like to thank all those who have given us permission for the reproduction of the photos, cartoons and other images that contribute so much to this book.

Finally, we thank the contributors for their timely submission of revised workshop papers and for their patient responses to our endless queries.

CONTRIBUTORS

Nicholas Barry is a Lecturer in Politics at La Trobe University. His research and teaching are in the areas of Australian politics, political institutions and political theory. He is currently working on a number of research projects relating to Australian political parties, constitutional conventions and inequality.

Ebony Bennett is the Deputy Director of The Australia Institute and has worked in federal politics for more than a decade. She has published research on gender and street harassment. She appears regularly as a commentator on *Sky News* and writes for *The Guardian* and Fairfax publications.

Andrea Carson is Associate Professor in the Department of Politics, Media and Philosophy at La Trobe University. Her research examines politics and the media, with special interests in investigative journalism, the media's role in a democracy and political communication. She has worked previously as a print journalist (*The Age*), in radio (ABC, RRR) and TV (as a producer of *7.30*).

Geoff Cockfield is Professor in Government and Economics and Executive Director of the Institute for Resilient Regions at the University of Southern Queensland. His research interests include rural politics, rural and regional development policy and natural resources management policy. He was the 2018–19 Fulbright Distinguished Chair in Agriculture and Life Sciences at Kansas State University.

Jennifer Curtin is Professor of Politics at the University of Auckland. She is co-editor of *Double Disillusion: The 2016 Australian Federal Election* (ANU Press, 2018) and of the forthcoming volume *A Populist Exception? The 2017 New Zealand General Election*. She is also co-author of *A Bark but No Bite: Inequality and the 2014 New Zealand Election* (ANU Press, 2017) and *Rebels with a Cause: Independents in Australian Politics* (UNSW Press, 2004).

Nick Economou is a Senior Lecturer in the School of Social Science at Monash University, where he teaches on Australian politics, elections and governance. His research interests include Australian national and State governance, electoral systems and federal, State and local elections, and the role and behaviour of Australia's political parties. Nick is a regular commentator on Australian politics and elections for media outlets including the ABC, 3AW, the BBC and various newspapers, and he writes for *The Conversation*.

Anika Gauja is an Associate Professor in the Department of Government and International Relations at the University of Sydney. Her research focuses on comparative party politics and organisation. She has also written extensively on Australian politics as co-author of *Powerscape: Contemporary Australian Politics* (Allen & Unwin, 2008), and co-editor of *Contemporary Australian Political Party Organisations* (Monash University Publishing, 2015) and *Double Disillusion: The 2016 Australian Federal Election* (ANU Press, 2018).

Zareh Ghazarian is a Senior Lecturer in Politics and International Relations in the School of Social Sciences at Monash University. His teaching and research interests include political parties, public policy and civic education. His most recent book is *The Making of a Party System: Minor Parties in the Australian Senate* (Monash University Publishing, 2015).

Murray Goot is Emeritus Professor in the Department of History, Politics and International Relations at Macquarie University and a panel member of the Inquiry into the Performance of the Opinion Polls at the 2019 Australian Federal Election, established by the Association of Market and Social Research Organisations. He is a Fellow of the Academy of the Social Sciences in Australia.

Antony Green is Chief Election Analyst with the Australian Broadcasting Corporation and, in the past three decades, has analysed more than 70 national, State and Territory elections. He is also an Adjunct Professor in the Department of Government and International Relations at the University of Sydney.

Simon Jackman (United States Studies Centre, University of Sydney) has published widely on American and Australian politics and statistical methods in the social sciences. In 2008–16, he was one of the principal investigators of the American National Election Studies. Jackman is a Fellow of the American Academy of Arts and Sciences, the Society for Political Methodology and the Academy of the Social Sciences in Australia.

Stewart Jackson is a Senior Lecturer in Politics at the University of Sydney. His main research interests are the Greens in the Asia-Pacific. He is the author of *The Australian Greens: From Activism to Australia's Third Party* (Melbourne University Publishing, 2016), and is currently working on a political biography of Jo Vallentine, the Greens' first senator.

Carol Johnson is Emerita Professor in the Department of Politics and International Relations at the University of Adelaide and a Fellow of the Academy of the Social Sciences in Australia. She has published extensively on Australian politics as well as on comparative issues of gender, sexuality and the politics of emotion. Her most recent book is *Social Democracy and the Crisis of Equality: Australian Social Democracy in a Changing World* (Springer, 2019).

Glenn Kefford is a Lecturer in Political Science in the School of Political Science and International Studies at the University of Queensland. His research focuses on political parties, elections and campaigning. He is the holder of an Australian Research Council Discovery Early Career Researcher Award for 2019–21, which explores online and offline campaigning by political parties in the 21st century.

Lucien Leon lectures in digital art at The Australian National University's School of Art and Design in Canberra. Lucien's political animations have been published in a variety of online and broadcast contexts, while his most recent publications explore the intersection between traditional and new media in the mediation of visual political satire, including case studies from Australia, the United States and the United Kingdom.

Michael Maley had a 30-year career at the Australian Electoral Commission, retiring in 2012 as Special Adviser, Electoral Reform and International Services. He has also worked as a consultant to the United Nations, the International Foundation for Electoral Systems, the International Institute for Democracy and Electoral Assistance and the Commonwealth Secretariat. He is a member of the Editorial

Board of the *Election Law Journal*, was awarded the Public Service Medal in 2001 and received the International Foundation for Electoral Systems' Joe C. Baxter Award in 2015.

Luke Mansillo is a PhD candidate in the Department of Government and International Relations and the US Studies Centre at the University of Sydney. In 2018, he was an associate in the Department of Government at Harvard University. He is interested in elections, political behaviour, public opinion and parties in Australia and other advanced democracies, in addition to quantitative social research design, and has published in the *Australian Journal of Political Science*.

Rob Manwaring is a Senior Lecturer at Flinders University in Adelaide. In 2018, his edited volume (with Paul Kennedy) *Why the Left Loses: The Decline of the Centre-Left in Comparative Perspective* was published by Policy Press. Rob teaches Australian politics and researches in the areas of labour and social-democratic politics.

Stephen Mills is Honorary Senior Lecturer with the School of Social and Political Sciences at the University of Sydney. He has written widely on election campaign management, party professionalisation and market research. He is a former journalist and was adviser to Prime Minister Bob Hawke.

Narelle Miragliotta is a Senior Lecturer in the Department of Politics and International Relations at Monash University. She has teaching and research interests covering different facets of Australian and liberal-democratic political institutions, including constitutions, parliaments, political parties and Australian elections and electoral systems. She is co-editor of *Contemporary Australian Political Party Organisations* (Monash University Publishing, 2015) and has been published in the *Australian Journal of Political Science* and *Parliamentary Affairs*.

Juliet Pietsch is Professor and Head of the School of Government and International Relations at Griffith University, specialising in race and ethnic politics and political sociology. Her recent research focuses on the political integration of migrants and ethnic minorities in Western immigrant countries and Southeast Asia. She is the author of *Race, Ethnicity, and the Participation Gap: Understanding Australia's Political Complexion* (University of Toronto Press, 2018) and co-editor of *Double Disillusion: The 2016 Australian Federal Election* (ANU Press, 2018).

Shaun Ratcliff is a Lecturer in Political Science at the US Studies Centre at the University of Sydney. His research focuses on using novel data sources to study the issue preferences and behaviour of political actors, including voters, interest groups and elites. He teaches on public opinion, political strategy and quantitative research methods. He has also worked in government and media relations and provided polling and statistical consulting for national political campaigns.

Ben Raue is an electoral and data analyst who writes about elections for the *Tally Room* and *The Guardian* and is an Adjunct Associate Lecturer in the Department of Government and International Relations at the University of Sydney. He has been writing about elections in Australia and around the world since 2008.

Will Sanders is a Senior Fellow at the Centre for Aboriginal Economic Policy Research at The Australian National University. He joined the North Australia Research Unit of The Australian National University in Darwin as a Research Assistant in 1981. He has been watching elections in the Northern Territory ever since and occasionally writing about them.

Marian Sawer is Emeritus Professor and Public Policy Fellow at The Australian National University and a Fellow of the Academy of the Social Sciences in Australia. She has led the Democratic Audit of Australia and has a longstanding interest in political finance. Her most recent book, coedited with Kerryn Baker, is *Gender Innovation in Political Science: New Norms, New Knowledge* (Palgrave, 2019).

Andrew Scott is Professor of Politics and Policy at Deakin University. He is a former trade union research officer and the author of five books and more than 30 other scholarly publications. His first book was *Fading Loyalties: The Australian Labor Party and the Working Class* (Pluto Press, 1991).

Jill Sheppard is a Lecturer in Politics at The Australian National University, researching why people participate in politics, what opinions they hold and why, and how both are shaped by political institutions and systems. She is involved in Australia's largest studies of public opinion and political behaviour, including the Australian Election Study and World Values Study. Before becoming an academic, Jill worked as an advisor to federal parliamentarians and she is interested in making sure that public opinion can rigorously inform public debate.

Marian Simms is Adjunct Professor at the Institute for Governance and Policy Analysis at the University of Canberra. She has held senior academic roles at The Australian National University, the University of Otago and Deakin University. She is a former president of the Australian Political Studies Association, former editor of the *Australian Journal of Political Science*, established the current partnership between ASSA and the election study group and has edited or co-edited six previous ASSA election studies. In 2003, Marian was awarded a Centenary Medal for her work on Australia's first federal election in 1901.

Rodney Smith is Professor of Australian Politics in the Department of Government and International Relations at the University of Sydney. He has written on a range of topics in Australian politics as co-editor of books such as *Contemporary Australian Political Party Organisations* (Monash University Publishing, 2015), *Contemporary Australian Politics: Theories, Practices and Issues* (Cambridge University Press, 2012) and *From Carr to Keneally: Labor in Office in NSW 1995–2011* (Allen & Unwin, 2012). He is Editor of the *Australasian Parliamentary Review* and the President of the Australian Political Studies Association for 2019–20.

Paul Strangio is an Associate Professor of Politics in the School of Social Sciences at Monash University. He has published widely on political leadership, including recently co-authoring a two-volume history of the Australian prime ministership. Since 2018, he has been the Visiting Cabinet Historian at the National Archives of Australia.

Marija Taflaga is a Lecturer and Director of the Centre for the Study of Australian Politics at The Australian National University. Her research focuses on Australian politics in comparative context, examining political parties' relationships with parliament and the executive. Marija also undertakes research in Australian political history and, more recently, in the area of the career paths of political elites.

James Walter is Emeritus Professor in Political Science in the School of Social Sciences at Monash University and a Fellow of the Academy of the Social Sciences in Australia. His chief publications are in the fields of leadership, biography, political ideas and policy, including a recent two-volume history of the Australian prime ministership (co-authored with Paul Strangio and Paul 't Hart) for which he was principal author of the contemporary volume.

John Wanna is Emeritus Professor at The Australian National University and at Griffith University. He was the foundation chair of public administration in the Australia and New Zealand School of Government and was its national research director. He has published widely on Australian politics and public policy and is a Fellow of the Academy of the Social Sciences in Australia.

John Warhurst first came to Canberra in 1978 and has written about federal elections for 40 years. He has written a weekly column for *The Canberra Times* for more than 20 years and is Emeritus Professor of Political Science at The Australian National University.

Paul Williams is a Senior Lecturer in Politics and Journalism at Griffith University's School of Humanities, Languages and Social Sciences. He is a weekly columnist with Brisbane's *Courier-Mail* newspaper and a frequent media commentator on Queensland politics. He has published widely on voter behaviour and political leadership in Australian scholarly journals.

Lawrie Zion is a Professor of Journalism at La Trobe University and Director of the university's Transforming Human Society Research Focus Area. Prior to joining La Trobe in 2006, he worked in the media for 18 years, including nine years at the ABC as a broadcaster and as a journalist for *The Age*, *The Australian* and numerous film publications. He currently leads the Australian Research Council–funded New Beats research project, which is investigating the career trajectories of journalists whose roles were made redundant between 2012 and 2014.

FOREWORD

What happened? That was the question most Australians were asking when facing the result of the May 2019 federal election. Even the victor described it as a miracle.

Scott Morrison became Australia's 30th prime minister against the predictions of all the national opinion polls. His Liberal–National Coalition had suffered a major swing in the Victorian State election just over six months earlier. He had himself been prime minister for only nine months, following the ousting of Malcolm Turnbull, which precipitated a by-election with another Liberal loss.

This volume investigates what happened. It is drawn from the contributions of 36 political scientists, analysts, journalists and commentators who took part in a post-election workshop sponsored by the Academy of the Social Sciences in Australia. It explores the new circumstances of this election. The loss of trust in political institutions seen across most Western democracies has been accompanied by the disengagement of citizens at least from the mainstream political process. We have seen the rise of populism, derision over 'fake news' and the way that social media fragments public discussion. And in the 2019 election we saw the influence of former federal MP Clive Palmer, who spent more money on the campaign than both major parties combined.

Morrison's Miracle provides in-depth analysis of the usual contributors to election wins and losses: patterns of voter behaviour and the campaign strategies of political parties and third parties. It also analyses regional variations in voting, the rise of Independents, the performance of the polls, the ideological contests and the role of the media. This is the ninth in the academy's election series covering federal campaigns. It builds on the preceding work and offers more in terms of comparing the 2019 election with those that went before.

I commend this book to all readers—scholars, practitioners, students and interested Australians—seeking to understand what happened in 2019. I congratulate and thank the editors for this important work.

Jane Hall
President
Academy of the Social Sciences in Australia

1

MORRISON'S MIRACLE: ANALYSING THE 2019 AUSTRALIAN FEDERAL ELECTION

Anika Gauja, Marian Sawer and Marian Simms

On the night of the 2019 election, Prime Minister Scott Morrison thanked the 'quiet Australians' for delivering a 'miracle' result, re-electing the Liberal–National Coalition and returning his government to power. Morrison was Australia's first Pentecostal prime minister and an exponent of the prosperity gospel, as well as miracles—redefining the Australian mantra of the 'fair go' as 'a fair go for those who have a go'. Morrison ended his victory speech with the words 'God bless Australia'—probably the first Australian leader to use such words since John Curtin in the depths of the Second World War.

The election result was very much at odds with expectations, given that national opinion polls had long been predicting a Labor win rather than the re-election of the centre-right Coalition. The backdrop was the declining level of trust in politicians and the media. Trust in politicians had reached its lowest level since first measured in Australia in 1969 (Cameron and Wynter 2018) and trust in the media was also at a low point (Edelman 2018). The discourse of 'fake news' was used to discredit news media, although the term was also used to describe disinformation campaigns spread on social media platforms for political purposes (Buckmaster and Wils 2019). Lack of trust and disengagement from party politics provided fertile ground for populist appeals and negative campaigning, particularly through social media. Labor leaders blamed the influence of populist parties and the cashed-up scare campaign around taxes, particularly the mythical 'death tax', for their defeat. Labor, with its plethora of policy offerings, seemed unable to cut through to disengaged and distrustful voters while simpler negative messaging was more successful.

Populist minor parties on the right, such as Pauline Hanson's One Nation (PHON) and Clive Palmer's United Australia Party (UAP), made extensive use of social media, including platforms such as Facebook. This reflected a global shift whereby radical right parties and organisations were more than matching the left in their use of digital technology. In addition, in 2019, the Liberal Party's social media strategy was more successful than Labor's—for example, gaining more than twice the number of views for its Facebook page. This was unlike the 2013 and 2016 federal elections when Labor and the Greens were notably more active than the Coalition on social media platforms such as Twitter (see Bruns and Moon 2018).

Few seats changed hands, with the governing Coalition gaining one additional seat to give it 77 of the 151 seats in the House of Representatives, while Labor lost one seat. Reflecting the loss of trust in the major parties, the share of the vote going to minor parties and Independents continued to rise in the House of Representatives, although there was a slight dip in their Senate share (from 35.5 per cent in 2016 to 33 per cent in 2019). PHON did particularly well in Queensland and its two Queensland senators will share the balance of power on the crossbench with four other senators when Labor and the Australian Greens oppose the government. The Greens held all their Senate positions, increasing their vote significantly in South Australia and Queensland, while the Labor vote collapsed in Queensland, where it won only one Senate seat. The Nick Xenophon Team (NXT), renamed the Centre Alliance, retained a lower house seat and had two continuing senators. Palmer's UAP ran an expensive campaign but failed to secure a seat; Cory Bernardi's party, the Australian Conservatives, was disbanded soon after the election, with Bernardi continuing to sit as an Independent senator up until his resignation from the Senate in January 2020.

The 'modern' gender gap in the voting characteristics of recent Australian elections continued in 2019, with women voting to the left of men— that is, the 2019 Australian Election Study (AES) showed women were again more likely than men to vote Labor, more likely to vote Green and significantly less likely than men to vote for the Coalition.[1] The shift of women to the left or, more accurately perhaps, the shift of men to the right, reflects broader social changes, including employed women now having a higher union density than men and taking leadership positions in the trade union movement.

Election themes

Our aim in this chapter is to highlight the key themes of the campaign as they emerged in our election workshop discussions. For many observers, the 2019 federal election appeared to be a watershed, awash as it was with huge amounts of money paying for negative campaign material and contributing to the loss of civility on the campaign trail. The trend to personalisation continued, with the emphasis on leaders or candidates rather than on the parties for which they were standing. At the same time, distrust and disengagement on the part of many voters contributed to the success of negative campaigning targeting leaders and candidates.

Digital technology had broad consequences in terms of the fragmentation of the public sphere and the fact that many voters accessed their political news from echo chambers that confirmed their own views rather than exposing them to a diversity of opinion and debate. Negative campaigning thrives in such echo chambers, in what is often characterised as a 'post-truth' environment, and digital technology gives added emphasis to visual elements such as memes and GIFs and the affect conveyed by visual images. One good example in the 2019 campaign was a photoshopped image of Bill Shorten in the bath posted by PHON with the words 'Bill couldn't run a bath let alone a country'. The intersection between populism, personalisation and digital technology is a major theme of this book, along with its relationship to voter distrust.

---

1   A larger proportion of female respondents (37 per cent) than male respondents (33 per cent) indicated that they voted for Labor. Similarly, 15 per cent of female respondents voted for the Greens, compared with 9 per cent of male respondents. This pattern was reversed for the Coalition, with 48 per cent of male respondents voting for the Liberal and National Coalition parties, compared with 38 per cent of women. Data from The Australian National University, *Australian Election Study 2019*, available from: australianelectionstudy.org.

Also contributing to voter distrust has been the laissez-faire attitude of the Australian Government towards the regulation of political finance and the consequent perceived purchase of political access and influence by 'a few big interests' at the expense of the people as a whole. The 2019 federal election campaign will be remembered for the more than $80 million spent by billionaire Clive Palmer—an outlay that delivered preferences for the Coalition but failed to win Palmer's UAP a seat. The role of private money in federal elections makes Australia increasingly out of step with campaign finance regulation in comparable democracies. The cost of paid electronic advertising—banned in many comparable democracies—has driven Australian political parties to chase ever-greater private donations (Sawer 2019). Both political donations and the negative advertising these buy increase distrust in politicians and political parties.

Compounding the distrust stemming from the access bought by political donations are the perceived 'rorts' or abuse of entitlements by politicians, such as charging private or party travel to the public purse. Posts on social media platforms about such rorts quickly go viral, as in the helicopter memes that brought down former Speaker of the House of Representatives Bronwyn Bishop (Sawer and Gauja 2016). Australia differs from comparable democracies not only in its laissez-faire attitude to the role of private money in elections, but also in its attitude to the use of public money, such as parliamentary allowances, for electioneering. Under 2017 legislation, travel by staffers to assist parliamentarians in their re-election, including travel until the day before election day to work at party campaign headquarters, may be considered official business.

Populist discourse feeds on the distrust of democratic representatives or 'career politicians' arising from the perceived abuse of public office. At the same time, populist discourse promotes suspicion of courts and tribunals, dismissing issues of governance and accountability as concerns of the 'Beltway' or the 'Canberra bubble'. In a video released after he became prime minister, Morrison invoked these sentiments when he said: 'The Canberra bubble is what happens down here, when people get all caught up with all sorts of gossip and rubbish, and that's probably why most of you switch off any time you hear a politician talk' (Coorey 2018).

Mobilising resentment of selected elites is a feature of both left-wing populism (directed against the 'big end of town') and the more successful right-wing populism (directed against special interests with supposed contempt for the values of ordinary citizens but a desire to spend their taxes). The latter form of populist discourse was very successfully wielded by former Prime Minister John Howard (see Sawer and Laycock 2009; Snow and Moffitt 2012). Such populist discourse was deployed relentlessly in the 2019 campaign by the Coalition in social media ads such as: 'Labor can't manage money, so they come after yours.'

The election result, while surprising to most, was perhaps 'overdetermined'—in other words, any one of a number of causes might have been sufficient to account for it. In addition to overly complex policy messages and an unpopular Labor leader, there was the populist discourse feeding off voter distrust, the ubiquitous negative campaigning funded by Palmer and other private donors and the media dominance of Rupert Murdoch's News Corp. Not only is the concentration of media ownership in Australia among the highest in the world, but also the Murdoch mastheads and *Sky News* overwhelmingly campaigned against Labor during the campaign.

While the ubiquitous negative campaigning was seen as a new low in Australian politics, there was at least one positive development: the 2019 election was the first since the 2001 'Tampa' election not to mobilise anti-Islamic fears (Jensen 2019: 44). The closest the Prime Minister came to these previous campaigns was the repeated commitment to 'keeping Australians safe'. Following the massacre of worshippers in two mosques in New Zealand in March, which drew attention to the links between anti-Islamic hate speech and violence, the Coalition eschewed the kind of fear campaign seen in preceding Australian elections. Candidates found to have expressed anti-Islamic views were more or less promptly disendorsed.

The themes of this election had much in common with those dominating recent European elections, including voter distrust, populism and the personalisation of politics. Hence this book brings in comparative perspectives wherever possible, as well as consideration of the type of reforms desirable to boost public confidence in political institutions. The changing techniques of political persuasion are subjected to close examination, as are the methodologies used for public opinion polling and the changing patterns of voter behaviour, including the shift to early voting. Overall, the book provides a comprehensive overview of the actors and campaigns in the 2019 federal election and the rules of the game and contexts in which it took place. The timetable of the election is shown in Table 1.1.

Table 1.1 2019 federal election timetable

11 April	Prime Minister announces the election will be held on 18 May Postal vote applications open Writs issued for the House and half-Senate elections
18 April	Electoral rolls close
21 April	'Bulk' (registered political parties) candidate nominations for the House of Representatives close
23 April	Nominations of all candidates close
24 April	Declaration of candidates; draw for positions on the ballots
29 April	Early voting, mobile voting and checks on declaration envelopes commence, but no vote counting until close of voting at 6 pm on 18 May
15 May	Postal vote applications close at 6 pm
18 May	Election day
31 May	All declaration (e.g. postal and absent) votes due
21 June	Writs due; Parliament must sit within 30 days

Source: AEC (2019).

The continuing tradition

As noted in the 2016 federal election book, *Double Disillusion*, Australian political scientists have produced election books or special issues of journals analysing federal election campaigns since 1958. This is the 17th of such volumes—a series supported since the 1996 election by the Academy of the Social Sciences in Australia (ASSA). After each election there is an academy-sponsored workshop identifying the key themes of the campaign as well as focusing on patterns of voter behaviour, the campaign strategies of political parties and third parties, the performance of the opinion polls, ideological contests and the role of the media. The current volume brings together 36 contributors, ranging from established to early career scholars, and has benefited from commentary by the political journalists and practitioners present at the federal election workshop.

To address the themes of voter distrust, personalisation, populism and digital disruption and to explain the result, this volume is divided into four parts:

1. The context, covering the rules of the game, the campaign, candidates and preselection, ideology and leadership, marginal seat polling and the national polls.

2. The results in the House, Senate, the States and Territories, and electoral behaviour.
3. The actors, including the political parties and third parties.
4. The media, including the traditional media, campaign communications and the visual campaign.

The first part of the book examines the campaign and its context, beginning with an overview by Marian Simms. Simms argues that Morrison inherited a party room dogged by instability, ideological divisions and personal rivalries and his task was to show that the 'uncertainty' in the Coalition was over. Morrison's subsequent presentation of himself as a political outsider—an 'accidental' leader—was an example of personalised politics, as was Bill Shorten's injection of family stories and personal questions to the audience. This personalised and charismatic style may be used by mainstream parties to compete with the smaller populist parties and Independents.

Simms suggests that, due to a number of factors, the campaign is not restricted to the period between the announcement of the election and election day. These factors include the advent of the continuous campaign (accelerated by social media), Australia's short election cycles (especially with State electoral matters bleeding into federal politics) and the politicisation of the federal Budget. Hence the chapter covers the campaign context: the 'long campaign', from about November 2018 to Budget week starting on 1 April 2019; and the 'real' campaign, from Budget day on 2 April through to polling day.

Simms shows that, alongside his personal style, Morrison managed to deliver a carefully crafted and highly focused campaign, based largely on the economy. He was bland about policies but sharp in his criticisms of the track record and plans of the Australian Labor Party (ALP). In stark contrast, Labor had been crafting policies since before the 2016 federal election under a broad redistributive agenda, which it said contrasted with the Coalition's plans to support the big end of town. Arguably, Labor's strategy of attacking the Liberals as representing corporate Australia failed miserably against Morrison's persona and his statements and activities with regard to congestion-busting/drought-breaking.

In the next chapter, 'The rules of the game', Marian Sawer and Michael Maley set out the ways in which the regulatory regime for federal elections has improved and the ways it has fallen behind best practice in comparable democracies. Enrolment practice has finally been modernised, so the electoral roll is more comprehensive than ever; previous resistance to making enrolment easier has faded. Less positive is the continuing lack of restrictions on campaign expenditure at the federal level and the further liberalisation of the use of parliamentary resources for electioneering. The lack of any 'truth in political advertising' provision at the federal level became the subject of debate with the prevalence of misleading and deceptive claims—in particular, concerning Labor's tax policy. The shift to social media, however, meant any attempt to regulate content was even more challenging. Notable in 2019 was the continued rise in early voting—an unforeseen consequence of much earlier changes to the *Commonwealth Electoral Act*. Just over 40 per cent of electors voted before polling day, including a significant number before the major parties held their campaign launches. This raised both deliberative concerns and concerns over a level playing field, considering the resources needed to have a presence at pre-polling centres for a three-week polling period.

In Chapter 4, 'Candidates and preselection ', Anika Gauja and Marija Taflaga argue that, while candidate selection is an extremely important process in determining the representativeness of the Australian Parliament, it is one in which relatively few people participate, being largely dominated by executives and factions and shrouded in secrecy. Using an original dataset created for the chapter, they show that, for the 2019 federal election, only a handful of preselection contests was actually competitive and the majority received no media coverage. Gauja and Taflaga document the most controversial contests and analyse the impact of gender. They show that, in 2019, only 34 per cent of those who stood for party preselection were women. Overall, a higher percentage of women candidates was elected to the Senate than to the House of Representatives, but the overall composition of both houses is still heavily determined by the fact that the majority of incumbent parliamentarians are men.

In 'Ideology and populism' (Chapter 5), Carol Johnson sees the 2019 election as distinctive in presenting voters with a clear ideological choice between, on the one hand, a well-developed policy agenda to address stagnating wages and rising inequalities and, on the other, neoliberal opposition to such tax-and-spend policies (albeit in a form that emphasised a 'fair go' for ordinary Australians). While there might have been this choice, Labor did not succeed in communicating it effectively and its own past policies of economic deregulation and dismantling centralised wage-fixing may have reduced trust in its capacity to deliver.

In 2019, Labor engaged in populist discourse against 'the big end of town' in particular. The Morrison team also engaged in populist discourse, mobilising the people against big government and the spending of their money ('I don't think the Government knows better than you do about where your money should go'). The emphasis was on attacking Labor and Johnson suggests the Coalition was increasingly aware of the difficulty of selling a more explicitly neoliberal agenda of its own. Morrison himself combined neoliberal ideological beliefs and the compatible Pentecostal 'prosperity gospel'.

Paul Strangio and James Walter argue in Chapter 6, 'The personalisation of the campaign', that the personalisation of the election contest was both a continuation of previous trends and the deliberate crafting of personae by the leaders—notably, Scott Morrison. Strangio and Walter show how Morrison was able to emerge from relative obscurity—a political unknown—to appear as a well-liked ordinary bloke (see also Kelly 2018). Shorten, in contrast, was well-known for his long track record as ALP leader and a senior minister before that. Somehow, Shorten's experience became a liability, especially given the perception of his history in unseating previous leaders and engaging in dubious union deals. The authors conclude Shorten was no Bob Hawke, resembling more the hapless Bill Hayden, who stood aside to enable Hawke's leadership in 1983.

In Chapter 7, 'National polling and other disasters', Luke Mansillo and Simon Jackman examine the failure of the national polls conducted before the election to anticipate the result. The national polls—which had been reasonably accurate predictors of election outcomes in recent years—powerfully shaped expectations among the public, journalists and politicians themselves that Labor would win the election. Mansillo and Jackman fit a 'state-space model' to the public opinion polls fielded between the 2016 and 2019 federal elections, identifying the estimated trajectory of voting intentions between the two elections, house effects (biases specific to each polling organisation) and the discontinuity in public opinion associated with the transition from Malcolm Turnbull to Morrison as prime minister in August 2018. Polling error in 2019 was largely associated with underestimating Coalition support, while overestimating support for minor parties, especially on the part of YouGov Australia. Some of this polling error could have been anticipated given the observed biases in polls fielded before the 2016 federal election (Jackman and Mansillo 2018), but most of the 2016–19 error was new. What was especially striking about the polling errors in 2019 was that: a) errors in estimates of first preferences did not 'wash out' when converted to two-party-preferred estimates, such that b) the resulting errors in the two-party-preferred estimates were large by historical standards, and c) they led to an incorrect prediction as to which party would form government, at which point larger-than-typical 'poll error' became a fully fledged crisis of confidence in polls and the polling industry. The chapter identifies pollster malpractice through 'herding'; published polls during the campaign period were far too close, suggesting adjustment of weighting procedures to match estimates from rival polling organisations.

In 'The perilous polling of single seats' (Chapter 8), Murray Goot forensically examines the opinion surveys undertaken in individual seats and, more often, in groups of seats. He discusses the decline in the number of such polls compared with previous elections and their methodological limitations and lack of transparency. Notably, not all single-seat polls are in the 'marginals' and may be undertaken for other reasons. For example, while the federal seat of Deakin was not marginal, it was considered potentially winnable by the ALP due to the anti-Liberal swing in the equivalent Victorian State seats. Goot notes that 'provincial' seats were overpolled compared with both rural and metropolitan ones. These polls overestimated both the ALP primary vote and the UAP primary vote. More worrying were the conflict-of-interest issues whereby a single company undertook polling for different clients who assumed the results were confirmatory rather than duplicated! Goot's chapter raises issues of 'trust' in both single-seat and national polls.

The second part of the book analyses the results of the 2019 federal election. This is done across four chapters, with chapters presenting a detailed breakdown of the House of Representatives and Senate results, a chapter analysing regional variations in the campaign and another chapter that explores patterns of individual voter behaviour. Such a multifaceted analysis is necessary to fully understand the complexity of Australian federal elections, which comprise two discrete elections using different voting systems—one for the House of Representatives and one for the Senate.[2] It is also necessary to understand the role and importance of regions in Australia's federated democracy and to appreciate the dynamics of class, age and ethnicity that underlie patterns of voting.

---

2   State senators have six-year terms, while House of Representatives terms are three years; typically, a House election coincides with a so-called half-Senate election.

In Chapter 9, Ben Raue presents the results of the House of Representatives vote, highlights the key contests in each of the States and Territories and explains the electoral redistributions and by-elections that took place during the previous parliamentary term. Raue reports that the primary vote for minor parties in the House in 2019 increased to a historic high of 25.2 per cent, and preferences (particularly those for Palmer's UAP and PHON) played an important role in the outcome of the election. The 2019 election was also notable for the growth in postal and pre-poll voting, which favoured the Coalition, and the gap in the two-party-preferred vote between those who voted early and those who voted on election day was wider than in the preceding six elections.

Reporting the results of the Senate contest, Antony Green analyses the impact of changes to the Senate voting system that were designed to make voting more transparent and proportionate by abolishing group voting tickets. The number of groups and candidates contesting the election fell compared with the previous half-Senate election in 2013. The new system also produced a result that achieved what it was intended to do: to favour political parties with a substantial vote before the allocation of preferences and to make it much more difficult for parties to be elected on the basis of preference deals.

The 2019 election was notable for the variation in electoral support for the Coalition and Labor among the Australian States, Territories and regions. In Chapter 11, Nick Economou, Zareh Ghazarian, Narelle Miragliotta, Will Sanders, Rodney Smith, John Warhurst and Paul Williams briefly analyse the campaign in the States and Territories. They discuss previous State and Territory election results, economic conditions, specific policy promises and campaign visits from the major party leaders. They highlight key contests and analyse notable regional variations within each jurisdiction.

In Chapter 12, on voter behaviour, Shaun Ratcliff, Jill Sheppard and Juliet Pietsch examine the impact of age, economic status and ethnicity on how Australians vote. Using new data from the Cooperative Australian Election Survey, they show that higher-income homeowners supported the Coalition, whereas lower-income renters voted for Labor. They argue that Labor's policy on housing affordability and inequity was an electoral liability; while support was concentrated among Labor voters, opposition was diffuse. The authors show that ethnic minorities did not favour the Coalition, nor did their views on same-sex marriage push them to vote for the Coalition parties in the election.

The third part of the book turns to the role of party actors and Independents in the campaign as well as third parties. In Chapter 14, Nicholas Barry explores continuities in the Liberal campaign such as the discursive strategy of identifying Labor with class warfare but also new elements such as the party's social media strategy, which was much more successful than in 2016. He describes Morrison as a 'conservative' who successfully brought together conservatives, moderates and former Turnbull supporters. He also examines the Liberal Party's 'women problem': its failure to put more women into parliament, their treatment while in parliament and the parallels with the underrepresentation of women in conservative parties in Europe and elsewhere. Meanwhile, the rural-based Coalition partner, the National Party, more than held its own despite the diminished rurality of its electorates, a leadership scandal, mismanagement of water allocations in the Murray–Darling Basin and the conflicting interests of miners and farmers elsewhere. Geoff Cockfield notes that among the policy dilemmas confronting the Nationals is that of migration, where the traditional social conservatism of the party has to be balanced with regional demands for labour for agricultural industries.

The hollowing out of support for centre-left parties across Europe forms the backdrop of Rob Manwaring's analysis of the structural factors affecting Labor, including the erosion of its support base in the unions. He also compares Labor and Coalition policies, noting how the relatively policy-rich offerings of Labor failed to gain traction compared with the concentrated negative message of the Coalition's campaign. It was a different story for the Greens, who were surging across Europe in the May elections for the European Parliament but making only relatively small gains in Australia. In Chapter 16, Stewart Jackson explores why climate change did not become—as expected—a key focus of the election. He finds a number of reasons: internal party problems, particularly in Victoria; the presidential-style campaign waged by Morrison against Shorten, which became the focus of attention; and the fact the Greens campaigned on a range of issues, not just climate change.

Minor populist parties on the right—such as PHON and Clive Palmer's UAP, Katter's Australian Party (KAP) and the Jacqui Lambie Network (JLN)—were catching up with the Greens in the scale of their social media and digital campaigning, which is something closely analysed by Glenn Kefford in Chapter 17. Electors continued to vote for a wide range of minor parties and Independents, with their choice depending on the State or region in which they lived. There was no evidence of any significant return to historical patterns of strong identification with the major parties.

The exploration by Jennifer Curtin and Jill Sheppard of the Independents' campaigns again highlights the disaffection with the major parties and the search for alternatives. In the rural Victorian seat of Indi, there was a unique community-based process to replace retiring Independent, Cathy McGowan. 'Voices of Indi' volunteers determined a succession process through which Helen Haines was chosen as preferred candidate and became the first Independent to succeed another in a federal electorate. Meanwhile in Warringah, Independent Zali Steggall was successful in defeating former prime minister Tony Abbott. The authors place her among a new group of socially progressive but economically conservative women Independents, alienated by the Liberal Party's lack of attention to climate policy and failure to develop a culture more inclusive of women. One such woman, Dr Kerryn Phelps, was unsuccessful in retaining the usually safe Liberal seat of Wentworth, which she had managed to win in a 2018 by-election.

Whereas unions were high-profile actors in the 2019 election, business was not, and is described by John Wanna in Chapter 19 as 'missing in action'. The slack, however, was taken up by business-oriented commentators— some from third parties and others from the media, including *Sky News* commentator and former Liberal Party adviser Chris Kenny. Big business was not active in the campaign, in contrast to preceding federal elections, and in some instances was supportive of ALP policy positions such as reviewing the level of payments of the Newstart allowance for the unemployed. Advertising and campaigning were conducted by other peak councils, such as the Australian Property Council and Master Builders Australia, which joined the chorus of opposition to the ALP's plans to abolish negative gearing and capital gains tax discounts.

In Chapter 20, Andrew Scott examines the role of a range of specific unions in the policy debates and advertising campaigns. The peak union body, the Australian Council of Trade Unions (ACTU), did not reach the highwater mark achieved in its 2007 election campaign, when it helped unseat then Prime Minister John Howard over his 'WorkChoices' industrial relations legislation.

In 2019, a number of feminised unions—in industries with a predominantly female workforce—ran strong campaigns. Scott discusses grassroots and advertising campaigns by nurses' and teachers' unions. The ACTU and the Victorian Trades Hall Council—the latter emboldened by the pro-Labor swing in the 2018 State election—undertook surveys and campaigns in targeted seats. Mining and energy interests effectively created a wedge between parts of the union movement and the ALP, so there were no united voices over big election issues such as the proposed Adani coalmine in central Queensland.

In Chapter 21, on third parties and think tanks, Ebony Bennett argues that activist group GetUp! used the same strategy it had used in 2016 but with limited success. It targeted 'right-wing blockers' in seven seats and campaigned in a further 22. Its main success was in the seat of Warringah, which saw the defeat of Abbott; small swings were achieved elsewhere. GetUp! itself also became a target, was forced to withdraw a tasteless advertisement, and was accused of bullying and harassment by Liberal candidate (now MP) Nicolle Flint.

A conservative counterpart, Advance Australia (AA), was formed in late 2018 and worked in the targeted seats of Warringah, Mayo, Indi and Flinders. AA's memorable 'Captain GetUp' was possibly more effective at promoting GetUp! than opposing it. Bennett also analyses the policy contributions of the think tanks The Australia Institute and the conservative Institute of Public Affairs (IPA).

The fourth part of the book examines the role of the media in the campaign, ranging from traditional print media to YouTube videos. In Chapter 22, Andrea Carson and Lawrie Zion find that the front-page emphasis on tax increases and Labor spending supported the Coalition's campaign narrative, particularly in the Murdoch mastheads and the *Australian Financial Review*. The Murdoch-owned *Sky News* also reinforced negative messages about Labor (and positive messages about PHON). The Coalition's social media strategy—particularly its use of video posts—was notably more successful than Labor's, attracting more than twice as many Facebook viewers. Social media also provided a platform enabling third parties and other actors, as well as the Coalition, to spread a fear campaign falsely claiming that Labor would introduce a 'death tax'.

In Chapter 23, Stephen Mills compares Liberal and Labor campaign communications strategies, finding that Labor adopted a 'challenger-style, policy-centred strategy incorporating a largely positive and broad-based message of change'. The Liberals, by contrast, adopted a largely negative incumbency-style strategy, policy-free and focused on leadership. This resulted in a campaign fought over the Opposition's policy rather than the record of the Coalition Government. Mills analyses how these campaign strategies were implemented—in particular, the flaws in Labor's campaign advertising compared with the simpler and more effective Liberal ads, including one in which a framed family photo is being squeezed in a rusty old vice called Labor. The pun used elsewhere was also effective: 'Labor: The Bill Australia can't afford.' Both parties had separate teams organised to deliver such messages through news media, electronic advertising and digital media, and Labor also had a separate team for direct voter contact (doorknocking and phone banks)—something into which the Coalition has traditionally put less effort. Despite Labor (and ACTU) experience with such fieldwork and its increased scale in 2019, it was relatively unsuccessful compared with the determined and highly negative incumbency campaign.

The visual elements in campaigning are of increasing importance and Lucien Leon analyses the contrasting functions of memes—familiar images transmitted with brief witty captions—in Chapter 24. While memes are often called the new political cartoons, they are also the form increasingly taken by everyday political engagement. However, they can be weaponised by political parties and have the capacity to polarise and misinform the electorate as they go viral. The intervention of political players had consolidated since 2016 and most of the memes featured in mainstream news media came from six Facebook groups, including Clive Palmer's Put Australia First, Australian Young Greens and Labor and Liberal–oriented groups. The memes circulating during the campaign focused on tax, the economy, climate change, Liberal leadership and distrust of Bill Shorten, and Leon argues they provided a reliable gauge of the electoral mood. A selection of memes, cartoons and videos is included in this chapter, illustrating responses to the campaign by political cartoonists, partisan players and engaged citizens.

Aftermath: Morrison's mandate

Bill Shorten's resignation from the ALP leadership on election night created speculation over his replacement; in the event, Anthony Albanese was the sole candidate when the nominations closed, and the three other leadership positions were also uncontested, with much behind-the-scenes discussion. The new ALP team comprised Anthony Albanese (NSW) as Leader, Richard Marles (Victoria) as Deputy Leader, Penny Wong (South Australia) as Senate Leader and Kristina Keneally (NSW) as Deputy Senate Leader. Shorten opted to remain an MP and is a member of Albanese's Shadow Cabinet, which comprises 12 women and 12 men.

Morrison's new ministry was sworn in on 29 May, with a mix of existing ministers and others in new roles—notably, Ken Wyatt as the first Aboriginal Minister for Indigenous Australians and Senator Bridget McKenzie as the first woman Minister for Agriculture. McKenzie did not last long in this position. She resigned in February 2020 and returned to the backbench after she was found to have breached the Statement of Ministerial Standards for her involvement in the sports grants scandal (Coorey 2020).

Ministers Josh Frydenberg (Treasurer) and Mathias Cormann (Senate Leader and Minister for Finance) would be responsible for delivering the Coalition tax cuts that passed the Senate on 4 July. While the delivery of personal tax cuts was Morrison's core promise, arguably his 'mandate' was open-ended.

References

Australian Electoral Commission (AEC). 2019. *2019 Federal Election Timetable*. Canberra: AEC. aec.gov.au/elections/federal_elections/2019/timetable.htm.

Bruns, Axel and Brenda Moon. 2018. 'Social Media in Australian Federal Elections: Comparing the 2013 and 2016 Campaigns'. *Journalism and Mass Communications Quarterly* 95(2): 425–48. doi.org/10.1177/1077699 018766505.

Buckmaster, Luke and Tyson Wils. 2019. 'Responding to fake news'. *Parliamentary Library Briefing Book*. Canberra: Commonwealth of Australia. www.aph.gov. au/About_Parliament/Parliamentary_Departments/Parliamentary_Library/ pubs/BriefingBook46p/FakeNews.

Cameron, Sarah and Thomas Wynter. 2018. 'Campaign Finance and Perceptions of Interest Group Influence in Australia'. *Political Science* 70(2): 169–88. doi.org/10.1080/00323187.2018.1562307.

Coorey, Phillip. 2018. 'Scott Morrison reminds us of "the things that matter"'. *Australian Financial Review*, 18 October. www.afr.com/politics/scott-morrison-reminds-us-of-the-things-that-matter-20181018-h16tme.

Coorey, Phillip. 2020. 'Jockeying begins after Bridget McKenzie resigns over sports rorts'. *Australian Financial Review*, 2 February. www.afr.com/politics/federal/bridget-mckenzie-resigns-over-sports-rorts-20200202-p53wzb.

Edelman, Richard. 2018. *2018 Edelman Trust Barometer: Global Report*. [Online]. www.edelman.com/sites/g/files/aatuss191/files/2018-10/2018_Edelman_Trust_Barometer_Global_Report_FEB.pdf.

Gauja, Anika, Peter Chen, Jennifer Curtin and Juliet Pietsch. 2018. *Double Disillusion: The 2016 Australian Federal Election*. Canberra: ANU Press. doi.org/10.22459/dd.04.2018.

Jackman, Simon and Luke Mansillo. 2018. 'The campaign that wasn't: Tracking public opinion over the 44th parliament and the 2016 election campaign'. In *Double Disillusion: The 2016 Australian Federal Election*, edited by Anika Gauja, Peter Chen, Jennifer Curtin and Juliet Pietsch, 133–56. Canberra: ANU Press. doi.org/10.22459/dd.04.2018.06.

Jensen, Erik. 2019. 'The Prosperity Gospel: How Scott Morrison Won and Bill Shorten Lost'. *Quarterly Essay* 74: 1–71.

Kelly, Shaun. 2018. 'Leave no trace: The story of Scott Morrison'. *The Monthly*, November: 22–33.

Savva, Niki. 2019. *Plots and Prayers: Malcolm Turnbull's Demise and Scott Morrison's Ascension*. Melbourne: Scribe Press.

Sawer, Marian. 2019. 'After Clive Palmer's $60 million campaign, limits on political advertising are more important than ever'. *The Conversation*, 21 May.

Sawer, Marian and Anika Gauja. 2016. 'Party rules: Promises and pitfalls'. In *Party Rules? Dilemmas of Political Party Regulation in Australia*, edited by Anika Gauja and Marian Sawer, 1–36. Canberra: ANU Press. doi.org/10.22459/PR.10.2016.01.

Sawer, Marian and David Laycock. 2009. 'Down with Elites and Up with Inequality: Market Populism in Australia and Canada'. *Commonwealth & Comparative Politics* 47(2): 133–50. doi.org/10.1080/14662040902842836.

Snow, Dave and Benjamin Moffitt. 2012. 'Straddling the Divide: Mainstream Populism and Conservatism in Howard's Australia and Harper's Canada'. *Commonwealth & Comparative Politics* 50(3): 271–92. doi.org/10.1080/14662043.2012.692922.

PART 1. CAMPAIGN AND CONTEXT

2

ELECTION CAMPAIGN OVERVIEW

Marian Simms[1]

Scott Morrison—reminiscent of Tony Abbott in the 2013 federal election—campaigned until the last moment of the 2019 election campaign, ending up in the marginal seat of Bass, Tasmania, on election morning, 18 May. The previous day, he had crisscrossed Queensland and finished in the marginal coastal seat of Gilmore in New South Wales. The Coalition was rewarded with one additional seat and majority government. The House of Representatives is finely balanced; the Coalition is a bad by-election away from relying on the Speaker's casting vote. While few seats changed hands in the election, the outcome was 'transformative'.

Some jurisdictions formally recognise that campaigning commences well before the actual election announcement; the United Kingdom, for example, acknowledges a 'pre-campaigning' period of about three months—generally known as the 'long' campaign (White 2015). In Australia, there was a clear policy divide between the major parties, with the Coalition promising tax cuts and the Australian Labor Party (ALP) supporting new welfare and energy initiatives funded by closing tax loopholes—a divide that had developed over several Budget cycles. In an era of the 'continuous campaign', most of Labor's new policies and the government's new expenditure commitments

1   Marian Simms was Executive Director, Social, Behavioural and Economic Sciences, at the Australian Research Council in the industry and education portfolios from 2011 to 2017. The views expressed here are her own. Marian is grateful for comments from Anika Gauja, John Wanna and other workshop participants.

were released well ahead of the election announcement. The 2019 election campaign, like the 2013 campaign and to a degree the 2016 one, was fought not 'principally on policy issues, but on personalities' (Johnson et al. 2015: 1; Gauja et al. 2018: 3).

This chapter is therefore divided into four parts: distinctive features of the overall campaign; the campaign context (the legacy of Malcolm Turnbull's prime ministership); the long campaign (from the beginning of Scott Morrison's prime ministership), covering critical issues and events well before Morrison called the election on 11 April 2019 for an 18 May House and half-Senate election; and the 'real' campaign, commencing with the federal Budget speech a week before the election was called.

Distinctive features of the campaign

The interrelated themes of the campaign were leadership, by-elections, State elections, opinion polls and the emergence of issues such as migration limits and refugees, urban infrastructure, housing affordability, religious freedom, the recognition of West Jerusalem as the capital of Israel, aged care, 'closing the gap' strategies, terrorism, the economy and specifically the Budget surplus, domestic violence, medical research, a levy on banks, taxation, emissions targets, the 'living wage' and Australian citizenship.[2] The politics of personality and different strands of populism were features of the 2019 election campaign. They are interrelated, as personalised parties led by charismatic leaders that attack mainstream parties and institutions as 'untrustworthy' are one kind of populism that fills a perceived representation gap (Taggart 2002: 62).

Prior to the election campaign and during the campaign itself, the use of social media was important. For example, claims about the ALP's alleged plans to introduce a 'death tax' were virulent on social media and were used in Liberal Party campaign advertising—as in the words of a campaign brochure distributed by the Canberra Liberals (2019): 'Labor will tax, your rent, your home, your car, your retirement—LABOR WILL TAX YOU TO DEATH.'[3]

---

2   This list is taken from formal policy announcements and major speeches by the Coalition and Labor leaders.

3   US Republican pollster Frank Luntz is generally credited with organising the widespread use of the term 'death tax' in the mid-1990s as a way of mobilising public opinion against estate taxes.

Shorten wasted valuable time during the election campaign issuing denials. Ultra-right groups played on fears that the ALP was anti-growth, anti-mining and anti-jobs, running social media campaigns through Facebook and producing social media posts on Corflute signs during the Longman by-election (28 July 2018).

In the lead-up to the election announcement, the Coalition, its associated groups and sections of the print and electronic media depicted the ALP's longstanding policies to remove tax breaks as plans to introduce 'new' taxes. This was from the Abbott playbook, borrowed from US Republican strategists, as in Abbott's claims in 2013 that Labor would put a big tax on everything (see Johnson et al. 2015) and his later attacks on Turnbull's 'tax on coal'. Retiring Liberal Member of Parliament (MP) Christopher Pyne letterboxed his electorate in Adelaide with pamphlets saying Labor's proposed negative gearing changes would create a 'housing tax' and a new recession. Conservative think tank the Institute of Public Affairs (IPA) also argued that the living wage policy would create a recession (Creighton 2019: 5).

The 2017–18 and 2018–19 federal Budgets had provided opportunities for the political leaders to articulate policies and develop themes; some issues had carried over from the 2016–17 Budget and the 2016 election. Clear differences emerged between the two sides of politics on fiscal policies, with the Coalition's flatter tax structures and corporate tax cuts versus Labor's slanting of tax reform towards lower-income workers. Labor would initiate a major review of the Newstart Allowance for the unemployed, which the Coalition strenuously opposed. The Coalition saw itself as providing opportunities, rewarding success and supporting business investment—in line with Turnbull's signature National Innovation and Science Agenda. The ALP could depict itself as the 'fair go' party versus the Coalition's 'mates' rates. Such a strategy may have looked effective against Turnbull but would not stick so easily against Morrison. See, for example, Shadow Minister for Finance Jim Chalmers's (2019) tweet about Minister for Finance Mathias Cormann and Prime Minister Morrison's travel 'perks' from corporate friends.

Turnbull had released an overarching signature policy and rearranged the Commonwealth bureaucracy to support this,[4] whereas Morrison and his opponent, Bill Shorten, made policy-oriented set-piece speeches (see Table 2.1).

4   The National Innovation and Science Agenda provided little 'new' money but considerable repurposing of funds, especially around research grants and business and university incentives.

While leadership remained an issue throughout the formal campaign, many of the pre-campaign issues were muted, while others re-emerged with intensity—notably, the economy, taxation, housing and urban infrastructure or 'congestion' and the Adani coalmine. Religion re-emerged in the third and final leaders' debate—only because the compere, the ABC's Sabra Lane, asked both leaders for their views on the recent sacking of rugby union player Israel Folau by Rugby Australia due to his comments on social media, inter alia, that gay people would go to hell.

A number of these key campaign issues had also played out during the by-elections held in 2017 and 2018.[5] Other issues—notably, the bad behaviour of the banks—did not provide a 'framework' for the 2019 election, despite journalist Paul Kelly's prediction (Kelly 2019: 1). Overall, the Coalition's strategy of accepting the banking royal commission's findings and 'moving on' reduced Labor's strategy of reminding voters that Morrison had opposed calls for a royal commission to 'nothing more than a populist whinge' (McIlroy 2019: 7).

The 2019 election would be fought along new boundaries, after a 2017–18 redistribution enlarged the House to 151 from 150 and gave Victoria and the Australian Capital Territory new seats, removing one from South Australia (see Raue, Chapter 9, this volume). This was thought likely to benefit the ALP, especially in Victoria, as Melbourne expanded into the regions, and the naming of new and existing seats was contentious.

The context: The Turnbull prime ministership

Malcolm Turnbull fared well after taking over the leadership from Tony Abbott in September 2015, especially in the preferred prime minister ratings of the opinion polls, where he overshadowed Bill Shorten. Such was Turnbull's standing it was widely anticipated he would call an early election. Instead, he persevered with a double-dissolution strategy over contentious industrial relations legislation and set a 55-day campaign. Turnbull came close to losing the 'unlosable' election; the Coalition scraped home with a narrow majority of 76 seats (see Gauja et al. 2018). Despite Shorten's personal unpopularity and the ALP's low primary vote, there was a solid two-party-preferred swing to Labor.

---

5   These were due mainly to MPs' ineligibility under Section 44(i) of the Australian Constitution.

2017

Turnbull's credibility had suffered a blow and he staggered through 2017 facing multiple challenges, not the least being the long-running imbroglio over the eligibility to sit in the parliament of a number of senior Coalition figures (along with minor party MPs) during 2017—an issue in which ALP figures came to be embroiled the following year after months of declaring the party had robust processes for checking candidate eligibility.

Sussan Ley, Turnbull's Minister for Health, Aged Care and Sport, had resigned her portfolio in January 2017 over some of her travel claims failing the 'pub test'. Travel issues had previously been a headache for the Abbott Government, ensnaring Abbott himself and National Party Leader and Deputy Prime Minister Barnaby Joyce. Then Speaker of the House of Representatives Bronwyn Bishop was forced to resign the speakership in 2015 over live footage of her arrival via helicopter at a regional golf course in late 2014. Abbott subsequently initiated a comprehensive review of 'parliamentary entitlements', which reported to Turnbull in 2016. As well as fuelling a lack of respect for and lack of trust in the federal parliament, these events potentially fed the perception that the Coalition was rorting the system and cavorting with the rich and famous while many constituents were doing it tough.

After the High Court found in October 2017 that National Party Leader Joyce was ineligible to sit in parliament,[6] his seat of New England was immediately declared vacant and writs were issued for a 2 December by-election.[7] Soon after, Liberal John Alexander resigned his Sydney seat of Bennelong, also over concerns relating to Section 44(i) of the Australian Constitution, and a by-election was set for 16 December.

The loss of two Coalition MPs sent Turnbull into minority government, relying on crossbenchers Rebekha Sharkie and Cathy McGowan during the last parliamentary session of 2017. Both Joyce and Alexander were returned, although Alexander suffered a 5.3 per cent negative swing in

---

6   The High Court sits as the Court of Disputed Returns on references from the House and/or Senate, the Australian Electoral Commission (AEC) or petitions from an eligible voter or candidate. See High Court (2017).

7   Joyce survived the by-election only to be caught in a major scandal in early 2018; he received a major telling off from Turnbull and was sent on enforced leave. An update to the Ministerial Code of Conduct—the Statement of Ministerial Standards—banned sexual relations between ministers and their staff.

the primary vote, whereas his opponent, the ALP's seasoned campaigner and former NSW premier Kristina Keneally, gained a positive swing. Her primary vote was up 7.3 per cent.

With the Coalition in minority government, Labor flexed its muscles in the House, again urging the Coalition to call a royal commission into the banks, following a Senate inquiry into the Australian Securities and Investments Commission (ASIC) in 2014 and media exposés of sharp practices by the banks especially regarding housing and farm finance.[8] Sections of the National Party were angry at the banks' mishandling of farm loans, were threatening a private member's bill and pushed the government to act, helped by the big banks requesting an inquiry. Finally, the Royal Commission into Misconduct in the Banking, Superannuation and Financial Services Industry was announced, in late November 2017 (Ziffer 2019: 4–7).[9]

2018

The eligibility issue recurred in 2018, this time implicating high-profile ALP MPs David Feeney and Katy Gallagher, among others; Feeney resigned and Senator Gallagher was found to be ineligible. The March by-election for Feeney's Victorian seat of Batman was won by his successor, Ged Kearney, a popular former union leader (see Scott, Chapter 20, this volume). A cluster of by-elections was scheduled for 'Super Saturday', 28 July, with nine-week campaigns. Both the timing and the length of the campaigns were controversial: there was a clash with the date long set for the ALP's national conference. Leader of the Opposition in the Senate, Penny Wong, quizzed the electoral commissioner at a Senate Estimates Committee hearing, declaring him to be partisan: 'The timeline in relation to this by-election is demonstrably, substantially different to the timelines which were applied in seats which were previously held by government members, which looks partisan' (see Brown 2018a).[10]

---

8   Bill Shorten had promised a royal commission into the banking and financial sector in the lead-up to the 2016 election.
9   The report was delivered in February 2019; subsequently, the CEO and the chair of the National Australia Bank announced their resignations. The former resigned almost immediately and the latter remained until a new chair was appointed.
10   Technically, the Speaker announces the dates of by-elections on advice from the AEC.

In the by-elections, four of the five seats were held by the ALP, while the fifth was held by the Centre Alliance: Braddon (Tas.), Justine Keay (ALP); Fremantle (WA), Josh Wilson (ALP);[11] Longman (Qld), Susan Lamb (ALP); Mayo (SA), Rebekha Sharkie (Centre Alliance); and Perth (WA), Patrick Gorman (ALP), who was running in place of former member Tim Hammond, who had resigned for family reasons.

The senators found to be ineligible were replaced by countback (on the complexities of this, see Sawer and Maley, Chapter 3, this volume). Some processes were complicated, such as the disqualification in New South Wales of Fiona Nash, whose replacement, Hollie Hughes, was also found to be ineligible; under Section 44(iv), the replacement was former military official Jim Molan (of the conservative wing of the NSW Liberal Party).[12]

The results of the July 2018 'Super Saturday' by-elections had negative outcomes for the Liberals. The ALP and Centre Alliance held on to their seats, with swings against the Liberals in all seats. The outcome was also detrimental to Turnbull's leadership, alongside other factors such as internal party and Coalition divisions over his signature National Energy Guarantee (NEG) policy,[13] and the retention on the Senate's agenda of the proposed corporate tax cuts for big business. In Longman (Qld), for example, the Liberals' private research showed locals were deeply unhappy about the proposed corporate tax cuts for big business benefiting the banks and about possible consequential health Budget cuts (Savva 2019: 203). In a complicated process, the Coalition had reshuffled the corporate tax package first mooted in the 2016 Budget, but as late as winter 2018, it was still hoping to pass the second tranche of tax cuts for businesses worth more than $50 million. In the event, Pauline Hanson withdrew her support for the corporate tax package ahead of the Longman by-election (on 28 July 2018). However, despite Hanson not campaigning in person—due to 'exhaustion'—and being replaced with a carboard cut-out figure of herself, Pauline Hanson's One Nation (PHON) received a swing of 6.49 per cent.

---

11   Wilson was brought in at the last minute for the 2016 election, as the original candidate had been disendorsed for failing to disclose two convictions (Foster 2016).

12   In December 2017, the Turnbull Government established an inquiry into Section 44 by the Joint Standing Committee on Electoral Matters. In May 2018, the committee recommended a referendum to change Section 44(i). Molan was relegated to an unwinnable spot for the 2019 Senate ticket and campaigned on a below-the-line strategy, in which he garnered more than 100,000 votes but was ultimately unsuccessful. However, in November 2019, Molan was selected by the NSW Liberal Party to fill a casual vacancy caused by the resignation of Senator Arthur Sinodinos.

13   The NEG comprised two elements: an energy price guarantee for consumers and an emissions target.

Arguably, the by-election wins created future problems for Labor. The ALP had issued or reissued policies throughout 2018, including the immediate abolition of franking credit cash refunds and the end of negative gearing for new investors in old stock rental properties from 2020. It had taken these and other policies to the 2018 by-elections and, in the case of its negative gearing reforms, to the 2016 election. Longman is a retirement-belt constituency and, although there was negative campaigning, Labor's primary vote had increased to nearly 40 per cent. Some negative campaigning was around Labor's links with the Greens, as per the polling booth placards put out by the ultra-right (and posted on Facebook): 'This year Bill Shorten, and Susan Lamb voted with the Greens 100% of the time (#THETRUTHMATTERS 2018)'. In the March 2018 Batman by-election in Victoria, the Greens pitched to conservative voters to preference Greens ahead of Labor on account of the ALP's franking credits policy (Carey 2018). Labor subsequently adjusted its 'no franking credits' policy to exclude all pensioners and part-pensioners.

Despite positive signs in 2018 for the Coalition, with the Liberals winning State elections in South Australia and Tasmania, the messiness of the Section 44 situation and the passing of the 30 bad polls milestone for Turnbull in April led to leadership rumblings—based on fears that the Coalition was heading for defeat at the next federal election, which was due by late May 2019.[14] Turnbull's public fight with Joyce over the latter's affair with a staffer had not helped relations with the National Party, which, for largely pragmatic reasons, resented the loss of Joyce—a strong grassroots campaigner—in February 2018. The marriage equality debate had already opened old wounds between progressives and social conservatives in the Coalition.

The promised personal tax cuts from the 2018–19 Budget went awry in the Senate as Pauline Hanson went cool on the package. The Turnbull–Morrison economics team had earlier backed away from the increase in the Medicare Levy for high-income earners proposed in the 2017–18 Budget. Labor had promised better tax cuts for low-income workers, an education funding package for the Technical and Further Education (TAFE) sector and more health infrastructure. Shorten's general philosophy in developing policy was 'transparency'—in terms of debating issues at the ALP's national conference and promulgating those policies with a unified team (Marr 2015: 2).

---

14   If a half-Senate election were to be held alongside the House election.

The ALP's retention of Longman in July with a 9 per cent swing against the Liberals, and a high PHON primary vote of 17 per cent, worried Queensland Liberals in nearby marginal seats, including the Minister for Home Affairs, Peter Dutton, in the Brisbane seat of Dickson. The fourth week of August 2018 was a political circus, resulting in Turnbull losing the leadership to Morrison on a second contest after Turnbull called a leadership 'spill' and saw off an initial challenge from Dutton (see Strangio and Walter, Chapter 6, this volume).

The long campaign: The Morrison prime ministership

2018

Malcolm Turnbull's resignation from parliament after he lost the prime ministership in August triggered a by-election in Wentworth (NSW) on 20 October 2018. Independent candidate Dr Kerryn Phelps won narrowly and took her seat in parliament on 26 November; the Morrison Government was in a minority.[15] Its minority status was reiterated the next day when Julia Banks—an outspoken critic of bullying by men within the Liberal Party and of the dumping of Turnbull—resigned from the Liberal Party and joined the crossbench (see Curtin and Sheppard, Chapter 18, this volume).[16] After the Wentworth by-election, the next major test of Morrison's performance was the Victorian State election of 24 November 2018; State Labor received a positive swing and moved into Liberal heartland seats. As outlined by Nick Economou et al. (Chapter 11, this volume), this was widely seen as indicating that, federally, the Liberals would have serious trouble in Victoria.

---

15   In August, as a protest against the Liberal leadership changes, Kevin Hogan, Nationals MP for Page, moved to the crossbench, while still attending National Party meetings and continuing to be a National Party MP; he promised supply and confidence. He was backed by National Party Leader, Michael McCormack.

16   Banks apparently did so without providing advance notice to the party leadership and while Morrison was giving a press conference. Banks was the only Coalition candidate to win a seat from the ALP in the 2016 election.

Table 2.1 The long campaign

Name/date	Event
Bill Shorten 29 October 2018	Address to the Lowy Institute, Sydney: 'The foreign policy of the next Labor Government'
Scott Morrison 19 November 2018	Bradfield Address, Sydney: migration limits, population policy and urban infrastructure
Bill Shorten 22 November 2018	Energy policy launch, Sydney, with Chris Bowen (Shadow Treasurer) and Mark Butler (Shadow Minister for Energy and Climate Change): emissions reductions, solar storage battery subsidy; NEG back on the table
Bill Shorten 16–18 December 2018	ALP National Conference, Adelaide: housing affordability theme
Treasurer Josh Frydenberg and Minister for Finance Mathias Cormann 17 December 2018	Mid-Year Economic and Fiscal Outlook (MYEFO) released: surplus foreshadowed by next financial year
Bill Shorten 14 January 2019	Announces $50 million for diabetes research; major funding boost for Kakadu National Park, Kakadu, Northern Territory (NT)
Scott Morrison 13 January 2019	Announces additional funding for Kakadu National Park (NT) and Australia Day citizenship policy at a press conference with Indigenous Country Liberal Party candidate Jacinta Price at Jabiru, which is surrounded by Kakadu
Scott Morrison 29 January 2019	Speech to Brothers Rugby Union Club, Brisbane: Coalition will deliver jobs and growth
Scott Morrison 11 February 2019	Address to National Press Club, Canberra: government to increase aged care funding by $662 million
Scott Morrison 5 March 2019	*Australian Financial Review* (*AFR*) Business Summit, Sydney: Labor would be bad for the economy
Bill Shorten 6 March 2019	*AFR* Business Summit speech, Sydney: next election would be a referendum on wages; ALP needed to work with business and unions
Bill Shorten 26 March 2019	'Living wage' policy press release
Bill Shorten 31 March 2019	Press release for 1 April: climate change, emissions reductions and waste strategies (Mark Butler's electric car target tweet the previous day)
Treasurer Josh Frydenberg 2 April 2019	Budget speech: infrastructure, tax cuts, support for business
Bill Shorten 4 April 2019	Budget reply speech: ALP opposed second and third stages of tax cuts; unveiled $2.3 billion cancer care package Address to Labor Business Forum, Canberra
Scott Morrison 5 April 2019	Royal Commission into Violence, Abuse, Neglect and Exploitation of People with Disability announced

Morrison, speaking after the resumption of parliament on 26 November, warned Shorten not to get too 'carried away' with the State election results, arguing the next federal election would be different—it would be Morrison versus Shorten. John Howard said Shorten was expecting a 'coronation' (Karp 2019). Morrison was active on the policy front— setting up an aged care royal commission (which commenced its work on 18 January 2019), dumping plans to raise the retirement age to 70 from 67 for aged pension eligibility, apologising in the parliament to victims of institutional child abuse and bringing Abbott and Joyce back into the fold with roving ambassadorial briefs for Indigenous affairs and the drought, respectively. The Commonwealth–State National Drought Summit was held at Old Parliament House in Canberra on 26 October 2018. Morrison's headland Project Sydney Bradfield Oration of 19 November (sponsored by Sydney's *Daily Telegraph*) supported limits on immigration and the bolstering of urban infrastructure in Sydney and north Queensland, among other places (see Morrison 2018).

Morrison attended to party discipline and, on 3 December, called a special meeting of the federal Parliamentary Liberal Party to change its rules to require a two-thirds majority to initiate any future leadership ballot. Morrison's Sydney Institute speech of 14 December 2018 promised to recognise West Jerusalem as the capital of Israel.

The ALP's national conference—postponed from July due to the clash with the Super Saturday by-elections—was held on 16–18 December 2018 in Adelaide—and in retrospect was a dress rehearsal for the ALP's 2019 policy launch on 5 May 2019. Social policies were highlighted, especially on housing affordability, and a compromise on refugees was announced (an increased intake overall but firm policy on strong borders). Shorten's set-piece speech was well received (e.g. Wright 2018). The conferral of life membership of the ALP on former prime ministers Kevin Rudd, Julia Gillard and Paul Keating foreshadowed their appearance at the ALP policy launch.

2019

Early in 2019, Morrison made policy announcements on jobs and economic growth, a boost to aged care expenditure, Indigenous education, emissions reduction and domestic violence, and attended a mosque open day. He established a review into 'best practices' for dealing with internal Liberal Party complaints, such as those over bullying; he cut permanent migration, gave a huge funding boost to regional infrastructure, including increased spending on Kakadu National Park and surrounding roads, and defended the Budget.

Most of these announcements were positive campaigning. There were two striking examples of the 'negative' Morrison: his address to the *Australian Financial Review* Business Summit (on 5 March), in which he made a scathing attack on Labor's economic credentials; and his appearance on the TV show *The Project* in late March, during which he attacked host Waleed Aly. Morrison was retaliating over Aly's recent claim that Morrison had used Islamophobia for political gain in 2010–11. In the wake of the Christchurch, New Zealand, terror attack of 15 March 2019, Morrison condemned anti-Muslim statements, denied the Coalition was anti-Muslim and saw to it that Liberal candidates who had made anti-Muslim comments were disendorsed.[17]

While candidates and preselection are discussed in Anika Gauja and Marija Taflaga's Chapter 4 (this volume), it is worthwhile mentioning Morrison's installation (via the NSW State Executive) of Indigenous business leader Warren Mundine in the marginal NSW coastal seat of Gilmore as a rare example of a questionable decision.[18]

The Nationals' Assistant Minister to the Deputy Prime Minister Andrew Broad resigned from the rural Victorian seat of Mallee in January 2019 following his resignation from the ministry (in December 2018) over a scandal exposed in the women's magazine *New Idea*. There were rumours that Bridget McKenzie, the Nationals' Deputy Leader, would resign from the Senate to contest Mallee or Indi; she had already moved her senate office to Wodonga in the electorate of Indi, from Bendigo (D'Agostino and Johnston 2018). Indi was held by popular Independent MP Cathy McGowan.

The results of the NSW State election on 23 March 2019 were more heartening for the federal Liberals, although not for their National Party counterparts, than the Victorian results, as the State Coalition government retained office. Subsequently, State ALP Leader Michael Daley was forced

---

17   He also carpeted the Turkish Ambassador over anti-Anzac comments made by the Turkish Prime Minister in response to the Christchurch shootings.

18   Gilmore had seen running factional battles between rival Liberal groups and, as an open seat, the National Party had endorsed a high-profile former MP. It was targeted by the ACTU as a potentially winnable seat.

to step down due to some historical anti-Asian remarks of his that had been recorded; it was some days before he announced he would not recontest. Labor went into the 2019 federal election campaign in New South Wales awkwardly, with a caretaker State leader.[19]

Ministerial retirements and new candidate picks dominated media discussion in the first quarter of 2019, as did speculation over whether various Turnbull-orientated Liberals would resign. Kelly O'Dwyer announced her intention to resign on Saturday, 19 January. Late the following week, Coalition ministers Michael Keenan and Nigel Scullion also announced they would not contest the upcoming election. Former Liberal MP for the marginal seat of Chisholm, Julia Banks, was running as an Independent for the Victorian seat of Flinders, which was held by Liberal Minister for Health, Greg Hunt—originally a 'moderate' but over time a supporter of conservatives Abbott and Dutton.[20] In February, former foreign minister and failed leadership contender Julie Bishop said she would not recontest the seat of Curtin (WA). The retirements of ministers Christopher Pyne and Steve Ciobo were confirmed on 2 March 2019, and former Army Reserve brigadier Linda Reynolds replaced Ciobo as Minister for Defence Industry on 4 March (and her shift to the Defence Ministry after the election, in place of Pyne, was foreshadowed). The Sunday papers featured Julie Bishop 'blaming' Pyne, as well as Mathias Cormann, for undermining her in the previous year's Liberal leadership ballot, claiming she would have been well-placed to win the May election (Spagnolo 2019). Former staunch Turnbull supporter and small business minister Craig Laundy announced his retirement in March—stepping down as the Member for Reid, which became an open seat and a venue for Coalition and Labor events. John Howard campaigned strongly on behalf of the new Liberal candidate in Reid, Fiona Martin (Clench 2019).

There were other high-profile announcements and retirements—notably, of Cathy McGowan, the Independent MP for Indi (announced via a tweet on 14 January). She had tweeted her successor's name, Helen Haines, the previous day. On 15 January, Rob Oakeshott (a former Independent

---

19   There were concerns about federal implications, especially for those seats with high proportions of Asian voters. The ALP's primary vote was 33 per cent and it won only two seats. The Coalition lost two National Party seats to the Shooters, Fishers and Farmers Party as part of a backlash over the problematic water policy.

20   Hunt supported Abbott in the 2015 Liberal Party leadership contest and Dutton in the 2019 Liberal leadership contest, from which Morrison emerged as Liberal leader.

Member for Lynne) stated via a video post on his website that he would run for the nearby seat of Cowper—sensing an opportunity with the sitting National Party MP retiring.

On the Labor side, Bill Shorten's campaign bus was launched, the ALP's National Executive signed off on factional picks for the 2019 election, Labor's primary vote in Newspoll fell from 41 to 38 and veteran ALP Senator Jacinta Collins announced she would not contest the next election, citing family and health reasons, and headed off to a senior role in the Catholic education sector.

As in late 2017 when Turnbull was briefly the prime minister of a minority government, Labor began to seize the political initiative. Shorten established a review of the recent catastrophic mass fish deaths in the Murray–Darling river system, commissioning the Australian Academy of Science to provide a timely report. Two days later, Morrison set up an independent inquiry into the fish deaths by the Commonwealth Agriculture Department.

The most significant example of governing while in opposition was the so-called Medevac legislation, which allowed the timely medical evacuation of ill people from Manus Island and Nauru, fulfilling a major campaigning plank of Phelps's and supported by Labor and the Independents on the Senate crossbench.[21] This was designed to be a humiliation for Morrison; instead, he gained the advantage, devising amendments to give power to the minister to assess transfers in a timely fashion. This was the first major occasion where Labor underestimated Morrison (Jensen 2019). Shortly after the Bill's passage at the beginning of March, Minister for Home Affairs Dutton reopened the asylum seeker camp on Christmas Island (off the north-west coast of Australia), predicting the arrival of many refugee boats now that medical transfers could easily guarantee entry to Australia.

Having announced its policies on excess franking credits (as amended) and negative gearing/capital gains tax discounts in 2018 and 2016, respectively, in February 2019, in the wake of the devastating banking royal commission's 'Hayne report', Labor announced its 'fairness fund' levy on banks. The levy would be used to support financial counselling for disadvantaged bank customers. *The Australian* newspaper labelled it a '$640 million hit on banks' (Brown 2019: 1).

---

21   Senators Hanson and Cory Bernardi opposed the 'Medevac' amendments to a government Bill in the Senate.

In March, Shorten and Chalmers said the election would be about wages, with the Fair Work Commission having a central role. The ALP's 'living wage' policy was released on 25 March 2019. It was attacked by the conservative IPA, which claimed it would push Australia into recession, and the negative gearing changes were also presented as a 'housing tax' that would create a bigger recession. Interestingly, the Chief Executive Officer of the Business Council of Australia (BCA), Jennifer Westacott, welcomed the living wage, and had earlier supported an increase in Newstart, alongside the Minerals Council of Australia.

At his speech to the *AFR* Business Summit in early March, Shorten pushed fair wages as his theme and accused the Prime Minister of denigrating workers in his speech the previous day; Shorten invoked the Hawke–Keating accord era while stepping away from a formal accord himself (see Table 2.1).

Labor fell in with the decision of the Coalition's Expenditure Review Committee (ERC) to restrict annual migration to 160,000, replacing the previous cap of 190,000 per annum. The Coalition would also develop an integrated settlement policy to ease congestion in Melbourne and Sydney. Labor reluctantly agreed while attacking the announcement as 'dog whistling'.

The leaking of footage showing PHON's Steve Dickson and James Ashby in the United States the previous September appearing to solicit a large donation from the National Rifle Association (NRA) was shown on Australian television in March; Bill Shorten questioned the Coalition's preferencing policy, while Morrison responded two days later, recommending Liberals preference PHON below Labor (Worthington 2019). Those LNP politicians in the National Party room, however, indicated they would not preference Labor above PHON.

The Greens (2019) outlined their environment policy in late March, foreshadowed by their Environment Spokesperson, Adam Bandt, depicting coal as the 'modern-day asbestos' (Brown 2018b). Former Greens leader Bob Brown led the anti-Adani convoy, arriving in Brisbane on 22 April for a rally outside Adani's offices: 'Ahead of the march, Brown hit out at media reports detailing posts made by a commenter on a private Facebook page likening people who support the Adani mine to "Nazis who worked in gas chambers"' (Layt 2019).

On 1 April, Shorten officially announced a new strategy on climate change, emissions targets and waste, building on the party's 2018 national platform (ALP 2018: 74–91).[22] The previous day, Shadow Minister for Climate Change and Energy, Mark Butler (2019), had tweeted the ALP's historic electric car policy: 50 per cent of new cars would be electric by 2030. The electric car policy and its costings provided a target for the Coalition.

The 'real' campaign: The 2019 Budget and the 2019 election campaign

The Treasurer's Budget speech on 2 April followed by his speech to the National Press Club on 3 April were well received and showed a degree of pragmatism—for example, by belatedly adding Newstart to the list of benefits to receive a special energy supplement payment of $75, in line with single pensioners.[23] The 'Budget bounce' of 2 percentage points was reflected in the next week's fortnightly Newspoll. The debate over the Budget marked the real beginning of the 2019 election campaign— notably, the delivery of the Budget was brought forward five to six weeks from the traditional date of the second Tuesday in May, to allow time for an election campaign for a late-May election. Morrison sought a mandate for the tax package, which, if the Coalition were re-elected, would be introduced immediately after the resumption of parliament. (On a different note, Morrison announced a royal commission into disability abuses at the end of Budget week.)

The ALP amended its taxation policy in line with some of the Budget surprises, such as the Coalition ditching the Budget repair levy for high-income earners, but retained the essentials of the tax policy taken to the 2018 ALP conference—notably, providing additional tax relief to those earning less than $40,000 (Shorten 2018).

A new expenditure item was the cancer care package, which became a theme of Labor's campaign strategy and a target for Frydenberg's attacks on the ALP's lack of economic credibility.

---

22 Shorten had pre-released the press statement on 31 March.
23 See ABC (2019a). Morrison ultimately blamed being in a minority government.

The expected election announcement did not happen on the weekend of 6–7 April; however, a few days later, Morrison said the Liberals would not run election advertisements on Good Friday, Easter Sunday or Anzac Day; Shorten agreed not to advertise on Good Friday or Anzac Day. Morrison announced the election on 11 April (see Table 2.2), releasing a video (Fernando and Palin 2019) and making a strong speech, which consolidated his recent Budget statements while repeating a strong negative line on Labor's policies (variants of this approach were replayed throughout the campaign by Morrison and were echoed by Treasurer Frydenberg [Lewis and Riordan 2019]):

> There is a clear choice … that will determine the economy that Australians live in, not just for the next three years but for the next decade … between the government that is delivering a strong economy and will continue to do so, or Bill Shorten's Labor party that we always know can't manage money, [between] lowering taxes for all Australians [and] Bill Shorten's Labor party that will impose higher taxes that will weigh down our economy. It's taken more than five years to turn around Labor's budget mess. Now is not the time to turn back. (ABC 2019b)

Labor responded with Shorten announcing via tweet a 'fair go' election and Deputy Leader Tanya Plibersek (2019) counteracting Morrison's claims regarding Labor's economic credentials and calculating that the mooted surplus would be built on a gross underspend in the National Disability Insurance Scheme (NDIS).

Table 2.2 The 'real' campaign

Name	Date	Event
Scott Morrison	11 April 2019	Visits Governor-General to call an election, Canberra. Speech: 'A strong economy' and 'lower … taxes' with the Coalition; 'Labor can't manage money' and will introduce 'higher taxes' (ABC 2019b).
Bill Shorten	11 April 2019	Tweet from Melbourne's Moonee Ponds: 'Bring it on! The "fair go" election'
Tanya Plibersek (Deputy Labor Leader)	11 April 2019	Media interview in Melbourne: Labor can manage the economy; Coalition's projected surplus for 2019–20 based on serious NDIS underspend
Independents	12 April 2019	NSW Liberal Party complaint to the Australian Electoral Commission alleging orchestration of the funding of four Independents: Zali Stegall (Warringah), Kerryn Phelps (Wentworth), Julia Banks (Flinders), Oliver Yates (Kooyong)

Name	Date	Event
Peter Dutton (Minister for Home Affairs/ Liberal candidate for Dickson)	13 April 2019	Apologises for 'gaffe' about disabled ALP candidate for Dickson, Ali France
Bill Shorten	14 April 2019	Rally for ALP volunteers, with Tanya Plibersek, Senator Kristina Keneally (former ALP NSW Premier), Chris Bowen (Shadow Treasurer) and Senator Penny Wong (Labor Leader in the Senate), Burwood, Sydney (seat of Reid): outlining local effects of ALP health policy, such as major upgrade of Concord Hospital, and defending tax changes — critiquing 'retiree tax' label
Bill Shorten	20 April 2019	Press release: attacking social media scare campaign about alleged Labor 'death tax'
Mathias Cormann (Minister for Finance and Liberal Senate Leader)	26 April 2019	Liberal preferences would not go to Fraser Anning (selected as a replacement for PHON's Malcolm Roberts, he became an Independent, subsequently joining KAP, from which he was expelled in October 2018 for his controversial inaugural speech)
Bill Shorten and Tanya Plibersek	26 April 2019	Labor's Women's Policy launch, Women's Hospital, Melbourne
Bill Shorten	28 April 2019	'Fair Go for Australia' rally, Box Hill, Melbourne: childcare support package, dental care for children and pensioner/health cards
Scott Morrison	28 April 2019	Western Sydney 'Congestion busting' rally at Homebush Stadium (seat of Reid), with NSW Premier, Gladys Berejiklian, and former prime minister John Howard
First Leaders' Debate	29 April 2019	Perth. Shorten won 52:12 of the audience vote; 11 were undecided
Pauline Hanson	30 April 2019	Steve Dickson resigns from PHON over release of secretly recorded footage of him meeting with NRA in New York. Hanson's tearful interview on Channel Nine's *A Current Affair* and other TV programs
Warringah Debate between Tony Abbott and Zali Steggall	2 May 2019	No winner declared; both seen by audience members as energetic and enthusiastic, and Steggall seen as the frontrunner in the campaign
Second Leaders' Debate	3 May 2019	Brisbane. Shorten won 43:41 of the audience vote; 16 were undecided
Bill Shorten	5 May 2019	ALP policy launch, 'A Fair Go', Brisbane: focus on health, tax cuts for small business, constitutional recognition for Indigenous Australians
	7 May 2019	'Mother of invention' front-page *Daily Telegraph* [Sydney] story accuses Shorten of omitting key facts from his election launch story about his mother's sacrifices for her family

Name	Date	Event
Third Leaders' Debate	8 May 2019	National Press Club, Canberra: testy exchanges between Shorten and Morrison
Scott Morrison	12 May 2019, Mother's Day	Liberal Party policy launch, 'Building Our Economy, Securing Your Future', Melbourne: major new promise of deposit guarantee scheme for first homebuyers (matched by Labor); attacks on Labor's so-called housing tax
Election day	16 May 2019	Melbourne's *Herald Sun* releases YouGov/Galaxy polls for 10 marginal seats showing outcome tightening and Liberals leading in Deakin and Flynn

At this stage, Morrison and Frydenberg were focusing on the economy, allowing resources minister Matt Canavan (see Doran and Sweeney 2019) and home affairs minister Peter Dutton to probe Labor's divisions over the Adani coalmine, which was proposed for the Galilee Basin in central Queensland (SBS 2019). While ALP Shadow Assistant Treasurer Andrew Leigh was sharply critical of Adani, Deputy Leader Tanya Plibersek was more nuanced, maintaining she and the party were sceptical, believing the benefits were 'overstated' and the detrimental environmental impacts 'understated' (quoted in Doran and Sweeney 2019). The ALP Member for Herbert (Qld), Cathy O'Toole (ABC 2019c), was a rare Labor voice defending Adani.

Based on the national published polls—especially their two-party-preferred vote—a united team and the careful development of a suite of policies over several years, Labor appeared to be in the ascendancy, whereas the Coalition had endured two leadership changes, disaffected frontbenchers and backbenchers and several scandals. There were few policy achievements and, arguably, the passage of the same-sex marriage legislation in December 2017—and the preceding postal survey—was forced on the Coalition.

The campaign effected a reversal, with the Coalition setting a clear agenda: to continue the approach started by Morrison late in 2018. The Coalition's main theme was set from the start: there was a stark choice between the Coalition, with its consistent track record on managing the economy and introducing lower taxes, and Labor's record of failing to manage the economy and introducing higher taxes. This theme was a continuation of the Coalition's line from early 2019, if not earlier. Labor was on the defensive from early in the campaign (see Zappavigna et al. 2019).

Both leaders—as discussed in other chapters of this volume—crafted policy announcements relevant to the specific location, and campaign expenditure focused on marginal seats (see Table 2.2 for key campaign events, the debates, party launches and themes). Labor (Shorten 2019) had committed to a strong women's policy compared with the Coalition.

The three formal debates were opportunities for both sides to press their policies and showcase their leadership styles. Shorten was 'engaging' well, especially in the first two debates, in which he opted for a personalised approach. Morrison seemed to have a checklist of issues to cover in these debates, such as franking credits, Labor's taxes and border protection (DailyBulletin.com.au 2019). His eagerness to expose Shorten's lack of economic credibility—as in the zinger question about the cost of electric vehicles in the first debate—did not resonate with the audience. Shorten's response was to frame Morrison as a leader who could not be trusted due to the preference deal with Clive Palmer's UAP announced a few days earlier. Shorten asked whether Palmer would be the next prime minister.

For the two debates on free-to-air television, audience figures were considerably higher than in 2016, suggesting a higher level of citizen engagement than was generally expected; the second debate, on *Sky News* (and *Night Sky*), compered by David Speers, had much lower figures but was rebroadcast on social media (see Moran and Rota 2019; Dyers 2019).

Shorten's personalised style was on display towards the end of his official policy launch on 5 May when he invoked his mother's story of hardship as inspiring his commitment to 'a fair go'. Sydney's *Daily Telegraph* ridiculed Shorten's depiction of his mother under the very negative headline of 'Mother of invention', which generated controversy, as the other Murdoch-owned tabloids had chosen not to run the story. Arguably Shorten's strongest speech was his concession speech on election night (ABC 2019d).

The Coalition's policy launch was held on the final Sunday of the campaign, in line with the longstanding convention that ministers may not claim travelling allowances from that day. The Mother's Day theme featured MP Sarah Henderson from the marginal Victorian seat of Corangamite (notionally Labor after the 2018 redistribution). Morrison's motto was 'Building our economy, securing your future'. He recited well-used themes, such as Labor's 'housing tax', and introduced a new deposit guarantee scheme for first homebuyers (immediately matched by Labor).

Morrison's quiet launch in Melbourne, with his immediate family and senior ministers, contrasted with Shorten's political family of colleagues and former Labor prime ministers—missing Bob Hawke, who was ill and passed away a week or so later. Kevin Rudd campaigned in Queensland. Former Liberal prime minister John Howard campaigned actively alongside Morrison and various marginal-seat MPs, saying Shorten would be the 'most left-wing Prime Minister since world war two' (Karp 2019).

The Labor team had spent much of the campaign on a defensive footing—defending its record on the economy, publicising its 'fairness' agenda and trying to explain its tax 'loopholes' reform as part of that fairness. Good policies were lost in the narrowcasting of the agenda by the Coalition, and other policies were criticised or dismissed—for example, in claims that Labor's free cancer treatment policy was ill advised as public treatment was already free, or that the electric car proposal was dictatorial and would be expensive, wasteful of energy and involve costly recharging stations. Even after the ALP costings were approved by the Parliamentary Budget Office on Friday, 10 May, Frydenberg and others airily dismissed the open-ended nature of the ALP's energy plan.

References

Australian Broadcasting Corporation (ABC). 2019a. 'Scott Morrison: Interview with Leigh Sales'. *7.30*, [ABC TV], 3 April.

Australian Broadcasting Corporation (ABC). 2019b. 'Prime Minister Scott Morrison calls election for May 18'. *ABC News*, 11 April. www.abc.net.au/news/2019-04-11/prime-minister-scott-morrison-calls-election/10991796.

Australian Broadcasting Corporation (ABC). 2019c. '"I welcome jobs to this city": Labor MP gives tacit approval to Adani mine'. *ABC News*, 2 May. www.abc.net.au/news/2019-05-02/cathy-otoole-on-adani-mine/11065730.

Australian Broadcasting Corporation (ABC). 2019d. 'Bill Shorten concedes defeat'. *ABC News*, 19 May. www.abc.net.au/news/2019-05-19/bill-shorten-concedes-defeat/11127302.

Australian Labor Party (ALP). 2018. *National Platform: A Fair Go for Australia*. Canberra: ALP.

Brown, Greg. 2018a. 'Politics now blog'. *The Australian*, 24 May. www.theaustralian.com.au/nation/politics/politicsnow-live-news-from-the-house-of-reps-the-senate/news-story/433beea4fed775419fe45ec8271a3f9c.

Brown, Greg. 2018b. 'Greens bid to outlaw thermal coal trade'. *The Australian*, 16 November. www.theaustralian.com.au/nation/politics/greens-bid-to-outlaw-thermal-coal-trade/news-story/139df9ecb034f699f81215eef0e32cae.

Brown, Greg. 2019. 'Shorten to hit banks with levy for $64 million'. *The Australian*, 25 February: 1.

Butler, Mark. 2019. 'BREAKING: Labor will implement OZ's first national electric vehicle policy …'. Twitter, 1 April. twitter.com/mark_butler_mp/status/1112435605588185088?lang=en.

Canberra Liberals. 2019. *Labor will tax you to death*. Election leaflet. Canberra: Canprint Communications.

Carey, Adam. 2018. 'Greens late pitch for conservatives'. *The Age*, [Melbourne], 17 March: 4.

Chalmers, Jim. 2019. Twitter feed, 19 February. twitter.com/JEChalmers/status/1098125063524515840.

Clench, Sam. 2019. 'John Howard makes awkward admission while campaigning in marginal Sydney seat'. *News.com.au*, 26 April. www.news.com.au/national/federal-election/john-howard-makes-awkward-admission-while-campaigning-in-marginal-sydney-seat/news-story/e7fb8a8b5d01019f437b417db556556a.

Creighton, Adam. 2019. 'IPA says living wage will push Australia in recession direction'. *The Australian*, 1 April: 5.

D'Agostino, Emma and David Johnston. 2018. 'Senator Bridget McKenzie to move office from Bendigo to Wodonga in 2019'. *Bendigo Advertiser*, 24 October. www.bendigoadvertiser.com.au/story/5720062/senior-liberal-fumes-over-bridget-mckenzies-office-move/.

DailyBulletin.com.au. 2019. 'Australian news: First leaders' debate'. [Transcript of the debate between Scott Morrison and Bill Shorten, Perth, 29 April]. NewsCompany.com.au. www.dailybulletin.com.au/news/44924-prime-minister-transcript-leaders-debate.

Doran, Matthew and Lucy Sweeney. 2019. 'Federal election 2019 live: Scott Morrison says voters have "clear choice" at May 18 poll'. *ABC News*, 11 April. www.abc.net.au/news/2019-04-11/federal-election-live-scott-morrison-calls-may-18-election-date/10968588.

Dyers, Glenn. 2019. 'Leaders' debate brings in the viewers (just don't ask Sky)'. *Crikey*, 9 May. www.crikey.com.au/2019/05/09/glenn-dyers-tv-ratings-581/.

Fernando, Gavin and Megan Palin. 2019. 'Prime Minister Scott Morrison confirms May 18 election date'. *News.com.au*, 15 April. www.news.com.au/finance/economy/federal-budget/federal-election-2019-what-you-need-to-know/newsstory/33eeb154fd2a407adf0f505d2d9173d4.

Foster, Brendan. 2016. 'After a comical start, Labor looks set for a romp in the seat of Fremantle'. *Sydney Morning Herald*, 8 June.

Gauja, Anika, Peter Chen, Jennifer Curtin and Juliet Pietsch. eds. 2018. *Double Disillusion: The 2016 Australian Federal Election*. Canberra: ANU Press. doi.org/10.22459/DD.04.2018.

High Court of Australia. 2017. *Submissions of the Hon. Barnaby Joyce MP*. 28 September. No. C15 of 2017. www.hcourt.gov.au/assets/cases/03-Canberra/c11-2017/Joyce_Submissions.pdf.

Jensen, Erik. 2019. 'The Prosperity Gospel: How Scott Morrison Won and Bill Shorten Lost'. *Quarterly Essay* 74: 1–71.

Johnson, Carol, John Wanna with Hsu-Ann Lee. eds. 2015. *Abbott's Gambit: The 2013 Australian Federal Election*. Canberra: ANU Press. doi.org/10.22459/AG.01.2015.

Karp, Paul. 2019. 'Shorten pledges billions for seniors' dental bills, childcare and educators' wage rise'. *The Guardian*, 28 April. www.theguardian.com/Australia-news/2019/apr/28/shorten-pledges-billions-for-seniors-dental-bills-childcare-and-educators-wage-rise.

Kelly, Paul. 2019. 'Banking report to provide "framework" for next election'. *The Australian*, 5 February: 1.

Layt, Stuart. 2019. 'We come in peace: Bob Brown says as thousands march in anti-Adani caravan'. *Brisbane Times*, 22 April. www.brisbanetimes.com.au/national/queensland/we-come-in-peace-bob-brown-says-as-thousands-march-in-anti-adani-caravan-20190422-p51g7i.html.

Lewis, Rosie and Primrose Riordan. 2019. 'Federal election 2019, campaign day 26'. *The Australian*, 7 May. www.theaustralian.com.au/nation/politics/federal-election-2019-campaign-day-26-bill-shorten-battles-newspoll-hit/news-story/0746ab1062e0153105f87dbb33d5c3dd.

McIlroy, Tom. 2019. 'The politics of banker bashing'. *Australian Financial Review*, 9–10 February: 17.

Marr, David. 2015. 'Faction Man: Bill Shorten's Path to Power'. *Quarterly Essay* 59: 1–109.

Moran, Robert and Genevieve Rota. 2019. 'Secondary coverage, primary interest for first election debate on Seven'. *Sydney Morning Herald*, 30 April.

Morrison, Scott. 2018. 'Project Sydney Bradfield Oration, Sydney, 19 November'. *YouTube*. www.youtube.com/watch?v=NCf8pK0NHk8.

'Radio interview—RN Drive Victoria—Thursday, 11 April 2019'. [Transcript]. www.tanyaplibersek.com/transcript_tanya_plibersek_radio_interview_rn_drive_victoria_thursday_11_april_2019.

Savva, Niki. 2019. *Plots and Prayers: Malcolm Turnbull's Demise and Scott Morrison's Ascension*. Melbourne: Scribe Press.

Shorten, Bill. 2018. 'A Fair Go for Australia, 15 December'. *YouTube*. www.youtube.com/watch?v=t_85rtWgaH0.

Shorten, Bill. 2019. 'Australian Women: Labor's Plan for Equality, Policy launch, Melbourne, 26 April'. www.billshorten.com.au/launch_of_australian_women_labor_s_plan_for_equality_melbourne_friday_26_april_2019.

Spagnolo, Joe. 2019. 'Julie Bishop: I was Liberals' best bet to beat Bill Shorten in federal election'. *West Australian* [Perth], 2 March. thewest.com.au/politics/federal-politics/julie-bishop-i-was-liberals-best-bet-to-beat-bill-shorten-in-federal-election-ng-b881123326z.

Special Broadcasting Service (SBS). 2019. 'Take politics out of Adani mine: Plibersek'. *SBS News*, 11 April. www.sbs.com.au/news/take-politics-out-of-adani-mine-plibersek.

Taggart, Paul. 2002. 'Populism and the pathology of representative politics'. In *Democracies and the Populist Challenge*, edited by Yves Meny and Yves Surel, 62–80. London: Palgrave Macmillan. doi.org/10.1057/9781403920072_4.

The Greens. 2019. *Renewable Economy & Climate Change*. Canberra: The Greens. greens.org.au/platform/renewables#repower.

#THETRUTHMATTERS. 2018. Longman by-election billboard.

White, Isobel. 2015. 'Regulation of candidates' campaign expenditure: The long and the short of it'. 14 January. London: House of Commons Library. commonslibrary.parliament.uk/parliament-and-elections/elections-elections/regulation-of-candidates-campaign-expenditure-the-long-and-the-short-of-it/.

Worthington, Brett. 2019. 'Scott Morrison confirms Liberals will preference One Nation lower than Labor at federal election'. *ABC News*, 28 March. www.abc.net.au/news/2019-03-28/one-nation-will-be-preferenced-lower-than-labor-pm-announces/10947720.

Wright, Tony. 2018. 'Don't blow this—not now: Bill Shorten's message at Labor's quasi election launch'. *Sydney Morning Herald*, 16 December. www.smh.com.au/politics/federal/don-t-blow-this-not-now-bill-shorten-s-message-at-labor-s-quasi-election-launch-20181216-p50mkn.htm.

Zappavigna, Adrianna, James Hall and AAP. 2019. 'Workers losing hundreds over Easter: Bill Shorten's pledge to restore penalty rates'. *News.com.au*, 20 April. www.news.com.au/national/politics/workers-losing-hundreds-over-easter-bill-shortens-pledge-to-restore-penalty-rates/news-story/f0f39240e58898d101eb4c3fdcc04900.

Ziffer, Daniel. 2019. *A Wunch of Bankers: A Year in the Hayne Royal Commission*. Melbourne: Scribe Press.

3

THE RULES OF THE GAME

Marian Sawer and Michael Maley

In 2019 the federal election campaign was awash with money as never before, prompting many to wonder whether billionaires could now buy elections in Australia and what exactly were the rules of the game. The money bought an onslaught of negative advertising and resulted in a substantial number of complaints to the Australian Electoral Commission (AEC). It prompts questions about how far Australia is now lagging behind best practice in the regulation of campaign finance and other aspects of electioneering in the digital age. As we shall see in this chapter, there are a number of ways in which Australia departs from the principles of the 'level playing field' for electoral competition, as laid down in international guidelines.

The *Commonwealth Electoral Act 1918* (the *Electoral Act*) has been the vehicle for some of Australia's most distinctive electoral reforms, including compulsory voting, preferential voting, single transferable vote proportional representation for Senate elections, independent electoral administration and a process for the redistribution of electoral boundaries that is widely recognised as one of the world's best. From its original length of 62 pages, the Act has grown over the century to its current length of 639 pages. Its growth reflects the increasing complexity of electoral processes but also a lack of trust that political parties will comply with the rules unless they are laid down in great legislative detail. In some areas, however, regulation has retreated—for example, the original limits on campaign expenditure were finally withdrawn in 1980.

Our aim here is not to describe the whole of the regulatory framework for the election, but rather to focus on parts that have been the subject of controversy and a focus for reform efforts. We will not include elements that are important but relatively uncontroversial, such as the redistribution process, which is covered in Chapter 9 of this volume. We deal with enrolment, political party registration, candidate nomination (and disendorsement), campaign funding and advertising, and early voting. We conclude with some reflections on current trends in federal electoral reform.

Enrolment

In April 2019, the AEC announced it had achieved 'the best electoral roll in history', with 96.8 per cent of eligible voters (more than 16 million) now enrolled.[1] Youth enrolment had also reached its highest level, with an estimated 88.8 per cent of eligible 18–24-year-olds enrolled (AEC 2019a).

That achievement was driven by major changes in the preceding 10 years. Prior to 2009, there was an antiquated system whereby names could be added to the electoral roll only after receipt of a hardcopy electoral enrolment form completed by the claimant. Then, in September 2009, an online 'SmartForm' was introduced, which could be downloaded from the AEC website, although it still had to be signed and lodged manually. Next, in July 2010, a process was introduced whereby a person already on the roll could update their details online, without having to lodge a hardcopy form. At last, in 2012, the *Electoral Act* was amended to permit the AEC to update electors' details on the roll and to add new electors to the roll without receiving an enrolment form from the elector at all. This represented a fundamental shift from the system that had applied for about a century and that had placed the onus on voters to get on the roll and update their details when they moved address. In 2019, approximately two-thirds of all electoral enrolment was done by the AEC (see Chapter 12, this volume).

---

1   It should be noted that an enrolment of 96 per cent of eligible voters was already claimed in 1903—the highest enrolment of a national population anywhere for democratic purposes—but it was admitted at the subsequent conference of Commonwealth electoral officers that there had been some overenrolment in two States (Sawer 2003: 53).

While the Liberal and National parties opposed the 2012 reforms in the parliament, the relevant provisions of the *Electoral Act* have been left untouched since the return of the Coalition to power in 2013, and it seems unlikely that attempts will be made to wind them back. Indeed, the Joint Standing Committee on Electoral Matters (JSCEM) has recommended, among other things, that the *Electoral Act* be amended 'to allow for online enrolment in all enrolment circumstances, provided that an appropriate digital identity verification process is in place' (JSCEM 2018b: 41).

Apart from improvements through the provision of online and automatic enrolment, there was a surge in youth enrolment before the 2017 same-sex marriage postal survey. While there was speculation that having a more complete roll would result in lower turnout (the percentage of people on the roll who actually vote), in fact the 2019 (House) turnout of 91.9 per cent was greater than the 91 per cent achieved in 2016.

Political party registration

There was widespread concern over the success at the 2013 Senate election of 'micro-parties' with little community support, such as the Australian Motoring Enthusiasts Party, which won a Senate seat in Victoria despite gaining only 0.5 per cent of the first-preference votes. The majority of the votes that elected these micro-party candidates came from supporters of other parties and were collected through a 'preference harvesting' strategy first attempted at the 1999 NSW Legislative Council election.

While the 2016 reforms to the Senate voting system (which abolished the group voting ticket system) put a stop to preference harvesting, the number of registered political parties did not drop between 2016 and 2019. New parties registered since the 2016 election include Love Australia or Leave (with a registered logo of a map of Australia stamped 'Full') and the Involuntary Medication Objectors (Vaccination/Fluoride) Party. The application fee for party registration has remained at $500, and the number of members required in support of an application has remained at 500. The provision made in the *Electoral Act* for an existing federal parliamentarian to be able to apply to register a party without meeting a requirement for a minimum number of party members has, however, looked increasingly anomalous.

When party registration was introduced in 1984, there was an assumption that any MPs or senators making an application for party registration would previously have been elected in their own right. The rate at which senators have recently been leaving the parties through which they were elected was not envisaged. Senator Fraser Anning provides a striking example: he was elected on the ticket of Pauline Hanson's One Nation (PHON) following the disqualification of Senator Malcolm Roberts in 2017 but decided to enter the Senate as an Independent. He then joined Katter's Australian Party (KAP) for a few months in 2018 but was expelled after making a widely criticised speech in the Senate in which he referred to the 'final solution to the immigration problem'. Because he was a senator, he was able to register Fraser Anning's Conservative National Party without any membership requirement and ran unsuccessfully for it in 2019. The JSCEM recommended in its report on the 2016 election that this anomaly be done away with, but it was still in existence in 2019.

Candidates and nominations

Typically, it is only at election time that details of electoral regulation are of much interest to the media and the public. However, the departure from the parliament of seven MPs and eight senators in 2017–18 as a result of breaches of Section 44 of the constitution, whether because they were found to be dual citizens or for other reasons, figured prominently in the news.

The various rulings of the High Court on the interpretation of Section 44 have served to clarify the law to some extent, but there are points that remain unclear. In particular, the mechanism applied in the case of a disqualified senator, under which the ballots are recounted as though the departed senator had never been on the ballot, means it is possible for another senator whose qualification is undisputed to fail to be elected in the recount (Bonham 2017). It is unclear at this point whether the High Court would declare such 'unelection' to be legally possible or whether it would instead treat such a senator's position as being beyond dispute.

While more senators than MPs lost their seats, the political impact of Section 44 was felt primarily in the House of Representatives, as previous High Court rulings meant the House vacancies had to be filled through by-elections—with seven ultimately held in an eight-month period—rather than a recount process. Of particular significance was the 'Super Saturday' of voting on 28 July 2018. This saw the government poll poorly in the Queensland seat of Longman, which was a catalyst for the removal of Malcolm Turnbull as prime minister, and a further by-election following his resignation from parliament, at which his seat of Wentworth was lost to an Independent (see Chapter 2, this volume).

The travails arising from Section 44 generated much debate and an inquiry and report by the JSCEM (2018a). One outcome was an amendment to the *Electoral Act*, requiring candidates to provide 'qualification checklists' to the AEC, covering in much more detail than previously anything that could impact on their qualification under Section 44. The checklists must be published, but the AEC has no power to reject a nomination on the strength of shortcomings in the checklist or associated documents, as long as all 'mandatory questions' in the checklist have been answered. On 24 April 2019, the AEC (2019b) did, however, announce in relation to a WA Senate candidate, Rodney Culleton, that given his previous disqualification by the High Court, it was referring his nomination form to the Australian Federal Police to examine whether a false statement had been made concerning his status as an undischarged bankrupt.

The mechanisms by which a challenge to a candidate's qualification may be put before the High Court have also been clarified in a 2018 case (*Alley v Gillespie*). The only processes for obtaining a High Court ruling now are a petition to the Court of Disputed Returns following an election or a referral from the relevant House of the parliament. In the final week of sittings of the 45th Parliament, each House adopted a bipartisan resolution setting out procedures to be followed before making such a referral. The effect of those would be to limit the court's involvement to cases referred on the basis of fresh information not disclosed in the relevant qualification checklist.

In the aftermath of the election, there was speculation on social media about whether the disqualification of a *defeated* candidate could be the basis for challenging an election in the Court of Disputed Returns. That scenario has been examined in detail by Graeme Orr (2015) and is highly unlikely.

Finally, it is noteworthy that 1,056 candidates stood for the House of Representatives in 2019—an increase from the 994 who stood in 2016. They were not deterred by the increase shortly before the election in the deposit required of candidates, raising it from $1,000 to $2,000 and bringing it into line with that payable by Senate candidates.

Disendorsements

The 2019 election was also notable for the number of cases in which a candidate whose endorsement by a party had been announced was subsequently 'disendorsed'. According to a running tally compiled by Kevin Bonham (2019), 33 intending candidates were disendorsed, resigned or withdrew from the election after it was announced, with 10 of those cases arising only after the close of nominations. A substantial number of the cases that arose before the close of nominations were the result of difficulties the candidates faced in confirming that they were not disqualified under Section 44. The cases arising after the close, on the other hand, flowed mainly from the discovery of sexist, anti-Muslim or homophobic statements they had made on social media. Bonham has argued plausibly that the onerous nature of Section 44 checking may have left party organisations with less time and fewer resources to check candidates' social media history thoroughly enough. High-profile casualties included (before the close of nominations) a former ALP MP for Fremantle and Commonwealth minister Melissa Parke; and (after the close) the Queensland leader of PHON and former State MP and minister, Steve Dickson.

The full implications of the disendorsement of a candidate after the close of nominations are not, however, clear. The *Electoral Act* makes no provision for such a step; a statement of disendorsement at that stage is essentially a political rather than a legal act. A candidate so 'disendorsed' remains on the ballot paper and is still shown as the candidate of the disendorsing party. In addition, votes for the candidate are still treated as votes for the party in the vote totals published by the AEC. A question the disendorsing parties generally left up in the air was how their disendorsed candidates would be treated post election should they win. As it happened, only one of the disendorsed candidates—the erstwhile Liberal candidate in Lyons—was running in a seat that the disendorsing party had any real chance of winning, and she did not in fact win.

Campaigning and electoral funding

The election was marked by an unusual level of controversy surrounding campaign activities and spending, electoral advertising and its authorisation and the level of regulation of such activities. Public funding for parties and candidates who received more than 4 per cent of the vote was introduced at the federal level in 1984 but failed in the objective of reducing party reliance on private funding. Under legislation enacted in 2018, the amount of public funding is currently $2.801 per vote or the amount of electoral expenditure, whichever is lower. The role of private money in Australian elections was highlighted by the ubiquitous campaign presence of billionaire Clive Palmer, founder and leader of the United Australia Party (UAP). With expenditure that dwarfed that of the major parties, he was able to flood the print media, airwaves, social media and billboards with his advertising. As Nielsen data show, between 1 September 2018 and 18 May 2019, Palmer spent $53.6 million on television, radio and newspaper advertising alone, while the Liberal Party spent $14.5 million and Labor $13.3 million (Figure 3.1).

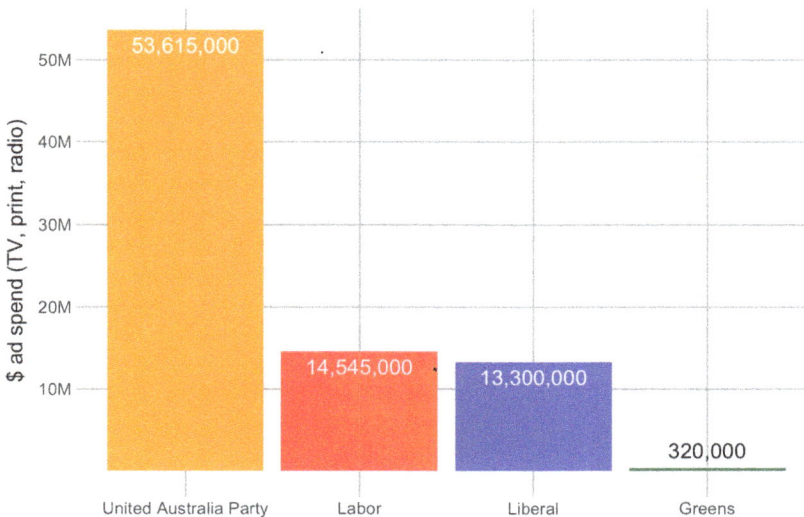

Figure 3.1 Political party advertising spending, 1 September 2018 – 18 May 2019

Source: Nielsen Ad Intel Portfolio, TV, print and radio ad spend, 1 September 2018 – 18 May 2019. Courtesy Nielsen.

In the final two weeks of the campaign, this was mostly negative advertising directed against Labor, using slogans such as 'Labor will hit us with an extra trillion dollars of taxes & costs. Tell Shifty he's dreaming.' Although Palmer's party polled only 3.4 per cent of the vote in the House of Representatives, with many candidates losing their deposits, he claimed success in defeating the ALP through the effect of his advertising and preference flows.

As noted above, since 1980, Australia has had no limits on campaign expenditure at the federal level, unlike most countries in the Organisation for Economic Co-operation and Development (OECD). Neither does it have limits on political donations at the federal level. Declared donations of more than $40 million were made for the 2016 federal election, quite apart from donations below the (high) disclosure threshold (Wood and Griffiths 2018: 10, 34). A dampener was put on campaign finance reform by the 1992 High Court decision in the case of *Australian Capital Television Pty Ltd v Commonwealth* that the Hawke Government's attempt to ban paid political advertising in the electronic media contravened an implied freedom of political communication.

Subsequent cases have, however, confirmed that the High Court will not necessarily strike down reasonable (proportionate) regulation of political finance. In 2015 in *McCloy v New South Wales*, the court upheld a cap on political donations and a ban on political donations by property developers, finding that the restrictions on freedom of political communication were defensible in the light of the benefits of ensuring the integrity of the political system and 'equality of opportunity to participate in the exercise of political sovereignty'.

The constitutionality of regulating political donations was reaffirmed in April 2019 by the High Court in the case of *Spence v Queensland*. The Commonwealth Parliament had passed amendments to the *Electoral Act* to enable Commonwealth law to override the tighter regulation of political donations at the State or Territory level. This provision (Section 302CA) was overturned by the High Court and Queensland's ban on developer donations was upheld, despite an attempt by the plaintiff, former Queensland Liberal National Party president Gary Spence, to argue it burdened the freedom of political communication.

The lack of any restrictions on the amount of political expenditure or political donations at the federal level, despite the High Court's recent rulings, has given rise to perceptions among voters that government is run primarily for the benefit of 'a few big interests'. In 2019, as in 2016, 56 per cent of respondents to the Australian Election Study believed this (Cameron and McAllister 2019: 16). Indicative of how far Australia has fallen behind in regulating the role of private money in elections, the Perceptions of Electoral Integrity survey now places Australia 26th out of 33 OECD countries on the campaign finance dimension (Cameron and Wynter 2018: 172). Highly regulated industries are the largest donors, and spikes in donations occur when policy changes are proposed affecting industries such as gambling or mining (Wood and Griffiths 2018: 42–43). The 2018 Democracy 2025 survey, conducted well before Palmer's cash splash, found that, of possible reforms to rebuild trust, by far the strongest support was for limits on political donations and campaign expenditure (Stoker et al. 2018: 44).

Another change enacted at the end of 2018 (apart from the reintroduction of campaign expenditure as the basis for public funding) was the banning of 'foreign' donations of more than $100 made for the purpose of funding electoral expenditure. The registration of foreign lobbyists was also required. Otherwise, there was a continuing lack of transparency about the sources of many donations, due to the high threshold for disclosure and other loopholes, such as allowing the splitting of donations between different divisions of a party. Forty per cent of the money received by political parties at the 2016 election had no identifiable source (Wood and Griffiths 2018: 31). Timeliness also continued to be a problem, with disclosures only published in the February following the financial year in which they were made (that is, up to 18 months after the donation was made) rather than the 'real-time' disclosure being adopted in other jurisdictions such as Queensland.

The use of public resources for campaigning

The laissez-faire approach adopted at the federal level to the use of private money in elections also extends to the use of government and parliamentary resources for campaign purposes. This is contrary to international standards that specify that party regulation should prevent incumbent parties or candidates from using state resources to obtain an unfair advantage (OSCE 2011). In Australia, incumbent governments regularly benefit from the use of government advertising for partisan purposes and spikes in such advertising occur in the run-up to elections. While guidelines in place since 2008 require campaigns to be objective and not directed at promoting party-political interests, this has done little to stop the use of emotive language and images to foster a positive impression of the incumbent government. In 2019, the government engaged in saturation advertising of its infrastructure programs and tax reforms in the period before the issue of the writs. For example: 'The Australian Government is building a better tax system, so hard-working Australians can keep more of their money' (Australian Government Campaign: bettertax.gov. au/campaign.html). There are also important benefits from the pork-barrelling associated with discretionary grants programs. It was estimated that, in the marginal Victorian seat of Corangamite, 41 promises were made on behalf of the Liberal candidate, adding up to $26,500 per voter (Wright and Irvine 2019; see also Chapter 11, this volume).

One use of parliamentary resources for political campaigning that was extraordinary even by relatively loose Australian standards was the setting up of a parliamentary inquiry into the opposition's tax reform policy. This was the House of Representatives Economics Committee inquiry into the implications of removing refundable tax credits, begun in September 2018. The chair set up a website in the committee's name, stoptheretirementtax. com, and used Twitter to direct people 'worried about Labor's retirement tax' to register on the website to attend hearings and make statements. Initially, those wishing to register were required to sign a petition opposing the Labor policy. The well-attended townhall-style meetings held around Australia at public expense proved highly successful in reframing Labor's proposed reform as a 'retirement' or 'retiree' tax. The committee's chair, Tim Wilson, justified his use of parliamentary resources by saying that the 'parliamentary purpose' was to 'campaign against a piece of policy' (Evershed and Knaus 2019).

Apart from this somewhat exceptional use of a parliamentary committee, all incumbent parliamentarians also benefit from resources such as electorate staff and parliamentary allowances. Many also benefit from 'personal employees'—staff employed under the *Members of Parliament (Staff) Act 1984 (MOP(S) Act)*. These 'personal employees' are normally employed by ministers, office holders, shadow ministers and former leaders, except in the case of crossbenchers. They are in addition to the four electorate staff to which each MP or senator is entitled. In February 2019, the government had 452 personal employees compared with 95 for the ALP Opposition and 17 for the Greens. In addition, three personal employees were provided for each of the crossbenchers in the Senate and the House of Representatives (increased to four after the 2019 election)—an indication of their significance in the balance of power. The Department of Finance website advises that employees under the *MOP(S) Act* are employed to assist with parliamentary duties, not for party-political purposes, and 'accordingly' may 'undertake activities in support of their employing senator or MP's re-election but not in support of the election or re-election of others'. These parliamentary resources are unequally distributed both between incumbent parties and, more especially, between candidates of such parties and candidates of other parties and Independents who do not have access to parliamentary resources.

Supposedly, such staff and allowances are provided for parliamentary and electorate purposes, with any other effects, such as promoting the re-election of the parliamentarian, only incidental. However, the use of allowances for electoral campaigning purposes has been normalised and has long been recognised as unfairly advantaging incumbents. In 2010, an independent review of parliamentary entitlements, appointed by the Rudd Government, recommended that access to printing and communications entitlements be removed from the date of the announcement of a federal election, along with travelling allowance for parliamentary staff working at party campaign headquarters. The review committee noted the latter created the 'not unreasonable perception that staff were engaged in party political business at public expense' (Belcher et al. 2010: 74–76).

No progress was made in implementing these particular recommendations. Indeed, the *Parliamentary Business Resources Act 2017* (*PBR Act*) and associated determinations made it clear that travel to assist parliamentarians in their re-election, including travel to work at party campaign headquarters, could be considered official business. Moreover, such travel-related resources for the hundreds of *MOP(S) Act* staff and electorate staff could be accessed until the day before polling day, unlike the previous convention that such travel be paid for by political parties in the period after their election campaign launches. Under the *PBR Act*, it was made clear that electioneering activities could be regarded as official business and hence undertaken at Commonwealth expense (IPEA 2019). The 2018 *Guidance on Caretaker Conventions* provided by the Department of the Prime Minister and Cabinet did, however, continue to refer to the 'long-standing convention that Ministers do not claim travelling allowance from the day of the Prime Minister's campaign launch to the day after polling day' (PM&C 2018: 7.2.5).

Under the *PBR Act*, the parliamentary allowances of federal parliamentarians (now called office expenses) could be spent on not just printed or other forms of communication, but also advertising on social media. However, an attempt in February 2019 by the government to remove a restriction on the use of office expenses for radio and television content was disallowed by the Senate in April. Australia remains out of step with comparable democracies such as Canada, New Zealand and the United Kingdom in allowing both the use of parliamentary allowances for electioneering and access to the services of the Parliamentary Library after parliament is dissolved. As already noted, this is contrary to the principle that incumbent parties or candidates should be prevented from using state resources to obtain unfair electoral advantage (Sawer and Gauja 2016: 11).

Authorisation of advertisements and deceptive advertising

A new requirement in the *Electoral Act* (since 2017) is for authorisation of advertising on social media. It is not yet clear how effective this will be, not least because, for all their expanded scope, the new provisions only cover certain forms of social media communication and do not apply to unpaid viral messages shared by people who are not 'disclosure entities' as defined in the Act. In addition, the 48-hour ban on advertising in broadcast media before election day does not apply to social media. There was a huge amount of negative advertising on social media on the Thursday and Friday before the 2019 election, including the ubiquitous 'death tax' advertising, with video clips of ALP frontbenchers saying the words 'death tax' when trying to deny the rumour of such a tax.

Although the AEC has entered into a cooperative arrangement with Facebook, there were almost 500 complaints about election advertising during the campaign, including 87 cases of advertising found by the AEC to have failed to meet the authorisation requirement (Knaus and Karp 2019).

At the federal level, the main requirement is that campaign advertisements be authorised and there is no requirement for 'truth in advertising'. The only prohibition of misleading advertising in the *Electoral Act* is restricted to the process of casting a vote. The prevalence of misleading and deceptive advertising during the campaign—particularly the torrent of claims on social media that the ALP intended to introduce a 'death tax'—led to renewed calls for broader regulation (Knaus and Evershed 2019; Murphy et al. 2019; Steketee 2019). When Essential Research undertook focus groups in June, it found that 'at least three members in each group thought the death tax was a real thing' (Lewis 2019). Two weeks before the election, there were also reports of unauthorised 'news' circulating in chat rooms on the Chinese-language platform WeChat to the effect that under an ALP government there would be an enormous increase in the number of refugees entering Australia, at the expense of taxpayers (see Chapter 14, this volume).

It needs to be emphasised that election campaigning based on the dissemination of deliberate falsehoods represents a fundamental challenge to the democratic process. Responding effectively to that challenge is, however, by no means straightforward (Maley 2019). Truth in advertising provisions have an interesting history in Australia. Prior to the second conscription referendum in 1917, the Hughes Government prohibited under the *War Precautions Act* the publication of 'any false statement of fact of a kind likely to affect the judgment of electors in relation to their votes'. In early 1984, the Hawke Government enacted a provision based on the 1917 regulation, which, however, was quickly repealed after the Joint Select Committee on Electoral Reform (1984) highlighted the difficulties involved in enforcing it. These included not only the danger of suppressing public debate, as in 1917, but also difficulty in classifying statements about the future as either true or false and the risk of turning campaigns into a lawyers' picnic. Until now, Australia's main experience with such provisions has arisen from the rules applying in South Australia (Renwick and Palese 2019: 22–30) and the Northern Territory.

An example of advertising that fell within the currently prohibited category was the Liberal Party signage at polling places in the Victorian electorates of Chisholm and Kooyong. The Chinese-language signs mimicked an AEC notice, using the same shade of purple, and told voters the 'correct' way to vote was to 'vote 1 Liberal Party' (see Plate 3.1). Faced with complaints on election day, the AEC noted that the authorisation requirements of the *Electoral Act* had not been breached (there was authorisation in tiny letters at the bottom of the signs) and that it did not have a monopoly on the use of particular colours. The publication of electoral matter in languages other than English, particularly on polling day, constitutes a significant challenge for electoral regulators. On 31 July 2019, the matter was taken to the Court of Disputed Returns. The results in Kooyong and Chisholm were challenged on the ground that the posters were in breach of the *Electoral Act* prohibition of misleading and deceptive conduct, with the mimicry of an AEC notice indicating an intention so to deceive. The court ultimately held the display of the posters to have been in breach of the law. However, to force a fresh election in such situations it must also be shown that the election outcomes were likely to have been affected (Orr 2019), and the court was not satisfied of that. A longer-term solution may be to amend Subsection 339(2) of the *Electoral Act* to prohibit use of material that could reasonably be taken to be an official AEC notice.

It is clear that the rise of social media has fundamentally changed the environment in which elections are conducted when compared with 1917 or even 1984, to the point where it would be virtually impossible for the truth of published statements to be comprehensively policed or even monitored. Short of closing internet access during election campaigns, it is hard to see progress being made on this issue.

Plate 3.1 Chisholm polling place sign mimicking an AEC notice
Photo: Courtesy of the Victorian Trades Hall Council.

Campaigning at polling places

The presence outside polling places of third-party campaigners, especially from the union movement and from organisations such as GetUp!, has long been a matter of concern to some Coalition figures. During the 44th Parliament (2013–16), the JSCEM commenced an inquiry into campaigning at polling places, but it lapsed on the dissolution of the parliament and was not resumed. After the 2019 election, it was reported (Norington 2019) that the re-elected Coalition Government was considering 'introducing rules to restrict spruikers outside polling booths to volunteers who are attached to registered parties and independent candidates'. Any such restriction would inevitably be challenged in the High Court as imposing an impermissible burden on the implied constitutional freedom of political communication.

Early voting, counting and results

In 2019, the incidence of early voting rose to unprecedented levels. The *Electoral Act* specifies seven modalities for voting before the day fixed for polling. Five of those (voting in the Antarctic, telephone voting by blind or vision-impaired electors and mobile polling in special hospitals, prisons and remote areas) are used by a relatively small and stable number of people. The remaining two—pre-poll and postal voting—reached record levels in 2019 (see Figure 3.2). The greatest boom came in the pre-poll numbers: 4,766,853 such votes were cast—31.6 per cent of votes cast in the election. Just over half of those pre-poll votes were cast in the five days immediately before polling day. Postal voting, however, also increased: 1,291,364 postal votes were received by the AEC, representing 8.6 per cent of those who voted.

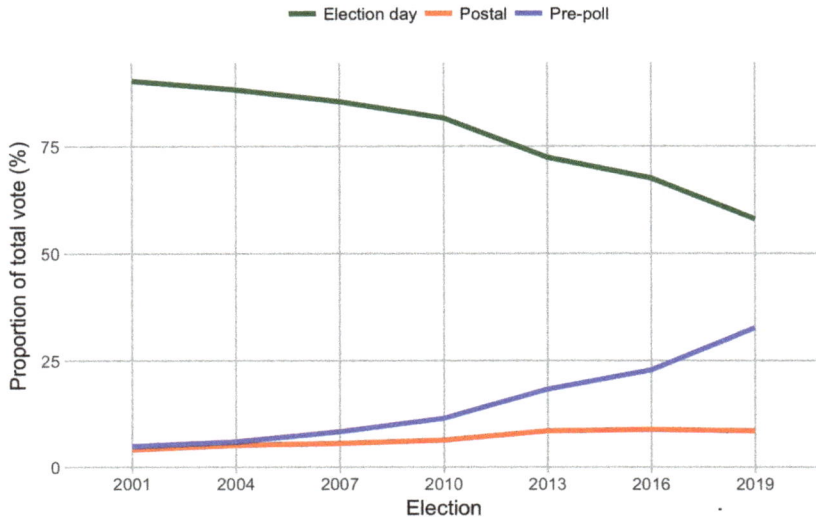

Figure 3.2 Proportion of House of Representatives votes by voting method

Source: Constructed by Ben Raue from AEC data.

This growth represented a continuation, but also an accentuation, of a trend developing over a long period. It had its roots in two significant changes to the *Electoral Act* in 1984. The first made it possible for an elector attending an AEC office to make an 'oral application for a postal vote' that could then be recorded on the spot. As this process became more popular, it was renamed 'pre-poll voting'. The second change relieved those seeking a postal vote of the obligation to state the specific ground on which they were applying. For all practical purposes, this meant that, from then on, anyone who wished to cast a postal vote rather than an ordinary vote for reasons of personal convenience could do so, not least because a number of the prescribed qualifications were purely within the knowledge of the voter, such as the voter's travel plans for election day, and could not be objectively tested. These changes were viewed at the time as ones of minor, primarily administrative, significance; where they would ultimately lead was certainly not foreseen.

By 2007, however, the rising popularity of early voting could not be denied. In the aftermath of that year's election, the AEC (2008: 41) argued to the JSCEM that:

> With close to 2 million votes being cast before polling day in 2007 (either at early voting centres, or through the post), it is now misleading to conceive of an election as taking place on a single polling day: there is, in fact, a polling period.

The AEC further put it to the committee that, in the face of the trend, there were basically three options open to the parliament: do nothing, attempt to wind back early voting or embrace the trend and be prepared to modify and resource the process to enhance its efficiency. The JSCEM (2009: 190–91) supported the third option, leading directly to another major change: pre-poll votes cast within a voter's own electoral division—which until then had had to be recorded and counted as declaration votes—could instead be cast as ordinary votes, making the pre-poll voting experience for such voters essentially identical to that of voting on polling day.

The point reached in 2019—with just over 40 per cent of votes recorded before polling day (see Figure 3.3)—has certainly generated concerns. One is the effect on the deliberative quality of election campaigning when large numbers of votes are cast before parties have released all their policies or even had their campaign launches (Mills and Drum 2019). Another is the concern about a level playing field, that a three-week period for pre-poll voting disadvantages Independent candidates and minor parties who may not have the resources to hand out how-to-vote cards at pre-polling centres for such a prolonged period.

In its report on the 2016 election, the JSCEM (2018b: 88) recommended that the *Electoral Act* be amended to restrict pre-poll voting to no more than two weeks before election day. Although there was no response in time for the 2019 election, the committee will certainly revisit the issue. But limiting the period for pre-poll voting is unlikely to make much difference to its growing popularity; in 2019, 86 per cent of pre-poll votes were cast in the fortnight before polling day anyway. In addition, the option voters now have of applying for a postal vote via the AEC website has made postal voting so easily accessible that restrictions on pre-poll voting could well have the effect of increasing postal voting, rather than encouraging a return to ordinary voting.

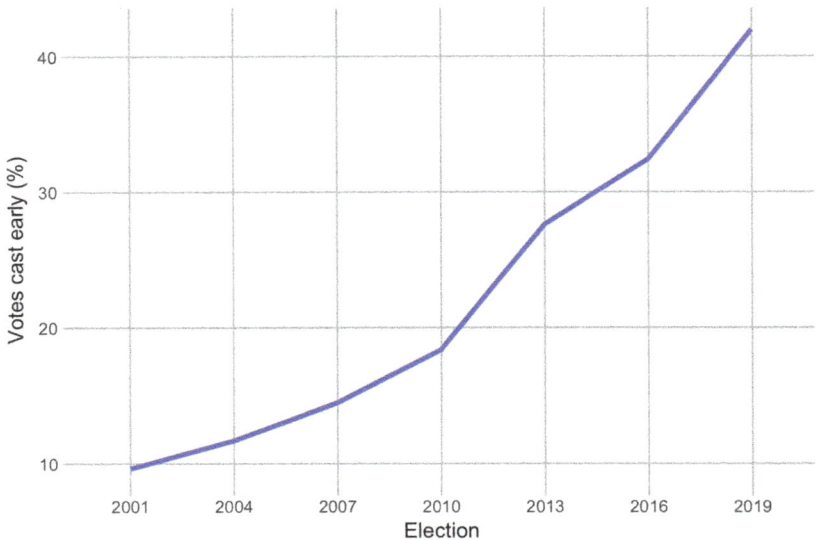

Figure 3.3 Rise in proportion of House of Representatives votes cast before election day

Source: Constructed by Ben Raue from AEC data.

The rise of early voting has created various difficulties for the AEC. With fewer people voting on polling day, it has come under pressure, including from the Australian National Audit Office (Brent 2014), to cut back on resourcing of polling booths; but if that were done too vigorously, it could lead to queueing and delays on polling day, which could tip the balance further in favour of more convenient early voting. At the same time, the AEC remains under pressure to deliver a result on the Saturday night of an election if possible; that now requires each electoral division to organise a discrete count of tens of thousands of pre-poll ordinary votes, staffed by a cohort of casuals separate from those who have worked at the polling booths during the day.

The 2019 count was also the subject of a High Court case (*Palmer & Ors v Australian Electoral Commission & Ors*) seeking to restrain the AEC from publishing the results of 'two-candidate-preferred' counts on election night until after 9.30 pm Australian Eastern Standard Time. This was the moment when the polls would close in the Territories of Christmas Island and Cocos (Keeling) Islands, three and a half hours after they closed on the eastern seaboard. Palmer argued that electors might be influenced by hearing these counts before voting but the court was unanimous in its view that the application should be dismissed. This is in line with the ongoing reluctance of the court to interfere with the very considerable latitude given by the constitution to parliament to devise electoral processes.

Trends in the rules of the game

The experience of the 2019 election highlights a number of regulatory issues arising from the rapidly changing electoral environment. Australia has now shifted from having a polling day to having a polling period. This change may turn out to be irreversible; it will be difficult to place restrictions on convenience voting when it has proved so popular. In addition, it is notable that, while the rise in early voting may encourage parties to release more policies in the early part of the campaign period, parties still tend to have their formal campaign 'launches' ridiculously close to polling day.

Another issue relates to timing. As noted earlier, the inquiry by the JSCEM into campaigning at polling places lapsed on the dissolution of the 44th Parliament, while the committee's report on the 2016 election took so long to produce that action to implement its recommendations proved impossible prior to the 2019 election. The comparative shortness of the federal parliamentary term is clearly a constraint, but the relatively leisurely approach to the conduct of inquiries and production of final reports taken by the committee in recent times does not bode well for its future as a vehicle of reform.

On the other hand, it is notable that some matters long the subject of partisan contestation seem to be slowly fading from the scene. For example, the issue of proof of identity for enrolment has essentially been resolved by technological change. In addition, a number of players with a US Republican Party–inspired reform agenda focused on the supposed dangers of electoral fraud have now left the political arena.

One major continuing issue is the failure to introduce political finance reform at the federal level and the way this undermines the efforts of States and Territories to reduce the influence of private money in elections. While the Greens and many nongovernmental organisations have long been campaigning for reform, and the ALP is now committed to caps on expenditure as well as much greater transparency around donations, there is little confidence that progress will be made under the federal Coalition, which has consistently opposed reforms in this area.

Finally, it is clear that the growth of social media, and the ways in which it rapidly evolves, gives rise to great difficulties both for the structuring and for the administration of appropriate schemes of regulation. At present, there seem to be no obvious solutions to these difficulties.

References

Alley v Gillespie [2018] HCA 11. 21 March 2018. classic.austlii.edu.au/au/cases/cth/HCA/2018/11.html.

Australian Capital Television Pty Ltd v Commonwealth [1992] HCA 1. 15 January 1992. classic.austlii.edu.au/au/cases/cth/HCA/1992/1.html.

Australian Electoral Commission (AEC). 2008. Submission 169. *Inquiry by the Joint Standing Committee on Electoral Matters (JSCEM) into the 2007 Federal Election*. Canberra: Parliament House. www.aph.gov.au/Parliamentary_Business/Committees/House_of_Representatives_Committees?url=em/elect07/subs/sub169.pdf.

Australian Electoral Commission (AEC). 2019a. *The best electoral roll in history*. Media release, 23 April. Canberra: AEC. www.aec.gov.au/media/media-releases/2019/04-23.htm.

Australian Electoral Commission (AEC). 2019b. *Statement from the Australian Electoral Commission: Mr Rodney Culleton—Candidate for the Western Australian Senate*. Media release, 24 April. Canberra: AEC. www.aec.gov.au/media/media-releases/2019/04-24a.htm.

Belcher, Barbara, John Conde, Jan Mason and Allan Fels. 2010. *Review of Parliamentary Entitlements: Committee Report*. Canberra: Commonwealth of Australia. www.finance.gov.au/publications/reviews/review-parliamentary-entitlements-committee-report.

Bonham, Kevin. 2017. 'Section 44: Could Parry peril unelect McKim?'. *Dr Kevin Bonham Blog* 31 October. kevinbonham.blogspot.com/2017/10/section-44-could-parry-peril-unelect.html#more.

Bonham, Kevin. 2019. 'Disendorsed, resigned or withdrawn candidates at the 2019 federal election'. *Dr Kevin Bonham Blog,* 3 May. kevinbonham.blogspot.com/2019/05/disendorsed-resigned-or-withdrawn.html.

Brent, Peter. 2014. 'Revenge of the auditors'. *The Australian*, 17 November. mumble.com.au/?p=2843.

Cameron, Sarah and Ian McAllister. 2019. *The 2019 Australian Federal Election: Results from the Australian Election Study*. Canberra: School of Politics and International Relations, College of Arts and Social Sciences, The Australian National University. australianelectionstudy.org/wp-content/uploads/The-2019-Australian-Federal-Election-Results-from-the-Australian-Election-Study.pdf.

Cameron, Sarah and Thomas Wynter. 2018. 'Campaign Finance and Perceptions of Interest Group Influence in Australia'. *Political Science* 70(2): 169–88. doi.org/10.1080/00323187.2018.1562307.

Department of the Prime Minister and Cabinet (PM&C). 2018. *Guidance on Caretaker Conventions*. Canberra: Australian Government. www.pmc.gov.au/resource-centre/government/guidance-caretaker-conventions.

Evershed, Nick and Christopher Knaus. 2019. 'Tim Wilson to assess at least 97 franking credit inquiry submissions he helped write'. *The Guardian*, 12 February. www.theguardian.com/australia-news/2019/feb/12/tim-wilson-to-assess-at-least-97-franking-credit-inquiry-submissions-he-helped-write.

Independent Parliamentary Expenses Authority (IPEA). 2019. *Election Period— Travel—High Level Guidance Note*. Canberra: Commonwealth of Australia. www.ipea.gov.au/sites/default/files/election_period_guidance_note_v1.pdf.

Joint Select Committee on Electoral Reform. 1984. *Joint Select Committee on Electoral Reform: Second Report*. August. Canberra: Commonwealth of Australia. www.aph.gov.au/Parliamentary_Business/Committees/House_of_Representatives_Committees?url=reports/1984/1984_pp198.pdf.

Joint Standing Committee on Electoral Matters (JSCEM). 2009. *Report on the Conduct of the 2007 Federal Election and Matters Related Thereto*. June. Canberra: Commonwealth of Australia. www.aph.gov.au/Parliamentary_Business/Committees/House_of_Representatives_Committees?url=em/elect07/report2/final.pdf.

Joint Standing Committee on Electoral Matters (JSCEM). 2018a. *Excluded: The Impact of Section 44 on Australian Democracy*. May. Canberra: Commonwealth of Australia. parlinfo.aph.gov.au/parlInfo/download/committees/reportjnt/024156/toc_pdf/Excluded.pdf;fileType=application%2Fpdf.

Joint Standing Committee on Electoral Matters (JSCEM). 2018b. *Report on the Conduct of the 2016 Federal Election and Matters Related Thereto*. November. Canberra: Commonwealth of Australia. parlinfo.aph.gov.au/parlInfo/download/committees/reportjnt/024085/toc_pdf/Reportonthe conductofthe2016federalelectionandmattersrelatedthereto.pdf;fileType=application%2Fpdf.

Knaus, Christopher and Nick Evershed. 2019. 'False election claims spark push for truth in political advertising laws'. *The Guardian*, 20 May. www.theguardian.com/australia-news/2019/may/20/false-election-claims-spark-push-for-truth-in-political-advertising-laws?CMP=share_btn_tw.

Knaus, Christopher and Paul Karp. 2019. 'Australian Electoral Commission finds 87 cases of election ads breaching law'. *The Guardian*, 22 May. www.theguardian.com/australia-news/2019/may/22/australian-electoral-commission-finds-87-cases-of-election-ads-breaching-law.

Lewis, Peter. 2019. 'How the internet led to division, distraction and civic disengagement'. *Big Ideas with Paul Barclay*, ABC RN, 1 July. www.abc.net.au/radionational/programs/bigideas/how-the-internet-created-division,-distraction-and-disengagemen/11225692.

McCloy v New South Wales [2015] HCA 34. 7 October. classic.austlii.edu.au/au/cases/cth/HCA/2015/34.html.

Maley, Michael. 2019. 'Home truths about political advertising'. *Inside Story*, 30 July. insidestory.org.au/home-truths-about-political-advertising/.

Mills, Stephen and Martin Drum. 2019. 'Three weeks of early voting has a significant effect on democracy. Here's why'. *The Conversation,* 29 April. theconversation.com/three-weeks-of-early-voting-has-a-significant-effect-on-democracy-heres-why-115909.

Murphy, Katherine, Christopher Knaus and Nick Evershed. 2019. '"It felt like a big tide": How the death tax lie infected Australia's election campaign'. *The Guardian*, 8 June. www.theguardian.com/australia-news/2019/jun/08/it-felt-like-a-big-tide-how-the-death-tax-lie-infected-australias-election-campaign.

Norington, Brad. 2019. 'GetUp put on notice over political links'. *The Australian*, 22 May. www.theaustralian.com.au/nation/politics/getup-put-on-notice-over-political-links/news-story/639c1086e5c4f6067b76027c5e96d156.

Organization for Security and Co-operation in Europe (OSCE). 2011. *Guidelines on Political Party Regulation*. Warsaw: OSCE Office for Democracy and Human Rights. www.osce.org/odihr/77812.

Orr, Graeme. 2015. 'Does an Unqualified but Losing Candidacy Upset an Election?'. *Election Law Journal* 14(4): 424–29. doi.org/10.1089/elj.2015.0336.

Orr, Graeme. 2019. 'High Court challenge in Kooyong and Chisholm unlikely to win, but may still land a blow'. *The Conversation*, 1 August. theconversation.com/high-court-challenge-in-kooyong-and-chisholm-unlikely-to-win-but-may-still-land-a-blow-121300.

Palmer & Ors v Australian Electoral Commission & Ors. 2019. B19/2019. www.hcourt.gov.au/cases/case_b19-2019.

Renwick, Alan and Michela Palese. 2019. *Doing Democracy Better: How Can Information and Discourse in Election and Referendum Campaigns in the UK Be Improved?* London: The Constitution Unit, University College London. www.ucl.ac.uk/constitution-unit/sites/constitution-unit/files/184_-_doing_ democracy_better.pdf.

Sawer, Marian. 2003. 'Enrolling the people: Electoral innovation in the new Commonwealth of Australia'. In *Realising Democracy: Electoral Law in Australia*, edited by George Williams, Bryan Mercurio and Graeme Orr, 52–65. Sydney: Federation Press.

Sawer, Marian and Anika Gauja. 2016. 'Party rules: Promises and pitfalls'. In *Party Rules? Dilemmas of Political Party Regulation in Australia*, edited by Anika Gauja and Marian Sawer, 1–35. Canberra: ANU Press. doi.org/10.22459/ PR.10.2016.01.

Spence v Queensland. [2019] HCA 15. 15 May. classic.austlii.edu.au/au/cases/ cth/HCA/2019/15.html.

Steketee, Mike. 2019. 'The slippery slope of officially sanctioned lying'. *Inside Story*, 12 July. insidestory.org.au/the-slippery-slope-of-officially-sanctioned-lying/.

Stoker, Gerry, Mark Evans and Max Halupka. 2018. *Trust and Democracy in Australia: Democratic Decline and Renewal*. Report No. 1, Democracy 2025. www.democracy2025.gov.au/documents/Democracy2025-report1.pdf.

Wood, Danielle and Kate Griffiths. 2018. *Who's in the Room? Access and Influence in Australian Politics*. Melbourne: Grattan Institute. grattan.edu.au/report/ whos-in-the-room/.

Wright, Shane and Jessica Irvine. 2019. 'Peak pork: The marginal seat where election promises add to $26,500 per voter'. *The Age*, [Melbourne], 15 May. www.theage.com.au/federal-election-2019/porkathon-at-26k-per-voter-20190514-p51n4j.html.

4

CANDIDATES AND PRE-SELECTION

Anika Gauja and Marija Taflaga

Between them, the Coalition parties, the ALP, the Greens and Pauline Hanson's One Nation (PHON) fielded 520 candidates in 151 House of Representatives seats for the 2019 Australian federal election. Candidate selection—more commonly known as 'pre-selection' in Australia—is the process by which a political party decides who will be its endorsed election candidates. It is a high-stakes activity, involving personal, professional and factional ambitions. Depending on how a party chooses its candidates, it is also one of the best opportunities party members have to exercise power within their parties and to indirectly influence public policy outcomes.

Candidate selection is equally important beyond political parties because it shapes the choice before voters, the composition of parliaments, the interests most likely to be heard in policy debates and legislative outcomes (Cross 2008: 598). As Hazan and Rahat (2010: 10) argue, 'candidate selection affects the fundamental nature of modern democratic politics and governance'. Yet, as Gallagher and Marsh (1988) contend, despite their importance in determining the composition of the legislature, candidate selection contests resemble the 'secret garden' of politics. Although political parties are defined by the *Commonwealth Electoral Act 1918* as organisations seeking to promote the election of one or more candidates to the House of Representatives and the Senate, they are not required to disclose how this selection takes place, nor are they mandated to use a particular method. While it is relatively straightforward to obtain information on the formal rules governing pre-selections through party rules and constitutions, finding any data on the contests themselves and how these rules are applied in particular cases is far more difficult.

For this chapter, we have created an original database of pre-selection contests and candidate data for the 2019 House of Representatives and Senate elections, compiled by the authors from local and national media accounts, party websites and AEC candidate information. The database covers the Coalition parties—the Liberal Party, the National Party and the Queensland Liberal National Party (LNP)—the ALP, the Greens and PHON in all 151 House of Representatives seats and the Senate tickets for these parties. It provides information on publicly reported pre-selections, whether the contest was competitive, who participated and who was selected as the official party candidate. We also collect information on all candidates selected, including incumbency and gender.

The chapter begins by analysing the number of reported and competitive House of Representatives pre-selection contests. It then outlines the variety of mechanisms used by Australian parties to select their candidates and the stages in the process. We then focus on the 33 pre-selection contests that were competitive—that is, contested by two or more candidates. We end by examining the democratic implications of pre-selection and analysing the candidates selected for the House of Representatives and Senate by incumbency and gender.

Pre-selection contests for the 2019 Australian federal election

Gallagher and Marsh's (1988) assertion that candidate selection is the 'secret garden' of politics is largely confirmed by our data. Of the 520 candidate selections we know occurred, we were able to find publicly reported information on only 326 contests (63 per cent). The presumption, then, is that the selection events that were not publicly reported on consisted of the routine endorsement of incumbent candidates—contests for which there were no challengers for the position—or selections made exclusively by a party executive (appointments), including those made at short notice with limited candidates available. In New South Wales, for example, the Liberal Party State Executive voted to endorse all sitting members (Murphy and Davies 2018). Only in 33 instances across Australia (6 per cent of the total pre-selection events) could we find evidence of a competitive pre-selection contest—that is, a selection with more than one candidate (Table 4.1). If we examine the number of competitive contests by State and Territory, the Australian Capital Territory is the clear outlier: 56 per cent of pre-selections in the Territory were competitive, compared with a maximum of 6 per cent in New South Wales, Queensland and Western Australia.

Table 4.1 Pre-selection contests for the 2019 Australian federal election (House of Representatives)

State or Territory	No. of electorates	No. of candidates/ pre-selection events	Reported pre-selections	Competitive contests
ACT	3	9	6	5
NSW	47	148	88	9
NT	2	6	3	0
Qld	30	119	67	7
SA	10	30	16	1
Tas.	5	20	18	1
Vic.	38	121	86	6
WA	16	67	42	4
Total	**151**	**520**	**326**	**33**

Source: Authors' own data.

Table 4.2 presents the number of competitive pre-selection contests for the House of Representatives, by party. The Liberal Party staged the greatest number of competitive pre-selection contests, by some margin. Although more Coalition parliamentarians retired before the election was called than did Labor parliamentarians,[1] this alone does not account for the difference. Part of the explanation may be the decision by Labor, which was the frontrunner, to quickly resolve damaging and messy pre-selection contests. The most extreme case of Labor's efforts to settle disputes internally occurred within its Victorian division, where a factional dispute broke out between the Left and the Right. Labor Leader Bill Shorten secured the intervention of Labor's powerful national executive to administer its pre-selections and imposed a $500 fee on candidates to suppress 'vexatious' factional candidacies (Brown 2018). PHON did not stage a single competitive contest, which is explained by the fact that candidates were chosen exclusively by the party's State and national

---

1   Ten Coalition lower house parliamentarians retired, compared with six Labor parliamentarians.

executives. The Greens held only one reported competitive lower house contest, in the Queensland seat of Brisbane. This could be explained by the relatively high cost of resourcing such contests and finding available candidates, which could be difficult for a smaller party to meet.

Table 4.2 Pre-selection contests by party: 2019 Australian federal election (House of Representatives)

Party	Reported pre-selections	Competitive contests	Ratio of competitive to reported contests (%)
LIB/LNP	106	21	20
ALP	67	9	13
Greens	83	1	1
PHON	51	0	0
National Party	19	2	11

Source: Authors' own data.

The diversity of pre-selection methods in Australia

Candidate selection is typically conducted in three stages: 1) establishing both the eligibility and the nomination of candidates (before the contest); 2) a selection process (during the contest); and 3) vetting and endorsement (after the contest). Parties retain high levels of control over candidates because they are the institutional interface between candidates and the AEC. All candidates, including incumbents, must be endorsed by their party before appearing on the ballot under the party name. As noted above, there is significant variation within, and between, the Australian political parties at all three of these stages.

The typical requirement for nomination in Australia is party membership, often for a minimum period (ranging from three months in the South Australian Liberal Party to three years in the Queensland ALP). Additional criteria that may be imposed include trade union membership (in the ALP), attendance at a minimum number of party meetings and nomination by a prescribed minimum number of party members. However, in almost all cases, party executive bodies can override these nomination requirements. For example, the NSW ALP Administration Committee can decide to waive minimum membership requirements if it considers 'there would be a significant advantage to the party if the member concerned was allowed to contest the selection ballot' (Rule no. 11). Political parties also exercise a power of veto over candidate nominations, which are subject to review. These powers can be extremely broad. For example, the South Australian Liberal executive may refuse to accept a nomination if it is in the 'best interests of the division and shall not be bound to give any reasons'. Therefore, despite the formal rules that govern candidacy requirements, political parties possess significant scope and flexibility to intervene where it may be electorally desirable to do so.

The easiest way of distinguishing between all the different ways of selecting candidates currently used by Australian parties is to focus on which groups or individuals are able to participate in making the decision (the 'selectorate') (see, for example, Cross and Gauja 2014). Selectorates can range from being highly exclusive, with candidates chosen by a single party leader, to highly inclusive, where a candidate might be selected in a primary-style pre-selection open to all voters in the region (see Hazan and Rahat 2010: 35).

Parties' pre-selection methods for their 2019 candidates spread across the entire spectrum. At one end of the spectrum are processes involving a rank-and-file vote. For example, the Labor and Liberal parties conduct rank-and-file pre-selection plebiscites in the Australian Capital Territory and the Northern Territory. Several parties, including the ALP and the National Party, have previously held more open selection contests involving participation from local communities (Gauja 2017), though this was not a feature of the 2019 pre-selections. A more common method is by a selection committee comprising representatives/delegates from various areas of the party organisation (for example, branches, parliamentarians, State council and so on). This is used by the West Australian Liberals to select candidates for the House of Representatives. At the other end of the spectrum are highly exclusive selection processes, such as that used by PHON. In Queensland, for example, candidates are selected by the party's four-person State executive. The national executive continues, however, to exercise significant discretion over the selection of candidates:

> The State Executive must ensure that best practices in relation to the vetting of Candidates [are] per instruction from the National Executive which may vary and change from time to time as deemed necessary in the best interests of the Party.[2]

---

2   Pauline Hanson's One Nation Queensland State Constitution 2017, s. 5.2.

Apart from the freedom given to State parties to implement their own selection processes as they see fit, many parties retain a significant degree of freedom in being able to alter those processes at short notice.

The final stage of the candidate selection process is receiving the endorsement of the party after the selection contest has taken place. As with nomination procedures, political parties possess the ability to intervene at this point to refuse endorsement. This can occur at both the State and the national levels. For example, the ALP's administrative committee in Queensland shall not endorse a candidate for public office if 'such person's record shows failure, without good and cogent reasons, to vote for and/or defend Labor's legislation or if that person's candidature may prejudice Labor's prospects'.[3] Party executives may also intervene to disendorse candidates after the close of nominations, which occurred in several instances in 2019 (see Sawer and Maley, Chapter 3, this volume). One Labor, two Greens and four Liberal Party lower house candidates were either disendorsed or resigned under pressure from the party after social media commentary was uncovered that revealed sexist, homophobic and racist comments.[4]

Candidate selection in the Senate operates differently from that in the House of Representatives. This is the product of different voting systems, which sees parties produce party list tickets. As parties are organised federally, there is variation across and within Australian Senate candidate selection procedures. However, as a general rule, Senate contests tend to be more centralised and have the greater potential to be influenced by the party's central office. Again, PHON represents one extreme, where the party appoints candidates, and the Greens are at the other, where some States hold party-wide membership ballots. For both these parties, it is the Senate contest that really matters. By contrast, the Liberal and Labor parties tend to use mixed systems, with a combination of membership representation and central organisational representatives (Cross and Gauja 2014), and have been disinclined to introduce radical reform of procedures (Miragliotta 2013).

---

3   2018 Rules of the Australian Labor Party (State of Queensland), s. 49(3).
4   ALP: Luke Creasey (Melbourne); Greens: Jay Dessi (Lalor), David Paull (Parkes); Liberal: Jeremy Hearn (Isaacs), Peter Killin (Wills), Jessica Whelan (Lyons) and Gurpal Singh (Scullin).

Senate contests are usually competitive, in so far as there is a competitive process for allocating winnable positions on the Senate ballot. What may not always occur is the entrance of non-incumbent candidates to this process. As parties are likely to secure, at best, three senators, the real contest on Senate tickets is to resolve the order of names. Senators, compared with members of the House, tend to have stronger backgrounds in the party organisation and are more likely to have had a 'careerist' trajectory into politics (van Onselen 2015; Miragliotta and Errington 2012). For this reason, Senate contests are regularly the cause of factional manoeuvrings, and it is through this lens that much scrutiny of Senate pre-selection contests arises in the news.

Notable pre-selection contests for the 2019 Australian federal election

House of Representatives

Table 4.3 provides the details of all the competitive pre-selection contests held by the major parties and the Greens for the 2019 House of Representatives election. As the table shows, a major reason for a competitive pre-selection is the retirement or resignation of a sitting parliamentarian.

The creation of the new seat of Bean in the Australian Capital Territory saw both the Liberals and Labor hold pre-selections in which multiple candidates contested. The ALP's pre-selection contest was won by David Smith, who had served in the Senate since May 2018, when Katy Gallagher was disqualified for failing to properly renounce her UK citizenship (for details on the citizenship crisis, see Taflaga and Curtin 2018, 2019). The Liberal Party pre-selected Ed Cocks, who competed with Jane Hiatt, a small business owner (Whyte 2018b). Following the resignation of the ALP's Gai Brodtmann in the seat of Canberra, competitive contests were also held by both parties in that seat. The ALP's contest was won by Alicia Payne, running against four men, in a contest that saw the intervention of the party's national executive to investigate the distribution of flyers making damaging claims against one of the candidates (Whyte 2018a). The pre-selected Liberal candidate, Mina Zaki, was plagued by allegations that she had not finalised the renunciation of her Afghan citizenship (Whyte 2019).

Table 4.3 Competitive pre-selection contests, House of Representatives, 2019

Seat	State/ Territory	Party	Chosen candidate	No. of candidates	Context	TPP swing (%)
Bean	ACT	ALP	David Smith	3	New seat	n.a.
Bean	ACT	LIB	Ed Cocks	2	New seat	n.a.
Canberra	ACT	ALP	Alicia Payne	5	Retiring MP	+4.1
Canberra	ACT	LIB	Mina Zaki	3	Retiring MP (other party)	−4.1
Fenner	ACT	LIB	Leanne Castley	2		+1.3
Cowper	NSW	NAT	Patrick Conaghan	3	Retiring MP	+2.2
Eden-Monaro	NSW	LIB	Fiona Kotvojs	5		+2.1
Gilmore	NSW	LIB	Grant Schultz*	2	Retiring MP	−3.3
Hughes	NSW	LIB	Craig Kelly**	2		+0.5
Lindsay	NSW	LIB	Melissa McIntosh	4	Retiring MP (other party)	+6.2
Mackellar	NSW	LIB	Jason Falinski**	2		−2.5
Page	NSW	ALP	Patrick Deegan	2		−7.1
Parramatta	NSW	LIB	Charles Camenzuli	3		+4.2
Reid	NSW	ALP	Sam Crosby	2	Retiring MP (other party)	+1.5
Bowman	Qld	LNP	Andrew Laming	2		+3.2
Brisbane	Qld	GRN	Andrew Bartlett	3		−1.0
Capricornia	Qld	ALP	Russell Robertson	2		−11.7
Dickson	Qld	ALP	Ali France	2		−2.9
Flynn	Qld	NAT	Ken O'Dowd	2		+7.6
Moncrieff	Qld	LNP	Angie Bell	5	Retiring MP	+0.8
Ryan	Qld	LNP	Julian Simmonds	2		−3.0
Mayo	SA	LIB	Georgina Downer	2		−2.2
Braddon	Tas.	LIB	Gavin Pearce	3		+4.8
Chisholm	Vic.	LIB	Gladys Liu	9	MP resigns from party	−2.3
Higgins	Vic.	LIB	Katie Allen	8	Retiring MP	−6.1

Seat	State/ Territory	Party	Chosen candidate	No. of candidates	Context	TPP swing (%)
Indi	Vic.	LIB	Steve Martin	3	Retiring MP (other party)	+4.1
Jagajaga	Vic.	ALP	Kate Thwaites	2	Retiring MP	+1.0
Macnamara	Vic.	LIB	Kate Ashmor	3	Retiring MP (other party)	−5.0
Mallee	Vic.	NAT	Anne Webster	6	Retiring MP	−3.6
Curtin	WA	LIB	Celia Hammond	5	Retiring MP	−6.4
Hasluck	WA	ALP	James Martin	3		−3.3
Moore	WA	LIB	Ian Goodenough	5		+0.6
Pearce	WA	ALP	Kim Travers	2		−3.9

n.a. not applicable

LIB = Liberal Party

NAT = National Party

GRN = Greens

* Grant Schultz was chosen by Liberal Party members as the candidate for Gilmore, but this was not endorsed by the State executive.

** Incumbent MP Craig Kelly was challenged by NSW State President Kent Johns, but Prime Minister Scott Morrison and the State executive intervened to endorse Kelly as the candidate. Incumbent Jason Falinski was also endorsed under this process (Murphy and Davies 2018).

Source: Compiled by the authors.

Several Liberal Party pre-selections in New South Wales were controversial. In Gilmore, local party members chose Grant Schultz as the preferred candidate, but this decision was overruled by the party's executive, which installed Warren Mundine as the official candidate (Fist 2019). Schultz consequently resigned from the party and contested the seat as an Independent. Labor's Fiona Phillips won the seat and the Liberals suffered a 16.1 per cent primary vote swing against Mundine. In both Hughes and Mackellar, the Liberal Party executive intervened to endorse the incumbent members, Craig Kelly and Jason Falinski, respectively, from challenges by local members. Interestingly, the Queensland LNP executive did not intervene in the seat of Ryan to re-endorse sitting MP Jane Prentice, who was beaten by local councillor and former staffer Julian Simmonds in a pre-selection challenge (McGowan 2018).

Women were selected in two competitive Liberal pre-selection contests, in the Victorian seats of Chisholm and Higgins. In Chisholm, Gladys Liu was selected from a field of nine candidates to replace Julia Banks, who resigned from the Liberal Party after making allegations of bullying against others in the party (Preiss 2018). In Higgins, paediatric gastroenterologist Dr Katie Allen was pre-selected to replace the retiring Kelly O'Dwyer (Kehoe 2019). In the West Australian seat of Curtin, former Curtin University vice-chancellor Celia Hammond was chosen to replace retiring Liberal Party minister Julie Bishop (Burrell 2019).

Senate

Several Senate selection contests proved controversial, highlighting continuing strife within some State party divisions. In the Victorian Liberal Party, pre-selections due to be held in May 2018 were cancelled at the eleventh hour as a result of manoeuvrings by the conservative faction within the State council (Norman 2018a). Moderate Senator Jane Hume was perceived to be the primary focus of the conservative faction's efforts to organise, though speculation that conservative MP Kevin Andrews would be unlikely to survive pre-selection was also reported. In August, the Victorian party automatically endorsed all sitting MPs, avoiding a vote of members (Crowe 2018), and in September, as one of his first acts as prime minister, Scott Morrison intervened to see both Victorian senators re-endorsed (Norman 2018b). When the remaining spots on the Victorian Liberal ticket were finalised remains unclear.

In New South Wales, both the Liberals and the Greens had competitive and controversial pre-selection processes. In New South Wales, incumbent senator and frontrunner for the NSW ticket, Jim Molan (right faction), was relegated to fourth—an unwinnable spot on the Coalition Senate ticket. The moderates Hollie Hughes and Andrew Bragg won 199 and 157 votes, respectively, to Molan's 141 votes. It was believed the surprise result was the consequence of centre-right faction leader Alex Hawke's withdrawal of support from Molan at the last minute (Hunter and Loussikian 2018). The Nationals pre-selected Perin Davey, who took the third spot on the ticket. This deal within the Coalition was viewed with bitterness, because many Nationals believed the third spot was unwinnable given the government's poor performance. Tensions were raised again when Senator Molan ran a below-the-line campaign that saw him garner 132,000 below-the-line votes (a record high) (Chang 2019; Grattan 2019). Despite the campaign's success, and the Coalition's strong performance, it was not enough; Davey was the only senator elected for the Nationals.

A major contest developed when left Greens Senator Lee Rhiannon was challenged by Mehreen Faruqi. Rhiannon's position within the Greens had come under pressure as a result of the NSW Greens' practice of binding members to vote in defiance of decisions made by the federal party. Rhiannon's actions had prompted her suspension from the Greens' party room until the NSW Greens undertook internal reforms (Gartrell 2017). Faruqi won pre-selection over Rhiannon with 60.7 per cent of the vote, in a result seen as a major blow for the left faction (Nicholls 2017).

Turning to other States, minor skirmishes between the factions broke out in the South Australian Labor Party. An unfavourable redistribution saw Mark Butler without a safe seat. The eventual deal between the left and right factions saw the left exchange one of its Senate spots in return for the seat of Adelaide, held by the retiring Kate Ellis of the right (Puddy et al. 2018). In Queensland, the LNP achieved generational renewal when controversial Senator Barry O'Sullivan failed to achieve endorsement and Senator Ian Macdonald was relegated to fourth position on the ticket (Owens 2018). Macdonald took the decision badly, declaring the party was failing to represent north Queensland, and urged supporters to vote for him below the line (AAP 2019). Similar concerns about regional representation were raised within the ALP, with members fearful of a takeover by Brisbane and the Construction, Forestry, Maritime, Mining and Energy Union (CFMMEU) (Killoran 2018). Finally, the unaligned Tasmanian Senator Lisa Singh was relegated to the fourth spot on Labor's ticket as a result of a factional deal between the right and left, despite winning second place on the membership ballot (Denholm 2018).

The consequences of pre-selection: Who contests and who is elected?

There is some debate among political scientists about whether women are disadvantaged in relatively more competitive and open selection contests (see, for example, Pruysers et al. 2017). Table 4.4 reports the proportion of women candidates who participated in pre-selection contests for the House of Representatives against the proportion of candidates who were chosen. Evidence from the 2019 Australian federal election pre-selections shows that, while women are still in the minority in such contests in the House, they are just as likely—if not more likely—to be selected as the party's official candidate.

This was the case for all parties except the Greens (for whom only one competitive pre-selection contest was publicly reported) for the House of Representatives. The ALP had the largest share of women as both pre-selection candidates and officially endorsed candidates (44 per cent), followed by the Liberal Party and the National Party—mirroring the partisan patterns of representation observed in the federal parliament (Hough 2019). The existence of Labor's quota rule, which see contests spilled if an insufficient number of women are put forward, likely drives the result for this party. For the Liberal Party, it may be the threat of intervention from State executives or the effect of public pressure given recent and sustained criticism of the low levels of female representation within that party (McMahon 2018).

Table 4.4 Competitive contests: Candidates by party and gender in the House of Representatives

Party	No. of House of Representatives pre-selection candidates			No. of House of Representatives candidates selected		
	M (No.)	F (No.)	Relative % of women	M (No.)	F (No.)	Relative % of women
ALP	14	9	39	5	4	44
LIB/LNP	42	23	35	11	8	42
Greens	2	1	33	1	0	0
Nationals	10	2	17	2	1	33
Total	**68**	**35**	**34**	**19**	**13**	**41**

Source: Compiled by the authors.

Table 4.5 Candidates nominated for the Senate compared with those elected

Party	Candidates at pre-selection					Elected to the Senate		
	Total no. of candidates	Total candidates selected	M (No.)	F (No.)	Relative % of women selected as candidates	M (No.)	F (No.)	Relative % of women
ALP	39	37	15	22	59	5	8	62
LIB/LNP	37	31	20	11	35	11	6	35
Greens	37	35	5	30	86	2	4	67
Nationals	8	8	3	5	62	0	1	100
PHON	12	12	9	3	25	1	0	0
Total	**133**	**123**	**52**	**71**	**58**	**19**	**18**	**50**

Source: Compiled by the authors.

Table 4.5 shows that women were a little more likely than men to be selected as Senate candidates and that they went on to win 50 per cent of the seats contested by the five parties considered in this chapter. However, this result is not distributed evenly across all parties. Labor nominated 22 (59 per cent) women and saw eight (62 per cent of their successful candidates) elected. Of the 35 candidates nominated by the Greens, 30 (86 per cent) were women, and they succeeded in electing six senators, 67 per cent of whom were women. The Greens' figures reflect the historically stronger performance of smaller parties in achieving women's representation. It may also reflect the party's policy platform and institutional organisation, which make it a more welcoming environment for women.

On the right, the results were mixed. The Nationals nominated more women than men (62 per cent) at this year's election. This may be because the party considered its chances of electoral success were limited because of the nature of its Coalition agreements with the Liberals. However, it succeeded in electing one woman, Perin Davey from New South Wales. The Liberal Party was once again the laggard; only 35 per cent of its nominations were women (a higher proportion than in the House) and it succeeded in electing six women (35 per cent).

The data presented in Table 4.6 illustrate the effect of incumbency. Women candidates make up a much higher proportion of non-incumbent candidates selected by each of the parties but perform better in the Senate than in the House. This reflects both the current gender imbalance in the federal legislature and historically observed stronger representation for women in the upper chamber. Both the Liberal Party and the ALP nominated a similar percentage of women non-incumbent candidates in the House, but only 15 per cent of Liberal MP incumbents were women. In the Senate, the situation was somewhat reversed: both parties had similar levels of women incumbents (50 per cent ALP versus 42 per cent Liberals), but Labor had one-third more women non-incumbents, reflecting a higher level of women's participation overall. Given the much greater likelihood that incumbents are re-elected, these patterns, especially in the lower house, arguably perpetuate rather than address gender disparities in the parliament. Indeed, following the result, women will make up 47 per cent of Labor parliamentarians and only 23 per cent of Liberal parliamentarians (Norman 2019).

Table 4.6 Candidates selected by incumbency, party and gender in the House of Representatives and the Senate

Party	Incumbent						Non-incumbent					
	House of Representatives			Senate			House of Representatives			Senate		
	M (No.)	F (No.)	Relative % of women	M (No.)	F (No.)	Relative % of women	M (No.)	F (No.)	Relative % of women	M (No.)	F (No.)	Relative % of women
ALP	35	25	42	5	5	50	49	43	47	10	17	63
LIB/LNP	52	9	15	7	5	42	45	39	46	14	6	30
Greens	1	0	0	2	4	67	84	63	43	0	0	0
Nationals	8	0	0	1	0	0	10	6	38	2	5	71
PHON	0	0	0	1	0	0	40	19	32	8	3	27
Total	**96**	**34**	**26**	**16**	**14**	**47**	**228**	**170**	**43**	**34**	**31**	**48**

Source: Compiled by the authors.

Conclusion

Although candidate selection is key to determining the composition of the legislature, Australian parties' pre-selection processes for the 2019 federal election illustrate the closed nature of the majority of these events. Only a tiny proportion of pre-selection contests could be considered competitive. In reality, the decision as to who will be a candidate is often determined by just a handful of people. For party pre-selections to the Senate, this democratic deficit is compounded by factional manoeuvring, culminating in this election, for the Liberal Party, in prime ministerial intervention in Victoria. Some pre-selections are contested, particularly those where an incumbent parliamentarian is retiring, but these are infrequent events. Given the public scepticism about and distrust of parties and politicians in Australia, the closed and secretive nature of pre-selection processes appear to amplify rather than resolve this problem.

Pre-selection contests also have concrete outcomes for the election of women to the federal parliament. On a positive note, our data show that where women do contest competitive pre-selection contests, they are not disadvantaged. However, the effect of incumbency (that is, a predominantly male parliament) continues to perpetuate the gender imbalance in the legislature. This effect is particularly pronounced for parties that have eschewed quotas. With the Coalition parties struggling to improve organisational practices and facilitate more opportunities for women, the underrepresentation of conservative women's voices in the legislature will continue to be an issue leading into the next election.

References

Australian Associated Press (AAP). 2019. 'Dumped LNP Senator urges vote 1 for him'. *The Canberra Times*, 2 May. www.canberratimes.com.au/story/6101535/dumped-lnp-senator-urges-vote-1-for-him/digital-subscription/.

Brown, Greg. 2018. 'ALP charges candidates $500 to appease factions'. *The Australian*, 24 July. www.theaustralian.com.au/news/alp-charges-candidates-500-to-appease-factions/news-story/dac3dd7aa550505f1b18f97d05e56af6.

Burrell, Andrew. 2019. 'Celia Hammond wins Liberal preselection for Curtin'. *The Australian*, 10 March. www.theaustralian.com.au/nation/politics/celia-hammond-wins-liberal-preselection-for-curtin/news-story/1fef2dbfcb2b07bc7df9049d375a4b94.

Chang, Charis. 2019. 'Jim Molan concedes defeat, admits he won't get a Senate seat'. *News.com.au*, 12 June. www.news.com.au/national/federal-election/jim-molan-concedes-defeat-admits-he-wont-get-a-senate-seat/news-story/dfcd912dfe56b7106b4e8eb4968c9095#.ewyav.

Cross, William. 2008. 'Democratic Norms and Party Candidate Selection: Taking Contextual Factors into Account'. *Party Politics* 14(5): 596–619. doi.org/10.1177/1354068808093392.

Cross, William and Anika Gauja. 2014. 'Designing Candidate Selection Methods: Exploring Diversity in Australian Political Parties'. *Australian Journal of Political Science* 49(1): 22–39. doi.org/10.1080/10361146.2013.873769.

Crowe, David. 2018. 'Victorian Liberal Party endorses all sitting federal MPs, avoiding members' vote'. *Sydney Morning Herald*, 2 August. www.smh.com.au/politics/federal/victorian-liberal-party-endorses-all-sitting-federal-mps-avoiding-members-vote-20180803-p4zv9e.html.

Denholm, Matthew. 2018. 'Push to rethink union boss power'. *The Australian*, 9 September. www.theaustralian.com.au/national-affairs/felled-labor-senator-urges-rethink-of-union-boss-party-power/news-story/1c77eb858f2e2d935d021bf75bccdf9f.

Fist, Rebecca. 2019. 'Gilmore hopeful Grant Schultz resigns from Liberal Party in disgust, will run as an independent'. *South Coast Register*, [Nowra], 22 January. www.southcoastregister.com.au/story/5864261/grant-schultz-resigns-as-liberal-party-abandons-democracy/.

Gallagher, Michael and Michael Marsh. eds. 1988. *Candidate Selection in Comparative Perspective: The Secret Garden of Politics*. London: SAGE Publications.

Gartrell, Adam. 2017. 'Lee Rhiannon suspended from Greens party room pending reform in NSW'. *Sydney Morning Herald*, 28 June. www.smh.com.au/politics/federal/lee-rhiannon-suspended-from-greens-party-room-pending-reform-in-nsw-20170628-gx05zq.html.

Gauja, Anika. 2017. *Party Reform: The Causes, Challenges and Consequences of Organizational Change*. Oxford: Oxford University Press. doi.org/10.1093/acprof:oso/9780198717164.001.0001.

Grattan, Michelle. 2019. 'Angry Nationals play payback in NSW Senate row'. *The Conversation*, 15 May. theconversation.com/angry-nationals-play-payback-in-nsw-senate-row-117208.

Hazan, Reuven and Gideon Rahat. 2010. *Democracy Within Parties: Candidate Selection Methods and their Political Consequences*. Oxford: Oxford University Press. doi.org/10.1093/acprof:oso/9780199572540.001.0001.

Hough, Anna. 2019. *Composition of Australian Parliaments by Party and Gender: A Quick Guide*. 1 July. Canberra: Parliamentary Library. www.aph.gov.au/About_Parliament/Parliamentary_Departments/Parliamentary_Library/pubs/rp/rp1920/Quick_Guides/CompositionPartyGender.

Hunter, Fergus and Kylar Loussikian. 2018. 'Surprise Liberal preselection result spells end of Jim Molan's Senate career'. *Sydney Morning Herald*, 24 November. www.smh.com.au/politics/federal/surprise-liberal-preselection-result-spells-end-of-jim-molan-s-senate-career-20181124-p50i3t.html.

Kehoe, John. 2019. 'Higgins Liberal pre-selection won by Dr Katie Allen'. *Australian Financial Review*, 24 February. www.afr.com/news/politics/national/higgins-liberal-preselection-won-by-dr-katie-allen-20190224-h1bnkd.

Killoran, Matthew. 2018. 'Regional Labor "revolt" over Senate seat fears'. *The Courier-Mail*, [Brisbane], 7 August.

McGowan, Michael. 2018. 'Jane Prentice loses LNP preselection for Queensland seat of Ryan'. *The Guardian*, 12 May. www.theguardian.com/australia-news/2018/may/12/jane-prentice-loses-lnp-preselection-for-queensland-seat-of-ryan.

McMahon, Neil. 2018. 'Q&A recap: Liberal Senator mocked after defending party's gender problem'. *Sydney Morning Herald*, 21 May. www.smh.com.au/entertainment/tv-and-radio/q-and-a-recap-liberal-senator-mocked-after-defending-party-s-gender-problem-20180522-p4zgo2.html.

Miragliotta, Narelle. 2013. 'Explaining the (Lack of) Use of Radical Candidate Selection Methods by Australia's Major Parties'. *Australian Journal of Politics & History* 59(1): 113–26. doi.org/10.1111/ajph.12007.

Miragliotta, Narelle and Wayne Errington. 2012. 'Legislative Recruitment and Models of Party Organisation: Evidence from Australia'. *The Journal of Legislative Studies* 18(1): 21–40. doi.org/10.1080/13572334.2012.646708.

Murphy, Katharine and Anne Davies. 2018. 'Craig Kelly saved from preselection after NSW party bows to PM'. *The Guardian*, 3 December. www.theguardian.com/australia-news/2018/dec/03/nsw-party-bows-to-morrison-pressure-to-save-craig-kelly-from-preselection.

Nicholls, Sean. 2017. 'Mehreen Faruqi defeats Lee Rhiannon after fierce battle for Greens Senate ballot'. *Sydney Morning Herald*, 25 November. www.smh. com.au/politics/federal/mehreen-faruqi-defeats-lee-rhiannon-after-fierce-battle-for-greens-senate-ballot-20171125-gzsrfz.html.

Norman, Jane. 2018a. 'Malcolm Turnbull openly defied by Victorian Liberals amid claims of a power struggle'. *ABC News*, 4 May. mobile.abc.net.au/ news/2018-05-04/malcolm-turnbull-being-openly-defied-by-the-victorian-liberals/9724974.

Norman, Jane. 2018b. 'Scott Morrison ends impasse over Victorian branch preselection of Jane Hume and James Paterson'. *ABC News*, 6 September. www.abc.net.au/news/2018-09-06/liberal-pre-selection-jane-hume-james-paterson-impasse-ends/10210388.

Norman, Jane. 2019. 'Women still underrepresented in parliament after 2019 federal election'. *ABC News*, 27 May. www.abc.net.au/news/2019-05-27/ women-still-underrepresented-in-parliament/11148020.

Owens, Jared. 2018. 'Macdonald, O'Sullivan dumped in LNP Senate preselection'. *The Australian*, 6 July. www.theaustralian.com.au/national-affairs/macdonald-osullivan-dumped-in-lnp-senate-preselection/news-story/ 724a09027ba309cd1a6edb4c46115296.

Preiss, Benjamin. 2018. 'Liberals choose party activist to replace Julia Banks in Chisholm'. *The Age*, [Melbourne], 26 October. www.theage.com.au/politics/ victoria/liberals-choose-party-activist-to-replace-julia-banks-in-chisholm-20181026-p50c8b.html.

Pruysers, Scott, William P. Cross, Anika Gauja and Gideon Rahat. 2017. 'Candidate selection rules and democratic outcomes: The impact of parties on women's representation'. In *Organizing Political Parties: Representation, Participation, and Power*, edited by Susan E. Scarrow, Paul D. Webb and Thomas Poguntke, 208–33. Oxford: Oxford University Press. doi.org/ 10.1093/oso/9780198758631.003.0009.

Puddy, Rebecca, Casey Briggs and Leah MacLennan. 2018. 'Labor's factions negotiate deal to keep Mark Butler in parliament'. *ABC News*, 18 July. www. abc.net.au/news/2018-07-18/preselection-plans-to-salvage-mark-butlers-place-in-parliament/10007358.

Taflaga, Marija and Jennifer Curtin. 2018. 'Australia: Political Development and Data for 2017'. *European Journal of Political Research Political Data Yearbook* 57(1): 14–22. doi.org/10.1111/2047-8852.12203.

Taflaga, Marija and Jennifer Curtin. 2019. 'Australia: Political Development and Data for 2018'. *European Journal of Political Research Political Data Yearbook* 58. doi.org/10.1111/2047-8852.12234.

van Onselen, Peter. 2015. *Professionals or Part-Timers? Major Party Senators in Australia*. Melbourne: Melbourne University Publishing.

Whyte, Sally. 2018a. 'Labor candidates chosen for Canberra and Bean'. *The Canberra Times*, 1 September. www.canberratimes.com.au/story/6012145/labor-candidates-chosen-for-canberra-and-bean/.

Whyte, Sally. 2018b. 'Ed Cocks preselected to represent Liberals in Bean'. *Sydney Morning Herald*, 28 September. www.smh.com.au/politics/federal/ed-cocks-preselected-to-represent-liberals-in-bean-20180928-p506ok.html.

Whyte, Sally. 2019. 'Federal election 2019: Expert says Canberra Liberal candidate Mina Zaki may be dual citizen'. *The Canberra Times*, 5 May. www.canberratimes.com.au/story/6106562/canberra-liberal-candidate-denies-citizenship-problem/.

5

IDEOLOGY AND POPULISM

Carol Johnson[1]

The 2019 Australian federal election campaign offered voters a clear ideological choice. However, this was largely due to Labor's ambitious agenda that sought to address issues of rising inequality and to increase government revenue to fund government services and benefits. The Liberal Party's 'small target' strategy articulated its more neoliberal ideological position largely via critiquing Labor's tax and spending policies. The election campaign also displayed elements of both left-wing and right-wing populism, in which 'we the people' are mobilised against a perceived predatory enemy: 'them'. In a shift away from neoliberal ideological perspectives, Labor depicted itself as representing the people (particularly the working and middle classes) against the more economically privileged 'top end of town'. Scott Morrison took a more neoliberal populist position, mobilising the people against big government by depicting himself as an ordinary bloke trying to stop Labor from ripping off and spending taxpayers' money. Two minor right-wing parties displayed more fully blown populist agendas and were a significant source of preferences for the Coalition Government—namely, Pauline Hanson's One Nation (PHON) and Clive Palmer's United Australia Party (UAP).

1   This chapter draws on some material from an Australian Research Council–funded project (DP140100168), 'Expanding equality: A historical perspective on developments and dilemmas in contemporary Australian social democracy'. My thanks to the discussants (Frank Bongiorno and Mark Evans), the convenors and other participants at the 2019 federal election workshop for their feedback on the initial draft of this chapter.

Given that much of the Liberals' campaign was focused on critiquing Labor's economic policy, this discussion will begin with an analysis of Labor's position, before moving to an analysis of the Liberals' position as the major party in the Coalition. It will then analyse the populism exhibited by PHON and the UAP. I argue, contrary to Jan-Werner Müller (2016), that it is important to identify populist elements in mainstream politicians' discourse even if they do not exhibit the full-blown populism displayed by minor parties such as PHON and the UAP or by iconoclastic politicians such as Donald Trump in the United States.

Labor

Labor had been developing its policies, focusing on creating a more equal society, since well before the 2016 election, although the 2019 campaign saw some new policies added (see Chapters 13 and 20, this volume). Labor pledged to improve wages and conditions in a time of wage stagnation and rising economic inequality, to support racial, ethnic and same-sex equality and to raise revenue to better fund government services, including in child care, health and dental care and education. In these respects, Labor was espousing a relatively traditional Australian social-democratic ideological agenda, albeit one that emphasised providing a 'living wage' (Shorten 2019b) rather than providing a welfare state as extensive as in some European social democracies (Castles 1985). However, it was a post-Whitlamite and 21st-century version of that agenda that addressed a range of inequality issues wider than just those of class (see further Johnson 2019). For reasons that will be discussed later in this chapter, Labor's broader equality agenda did not become a major issue during the election in terms of the key debating points between the Liberals and Labor, although some anti-Labor forces did raise issues regarding Labor's support for lesbian, gay, bisexual, transgender, queer and intersex (LGBTQI) rights. Rather, the debate between the two major parties during the election campaign focused on critiquing Labor's tax policies, and those are what will be discussed in most detail in this chapter. Indeed, one of Labor's problems in the campaign was that it had difficulty framing the debate around its chosen issues, rather than ones highlighted by the Liberals.

Although some media commentators characterised Labor's tax policies as involving a radical move to the left, they were often merely winding back tax concessions and loopholes that had been introduced by the Howard Government during the heady days of the mining boom. For example, Howard had changed Keating-era legislation to provide franking credits to those who had not paid tax and had reduced Labor's capital gains tax. Similarly, the Hawke–Keating Government had originally tried to abolish negative gearing altogether before industry pressure made them reintroduce it. The real estate and housing industries also campaigned against Labor's negative gearing and capital gains tax changes in 2019 (see Wanna, Chapter 19, this volume).

Nonetheless, Labor's ideological position differed from that espoused during the Hawke and Keating years, despite both past Labor leaders' endorsement of Bill Shorten (Hawke and Keating 2019). Labor under Shorten did not emphasise the positive role of the market and private business in the way Hawke and Keating had. Rather, Shorten (2019b) focused on addressing issues of rising economic inequality. He argued 'that capital in this country is taxed very lightly, but income is taxed very heavily', which had major implications for ordinary Australians, from young people to pensioners (ABC 2019b). Meanwhile, Shorten stated that government spending benefited the privileged:

> When you say 'big spending', let's tell the truth here—this government is spending money. They spend it in tax cuts— $77 billion for the top tier of tax earners. They spent three years trying to give away $80 billion to the big end of town in corporate tax cuts. (ABC 2019c)

Shorten also argued that 'income has been redistributed from wages to profits' (quoted in Hartcher 2019). Labor emphasised the need to raise wages given wage stagnation and also the need to tackle the gender wage gap (NewCompany.com.au 2019b), including via government-funded wage subsidies in the female-dominated areas of early childhood education and care work. Labor's position on industrial relations also marked an ideological shift from the neoliberal-influenced Hawke and Keating years (as well as aspects of the Gillard years), particularly in regard to deficiencies in the existing enterprise bargaining regime and other rules constraining unions, including restrictions on pattern bargaining (see further Johnson 2019: 125–29). While Shorten claimed he would work with business, among others, in the spirit of Hawke and

Keating's accord (Shorten 2019a), he seemed to overlook the fact Hawke and Keating had offered business wage restraint initially (and later real wage cuts), subsidised by government spending on the social wage, and had also overseen a major transfer from wages to profits (see further Johnson 2019: 118–20). By contrast, Shorten tried to reframe the idea of what good economic management was, arguing: 'This government loves to talk about a strong economy but strong for who? Corporate profits are up 39 per cent but wages are only up 5 per cent' (ABC 2019b). However, Shorten argued on a number of occasions that increasing wages would be good for the economy because 'more money in the pockets of wage-earners, means more trade for shops in the high street and more confidence across the board. That is what we call a win-win, good for business, good for workers, and good for Australia' (Shorten 2019b).

Nonetheless, as in the 2016 election campaign (see Johnson 2016: 63–64, 73) and despite increased attempts to talk to business leaders (see Chapter 19, this volume), in 2019, Labor arguably did not make a frequent enough case that its policies would benefit both labour and at least some key sections of capital. Yet, that argument had long been a central part of Labor's traditional social harmony ideology (see further Johnson 1989: 4, 24, 102), helping make their case for Labor being better economic managers of a capitalist economy than the Liberals. Such issues pose a challenge for reforming social-democratic governments because they can be important to the many voters whose jobs and incomes are dependent on private sector investment. Yet, once again, in partially moving beyond its neoliberal positions of the 1980s and 1990s, Labor seemed to have forgotten how it had previously nuanced its economic management arguments. While previous Labor governments had sometimes evoked populist arguments to target particular sections of capital—for example, the banks under Ben Chifley or the multinationals under Gough Whitlam—generally they had argued that their policies would benefit both the economy as a whole and other key sections of capital, for example, the Australian manufacturing industry (Love 1984: 165–81; Johnson 1989: 21–26, 55–62).

Furthermore, Labor also failed to make a strong case during the election campaign for the economic management credentials of previous Labor governments. Instead, Labor tended to rely on its argument that it had made the tough revenue-raising decisions that would produce bigger surpluses than the Liberals and a greater reduction in debt (Bowen 2019). Yet Labor could have made a stronger case that its Keynesian stimulus policies during the Global Financial Crisis had helped to save the Australian economy from recession and that the Rudd and Gillard deficits were relatively low by international standards at the time and largely due to falling revenue (see, for example, the claims by Rudd 2013; Swan 2012). Interestingly, Paul Keating (and a then terminally ill Hawke) seemed to recognise the need to defend Labor's past economic policies more than Labor's current leadership team (Hawke and Keating 2019). Labor officials subsequently acknowledged that their advertising failed to counter some of the key Liberal critiques of their policies, which will be discussed below (Jensen 2019: 68). Meanwhile, Labor's key positive arguments were lost in a mass of policy detail (see Chapters 13 and 23, this volume).

The Liberals

By contrast, the Liberals mounted a small-target campaign around a number of key themes and images. While neoliberal ideology still underpinned their position, especially in regard to critiquing big-spending and big-taxing governments, it was in a restricted, more palatable form that suggested the Liberals were increasingly aware of the difficulties of selling more explicit neoliberal ideology to the broader electorate (see Huntley 2019). Rather, the Liberals focused on undercutting Labor's slogans, as listed on the ALP website of 18 May 2019, of supporting 'a fair go for Australia' and 'standing up for middle and working Australia' against the 'top' or 'big' end of town.

First, after by-election losses, the Liberals advocated tax cuts for lower-income earners to challenge those proposed by Labor (Bowen 2019). The Liberals also reaffirmed that they would not take their previously proposed tax cuts for big business to the election. Significantly, Morrison (ABC 2019a) admitted that corporate tax cuts did not have public support and business needed to rebuild public trust, although it was claimed that his alternative tax agenda would still disproportionately benefit higher-income earners and undermine progressive taxation rates in the longer term (RMIT ABC Fact Check 2019).

Second, the Liberals argued that it was actually Labor that was being unfair. Morrison's slogan, 'A fair go for those who have a go' (Morrison 2019d), suggested the Coalition Government was the real supporter of fairness while Labor would be spending taxpayers' hard-earned money on those who were less worthy—for example, welfare recipients. In short, Morrison was potentially mobilising *ressentiment* against welfare recipients (see further Hoggett et al. 2013). Morrison's neoliberal position here was also compatible with the Pentecostal 'prosperity gospel' (see further Wrenn 2019: 426) in which those who believe in God are rewarded by being wealthy while 'the ungodly become poor' (Almond 2019).[2] In a very successful scare campaign, the Liberals contentiously branded Labor's measures designed to close expensive tax concessions and loopholes as new 'taxes' (Henriques-Gomes and Koukoulas 2019), suggesting they would have a much broader impact than Labor claimed was the case (LP 2019a). Labor's franked dividend policies were branded the 'retiree tax', while its negative gearing measures were branded the 'housing tax', with claims the latter would both reduce house values and increase rents. In addition, Coalition advertisements erroneously suggested that Labor planned to introduce a 'death tax' on inheritance. The clear message of a suite of Liberal Party advertisements was that a Labor government would be a risk to voters' standard of living and the economy in troubling global economic times (LP 2019b). Meanwhile, Labor's big spending on the suite of policies discussed earlier was criticised. Labor was 'The Bill Australia can't afford' (LP 2019b). In short, the Liberals ran an effective campaign with simple and consistent messages that were designed to cut through and played on feelings of economic insecurity.

Fourth, Scott Morrison undermined Labor's argument that the Coalition Government supported the 'top end of town' by depicting himself as 'ScoMo', an ordinary Australian, the daggy dad from the suburbs who loved sport and having a beer down the pub. Morrison also mobilised his suburban dad persona to criticise Labor's environmental policies, arguing, for example, that Labor's electric car policy would 'end the weekend' given that, unlike the four-wheel-drives that families loved, the electric cars Shorten advocated people buy would not tow a trailer or boat or 'get you to your favourite camping spot with your family' (quoted in Remeikis 2019). While Turnbull's wealthy, elitist image potentially reinforced Labor's narrative, Morrison's image intentionally undercut it. Furthermore, unlike Turnbull in 2016, Morrison did not repeatedly denounce Labor as anti-business or emphasise the trickle-down benefits of corporate tax cuts, despite his own previous statements (cited in Hutchens 2017). Indeed, as already mentioned, he had acknowledged that business had to rebuild

---

2   For a more detailed analysis of the impact of Pentecostalism on Morrison, see Almond (2019).

public trust after various scandals, including the findings of the banking royal commission that he had originally strongly opposed establishing. Instead of being associated with big business, Morrison had previously made a point of identifying himself with the 'quiet Australians'—those Australians who were not 'shouty voices on the fringes telling us what we're supposed to be angry and outraged about' but instead getting on with their everyday lives, working hard while looking after their families and supporting their local communities (Morrison 2019a). He argued that, while Labor was going on about division and 'class war', the job of Liberals was to get on with governing and to provide Australians with the basic services they needed (Morrison 2019a).

Nonetheless, there were still neoliberal underpinnings to the Liberals' arguments, including the populist ones mobilising the people against big government. They evoked the old neoliberal positions that the source of exploitation of ordinary people lies in the state ripping off their money (rather than exploitation in the labour market) and that the best way of improving voters' income is therefore to give them tax cuts. While the Coalition Government claimed to be returning the Budget to surplus, Labor was depicted as the party of debt: 'Labor can't manage money: That's why they are coming after yours' (LP 2019a). Similarly, Morrison raised old neoliberal arguments about reward and choice, arguing:

> All Australians who work hard should … keep more of what they earn … when it's in your hands, you're making the choices about where it's spent. I don't think the Government knows better than you do about where your money should go. That's why I believe in lower taxes for everybody. (Morrison, in NewCompany. com.au 2019a)

Morrison also depicted himself as supporting a neoliberal aspirational and self-reliant citizen as opposed to 'Bill Shorten, who just wants to tax all of those aspirations more' (Morrison 2019b).

However, some previous aspects of the neoliberal agenda were downplayed during the election campaign, including Howard-era culture war arguments that elite, politically correct 'special interests' were ripping off taxpayers (Hindess and Sawer 2004: 9). Despite his own socially conservative ideology, and the previously cited references to his 'quiet Australians' eschewing 'shouty voices on the fringes', Morrison avoided issues that would unleash divisions between conservatives and moderates within the Liberal Party or antagonise former moderate Turnbull voters. It also seems likely that Liberal pollsters had picked up a more progressive mood for change in large sections of the electorate that they were trying to neutralise (Huntley 2019). Consequently, Morrison emphasised the number of women in his Cabinet and claimed that he believed in 'an Australia where you are accepted and acknowledged, regardless of your age, your ethnicity, your religion, your gender, your sexuality, your level of ability, or your wealth or your income' (Morrison 2019b). Meanwhile, the Christchurch (New Zealand) massacre had highlighted the risks of evoking ethnic and racial divisions.

Morrison's previous culture war interventions over issues ranging from the role of Captain Cook in Australian history (Morrison 2019c) to critiques of 'gender whisperers' in schools (Morrison 2018b) were largely put on hold. For example, Morrison sidestepped a question about Tasmanian legislation that would make specifying a gender on birth certificates optional, by supporting State sovereignty (Norman 2019). In the 2016 campaign, Morrison had highlighted claims of discrimination against Christians. Yet, in the 2019 Third Leaders' Debate, it was Shorten who stated that rugby player Israel Folau should not be sacked for proclaiming that homosexuals would go to hell while Morrison was more circumspect (NewCompany.com.au 2019b). Rather, Morrison relied on an image of his worshipping in his Pentecostal church, with arm raised, to reassure conservative Christian voters. Campaigning over such issues tended to be left to conservative community groups and to News Corp. Various religious leaders claimed that their campaigns over so-called religious freedom (including the right for religious schools to sack teachers who did not endorse their ethos) had reduced Labor's vote (Kelly and Shanahan 2019). An article in *The Australian* also accused Shorten of having ignited an 'unholy war' (Kelly 2019) and of illegitimately targeting Morrison's religious beliefs when Shorten expressed surprise that Morrison had initially evaded answering a journalist's question regarding his own views on whether gays went to hell (Crowe 2019).

Although Morrison eventually stated that he did not believe gays went to hell, he had opposed same-sex marriage and was one of the MPs who abstained from voting on the issue in parliament after the public voted overwhelmingly in favour during the postal plebiscite. It was noticeable that Morrison's speeches during the election campaign rarely evoked the biblical allusions that had peppered some of his previous speeches (for example, Morrison 2018a). However, Morrison's faith was very evident in his election victory speech, which was unusually religious in tone by Australian standards. Morrison (2019e) wished Bill Shorten and his family 'God's blessing', while affirming that he had 'always believed in miracles' and 'tonight we've been delivered another one'. Morrison ended his speech with the words: 'God bless Australia.'[3]

Minor parties and populism

While this chapter has argued that both the Labor and the Liberal campaigns reflected some populist elements, the ideological position of PHON and the UAP more closely meet Mudde's (2017: 4) definition of full-blown populism, including 'an ideology that considers society to be ultimately separated into two homogenous and antagonistic groups, the "pure people" and "the corrupt elite"'. While the Greens' preferences generally favoured Labor, the Coalition's formal and informal preference arrangements with PHON and the UAP enabled it to benefit from more explicitly right-wing populist agendas, without having to enunciate them itself.

Morrison justified the Coalition's preference deal with Clive Palmer (and indirectly, the preference deals some Queensland LNP members agreed with PHON) by suggesting the Greens' environmental and climate change policies were a greater threat to Australia than Clive Palmer (Shanahan and Kelly 2019). The Greens' policies would exacerbate Labor policies on climate change that Liberals had already suggested would ruin the economy and cost working-class jobs in the mining sector (Canavan, cited in Livingston and Osbourne 2019).

Pauline Hanson has been described as the 'the quintessential radical right-wing populist', who anticipated the mobilisation of anti-elitism and opposition to foreign immigration that have 'become central to current radical right wing populist discourse' (Betz 2019; see also Grant et al. 2019). Her party's 2019 election campaign policies continued this tradition. For example, PHON supported removing Australia from the international refugee convention, massively reducing the immigration intake and introducing a Trump-style travel ban for people from 'extremist' countries (PHON n.d.).

---

3   According to Middleton (2019), Morrison's commonly used expression 'How good is …', which also featured prominently in the speech, references a common Pentecostal expression, 'How good is God?'.

The UAP's mining magnate leader, Clive Palmer, funded an approximately $60 million advertising campaign that particularly targeted Labor's tax agenda, depicting it as ripping off ordinary Australians (Palmer 2019). The UAP is a sometimes unusual populist party—for example, UAP policy supported increasing the parliamentary representation of women (UAP 2019b). Nonetheless, the UAP's populism was evident in its rhetoric that the party would 'make Australia great again' by standing up for the people against self-interested politicians (Palmer 2019). In particular, the UAP argued that the existing political elite had been selling out Australia to Chinese commercial interests and the Chinese Communist Government might try to take over the country (UAP 2019a; Loomes 2019). Fear of China has been mobilised by other populists internationally—most prominently by Donald Trump.

Despite PHON and UAP preferences assisting the Coalition in retaining government, radical right-wing populism has not had as much electoral success in Australia as in some European and Asian countries. PHON won one Senate seat; the UAP won no seats.

Conclusion

As the overall analysis in this book establishes, election outcomes are usually determined by multiple factors. This chapter suggests that Labor lost the 2019 election in part because it did not win the ideological contest over the discursive framing of economic issues. Labor believed it could win the economic arguments because economic inequality was rising and wages were stagnating. Labor was convinced that only a relatively small number of voters would be negatively financially impacted by its election policies while far more would benefit from the revenue raised. However, the Liberals ran an effective campaign that succeeded in convincing sufficient numbers of voters that Labor's policies would impact detrimentally on most Australians and that the real risk to people's living standards was big-taxing and big-spending government. In so doing, the Liberals drew on neoliberal ideological positions that Labor had itself once reinforced, including cutting taxes. Previous Labor governments had also arguably inadvertently undermined many voters' confidence in the ability of governments to improve standards of living. As Robinson (2019) has noted: 'In the 1990s, Labor had laid waste to the institutions of centralised wage-fixation and economic regulation that established for many otherwise conservative voters a plausible linkage between politics and material conditions.' Labor also did not manage to convince sufficient voters that it could improve their standard of living by managing a capitalist economy effectively. In statements more in tune with classic Labor social harmony ideology that has been discussed earlier, new Labor Leader, Anthony Albanese, argued that: 'The language used was terrible … unions and employers have a common interest. Successful businesses are a precondition for employing more workers' (quoted in Benson et al. 2019). The new Shadow Treasurer, Jim Chalmers, concurred that some of the language used, such as 'top end of town', did not strike the right chord in the Australian community (ABC 2019d). In other words, key Labor figures now believe that Labor's attempts at using elements of populism, by mobilising the people against the 'big' or 'top' end of town, were counterproductive. By contrast, the Liberals' use of populist strategies, especially mobilising the people against big government, appears to have cut through more effectively.

Labor's failure to win the economic arguments against a pared down and more electorally palatable version of neoliberalism potentially has lessons for social-democrats pursuing more left-wing policies in the United Kingdom and Europe, for left-wing Democrats in the United States and for those advocating left-wing forms of populism (Mouffe 2018: 66, 92). However, the right is not unscathed. While its critique of Labor policies succeeded, it is not clear how much of the government's broader economic narrative remains, or what levers a government promising surpluses will be able to pull to manage the economic difficulties that lie ahead.

References

Almond, Philip. 2019. 'Five aspects of Pentecostalism that shed light on Scott Morrison's politics'. *The Conversation,* 23 May. theconversation.com/five-aspects-of-pentecostalism-that-shed-light-on-scott-morrisons-politics-117511.

Australian Broadcasting Corporation (ABC). 2019a. 'Scott Morrison discusses the Budget and the imminent election'. *7.30*, [ABC TV interview transcript], 3 April. www.abc.net.au/7.30/scott-morrison-discusses-the-budget-and-the/10968622.

Australian Broadcasting Corporation (ABC). 2019b. 'Opposition leader Bill Shorten discusses Labor's election promises'. *7.30*, [ABC TV interview transcript], 1 May. www.abc.net.au/7.30/opposition-leader-bill-shorten-discusses-labors/11064844.

Australian Broadcasting Corporation (ABC). 2019c. 'Bill Shorten on Q&A'. *Q&A*, [ABC TV program transcript], 6 May. www.abc.net.au/qanda/2019-06-05/11037828.

Australian Broadcasting Corporation (ABC). 2019d. 'Jim Chalmers joins Insiders'. *Insiders*, [ABC TV interview transcript], 23 June. www.abc.net.au/insiders/jim-chalmers-joins-insiders/11238976.

Benson, Simon, Greg Brown and Michael McKenna. 2019. 'Albanese vows to end Labor's class-war rhetoric'. *The Australian*, 23 May. www.theaustralian.com.au/nation/politics/albanese-vows-to-end-labors-classwar-rhetoric/news-story/5dccd3b687017f55145bdf4750be803c.

Betz, Hans-Georg. 2019. 'Australia's own brand of radical populism'. Blog post, 22 June. Centre for Analysis of the Radical Right. www.radicalrightanalysis.com/2019/06/22/australias-own-brand-of-radical-populism/.

Bowen, Chris. 2019. 'Address to the National Press Club, Canberra, 10 April'. [Transcript]. www.chrisbowen.net/transcriptsspeeches/address-to-the-national-press-club-wednesday-10-april-2019/.

Castles, Frank. 1985. *The Working Class and Welfare: Reflections on the Political Development of the Welfare State in Australia and New Zealand, 1890–1980*. Sydney: Allen & Unwin.

Crowe, David. 2019. 'Morrison accuses Shorten of taking a cheap shot over gays going to hell'. *Sydney Morning Herald*, 14 May. www.smh.com.au/federal-election-2019/govern-for-all-shorten-takes-aim-at-morrison-over-gays-going-to-hell-20190514-p51n3k.html.

Grant, Bligh, Tod Moore and Tony Lynch. eds. 2019. *The Rise of Right Populism: Pauline Hanson's One Nation and Australian Politics*. Singapore: Springer. doi.org/10.1007/978-981-13-2670-7.

Hartcher, Peter. 2019. 'Could Bill Shorten be the saviour of capitalism?'. *Sydney Morning Herald*, 27 April: 34. www.smh.com.au/federal-election-2019/could-bill-shorten-be-the-saviour-of-capitalism-20190426-p51hny.html.

Hawke, Bob and Paul Keating. 2019. 'Scott Morrison is flying in the face of history with his fallacious claim'. *Sydney Morning Herald*, 8 May. www.smh.com.au/federal-election-2019/scott-morrison-is-flying-in-the-face-of-history-with-his-fallacious-claim-20190507-p51kts.html.

Henriques-Gomes, Luke and Stephen Koukoulas. 2019. 'Are any of the Coalition's claims of new Labor taxes actually true?'. *The Guardian*, 14 May. www.theguardian.com/australia-news/2019/may/14/are-any-of-the-coalitions-claims-of-new-labor-taxes-actually-true.

Hindess, Barry and Marian Sawer. 2004. 'Introduction'. In *Us and Them: Anti-Elitism in Australia*, edited by Marian Sawer and Barry Hindess, 1–13. Perth: API Network, Australia Research Institute, Curtin University of Technology.

Hoggett, Paul, Hen Wilkinson and Phoebe Beedell. 2013. 'Fairness and the Politics of Resentment'. *Journal of Social Policy* 42(3): 567–85. doi.org/10.1017/S0047279413000056.

Huntley, Rebecca. 2019. 'Australia Fair: Listening to the Nation'. *Quarterly Essay* 73: 1–64.

Hutchens, Gareth. 2017. 'Scott Morrison says Australia needs tax cuts to offset hit from US cuts'. *The Guardian*, 21 December. www.theguardian.com/australia-news/2017/dec/21/scott-morrison-says-australia-needs-tax-cuts-to-offset-hit-from-us-cuts.

Jensen, Erik. 2019. 'The Prosperity Gospel: How Scott Morrison Won and Bill Shorten Lost'. *Quarterly Essay* 74: 1–71.

Johnson, Carol. 1989. *The Labor Legacy: Curtin, Chifley, Whitlam, Hawke*. Sydney: Allen & Unwin.

Johnson, Carol. 2016. 'The ideological context: Election 2016'. In *Double Disillusion: The 2016 Australian Federal Election*, edited by Anika Gauja, Peter Chen, Jennifer Curtin and Juliet Pietsch, 59–80. Canberra: ANU Press. doi.org/10.22459/DD.04.2018.03.

Johnson, Carol. 2019. *Social Democracy and the Crisis of Equality: Australian Social Democracy in Changing Times*. Singapore: Springer. doi.org/10.1007/978-981-13-6299-6.

Kelly, Joe. 2019. 'Shorten ignites unholy war by targeting Morrison's religion'. *The Australian*, 5 May. www.theaustralian.com.au/nation/politics/shorten-ignites-unholy-war-by-targeting-morrisons-religion/news-story/81db40d09c08f86b39f1ebd6e63d7ab0.

Kelly, Joe and Angela Shanahan. 2019. 'Religious freedom fears swayed poll, clerics claim'. *The Australian*, 22 May: 5.

Liberal Party of Australia (LP). 2019a. 'Labor can't manage money: That's why they are coming after yours'. Campaign flyer distributed in the electorate of Adelaide, 2019 election campaign.

Liberal Party of Australia (LP). 2019b. Liberal Party of Australia YouTube Channel. www.youtube.com/channel/UC3rLL1h9swUpQszCPJPVoOg.

Livingston, Angus and Paul Osborne. 2019. 'Morrison government approves groundwater plan for Adani coal mine'. *West Australian*, [Perth], 9 April. thewest.com.au/business/coal/morrison-government-approves-groundwater-plan-for-adani-coal-mine-ng-b881163037z.

Loomes, Phoebe. 2019. 'Clive Palmer's newest ad picked apart by experts in politics and defence'. *News.com.au*, 18 February. www.news.com.au/national/federal-election/clive-palmers-newest-ad-picked-apart-by-experts-in-politics-and-defence/news-story/41b84f2461d77f02784ce87dcebf94f1.

Love, Peter. 1984. *Labour and the Money Power: Australian Labour Populism, 1890–1950*. Melbourne: Melbourne University Press.

Middleton, Karen. 2019. 'Shorten loses again, trying to undermine Albanese leadership'. *The Saturday Paper*, [Melbourne], 25–31 May. www.thesaturdaypaper.com.au/news/politics/2019/05/25/shorten-loses-again-trying-under mine-albanese-leadership/15587064008188?cb=1558846607.

Morrison, Scott. 2018a. 'Address: Official opening of the Howard Library, Old Parliament House, Canberra, 4 December'. [Transcript]. www.pm.gov.au/media/address-official-opening-howard-library.

Morrison, Scott. 2018b. 'We do not need "gender whisperers" in our schools. Let kids be kids'. Twitter, 4 September. twitter.com/ScottMorrisonMP/status/1037100764294836224.

Morrison, Scott. 2019a. '2019 Sir Robert Menzies Lecture, speech, Melbourne, 12 March'. [Transcript]. Canberra: Liberal Party of Australia. www.liberal.org.au/latest-news/2019/03/12/2019-sir-robert-menzies-lecture.

Morrison, Scott. 2019b. 'Coalition campaign launch, speech, Melbourne, 12 May'. [Transcript]. Canberra: Liberal Party of Australia. www.liberal.org.au/latest-news/2019/05/12/coalition-campaign-launch.

Morrison, Scott. 2019c. *Honouring Captain James Cook's voyage*. Media release, 22 January. Canberra: Prime Minister of Australia. www.pm.gov.au/media/honouring-captain-james-cooks-voyage.

Morrison, Scott. 2019d. 'Doorstop, Googong, NSW, 4 April'. [Transcript]. Canberra: Prime Minister of Australia. www.pm.gov.au/media/doorstop-googong-nsw.

Morrison, Scott. 2019e. 'Speech, Sydney, 18 May'. [Transcript]. Canberra: Prime Minister of Australia. www.pm.gov.au/media/speech-sydney.

Mouffe, Chantal. 2018. *For a Left Populism*. London: Verso.

Mudde, Cas. 2017. 'Introduction to the populist radical right'. In *The Populist Radical Right: A Reader*, edited by Cas Mudde, 1–10. London: Routledge. doi.org/10.4324/9781315514574.

Müller, Jan-Werner. 2016. *What is Populism?* Philadelphia: University of Pennsylvania Press.

NewCompany.com.au. 2019a. 'Leaders' debate—Brisbane'. [Transcript of the second leaders' debate between Scott Morrison and Bill Shorten, Brisbane, 3 May]. *Daily Bulletin*, 4 May. www.dailybulletin.com.au/news/45090-leader-s-debate-brisbane.

NewCompany.com.au. 2019b. 'Prime Minister, leaders' debate—National Press Club, Canberra'. [Transcript of the third leaders' debate between Scott Morrison and Bill Shorten, Canberra, 8 May]. *Daily Bulletin*, 9 May. www.dailybulletin.com.au/news/45230-prime-minister-leaders-debate-national-press-club-canberra.

Norman, Jane. 2019. 'Scott Morrison's re-election strategy relies on him passing the "pub test"'. *ABC News*, 24 April. www.abc.net.au/news/2019-04-24/election-2019-analysis-morrison-campaign-strategy-the-pub-test/11035336.

Palmer, Clive. 2019. '2019 election launch and policy speech, delivered by federal leader Clive Palmer, United Australia Party campaign launch, 30 April'. Brisbane: UAP. www.unitedaustraliaparty.org.au/2019-election-launch-and-policy-speech/.

Pauline Hanson's One Nation (PHON). n.d. 'Asylum seekers and refugees'. [Online]. www.onenation.org.au/policies/asylum-seekers-and-refugees/.

Remeikis, Amy, 2019. '"Shorten wants to end the weekend": Morrison attacks Labor's electric vehicle policy'. *The Guardian*, 7 April. www.theguardian.com/australia-news/2019/apr/07/shorten-wants-to-end-the-weekend-morrison-attacks-labors-electric-vehicle-policy.

RMIT ABC Fact Check. 2019. 'Fact Check: Will $77 billion worth of Coalition tax cuts go to people earning more than $180,000?'. *ABC News*, 14 June. www.abc.net.au/news/2019-05-09/federal-election-fact-check-cost-of-coalition-tax-cuts/11092856.

Robinson, Geoffrey. 2019. 'Labor's election defeat reveals its continued inability to convince people it can make their lives better'. *The Conversation,* 19 May. theconversation.com/labors-election-defeat-reveals-its-continued-inability-to-convince-people-it-can-make-their-lives-better-117082.

Rudd, Kevin. 2013. 'The Australian economy in transition: Building a new national competitiveness agenda, speech, Canberra, 11 July'. [Transcript]. Canberra: Prime Minister of Australia. pandora.nla.gov.au/pan/79983/20130830-1433/www.pm.gov.au/press-office/address-national-press-club.html.

Shanahan, Dennis and Paul Kelly. 2019. 'Greens "a greater threat than Palmer", says Morrison'. *The Australian*, 11 May. www.theaustralian.com.au/nation/politics/greens-a-greater-threat-than-palmer-says-morrison/news-story/95d00971932a256a0a0ea0407a2ba805.

Shorten, Bill. 2019a. 'Address to the *Australian Financial Review* Business Summit, Sydney, 6 March'. [Transcript]. Canberra: ALP. www.billshorten.com.au/address_to_the_australian_financial_review_business_summit_sydney_wednesday_6_march_2019.

Shorten, Bill. 2019b. 'Address to ALP campaign launch, Brisbane, 5 May'. [Transcript]. Canberra: ALP. www.billshorten.com.au/address_to_alp_campaign_launch_brisbane_sunday_5_may_2019.

Swan, Wayne. 2012. 'The Budget and the fair go in the Asian century, National Press Club Post-Budget Address, Canberra, 9 May'. [Transcript]. Canberra: The Treasury. webarchive.nla.gov.au/awa/20120919122124/http://pandora.nla.gov.au/pan/121071/20120919-1629/www.treasurer.gov.au/wmsDisplayDocsf966.html.

United Australia Party (UAP). 2019a. *Palmer blasts WA Government for allowing Chinese control of Australian airports.* Media release, 31 January. Brisbane: UAP. www.unitedaustraliaparty.org.au/palmer-blasts-wa-government-for-allowing-chinese-control-of-australian-airports/.

United Australia Party (UAP). 2019b. *Women need a stronger voice in our parliament: If Canada can do it, why can't we?* Campaign flyer. Brisbane: UAP. www.unitedaustraliaparty.org.au/wp-content/uploads/2019/02/3_Gender Equality.pdf.

Wrenn, Mary V. 2019. 'Consecrating Capitalism: The United States Prosperity Gospel and Neoliberalism'. *Journal of Economic Issues* 53(2): 425–32. doi.org/10.1080/00213624.2019.1594528.

6

THE PERSONALISATION
OF THE CAMPAIGN

Paul Strangio and James Walter

This chapter considers the characteristics of the leaders of the major parties, Scott Morrison and Bill Shorten, the circumstances with which they were confronted and the way opportunities were seized or lost to confound the widespread expectations that had preceded the 2019 election campaign.

The media's inordinately 'leader-centric' bias in campaign reporting is long-established. Yet it might have been thought that the bitter experience of leadership turmoil in both parties of government over the previous decade would have put a brake on public expectations that the 'right' leader would provide the solution to present dilemmas. Indeed, some commentators remarked that 'Australia has had enough of messianic leaders for a while' (Hartcher 2019a). The Labor Party's campaign—choreographed as a team effort—seemed apt if such a transition in leadership style proved better attuned to the zeitgeist. For their part, Liberal Party MPs were reportedly unhappy with the 'presidential' aspect of Malcolm Turnbull's campaign at the 2016 election and reluctant to see a reversion to the leader 'standing in' for the party (Crowe 2019). And yet, this was precisely what defined the campaign, as Morrison, 'the Messiah from the Shire', contrived what had seemed an improbable victory. Leader-centrism appears once more to have been endorsed.

Observers argued that Morrison had 'to carry the operation because there's no alternative' (Murphy 2019b). On the other hand, it rapidly became apparent that playing the lone fighter, battling the odds against what appeared to be an ascendant Labor Party, suited Morrison's combative temperament and played to his strong suit. He proved a formidable campaigner—energised on the hustings, a big personality and 'a natural one-man-band, filling the stage, pounding the drums' (Grattan 2019b). Morrison the extrovert's love of such showmanship, combined with a capacity to play the everyman, chatting amiably with all-comers on the campaign trail, contrasted with Shorten's more wooden persona. It was not that Shorten lacked people skills, but he was most adept in small groups and face-to-face encounters in which his ability to persuade and negotiate had been honed during his work as a senior trade union official. He only rarely managed to translate those skills on to bigger stages.

Shorten was further constrained from matching the leadership grandiosity of the Morrison campaign by his perennially poor popularity ratings. Possessing neither an easy appeal nor magnetism, he had also been dogged by a perception of shiftiness originating from his part in bringing down two former Labor prime ministers, Kevin Rudd and Julia Gillard. The settled, unflattering view of Shorten as a factional machine man accentuated the contrast with the cleanskin and everyman Morrison. Yet Shorten's team-orientated approach was also a product of his background and instinct. As Labor leader, he had applied his union experience in orchestrating groups and negotiating deals to cauterise the party's wounds from the infighting of 2010–13. Together with a unified Shadow Cabinet, Shorten had developed an extensive policy agenda (see also Manwaring, Chapter 13, and Scott, Chapter 20, this volume). Now he would present as a team director—or 'coach', as he liked to characterise his leadership role—consistently flanked by senior colleagues who shared the articulation of Labor's ambitious program.

The scene was set, then, for an unusually clear differentiation between what the Coalition and Labor offered the public and how the leaders presented. Nothing illuminated the distinctions more starkly than the campaign launches of the major parties. Shorten joined his entire Shadow Cabinet on stage, foreshadowing a raft of policies packaged as delivering fairness and equality, with past Labor prime ministers in the front row, including the recent mortal enemies, Rudd and Gillard, to prove that old divisions had been transcended. In contrast, despite introductory speeches by a handful of others, the dominant image of the Liberal Party launch was of Morrison alone on the stage, with only his family for support at the end, speaking of the 'promise of being Australian' and allowing Australians 'quietly going about their lives, to realise their simple, honest and decent aspirations—quiet, hardworking Australians'. It was, in effect, a launch of Scott Morrison, aiming to consolidate the personalisation to which the entire campaign had been directed. The result would amount to a test case of the appeal of leader pre-eminence versus collaborative leadership in the electorate—or at least the capacity of Morrison and Shorten to 'sell' the relative advantages of each.

The creation of 'ScoMo'

In the course of a 12-year career in federal politics, Scott Morrison perfected the technique of presenting a public persona—hardworking, capable, approachable, positive and straightforward—that plays to advantage on the political stage, but masks the driven, ambitious political operator, adopting whatever tactic suits his ends in pursuing his objectives. Despite an early career in marketing, which peaked with his appointment (by the Howard Government) as inaugural director of Tourism Australia (2004–06), he entered politics as a political apparatchik, having served as director of the NSW Liberal Party (2000–04) before winning a controversial pre-selection battle for the NSW seat of Cook in 2006. Morrison was elected to the Commonwealth Parliament in 2007.

That pre-selection process was an early manifestation of Morrison's predilection for hardball politics. Competing against Michael Towke, Morrison lost the first round of voting 82 votes to eight. Immediately, a series of damaging stories in Sydney's *Daily Telegraph*, and an equally damaging file presented to the NSW party executive, put paid to Towke's ambitions; Morrison was endorsed. Labor Party MP and fixer Senator Sam Dastyari had compiled the file but said he handed over the material to Morrison's 'factional lieutenants', remarking later: 'I would never underestimate Scott Morrison because I would never underestimate a guy who would turn to one of his political opponents to take out one of his own … a guy who will do that will do anything' (see Martin 2019).

A modus operandi had been established: Morrison was adept at attracting supporters who, as in this case, would play crucial roles in later episodes that furthered his career, but allowed plausible deniability about his own agency in what transpired. Thus, when Malcolm Turnbull challenged Tony Abbott in 2015, Morrison demonstrated his support for the leader—even showing his vote for Abbott to colleagues—but let his parliamentary supporters vote for Turnbull (Kelly 2018: 25). 'If he had wanted his supporters to back Tony', said a senior Liberal, 'it would have happened' (Snow 2019a: 33). Likewise, in the remarkable events of late August 2018 that saw Turnbull deposed,

Morrison was represented as 'the accidental prime minister', only standing for the position when Turnbull realised his leadership was beyond salvation and released him to do so. Yet the double dealing of Morrison's supporters in the initial ballot precipitated by Peter Dutton that undermined Turnbull, and in contriving to edge out Julie Bishop while ensuring the defeat of Dutton in the second ballot, later became known (Savva 2019b; Sky News 2019; Williams 2019).

As a senior minister in both the Abbott and the Turnbull Coalition Cabinets, Morrison had shown himself to be tough, pragmatic and adaptable. As Minister for Immigration and Border Protection (2013–14), he took pride in having devised, with former major-general and later Senator Jim Molan (see Chapter 2, this volume), Operation Sovereign Borders to stop asylum seeker boats. Insiders thought he pursued policy aggressively, sometimes as a hard man, with a predilection for secrecy, and used his authority to lean on others. As Minister for Social Services (2014–15), he adopted a more 'caring' demeanour as a negotiator with the welfare lobby. Then as Treasurer (2015–18), he changed gear again to seem the enlightened technocrat. His technique for dealing with controversy was to invent a rationale that prevented him answering questions, or, if they could not be avoided, to imply he had no personal responsibility for events: 'I did the job that I had to do in that situation' (see Kelly 2018: 25). While competent and reliable with a prodigious appetite for work and impatience with anyone who got in his way, Morrison was not, according to a leading business figure, 'a particularly deep thinker … he is very transactional' (quoted in Snow 2019a: 33).

Sean Kelly argues that Morrison developed a capacity to do whatever was needed to scramble through the ranks while revealing as little as possible, leaving no trace. It allowed him to assume the prime ministership as a cleanskin, free of the taint of political wheeling and dealing. The cost was that he remained relatively unknown. The solution, however, was to be found in the consolidation of a persona that had started to take shape as Morrison got closer to the top of the game: 'ScoMo'.

ScoMo—a self-deprecatory nickname redolent of locker room banter— is the tag of an 'ordinary bloke', albeit one doing an extraordinary job. It is an appellation peculiarly suited to the story being constructed around the Morrison persona. In the frantic months before the campaign proper, Morrison turned to filling in the clutter-free outline of ScoMo with the broad brushstrokes that would characterise his campaign performance (see Kelly 2018: 30).

ScoMo signified authenticity, and Morrison's supporters supplied the details. Of the daggy, blokey, suburban dad schtick that became the abiding impression of ScoMo, friend (and former Howard staffer) Dave Gazard insisted:

> What you see is what you get. He wants to go to the footy, he wants to see the Sharks [his rugby team], he walks around in a T-shirt and shorts, he wears a baseball cap, he goes to church. That is him … He is the son of a cop, grew up in suburban Sydney, a curry night cooking at home is his idea of a great night. He is a pretty normal guy. (Snow 2019a: 33)

The ScoMo persona also benefited from Morrison's avowed religiosity. While not unique among Australian politicians in professing his Christian faith, Morrison was unusual among prime ministers in his adherence to an evangelical creed, Pentecostalism. For him, however, it was a private issue, a matter of faith and conduct, not a 'policy handbook' (see Snow 2019a: 33). Questions about the disparity between the harsh border regime he had instituted and 'Christian compassion', or about policies directed to material acquisition for the enterprising while welfare provision was trimmed, could be subsumed by Pentecostalism's focus on God and the hereafter, attention to personal salvation rather than collective justice, preferment for those who have been 'saved' and belief that material success flows to the godly (Almond 2019). Hardball politics could be justified in the battle against evil. However, Morrison showed little inclination to proselytise; it did not fit the relaxed, suburban dad schtick he was developing. Yet the sincerity of his beliefs could be read as a manifestation of principle—a shield against the charge of being a calculating opportunist (see Boyce 2019).

What you see is what you get—well, not exactly, as we argue, but ScoMo was the screen that made the hitherto anonymous prime minister someone to whom you could relate and obscured what he had done to get to the top. It replaced the tarnished Liberal brand: 'The government brand became Morrison himself' (Crowe 2019: 6). It signalled the Coalition's connection to and understanding of 'quiet Australians'. It was given momentum by Morrison's self-belief; he could persuade himself of any position that he determined to be right and he believed in the schtick. And it facilitated the relentless simplification of the Coalition's campaign as a contest between ScoMo and Shorten.

Morrison, the campaigner

Once the campaign was under way, Morrison proved remarkably effective on the road. His self-confidence and determination were manifest, but the affable ScoMo was careful to appear positive rather than confrontational in these settings. The impression of authenticity was all important. Constantly travelling between different settings, cities, States and marginal seats, his stamina and task orientation were extraordinary.

His savvy marketing skills and long-established habit of controlling communication served him well. Ready with simplistic slogans and aphorisms ('If you have a go, you'll get a go!'), but adept in smothering unwelcome questions with verbosity and talking over the top of his interlocutors (see, for example, ABC 2019b), he stayed relentlessly on message. The core of the message was always the assertion of the danger of a Labor victory, summed up by the slogan 'The Bill you can't afford', which had been workshopped by the Liberal campaign team. The tactic was to turn every question into a question about the Labor Party, its ambitious program and especially its leader: 'It's a choice between me and Bill Shorten, nothing else', Morrison said repeatedly, including at his campaign launch.

This emphasis on personalisation was calculated to disrupt Labor's efforts to focus the debate on policy. Such commitments as Morrison made were inordinately general—'It is my vision … to keep the promise of Australia'—and typically framed as a counter to the Labor risk: tax cuts against Labor's 'class warfare' tax reform proposals; cheaper energy versus Labor's unrealistic emissions abatement targets and reckless commitment to costly transitions in energy supply; cuts to immigration (with many references to Labor's failure to secure the borders); and maintenance of a sound economy, 'back in the black', as opposed to Labor's alleged incapacity to manage money. There was, however, no broader agenda. In three leaders' debates, Shorten tried to target this lack, but as Katherine Murphy observed:

> The Liberal leader has a well-honed talent for getting out from under … Morrison is a politician who thinks like a campaign director and carries an invisibility cloak. Going up against Morrison in a head-to-head is a bit like wrestling smoke. (Murphy 2019b)

Instead, Shorten was pushed back by Morrison's interjections and questions into elaborating the detail of Labor's policies, leaving himself open to interrogation on costings and equivocation on issues that were not yet fully resolved. Arguably, the constant disruption and confrontation in which Morrison indulged during the debates—including standing over Shorten in the final debate, which prompted the riposte, 'You're a classic space invader'—worked against the affable ScoMo persona; the studio audiences gave the debates to Shorten. But, interestingly, the response of television viewers appeared to contradict that of those in the room, perhaps indicating the doubts among voters about Labor's ambition and an appreciation of Morrison's efforts to force Shorten to 'come clean'.

While Morrison was the star performer, holding the stage, both the content and the targeting of what he presented relied on the ground campaign run by the Liberal Party's Federal Director, Andrew Hirst, and his deployment of key operatives from the polling and research firm Crosby Textor Group (C|T), which had been associated from its beginnings with the Liberal Party. Hirst, who had worked for Abbott and later for C|T, called on particular C|T colleagues to assist the Liberal campaign. Their skill was in the polling that indicated the path to victory in marginal seats, in social media targeting of people most likely to respond to the Coalition's message and in the tactics of the negative campaign (Bourke 2019; Lau and Rovner 2009; Martin 2004; and see Chapter 23, this volume).

While Liberal strategists claimed that Morrison effectively tapped into the aspirations of middle Australia (see Snow 2019c), the reality was more complicated and illustrated how targeted messaging, fostering negative affect, drew on social division and fostered the aggregation of localised resentment. Middle Australia's aspirations were not the drivers; the schism was between young workers in the cities and retirees and underemployed people in the regions. It was the fears of the latter to which the Coalition spoke, and it was in these regions that Morrison was most active (Dennis 2019; Megalogenis 2019; and Part 2 of this volume).

Bill Shorten: The unequal protégé?

Two days before polling day came news of the passing of Labor's longest-serving prime minister, Bob Hawke. The loss of a Labor legend and the parallels in background between Shorten and Hawke meant that conjecture focused particularly on how it might influence voter sentiment towards the Opposition. In his 2016 memoir cum personal political manifesto, Shorten had written that his political coming of age occurred in the early 1980s, coinciding with the election to office of the Hawke Government (Shorten 2016: 23–27). He was, in other words, a Hawke-era Laborite. Shorten's pre-parliamentary career as an Australian Workers' Union (AWU) official, culminating in a high-profile stint as its national secretary, had long invited comparisons with Hawke. It was during his time in the trade union movement, according to Shorten, that he fashioned an operating style of consensus leadership that was also redolent of Hawke. Considering these symmetries between the men, the timing of Hawke's passing—on the cusp of what was widely anticipated to be a likely Shorten victory—had almost a providential feel.

Yet, ironically, the Shorten campaign of 2019 was, in its fundamentals, designed around the reality that he was no Hawke. His leadership path to the contest more closely resembled, if anything, that of the rival Hawke dramatically deposed on the day of the calling of the 1983 federal election, the luckless Bill Hayden (for an account of these events, see Kelly 1984). Like Hayden, Shorten had inherited the leadership following a demoralising Labor election loss (albeit in Hayden's case he became leader following the second of two landslide Labor defeats suffered under Gough Whitlam in 1975 and 1977). Like Hayden, Shorten had made substantial ground in his first election as leader to place Labor within striking distance of government. Both had won regard for building around them a stable and united shadow ministerial team and for overseeing a substantial renovation of Labor's policy program. Like Hayden, however, Shorten was continuously dogged by questions about his lack of personal appeal to the electorate. Both men were the butt of regular criticism for their stolid communication style and ungainly appearance. In Hayden's case, the nagging doubts caused by his relative unpopularity were ultimately what precipitated him being pressured by his parliamentary colleagues to step aside for Hawke on the day that Malcolm Fraser (caught out by the Labor leadership change) triggered the 1983 election. In words that became part of Australian political folklore, Hayden bitterly declared at his parting press conference: 'I believe that a drover's dog could lead the Labor Party to victory the way the country is and the way the opinion polls are' (quoted in Kelly 1984: 388).

The difference in 2019 was that Labor had no Hawke-like messiah waiting in the wings and, even if there had been an obvious charismatic alternative, the party's revised 2013 rules for the selection and deselection of leaders would have impeded any five-minutes-to-midnight change. For Labor, it was the unpopular Shorten or bust. To put it another way, the Labor campaign became a test of whether the so-called drover's dog could actually win (Strangio 2019).

The Shorten campaign: The weight of expectation

Amid the leadership instability that had been a defining feature of Australian politics over the previous decade, Shorten stood out as an exception as he embarked on the 2019 election campaign. In his nearly six years as Labor leader, he had been pitted against three different Coalition prime ministers and he was the first Opposition leader to enjoy such security of tenure since Kim Beazley (1996–2001). Before that, Whitlam, Arthur Calwell, H.V. Evatt and Robert Menzies were the only other Opposition leaders since the Second World War to have gone to the electors in at least two consecutive elections, and of them, only Whitlam and Menzies became prime minister. Yet, unlike Shorten, neither of these two giants of Australian politics had been directly crowned Opposition leader following their party's loss of government. In that respect, Shorten was attempting to create his own piece of political history at the 2019 election.

If Morrison's persona was a work in progress in the minds of voters, Shorten's comparative longevity as Opposition leader meant he was a known commodity within the electorate. A trawl through past Newspolls confirms that his leadership ratings were chronically poor. Apart from a brief honeymoon in the months following his election as Opposition leader in October 2013, approval of his performance had outstripped disapproval only on a handful of occasions and then only barely. He had mostly trailed badly on the question of preferred prime minister. Eventually, the Labor Party's own post-election review conceded that Shorten's unpopularity contributed to the election loss (Emerson and Weatherill 2019: 8, 24–26).

The results of the 2016 Australian Election Study (AES) provide insight into the nature of Shorten's image problem among voters. Though Shorten scored creditably on the qualities of intelligence and knowledgeability (albeit not as highly as Turnbull), survey respondents marked him low on the qualities of honesty, trustworthiness and inspirational leadership

(Bean 2018: 244). Leadership trait polling on the leaders on the cusp of the 2019 campaign suggested this perception issue for Shorten was baked in. While the characteristics most associated with Morrison were 'well intentioned', followed by 'smug' and 'arrogant', for Shorten, it was 'untrustworthy' (Bickers 2019). The responses to the leaders by voter focus groups initiated by *The Age* and *The Sydney Morning Herald* suggested Shorten received some kudos for his doggedness and policy initiative. Yet the comment about Shorten that was singled out as having elicited 'knowing laughter and nodding' was that 'he's someone you'd like to punch in the head, really' (T. Wright 2019; Hartcher 2019b). Arguably, the publication of this was as revealing of a blithe normalising of incivility in public discourse as it was of sentiment towards the Labor leader.

Despite the liability of his unpopularity, Shorten entered the campaign favoured by the polls, the pundits and the bookies to become prime minister. In a series of profiles preceding and coinciding with the calling of the election, a motif was that of Shorten as a collegial leader anchored firmly in his party: 'Shorten is in fact selling Labor, not himself. The "team" dominates the talking points, and the "team" flanks Shorten ... 2019, for Labor, is a brand campaign, not a presidential one' (Murphy 2019a). Shorten consistently constructed his own leadership in those terms: 'The Labor Party is too big to be run by one person. The country is too big to be run by a messiah or by a dictator or by a one-trick pony' (Bramston 2019a). 'I'm not going to be a messiah. I don't believe in the ... authoritarian strongman' (ABC 2019a). It was a theme that reprised 2016 yet Shorten also emphasised it was an approach to leadership that had been confirmed by his experience over the previous six years. He stressed that Opposition had tested him and he had 'learnt a lot about myself ... These days I listen a lot more than I talk' (Bramston 2019a).

The delegation of policy initiative extended to ambitious elements of Labor's policy program such as negative gearing reform and the abolition of tax credits on franked dividends (see also Simms, Chapter 2, and Manwaring, Chapter 13, this volume). It was said that Shorten had required significant persuasion and time to embrace these and other measures. He explained it this way: 'I'm willing to take policy risks after I have thought about all the angles' (Snow 2019b). The boldness of the program implied confidence in Labor's position. But, according to Shorten, it was also informed by recent political history, particularly the predicament in which the Coalition found itself in 2013 after it won office on the back of an Abbott-led crusade that accentuated the negative and was threadbare in constructive policies. Shorten compared recent incoming governments and prime ministers to 'the proverbial dog that caught the truck. What do we do now?' (quoted in Tingle 2019: 30).

Favouritism imposed a heavy weight of expectation on Shorten and, in combination with the party's substantial reform agenda, it would be noted that this impacted on the dynamics of the campaign: the onus of proof was inverted, with the Opposition leader viewed more akin to an incumbent than a prime ministerial aspirant (Aly 2019). Shorten's campaign inner circle comprised his deputy, Tanya Plibersek, shadow treasurer Chris Bowen and Labor's Senate Leader, Penny Wong (Bramston 2019b). Wong's fellow Senator Kristina Keneally was 'captain' of the campaign's 'Bill Bus' and was described as playing a mix of 'confidant, sounding board, media wrangler, morale booster and, where necessary, attack dog' (S. Wright 2019). While behind the scenes men were equally integral to Shorten's campaign team—it was reported his chief of staff, Ryan Liddell, was the person he trusted above anyone else (Bramston 2019b)— the public prominence of women in Shorten's entourage was not lost on commentators (for example, Overington 2019). This culminated at Labor's official launch when Shorten was introduced by a quartet of women: Queensland Premier, Annastacia Palaszczuk, Wong, Plibersek and his wife, Chloe. The launch itself represented a celebration of Shorten's achievements in healing the party's wounds of 2010–13, building a unified team and enabling a comprehensive program as telegraphed by the choreographed images of the joint entrance of Rudd and Gillard and of Shorten accompanied on stage post policy speech by his entire shadow ministry. The program was described as 'the sum of their collective effort, not a postscript trailing a presidential figure' (Murphy 2019c).

For all the determined construction of Shorten as a team captain, modern election campaigns inevitably default to a principal spokesperson. Shorten began scratchily in that light, fumbling details on complex areas such as superannuation and the costings of Labor's climate policy. Though minor missteps, they were eagerly seized on by his critics in the News Corp media (for example, Kenny 2019; see also Wanna, Chapter 19, this volume). Shorten subsequently conceded an initial sluggishness: 'The first week of the campaign smartened me up. I stepped up a gear, no question … [I realised] the years of policy work itself won't do the story … I need to tell the story' (Snow 2019b). In retrospect at least, a failure to distil a focused, readily understood and reassuring narrative from Labor's extensive agenda would be recognised as a weakness of

Shorten's presentation throughout the campaign: 'I didn't hear Shorten, as his party's chief storyteller, tell a persuasive story about his policies … [by polling day] what most voters had seen and heard from Labor was clutter' (Carney 2019).

Shorten was judged by studio audiences to have bested Morrison in the first two of the three televised leadership debates (see above) and a reasonable assessment of the final contest hosted by the ABC was that the Prime Minister was 'across detail' whereas his opponent was 'more emotive and vibrant' (Shanahan 2019). Probably Shorten's most arresting media performance of the campaign was a solo appearance on the ABC's *Q&A* program in which he gave flesh to his aspiration to provide equality of opportunity for all Australians by relating the story of his mother's unfulfilled career aspirations, which also featured in his campaign launch (McMahon 2019). That moment became engulfed in controversy when Sydney's *Daily Telegraph* and some other Murdoch tabloids ran a tawdry story cavilling at the accuracy of Shorten's account of his mother's employment history (Caldwell 2019)—an overreach that inspired an emotional rebuttal by the Opposition leader and elicited public sympathy for him from Morrison, although the Prime Minister shrewdly used it to reinforce his core campaign message by declaring that the election was 'not about our families … it's about the choice between Bill Shorten and myself as prime minister' (Worthington 2019). The veteran journalist Michelle Grattan wrote that, in the wake of Shorten's passionate denunciation of the News Corp report, some 'old Labor hands' were comparing it to his appearances during the 2006 Beaconsfield mine disaster when, as an AWU official, he had first captured national attention. Shorten, who 'over the years has been unable to persuade voters to like him', observed Grattan (2019a), 'had suddenly been humanised'.

By election day, the final opinion polls showed Shorten's leadership ratings had inched up during the campaign but were still in the negative. Yet with Labor maintaining a decisive edge in the two-party-preferred estimates, he remained overwhelming favourite to become prime minister. In the meantime, two events 48 hours out from polling day—one planned (Shorten delivering his last major set piece address at Blacktown Hall, the scene of Whitlam's famous 1972 campaign launch) and one unforeseen (the announcement of Hawke's death that same evening)—had the combined effect of reinforcing the impression of a campaign and a leader firmly in the embrace of Labor history. On polling morning, another veteran commentator, Paul Kelly, while sharing the expectation that Shorten was likely to lead his party to victory, nonetheless noted ominously that he had failed to engender inspiration to the last: 'At the end Shorten … invoked the Whitlam spirit trying to energise his campaign and inject it with the 1972 "it's time" enthusiasm that it has manifestly been missing' (Kelly 2019a).

Conclusion

The drover's dog could not win. In the post-mortems that followed Labor's unexpected defeat, including that conducted by his own party, Shorten's lack of personal appeal was identified as a significant contributing factor. One columnist demanded: 'How was it possible the party saddled itself with a leader who, by any reasonable measure, was one of the least popular and most distrusted politicians in the entire country' (Walker 2019). It was an assessment backed by suggestions since before the campaign and acknowledged by Labor retrospectively that Shorten was particularly poorly received in Queensland (Savva 2019a; Emerson and Weatherill 2019: 26)—the State that was instrumental in the party's defeat. Liberal insiders divulged the fact that pivotal to the Coalition's revival strategy and victory had been the twin targeting of Shorten's leadership and Labor's tax reform measures as encapsulated in the slogan: 'The Bill you can't afford' (Bourke 2019; Markson and Devine 2019). The post-mortems— again, including the party's own—also attached blame to Labor's policy overreach, but here, too, Shorten was implicated both for misreading the electorate's mood and for his deficiencies in translating that program into a clear and compelling case for change.

There was speculation following the election that Shorten might not have been fully reconciled to elements of Labor's election agenda and that his support for them had been the price 'to buttress his leadership internally' (Kelly 2019b). This notion added to an impression—accentuated in hindsight—that Shorten had effaced himself in relation to his party by his campaign: running on an audacious reform agenda that belied his natural political caution and eschewing predominance in favour of the team. This conjured up an observation made at the time of the 2016 election about the test that still lay ahead for Shorten as Labor leader. He had proved himself skilled at harnessing the talents of his colleagues and tending to relationships within the party, but the finest Labor leaders had balanced that art with being 'prepared, where necessary, to cajole and impose their will on the party', to transcend it by building an autonomous following to augment its appeal (Strangio 2016). Fatally weakened by his inability to create a connection with the public, Shorten had never managed that evolution. Instead, as one commentator noted at the start of the 2019 campaign, his time at the head of the party was 'a study of recessing himself in the Labor leadership' (Murphy 2019a).

On the other hand, the Coalition victory was an unambiguous triumph for Scott Morrison—success against expectations. Where Labor had counted on a program-driven appeal, the Coalition eschewed policy detail for tactics: the creation of doubt about everything Labor proposed, sophisticated social media analytics and the presentation of a leader who claimed sound economic management and emphasised his understanding of the challenges and the aspirations of 'quiet Australians'.

The election outcome highlights the disparity between the expectations of political insiders and those of the many for whom the demands of daily life dominate and who seek short cuts to simplify their decision and a leader whose message substantiates their concerns or clarifies options. The gamble on personalisation worked; Morrison proved just such a leader. Despite his rise in the party, he had contrived to remain an enigma. Relatively unknown outside the 'Canberra bubble', he could construct a persona—ScoMo—attuned to the needs of the campaign: the ordinary bloke who understood common people and could give substance to their concerns by amplifying doubts about Shorten, his all-too-well-known opponent.

The circumstances of the 2019 election result—the pronounced personalisation of the Coalition's campaign and the thinness of its re-election policy program—undeniably bestowed on Morrison enormous authority and unusual latitude. As well placed as any leader to end the prime ministerial instability that has been a defining feature of Australian politics for a decade, his task would now be to capitalise on that opportunity.

References

Almond, Philip C. 2019. 'Five aspects of Pentecostalism that shed light on Scott Morrison's politics'. *The Conversation,* 23 May. theconversation.com/five-aspects-of-pentecostalism-that-shed-light-on-scott-morrisons-politics-117511.

Aly, Waleed. 2019. 'Why Shorten's mum is pivotal'. *Sydney Morning Herald,* 10 May: 22.

Australian Broadcasting Corporation (ABC). 2019a. 'Bill Shorten on Q&A'. *Q&A,* [ABC TV], 6 May. www.abc.net.au/qanda/2019-06-05/11037828.

Australian Broadcasting Corporation (ABC). 2019b. 'Prime Minister Scott Morrison discusses the Coalition's policies'. *7.30,* [ABC TV], 6 May. www.abc.net.au/7.30/scott-morrison-discusses-the-coalitions-policies/11085546.

Bean, Clive. 2018. 'Changing leaders, "Mediscare" and business as usual: Electoral behaviour'. In *Double Disillusion: The 2016 Australian Federal Election*, edited by Anika Gauja, Peter Chen, Jennifer Curtin and Juliet Pietsch, 235–53. Canberra: ANU Press. doi.org/10.22459/DD.04.2018.10.

Bickers, Claire. 2019. 'It's smug versus dodgy'. *Herald Sun,* [Melbourne], 6 April: 16.

Bourke, Latika. 2019. 'Beating Labor at their own game'. *Sunday Age,* [Melbourne], 26 May: 12.

Boyce, James. 2019. 'The Devil and Scott Morrison: What do we know about the Prime Minister's Pentecostalism?'. *The Monthly,* February: 10–14.

Bramston, Troy. 2019a. 'New era ambition of wannabe PM'. *Weekend Australian,* [Inquirer], 23–24 March: 11–12.

Bramston, Troy. 2019b. 'Shorten squad at the ready, waiting for the call'. *Weekend Australian,* 6–7 April: 6.

Caldwell, Anna. 2019. 'Shorten's mother of all lapses'. *Daily Telegraph,* [Sydney], 8 May: 4–5.

Carney, Shaun. 2019. 'Labor was a victim of policy clutter'. *Herald Sun,* [Melbourne], 21 May: 20.

Crowe, David. 2019. 'Liberal's campaign was defined by desperate ploys'. *Sunday Age,* [Melbourne], 19 May: 6.

Denniss, Richard. 2019. 'The Morrison election: What we know now'. *The Monthly*, June. www.themonthly.com.au/issue/2019/june/1559397600/richard-denniss/morrison-election-what-we-know-now.

Emerson, Craig and Jay Weatherill. 2019. *Review of Labor's 2019 Election Campaign*. Canberra: ALP. alp.org.au/media/2043/alp-campaign-review-2019.pdf.

Grattan, Michelle. 2019a. 'Another moment of "connection" for Bill Shorten'. *The Canberra Times*, 11 May. www.canberratimes.com.au/story/6118232/another-moment-of-connection-for-bill-shorten/.

Grattan, Michelle. 2019b. 'Against the odds, Scott Morrison wants to be returned as Prime Minister. But who the bloody hell is he?'. *The Conversation*, 13 May. theconversation.com/against-the-odds-scott-morrison-wants-to-be-returned-as-prime-minister-but-who-the-bloody-hell-is-he-116732.

Hartcher, Peter. 2019a. 'Depressing contest means we have to consider the choice of parties and policies, not personalities'. *Sydney Morning Herald*, 11 April. www.smh.com.au/politics/federal/depressing-contest-means-we-have-to-consider-the-choice-of-parties-and-policies-not-personalities-20190410-p51cya.html.

Hartcher, Peter. 2019b. 'Focus groups flag danger for leaders'. *The Age*, [Melbourne], 4 May: 12.

Kelly, Paul. 1984. *The Hawke Ascendancy: A Definitive Account of its Origins and Climax 1975–1983*. Sydney: Angus & Robertson.

Kelly, Paul. 2019a. 'Radical trap of a Shorten win'. *Weekend Australian*, [Inquirer], 18–19 May: 34.

Kelly, Paul. 2019b. 'Post-material push cannot conquer the nation'. *The Australian*, 12 June: 12.

Kelly, Sean. 2018. 'Leave no trace: The story of Scott Morrison'. *The Monthly*, November: 22–33.

Kenny, Chris. 2019. 'Shorten's blunders deplete his charge'. *Weekend Australian*, [Inquirer], 20–21 April: 19.

Lau, Richard R. and Ivy Brown Rovner. 2009. 'Negative Campaigning'. *Annual Review of Political Science* 12: 285–306. doi.org/10.1146/annurev.polisci.10.071905.101448.

McMahon, Neil. 2019. 'Q&A: Bill Shorten utters the most powerful and personal sentence of the campaign'. *Sydney Morning Herald*, 7 May. www.smh.com.au/entertainment/tv-and-radio/q-and-a-bill-shorten-utters-the-most-powerful-and-personal-sentence-of-the-campaign-20190507-p51kp6.html.

Markson, Sharri and Miranda Devine. 2019. 'How Scomo pulled off a miracle'. *Daily Telegraph*, [Sydney], 25 May: 42.

Martin, Paul S. 2004. 'Inside the Black Box of Negative Campaign Effects: Three Reasons Why Negative Campaigns Mobilize'. *Political Psychology* 25(4): 545–62. doi.org/10.1111/j.1467-9221.2004.00386.x.

Martin, Sarah. 2019. 'Scott Morrison: "Master of the middle" may pull the Coalition out of a muddle'. *The Guardian*, 21 April. www.theguardian.com/australia-news/2019/apr/21/scott-morrison-master-of-the-middle-may-pull-coalition-out-of-a-muddle?CMP=Share_i%E2%80%A6.

Megalogenis, George. 2019. '2019 Election: The shock of the new normal—Why the election result shouldn't have surprised the major parties'. *The Monthly*, June. www.themonthly.com.au/issue/2019/june/1559397600/george-megalogenis/2019-election-shock-new-normal.

Murphy, Katharine. 2019a. 'Labor's path to victory is open—but have voters made peace with Bill Shorten?'. *The Guardian*, 11 April. www.theguardian.com/australia-news/2019/apr/11/labors-path-to-victory-is-open-but-have-voters-made-peace-with-bill-shorten.

Murphy, Katharine. 2019b. 'How Shorten the redeemer met Morrison the disruptor—and decided to fight back'. *The Guardian*, 20 April. www.theguardian.com/australia-news/2019/apr/20/how-shorten-the-redeemer-met-morrison-the-disruptor-and-decided-to-fight-back?CMP.

Murphy, Katharine. 2019c. 'Former PMs bury the hatchet in show of unity at Labor campaign launch'. *The Guardian*, 5 May. www.theguardian.com/australia-news/2019/may/05/former-pms-bury-the-hatchet-in-show-of-unity-at-labor-campaign-launch.

Overington, Caroline. 2019. 'Bill's entourage hints at female-voter problem'. *The Australian*, 17 April: 5.

Savva, Niki. 2019a. 'Libs are lucky: What if Labor had a popular leader?'. *The Australian*, 14 March: 12.

Savva, Niki. 2019b. *Plots and Prayers: Malcolm Turnbull's Demise and Scott Morrison's Ascension*. Melbourne: Scribe Press.

Shanahan, Dennis. 2019. 'ScoMo's details v Bill's emotions'. *The Australian*, 9 May: 1.

Shorten, Bill. 2016. *For the Common Good: Reflections on Australia's Future*. Melbourne: Melbourne University Press.

Sky News. 2019. 'Bad blood/new blood'. *Sky News*, 25–26 June.

Snow, Deborah. 2019a. 'Can this man pick up the pieces?'. *The Age*, [Melbourne], 4 May: 32–33.

Snow, Deborah. 2019b. 'Bill Shorten's final dash in the long road to the top'. *Sun Herald*, [Melbourne], 12 May: 11–12.

Snow, Deborah. 2019c. 'How Morrison effectively tapped into middle Australia'. *The Age*, [Melbourne], 20 May. www.theage.com.au/federal-election-2019/how-morrison-successfully-tapped-into-middle-australia-20190519-p51p1c.html.

Strangio, Paul. 2016. 'Shorten the consensus leader unites a fractured Labor, but it may not quite be enough'. *The Conversation*, 30 June. theconversation.com/shorten-the-consensus-leader-unites-a-fractured-labor-but-it-may-not-quite-be-enough-61741.

Strangio, Paul. 2019. 'After six years as Opposition Leader, history beckons Bill Shorten. Will the "drover's dog" have its day?'. *The Conversation,* 13 May. theconversation.com/after-six-years-as-opposition-leader-history-beckons-bill-shorten-will-the-drovers-dog-have-its-day-115490.

Tingle, Laura. 2019. 'Between fear and ideas: Bill Shorten on the road ahead'. *The Monthly*, March: 19–30.

Walker, Tony. 2019. 'Shorten failed to sell complex reform program'. *The Age*, [Melbourne], 20 May: 26.

Williams, Pamela. 2019. 'The war on Malcolm: Behind the scenes of an overthrow'. *The Monthly*, February: 22–41.

Worthington, Brett. 2019. 'Bill Shorten accuses the Daily Telegraph of "new low" for federal election story on his mother'. *ABC News*, 8 May. www.abc.net.au/news/2019-05-08/bill-shorten-slams-daily-telegraph-federal-election-mother-story/11090238.

Wright, Shane. 2019. 'The rise and rise of Kristina Keneally inside Bill Shorten's inner circle'. *Sydney Morning Herald*, 13 April. www.smh.com.au/federal-election-2019/the-rise-and-rise-of-kristina-keneally-inside-bill-shorten-s-inner-circle-20190413-p51duq.html.

Wright, Tony. 2019. 'Stumped for words: Melburnian panel finds little love for top pollies'. *The Age*, [Melbourne], 4 May: 12.

7

NATIONAL POLLING AND OTHER DISASTERS

Luke Mansillo and Simon Jackman

Perhaps one of the most important and unexpected features of the 2019 Australian federal election was the fact that public polls 'got it wrong'. Polls pointing to a Labor win dominated pre-election prognostication, while lamentations and dissection of polling error dominated post-election analysis.

As we argue below, polling errors in the 2019 election were large, but not completely unprecedented. Following generally good performances in 2016 and 2013, few commentators or analysts recalled that the 2010 election saw large errors in the polls. What was especially noteworthy about 2019 was the consistency of the poll results indicating Labor would win, and the extent to which Australian political actors—politicians, media and the public—'locked in' behind these poll-shaped but wrong expectations that had shaped the content and conduct of Australian politics not just during the election campaign, but also for some years previously.

The large and extensive influence of polls on mass and elite politics is well documented in the political science literature. Polls shape how elites develop and implement public policy (Burstein 2003), how they decide whether to engage in leadership ructions (Brown 1992) and the decisions of individual politicians to resign from politics (Stone et al. 2010). We note that 13 Liberal–National Coalition parliamentarians retired ahead of the

2019 election, nine of them from the ministry. Individual and corporate donors also rely on the polls in assessing whether, and to whom, to make campaign contributions (Fuchs et al. 2000).

Polls also provide politicians with opportunities to advance issues and agendas on behalf of their constituencies or their parties or to serve more personal causes, such as leadership ambitions (Meyer and Minkoff 2004; Petersen et al. 2008). Critically, in Westminster systems—in which party leadership is in some sense under constant scrutiny, coupled with the advent of a more 'presidentialised' prime ministership (Hart 1992; see also Chapter 6, this volume)—polling has taken on even greater political significance. Polls provide backbenchers from marginal seats with a regular barometer of their party's chances at the next election. Indeed, a key feature of Australian politics over the past decade has been the way poll results have driven leadership challenges and turnover, with profound consequences for who governs and how they govern.

Hence, understanding the magnitude and sources of polling error in the 2019 Australian election is not a mere technical exercise, but is fundamental to understanding Australian politics, policies and leaders.

Estimating poll bias

We begin by estimating the magnitude of the polls' errors, or biases, in the 2019 election cycle. We rely on a methodology that one of us helped pioneer (Jackman 2005, 2009) and is used widely by polling analysts in Australia (Mark the Ballot 2017) and internationally (Ellis 2017; Pickup et al. 2011). We previously deployed this modelling strategy to analyse polls leading up to the 2016 Australian federal election (Jackman and Mansillo 2018).

We fit a statistical model to public polls fielded between the 2016 and 2019 elections. For each poll, we usually observe the following: 1) estimates of voting intentions, which are typically reported as an integer percentage; 2) the field dates; 3) the number of poll respondents; 4) the population of interest (typically, all adult Australian citizens); and 5) the identity of the polling company conducting the poll. Most media reports of polls do not contain even this much information. Sometimes reports omit information such as the number of respondents or field dates, sampling methodologies and weighting procedures applied after data collection, which almost never appear in media reports of polls or in the polling companies' description of their methods.

Nonetheless, with this basic information from a series of polls, we set about recovering the day-by-day trajectory of voting intentions between the 2016 and 2019 elections. Let t index the $T = 1,051$ days between the 2016 and 2019 elections and let ξ_t denote true (but 'latent' or indirectly observed) voting intentions on day t. Of great utility is that ξ is revealed on election day, both in 2016 and in 2019 on days $t = 1$ and $t = T = 1,051$, once the AEC publishes final election results.[1] These two election day 'endpoint' observations serve as 'anchors' or fixed points that let us reconstruct the trajectory of voting intentions from observed polls, at the same time as we estimate and correct for biases in the polls.

Poll p fielded on day t by polling company j supplies an estimate of ξ_t, reported as proportion $y_p \in [0,1]$ (conventionally reported after rounding to two digits of precision), with sample size n_p. We assume that the variance of each poll estimate is $V_{p(t)} = y_p(1 - y_p)/n_{p(t)}$, which is a reasonable approximation absent detailed information about the polls' sampling and weighting methodologies.[2]

Each poll result, y_p, is assumed to be a sum of the true but unobserved state of voting intentions on the corresponding day, $\xi_{t(p)}$, and the bias of the corresponding pollster, denoted as $\delta_{j(p)}$.[3] Averaging over the random error produced by sampling, we assume $E(y_p) = \xi_{t(p)} + \delta_{j(p)}$. For polls with the sample sizes considered here, we can conveniently assume a normal law for the poll results—that is, $y_p \sim N(\xi_{t(p)} + \delta_{j(p)}, V_p)$.[4]

---

1   Treating the published election results as errorless measures of the corresponding ξ_t assumes no meaningful errors in the national vote counts nor any sizeable electoral fraud; these assumptions seem valid in the context of both the 2016 and the 2019 Australian federal elections.

2   This variance can be interpreted as a measure of the uncertainty one possesses about true voting intentions, ξ_t, given an unbiased poll of sample size n_p acquired via simple random sampling. If 1) poll p is biased or 2) simple random sampling was not deployed, the actual variance will differ slightly from the expression in the text.

3   We use the notation $t(p)$ to refer to the day(s) in which poll p was in the field and $j(p)$ to refer to the polling house j that fielded poll p. The total sample of a poll n_p we divide by $t(p)$ days in poll p to give the incorporate information from each over each day of fielding with the correct precision. This produces a smoother estimate of voting intentions than the previous attempts that used the median date of fielding (Jackman 2005; Jackman and Mansillo 2018).

4   Most polls have a multiday field period, which we accommodate with the following procedure. A poll fielded between days t and $t + r$ is modelled as a function of $\xi_t, \ldots, \xi_{t+r}$, spreading the polls' sample $n_{(p)}$ uniformly over the $r + 1$ field days; this 'per field day' sample size, $n_p/(r + 1)$, appears in the denominator of the expression for $V_{(p)}$ given in the previous paragraph.

The model also exploits the fact that, despite political upheavals such as leadership spills, voting intentions change relatively slowly. We assume that a priori voting intentions on day t are, on average, unchanged from the previous day. Day-to-day changes in the ξ_t follow a normal distribution, with a small but unknown variance, ω^2—that is, $\xi_t \sim N(\xi_{t-1}, \omega^2)$. We augment the model to include a discontinuity (or 'jump') on 28 August 2018, the day Morrison replaced Turnbull as Liberal leader and prime minister.[5]

The inferential task is to recover estimates of: 1) the sequence of latent voting intentions, $\{\xi_t\}$; 2) the house effects, δ_j; 3) the innovation variance parameter, ω^2; and 4) the discontinuity parameter, γ. Technical details on estimation and underlying computation appear in Jackman (2009). We derive estimates separately for the ALP, Liberal–National Coalition, the Australian Greens and other primary voting intentions as well as two-party-preferred voting intentions.

Data

First, we analyse a dataset of 226 polls, fielded between the 2016 and 2019 elections. These polls span six distinct polling companies and methodology sets, shown in Table 7.1. We treat three Galaxy polls fielded in 2019 as in the 'Newspoll' category, as they were fielded a considerable time after YouGov had acquired Galaxy but with the identical online and interactive voice response (IVR) interview modes that Galaxy Research had used for the Newspoll-branded polls commissioned by *The Australian* newspaper.

The 12 YouGov/Fifty Acres–branded polls were conducted online, administered to respondents drawn from the YouGov national panel, with quota sampling designed to produce a nationally representative sample with respect to age, gender and region. YouGov partnered with Fifty Acres, a government and public relations firm, to produce these polls. Public polling is highly concentrated in the hands of a small number of firms; weekly polls from Essential are the sole, high-frequency alternative to Newspoll/Galaxy/YouGov polls. The Newspoll/Galaxy polls use a combination of IVR phone and online panel surveys (details of the

---

5   On that day the model becomes $\xi_t \sim N(\xi_{t-1} + \gamma, \omega^2)$, in which γ is the jump parameter. We make no a priori assumption as to whether γ is positive or negative.

proportions of each are not public knowledge), while Essential uses only online panel surveys and Ipsos uses live-interviewer computer-assisted telephone interviewing surveys. The few Roy Morgan polls were all conducted with face-to-face interviews as part of their regular consumer and market research surveys.

To establish historical benchmarks for the errors of the 2019 polls, we also analyse a dataset of 1,624 polls, fielded between the 2004 and 2019 elections. The analysis described above is repeated for the four prior parliamentary periods.

Table 7.1 Polls by survey house

Survey house	No. of polls
Essential	108
Ipsos	18
Newspoll	61
ReachTEL	15
Roy Morgan (Face-to-Face)	12
YouGov	12

Source: Authors' calculations.

Estimated trajectories of voting intentions, 2016–19

The circular symbols in Figure 7.1 correspond to estimates from public polls of the ALP's share of first-preference vote intentions, 2016 to 2019. The two horizontal reference lines indicate the 2016 and 2019 election results, with Labor winning 34.7 per cent and 33.3 per cent of first preferences, respectively. The darker, thicker line undulating across the graph is the output of our model, the sequence of daily estimates of ξ_t between the 2016 and 2019 elections; the effect of the 'endpoint' constraints are clearly visible, with the estimates of true public opinion beginning and terminating on the observed, actual 2016 and 2019 election results.

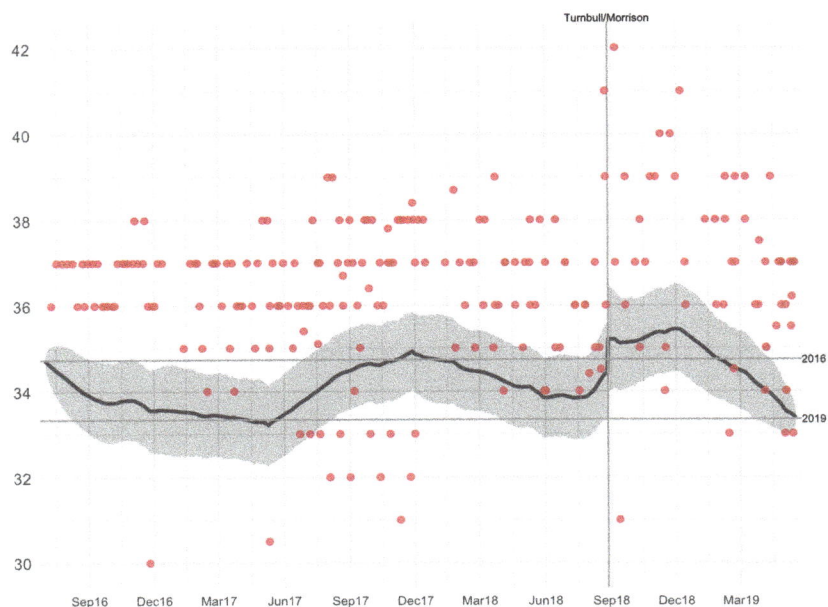

Figure 7.1 ALP first-preference voting intentions between the 2016 and 2019 federal elections

Notes: The darker, thicker line is the output of our model, connecting the daily estimates of the true state of public opinion, given our model and the observed 2016 and 2019 election results; the shaded region is a pointwise 95 per cent credibility interval around the daily estimates. Circles are poll results, used as input to our model.

Source: Authors' calculations.

Figure 7.1 also makes clear that the polls typically overestimated Labor's share of the vote; the bulk of the polls lie well above the estimated true state of public opinion. Observe also—with the benefit of hindsight—that: 1) at no point between the 2016 and 2019 elections was Labor's share of first preferences any stronger than in the 2016 election, even in the immediate aftermath of the Turnbull-to-Morrison leadership transition; and 2) there was a steep deterioration in Labor's first-preference vote share in the six months leading up to the 2019 election, of about 1.8 percentage points. This fall in support for Labor is more than twice the boost in Labor voting intentions that occurred at the time of the Turnbull–Morrison transition.

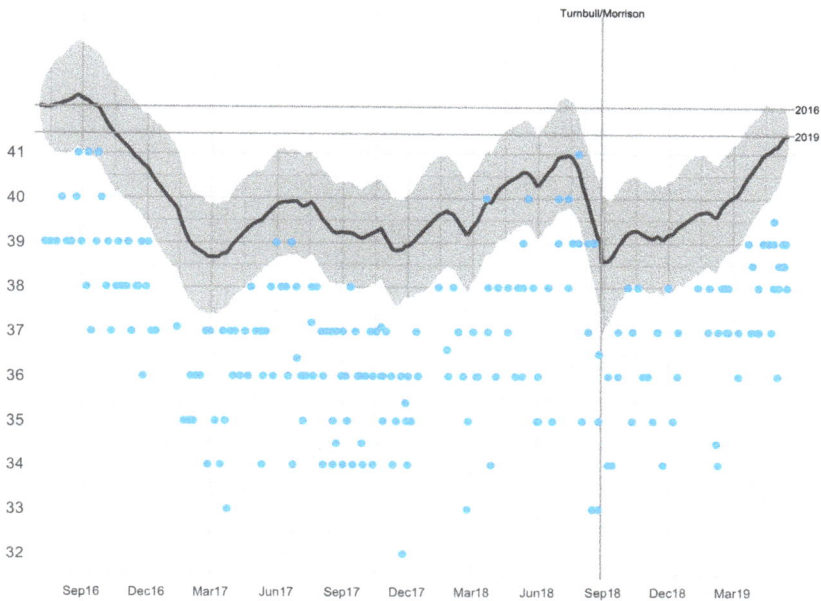

Figure 7.2 Coalition first-preference voting intentions between the 2016 and 2019 federal elections

Notes: The darker, thicker line is the output of our model, connecting the daily estimates of the true state of public opinion, given our model and the observed 2016 and 2019 election results; the shaded region is a pointwise 95 per cent credibility interval around the daily estimates. Circles are poll results, used as input to our model.

Source: Authors' calculations.

The equivalent graph for Coalition voting intentions is shown in Figure 7.2. Just as the polls tended to overstate the true level of Labor support, support for the Coalition was almost always understated, with almost all of the polls (the points in Figure 7.2) lying below the estimated true level of Coalition support.

Again, with the benefit of hindsight, we see that Coalition support did fall in the months immediately after the July 2016 election, stabilising around the 39 per cent level for most of 2017 (some 3 percentage points below the 2016 election result). A modest recovery in 2018 was reversed in the months preceding the Liberal leadership transition in August 2018. Over the course of Morrison's tenure, Coalition support recovered more than 2 percentage points, from 39 per cent to the 41.4 per cent result obtained at the May 2019 election.

Critically, not a single public poll reported Coalition first-preference support above 39.5 per cent in the period between Morrison becoming leader in August 2018 and the May 2019 election—far below the actual level of Coalition support during this period and indicative of the magnitude of poll bias in the 2016–19 cycle. It is understandable how this fed low expectations for the Coalition's electoral prospects. In previous work, Jackman (1994) applied the Tufte (1973) log-vote share on log-seat share model to Australian federal elections between 1949 and 1993 and found the typical value for the Coalition to win 50 per cent of House of Representatives seats is 49.1 per cent of the two-party-preferred vote.[6] Only for the briefest point after Morrison became the prime minister in August 2018 was the Coalition past this critical threshold.

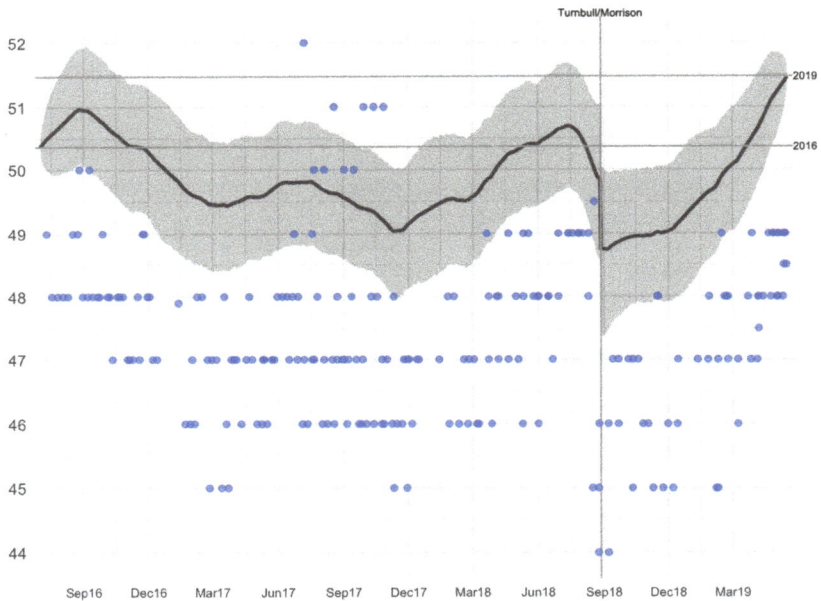

Figure 7.3 Coalition two-party-preferred voting intentions between the 2016 and 2019 federal elections

Notes: The darker, thicker line is the output of our model, connecting the daily estimates of the true state of public opinion, given our model and the observed 2016 and 2019 election results; the shaded region is a pointwise 95 per cent credibility interval around the daily estimates. Circles are poll results, used as input to our model.

Source: Authors' calculations.

---

6   This was found to be invariant in Jackman (2009) and Mansillo and Evershed (2016) with the addition of more data.

A similar set of findings holds with even greater force for Coalition two-party-preferred support, shown in Figure 7.3. Few polls overestimated Coalition support; most estimated the Coalition to be underperforming relative to its 2016 two-party-preferred result. The polls did pick up a recovery in Coalition two-party-preferred support over the course of Morrison's tenure, but generally were biased by a considerable margin.

Pollster biases

Estimates of the biases specific to each polling organisation—the 'house effects' or δ parameters in our model—appear in Figures 7.4 and 7.5. Of the six polling organisations considered, four systematically overestimated Labor's first preferences: Morgan, ReachTEL, Essential and Newspoll. YouGov and Ipsos did not overestimate Labor's vote share but both organisations did underestimate Coalition first preferences, as did *every* polling organisation. The underestimates of Coalition first preferences are large in several cases, reaching almost 5 percentage points for YouGov, more than 4 percentage points for ReachTEL and 3 percentage points for Newspoll. Newspoll also overestimated support for the Australian Greens by 1 percentage point.

YouGov's large underestimate of Coalition first preferences is accompanied by a large overestimate of support for minor parties and Independents, by almost 5 percentage points. This bias is the largest polling error we observe for minor parties and Independents and is large relative to the actual level of support for minor parties and Independents in 2019 (14.8 per cent). Experimental methods may be a useful strategy for future research to identify whether such bias was a product of errors of representation or errors of measurement.

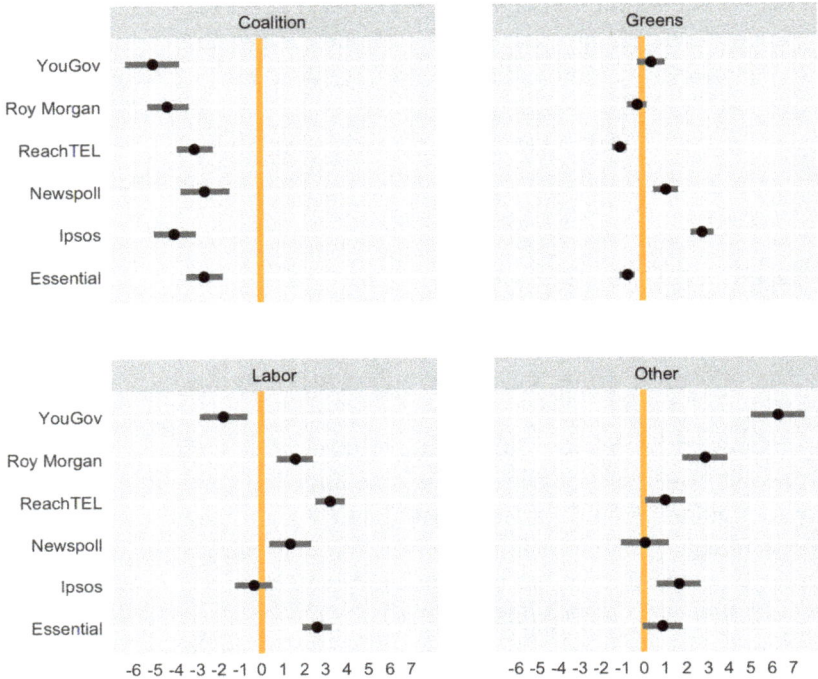

Figure 7.4 First-preference voting intentions house effects, 2016–19

Notes: Each point indicates an estimate of each polling organisation's bias with respect to the first preferences for the indicated party; horizontal bars cover 95 per cent credible intervals. Positive quantities are overestimates; negative quantities are underestimates.

Source: Authors' calculations.

Bias with respect to two-party-preferred voting intentions is shown in Figure 7.5. Consistent with Figure 7.3, all survey organisations, except YouGov, systematically underestimated the Coalition's share of the two-party-preferred vote, and by large margins: 2.5 to 3 percentage points. One possible source of Newspoll's underestimation of Coalition two-party-preferred support could be the assumption that only 60 per cent of PHON's preferences would flow to the Coalition. As it transpired, about 65 per cent of PHON preferences made their way to the Coalition from its 59 registered candidates, who secured 3.08 per cent of the national vote (see Chapters 4, 8 and 17, this volume); PHON did not run candidates in the other 92 seats. Even if PHON had fielded candidates in every seat and secured the same vote share, it would have secured 7.88 per cent of the vote (similar to where Newspoll and Essential placed the party in March 2019). This overestimate of PHON support—

and the minor underestimate of preference flows to the Coalition—explains a mere 0.4 percentage points of Newspoll's two-party-preferred 2.5 percentage point underestimate.

We also note that, despite considerable variability in biases with respect to first-preference voting intentions (see Figure 7.5), there is far less variation in two-party-preferred bias across survey organisations. This finding is provocative, suggesting less dispersion across polling companies in two-party-preferred estimates relative to the variation in first-preference poll estimates. Two possible mechanisms for this are: 1) first-preference errors might fortuitously 'cancel out' when converted to two-party-preferred estimates, as appears to be the case with YouGov; or 2) pollsters use the mapping from first preferences to two-party-preferred—and assumptions about preference flows—to shade their results towards an industry consensus, which is an instance of the phenomenon known as 'herding'.

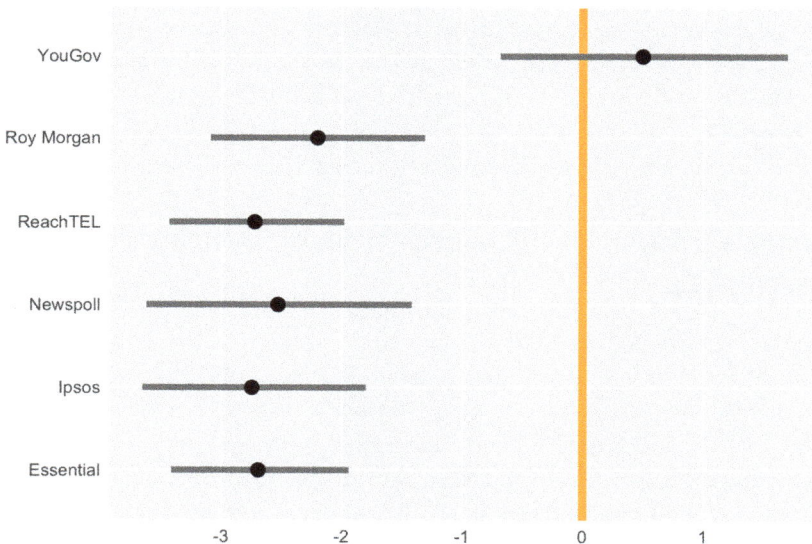

Figure 7.5 Coalition two-party-preferred voting intentions house effects, 2016–19

Notes: Each point indicates an estimate of each polling organisation's bias; horizontal bars cover 95 per cent credible intervals. Positive quantities are overestimates; negative quantities are underestimates.

Source: Authors' calculations.

Herding

Herding by pollsters has been observed at general elections in the United States (Panagopoulos et al. 2018), the United Kingdom (Sturgis et al. 2016), Canada (Whiteley 2016) and France (Evans and Ivaldi 2018). Herding is common in professions such as stock trading (Rülke et al. 2016) because of the incentive structures at play. There is safety in numbers: better to all be wrong together than risk being alone publishing a poll estimating an outcome wildly distant from the actual result. It requires a great deal of confidence for a pollster to take that sort of risk. Lonergan Research's Chris Lonergan admitted being embarrassed and jettisoning a poll he conducted because 'no one wants to release a poll that is wildly out of step ... we didn't want to be seen as having an inaccurate poll' (Koziol 2019).

Call it herding, harmonisation or looking over your shoulder; pollsters take stock of the competition and the available information each election cycle. This can be achieved by either not publishing the results of a poll conducted, such as in the Lonergan case, or 'deliberately adjust[ing] their methodology to produce certain results' (Prosser and Mellon 2018), which in effect suggests pollsters were playing the *weighting* game.

House effects in 2019 are large by historical standards

We gain historical perspective on 2019 polling errors by repeating this analysis with polls published prior to the 2007, 2010, 2013 and 2016 elections, utilising the same statistical model described above.[7] Newspoll before July 2015 was conducted with live phone interviews and we distinguish this from the subsequent period when Newspoll was conducted with online panel and IVR interview and sampling methods. Nielsen polls, employing live phone interviews, ceased in July 2014.

---

7   The models include discontinuities for Kevin Rudd becoming the Labor leader (replacing Kim Beazley), Julia Gillard becoming prime minister (replacing Rudd), Rudd ousting Gillard to become prime minister again and the Abbott to Turnbull transition.

Comparing the 2019 two-party-preferred house effects with historical elections in Figure 7.6, it is clear that most pollsters, with the exception of YouGov, had very large misses. What is sobering is that, in 2010, every pollster managed to underestimate the Coalition's two-party-preferred vote. Newspoll was only 0.75 percentage points worse in 2019 than its 2010 performance. Essential and Roy Morgan in 2010 had estimates worse than any poll in 2019. The polls plainly 'got it wrong' across the board in 2019, as in 2010; biased estimates are not unique to 2019.

For the major parties' primary votes, we find little improvement in Figures 7.7 and 7.8. Every pollster underestimated the Coalition's primary vote and only YouGov, ReachTEL and Ipsos did so considerably more than the median house bias for the five elections. The last time Newspoll had not systematically underestimated the Coalition's primary vote was for the 2007 election. Ipsos's estimate for Labor deteriorated markedly between 2016 and 2019.

The general difficulty pollsters had in 2019 was underestimating the Coalition's primary vote—a similarity with 2010, when all pollsters systematically underestimated it, too. One avenue for future research would be to assess the available historical information on how the rate of undecided voters and their treatment affect the estimates of vote choice. Gelman et al. (2016) found during the 2012 US presidential election campaign that the swinging voter was mythical, with the swings observed in the polls related to the contacted sample's partisan enthusiasm and willingness to participate in surveys during the election campaign. Events in an election campaign can elicit survey bias as an artefact of sampling non-response, with their primes conditioning partisan response rates. It is more than plausible that a government's messy internal party turmoil could affect Australian partisans in a similar way to American partisans responding to their party candidate's performance in a presidential debate and associated media commentary. It is arguably more possible, since the breakdown of civil political norms—that is, the ousting of prime ministers—should elicit more ire than a comparatively poor television debate performance. If Labor partisan willingness to be polled was dampened after Julia Gillard became prime minister in 2010 and Coalition partisan willingness to be polled was dampened after Morrison became prime minister in 2018, there should be a relationship between the number of reported uncommitted respondents and the underestimates of the respective parties. This is not limited to leadership altercations; many other things could depress partisan spirits.

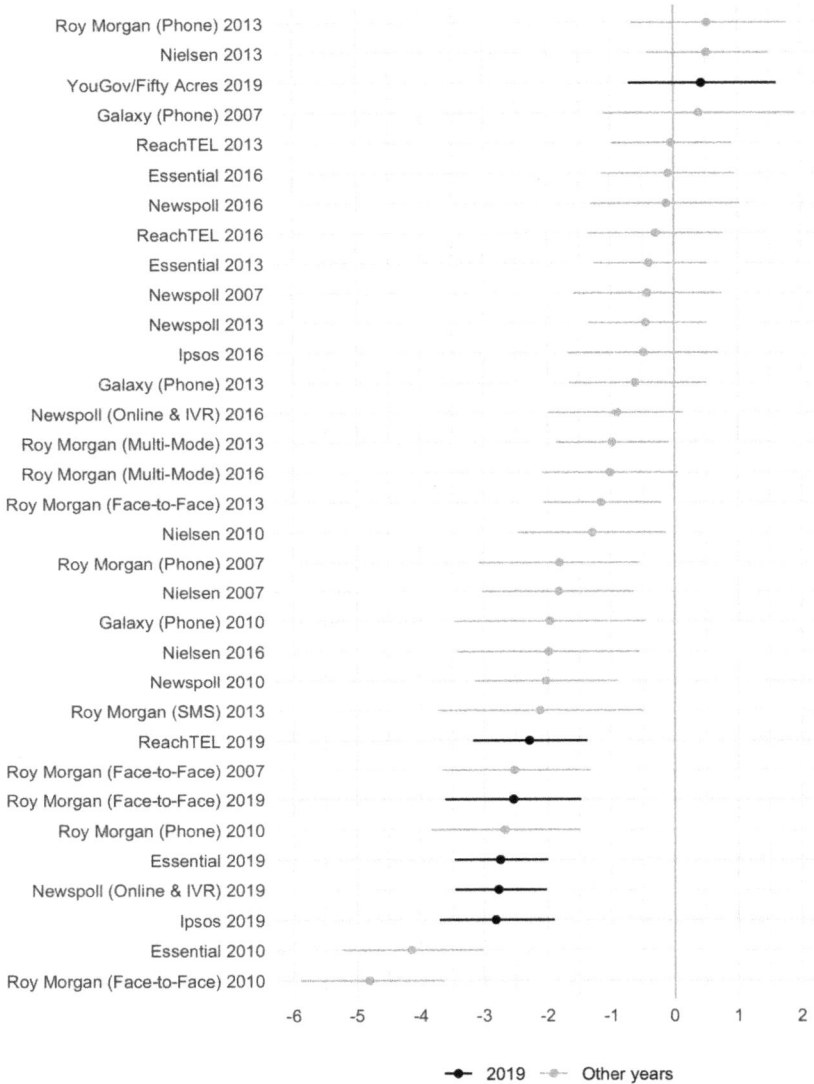

Figure 7.6 Coalition two-party-preferred voting intentions historical house effects, 2004–19

Notes: Each point indicates an estimate of each polling organisation's bias; horizontal bars cover 95 per cent credible intervals. Positive quantities are overestimates; negative quantities are underestimates.

Source: Authors' calculations.

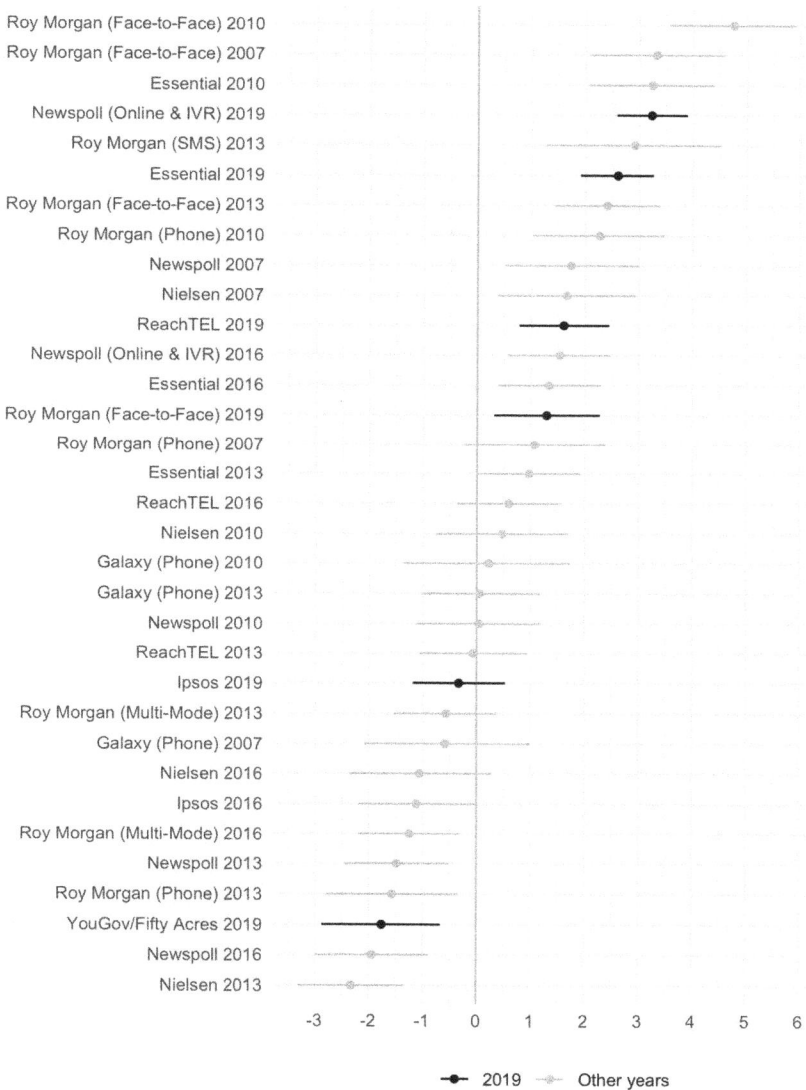

Figure 7.7 Labor first-preference voting intentions historical house effects, 2004–19

Notes: Each point indicates an estimate of each polling organisation's bias; horizontal bars cover 95 per cent credible intervals. Positive quantities are overestimates; negative quantities are underestimates.

Source: Authors' calculations.

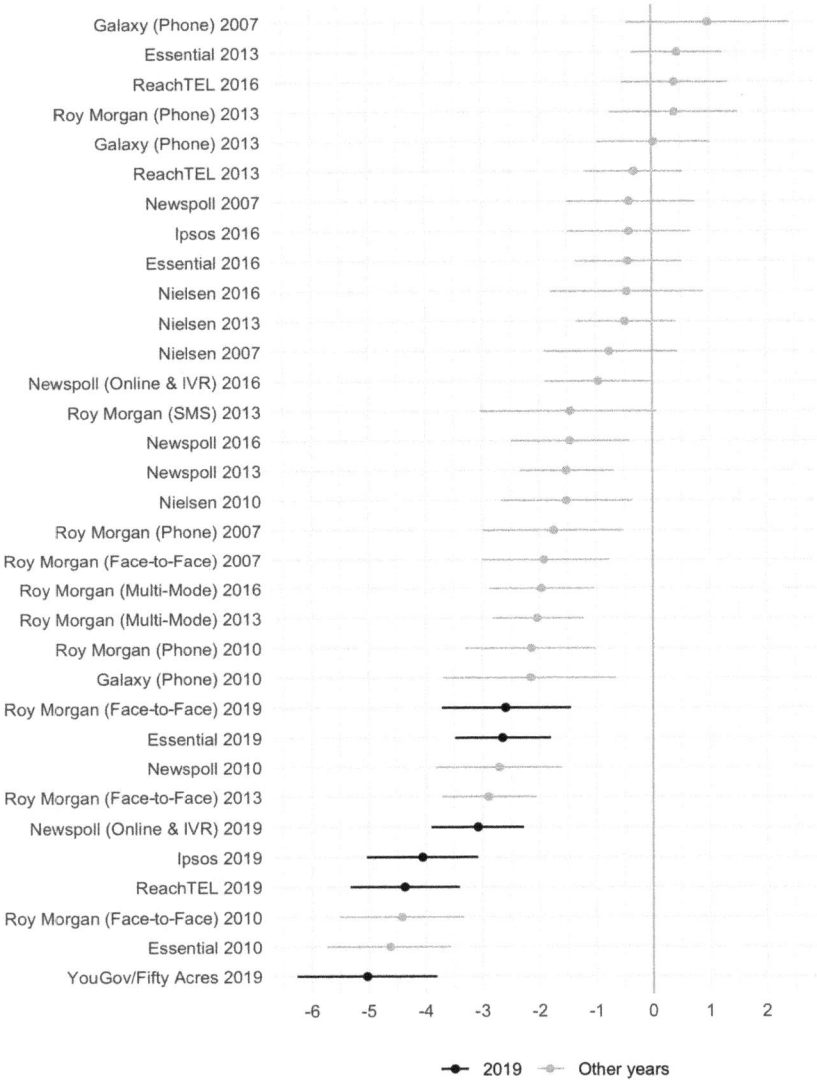

Figure 7.8 Coalition first-preference voting intentions historical house effects, 2004–19

Notes: Each point indicates an estimate of each polling organisation's bias; horizontal bars cover 95 per cent credible intervals. Positive quantities are overestimates; negative quantities are underestimates.

Source: Authors' calculations.

What is herding and how can we detect it?

As mentioned before, pollsters are susceptible to herding. In the case of election polling, pollsters who stray from the herd and meet an unexpected election result will suffer very real commercial consequences: vanishing clients. For pollster survival, it is safer to be in the herd than alone in the field.

Survey houses have a few choices about weighting once data have been collected and before publishing the results. Very few pollsters state which variables, such as age and gender, go into their weights, and none is open about how these weighting covariates are cut. For instance, age is a continuous variable that can be cut at different points on the population age structure into different groups with different sizes. Whether the data collected on these covariates are imbalanced (or what degree of imbalance exists), the public is not told. There are trade-offs that must be made when weighting. However, there comes a point when increasing weight complexity (and its variance), while reducing the estimate's bias, induces more error than the amount of bias removed. This opaque corner of polling should be made more transparent. The paucity of detail—such as what exactly is in the weighting scheme's 'secret sauce'—is a norm in Australian political polling, allowing pollsters to get away with shoddy workmanship undetected before an election.

Theory: Herding manifests as underdispersion

We leverage one of the oldest and most well-known theorems in statistics, the Central Limit Theorem (CLT), to test for herding in the polls immediately before the past five elections. Polls that herd should be underdispersed, displaying less variability than what we should see under the CLT. Suppose the true level of voting intentions is $\pi \in [0,1]$, a proportion between 0 and 1. Then via the CLT,[8] a series of unbiased, simple random samples of size n will produce estimates of π denoted by $\hat{\pi}$ that follow a normal distribution with mean π and variance $V(\hat{\pi}) = \pi(1 - \pi)/n$.

---

8   Or actually, a special case of the CLT, the De Moivre–Laplace Theorem, dating to 1738 in the case of Abraham de Moivre and 1820 for Pierre-Simon Laplace's celebrated *Théorie analytique des probabilités*.

Putting to one side the bias that we have already analysed, we now compare the observed dispersion of the polls with the theoretically expected dispersion, given: 1) the polls' stated sample sizes, n_p; and 2) an assumption about π, that voting intentions are generally unchanged from the days immediately preceding election day to the day of the election. In particular, we assume no change in voting intentions for d days prior to the election. Let $D(d)$ denote the set of polls fielded within d days of the election, with the standard deviation of those polls' estimates of π denoted as $s_d \equiv s_{D(d)}(\hat{\pi})$. We then repeat the following calculations over a range of values of d: 1) simulate poll results for each poll, $p \in D(d)$—that is, $y_p^* \sim N(\pi, V_p)$, $V_p = \pi(1-\pi)/n_p$; 2) round each y_p to the same degree of precision as in the corresponding reported poll; and 3) compute s_d^*, the standard deviation of y_p^*. We then see—over many repetitions of the preceding steps—the rate at which $s_d^* > s_D(d)$. That is, is the variability of actual polls, D, smaller, larger or indistinguishable from what the CLT tells us we should see under simple random sampling? We apply this procedure to polls from the past five election campaigns.

Strong evidence of underdispersion in the Coalition's primary and two-party-preferred polling

The major party primary and two-party-preferred voting intentions are plotted in Figure 7.9. The dispersion of polls estimating the two-party-preferred vote in 2019 is well below what the CLT would require. This is indicated by the black line being below the shaded 95 per cent credibility intervals of where the optimum amount of dispersion would be given the estimates published and the sample sizes involved. The two-party-preferred estimates' dispersions were mostly within the optimum bands for the 2013 and 2016 elections but not for the 2010 and 2007 elections, which were overdispersed for the most part.[9] There were large biases observed for these years (see Figure 7.6).

---

9   In 2013, pollsters transitioned from overdispersion to underdispersion, suggesting herding occurred as the election neared.

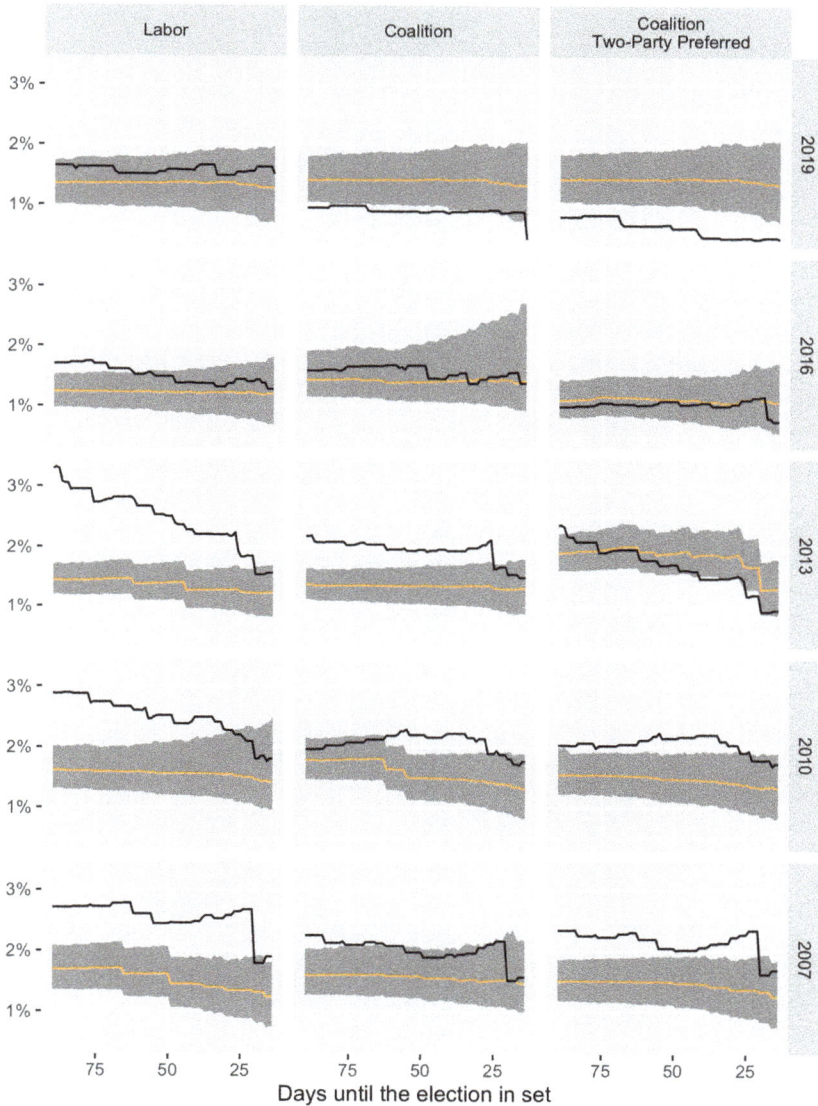

Figure 7.9 Dispersion before an election, 2004–19

Notes: For the polls conducted within each set of days until the election, the black line represents the observed dispersion in the polls and the orange line represents the theoretically expected dispersion. The poll dispersion coverage period sets take the value of 14 through to 90 days before each election.

Source: Authors' calculations.

For the 2019 major party votes, only the Coalition's primary vote was underdispersed, but less than the two-party-preferred, while estimates for Labor's support were as theoretically expected. There is a fair amount of overdispersion in historical primary votes; for the 2010 and 2013 elections, recent leadership changes made actual change to voter intensions plausible, especially for Labor partisans. The overdispersion observed might alternatively be suggestive of the non-response bias issues Gelman et al. (2016) identify, which pollsters, given their limited options, have attempted to paper over with extreme weights (Ansolabehere and Rivers 2013; Rosenbaum and Rubin 1983), inducing more variance and thereby error while reducing the observed bias in an imbalanced sample.

Conclusion: Polls and other disasters

The polls certainly missed the mark in 2019. The poll errors in 2019 were large and persistent across the 2016–19 cycle, shaping expectations about the election outcome with consequences for the way politics was conducted towards the election, spanning substantive matters such as policy debates and the parliament's agenda, through to media coverage and politicians' career decisions.

While large and enduring—and hence of immense political consequence—the magnitude of the poll errors in 2019 was not unprecedented. Our analysis of historical poll errors in Australian federal elections reveals that there were large poll errors in 2010. Any discussion of poll error in that election cycle was displaced with intense media interest in the fact that the 2010 election produced the first hung Commonwealth Parliament since 1940. Good poll performance in the 2013 and 2016 election cycles further helped to erase the prospect—and reality—of poll error from collective political memory. Hence, we have the alchemy of the 2019 election cycle, in the transformation of the uncertainty in random sampling, which produces estimates of public opinion into certainty.

Part of this alchemy was herding among the polls—a clustering of poll results reflecting the shared consensus that Labor would win the election. We provide clear evidence of underdispersion in the polls fielded in the lead-up to the 2019 election—a signature of herding. As unprofessional as herding may seem—and is—the commercial imperatives for it are clear. But the 2019 election cycle also makes clear the harm to the polity that follows when herding and poll bias occur at once. Pollsters might not be able to do much about the latter. Bias only manifests ex ante, but herding happens along the way.

We also note the steady shift in Australian polling from live interviewer, random-digit dialling methods to the use of other survey modes such as pre-recruited panels of respondents taking surveys online, IVR or 'robo polls' and SMS or Facebook Messenger polls. Faster and less expensive ways of conducting surveys do present considerable challenges for data quality.

These newer survey modes are almost surely more susceptible than older methods to errors of coverage (are all members of the target population capable of being reached with a given sampling technology and its specific implementation?) and non-response bias (after contact, the decision about whether to participate in the survey is correlated with variables being measured by the survey). Remediating these biases usually involves weighting after data collection, with reference to a trusted data source such as the Australian census. But what variables are pollsters to weight on, and how aggressively to do this? And, until an election reveals the true state of voting intentions, survey companies are flying blind when deploying new survey modes. The temptation to look over one's shoulder at the competition in this environment must be immense, as is the scope for doing so given the vast array of choices to be made when weighting data.

We invoke an adage applicable in many fields of science: sunlight is the best disinfectant. That is, there is a strong scientific case—and perhaps a commercial case as well—for greater transparency in how poll data are collected and weighted to ensure representativeness. We note that long-time pollster John Stirton (2019: 310–13) has called for urgent reform in this direction.

Given the errors in the 2019 election, there would seem to be a strong normative case, too, for Australia's pollsters pulling back the curtain, even a little, to help us better understand why and how they generate the numbers they do. The quality of political discussion, the salience and content of the nation's policy agenda—indeed, the health of Australian democracy—would gain from a commitment to this transparency around the polling of Australian public opinion.

References

Ansolabehere, Stephen and Douglas Rivers. 2013. 'Cooperative Survey Research.' *Annual Review of Political Science* 16: 307–29. doi.org/10.1146/annurev-polisci-022811-160625.

Brown, J. Andrew. 1992. 'The Major Effect: Changes in Party Leadership and Party Popularity'. *Parliamentary Affairs* 45(4): 545–64. doi.org/10.1093/oxfordjournals.pa.a052382.

Burstein, Paul. 2003. 'The Impact of Public Opinion on Public Policy: A Review and An Agenda'. *Political Research Quarterly* 56(1): 29–40. doi.org/10.1177/106591290305600103.

Ellis, Peter. 2017. 'State-space modelling of the Australian 2007 federal election'. *Free Range Statistics Blog*, 24 June. freerangestats.info/blog/2017/06/24/oz-polls-statespace.

Evans, Jocelyn and Gilles Ivaldi. 2018. 'Forecasting and polling.' In *The 2017 French Presidential Elections*, edited by Joycelyn Evans and Gilles Ivaldi, 123–47. Cham, Switzerland: Springer. doi.org/10.1007/978-3-319-68327-0_6.

Fuchs, Ester R., E. Scott Adler and Lincoln A. Mitchell. 2000. 'Win, Place, Show: Public Opinion Polls and Campaign Contributions in a New York City Election'. *Urban Affairs Review* 35(4): 479–501. doi.org/10.1177/10780870022184499.

Gelman, Andrew, Sharad Goel, Douglas Rivers and David Rothschild. 2016. 'The Mythical Swing Voter'. *Quarterly Journal of Political Science* 11(1): 103–30. doi.org/10.1561/100.00015031.

Hart, John. 1992. 'An Australian president? A comparative perspective'. In *Menzies to Keating: The Development of the Australian Prime Ministership*, edited by Patrick Weller, 183–201. Melbourne: Melbourne University Press.

Jackman, Simon. 1994. 'Measuring Electoral Bias: Australia, 1949–93'. *British Journal of Political Science* 24(3): 319–57. doi.org/10.1017/s000712340000688.

Jackman, Simon. 2005. 'Pooling the Polls Over An Election Campaign'. *Australian Journal of Political Science* 40(4): 499–517. doi.org/10.1080/10361140500302472.

Jackman, Simon. 2009. *Bayesian Analysis for the Social Sciences*. Hoboken, NJ: John Wiley & Sons. doi.org/10.1002/9780470686621.

Jackman, Simon and Luke Mansillo. 2018. 'The campaign that wasn't: Tracking public opinion over the 44th Parliament and the 2016 election campaign'. In *Double Disillusion: The 2016 Australian Federal Election*, edited by Anika Gauja, Peter Chen, Jennifer Curtin and Juliet Pietsch, 133–56. Canberra: ANU Press. doi.org/10.22459/DD.04.2018.06.

Koziol, Michael. 2019. '"Embarrassed" pollster ripped up poll that showed Labor losing election'. *Sydney Morning Herald*, 9 June. www.smh.com.au/politics/ federal/embarrassed-pollster-ripped-up-poll-that-showed-labor-losing- election-20190604-p51u9v.html.

Mansillo, Luke and Nick Evershed. 2016. 'Pooling the polls: How we're tracking opinion polling for the Australian election'. *The Guardian*, 8 May. www. theguardian.com/australia-news/datablog/2016/may/08/pooling-the-polls- how-were-tracking-opinion-polling-for-the-australian-election.

Mark the Ballot. 2017. 'Bayesian aggregation'. *Mark the Ballot Blog*. marktheballot. blogspot.com/p/the.html.

Meyer, David S. and Debra C. Minkoff. 2004. 'Conceptualizing Political Opportunity'. *Social Forces* 82(4): 1457–92. doi.org/10.1353/sof.2004.0082.

Panagopoulos, Costas, Kyle Endres and Aaron C. Weinschenk. 2018. 'Preelection Poll Accuracy and Bias in the 2016 US General Elections'. *Journal of Elections, Public Opinion and Parties* 28(2): 157–72. doi.org/10.1080/17457289.2018. 1441850.

Petersen, Jürgen, Sibylle Hardmeier and Bruno Wüest. 2008. 'Polls as Public– Politic Linkage: A Comparative Analysis of Poll Use and Roles of MPs in Parliamentary Debate'. *The Journal of Legislative Studies* 14(3): 315–38. doi.org/10.1080/13572330802259509.

Pickup, Mark, J. Scott Matthews, Will Jennings, Robert Ford and Stephen D. Fisher. 2011. 'Why Did the Polls Overestimate Liberal Democrat Support? Sources of Polling Error in the 2010 British General Election'. *Journal of Elections, Public Opinion and Parties* 21(2): 179–209. doi.org/10.1080/174 57289.2011.563309.

Prosser, Christopher and Jonathan Mellon. 2018. 'The Twilight of the Polls? A Review of Trends in Polling Accuracy and the Causes of Polling Misses'. *Government and Opposition* 53(4): 757–90. doi.org/10.1017/gov.2018.7.

Rosenbaum, Paul R. and Donald B. Rubin. 1983. 'The Central Role of the Propensity Score in Observational Studies for Causal Effects'. *Biometrika* 70(1): 41–55. doi.org/10.1093/biomet/70.1.41.

Rülke, Jan-Christoph, Maria Silgoner and Julia Wörz. 2016. 'Herding Behavior of Business Cycle Forecasters'. *International Journal of Forecasting* 32(1): 23–33. doi.org/10.1016/j.ijforecast.2015.02.004.

Stirton, John. 2019. 'Why the polls got it wrong'. In *From Turnbull to Morrison: The Trust Divide*, edited by Mark Evans, Michelle Grattan and Brendan McCaffrie, 307–13. Melbourne: Melbourne University Press.

Stone, Walter J., Sarah A. Fulton, Cherie D. Maestas and L. Sandy Maisel. 2010. 'Incumbency Reconsidered: Prospects, Strategic Retirement, and Incumbent Quality in US House Elections'. *The Journal of Politics* 72(1): 178–90. doi.org/10.1017/s0022381609990557.

Sturgis, Patrick, Nick Baker, Mario Callegaro, Stephen Fisher, Jane Green, Will Jennings, Jouni Kuha, Ben Lauderdale and Patten Smith. 2016. 'Report of the Inquiry into the 2015 British General Election Opinion Polls'. *Journal of the Royal Statistical Society: Series A (Statistics in Society)* 181(3): 757–81. doi.org/10.1111/rssa.12329.

Tufte, Edward R. 1973. 'The Relationship Between Seats and Votes in Two-Party Systems'. *American Political Science Review* 67(2): 540–54. doi.org/10.2307/1958782.

Whiteley, Paul. 2016. 'Why Did the Polls Get It Wrong in the 2015 General Election? Evaluating the Inquiry into Pre-Election Polls'. *The Political Quarterly* 87(3): 437–42. doi.org/10.1111/1467-923X.12274.

8

THE PERILOUS POLLING OF SINGLE SEATS

Murray Goot[1]

For a contest that was to be decided, many insisted, by hand-to-hand combat in various seats, we might have expected commentators on the progress of the 2019 election campaign to have focused on the polling in particular seats rather than on the national polls. But they did not. While there were, as there long has been, many fewer national polls than single-seat polls— mostly, though not entirely, in seats classified officially as 'marginal'—when it came to anticipating the outcome, the scorecards from the single-seat polls certainly did not displace the traditional focus on the national polls.

Given the media's interest in contests where Coalition MPs were under threat from Independents or the Greens, and in contests where Coalition candidates were mounting credible challenges against Independent MPs, we might also have expected the media to have commissioned polls in a number of these seats. But only in Mayo (SA), where Rebekha Sharkie (Centre Alliance) was facing a Liberal challenge to regain the seat, was there any media-sponsored polling in seats of this kind.

1   My thanks to Kevin Bonham, William Bowe; David Briggs, Angela Smith and Campbell White at YouGov Galaxy; David Bednall, Andrew Bunn, Jessica Elgood at Ipsos; Carol Johnson, Malcolm Mackerras, Gary Morgan of Roy Morgan Research; Marian Simms, Mark Textor of the C|T Group; James Stewart from uComms; John Utting of Utting Research; and a number of journalists who would probably prefer to remain unnamed. The author is a panel member of the Inquiry into the Performance of the Opinion Polls at the 2019 Australian Federal Election, established by the Association of Market and Social Research Organisations. The views expressed in this chapter, however, are his own. The research was supported by the Australian Research Council under DP150102968.

At the same time, we might have expected polls in single seats, with their smaller samples, to have performed more poorly than the national polls. While many did perform more poorly, almost as many performed better. The single-seat polls that proved the best guides, on average, were those conducted in New South Wales and in Victoria; in New South Wales, they were more accurate than the national polls. The worst polls—much worse than could be explained by sample size alone—were the single-seat polls conducted in Queensland and Western Australia, which were the States where the Coalition did best. It was in these States that the national polls may have been the poorest guides as well.

In this chapter—in addition to noting how many single-seat polls there were, which seats were polled and how well the polls did in comparison with the national polls—I ask: who commissioned the polls in single seats (the major media groups), when were they conducted (mostly, towards the end of the campaign and not more than once) and which market research firms conducted them (just two; one, arguably, with a conflict of interest). I set out what pollsters reported about their respondents' vote choice: first preferences and two-party preferred—a measure that was pollster-constructed. I look at how closely the polls came to forecasting the results in individual seats, either in terms of their proximity to the final figures (a statistician's measure) or in terms of picking the winners (a journalist's concern). That 'the polls' got it wrong is a judgement based, for the most part, on the national polls. Would the view of the polls' performance be different were it based on the single-seat polls?

I also review various accounts of where the single-seat polls went wrong: late deciders, samples too small, the 'undecided' ignored and margins of sampling error not adequality acknowledged. I conclude by asking how these polls could have performed better; and, in commissioning and publishing them, how the media could have better managed their risks. The answers to both questions suggest that not a lot is likely to change.

The polls: For whom, where and when

During election campaigns, polls help sell newspapers. If they can afford it—and most metropolitan mastheads can—the press, and occasionally a television network, commission polls of various kinds and promote them as 'exclusives'. During the 2019 campaign, the results of 18 national polls were published, each with its own estimate of how Australians would vote. Six were commissioned by *The Australian*, the national daily owned by News Corp Australia; two by the *Australian Financial Review* (*AFR*), *Sydney Morning Herald* and Melbourne *Age*, which were formerly owned by Fairfax but are now owned by Nine Entertainment; and two by News Corp's metropolitan mastheads the *Daily Telegraph* (NSW), *Herald-Sun* (Victoria), *The Courier-Mail* (Queensland), *The Advertiser* (South Australia) and the *Mercury* (Tasmania). The other eight were conducted by market research firms with no media contracts: five by Roy Morgan Research and three by Essential Research, which released its results to *The Guardian* (see Table 8.1).

Over the same period, News Corp, Seven West Media and Network 10 released, in varying detail, the results of 43 single-seat polls conducted in 35 seats (Appendix Tables A8.1–A8.3); of these, 32 were marginal seats. Ten days after the election had been called, Newspoll ran polls for *The Australian* in Pearce (WA), Herbert (Qld), Deakin (Vic.) and Lindsay (NSW). A week or so out from the election, on 9–11 May, it followed up with polls in Herbert and Lindsay and two other seats, Corangamite (Vic.) and Bass (Tas.). Mid-campaign, YouGov Galaxy conducted polls for Seven West Media in three West Australian seats (Cowan, Pearce and Swan), following up on the final Tuesday and Wednesday of the campaign with polls in these seats and two others (Hasluck and Stirling). On Monday and Tuesday of the final week of the campaign, YouGov Galaxy conducted polls in 11 'crucial seats'—Dickson, Flynn, Forde, Herbert and Leichhardt (Qld); Deakin, Higgins and La Trobe (Vic.); and Gilmore, Macquarie and Reid (NSW)—for the News Corp Australia Network. The results of these polls were released one by one, hour by hour, from 10 am Eastern Standard Time the day before the election (News Corp Australia Network 2019), a pattern designed to encourage interested readers to take out a subscription to the relevant masthead. First—and last—out of the blocks was uComms, commissioned by News Corp's *Geelong Advertiser*, shortly after the election was called, to test opinion in the very marginal seat of Corangamite (Vic.) in which the newspaper circulated (Jefferson 2019, the poll mistakenly attributed to ReachTEL), and to test opinion for Network 10's *The Project*, shortly before the election, in 12 seats (including Corangamite) drawn from all six States. Every poll was a robo-poll, using interactive voice recognition (IVR), with questions asked on the telephone, but not by a live interviewer, and answered by someone in the household, though not necessarily the person from whom the pollster wants to hear.

Table 8.1 Electorates in which polls were conducted during the election campaign, 10 April – 18 May 2019

Electorate	State	Region[a]	Party	TPP margin		Media sponsors	Left sponsors	
				ALP	Coalition		ALP	ACTU
Banks	NSW	Inner metro	LIB		1.5			+
Eden-Monaro	NSW	Rural	ALP	3.0			+	
Gilmore	NSW	Rural	LIB		0.8	Galaxy		+
Lindsay	NSW	Outer metro	ALP	1.1		Newspoll	+	
Macquarie	NSW	Provincial	ALP	2.2		Galaxy		
Page	NSW	Rural	LIB		2.3	uComms	+	
Reid	NSW	Inner metro	LIB		4.7	Galaxy, uComms	+	+
Robertson	NSW	Provincial	LIB		1.2		+	+
Casey	Vic.	Outer metro	LIB		4.6	uComms		
Chisholm	Vic.	Inner metro	LIB		3.0		+	
Corangamite	Vic.	Provincial	ALP	0.1		Newspoll, uComms	+	+
Deakin	Vic.	Outer metro	LIB		6.5*	Galaxy, Newspoll	+	
Dunkley	Vic.	Outer metro	ALP	1.2			+	+
Higgins	Vic.	Inner metro	LIB		10.1*	Galaxy, uComms		
La Trobe	Vic.	Outer metro	LIB		3.2	Galaxy	+	
Capricornia	Qld	Provincial	LNP		0.6			
Dickson	Qld	Outer metro	LNP		1.8	Galaxy, uComms	+	+
Flynn	Qld	Rural	LNP		1.1	Galaxy	+	+
Forde	Qld	Outer metro	LNP		0.7	Galaxy, uComms		+

Electorate	State	Region#	Party	TPP margin		Media sponsors	Left sponsors	
				ALP	Coalition		ALP	ACTU
Griffith	Qld	Inner metro	ALP	1.5			+	
Herbert	Qld	Provincial	ALP	0.1		Galaxy, Newspoll	+	‡
Leichhardt	Qld	Rural	LNP		4.1	Galaxy, uComms	+	‡
Longman	Qld	Provincial	ALP	0.8			+	
Petrie	Qld	Outer metro	LNP		1.7		+	‡
Boothby	SA	Outer metro#	Liberal		2.8	Galaxy, uComms	+	‡
Mayo	SA	Rural	CA		[3.7]	Galaxy		
Sturt	SA	Inner metro	LIB		5.4	Galaxy		
Cowan	WA	Outer metro	ALP	0.7		Galaxy		
Hasluck	WA	Outer metro	LIB		2.1	Galaxy, uComms	+	‡
Pearce	WA	Outer metro	LIB		3.7	Galaxy, Newspoll, uComms		
Perth	WA	Inner metro	LIB		3.4	Galaxy		
Stirling	WA	Inner metro	LIB		6.2*	Galaxy	+	
Swan	WA	Inner metro	LIB		3.6	Galaxy	+	‡
Bass	Tas.	Provincial	ALP	5.5		Newspoll		‡
Braddon	Tas.	Rural	ALP	1.8		uComms	+	‡

* Not classified as 'marginal' by the AEC.

AEC, 'Demographic Classification of Electoral Divisions' (www.aec.gov. au/Electorates/maps.htm).

+ indicates ALP polling in that seat.

‡ indicates ACTU polling in that seat.

Note: Shaded rows represent seats polled for a media organisation and one other organisation.

Sources: YouGov for Galaxy and Newspoll; Maiden (2019) for Labor's targets by region; Karp (2019) for the ACTU's targeted seats; Mackerras (2019) for the two-party-preferred margins.

Having one firm (Galaxy, in 2016; YouGov, in 2019) using identical methods and responsible for two brands—Newspoll and YouGov Galaxy—raised potential conflicts of interest. In seats polled by both, could the results published under one brand be very different from those published under the other? Three seats—Deakin (Vic.), Herbert (Qld) and Pearce (WA)—were polled and sometimes repolled by both Newspoll and YouGov Galaxy (Table 8.1). But they were polled by one, followed by the other, either two weeks apart (Pearce) or four weeks apart (Deakin, Herbert). This may have avoided questions being raised about inconsistent results, but where the results were consistent it risked raising the question of herding. That few seats were polled by both Newspoll and YouGov Galaxy could be read in different ways: reassuringly, as an outcome that minimised any conflict; worryingly, as a sign of how the conflict constrained seat selection; or as sheer coincidence, determined not by two not-very-independent polling operations, but by two entirely separate clients.

Of greater concern to *The Australian* was its discovery—though not until after the election—that YouGov Galaxy had been doing Labor's single-seat polling as well. The pollster's failure to disclose its involvement with Labor meant that journalists who thought they were cross-checking Newspoll's figures with an independent source (Labor) were doing nothing of the kind. Liberal sources expressed their disbelief in the figures Newspoll was producing for *The Australian* since they were at odds with the figures the Crosby Textor Group (C|T) was generating for the Liberals. Labor sources, on the other hand, were happy to confirm that the single-seat figures Newspoll was reporting were very like their own. Journalists either did not ask who was doing Labor's polling or were not told.

In terms of which outlets commissioned polls and from which pollsters, the contrast with 2016 was marked. In 2016, no polls were commissioned by Seven West Media or the News Corp Australia network, and uComms did not exist. News Corp's metropolitan mastheads commissioned single-seat polls of their own, either from YouGov Galaxy or from ReachTEL; the latter had also polled for *7 News* and Fairfax Media (subsequently, part of Nine Entertainment). In 2019, ReachTEL conducted no polls; in 2016, it conducted polls in 21 seats. In 2019, Morgan undertook no single-seat polling; in 2016, it had conducted polls in 31 seats (Goot 2018: 117–22).

As remarkable as the decline—from 47 in 2016 to 26—in the number of seats polled was the decline in the number seats polled more than once, which was down from 18 (including three polled as many as four times) in 2016 to 11 (only one polled four times). Long gone were the days when, courtesy of one pollster or another, a seat might be polled up to eight times (Goot 2009: 123). Filling the gaps, journalists paid increasing attention to what they could glean about the state of play from the political parties, interest groups or other 'activists'.

The decline in the number of single-seat polls the media commissioned, and the reduction in the number of seats they polled more than once, reflects cost pressures and concerns about the credibility of single-seat polls. Costs—a perennial consideration—had been pressing on media managers with increasing force, notwithstanding that robo-polls are cheap compared with traditional methods. Credibility, by contrast, was a relatively new concern. Whereas journalists not so long ago would express regret at the inability of their organisations to fund more single-seat polls, now they were more inclined to qualify their reports by referring to the unreliability of such polls (for the most forensic analysis, see Jackman and Mansillo 2018: 149).

The seats

Of the seats requiring a swing of less than 6 percentage points to change—the AEC's definition of a marginal seat—21 were held by the Coalition and 22 by Labor (including Corangamite and Dunkley, which were notionally Labor as a result of a redistribution). Yet the seats that were polled were not drawn in equal numbers from the two sides. Nor would one expect them to be. The election, after all, was a contest that Labor was expected to win—an expectation due in no small measure to an uninterrupted string of national polls that showed Labor ahead. Consequently, the number of Liberal seats polled (23) was twice the number of Labor seats (11)—the ratio being constant for YouGov Galaxy, Newspoll and uComms. The number of Liberal seats polled at least twice (eight) was four times the corresponding number of Labor seats.

Though most of the seats polled were marginal, they were not always the most marginal. Seats polled for Seven West Media included two that required swings of close to 4 percentage points but excluded one (Perth) that required a swing closer to 3 percentage points. *The Australian* organised polls in the third most marginal Liberal seat in Western Australia; the most marginal Labor seats in Queensland, Victoria and New South Wales; a Liberal seat in Victoria (Deakin) that was not classified as marginal; and a seat (Bass) that was Labor's second most marginal, not its most marginal, seat in Tasmania. News Corp chose Labor's most marginal seat in Queensland (Herbert) plus the Coalition's eighth most marginal (Leichhardt) and three of its four most marginal seats, but not its most marginal (Capricornia); three Liberal seats in Victoria, only one of them (La Trobe) a marginal seat; and in New South Wales, Labor's second most marginal seat (Macquarie) plus the Liberals' most marginal (Gilmore) and fourth most marginal seat (Reid). Network 10's *The Project* chose Page—the only National Party seat to figure in any of the single-seat polling—and Reid, which were, respectively, the second and fourth most marginal Coalition seats in New South Wales; Casey and Higgins (as well as Corangamite), which were the third and 13th most marginal Liberal seats in Victoria; Dickson, Forde and Leichhardt, which were the second, fourth and eighth most marginal LNP seats in Queensland; Hasluck and Pearce, the most marginal and third most marginal Liberal seats in Western Australia; and Boothby and Braddon, the most marginal Liberal and Labor seats in South Australia and Tasmania, respectively.

Notable for their absence were Warringah (NSW), where former prime minister Tony Abbott was being challenged (successfully) by Zali Steggall (Independent); and Kooyong (Vic.), where the Treasurer, Josh Frydenberg (Liberal), was being challenged (unsuccessfully) by Julian Burnside (the Greens). Also ignored were Wentworth (NSW), where Kerryn Phelps (Independent) was being challenged (successfully) by Dave Sharma (Liberal); and Indi (Vic.), where Helen Haines (Independent), hoping to succeed Cathy McGowan (Independent), was being challenged (unsuccessfully) by Steve Martin (Liberal). These contests (discussed by Curtin and Sheppard, Chapter 18, this volume) involved Independent candidates who were women.

The National Party seats ignored included some considered to be at risk from independents—chief among them: New England (NSW), where former deputy prime minister Barnaby Joyce was being challenged (unsuccessfully) by Adam Blakester (Independent); and Cowper (NSW), where the newly pre-selected National Party candidate Patrick Conaghan was being challenged (unsuccessfully) by the former member for Lyne, Rob Oakeshott (Independent).

Across the largest States, the polls were relatively thinly spread; across the smaller States, the coverage was greater. In the most populous States, the number of seats polled—New South Wales (eight), Victoria (seven), Queensland (nine) and Western Australia (six)—was roughly the same. Across the remainder—South Australia (three) and Tasmania (two)—it was numerically smaller but disproportionately large. Inner metropolitan and outer metropolitan seats, each of which accounted for 26 per cent of the seats in the outgoing House, were slightly underrepresented in the media polls; each made up about 30 per cent of the seats. Underrepresented, too, were rural seats (18 per cent) that made up one-quarter of the outgoing House. Overrepresented were provincial seats: 30 per cent of the seats polled, but only half that proportion on the floor of the House (see Table 8.1). If seat selection is any guide, the media thought this election was not going to be decided only in the metropolitan suburbs, let alone in the metropolitan suburbs of the largest States.

Sharing an assumption that this was an election at which more Liberal than Labor seats would fall, there was considerable overlap between the seats the media polled and the seats polled by the ALP and the ACTU. (The Liberal Party's list of target seats was tightly guarded). Of all 20 seats polled by the ALP, 70 per cent were also polled for the media; of the 16 seats polled by the ACTU, the proportion polled for the media was almost the same. Of the 26 seats polled by either the ALP or the ACTU, less than 40 per cent were the same (Table 8.1)—a division of labour or a disagreement among allies about which seats offered the greater prospect?

The results

How well did the polls do in the single seats chosen by the media? The standard way of answering this question—standard for a statistician, if not for a journalist—is to look at the size of the differences between what the polls reported and what the election results showed. Standard for a journalist, if not for a statistician, is to look at whether the polls predicted the winners. We can run these tests for Newspoll and YouGov Galaxy, but we cannot run them for uComms since it produced no estimate of the first preferences, seat by seat, that took account of how the 'undecided' might divide, nor a seat-by-seat estimate of the two-party-preferred vote.

Looking only at those polls completed in the final week of the campaign—the 16 conducted by YouGov Galaxy and the four by Newspoll—the errors seem grim. Two-party preferred, the mean difference between the polls' estimates and the actual results was 4.1 percentage points for YouGov Galaxy and 3.0 percentage points for Newspoll; the median differences—3.8 percentage points (YouGov Galaxy) and 2.9 percentage points (Newspoll)—were very similar (Table 8.2).

Table 8.2 Differences between the polls' estimate of party support and the actual vote in single seats, two-party preferred, Galaxy and Newspoll (percentage points)

Pollster	Fieldwork[+]	Seats	Mean	Median
YouGov Galaxy	13–15 May	16	4.1	3.8
Newspoll	9–12 May	4	3.0	2.9

[+] Polls concluded more than 10 days before the election are excluded.

Sources: See Appendix Table A8.1 for YouGov Galaxy; Table A8.2 for Newspoll.

In Queensland, as Table 8.3 shows, the errors were considerably higher, 6 percentage points, on average; in Victoria (2.6), Tasmania (2.4) and New South Wales (1.7), they were markedly lower; and in Western Australia (4.3), they sat around the mean. In almost every case, the polls underestimated the Coalition's share of the two-party-preferred vote. Ipsos, the only polling organisation to have released State-by-State breaks from its final national poll, showed a similar pattern, with its biggest underestimate of the Coalition's two-party-preferred vote being for Tasmania (7.5 percentage points), followed by Queensland (5.7), Western Australia (4.6), South Australia and the Northern Territory (about 3.1), New South Wales (1.1) and Victoria (where it overestimated, not underestimated, the Coalition's two-party-preferred vote by 1.1 percentage points).

Table 8.3 Mean overestimates (+) or underestimates (–) of the two-party-preferred and first-preference vote in single seats, by party, Galaxy and Newspoll (percentage points)

Seats		TPP	First preferences					
State	No.	(Coalition)	ALP	Coalition	Greens	UAP	PHON	Other
WA	5	−4.3	+6.0	−2.7	−2.3	+1.2	−1.6	−0.6
Qld	6	−6.0	+5.7	−2.1	−1.4	+3.2	−5.2	−2.9
Vic.	4	−2.6	+0.8	−2.5	+1.8	+1.7	-	−0.6
NSW	4	−1.7	+0.5	−2.1	−1.5	+2.1	-	−0.8
Tas.	1	−2.4	+4.3	−2.3	−0.5	−0.9	-	−0.6

- PHON had no candidates in seats polled in Victoria, New South Wales and Tasmania.

Sources: See Appendix Table A8.1 for YouGov Galaxy; and Table A8.2 for Newspoll.

The main source of the differences between the polls' estimates and the election results, not surprisingly, was the polls' estimates of Labor's first preferences—and, to a lesser degree, the first preferences won by Clive Palmer's UAP. As Table 8.3 shows, polls conducted in single seats overestimated Labor's share of the vote—most egregiously in Western Australia (6 percentage points, on average), Queensland (5.7) and Tasmania (4.3), though hardly at all in Victoria (0.8) or New South Wales (0.5). The polls overestimated support for the UAP in Queensland (3.2 percentage points), but also in New South Wales (2.1), Victoria (1.7) and Western Australia (1.2). Conversely, the same polls underestimated support for the Coalition (the size of the errors being fairly uniform), the Greens (except in Victoria, where it overestimated them) and PHON—especially in Queensland. The contrast with 2016, when the polls underestimated Labor's support and overestimated support for the Coalition (Jackman and Mansillo 2018: 146), is striking.

Were the pollsters caught out by not polling closer to the election? If any of them thought this, none of them said it—and with good reason. Despite polling earlier, Newspoll (9–12 May) was closer to the mark in its seats than was YouGov Galaxy (13–15 May) in its seats (see also Jackman and Mansillo 2018: 150). Indeed, in two South Australian seats (Boothby and Mayo) polled before the final week of the campaign, YouGov Galaxy got closer to the mark than it did in most of the seats it polled during the final week (Appendix Table A8.1). During the final seven days of the campaign, only Newspoll conducted more than one national poll. It showed no tightening—if anything, the reverse (Benson 2019c).

After the election, at least one pollster wondered whether the (national) polls had erred in assuming the 'don't knows' would split along the same lines as other respondents (Lewis 2019). Did the 'don't knows' break disproportionately in favour of the Coalition? Evidence from two national post-election surveys suggests they did not. A JWS poll shows virtually no difference in the proportion of Coalition (39 per cent) and Labor respondents (37 per cent) who said they had decided on their vote in the final week, including on election day (JWS 2019: 10–11). Even if we ignore the fact that 49 per cent of Greens respondents also said they had decided late, these figures do not point to late deciders disproportionately favouring the Coalition. An Essential poll shows those who made up their mind on election day favoured the Coalition (38 per cent) over Labor (27 per cent). From this, *The Guardian* inferred that the Coalition did especially well from late deciders (Murphy 2019). But the figures showing that, of those who voted either Coalition or Labor at the last minute, 58 per cent voted Coalition and 42 per cent voted Labor almost exactly match the 41.4:33.3 division (equivalent to 55:45) in the share of the vote recorded by the Coalition and Labor at the election (Goot 2019).

Had pollsters found some defensible way of allocating most of the 'don't knows' to the Coalition, they would have reduced the differences between their figures and the election results in both the single-seat polls and the national polls. But to have really made a difference—to have closed the gap by 1 or 2 percentage points—the 'don't knows' would have needed to be much bigger than 1 or 2 per cent. In the 16 single-seat polls produced by YouGov Galaxy, 10 reported a 'don't know' figure of just 1 or 2 per cent. Of the four single-seat polls conducted by Newspoll, only one reported a figure for the 'don't knows'; it was 1 per cent. True, the figures for the 'undecided' published by uComms averaged 5 per cent (Appendix Table A8.3), but these derived from responses to uComms' initial question ('Which of the following parties will receive your first-preference vote?'), not from responses to this question plus the follow-up asked of the 'undecided' about the party or individual they had 'even a slight leaning' towards—a 'leaner' having preceded the figures published by YouGov Galaxy and Newspoll with which the uComms figures need to be compared.

Whether, ideally, 'don't knows' should be pushed—asked a 'leaner'—is a separate matter. Is reducing the 'undecided' to no more than 1 or 2 per cent of the sample really credible, when none of the national polls had a final 'undecided' of less than 4 per cent and at a time when so many respondents appeared to be uncertain about their choice? According to the post-election poll conducted by Essential, 26 per cent of voters did not make up their mind until the final week(s) of the campaign (Murphy 2019). JWS Research (2019) estimated that the proportion who made up their mind in the final week was as high as 40 per cent.

A quite different way of looking at the performance of the polls is to consider how accurately they anticipated who would win each seat. 'We were the most accurate in showing the seats likely to be won or lost in Queensland', said David Briggs, managing director of YouGov Galaxy, and in 'showing that Labor were not picking up seats they needed there' (quoted in Tabakoff 2019). However, since: 1) Briggs ran the only company polling single seats and producing figures that could be compared with the election results (uComms did not allocate the 'undecided'); 2) YouGov Galaxy had the Coalition ahead in only two of the four Queensland seats in which it polled; and 3) Labor not only failed to win seats in Queensland, but also lost two seats (in only one of which either YouGov Galaxy or Newspoll polled), it is difficult to see Briggs's claim amounting to much.

Neither YouGov Galaxy nor Newspoll made as bad a fist of it as they might have made. None of the seats polled by YouGov Galaxy and only one of the seats (Bass) polled by Newspoll had Labor winning seats they were not going to win, and neither YouGov Galaxy nor Newspoll had the Coalition losing seats they were not going to lose. The problem with YouGov Galaxy was having five of its 16 seats on an estimated two-party preferred of 50:50—seats that the Coalition went on to win (as Appendix Table A8.1 shows) either comfortably (Swan, 52.8 per cent; La Trobe, 54.5 per cent) or handsomely (Hasluck, 55.2 per cent; Herbert, 58.4 per cent; and Forde, 58.6 per cent).

Conclusion

Not for the first time in an Australian election, many thought the contest would be decided by local battles in individual seats (see, for example, Simms 1997). Not for the first time, some thought they discerned in this something new; one journalist wrote of a 'new hyper-localism' in political campaigning (Irvine 2019). And not for the first time in an Australian election, the single-seat polling proved neither particularly accurate in estimating vote shares (first preferences or the two-party preferred) nor especially good at forecasting which party in the various seats would win. Since elections allow polls to showcase their value, failing to come up with a tolerably good estimate of the vote shares or failing to predict a number of the winners is no small thing.

What might be done to improve them? One suggestion—dating from the early days of polling—is that pollsters, and the press, do more to emphasise the fact that polls provide estimates, not precise measures. At a meeting of Gallup Poll directors held after the 1948 American polling debacle, the director of the Italian Institute of Public Opinion announced that at the next election he would 'give the figures ±3'; if the figure in the poll was 50, he would report it as lying in the range 47–53. Piero Luzzatto Fegiz was intending to draw his readers' attention not to a poll's sampling error, but to the vagaries of electoral turnout (Gallup 1949: 8)—a source of non-sampling error. No matter. Would Australian readers have been happy to be told that the 50:50 results YouGov Galaxy reported in so many seats did not mean they were all on a 'knife-edge', but that there was a 95 per cent probability (with a sample size of about 500) that the two-party vote was somewhere between 54.5 (ALP) and 45.5 (Coalition), which would be a comfortable win for Labor, and 45.5 (ALP) and 54.5 (Coalition), which would be a comfortable win for the Coalition? Hardly. A poll on the eve of an election that does not double as a predictive device is a poll that has little commercial value. There is a reason for 'margins of error' being buried in the fine print, for the meaning of the phrase not being clarified and for the possible sources of *non*-sampling error passing without mention.

Thinking about ways of handling the 'don't knows', other than by assuming they will divide in much the same way as other respondents, makes more sense. At the same meeting of the 'Gallup family', George Gallup stressed that at the next American election:

> He would say 'The decided will vote in this way …' and then devote two or three paragraphs to explaining the problem of the undecided vote—e.g. how it could be reduced by a 'leaning' question and how the rest could be distributed—e.g. (a) in the same proportions as the rest of the vote, or by past preference.

He might even say to the reader:

> 'Here are the latest figures: this is what the (sampled) electorate said 7 days before the election day. What's your guess what will happen? Which party will gain votes, which one [will] lose, what will the net result be?' … In other words, let the reader actively participate in the game so that it isn't Dr Gallup but the reader himself who will get the laurels … or eat crow. (Gallup 1949: 5–6)

Reflecting on the performance of the Australian polls 70 years later, Peter Lewis, managing director of Essential, suggested that pollsters could have published a set of percentages for each party *and* the 'don't knows' that added to 100 rather than a set of percentages that added to 100 *excluding* the 'don't knows' (Lewis 2019). Whether pollsters would have been better advised to report the 'don't knows' after the 'leaner' or without the 'leaner', Lewis did not say. Publishing a set of percentages for each party *and* the 'don't knows' without a 'leaner', seat by seat, that added to 100 was precisely what uComms had done. However, while having pollsters report figures in this way might guarantee they were never wrong, it would hardly allow them to claim that they ever got it right.

The media, too, is in the prediction business—a business parasitic on the polls. Much media coverage is framed in terms of which of the parties is ahead, which is behind and whether the gap is opening or closing. It follows that few would want to publish seat-by-seat figures of the kind uComms produced for Channel 10; uComms did not produce a set of individual seat figures that excluded the 'don't knows', though it did publish a two-party-preferred figure for the 12 seats overall (putting the Coalition ahead 52:48) after pressing the 'don't knows' with a 'leaner' and excluding any who remained 'undecided'. In these seats, the Coalition would prevail, 54.5:45.5. Underestimating the Coalition's vote by 2.5 percentage points (54.5, not 52) put uComms on a par with the underestimates made by the national polls (Appendix Table A8.4).

Pollsters who do not predict the winner are asked by the media to explain—or, in the case of Ipsos (arguably the best of the national polls), do not have their contract renewed. Gallup thought the public's belief that pre-election polling had but one purpose—'to pick the winner'—was 'a misconception' (Gallup 1949: 5). But if that was the case, it was a misconception pollsters knew they lived by—one they could never hope to correct and still expect to have newspaper contracts at election time. Not that a pollster has ever been sacked on the basis of their single-seat polls, only on the basis of their nationwide polls.

On this occasion, the single-seat polls were never sufficiently extensive, consistent or reliable to override the message delivered by the national polls—all of them having delivered the same message for a long time. At the beginning of the final week of the campaign, *The Australian*, under the heading 'Marginals tumble into Coalition ledger but Labor clings to winning lead', published the results of its final single-seat polls (Benson 2019a). On election day, under the heading 'Voters' bob each way', it published the results of its final national poll. 'Despite the half-point break towards Labor in the final week', Simon Benson (2019c) reported, 'party strategists on both sides believe the swing is patchy and "hand-to-hand" battles in about 20 seats will decide the election'. The two headlines, and accompanying stories, captured much that was problematic in the way the polls were covered: the vision, however prescient, of marginal seats tumbling to the Coalition when only four had been polled, two of them showing Labor ahead; the idea that polls could measure changes of 0.5 percentage point, despite a footnote about a sampling error of ±1.8 percentage points, which, as it happens, was precisely the size of Newspoll's median error between 1993 and 2010 (Goot 2012: 106); and the suggestion that a lead in the polls meant a lead in the seats—something that had not held true in two of the previous 10 elections, in 1998 and 1990.

That pollsters are not well enough resourced to do their job well seems clear. They may need to improve their sampling frames or change sampling modes, boost their response rates (currently in single figures for IVR), especially among the disengaged, and attend to the way they weight their data (including education, and possibly religion, might help). To do this, they will need to ask more questions. They should include questions that better inform their readers, including questions that allow them to distinguish between respondents firmly committed to their vote choice and respondents who are not. Getting the polls off the hook may also require a change in the way journalists understand and report the polls. At the risk of adding another poor prediction to an already large pile, my guess is that most of these problems are unlikely to be resolved. Unlike pollsters with their predictions, however, I would be happy to be wrong.

References

Benson, Simon. 2019a. 'Kingmaker: Palmer's campaign hits pay dirt'. *The Australian*, 23 April.

Benson, Simon. 2019b. 'Marginals tumble into Coalition ledger but Labor clings to winning lead'. *The Australian*, 13 May.

Benson, Simon. 2019c. 'Voters' bob each way'. *Weekend Australian*, 18–19 May.

Coorey, Phillip. 2019. 'Labor clings to shrinking lead', *Australian Financial Review*, 17 May.

Crowe, David. 2019. 'Labor retains the edge but Coalition claws back ground', *Sydney Morning Herald*, 17 May.

Essential Media. 2019. *Essential Report*. www.essentialvision.com.au/category/essentialreport.

Gallup. 1949. 'Gallup Conference: Paris 3, 4, 5 & 6 Sept. 1949'. Minutes. Roy Morgan Papers.

Goot, Murray. 2009. 'Getting it Wrong While Getting It Right: The Polls, the Press and the 2007 Australian Election'. *Australian Cultural History* 27(2): 115–33. doi.org/10.1080/07288430903164769.

Goot, Murray. 2012. 'To the second decimal point: How the polls vied to predict the national vote, monitor the marginals and second-guess the Senate'. In *Julia 2010: The Caretaker Election*, edited by Marian Simms and John Wanna, 85–110. Canberra: ANU E Press. doi.org/10.22459/J2010.02.2012.06.

Goot, Murray. 2018. 'National polls, marginal seats and campaign effects'. In *Double Disillusion: The 2016 Federal Election*, edited by Anika Gauja, Peter Chen, Jennifer Curtin and Juliet Pietsch, 107–32. Canberra: ANU Press. doi.org/10.22459/DD.04.2018.05.

Goot, Murray. 2019. 'Did late deciders confound the polls?'. *Inside Story*, 19 September. insidestory.org.au/did-late-deciders-confound-the-polls/.

Ipsos. 2019. *Fairfax Ipsos Poll: National Poll (12–15 May 2019)*. 16 May. Sydney: Ipsos Australia.

Irvine, Jessica. 2019. 'Dunny deeds buy your votes, but not dirt cheap'. *Sydney Morning Herald*, 16 May.

Jackman, Simon and Luke Mansillo. 2018. 'The campaign that wasn't: Tracking public opinion over the 44th Parliament and the 2016 election campaign'. In *Double Disillusion: The 2016 Federal Election*, edited by Anika Gauja, Peter Chen, Jennifer Curtin and Juliet Pietsch, 133–56. Canberra: ANU Press. doi.org/10.22459/DD.04.2018.06.

Jefferson, Andrew. 2019. 'Sarah Henderson on track to retain Corangamite according to new poll figures'. *Geelong Advertiser*, 20 April. www.geelongadvertiser.com.au/news/geelong/sarah-henderson-on-track-to-retain-corangamite-according-to-new-poll-figures/news-story [page discontinued].

JWS. 2019. *Post-election survey shows detail behind Saturday's surprising election result*. Sydney: JWS Research. jwsresearch.com/2019/05/24/post-election-survey-shows-detail-behind-saturdays-surprising-election-result/.

Karp, Paul. 2019. '"Breaking down the myths": Blue-ribbon Liberal seats on unions' long target list'. *The Guardian*, 20 April. www.theguardian.com/australia-news/2019/apr/20/breaking-down-the-myths-blue-ribbon-liberal-seats-on-unions-long-target-list.

Lewis, Peter. 2019. 'As pollsters, we are rightly in the firing line after the Australian election. What happened?'. *The Guardian*, 21 May. www.theguardian.com/commentisfree/2019/may/21/as-pollsters-we-are-rightly-in-the-firing-line-after-the-australian-election-what-happened.

Mackerras, Malcolm. 2019. 'Federal Pendulum 2019 election result'. *Unrepresentative Swill*, [Blog]. www.malcolmmackerras.com/mackerras-pendulums.

Maiden, Samantha. 2019. 'Newspoll pollster also behind ALP's flawed election research'. *The New Daily*, 20 May. thenewdaily.com.au/news/election-2019/2019/05/20/Labor-polls-election-loss.

Murphy, Katharine. 2019. 'Post-election research shows 11% of voters made up their mind on polling day'. *The Guardian*, 4 June. www.theguardian.com/australia-news/2019/jun/04/post-election-research-shows-11-of-voters-made-up-their-mind-on-polling-day.

News Corp Australia Network. 2019. 'Federal election 2019: New polls in ten crucial electorates to reveal likely winner'. *PerthNow*, 17 May. www.perthnow.com.au/news/australia/election-2019-opinion-polls-in-ten-crucial-electorates-to-reveal-likely-election-winner-ng-e42b7b35ca2e3a9a3af7dd2aaf381566.

Roy Morgan. 2019. 'ALP regains initiative with a week to go: ALP 52% cf. L-NP 48%', 14 May, Finding No. 7975. www.roymorgan.com/findings/7975-alp-regains-initiative-with-a-week-to-go-201905140553.

Simms, Marian. 1997. '"All politics is local politics": Candidates and campaigning in the 1996 election'. In *The Politics of Retribution: The 1996 Federal Election*, edited by Clive Bean, Marian Simms, Scott Bennett and John Warhurst, 47–54. Sydney: Allen & Unwin.

Tabakoff, Nick. 2019. 'The diary'. *The Australian*, 15 July.

Appendix 8.1

Table A8.1 Marginal seat polling, YouGov Galaxy, campaign period, 10 April – 18 May 2019 (percentages)

Fieldwork	Client	State (party)	No.	Seat	First preferences						Other		TPP (LNP)			
					ALP	Coalition	Greens	UAP	PHON	Other	Inf	DK	2016	Est. 2019	Actual 2019	Diff.
		WA (ALP)	2016	Cowan	41.7	42.2	7.6	-	-	8.5	5.5		49.3	49		
1 May	Seven West Media*		(506)		41	40	6	4	4	5		[2]		49		
14–15 May	Seven West Media*		(528)		42	38	8	2	5	5		[3]		47√		
			2019		38.1	39.4	10.1	2.6	5.6	4.2	5.4				49.2	
			Diff.		+3.9	-1.4	-2.1	-0.6	-0.6	+0.8						-2.2
		WA (LIB)	2016	Pearce	34.3	45.4	11.0	-	-	9.3	4.6		53.6			
1 May	Seven West Media*		(525)		35	40	11	2	5	7		[1]		51		
14–15 May	Seven West Media*		(545)		36	42	10	4	3	5		[3]		51√		
			2019		29.1	43.7	8.7	2.5	8.2	7.8	6.9				57.5	
			Diff.		+6.9	-1.7	+1.3	+1.5	-5.2	-2.8						-6.5
		WA (LIB)	2016	Swan	33.0	48.2	15.0	-	-	3.8	3.6		53.6			
1 May	Seven West Media*		(504)		37	44	11	4	1	3		[4]		51		

167

Fieldwork	Client	State (party)	No.	Seat	First preferences						Other		TPP (LNP)			
					ALP	Coalition	Greens	UAP	PHON	Other	Inf	DK	2016	Est. 2019	Actual 2019	Diff.
14–15 May	Seven West Media*		(508)		38	41	9	5	2	5		[5]		50		
			2019		33.3	44.7	12.3	1.8	2.4	5.6	5.8				52.8	
			Diff.		+4.7	-3.7	-3.3	+3.2	-0.4	-0.6						-2.8
		WA (LIB)	2016	Hasluck	35.3	44.9	12.7	-	-	7.1	4.0		52.1			
14–15 May	Seven West Media*		(501)		36	39	9	5	5	6		[2]		50		
			2019		30.6	43.7	11.4	2.3	5.3	6.7	5.4				55.2	
			Diff.		+5.4	-4.7	-2.4	+2.7	-0.3	-0.7						-5.2
		WA (LIB)	2016	Stirling	32.2	49.5	11.7	-	-	6.6	5.1		56.1			
14–15 May	Seven West Media*		(517)		41	45	7	1	2	4		[2]		51√		
			2019		31.9	47.1	11.9	1.8	3.6	3.7	4.6				55.8	
			Diff		+9.1	-2.1	-4.9	-0.8	-1.6	+0.3						-4.8
		Qld (LNP)	2016	Dickson	35.0	44.7	9.8	-	-	10.5	3.4		51.7			
13–14 May	News Corp Aust.		(542)		35	41	10	9	3	2		[4]		51√		
			2019		31.3	46.0	9.9	2.2	5.2	5.4	4.4				54.7	
			Diff		+3.7	-5.0	+0.1	+6.8	-2.2	-3.4						-3.7
		Qld (LNP)	2016	Flynn	33.4	37.1	2.8	-	17.2	9.6	5.4		51.0			

Fieldwork	Client	State (party)	No.	Seat	First preferences						Other			TPP (LNP)		
					ALP	Coalition	Greens	UAP	PHON	Other	Inf	DK	2016	Est. 2019	Actual 2019	Diff.
13–14 May	News Corp Aust.		(508)		33	37	3	11	7	9		[2]		53√		
			2019		28.7	37.9	3.0	4.2	19.6	6.6	5.8				58.6	
			Diff.		+4.3	–0.9	0.0	+6.8	–12.6	+2.4						–5.6
		Qld (LNP)	2016	Forde	37.6	40.6	6.4	–	–	15.4	5.1		50.6			
13–14 May	News Corp Aust.		(567)		41	42	5	4	7	1		[5]		50		
			2019		29.5	43.5	8.7	4.1	11.8	2.4	4.6				58.6	
			Diff.		+10.5	–1.5	–3.7	–0.1	–4.8	–1.4						–8.6
		Qld (ALP)	2016	Herbert	30.5	35.5	6.3	–	13.5	6.9 KAP 7.3 Other	6.9		50.0			
13–14 May	News Corp Aust.		(506)		31	32	5	9	6	14 KAP 3 Other		[1]		50		
			2019		25.4	37.2	7.3	5.7	11.1	11.1 KAP 9.8 Other	5.9				58.4	
			Diff.		+5.6	–5.2	–2.3	+3.3	–5.1	+2.9 KAP –6.8 Other						–8.4
		Qld (ALP)	2016	Leichhardt	28.1	39.5	8.8	–	7.5	4.3 KAP 11.8 Oth	7.3		54.0			
13–14 May	News Corp Aust.		(634)		34	40	8	5	4	7 KAP 2 Other		[1]		51√		

169

Fieldwork	Client	State (party)	No.	Seat	Period	ALP	Coalition	Greens	UAP	PHON	Other	Other — Inf	Other — DK	TPP (LNP) — 2016	TPP (LNP) — Est. 2019	TPP (LNP) — Actual 2019	TPP (LNP) — Diff.
13–14 May	News Corp Aust.	Vic. (LIB)	(540)	Deakin	2019	28.8	37.6	10.4	4.0	6.1	8.2 KAP / 5.1 Other	6.4			51√	54.2	
					Diff.	+5.2	+2.4	−2.4	+1.0	−2.1	−1.2 KAP / −3.1 Other	−2.1					−3.2
					2016	30.1	50.3	11.3	–	–	8.3	3.0	[2]	56.4			
13–14 May	News Corp Aust.	Vic. (LIB)	(538)	Higgins	2019	37	44	9	4	–	6	4.1			52√	54.8	
					Diff.	18	45	29	4	–	8.6	−2.6					−3.8
					2016	16.5	51.6	24.2	–	–	7.7	3.8	[1]	57.4			
13–14 May	News Corp Aust.	Vic. (LIB)	(541)	La Trobe	2019	25.3	48.1	22.2	1.3	–	3.0	2.0			50	54.1	
					Diff.	−7.3	−3.1	+6.8	+2.7	–	+1.0						−2.1
					2016	32.1	44.1	8.3	–	–	15.5	5.7	[1]	53.2			
		SA (LIB)		Boothby	2019	39	43	7	3	–	8					54.5	
					Diff.	34.5	45.8	7.8	2.6	–	4.5	4.5					−4.5
					2016	+4.5	+2.8	−0.8	+0.4	–	+3.5						
					2016	26.9	41.7	8.2	–	18.5 Xen.	4.7			52.7			

Fieldwork	Client	State (party)	No.	Seat	First preferences						Other		TPP (LNP)			
					ALP	Coalition	Greens	UAP	PHON	Other	Inf	DK	2016	Est. 2019	Actual 2019	Diff.
9 May	The Advertiser		(520)		37	47	9	3	-	4		[2]		53√		
			2019		34.6	45.2	12.0	1.9	-	6.3	4.7				51.4	
			Diff.		+2.4	+1.8	-3.0	+1.1	-	-2.3						+1.6
		SA (LIB)	2016	Mayo	16.7	32.9	8.1	-	32.9	5.6			52.9	CA	CA	
2 May	The Advertiser		(557)		7	38	7	3	43	2		[1]		57√		
			2019		13.7	37.7	9.3	3.2	34.2	2.0	3.1				55.1	
			Diff.		-6.7	+0.3	-2.3	-0.2	+8.8	-						+1.9
		SA (LIB)	2016	Sturt	23.2	44.4	7.6	-	19.9	4.8			55.4			
24 April	The Advertiser		(557)		35	42	6	9	-	8		[2]		53√		
			2019		29.9	50.6	11.2	2.4	-	6.0	5.4				56.9	
			Diff.		+5.1	-8.6	-5.2	+6.6	-	+2.0						-3.9
		NSW (LIB)	2016	Gilmore	39.2	45.3	10.5	-	ON	5.0	4.1		50.7			
13–14 May	News Corp Aust.		[540]		40	26 LIB 17 NAT	7	2	-	8		[2]		48√		
			2019		36.2	29.2 LIB 12.7 NAT	9.8	3.4	-	8.8	5.2				47.5	

Fieldwork	Client	State (party)	No.	Seat	First preferences						Other		TPP (LNP)			
					ALP	Coalition	Greens	UAP	PHON	Other	Inf	DK	2016	Est. 2019	Actual 2019	Diff.
			Diff.		+3.8	–3.2 LIB +4.3 NAT	–2.8	–1.4	–	–0.8						+0.5
13–14 May	News Corp Aust.	NSW (ALP)	2016	Macquarie	35.5	38.2	11.2	–	–	15.1	6.5		47.8			
			[540]		43	42	8	5	–	2		[1]		47√		
			2019		38.3	44.9	9.1	4.0	–	3.7	4.3				49.9	
			Diff.		+4.7	–2.9	–1.1	+1.0	–	–1.7						–2.9
13–14 May	News Corp Aust.	NSW (LIB)	2016	Reid	36.3	48.8	8.5	–	–	6.4	5.0		54.7			
			[540]		36	44	7	6	–	7		[5]		52√		
			2019		37.2	48.3	8.1	1.9	–	4.5	6.1				53.2	
			Diff.		–1.2	–4.3	–1.1	+4.1	–	+2.5						–1.2

- No candidate

* Published in either the *West Australian* or the *Sunday Times*.

√ Predicts the winner

Source: YouGov Galaxy.

Table A8.2 Marginal seat polling, Newspoll, campaign period, 10 April – 18 May 2019 (percentages)

Fieldwork	State (party)	No.	Seat	First Preferences						Other		TPP (Coalition)*			
				ALP	Coalition	Greens	UAP	PHON	Other	Inf.	[DK]	2016	Est.	Actual	Diff.
	WA (LIB)	2016	Pearce	34.3	45.4	11.0	-	-	9.3	4.6		53.6			
20 April		(509)		36	40	8	8	6	2		[2]		50		
		2019		29.1	43.7	8.7	2.5	8.2	7.8	6.9				57.5	
		Diff.		+6.9	-3.7	-0.8	+5.5	-2.2	-5.8						-7.5
	Qld (LIB)	2016	Herbert	30.5	35.5	6.3	-	13.5	6.9 KAP 7.3	6.9		50.0			
20 April		(529)		29	31	5	14	9	19 KAP 2		[2]		50		
9–11 May		(550)		30	35	7	7	7	13 KAP 1		n.s.		52√		
		2019		25.4	37.2	7.3	5.7	11.1	11.1 KAP 9.8	5.9				58.4	
		Diff.		+4.6	-2.2	-0.3	+1.3	-4.1	+1.9 KAP -8.8						-6.4
	Vic. (LIB)	2016	Deakin	30.1	50.3	11.3	-	-	8.3	3.0		56.4			
20 April		(535)		39	46	8	5	-	2		[1]		51√		
		2019		32.6	47.8	8.9	2.1	-	8.6	4.1				54.8	
		Diff.		+6.4	-1.8	-0.9	+2.9	-	-6.6						-3.8

173

Fieldwork	State (party)	No.	Seat	First Preferences						Other		TPP (Coalition)*			
				ALP	Coalition	Greens	UAP	PHON	Other	Inf.	[DK]	2016	Est.	Actual	Diff.
	Vic. (ALP)#	2016	Corangamite	34.1	43.7	12.1	-	-	10.1	4.7		50.0			
9–11 May		(573)		37	42	10	4	-	7		n.s.		49√		
		2019		35.5	42.4	8.9	2.2	-	11.0	4.0				49	
		Diff.		+1.5	-0.4	+1.1	+1.8	-	-4.0						0.0
	NSW (ALP)	2016	Lindsay	41.1	39.3	3.6	-	-	16.0	11.8		48.9			
20 April		(618)		40	41	4	7	-	8		[1]		49		
9–11 May		(577)		39	44	4	6	-	7		n.s.		52√		
		2019		35.6	46.5	4.8	1.4	-	10.2	11.1				55.2	
		Diff.		+3.4	-2.5	-0.8	+4.6	-	-3.2						-3.2
	Tas. (ALP)	2016	Bass	39.7	39.2	11.1	-	-	10.0	4.0		44.6			
9–11 May		(503)		39	40	10	4	-	7		n.s.		48		
		2019		34.7	42.3	10.5	4.9	-	7.6	4.5				50.4	
		Diff.		+4.3	-2.3	-0.5	-0.9	-	-0.6						-2.4

* Based on recent federal and State elections.

Won by the Liberals; notionally Labor on new boundaries.

√ Predicts the winner

n.s. = not stated

Sources: For 20 April, Benson (2019a); for 9–11 May, Benson (2019b).

Table A8.3 Marginal seat polling, uComms, 16 May 2019 (percentages)

State	Seat	Party	2016 TPP (Coalition)	First preferences									TPP (Coalition)	N.
				ALP	LNP	Greens	KAP	PHON	UAP	Ind.	Other minor	Undecided		
NSW	Page	LIB	52.3	32.6	35.1	11.3	–	–	3.3	6.0	5.6	6.1	n.s.	n.s.
NSW	Reid	LIB	54.7	38.6	43.5	6.6	–	–	1.3		5.5	4.5	n.s.	n.s.
Vic.	Casey	LIB	54.6	29.4	36.9	12.4	–	–	6.2	4.7	2.4	8.0	n.s.	n.s.
Vic.	Corangamite	ALP*	49.9	32.6	37.0	9.4	–	–	5.3	6.0	5.3	2.4	n.s.	n.s.
Vic.	Higgins	LIB	60.1	24.1	42.8	20.2	–	–	1.8	–	4.6	6.4	n.s.	n.s.
Qld	Dickson	LNP	51.8	32.0	41.4	10.4	–	4.0	3.6	2.4	1.9	4.3	n.s.	n.s.
Qld	Forde	LNP	50.7	31.1	37.2	7.9	–	11.1	6.7	–	3.3	2.7	n.s.	n.s.
Qld	Leichhardt	LNP	54.1	28.8	32.0	9.4	8.4	9.7	3.9	2.3	1.9	3.5	n.s.	n.s.
SA	Boothby	LIB	52.8	33.3	38.2	8.6	–	–	4.9	4.0	3.3	7.7	n.s.	n.s.
WA	Hasluck	LIB	52.1	32.1	40.9	10.2	–	3.3	2.2	3.5	2.8	4.9	n.s.	n.s.
WA	Pearce	LIB	53.7	28.4	37.0	7.6	–	8.8	1.2	4.2	5.1	7.9	n.s.	n.s.
Tas.	Braddon	ALP	48.2	31.4	35.6	6.9	–	6.9	4.1	8.5	3.0	3.7	n.s.	n.s.

* Won by the Liberals; notionally Labor on new boundaries.

n.s. = not stated

Question: 'For the federal election to be held on Saturday, which of the following parties will receive your first preference vote?'

Source: uComms for *The Project*, Network 10.

175

Table A8.4 Final national polls for the House of Representatives, by party, 2019 (percentages)

Poll	Mode	Fieldwork	LIB*/NAT/LNP	ALP	Greens	UAP	PHON	Other/Ind.~	DK	No.	Avg. diff.^	TPP# (LNP)	TPP# diff.
Essential	Online	10–14 May	(36.2/3.6) 38.5	36.2	9.1	n.s.	6.6	9.6	[8]	(1,201)	1.5	48.5	–3.0
Ipsos	CATI (landline + mobile)	12–15 May	(36/3) 39.0	33	13	3	4.	8	[7]	(1,842)	1.4	49	–2.5
YouGov Galaxy	Online	12–15 May	39	37	9	3	3	9	[7]	(1,004)	1.9	49	–2.5
Newspoll‡	Online + IVR landline	14–17 May	38	37	9	5	3	8	[4]	(3,038)	2.4	48.5	–3.0
Roy Morgan	Face-to-face	??–14 May	38.5	35.5	10	3.5	4	8.5	[5]	(1,265)	1.7	48	–3.5
Election		18 May	(36.9/4.5) 41.4	33.3	10.4	3.4	3.1	8.4				51.5	

n.s. = either not asked or not reported

* Liberal Party + Liberal National Party (Queensland) + Country Liberal Party (Northern Territory)

Two-party preferred (TPP) based on the distribution of minor party preferences at the 2016 election except for: Newspoll, 'based on recent federal and State elections'; except for Morgan, which reported a TPP based on stated preferences; and for Ipsos, which reported a TPP based on 2016 preferences and reported preferences (49:51 in both cases).

~ Based on four categories of response: LNP, ALP, Greens and Other.

‡ Excludes Northern Territory and the Australian Capital Territory for landline

Note: Numbers in brackets in the LIB/NAT/LNP cell (36.2/3.6), as published by Essential, are incorrect since they cannot be reconciled with the overall and correct (LNP) figure of 38.5.

Source: Essential Media (2019) and Lewis (2019) for the 'undecided'; Crowe (2019), Coorey (2019) and Jessica Elgood for Ipsos; YouGov Galaxy; Benson (2019c), for Newspoll; and Roy Morgan (2019).

PART 2.
THE RESULTS

9

HOUSE OF REPRESENTATIVES RESULTS

Ben Raue

The Liberal–National Coalition Government obtained a small swing towards it at the 2019 Australian federal election, gaining a handful of seats. This result restored the government's narrow majority, which now stands at 77 (of 151) seats. This is an increase of one from 2016, although the government had subsequently lost that majority through various by-elections in the final months of the previous parliament. This chapter covers the results of the 2019 election in the House of Representatives (the House), in individual seats and looking at the overall trends in terms of preference flows, the impact of early voting and the varying swings across the country.

2016 election

To place the 2019 House results in context, it is worth recapping the main results of the previous election. In 2016, the first-term Coalition Government went into the election with a sizeable majority, but the loss of 14 seats left it with the slimmest of majorities. The Coalition won 76 seats in the House of Representatives. Labor won 69 seats, which was a net gain of 14 seats. The Greens and Katter's Australian Party (KAP) retained one seat each, as did two Independent MPs. The Nick Xenophon

Team (NXT) also gained a single seat in the House of Representatives. The Coalition suffered a swing of 3.5 per cent against it on primary votes. Labor gained a 1.3 per cent swing, alongside a 1.6 per cent swing to the Greens. The NXT gained 1.9 per cent in its first outing. The Palmer United Party (PUP), which had polled 5.5 per cent in 2013, ran in only one electorate and polled 0.4 per cent in that seat.

Table 9.1 Results of the 2016 federal election by party

Party	Votes	Percentage	Swing	Seats	Seat change
Liberal–National Coalition	5,693,605	42.04	–3.51	76	–14
ALP	4,702,296	34.73	1.35	69	14
Greens	1,385,650	10.23	1.58	1	0
NXT	250,333	1.85	1.85	1	1
KAP	72,879	0.54	–0.50	1	0
PUP	315	0.00	–5.49	0	–1
Independents	380,712	2.81	1.44	2	0
Other	1,055,311	7.79	3.28	0	0

Source: Compiled by author from Australian Electoral Commission data (AEC 2016g, 2016c).

Redistribution of electoral boundaries

Redistributions in Australia are conducted independently of political parties and partisan officials, and electoral boundaries are drawn with little regard to their political impact. Australia does not see the partisan decision-making that is present in many States in the United States or the gerrymandered electoral boundaries those decisions produce (see Newton-Farrelly 2015).

Electoral redistributions are required when one of three criteria is met:

- The number of members to which a State or Territory is entitled changes.
- Seven years has elapsed since the last redistribution process.
- The number of electors in more than one-third of electorates deviates from the average divisional enrolment by more than 10 per cent for a period of more than two months.

In the term of parliament prior to the 2019 federal election, the House of Representatives electoral boundaries were redrawn in six of eight jurisdictions: Victoria, Queensland, South Australia, Tasmania, the Australian Capital Territory and the Northern Territory. The changes were minor in Queensland, Tasmania and the Northern Territory, but were much more dramatic in Victoria, South Australia and the Australian Capital Territory.

Redistributions in Queensland, Tasmania and the Northern Territory were triggered due to seven years passing since the last redistribution. The number of electorates did not change in any of these jurisdictions, and no seat experienced sufficient changes to shift the electorate's notional status from one party to another. The Hobart-based electorate of Denison in Tasmania was renamed 'Clark'. In Victoria, South Australia and the Australian Capital Territory, redistributions were necessary as these jurisdictions' entitlements for members had changed. The entitlement of members for each State and Territory was calculated in August 2017, and it was found that Victoria's entitlement had increased from 37 to 38 members, while South Australia's entitlement dropped from 11 to 10 and that of the Australian Capital Territory increased from two to three.

This change in entitlements necessitated significant redrawing of the electoral boundaries in these three jurisdictions. Two new notionally Labor electorates were created: the seat of Canberra in the Australian Capital Territory and the seat of Fraser in Victoria. The Labor-held seat of Port Adelaide in South Australia was abolished. Two Liberal-held seats in Victoria were redrawn as notionally Labor seats: Corangamite and Dunkley. These changes resulted in a net gain of three seats for Labor and a net increase of one seat overall. This left the governing Coalition with just 74 seats, alongside 72 for Labor and five for minor parties and Independents.

By-elections

Nine federal by-elections were held during the 2016–19 parliamentary term. This was the second-largest number of by-elections held during a single parliamentary term, only exceeded by the 10 held during the term of the 20th parliament from 1951 to 1954. Seven of these nine by-elections were triggered by the sitting member falling foul of the prohibition on candidates being elected if they held foreign citizenship (see Chapter 3, this volume), while the two others were caused by the local member's retirement.

Table 9.2 By-elections held during the 2016–19 parliamentary term

Electorate	Date	Outgoing MP	Result
New England	2 December 2017	Barnaby Joyce (NAT)	+7.2% to NAT (2CP)
Bennelong	16 December 2017	John Alexander (LIB)	+4.8% to ALP (2CP)
Batman	17 March 2018	David Feeney (ALP)	+3.4% to ALP (2CP)
Braddon	28 July 2018	Justine Keay (ALP)	+0.1% to ALP (2CP)
Fremantle	28 July 2018	Josh Wilson (ALP)	+11.6% to ALP (primary)
Longman	28 July 2018	Susan Lamb (ALP)	+3.7% to ALP (2CP)
Mayo	28 July 2018	Rebekha Sharkie (CA)	+2.6% to CA (2CP)
Perth	28 July 2018	Tim Hammond (ALP)	+2.0% to ALP (primary)
Wentworth	20 October 2018	Malcolm Turnbull (LIB)	51.2% to Ind. (2CP)

CA = Centre Alliance
2CP = two-candidate preferred
Source: Compiled by author from AEC data.

The first by-election, in the NSW seat of New England, was triggered in October 2017 when the High Court ruled that four senators and Deputy Prime Minister Barnaby Joyce were ineligible to be elected at the time of their nomination in 2016. Joyce was comfortably re-elected in December with almost 65 per cent of the primary vote and 73.6 per cent of the two-party-preferred vote, which was a swing of 7.2 per cent since 2016. Liberal MP John Alexander and Labor MP David Feeney both resigned from parliament prior to any High Court ruling that would have disqualified them. Alexander was re-elected to his seat of Bennelong (NSW) in December 2017 despite a 4.8 per cent two-candidate-preferred swing that halved his margin. Feeney did not run for re-election and his seat of Batman (in Victoria) was won by Labor candidate Ged Kearney with a 3.35 per cent two-candidate-preferred swing against the Greens from the March 2018 by-election.

A series of five by-elections was triggered for 28 July 2018. Four of the sitting members resigned due to irregularities with their renunciation of citizenship prior to the 2016 election, while the fifth member (Tim Hammond in Perth) chose to retire for reasons unrelated to any citizenship problem. All five of these by-elections saw the incumbent party gain a swing towards it. Sitting Labor MPs Justine Keay (Braddon), Josh Wilson (Fremantle) and Susan Lamb (Longman) all gained swings, as did new Labor candidate Patrick Gorman in Perth and Centre Alliance (CA) MP Rebekha Sharkie in Mayo.

The final by-election of the term was triggered in late 2018 by the removal of Malcolm Turnbull as Liberal leader and thus as prime minister. Turnbull resigned from parliament a week after his removal from office, necessitating a by-election in his seat of Wentworth in New South Wales. The subsequent by-election was won by Independent candidate Kerryn Phelps with 51.2 per cent of the two-candidate-preferred vote.

Candidate nominations

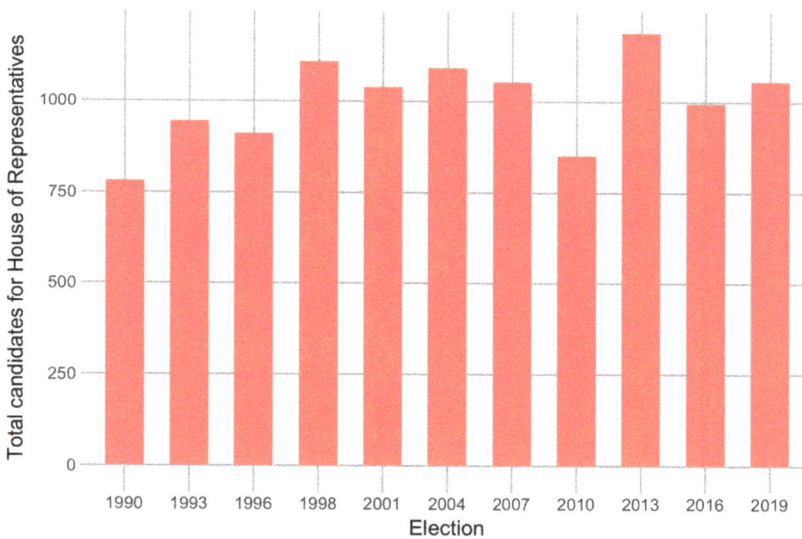

Figure 9.1 Total House of Representatives candidates per election, 1990–2019

Sources: Raue (2013); AEC data (2016e, 2019h).

Despite an increase in the nomination deposit for the House of Representatives, from $1,000 to $2,000 (see Chapter 3, this volume), 1,056 candidates nominated to run for the 151 House of Representatives seats at the 2019 federal election. This was roughly in line with the norm for elections since 1998, although it was an increase of 62 candidates from 2016 (see Figure 9.1). Labor, the Greens and the UAP each nominated a full slate of 151 candidates. The Liberal–National Coalition ran 162 candidates, thanks to the Liberal and National parties running candidates against each other in 11 seats. A total of 97 Independents ran for election, along with 344 members of other parties, including 59 members of

PHON, 48 members of Fraser Anning's Conservative National Party and 46 members of the Animal Justice Party. The 2019 Australian federal election was notable for the abnormally large number of candidates disendorsed by their party, either before or after the close of nominations, with 10 candidates disendorsed by their party following the close of nominations (see further, Chapters 3 and 4, this volume).

National result

The election produced a mixed result. Both the Coalition and Labor suffered negative primary vote swings. A majority of seats swung towards the Coalition on a two-party-preferred basis, but a substantial number of seats swung towards Labor. The Coalition polled 51.53 per cent of the two-party-preferred vote, which was a swing of 1.17 per cent from 2016 (Table 9.3). The Greens' primary vote stayed steady at 10.2 per cent, while there was a vote of more than 3 per cent each for the UAP and PHON (a swing of 1.8 per cent for the latter). More than one-quarter of all formal votes were cast for minor parties or Independents, which is the highest recorded in the House of Representatives under the modern party system, exceeding the previous record of 23.5 per cent at the 2016 election (see Chapter 17, this volume).

Table 9.3 Results of the 2019 federal election by party

Party	Votes	Percentage	Swing	Seats	Seat change
Liberal–National Coalition	5,906,875	41.44	–0.60	77	1
ALP	4,752,160	33.34	–1.39	68	–1
Greens	1,482,923	10.40	0.17	1	0
UAP	488,817	3.43	3.43	0	0
PHON	438,587	3.08	1.79	0	0
KAP	69,736	0.49	–0.05	1	0
CA	46,931	0.33	–1.52	1	0
Independents	479,836	3.37	0.56	3	1
Other	587,528	4.12	0.25	0	0

Source: Compiled by author from AEC data (2019c, 2019g).

Seats changing hands

As discussed, the redistributions that occurred prior to the election resulted in the Coalition losing two notional seats and Labor gaining three notional seats. As shown in Table 9.4, at the 2019 election, the Coalition gained five seats from Labor, while Labor gained one seat from the Coalition, resulting in a net gain of four seats for the Coalition. The Coalition also won back the seat of Wentworth, which was lost to an Independent in the 2018 by-election, but lost the nearby seat of Warringah to another Independent. Therefore, compared with the 2016 election result, there was a net increase of one seat for the Coalition and a net loss of one seat for Labor. The Greens, KAP and Centre Alliance each retained one seat, while two other seats were retained by Independents.

Table 9.4 Seats that changed party at the 2019 election

Seat	State	Incumbent	Winner	Margin (%)
Bass	Tas.	ALP	LIB	0.4
Braddon	Tas.	ALP	LIB	3.2
Corangamite*	Vic.	LIB	ALP	1.0
Dunkley*	Vic.	LIB	ALP	2.6
Gilmore	NSW	LIB	ALP	2.5
Herbert	Qld	ALP	LNP	8.4
Lindsay	NSW	ALP	LIB	5.2
Longman	Qld	ALP	LNP	3.3
Warringah	NSW	LIB	Independent	7.2
Wentworth	NSW	Independent	LIB	1.5

* Seat was redistributed prior to the 2019 election.
Source: Compiled by author from AEC data (2019l).

Differences between States

There were big differences in the election results between different States, with swings in different directions producing larger than normal gaps between the larger States (Table 9.5). Labor won the two-party-preferred vote in three States, with Labor polling particularly strongly in Victoria. The Coalition also won a majority in three States, with a particularly strong result in Queensland. This result was the continuation of a recent trend that had seen Victoria pull ahead as a strong Labor State, while Queensland moved towards the Coalition and New South Wales positioned itself as close to the centre of Australian politics (see further, Chapter 11, this volume).

Table 9.5 Two-party-preferred vote by State

State	ALP TPP	Coalition TPP	Swing to Coalition
NSW	48.22	51.78	1.26
Vic.	53.14	46.86	−1.30
Qld	41.56	58.44	4.34
WA	44.45	55.55	0.90
SA	50.71	49.29	1.57
Tas.	55.96	44.04	1.40
ACT	61.61	38.39	−0.49
NT	54.20	45.80	2.87
Australia	48.47	51.53	1.17

Source: AEC (2019i).

Figure 9.2 shows the difference between Labor's two-party-preferred vote in each State and its two-party-preferred vote in the remainder of the nation since 1958 for the three largest States.

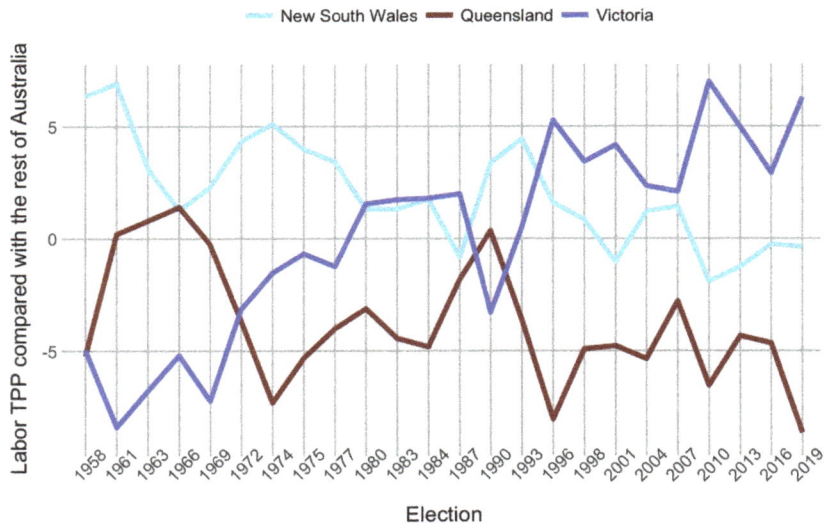

Figure 9.2 Labor two-party-preferred vote in each State compared with the remainder of the country, 1958–2019

Source: Constructed by the author from data provided by Antony Green.

The Coalition performed better in Queensland than in the remainder of the nation in 2019 than at any other election in the past six decades. Labor polled 6 per cent better in Victoria than in the remainder of the nation, which was just slightly below its relative performance in that State in 2010. Labor has traditionally underperformed in Victoria and overperformed in New South Wales, but there has been a long-term trend that has seen Labor improve in Victoria and lose ground in New South Wales, which now looks about average compared with the remainder of the country. Meanwhile, Queensland has become a State in which Labor consistently underperforms, with a particularly large gap in the two-party-preferred vote in 2019.

Reversal of 2016 swings

There was variation in swings not just between States, but also between different electorates within each State. The Coalition gained a swing on two-party-preferred votes in 92 electorates, while Labor gained a swing in the other 59 electorates. Labor generally gained more of a swing in more affluent and better-educated areas, while the Coalition tended to gain ground in less affluent areas (Evershed 2019). This manifested geographically in swings to Labor in more inner-city electorates (both Labor and Liberal seats), while the Coalition gained ground in outer suburban areas and rural electorates (such as northern Tasmania and northern Queensland) (see Chapter 11, this volume). These swings in part reversed some of the stronger trends at the 2016 election, which saw the Coalition do particularly badly in some of the same areas where they gained ground in 2016. For example, a 10.1 per cent swing to Labor in Bass in 2016 was partly cancelled out by a 5.9 per cent swing to the Liberal Party in 2019.

The impact of preferences

The continued increase in support for minor parties and Independents means that preferences are becoming increasingly important in deciding winners in individual electorates. One-quarter of all formal votes in the House of Representatives were cast for candidates other than the Coalition or Labor, which is the highest it has been under the modern party system. This figure has been steadily climbing from just 14.5 per cent in 2007.

Labor won 58.6 per cent of preference flows, which is down from 62.2 per cent in 2016. This partly reflects the increased vote for right-wing minor parties such as PHON and the UAP. About 65 per cent of preferences from voters who gave their first preference to these two parties favoured the Coalition over Labor, while 82 per cent of Greens voters favoured Labor over the Coalition. As a comparison, just over 50 per cent of PHON voters preferenced the Coalition in 2016, while less than 54 per cent of voters for the PUP preferenced the Coalition over Labor in the PUP's last iteration in 2013.

Figure 9.3 shows there was a slight increase in the number of seats for which it was necessary to distribute preferences. The winning candidate polled less than half of the formal vote in 105 of 151 seats—up from 102 of 150 seats at the 2016 election. While preferences were necessary to decide the result in more than 100 seats, the candidate leading on primary votes went on to win in almost every case. There were 12 electorates where the candidate leading on primary votes did not win. In 10 of these seats, the Labor candidate overtook the Coalition candidate. The Liberal candidate was overtaken by the Centre Alliance candidate in Mayo and by an Independent candidate in Indi.

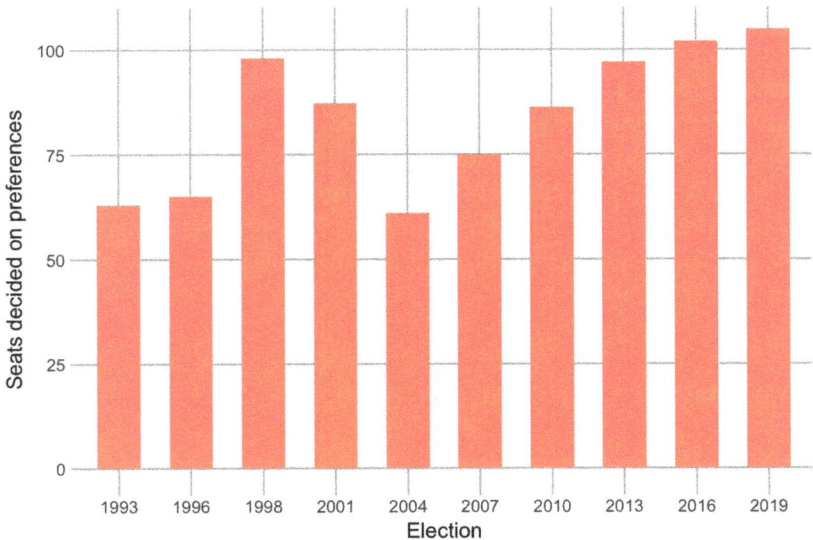

Figure 9.3 Seats decided on preferences, 1993–2019

Sources: Constructed by the author from AEC data (1998, 2001, 2004d, 2007d, 2010e, 2013e, 2016h, 2019h).

Difference between election day and early votes

There has been a significant increase in the proportion of votes cast before election day, primarily via pre-poll voting. The proportion of formal votes cast via pre-poll increased from 4.9 per cent in 2001 to 32.7 per cent in 2019. Postal voting also experienced an increase, from 4.1 per cent in 2001 to 8.5 per cent in 2019, with most of the growth taking place between 2007 and 2013 (see Chapter 3, this volume).

The Coalition has tended to do consistently better among early voters, and the increasing volume of early voters has not shifted this trend. The gap between the two-party-preferred vote among voters who cast their votes early and that among those who voted on election day was wider in 2019 than in any election since at least 2001 (Table 9.6). The Coalition polled 5.3 per cent better on the early vote than on election day, which compares with a gap of 4.8 per cent in 2016 and a gap as low as 3.8 per cent in 2007.

Table 9.6 Labor two-party-preferred vote before and on election day (percentage)

Election	ALP TPP election day	ALP TPP early vote	Difference	Proportion voting on election day
2001	49.5	44.8	4.6	90.4
2004	47.7	43.8	3.9	88.3
2007	53.2	49.5	3.8	85.5
2010	50.9	46.7	4.2	81.6
2013	47.8	43.1	4.7	72.4
2016	51.2	46.4	4.8	67.6
2019	50.7	45.4	5.3	58.0

Sources: Compiled by the author from AEC data (2004a, 2004b, 2007a, 2007b, 2010a, 2010b, 2013a, 2013b, 2016a, 2016b, 2019a, 2019b).

As Table 9.6 and Figure 9.4 illustrate, Labor has not won the early vote at any of the past seven elections, coming closest when they polled 49.5 per cent of the two-party-preferred vote in 2007. Yet that constituency has become much larger since 2007, and this growth in the early vote has not made these voters look any more like election-day voters. Labor managed to win a majority of the election-day vote in both 2016 and 2019, despite losing the overall two-party-preferred vote at both elections, thanks to a large differential with the early vote. This emphasises the importance of the early vote for deciding elections. With almost half of voters casting their vote early, a dominant position for the Coalition on the early vote can win elections even when Labor wins a majority on election day.

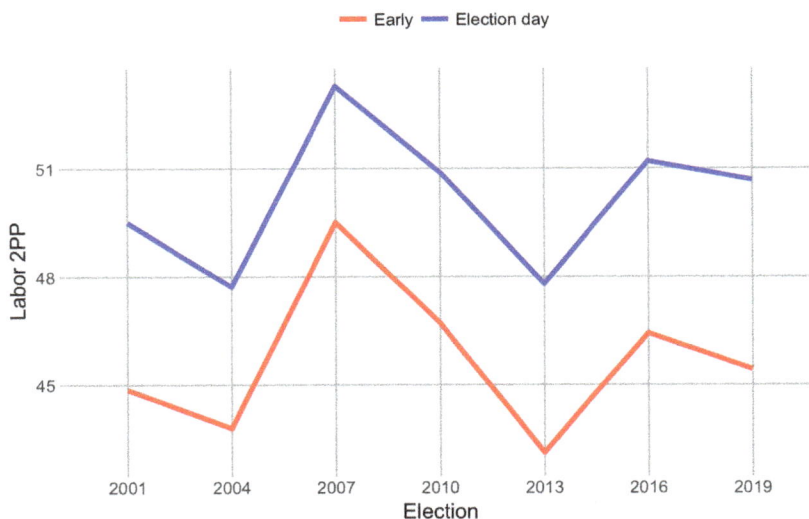

Figure 9.4 Labor two-party-preferred vote before and on election day

Notes: Election-day votes include ordinary, absent and provisional votes. Early votes include remote, mobile, special hospital, pre-poll and postal votes.

Sources: Compiled by the author from AEC data (2004a, 2004b, 2007a, 2007b, 2010a, 2010b, 2013a, 2013b, 2016a, 2016b, 2019a, 2019b).

Informal votes

There was an increase in informal votes at the 2019 election compared with the previous election, although the rate was still lower than it was at the 2010 and 2013 elections (Figure 9.5). The rate of informal voting in 2019 was 5.54 per cent of all votes cast for the House of Representatives. This was an increase from a rate of 5.05 per cent in 2016, but still less than the 5.55 per cent and 5.91 per cent recorded at the 2010 and 2013 elections, respectively. Despite an increase in informal votes, the effective participation rate increased again, as it did at the 2013 and 2016 elections. Some 84 per cent of all Australians who were eligible to vote cast a formal ballot in 2019—up from 80 per cent in 2010.

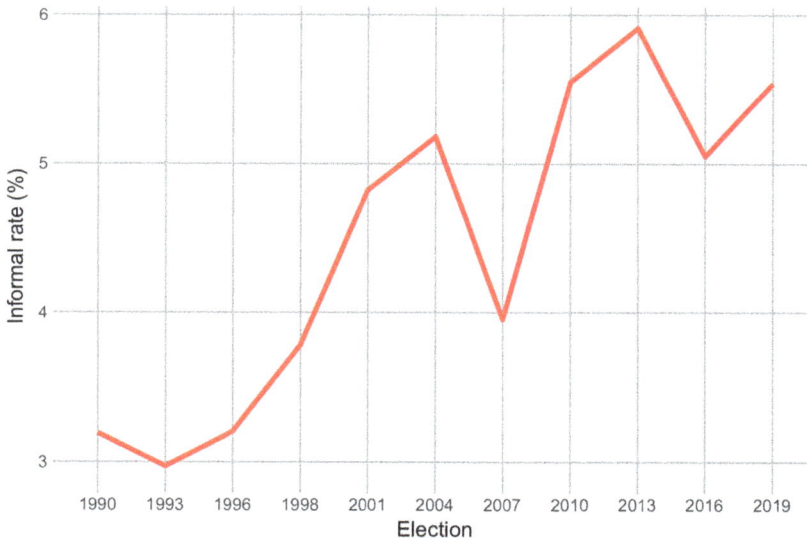

Figure 9.5 Informal voting rate at federal elections, 1990–2019
Sources: Constructed by the author from Carr (1990); and AEC (1998, 2001, 2004c, 2007c, 2010c, 2013c, 2016d, 2019d).

These trends varied significantly by State. In New South Wales, 7 per cent of all votes were informal, while the next highest rate was 5.4 per cent, in Western Australia. Victoria experienced a decline in the informal rate while the rate in Western Australia was a significant increase. New South Wales still has a higher effective participation rate than Queensland, Western Australia and the Northern Territory despite a much higher informal rate (Table 9.7).

Table 9.7 Informal voting rate by State (per cent)

State/Territory	Informal rate	Informal rate change	Effective participation rate
NSW	7.01	0.84	84.14
Vic.	4.66	−0.11	85.39
Qld	4.95	0.25	82.81
WA	5.44	1.44	81.77
SA	4.81	0.63	85.97
Tas.	4.39	0.40	87.67
ACT	3.49	0.72	89.13
NT	4.69	−2.66	62.23
National	**5.54**	**0.48**	**84.04**

Sources: Compiled by the author from AEC (2019d, 2019j, 2019k).

Labor–Coalition contests: State by State

New South Wales

There were 10 NSW seats held by Labor and the Coalition on margins of less than 6 per cent prior to the 2019 election. Two of these seats changed hands, with the Liberal Party and the ALP each gaining one seat off the other. Labor's Fiona Phillips gained the South Coast electorate of Gilmore with a 3.3 per cent two-party-preferred swing, while Liberal candidate Melissa McIntosh gained the Western Sydney electorate of Lindsay with a 6.2 per cent swing, finishing up with 55 per cent of the two-party-preferred vote. Sitting member effects played out badly in both seats, with Emma Husar removed as the Labor candidate in Lindsay after one term and Ann Sudmalis stepping down as Liberal MP in Gilmore, leading to both Coalition parties running along with an ex-Liberal Independent.

The Liberal Party gained swings across Western Sydney and came close to winning the seat of Macquarie, where Labor's Susan Templeman won a second term by just 371 votes (with 50.2 per cent of the two-party-preferred vote), following a 2 per cent swing to the Liberal Party. Labor also suffered swings in other Western Sydney seats, with Greenway and Parramatta pushed into the marginal seat category. Labor also suffered swings on the Central Coast and in the Hunter region. Swings of 9.5 per cent, 5.7 per cent and 5.5 per cent in the seats of Hunter, Paterson and Shortland, respectively, put all three of these Hunter region seats into the marginal seat category, while Labor's hold on Dobell was weakened and the Liberals' hold on Robertson was strengthened by a swing of just over 3 per cent. Labor frontbencher Joel Fitzgibbon was left with a margin of only 3 per cent in his seat of Hunter following a vote of 21.6 per cent for PHON—the highest vote for that party in any House of Representatives electorate.

Labor held hopes of making gains in two mid-suburban Liberal seats in more multicultural parts of Sydney, but made only modest gains in one of these seats, with a 1.5 per cent swing in Reid, where sitting Liberal MP Craig Laundy had retired. Liberal minister David Coleman did much better in the southern Sydney electorate of Banks, bolstering his 1.4 per cent margin with a 4.8 per cent swing. Labor retained two marginal seats in more regional parts of New South Wales, narrowly retaining the south-eastern seat of Eden-Monaro in the face of a 2.1 per cent swing, and also retaining the far north coast electorate of Richmond after a very small swing to Labor MP Justine Elliot. Nationals MP Kevin Hogan strengthened his hold on the neighbouring seat of Page with a 7.2 per cent swing.

Victoria

Most of the interesting contests in Victoria took place in seats held by the Liberal Party, but very few seats changed hands. Labor won two seats that had been redrawn into notionally Labor seats prior to the election and gained a 1 per cent swing in Corangamite and a 1.7 per cent swing in Dunkley, strengthening its hold in two Liberal-held seats that had been redrawn with Labor majorities. The Liberal Party suffered swings but held on to two key seats in the eastern suburbs of Melbourne. Liberal MP Michael Sukkar suffered a 1.7 per cent swing in Deakin, while in the neighbouring seat of Chisholm new Liberal candidate Gladys Liu was elected despite a 2.3 per cent swing to Labor.

A big boost in Labor's primary vote saw it pull ahead of the Greens in the inner eastern Melbourne seat of Higgins, where Liberal MP Kelly O'Dwyer had retired. Labor gained a 6.1 per cent swing on a two-party-preferred basis, leaving new Liberal MP Katie Allen holding her newly marginal seat by just 3.9 per cent. Three other marginal seats, on the outer fringe of Melbourne, did not move as much. Senior Liberal minister Greg Hunt suffered a 1.4 per cent swing against him in Flinders, while fellow Liberals gained small swings towards them in the outer eastern seats of Casey and La Trobe.

Queensland

Queensland is famous for a large proportion of its electorates being marginal, and this was certainly true in 2019, although large swings in a series of Queensland's marginal seats means there will be fewer marginal seats in the State at the next election. A lot of attention was focused on a string of five marginal seats on the central and northern coast, stretching from Gladstone to Cape York. Four of these five seats were held by the Liberal National Party (LNP), with the Townsville-area seat of Herbert won by the slimmest of margins by Labor's Cathy O'Toole in 2016. Big swings to the LNP in four of these seats saw them regain Herbert with an 8.4 per cent swing and strengthen their hold in Capricornia (11.7 per cent swing), Dawson (11.2 per cent) and Flynn (7.6 per cent). The LNP's Warren Entsch was re-elected in the far northern seat of Leichhardt by a 4.2 per cent margin, with a swing of just 0.2 per cent.

The LNP also gained sizeable swings in three marginal seats on the outer northern fringes of Brisbane, regaining the Labor seat of Longman with a 4.1 per cent swing and retaining Petrie with a 6.8 per cent swing and Dickson with a 3 per cent swing. The LNP's Bert van Manen pushed his Logan-area seat of Forde out of the marginal seat category with a swing of 8 per cent.

Two Labor seats closer to central Brisbane were made more marginal thanks to swings to the LNP. Labor suffered a 2.1 per cent swing in Moreton and a 5 per cent swing in Lilley. Labor just held on, by a 0.4 per cent margin, in Lilley following the retirement of former treasurer and deputy prime minister Wayne Swan. Labor did better in the inner-city seats of Brisbane and Griffith. Labor MP Terri Butler increased her margin by 1.4 per cent in Griffith, while LNP MP Trevor Evans had 1.1 per cent shaved off his margin in Brisbane.

Western Australia

The Liberal Party gained a swing of just under 1 per cent of the two-party-preferred vote in Western Australia, but most seats experienced only small swings, with no seats changing hands. Of the five seats held by margins of less than 6 per cent prior to the election, there were swings to Labor in three and swings to the Liberal Party in the other two. Labor gained a swing in its two marginal seats but suffered negative swings in its safer seats. Anne Aly gained a small, 0.15 per cent swing in Cowan, while Patrick Gorman gained a 1.6 per cent swing in Perth. The Liberal Party suffered a small, 0.9 per cent swing in Steve Irons's seat of Swan but gained swings in excess of 3 per cent in both Pearce and Hasluck.

South Australia

Both major parties gained large swings in South Australia due to the reduced presence of the Centre Alliance (previously called the Nick Xenophon Team), which polled 4.4 per cent, compared with more than 21 per cent at the 2016 election. No seats in South Australia changed hands. There was only one marginal seat, which was a contest between Labor and Liberal, in Liberal MP Nicolle Flint's seat of Boothby. She held this seat by a 2.7 per cent margin prior to the election, and this margin was reduced to 1.4 per cent.

Tasmania

The Coalition bounced back from a poor performance in Tasmania in 2016, gaining two seats and a two-party-preferred swing of 1.4 per cent Statewide. Liberal candidates Bridget Archer and Gavin Pearce, respectively, won their northern Tasmanian seats of Bass and Braddon with two-party-preferred swings of 5.8 per cent and 4.8 per cent. The Liberal candidate for Lyons, Jessica Whelan, was disendorsed shortly after the close of nominations, leading to the Liberal Party supporting the Nationals candidate, Deanna Hutchinson, who managed 15.7 per cent, but it was not enough to overtake the official Liberal candidate.

Australian Capital Territory

Labor retained all three ACT electorates, gaining a 4.1 per cent swing in the newly created inner-city electorate of Canberra while suffering swings of 1.3 per cent in the two outer suburban electorates of Bean and Fenner.

Northern Territory

Labor retained the two electorates in the Northern Territory but suffered swings to the Country Liberal Party (CLP) in both. The CLP gained a two-party-preferred swing of 3 per cent in the Darwin-area electorate of Solomon and gained a 2.7 per cent swing in the vast electorate of Lingiari.

Non-classic contests

The AEC defines a seat as 'non-classic' if the final two candidates after the distribution of preferences are not a Labor candidate and a Coalition candidate. Non-classic seats can include races where an Independent or minor party comes in the top two or where the final distribution of preferences is between two Coalition candidates.

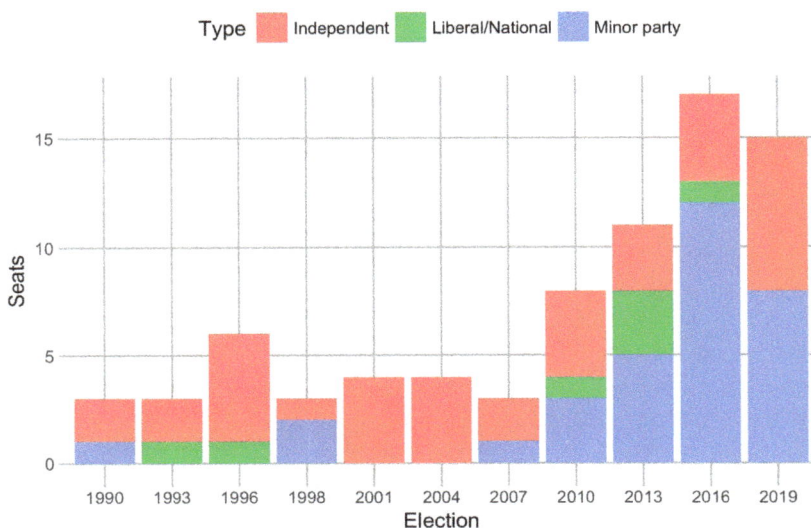

Figure 9.6 Non-classic races in federal elections, 1990–2019

Sources: Constructed by the author from Carr (1990); and AEC (1998, 2001, 2004a, 2007a, 2010d, 2013d, 2016f, 2019f).

The number of non-classic contests peaked at 17 of 150 seats at the 2016 federal election after a steady climb since 2010 (Figure 9.6). It declined slightly in 2019, down to 15 of 151 seats. There were seven contests in which an Independent made it to the top two, which is the highest number over the period analysed. There was a decline in the number of contests involving a minor party in the top two—down from 12 to eight. This decline was primarily due to the absence of the NXT. The NXT had come in the top two in four electorates in 2016, while its successor party came in the top two in only a single seat. The Greens also made it to the final count in only five seats in 2019, down from six.

Contests between the Liberal Party and the Nationals

The Liberal Party and the Nationals ran against each other in 11 seats, but in most cases only one of the two candidates was a serious contender. In addition to Gilmore and Lyons (mentioned above), which were ultimately won by Labor, the only other seat worth mentioning is Mallee. Mallee covers the north-western corner of Victoria and was held by retiring Nationals MP Andrew Broad. His retirement opened the door for the Liberal Party to contest the seat, along with Labor and two relatively prominent Independents. The Liberal Party narrowly outpolled Labor on primary votes to come second but was narrowly overtaken by Labor on the distribution of preferences.

The Greens

The Greens contested every electorate, but there was only a handful of seats where they made the top two and had any chance of winning, most of them in a contiguous area in inner Melbourne. Greens MP Adam Bandt further solidified his hold on the seat of Melbourne, with 71.8 per cent of the two-candidate-preferred count. Julian Burnside came second in the inner eastern seat of Kooyong, trailing Liberal Party Deputy Leader, Josh Frydenberg, with 44.3 per cent of the two-candidate-preferred vote. The Greens had come second in the neighbouring seat of Higgins in 2016, but a big surge in the Labor vote and a small drop in the Greens vote saw them fall into third place here. The Greens also went backwards in two inner northern seats, which had been their closest chances in 2016. They suffered a 3.2 per cent swing in Wills and a much larger, 13.4 per cent swing in neighbouring Cooper (previously named Batman).

Other minor parties and Independents

Three other minor party candidates made it to the final two in the distribution of preferences. Bob Katter was re-elected for a 10th term as Member for Kennedy, representing his KAP, with a 2.3 per cent swing. Rebekha Sharkie won a second full term as Member for Mayo representing the Centre Alliance, with a 2.2 per cent swing (although this was less than the margin she achieved at the 2018 by-election). Rosemary Moulden, running for Pauline Hanson's One Nation, polled 27.5 per cent of the two-candidate-preferred vote in Maranoa.

197

Independents came in the top two in seven electorates and three of those Independents were elected. Incumbent MP Andrew Wilkie was easily re-elected in his Hobart-area electorate of Clark with a 4.4 per cent swing. Cathy McGowan retired from her northern Victorian electorate of Indi, and endorsed fellow Independent Helen Haines, who won the seat with 51.4 per cent of the two-candidate-preferred vote (a 4.1 per cent swing compared with McGowan in 2016). Zali Steggall defeated former Liberal prime minister Tony Abbott in his northern Sydney seat of Warringah, with 57.2 per cent of the two-candidate-preferred vote. Kerryn Phelps was unsuccessful in her eastern suburbs electorate of Wentworth, losing to Liberal candidate Dave Sharma after defeating him in the 2018 by-election. Phelps managed 48.7 per cent of the two-candidate-preferred vote in 2019.

Former Independent MP Rob Oakeshott made a second attempt at a comeback in the NSW north coast seat of Cowper but fell short with just 43.2 per cent of the two-candidate-preferred vote. Independents also challenged Coalition MPs in two other seats, along the Murray River. Albury Mayor Kevin Mack came second in the southern NSW electorate of Farrer, polling 39.1 per cent of the two-candidate-preferred vote. Two Independents ran in the north-western Victorian seat of Mallee, polling almost 20 per cent between them but falling short of winning the seat.

Conclusion

The 2019 federal election produced a result that was very similar to that of the previous election in 2016, with a slim majority for the Coalition counterpoised against a large crossbench and a relatively strong Labor Opposition. Yet the interpretation of this result has typically been very different, thanks to high expectations for Labor in the context of poor government polling. Apart from the slim victory for the Coalition, the other major development in the 2019 election was the continuing slow growth of the minor party vote, with a record high number of votes cast for minor parties or Independents and six crossbench members elected to the House of Representatives. This relatively close election result sets up the next election as one that is very winnable for either major party and leaves the government with a stable but not strong majority for the next three years.

References

Australian Electoral Commission (AEC). 1998. 'Election statistics on CD-ROM'. [Online]. Canberra: AEC. www.aec.gov.au/About_AEC/Publications/ statistics/files/aec-1993-1996-1998-election-statistics.zip.

Australian Electoral Commission (AEC). 2001. 'Election results'. *Election 2001.* Canberra: AEC. www.aec.gov.au/About_AEC/Publications/statistics/files/aec-2001-election-statistics.zip.

Australian Electoral Commission (AEC). 2004a. '2004 Federal Election House of Representatives two candidate preferred by candidate by vote type'. *Virtual Tally Room.* Canberra: AEC. results.aec.gov.au/12246/results/Downloads/ HouseTcpByCandidateByVoteTypeDownload-12246.csv.

Australian Electoral Commission (AEC). 2004b. '2004 Federal Election House of Representatives two party preferred by polling place'. *Virtual Tally Room.* Canberra: AEC. results.aec.gov.au/12246/results/Downloads/HouseTppBy PollingPlaceDownload-12246.csv.

Australian Electoral Commission (AEC). 2004c. 'House of Representatives: informal votes by State'. *Virtual Tally Room.* Canberra: AEC. results.aec.gov. au/12246/results/HouseInformalByState-12246.htm.

Australian Electoral Commission (AEC). 2004d. 'House of Representatives: Seats decided on preferences'. *Virtual Tally Room.* Canberra: AEC. results.aec. gov.au/12246/results/HouseSeatsDecidedOnPrefs-12246-NAT.htm.

Australian Electoral Commission (AEC). 2007a. '2007 Federal Election House of Representatives two candidate preferred by candidate by vote type'. *Virtual Tally Room.* Canberra: AEC. results.aec.gov.au/13745/Website/Downloads/ HouseTcpByCandidateByVoteTypeDownload-13745.csv.

Australian Electoral Commission (AEC). 2007b. '2007 Federal Election House of Representatives two party preferred by polling place'. *Virtual Tally Room.* Canberra: AEC. results.aec.gov.au/13745/Website/Downloads/HouseTppBy PollingPlaceDownload-13745.csv.

Australian Electoral Commission (AEC). 2007c. 'House of Representatives: Informal votes by State'. *Virtual Tally Room.* Canberra: AEC. results.aec.gov.au/ 13745/Website/HouseInformalByState-13745.htm.

Australian Electoral Commission (AEC). 2007d. 'House of Representatives: Seats decided on preferences'. *Virtual Tally Room.* Canberra: AEC. results.aec. gov.au/13745/Website/HouseSeatsDecidedOnPrefs-13745-NAT.htm.

Australian Electoral Commission (AEC). 2010a. '2010 Federal Election House of Representatives two candidate preferred by candidate by vote type'. *Virtual Tally Room*. Canberra: AEC. results.aec.gov.au/15508/Website/Downloads/HouseTcpByCandidateByVoteTypeDownload-15508.csv.

Australian Electoral Commission (AEC). 2010b. '2010 Federal Election House of Representatives two party preferred by polling place'. *Virtual Tally Room*. Canberra: AEC. results.aec.gov.au/15508/Website/Downloads/HouseTppByPollingPlaceDownload-15508.csv.

Australian Electoral Commission (AEC). 2010c. 'House of Representatives: Informal votes by State'. *Virtual Tally Room*. Canberra: AEC. results.aec.gov.au/15508/Website/HouseInformalByState-15508.htm.

Australian Electoral Commission (AEC). 2010d. 'House of Representatives: Non-classic divisions'. *Virtual Tally Room*. Canberra: AEC. results.aec.gov.au/15508/Website/HouseNonClassicDivisions-15508-NAT.htm.

Australian Electoral Commission (AEC). 2010e. 'House of Representatives: Seats decided on preferences'. *Virtual Tally Room*. Canberra: AEC. results.aec.gov.au/15508/Website/HouseSeatsDecidedOnPrefs-15508-NAT.htm.

Australian Electoral Commission (AEC). 2013a. '2013 Federal Election House of Representatives two candidate preferred by candidate by vote type'. *Virtual Tally Room*. Canberra: AEC. results.aec.gov.au/17496/Website/Downloads/HouseTcpByCandidateByVoteTypeDownload-17496.csv.

Australian Electoral Commission (AEC). 2013b. '2013 Federal Election House of Representatives two party preferred by polling place'. *Virtual Tally Room*. Canberra: AEC. results.aec.gov.au/17496/Website/Downloads/HouseTppByPollingPlaceDownload-17496.csv.

Australian Electoral Commission (AEC). 2013c. 'House of Representatives: Informal votes by State'. *Virtual Tally Room*. Canberra: AEC. results.aec.gov.au/17496/Website/HouseInformalByState-17496.htm.

Australian Electoral Commission (AEC). 2013d. 'House of Representatives: Non-classic divisions. *Virtual Tally Room*. Canberra: AEC. results.aec.gov.au/17496/Website/HouseNonClassicDivisions-17496-NAT.htm. '

Australian Electoral Commission (AEC). 2013e. 'House of Representatives: Seats decided on preferences'. *Virtual Tally Room*. Canberra: AEC. results.aec.gov.au/17496/Website/HouseSeatsDecidedOnPrefs-17496-NAT.htm.

Australian Electoral Commission (AEC). 2016a. '2016 Federal Election House of Representatives two party preferred by division by vote type'. *Tally Room 2016 Federal Election*. Canberra: AEC. results.aec.gov.au/20499/Website/Downloads/HouseTppByDivisionByVoteTypeDownload-20499.csv.

Australian Electoral Commission (AEC). 2016b. '2016 Federal Election House of Representatives two party preferred by polling place'. *Tally Room 2016 Federal Election*. Canberra: AEC. results.aec.gov.au/20499/Website/Downloads/House TppByPollingPlaceDownload-20499.csv.

Australian Electoral Commission (AEC). 2016c. 'House of Representatives: First preferences by party'. *Tally Room 2016 Federal Election*. Canberra: AEC. results. aec.gov.au/20499/Website/HouseStateFirstPrefsByParty-20499-NAT.htm.

Australian Electoral Commission (AEC). 2016d. 'House of Representatives: Informal votes by State'. *Tally Room 2016 Federal Election*. Canberra: AEC. results.aec.gov.au/20499/Website/HouseInformalByState-20499.htm.

Australian Electoral Commission (AEC). 2016e. 'House of Representatives: Nominations by State'. *Tally Room 2016 Federal Election*. Canberra: AEC. results.aec.gov.au/20499/Website/HouseNominationsByState-20499.htm.

Australian Electoral Commission (AEC). 2016f. 'House of Representatives: Non-classic divisions'. *Tally Room 2016 Federal Election*. Canberra: AEC. results.aec.gov.au/20499/Website/HouseNonClassicDivisions-20499.htm.

Australian Electoral Commission (AEC). 2016g. 'House of Representatives: Party representation'. *Tally Room 2016 Federal Election*. Canberra: AEC. results.aec. gov.au/20499/Website/HousePartyRepresentationLeading-20499.htm.

Australian Electoral Commission (AEC). 2016h. 'House of Representatives: Seats decided on preferences'. *Tally Room 2016 Federal Election*. Canberra: AEC. results.aec.gov.au/20499/Website/HouseSeatsDecidedOnPrefs-20499.htm.

Australian Electoral Commission (AEC). 2019a. '2019 Federal Election House of Representatives two party preferred by division by vote type'. *Tally Room 2019 Federal Election*. Canberra: AEC. results.aec.gov.au/24310/Website/ Downloads/HouseTppByDivisionByVoteTypeDownload-24310.csv.

Australian Electoral Commission (AEC). 2019b. '2019 Federal Election House of Representatives two party preferred by polling place'. *Tally Room 2019 Federal Election*. Canberra: AEC. results.aec.gov.au/24310/Website/Downloads/House TppByPollingPlaceDownload-24310.csv.

Australian Electoral Commission (AEC). 2019c. 'House of Representatives: First preferences by party'. *Tally Room 2019 Federal Election*. Canberra: AEC. results. aec.gov.au/24310/Website/HouseStateFirstPrefsByParty-24310-NAT.htm.

Australian Electoral Commission (AEC). 2019d. 'House of Representatives: Informal votes by State'. *Tally Room 2019 Federal Election*. Canberra: AEC. results.aec.gov.au/24310/Website/HouseInformalByState-24310.htm.

Australian Electoral Commission (AEC). 2019e. 'House of Representatives: Nominations by State'. *Tally Room 2019 Federal Election*. Canberra: AEC. results.aec.gov.au/24310/Website/HouseNominationsByState-24310.htm.

Australian Electoral Commission (AEC). 2019f. 'House of Representatives: Non-classic divisions'. *Tally Room 2019 Federal Election*. Canberra: AEC. results.aec.gov.au/24310/Website/HouseNonClassicDivisions-24310.htm.

Australian Electoral Commission (AEC). 2019g. 'House of Representatives: Party representation'. *Tally Room 2019 Federal Election*. Canberra: AEC. results.aec. gov.au/24310/Website/HousePartyRepresentationLeading-24310.htm.

Australian Electoral Commission (AEC). 2019h. 'House of Representatives: Seats decided on preferences'. *Tally Room 2019 Federal Election*. Canberra: AEC. results.aec.gov.au/24310/Website/HouseSeatsDecidedOnPrefs-24310.htm.

Australian Electoral Commission (AEC). 2019i. 'House of Representatives: Two party preferred by state'. *Tally Room 2019 Federal Election*. Canberra: AEC. results.aec.gov.au/24310/Website/HouseTppByState-24310.htm.

Australian Electoral Commission (AEC). 2019j. 'House of Representatives: Turnout by State'. *Tally Room 2019 Federal Election*. Canberra: AEC. results. aec.gov.au/24310/Website/HouseTurnoutByState-24310.htm.

Australian Electoral Commission (AEC). 2019k. 'House of Representatives: Size of the electoral roll and enrolment rate 2019'. *Tally Room 2019 Federal Election*. Canberra: AEC. www.aec.gov.au/Enrolling_to_vote/Enrolment_stats/national/2019.htm.

Australian Electoral Commission (AEC) 2019l. 'House of Representatives: Seat summary'. *Tally Room 2019 Federal Election*. Canberra: AEC. results.aec.gov. au/24310/Website/HouseSeatSummary-24310.htm.

Carr, Adam. 1990. 'The House of Representatives: Australian legislative election of 24 March 1990'. *Psephos: Adam Carr's Election Archive*. [Online]. psephos. adam-carr.net/countries/a/australia/1990/1990reps1.txt.

Evershed, Nick. 2019. 'The eight charts that help explain why the Coalition won the 2019 Australian election'. *The Guardian*, 21 May. www.theguardian.com/news/datablog/2019/may/22/the-eight-charts-that-help-explain-why-the-coalition-won-the-2019-australian-election.

Newton-Farrelly, Jenni. 2015. *Fairness and Equality: Drawing Election Districts in Australia*. Melbourne: Australian Scholarly Publishing.

Raue, Ben. 2013. 'Nominations announced: Final update'. *The Tally Room*, 11 June. www.tallyroom.com.au/29634.

10

THE SENATE RESULT

Antony Green

The Morrison Government's narrow re-election was accompanied by a significant strengthening of its position in the Senate. The Coalition gained four seats from non-Green minor parties and reduced the number of minor parties from eight to four. These gains allowed the Coalition's numbers to draw level with the unchanged representation of Labor and the Greens. Combined with the smaller crossbench, this will simplify the government's task of passing legislation through the new Senate.

When the Greens vote with Labor, the Morrison Government will need support from four of the six non-Greens senators to pass legislation, or three of five after former Liberal Senator Cory Bernardi resigned from the Senate.[1] This compares with six of the eight non-Greens crossbenchers in the government's first term in office and nine of 11 in its second. The Coalition's gains also leave Labor and the Greens with less scope to initiate Senate committees aimed at embarrassing the government.

---

1   South Australian Senator Cory Bernardi was elected as a Liberal in 2016 and allocated a six-year term. He resigned from the party in February 2017 and registered a new party, the Australian Conservatives. Bernardi deregistered his party after the election and resigned from the Senate in January 2020. As required by Section 15 of the Constitution, Bernardi's replacement was Liberal.

Table 10.1 Composition of the Senate, 2014–2022

Senate term	Coalition	Labor	Greens	Others
2014–16	33	25	10	8
2016–19	30	26	9	11
2019–22	35	26	9	6

Note: Party representation is based on the first sitting of newly elected senators and does not take into account subsequent changes in party membership.

Source: Party representation calculated by author from AEC results.

As will be explained in this chapter, the Coalition's improved position was not due to changes in voter support for the Coalition or minor parties. The government's gains stemmed from two issues related to the mechanics of Senate elections. The first was the large number of crossbench senators facing re-election, having been allocated three-year terms after the 2016 double-dissolution election. The second flowed from new electoral rules that were first used at the 2016 election, but the political impact of which could be tested only by their first use at a half-Senate election.

The Senate electoral changes ended full preferential voting, transferred control of interparty preferences from parties to voters and gave voters more options to pick and choose between candidates on party lists. As will be shown, the 2019 results matched expectations that the changes would increase the importance of voters' first-preference choice while diminishing the role of preferences from excluded parties and candidates.

Some background on Senate elections

The two chambers of the Australian Parliament have always been elected with different representational bases and using different electoral systems. Representation by State in the House of Representatives is based on population, but original States have equal representation in the Senate. Since 1903, the House has been elected from single-member electorates, while the Senate has been elected from Statewide multi-member electorates, using proportional representation by single transferable vote (PR-STV) since 1949. Significant changes to the operation of PR-STV were introduced in 1984 and 2016.

Electors complete separate ballot papers for House and Senate elections and, while terms for the two chambers are not tied, elections are usually held on the same day.[2] The Australian Constitution includes a deadlock provision allowing a 'double dissolution' in which the Senate's fixed terms can be broken, sending the House and the whole Senate to election together.

Candidates have been grouped on the Senate ballot paper since 1922, with parties determining the order in which their candidates are listed since 1940. Most votes are cast for the top of each party's ticket, and the trickle down of preferences means PR-STV within parties generally operates as a form of party list proportional representation (List-PR). PR-STV diverges from List-PR in the allocation of seats to parties with a remaining vote of less than a quota. Where List-PR usually uses highest remainder or highest average methods to allocate final seats, Senate PR-STV fills the final seats by distributing preferences from excluded parties and candidates. The ability of parties to influence or control the flow of preferences on exclusion therefore determines how much PR-STV deviates from simple List-PR.[3]

Before 1984 there were no party names on ballot papers and voters were required to express a sequence of preferences for all candidates on the ballot paper. Only parties that actively campaigned by distributing how-to-vote material could hope to influence the flow of interparty preferences. Most minor parties struggled to influence results by preferences.

Changes introduced in 1984 created strong control over interparty preferences, delivering the same power to both major and minor parties. A thick horizontal line was included on the ballot paper, providing an area 'above the line' where voters could mark one party box that was imputed to carry the complete list of preferences of that party, or electors could vote for candidates as before by expressing preferences for all candidates listed 'below the line'. An example of the current ballot paper is shown in Figure 10.1, differing from the pre-2016 version by including party logos and new instructions.

---

2   All 18 elections since 1974 have been joint elections, 13 as House and half-senate elections and five as double dissolutions.
3   Background on the development of Australia's electoral system can be found in Farrell and McAllister (2006), while the more recent Senate changes introduced in 2016 are explored in Green (2018) and McAllister and Muller (2019).

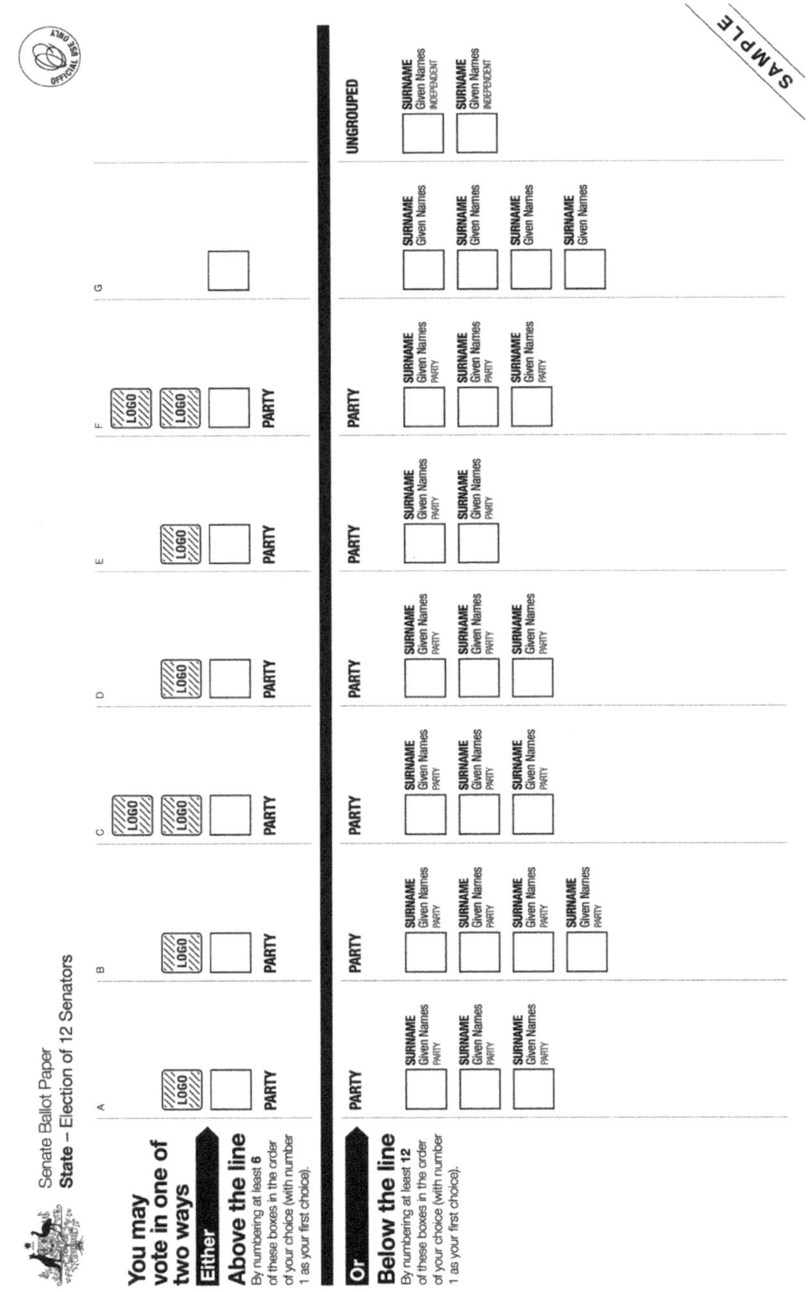

Figure 10.1 Example of the Senate ballot paper
Source: AEC.

The asymmetry in effort between the two voting methods herded voters into accepting the party tickets—a problem made worse as the number of candidates and parties contesting elections increased. With 98 per cent of major party votes and 90 per cent of minor party votes completed above the line, parties gained almost total control over interparty preferences. By the 2013 Senate election, the ever-increasing number of parties contesting Senate elections and the growing complexity of preference tickets lodged resulted in nine of the 36 State senators being elected from trailing positions on preferences, with several leap-frogging to victory from very low first-preference tallies (Green 2018). Group voting tickets (GVTs) were therefore increasing the divergence between PR-STV and List-PR outcomes.

The 2013 result led to changes that were introduced ahead of the 2016 double-dissolution election. Party logos were added but the divided ballot paper was retained. Group voting tickets were abolished, ending the ability of parties to control interparty preferences. Voters were given a new option to express preferences for parties by numbering at least six boxes above the line, and parties reverted to the pre-1984 situation of influencing preferences by handing out how-to-vote recommendations. Full preferential voting below the line was ended, with voters only needing to express preferences for at least 12 candidates. Generous savings provisions were included to prevent a rise in informal votes.

By passing control of interparty preferences to voters and giving voters more options to exhaust their preferences, the new system increased the importance of first-preference votes and diminished the ability of parties to engineer victories after trailing on first preferences. How the system would work in practice was masked by the calling of a double-dissolution election in 2016, which aided the election of minor parties by lowering the quota from 14.3 to 7.7 per cent.

Before examining how the new Senate electoral system worked in 2019, it is important to first look at the impact of the allocation of new Senate terms after the 2016 election, as well as the votes recorded by States and Territories at the 2019 election.

The consequences of the 2016 double dissolution

The 2016 double-dissolution election spilled all 76 Senate seats: 12 per State plus the four Territory senators. At the first sitting following the election, the rotation of terms was re-established by all State senators being allocated to either six-year terms ending in 2022 or three-year terms facing re-election in 2019. Terms were allocated on the order of election—a decision that resulted in the majority of minor party senators being allocated short terms, facing re-election in 2019.

Between 2016 and 2019, more than one-quarter of Senate representation changed through retirement or disqualification. Of the 76 senators elected in 2016, only 56 served a full three years. There were 20 departures from the chamber, including 10 senators disqualified under Section 44 of the Constitution—eight for citizenship issues and one each for a criminal offence and pecuniary interests (see Chapter 3, this volume). Retirements and other casual vacancies were filled by State parliaments appointing replacements from the same party. Disqualified candidates were replaced through a recount, with more senators disqualified in one term than had been disqualified in the previous 115 years.

The recounts caused a number of senators' terms to be reallocated in February 2018. There were also several changes in party affiliation during the term. Table 10.2 summarises the party composition of the Senate at the 2019 election, breaking the numbers into continuing members and three-year and Territory senators facing re-election in 2019.

Table 10.2 Composition of the Senate at the 2019 election

Senate as it finished	Coalition	Labor	Greens	Others
Six-year senators	16	13	3	4
Three-year senators	13	11	6	6
Territory senators	2	2	0	0
Total	31	26	9	10

Source: Calculated by author based on party representation ahead of the 2019 election.

Twelve crossbench senators faced re-election, including one Greens senator in every State. Three crossbenchers faced election in New South Wales, two in the other four mainland States and one in Tasmania. It has been unusual for half-Senate elections to return more than one crossbencher per State, with only seven of 54 contests between 1990 and 2013 electing more than one crossbencher, four of those due to the complex GVT preference deals at the 2013 election. The allocation of seats combined with the new Senate electoral system decreased the chances of multiple minor party senators being elected in any State.

The 2019 result

Table 10.3 summarises the overall change in votes and seat numbers produced by the 2019 Senate election. The government had a net gain of four seats at the expense of the crossbench, with overall numbers for Labor and the Greens unchanged.

Table 10.3 2019 election results

Senate as elected	Votes (%)	Change	Seats won	Change	New Senate
Coalition	38.0	+2.8	19	+4	35
ALP	28.8	−1.0	13	0	26
Greens	10.2	+1.6	6	0	9
PHON	5.4	+1.1	1	−1	2
UAP	2.4	+2.4	0	0	0
CA	0.2	−3.1	0	0	2
Others	15.1	−3.8	1	−3	2

Source: AEC.

The Coalition won three of the six vacancies in the five mainland States, two in Tasmania and one each in the two Territories. Compared with the outgoing Senate, in the new Senate, the Coalition gained seats from the crossbench in New South Wales, Victoria and Western Australia. The Liberal Party gained a seat from Labor in Queensland and Tasmania, though this second gain was cancelled out by the National Party losing its seat to Jacqui Lambie (of the Jacqui Lambie Network, or JLN).

Labor's Senate vote share was a further decline from the already low votes recorded in 2013 and 2016. Labor gained two seats, one each from the crossbench in New South Wales and South Australia, but lost seats to the Coalition in Queensland and Tasmania. Labor's vote was below 30 per cent in New South Wales, Queensland and Western Australia, falling short of two quotas in the last two States. Labor's vote was so low in Queensland that the party elected only one senator—its surplus beyond one quota, trailing the Greens.

The Greens retained all six seats and increased their vote, polling 9.9 per cent or higher in every State except New South Wales. The Greens did not achieve a quota on first preferences in any State, but in every State the party's vote in quotas was high enough to win seats where Labor fell significantly short of electing an extra member with its surplus quota.

The PHON increased its vote, finishing third ahead of the Greens in Queensland, fourth in the other mainland States and fifth behind the JLN in Tasmania. Only Queensland returned a PHON Senator, Malcolm Roberts, who won the seat he had been disqualified from in 2017, while the party lost its seat in Western Australia. Roberts's replacement in Queensland, Fraser Anning, and Brian Burston in New South Wales both defected and contested the 2019 election for other parties.

Support for the Centre Alliance (formerly the Nick Xenophon Team, or NXT) collapsed without the high-profile presence of Nick Xenophon's name on the ballot paper. Despite a massive advertising spend (see Chapter 17, this volume), the UAP polled only 2.4 per cent; its highest vote was 3.5 per cent in Queensland, where Clive Palmer was the party's leading Senate candidate.

Results by State

New South Wales

Table 10.4 Senate results: New South Wales

Party	Vote by party (%)			Senators allocated/elected		
	2013	2016	2019	2013	2016	2019
LIB/NAT	34.2	35.9	38.6	3	2	3
ALP	31.6	31.3	29.8	2	1	2
Greens	7.8	7.4	8.7	0	1	1
Liberal Democrats	9.5	3.1	1.9	1	1	0
PUP (2013–16)/UAP (2019)	3.4	0.1	1.5	0	1	0
PHON	1.2	4.1	5.0	0	0	0
Others	12.3	18.1	14.5	0	0	0

Notes: The 2016 column shows senators allocated to short terms by a Senate motion in February 2018; Senator Burston switched from One Nation to the UAP in June 2018.
Source: Party totals accumulated by author from AEC results.

The reallocation of Senate terms resulted in three minor party senators facing re-election, two Coalition and only one Labor senator. Despite polling a record low of 29.8 per cent (2.09 quotas), Labor was able to gain a seat at the expense of the crossbench.

The Coalition's vote rose compared with the previous election, polling 2.70 quotas and electing three senators. Nationals Senator John Williams retired and sitting Liberal Jim Molan was demoted to fourth on the Coalition ticket. Molan mounted a vigorous campaign encouraging Liberal supporters to vote for him below the line and polled a record 137,325 below-the-line votes (see Chapter 4, this volume). This was 2.9 per cent of all votes and 7.6 per cent of Coalition votes, but not nearly enough to elect him ahead of the three Coalition candidates above him.

The Greens retained their single seat, but the other two crossbenchers were defeated. Burston was defeated as a UAP candidate after being elected for One Nation in 2016. The Liberal Democrats lost the seat they had held for two terms. The name confusion with the Liberal Party that had previously advantaged the Liberal Democrats diminished after the party drew column R, well to the right of the 'Liberals and Nationals'. The Liberal Democrats had polled more strongly when to the left of the Liberal Party on the ballot paper, polling 9.5 per cent from column A in 2013 and 3.1 per cent from column D in 2016.

On first preferences, the Coalition polled 2.70 quotas, Labor 2.09, the Greens 0.61, PHON 0.35 and the other parties combined, 1.26 quotas. At the end of the count with two vacancies to fill, the Coalition had 0.97 quotas, the Greens 0.96 and PHON 0.68, with 0.39 quota of votes exhausted. The Coalition and the Greens candidates would have reached a quota had PHON been excluded. Of all minor party and Labor preferences distributed, 20.5 per cent flowed to the Coalition, 25.8 per cent to the Greens, 24.6 per cent to PHON and 29.1 per cent was exhausted.

Victoria

Table 10.5 Senate results: Victoria

Party	Vote by party (%)			Senators allocated/elected		
	2013	2016	2019	2013	2016	2019
LIB/NAT	40.1	33.1	35.9	2	2	3
ALP	32.5	30.7	31.1	2	2	2
Greens	10.8	10.9	10.6	1	1	1
AMEP	0.5	0.9	0.0	1	0	0
PHON	0.0	1.8	2.9	0	0	0
Derryn Hinch's Justice Party	0.0	6.1	2.8	0	1	0
PUP (2013–16)/UAP (2019)	3.7	0.3	2.5	0	0	0
Others	12.4	16.2	14.2	0	0	0

AMEP = Australian Motoring Enthusiasts Party

Note: The 2016 column shows senators allocated to short terms by a Senate motion in February 2018.

Source: Party totals accumulated by author from AEC results.

Justice Party Senator Derryn Hinch was defeated, with his seat won by the Liberal Party. Hinch had benefited from appearing in column A in 2016, but his vote more than halved after drawing Column I in 2019. Labor and the Greens retained their representation with around the same vote share as at the previous two elections.

The Coalition polled 2.51 quotas, Labor 2.18, the Greens 0.74, PHON and Derryn Hinch 0.20 each and all other parties together polled 1.17 quotas. After electing the first four senators, by count 355, only five parties remained: the Greens on 0.98 quotas, the Coalition on 0.76, Labor in fifth place on 0.33, having been passed by Hinch on 0.37, and PHON on 0.38. The exclusion of Labor's surplus elected the Greens' Janet Rice to the fifth vacancy and pushed Hinch ahead of PHON. At the end of the count, the third Liberal candidate had reached 0.93 quotas, Hinch held 0.58 quotas, with 0.49 quotas of votes exhausted.

The Victorian result demonstrated how the new Senate electoral system changed the dynamics of preferences. In 2013, the third Liberal candidate, Helen Kroger on 0.81 quotas, had been caught and passed by Ricky Muir of the Australian Motoring Enthusiasts Party (AMEP), who polled only 0.05 quotas (Green 2014). The ability of minor parties to use GVTs to direct preferences to Muir allowed him to pass Kroger. Without GVTs in 2019, more than 20 per cent of minor party voters directed preferences to the Liberal Party and more than 40 per cent of minor party preferences were exhausted before choosing between Hinch and the Coalition. Despite polling 4.2 per cent lower than in 2013, the Liberal Party in 2019 was not passed on preferences.

Queensland

Table 10.6 Senate results: Queensland

Party	Vote by party (%)			Senators allocated/elected		
	2013	2016	2019	2013	2016	2019
LNP	41.4	35.3	38.9	3	2	3
ALP	28.5	26.3	22.6	2	2	1
Greens	6.0	6.9	9.9	0	1	1
PUP (2013–16)/UAP (2019)	9.9	0.2	3.5	1	0	0
PHON	0.6	9.2	10.3	0	0	1
Others	13.6	22.1	14.8	0	1	0

Notes: The 2016 column shows senators allocated to short terms by a Senate motion in February 2018; the 2016 PHON seat filled by Fraser Anning on recount is shown as 'Others' held.
Source: Party totals accumulated by author from AEC results.

In Queensland, the Liberal National Party (LNP) gained a seat as Labor's vote collapsed to 22.6 per cent, with the party losing a seat and returning only one senator. The LNP polled 2.72 quotas, PHON 0.72, the Greens 0.70, Labor 1.58 and all other parties together 1.28 quotas. To the point where only the main four parties remained, 31.9 per cent of minor party preferences flowed to PHON, 20.8 per cent to the LNP, 18.9 per cent to the Greens and 12.7 per cent to Labor, with 15.7 per cent exhausting.

UAP preferences elected PHON's Malcolm Roberts, who won the seat he had lost in 2017 by disqualification. His surplus elected the third LNP candidate, after which the Greens were declared elected without the second Labor candidate being excluded.

Anning, who had replaced Roberts in the Senate but never sat with PHON, was defeated with 1.3 per cent of the vote for his new Fraser Anning's Conservative National Party.

Western Australia

Table 10.7 Senate results: Western Australia

Party	Vote by party (%)			Senators allocated/elected		
	2013	2016	2019	2013	2016	2019
LIB	39.2	38.5	40.9	3	2	3
NAT	5.1	2.5	1.4	0	0	0
ALP	26.6	28.3	27.6	1	2	2
Greens	9.5	10.5	11.8	1	1	1
PUP (2013–16)/UAP (2019)	5.0	0.4	1.7	0	0	0
SPRT	0.2	0.0	0.0	1	0	0
PHON	0.0	4.0	5.9	0	1	0
Others	14.4	15.8	10.7	0	0	0

SPRT = Australian Sports Party

Notes: The 2016 column shows senators allocated to short terms by a Senate motion in February 2018; the 2013 result is based on original Senate election, not the 2014 re-election.

Source: Party totals accumulated by author from AEC results.

Defending only two seats, the Liberal Party polled 2.86 quotas and gained a third senator at the expense of PHON's Peter Georgiou, who finished fourth with 0.41 quotas. Labor polled 1.93 quotas and elected two senators, while the Greens' Jordon Steele-John was re-elected to the short-term vacancy allocated to him after he replaced the disqualified Scott Ludlam.

At the original 2013 Senate election—subsequently voided and rerun— Labor had polled 1.86 quotas, the Greens 0.66 quotas and the Australian Sports Party 0.02 quotas. Complex preference flows delivered the final two vacancies to the Sports Party and the Greens despite Labor's significant lead on first preferences. Under the Senate's new electoral system, it was impossible for a minor party to corral preferences from other minor parties in the same way.

South Australia

Table 10.8 Senate results: South Australia

Party	Vote by party (%)			Senators allocated/elected		
	2013	2016	2019	2013	2016	2019
LIB	27.5	32.6	37.8	2	3	3
ALP	22.7	27.3	30.4	1	1	2
Greens	7.1	5.9	10.9	1	1	1
NXT/CA	24.9	21.8	2.6	1	0	0
Family First	3.8	2.8	0.0	1	0	0
PHON	0.0	3.0	4.9	0	0	0
PUP (2013–16)/UAP (2019)	2.6	0.1	3.0	0	0	0
Others	11.4	6.5	10.4	0	1	0

Notes: The 2016 column shows senators allocated to short terms by a Senate motion in February 2018, and also incorporates changes in party membership.

Source: Party totals accumulated by author from AEC results.

At the 2013 and 2016 elections, the South Australian Senate contest was heavily influenced by the success of the NXT. Xenophon's resignation in 2017 to contest the South Australian State election saw the party renamed the Centre Alliance. Without Xenophon's name on the ballot paper, the Centre Alliance's vote collapsed and the party was unable to re-elect Skye Kakoschke-Moore, who had been disqualified in 2017 and replaced with party defector Tim Storer. Storer did not contest the 2019 election.

Family First's Bob Day had won the final seat at the 2016 election, but after his disqualification in 2017, Family First folded into the Australian Conservatives, while Day's replacement, Lucy Gichuhi, eventually joined the Liberal Party. She was defeated in 2019 from the unwinnable fourth position on the Liberal ticket.

The Liberal Party polled 2.65 quotas, Labor 2.13, the Greens 0.76, PHON 0.34 and all other parties 1.12 quotas. Labor's exclusion elected the Greens, the Liberal's third candidate was elected after the exclusion of the Centre Alliance and the UAP, while PHON was left with 0.69 quotas at the end of the count.

Tasmania

Table 10.9 Senate results: Tasmania

Party	Vote by party (%)			Senators allocated/elected		
	2013	2016	2019	2013	2016	2019
LIB	37.5	32.5	31.5	2	1	2
NAT	0.0	0.0	1.1	0	1	0
ALP	32.8	33.6	30.6	2	3	2
Greens	11.7	11.2	12.6	1	1	1
PUP (2013–16)/UAP (2019)	6.6	0.7	2.6	1	0	0
PHON	0.0	2.6	3.5	0	0	0
JLN	0.0	8.3	8.9	0	0	1
Others	11.4	11.1	9.2	0	0	0

Notes: The 2016 column shows senators allocated to short terms by a Senate motion in February 2018, and also incorporates changes in party membership.

Source: Party totals accumulated by author from AEC results.

The disqualification of Jacqui Lambie on citizenship grounds rearranged Tasmania's Senate representation. Lambie had been elected to a six-year position, but the recount following her disqualification elected Steve Martin to a three-year vacancy, while a third Liberal was elevated to a six-year seat. Once elected, Martin declined to resign in Lambie's favour and later joined the National Party. Martin was defeated by Lambie at the 2019 election while the Liberal Party gained a seat from Labor, replacing the Nationals seat lost by Martin.

Long experience with the Hare-Clark electoral system at Tasmanian State elections result in a higher rate of voters venturing to vote for candidates below the line. Nationally, 7.3 per cent of ballot papers were below-the-line votes compared with 27.1 per cent in Tasmania—down slightly from 28.1 per cent in 2016. The Liberal Party polled 2.20 quotas, Labor 2.14, the Greens 0.88, the JLN 0.62, PHON 0.24 and all others 0.92.

In 2016, Labor's Lisa Singh was demoted to the normally unwinnable sixth position on the Labor ticket, but she polled 6.1 per cent of the vote below the line and won re-election ahead of higher-placed Labor candidates. In 2019, Singh was demoted to the unwinnable fourth position and polled a similar 5.7 per cent, but with the higher quota at a half-Senate election, was unable to pass higher-placed Labor candidates.

Reaction to the electoral changes by parties and candidates

Between 1984 and 2013, parties learnt how to use the GVT system to their advantage. Over time, more and more minor parties nominated for election, secure in their ability to exchange preferences and aggregate their votes via GVTs. The rapid increase in ballot paper groups after 2007 was a sign of how minor parties were using the GVT system. The new Senate system ended guaranteed preference flows and added a disincentive to low-polling and like-minded parties competing against each other. The decline in groups nominating since 2013 illustrates the impact of the new system (Table 10.10).

Table 10.10 Groups contesting Senate election, by State

Year	NSW	Vic.	Qld	WA	SA	Tas.	ACT	NT	Total
2007	25	23	24	21	19	11	8	5	136
2010	32	21	23	22	18	10	4	6	136
2013	44	39	36	27	33	23	13	12	227
2016	41	38	38	28	23	21	10	7	206
2019	35	31	26	23	16	16	7	9	163

Source: AEC nominations.

Some of the decline in groups' numbers was caused by the decline in the number of parties contesting every State. Previously, minor parties might have concentrated on one State but nominated candidates in other States to increase the pool of minor party votes. With the end of GVTs, the significant decline in groups at the 2019 election was due to fewer parties contesting every State. Table 10.11 tallies how many States parties contested.

Table 10.11 Number of smaller parties contesting one or more States, 2013 and 2019

Number of smaller parties contesting		
No. of States contested	2013	2019
1	9	15
2	5	6
3	4	9
4	6	1
5	7	1
6	14	10

Note: Totals do not include Labor, the Coalition or the Greens.

Source: AEC nominations, calculations by author.

Where in 2013 there were 27 minor parties that contested four or more States, in 2016 there were only 12. This withdrawal partly explains the decline in groups contesting. Where previously small parties were encouraged to contest every State to build the pool of minor party votes for preference harvesting, the tactic was self-defeating with the abolition of GVTs.

Reaction to the electoral changes: How the maths worked

The impact of preferences on Senate results can be estimated by comparing the number of elected members under Senate PR-STV with those that would have been elected under an alternative non-preferential system. The best comparison is with List-PR using a highest remainder method of allocating final seats. Under this List-PR method, members are elected either with filled quotas or with highest remainders—that is, leading partial quotas. The difference between an estimated List-PR Senate result and the actual PR-STV result is a measure of the impact of preferences, shown by the number of senators elected from trailing partial quotas. How much a PR-STV result will deviate from a modelled List-PR outcome depends on the strength of interparty preference flows.

Writing about the changes to the Senate's electoral system, Green (2018: 200) noted:

> The 2016 electoral changes effectively weighted the system in favour of highest remainders, first by weakening interparty transfers as the number of ballot papers exhausting preferences increased, and second by the abolition of group-voting tickets, ending party control over interparty transfers.

The hypothesis that the Senate's new electoral system weights the allocation of final seats in favour of highest remainders can be tested using the results of the 2013 and 2019 half-Senate elections. The results of both elections are compared with possible outcomes had the election been conducted using List-PR with a highest remainder method of allocating final seats.

A summary of the comparisons is provided in Table 10.12. It shows that nine senators were elected from trailing partial quotas in 2013, but no trailing parties were elected under the new system in 2019. With the new electoral system having weaker party control over preferences and a greater number of exhausted preferences, it behaves more like List-PR than the former Senate system under GVTs.

Table 10.12 Comparison of PR-STV and simulated List-PR results

	2013 Senators elected	2019 Senators elected
Filled quotas	21	22
Highest remainder	6	14
Trailing wins	9	0

Note: Excludes the four Territory senators.
Source: Calculations by author.

More detail on the 14 senators elected from leading partial quotas in 2019 is shown in Table 10.13. On the left are the partial quotas and parties for successful senators, while on the right are the highest polling unelected candidates and parties.

Table 10.13 2019 election: Success from partial quotas

State	Elected party and partial quota			Unelected party and partial quota	
NSW	0.70 LIB	0.61 GRN		0.35 PHON	
Vic.	0.74 GRN	0.51 LIB		0.20 PHON	0.20 DHJP
Qld	0.72 LNP	0.72 PHON	0.70 GRN	0.58 ALP	
WA	0.93 ALP	0.86 LIB	0.83 GRN	0.41 PHON	
SA	0.76 GRN	0.65 LIB		0.34 PHON	
Tas.	0.88 GRN	0.62 JLN		0.24 PHON	

Notes: DHJP refers to Derryn Hinch's Justice Party and GRN to the Australian Greens.
Source: AEC election results, calculations by author.

Of the 15 parties with a partial quota above 0.5 at the start of the count, only Labor in Queensland failed to win a seat. That was a contest in which four parties started with more than 0.5 partial quotas in a race for three seats. In the other five States, the partial quota for the next party in order—in each case, PHON—ranged from 0.20 quotas to 0.41 quotas, which were all well short of the partial quota of the sixth elected party.

It was a very different pattern in 2013 when every State except Queensland saw candidates elected from trailing partial quotas (shown in Table 10.14 by underlined text). In Victoria, the ratio of the lowest elected party to the highest defeated candidate was 0.04 to 0.81 quotas, and in Western Australia, 0.02 to 0.86 quotas.

Table 10.14 2013 election: Success from partial quotas

State	Elected party and partial quota			Highest unelected parties and quotas		
NSW	0.67 LDP	**0.39 L/NP**		0.55 GRN		
Vic.	**0.76 GRN**	**0.04 AMEP**		0.81 LIB		
Qld	0.90 LNP	0.69 PUP		0.42 GRN		
WA	**0.74 LIB**	**0.66 GRN**	**0.02 SPRT**	0.86 ALP	0.35 PUP	0.35 NAT
SA	0.92 LIB	**0.50 GRN**	**0.26 FFP**	0.74 NXT	0.59 ALP	
Tas.	0.82 GRN	**0.46 PUP**		0.63 LIB		

Notes: Bold text indicates parties successful from trailing partial quotas; WA result based on the original 2013 Senate result, not the 2014 re-election; LDP refers to the Liberal Democratic Party, L/NP to the Liberal–National Party Coalition (NSW) and FFP to the Family First Party.

Source: AEC election results, calculations by the author.

Table 10.15 categorises all successful and unsuccessful parties based on their initial partial quota.

Table 10.15 Elected and defeated senators based on partial quotas: 2013 and 2019 elections

	Number of successful and unsuccessful groups			
	2013 election		2019 election	
Partial quota value	Successful	Unsuccessful	Successful	Unsuccessful
0.9 to < 1.0 (14.3%)	2	0	1	0
0.8 to < 0.9 (12.9%)	2	2	3	0
0.7 to < 0.8 (11.4%)	2	1	4	0
0.6 to < 0.7 (10.0%)	3	1	5	0
0.5 to < 0.6 (8.6%)	0	2	1	1
0.4 to < 0.5 (7.1%)	2	1	0	1
0.3 to < 0.4 (5.7%)	1	2	0	2
0.2 to < 0.3 (4.3%)	1	8	0	4
0.1 to < 0.2 (2.9%)	0	9	0	27
< 0.1 (1.5%)	2	159	0	100

Note: Based on the original 2013 Senate election in Western Australia, not the 2014 re-election.

Source: AEC results, calculations by the author.

As noted earlier, 14 of the 15 parties that began the 2019 count with a partial quota above 0.50 were elected. The 15th, Labor in Queensland, was unsuccessful, as was every party that began the count with a partial quota under 0.50. This contrasts starkly with the 2013 result under GVTs. In 2013, there were six parties that were unsuccessful that started the count with more than 0.50 partial quotas. There were six parties successful after starting with a partial quota under 0.50 quotas. The most notorious cases were Ricky Muir in Victoria (AMEP) and Wayne Dropulich in Western Australia (SPRT), who leap-frogged to victory from less than 0.1 quotas.

Conclusion

This analysis confirms that the new Senate system weights the allocation of final seats in favour of parties with the highest remainders on first preferences. The abolition of GVTs, combined with the ending of full preferential voting, has weakened interparty preference flows. The new system does not prevent parties trailing on initial partial quotas from winning, but it does advantage parties that attract a significant first-preference vote and disadvantage those that rely primarily on attracting further preferences from other parties.

References

Farrell, David M. and Ian McAllister. 2006. *The Australian Electoral System: Origins, Variations and Consequences*. Sydney: UNSW Press.

Green, Antony. 2014. 'Ricky Muir's strange path to the Senate'. *Antony Green's Election Blog*, 7 August. www.abc.net.au/news/2014-08-07/ricky-muirs-strange-path-to-the-senate/9388474.

Green, Antony. 2018. 'The Senate results'. In *Double Disillusion: The 2016 Australian Federal Election*, edited by Anika Gauja, Peter Chen, Jennifer Curtin and Juliet Pietsch, 185–209. Canberra: ANU Press. doi.org/10.22459/DD.04.2018.08.

McAllister, Ian and Damon Muller. 2019. 'Electing the Australian Senate: Evaluating the 2016 Reforms'. *Political Science* 70(2): 151–68. doi.org/10.1080/00323187.2018.1561153.

11

THE ELECTION IN THE STATES, TERRITORIES AND REGIONS

Nick Economou, Zareh Ghazarian, Narelle Miragliotta,
Will Sanders, Rodney Smith, John Warhurst
and Paul Williams

In this chapter, we contextualise the regional variation in the 2019 election results by focusing on some of the local factors that influenced the campaign and the outcomes in each of the Australian States and Territories. While the States and Territories appear to have some influence on federal election outcomes, the reasons for this remain unclear (Martinez i Coma and Smith 2018). Investigating the diversity of election campaign issues, events and styles across Australia, we examine, where relevant, previous State and Territory election results, economic conditions, specific policy promises and campaign visits from the major party leaders, and analyse notable regional variations within each jurisdiction. A number of competitive 'battleground' seats are highlighted, which are seen as important for the overall outcome of the election, drawing significant resources from the major parties and attracting substantial media attention during the campaign.

New South Wales
By Rodney Smith

Apart from the fact that it provided around one-third of the 151 members of the House of Representatives, New South Wales was particularly important in 2019 because it contained a large proportion of marginal seats. The 2016 federal election left the major parties evenly balanced in New South Wales, with Labor holding 24 seats against the Coalition's 23 seats. By the 2019 federal election, the Liberal Party had narrowly lost the seat of Wentworth to the Independent Kerryn Phelps in a by-election caused by Malcolm Turnbull's resignation from parliament. Based on the 2016 results, swings to Labor of 2.5 per cent would take four NSW seats from the Coalition (Gilmore, Robertson, Banks and Page). On the other hand, if the Coalition managed swings towards it of 2.5 per cent, Labor would lose two NSW seats (Lindsay and Macquarie). Finally, a 1.1 per cent swing to the Liberals would see them regain Wentworth. Thus, New South Wales contained seven of the 23 marginal seats most likely to be critical to the 2019 outcome—more than any State except Queensland, which had eight.

Contextual factors

Two factors that might be important in explaining the results of the election are State economic conditions and State politics. In 2019, neither of these suggested that Labor would make significant gains against the Coalition in New South Wales.

For 18 months after the July 2016 federal election, the NSW economy performed strongly relative to the other States; however, it began to show some signs of weakening prior to the 2019 federal election. The annual percentage increase in gross State product to July 2018 in New South Wales was the lowest of all States and Territories, at 1 per cent (ABS 2018). The economic growth that did occur in New South Wales was uneven. The construction sector, driven partly by the NSW Government's heavy investment in public infrastructure projects (NSW 2018), contributed very visibly to the State's economic growth. However, the NSW agricultural sector contracted significantly (ABS 2018). To the extent that swinging voters judge governments retrospectively on their economic performance (Fiorina 1981), rather than voting on probable future economic conditions, the economic position of New South Wales gave them little cause to punish the federal Coalition.

The vagaries of election cycles produced the unusual circumstance of both national and NSW Coalition governments attempting to win third terms in the first half of 2019. The NSW fixed-term election was set for 23 March. Ultimately, the Coalition was returned to government in New South Wales with a slim majority, winning 48 of the 93 seats in the NSW Legislative Assembly. It recorded a first-preference legislative assembly vote of 41.6 per cent—down 4.1 per cent on the 2015 result. Labor barely improved its position, winning 33.3 per cent of the first-preference votes—down 0.8 per cent from 2015—and a notional two-party-preferred swing of 2.3 per cent across the State.

What were the implications of this result for the federal contest? Labor's failure to make large gains at State level suggested the Coalition might be able to hold on to its federal NSW seats. Labor did not achieve first-preference or two-party-preferred swings of real magnitude in any NSW region except northern Sydney, where the Liberals could be expected to retain their seats easily. The NSW win undoubtedly boosted Coalition morale, particularly within the Liberal Party. It paved the way for the Coalition to make infrastructure commitments during the federal campaign that would receive wholehearted support from the newly elected State Liberal Premier. Moreover, the Coalition's NSW campaign theme, that Labor would ruin the State's strong budgetary position, suggested the way the Coalition might campaign effectively against Labor at the federal poll.

The campaign in New South Wales

As in 2016, in 2019 the major party leaders visited NSW electorates for policy announcements more often than they did electorates in the other States and Territories (see Table 11.1; and Martinez i Coma and Smith 2018: 220). The difference between 2016 and 2019 is that in 2016 Bill Shorten made as many visits to NSW electorates as did his Liberal opponent, Malcolm Turnbull, while in 2019, Shorten was much less visible in New South Wales than Scott Morrison. Morrison's first visit of the campaign, on 11 April, was to the marginal Labor seat of Lindsay, in Sydney's west, while Shorten began his campaign in Deakin (see 'Victoria', below)—a relatively safe Liberal seat in Melbourne's east. These starting points could simply have been due to home State convenience (Morrison being from Sydney and Shorten from Melbourne); however, Shorten's relative lack of attention to New South Wales in

2019 appears to have been strategic. Shorten's last major campaign event was a meeting at Blacktown Town Hall in Sydney's west—a venue made iconic by Gough Whitlam's 'It's Time' campaign speech in 1972 (Chan 2019). Nonetheless, Table 11.1 shows that Morrison campaigned more frequently than Shorten in New South Wales, while Shorten focused more of his campaigning on Queensland, where polling suggested Labor might pick up more seats (see below). The two leaders gave roughly the same amounts of attention to the other States and Territories.

Table 11.1 Leaders' electorate visits by State and Territory

	Morrison	Shorten	McCormack	Total
NSW	23	14	12	49 (37 M + S)
Qld	11	16	7	34 (27 M + S)
Vic.	15	16	4	35 (31 M + S)
WA	10	8	0	18 (18 M + S)
SA	5	5	0	10 (10 M + S)
Tas.	9	7	3	19 (16 M + S)
ACT	0	0	0	0 (0 M + S)
NT	2	2	0	4 (4 M + S)
Totals	**75**	**68**	**27**	**170 (143 M + S)**

Source: Calculated from Worthington (2019).

Despite frequent news media commentary to the effect that Western Sydney was a key 'battleground' in the election, the leaders spent relatively little time there. Morrison made six visits to Western Sydney electorates, three of them to Lindsay. Shorten made just two visits to Western Sydney electorates (Lindsay and Greenway). Most electorates in Western Sydney went unvisited by either leader. Both leaders made more visits to inner Sydney electorates, particularly Reid, which each of them visited for five events (see Table 11.2).

The only electorates outside Sydney visited by both leaders were the marginal seats of Gilmore on the NSW South Coast and Robertson on the Central Coast. As might have been expected, National Party Leader Michael McCormack focused his attention on coastal and inland rural seats, including his own seat of Riverina.

Table 11.2 Leaders' electorate visits by NSW region

	Morrison	Shorten	McCormack	Unvisited electorates*	Contested electorates**	Total
Inner Sydney	8	6	0	1	2	5
Northern Sydney	0	1	0	4	0	5
Southern Sydney	2	0	0	2	0	4
Western Sydney	6	2	0	8	1	12
Central Coast	2	3	0	0	1	2
Hunter/ Illawarra	1	0	0	5	0	6
Coastal rural	3	2	5	3	1	6
Inland rural	1	0	7	4	0	7
Total	**23**	**14**	**12**	**27**	**5**	**47**

* Electorates not visited by Labor or Coalition leaders during the campaign.

** Electorates that both Labor and Coalition leaders visited to make announcements and campaign.

Source: Calculated from Worthington (2019).

In 2019, the major parties seemed to do less to target particular regions with policy packages than they had in 2016 (Martinez i Coma and Smith 2018: 221–22). The Liberal Party did package policies for four specific regions, including one addressed to Western Sydney.[1] Labor did not produce policy packages specifically for any NSW regions but included State-by-State breakdowns of some of its funding promises—for example, on education and infrastructure (ALP 2019a, 2019b). On key policies affecting specific regions, such as the development of the Western Sydney airport, the major parties' promises were quite similar (Liberal Party of Australia 2019b; ALP 2019b). Most of the parties' policies were directed generally at the national electorate. This was also true of 2016; however, in 2019, the parties seemed to expect voters to do more work to find out how policies might affect their own areas.

---

1   The other regional packages covered Tasmania, the Northern Territory and Central Queensland (Liberal Party of Australia 2019a).

Regional results

The overall results in New South Wales showed little change from either the 2016 federal election results or the March 2019 NSW State election. In two-party-preferred terms, the Coalition only lost votes to Labor in inner and northern Sydney—both areas where the Liberal Party could afford to lose votes. In Western Sydney, the Liberal Party gained ground in both its average first-preference vote (up 3 per cent) and against Labor in two-party-preferred terms (up 2.7 per cent). The 47.1 per cent average two-party-preferred Liberal vote in Western Sydney was high enough to undermine the still common idea that the diverse region of Western Sydney is a 'Labor heartland'. Outside Sydney, there were relatively few changes in votes. Overall, very few seats changed hands in New South Wales. Labor won Gilmore from the Liberals with a swing of 3.3 per cent but suffered swings against it in all the other marginal NSW seats, including Lindsay, which it lost. In both Gilmore and Lindsay, the incumbent MPs did not recontest their seats in controversial circumstances. This provides part of the explanation for the results in these seats; however, Labor's general failure to make up ground in marginal NSW seats was the larger and more important factor at work.

Victoria
By Nick Economou and Zareh Ghazarian

Since the 1993 federal election, Victoria has been a State in which the ALP has been the party preferred by the majority of voters. Given the persistent two-party majorities for Labor and notwithstanding the two-party swings that occur between elections, it is rare for anything other than a small number of ultra-marginal seats to change hands between the major parties in Victoria. The 2019 contest conforms with this dominant pattern.

Contextual factors

The expectation that the Liberals and Nationals were in some trouble in Victoria owed something to the State election held in November 2018. This election resulted in a landslide Labor victory in which there were significant swings to Labor in previously strong Liberal-voting districts in Melbourne's eastern suburbs and in the southeastern suburban growth corridor. The assumption was that the State election result was driven in no small way by voter response to events in federal politics in which Malcolm Turnbull had lost the prime ministership as a result of manoeuvring by ultra-conservative Liberals such as Michael Sukkar, the sitting Member for Deakin. Further, the Liberal members for Chisholm and Higgins, Julia Banks and Kelly O'Dwyer, had resigned from the Liberal Party citing a culture of male bullying. This, in turn, had flushed out Liberal Party State President Michael Kroger, who had to defend his party's reputation at the very time he was also involved in a major intraparty battle with the Cormack Foundation in a bid to gain access to campaign funds.

The campaign in Victoria

Labor's interest in the State was inevitable given that Opposition leader Bill Shorten held a Victorian seat (the western suburban division of Maribyrnong). Shorten was clearly of a mind to replicate the approach of his State colleague, Premier Daniel Andrews, as he travelled across metropolitan Melbourne promising federal support for a slew of transport infrastructure projects, the most ambitious of which was a proposal to construct a massive underground rail loop traversing the middle suburbs. Not to be outdone, Prime Minister Scott Morrison travelled to Corangamite to promise federal support to build a very fast rail connection between Geelong and Melbourne. Labor tried to up the ante with a promise to pour taxpayer funds into the Australian Football League stadium at Kardinia Park, also in Geelong. Back in Melbourne, Morrison committed federal funds to the construction of the infamous East–West Link—the proposed freeway to be tunnelled under the Greens-voting inner suburb of Carlton that the State Labor Government had refused to consider building.

Regional results

At the beginning of the election and at its conclusion, Labor held 21 seats in Victoria, the Liberals 12 seats, the Nationals three seats, the Greens one and there was one Independent. Save for a few new faces due to take their place on the back benches of the House of Representatives, nothing much changed.

Of course, the fact that there was no substantive change to the 2016 result was in fact the important outcome in the context of the general election result. Predictions of a Labor victory in the national contest were based on an assumption of a shift of Liberal seats to Labor occurring in a State such as Victoria. The expectation of such an outcome was driven by two electoral events preceding the 2019 national vote. First, Victoria was the State in which there was strongest support for same-sex marriage, with 65 per cent of Victorians voting 'yes' in the postal survey held in 2017. This suggested the State would reject the Coalition at the national level, especially as it was led by prominent socially conservative figures who had toppled the progressive Turnbull. Second, federal Labor's hopes of a strong performance in Victoria were buoyed by the significant realignment of voter support from Liberal to Labor in previously strong Liberal seats in the 2018 State election.

The fact that the expected Labor swing did not eventuate suggests either the 2018 State election was a ringing endorsement of the State Labor Government and its premier or something happened in between the State and federal elections to prevent the expected federal realignment occurring. The results from the 2019 federal contest do not give any clear insights as to what happened between the two elections other than to show that, at least in terms of the primary vote, it was the UAP that received the biggest swing, after which Independents and Labor received the next best swings. A review of the two-party swings by electoral division does not give much insight either, other than to highlight that, while there were swings to Labor in some of the Liberal Party's most marginal seats, they were nowhere near enough to result in a transfer of seats. Expectations of non–major party success were also unmet and the one incumbent Independent had to withstand a 4 per cent swing against her.

The reality of the Victorian result was that it was more akin to a confirming election than a government-changing election in that the result in 2019 was almost the same as it had been in 2016, notwithstanding all that had happened in the national political debate over that three-year cycle. The swing to Labor in Victoria in 2019 was negligible and certainly not of sufficient dimensions to result in a transfer of seats. All the other predictions of non–major party success by Greens and/or Independents also proved to be wrong. In accounting for the Victorian result, it is worth remembering that the 2019 outcome—in which Labor won the Statewide two-party vote but few, if any, seats changed hands—follows a longstanding pattern in Australian electoral politics.

Queensland

By Paul Williams

The unexpected result of the 2019 federal election campaign in Queensland, in defiance of reputable public opinion polls, marks it out as one of historical significance. News media narratives once again framed Queensland as a key battleground State but no published poll correctly forecast Labor's 26.7 per cent primary vote—the federal party's worst result in Queensland since 1901 and equivalent to the decimation of Anna Bligh's Labor Government in 2012.

The 2019 election supported the 'Queensland is different' thesis (Murphy 1978; McQueen 1979; Charlton 1983; Williams 2009, 2011). As a 'frontier' State—where agriculture, pastoralism and especially mining make up the core of economic activity and forge a political culture far removed from the 'Sydney–Melbourne–Canberra triangle'—regional Queensland shares characteristics with regional Tasmania, Western Australia, the Northern Territory and parts of New South Wales (for example, the seat of Hunter). But Queensland ultimately remains different given its status as Australia's most decentralised State, where more voters live outside the capital city than within it. Queensland comprises six regions, each exercising distinct electoral behaviours: Brisbane, Brisbane fringe, Gold Coast, Sunshine Coast, eastern provincial and western rural (Williams 2018b). Understanding this diversity, and how minor populist parties (and parts of the LNP) exploit those differences, is therefore essential to unpacking Queensland's role in the 2019 federal election.

Queensland voters—especially regional voters who have long bristled at post-material environmentalist and human rights policy agendas supplanting economic priorities—were primed for a conservative backlash long before the 2019 campaign began. From issues that much of regional Queensland found antithetical or irrelevant—of which anger at strict controls on tree-clearing and lower than average support for same-sex marriage are obvious manifestations—to major party leadership that failed to resonate with regional Australia, the 45th Parliament proved fertile ground for new conservative and populist leadership to take root in Queensland. More specifically, the seeds of the LNP's Queensland surge were sown overwhelmingly by two factors: Scott Morrison's accessible, pragmatic and occasionally populist leadership style, which contrasted strongly with Bill Shorten's apparently aloof and mistrusted persona;

and material economic concerns—of which the Adani coalmine and its promise of regional employment were merely one element—that saw voters reject both environmental concerns and Labor's arguably complicated and poorly defended tax policy in favour of what appeared to be the Coalition's pledge to keep taxes lower.

Contextual factors

At the 2017 State election, a relatively popular State Labor Government under Annastacia Palaszczuk increased its seat share. The LNP, by contrast, suffered a 7.6 per cent primary swing and won just 33.7 per cent of the primary vote (Williams 2018a). However, the Queensland economy throughout the 45th Parliament continued to suffer a post-mining slump that saw State unemployment hover around 6 per cent—higher than the national average—with regional unemployment around twice that, and youth unemployment in seats such as Herbert approaching 20 per cent (QGSO 2019; Brown 2019). Moreover, the collapse of Clive Palmer's Queensland Nickel in 2016—with $70 million long owed to workers in and around Townsville—made the mining downturn particularly piquant for north Queensland. Add the fact that wage growth had barely kept pace with inflation during a 'per capita recession' (Commins 2019) and regional Queensland promised a perfect storm for a regional blue-collar backlash against a federal Coalition that spruiked a buoyant national economy but delivered little household prosperity.

Despite the Adani coalmine anecdotally playing a pivotal role in Labor's defeat in regional Queensland, voter salience regarding this thorny issue did not initially appear high. Opinion polls during the 2017 State campaign indicated, for example, that just 17 per cent of voters rated the issue as important (Marszalek 2017; Williams 2018a). And when voters did show interest, public opinion appeared to be turning against the mine. Indeed, Palaszczuk enjoyed a mid-campaign fillip when she pledged to veto any federal public money being allocated to Adani for infrastructure. By early 2019, a YouGov-Galaxy poll found 51 per cent of Queenslanders supported coalmining generally, but just 37 per cent endorsed the Adani project specifically (Killoran 2019). In that sense, the Adani issue appeared to be totemic: while only a minority of Queenslanders were passionate about the Adani project specifically—which was not unexpected given publicised threats to groundwater, the Great Barrier Reef and the black-throated finch—regional voters saw the project as a lifeline to community revival. The fact Queenslanders rated material economic interests more highly than the environment—the reverse of the Australian average—is evidenced in Table 11.3.

Table 11.3 Critical issues for voters, Queensland and Australia, 2019 (per cent)

Issue	Queensland	Australia
Economy	27	23
Environment	24	29
Superannuation/pensions	8	8

Note: Per cent of respondents who identified these issues as most important to them in the 2019 election.
Source: Hanrahan (2019).

Notwithstanding these data, Adani's polarising effect clearly shaped voting intentions in all 30 Queensland seats (and in many outside Queensland), with Adani enjoying its strongest salience in the five seats closest to the mine's site in the Galilee Basin: Capricornia (the mine's location), Herbert, Dawson, Flynn and Maranoa. In Flynn—held by the LNP by just 1 percentage point—a YouGov-Galaxy poll found 55 per cent of voters (including one-third of Labor voters) rated the Adani mine as 'vital' for the future of central Queensland (Viellaris 2019).

The campaign in Queensland

Scott Morrison spent one-third of his campaign in Queensland—mostly in the regions—which was more than any other State except New South Wales. On successive tours, the Prime Minister pledged road infrastructure and repeated his mantra that Labor's $387 billion tax plan—including a so-called retirement tax and allegations of 'death duties'—would cripple Australia (Hewett 2019). Consequently, a YouGov-Galaxy poll found 59 per cent of all Queensland voters, and 27 per cent of Labor voters, preferred the Coalition's tax plan, compared with just 26 per cent of all Queensland voters who supported Labor's (Killoran and Smethurst 2019). In total, Morrison—including in a late blitz during the campaign's final week—visited the seats of Herbert, Flynn and Brisbane three times, Capricornia twice and Forde, Petrie, Longman and Leichhardt once each.

Aware of Queensland's capacity to make or break his campaign, Shorten also focused heavily on Queensland, and launched his Queensland campaign in Brisbane on 5 May. Curiously, the Opposition leader waited until the final week to visit Labor's most marginal seat of Herbert. Nonetheless, Shorten continued to campaign on his ability to deliver fairness while governing with unity and stability, but poorly defended policies on tax and Adani plagued him. While supporting mining generally, for example, Shorten refused to sign a Construction, Forestry, Maritime, Mining and Energy Union (CFMMEU) pledge to guarantee the Adani project and he maintained his right to review any Queensland Government approval (McKay 2019).

The Greens' campaign produced an unintended effect on regional Queenslanders contemplating a Labor vote. The 'Stop Adani' convoy— which travelled for 18 days under the tutelage of former Greens leader Bob Brown from Tasmania to Brisbane and then to Clermont, the heart of the Adani site, before moving to Canberra—raised the ire of regional Queenslanders in the five 'Adani' seats. Vilified as southern 'blow-ins', the Greens-led convoy galvanised local resentment toward 'outsiders', allowed a vacillating Labor Party to be conflated with Greens policies and ultimately fuelled Morrison's pleas for locals to reject a progressive policy agenda. Once again, even those in regional Queensland ambivalent about the mine would have seen Adani's approval as a totemic rejection of 'outsider' interference.

Regional results

While acknowledging the limitations of applying regional analysis to geographically large federal electorates that inevitably overlap criterion borders, Table 11.4 reveals Labor lost disproportionate support across the Brisbane fringe and in provincial towns along the eastern seaboard—each long considered blue-collar Labor heartlands (Williams 2018a, 2018b). Labor can take some comfort from the fact its losses were more moderate across Brisbane's middle-class suburbs. While swings against Labor were moderate also on the Gold and Sunshine coasts and in rural Queensland, the fact these moved from already low Labor bases provided the party no succour. The LNP, conversely, hardly improved its position in suburban Brisbane or rural Queensland, it declined in its Gold Coast heartland and made only modest gains in the Brisbane fringe. None of these results allows the LNP to rest on its laurels. Dramatically improved results, at Labor's expense, for PHON in all regions (especially the Brisbane fringe but not western rural) and for the UAP in all regions except Brisbane city, delivered gains to the LNP via preferences. Interestingly, PHON and the UAP performed better in Sunshine Coast seats than in Gold Coast seats.

Table 11.4 Queensland primary vote and swing, by region, 2019 federal election (per cent)

Region (no. of seats)	Labor (swing)	LNP (swing)	PHON (swing)	Greens (swing)	UAP (swing)	Other (swing)
Brisbane (6)	30.3 (−2.6)	44.8 (+0.4)	3.3 (+3.3)	18.2 (+3.2)	1.9 (+1.9)	1.5 (−6.2)
Brisbane fringe (8)	33.5 (−5.9)	40.0 (+1.3)	9.6 (+5.5)	9.4 (+2.1)	3.3 (+3.3)	4.2 (−6.3)
Gold Coast (3)	23.3 (−2.7)	49.5 (−4.2)	7.0 (+3.0)	9.9 (+0.6)	4.0 (+4.0)	6.3 (−0.7)
Sunshine Coast (2)	21.9 (−1.6)	49.8 (+1.5)	8.3 (+3.2)	12.5 (0.0)	3.3 (+3.3)	4.2 (−6.4)
Eastern provincial (7)	24.5 (−5.8)	41.3 (−0.3)	13.2 (+2.8)	6.2 (+0.6)	4.4 (+4.4)	10.4 (−1.7)
Western rural (4)	17.5 (−3.2)	45.5 (+1.0)	10.4 (+0.7)	6.0 (+0.4)	4.8 (+4.8)	15.8 (−3.7)

Note: Divisions are Brisbane (Brisbane, Bonner, Griffith, Lilley, Moreton, Ryan); Brisbane fringe (Blair, Bowman, Dickson, Forde, Longman, Oxley, Petrie, Rankin); Gold Coast (Fadden, McPherson, Moncrieff); Sunshine Coast (Fairfax, Fisher); eastern provincial (Capricornia, Dawson, Flynn, Herbert, Hinkler, Leichhardt, Wide Bay); western rural (Groom, Kennedy, Maranoa, Wright).

Source: Author's calculations from AEC (2019a).

Table 11.5 Comparing 'Adani' seat and Queensland results, primary vote and swing, 2019 federal election (per cent)

Party	'Adani' seat primary (swing)	'Adani' seat TPP (swing)	Queensland primary (swing)	Queensland TPP (swing)
LNP	42.8 (+2.0)	63.9 (+9.4)	43.7 (+0.5)	57.7 (+3.6)
ALP	22.8 (−7.8)	36.1 (−9.4)	26.7 (−4.2)	42.3 (−3.6)
PHON	15.1 (+8.8)	-	8.9 (+3.3)	-
Greens	4.6 (+0.8)	-	10.3 (+1.5)	-
UAP	4.4 (+4.4)	-	3.5 (+3.5)	-
Other	10.3 (−8.2)	-	6.9 (−4.6)	-

- not applicable

Note: The five 'Adani' seats are Capricornia, Herbert, Dawson, Flynn and Maranoa.

Source: Author's calculations from AEC (2019a).

Table 11.5 indicates that while the five Adani seats produced primary swings to the LNP only slightly larger than the Queensland mean, those same seats saw huge two-party-preferred swings—via populist right preferences—almost three times the Queensland average. The table also reveals a significant spike in PHON support—again, largely from an increased field—and levels of UAP support higher than the Queensland average. Overall, these data, including the modest increase in the Greens' vote, support the claim that Adani was a highly salient, indeed polarising, issue in central Queensland.

Western Australia
By Narelle Miragliotta

Western Australia was one of three key battleground States in 2019. This time around, Labor had grounds to believe that the State, which had long eluded the party, might finally deliver for it. At the 2016 federal election, Labor had enjoyed a modest but notable improvement in its primary vote (an increase of 3.7 per cent), signifying that a possible correction was occurring. And, at the March 2017 State election, the State Labor Party, led by Mark McGowan, achieved a swing of 9.1 per cent in its primary vote, claiming government.

Labor entered this contest with hopes of retaining its five existing electorates and also securing five additional seats: Hasluck (held by Ken Wyatt, then Minister for Senior Australians and Aged Care and Minister for Indigenous Health), Swan, Stirling (in which the incumbent, Michael Keane, resigned), Pearce (held by Attorney-General, Christian Porter) and Canning. Of these seats, $500,000 was spent on the campaign to win the inner metropolitan seat of Swan (Scarr 2019b). Labor's candidate, Hannah Beazley, was considered a strong prospect to secure the seat formerly held by her father, Kim Beazley, between 1980 and 1996.

The campaign in Western Australia

The importance of Western Australia to a Labor victory was reflected in the increased campaign visits Bill Shorten made to the State (12 per cent, up from 9 per cent in 2016), the promise to hold a historic summit of business and unions in Western Australia if elected (Lewis 2019: 9) and a $105 million pledge towards defence industry infrastructure for West Australian shipyards. Labor also sought to leverage the popularity of the State Labor Premier and the strong economic credentials of the State government, which, against expectations, delivered a $553 million surplus in its May Budget (Hondros et al. 2019).

While the underlying conditions for Labor in the State were encouraging, the Liberals were in full defensive mode. Scott Morrison visited Western Australia regularly throughout the campaign and was quick to flatter West Australian voters with his declaration that he would live in the west if he did not already call New South Wales home (Scarr 2019a). The Morrison Government was also able to take credit for increasing Western Australia's share of the goods and services tax (GST) and placing a floor under future GST allocations—long a sore point for the State (Laschon 2018). Moreover, the Liberals came to the State bearing various infrastructure projects totalling $1.4 billion, including a $349 million upgrade to the Tonkin Highway that would benefit voters in four of the party's marginal electorates, including Labor's most marginal seat of Cowan (Blaxendale and Varga 2019: 6).

There were also indications that some of Labor's policies might frustrate its much-hoped-for recovery. Polling of voters conducted in four marginal seats for the Liberals by MediaReach suggested that voters in these electorates believed Labor's proposed changes to negative gearing would likely cause property prices to fall or stagnate, and also do little to improve young people's access to the property market (Scarr and Hennessy 2019).

Regional results

It became apparent on election night that Labor's confidence of a resurgence in the State was misplaced. The gains achieved by Labor in 2016 almost evaporated in 2019. While the swing against the party's two-party-preferred vote was slim (0.9 per cent), its primary vote suffered a larger, 2.7 per cent swing against it, falling to 29.8 per cent—the second worst State-level performance for Labor.

Although federal Labor retained its five existing West Australian seats, the outcome suggests the malaise runs deep. The last time Labor attained seat parity with the Liberals in the State was in 1998 and the last time it held a plurality of West Australian electorates was in 1990. As Table 11.6 shows, the strongest swings recorded against Labor were in outer metropolitan electorates, followed by rural seats. Between them, these electorates constitute 10 of Western Australia's 16 seats. And while the average size of the swing against Labor in the inner metropolitan electorates was less severe, it comes off an already low base. In the inner metropolitan seats where the Greens averaged 14.3 per cent of the primary vote, the minor party entrenched its status as Labor's curse and saviour.

Table 11.6 West Australian election results by seat demographic

	Inner metropolitan	Outer metropolitan	Rural
Liberal average first-preference vote	45.03	41.47	46.27
Liberal average first-preference swing	–3.25	–2.08	1.65
Labor average first-preference vote	30.19	33.00	21.30
Labor average first-preference swing	–0.28	–5.81	–2.02
Greens average first-preference vote	14.32	10.05	9.79
Greens average first-preference swing	–0.34	–1.40	–1.00
Other average first-preference vote	10.12	15.46	22.55
Other average first-preference swing	4.13	8.36	1.28

Source: Author's calculation from AEC (2019b).

South Australia
By Narelle Miragliotta

One journalist lamented during the campaign that 'the arithmetic' did not favour South Australia in 2019 (Wills 2019b: 44). This assessment is difficult to disagree with entirely. South Australia has only ever returned a comparatively small number of federal lower house seats but, following the 2017–18 redistribution, its share of seats contracted further, from 11 to 10 (see further, Chapter 9, this volume). In the final analysis, only one seat was identified as vulnerable following the redistribution, the seat of Boothby, held by the Liberal incumbent, Nicolle Flint, on a margin of 2.7 per cent. Flint gained notoriety over her decision to sign the petition that led to the unseating of Malcolm Turnbull. This brought Flint unwanted attention, especially from GetUp!, which designated her one of the six 'hard right wreckers' that it campaigned against (Gailberger 2019a: 10).

But with only one seat truly competitive, the federal leaders did not spend significant time campaigning in the State. Over the course of the campaign, the two leaders visited South Australia five times apiece; in comparison, they made 16 stops in total to Tasmania (see Table 11.1). This did not mean, however, that either party ignored the State or Boothby, where the combined major party pre-election spending commitments for the marginal seat totalled $400 million (Wills 2019a: 6). Similarly, the Liberals—seeking to strengthen their prospects in Sturt, vacated by Christopher Pyne—committed $100 million in funding for three road projects in that electorate (Blaxendale and Varga 2019: 6). Labor sought to distinguish its party by, among other things, pledging to commission an independent study into the potential impact of an oil spill in the Great Australian Bight (Gailberger 2019b: 6).

Further reducing the urgency for the major parties was the absence of the NXT and, more particularly, its leader and founder, Nick Xenophon. Although the NXT was rebadged as the Centre Alliance when Xenophon quit politics in 2018, the new party, in his absence, was a more muted force, fielding only three lower house and two Senate candidates.

Table 11.7 South Australian election results by seat demographic

	Inner metropolitan	Outer metropolitan	Rural
Liberal average first-preference vote	38.80	34.63	48.72
Liberal average first-preference swing	5.21	4.68	7.29
Labor average first-preference vote	40.95	44.64	19.16
Labor average first-preference swing	4.03	6.40	0.63
Greens average first-preference vote	11.70	9.22	6.90
Greens average first-preference swing	4.27	3.45	2.08
Other average first-preference vote	8.48	25.20	11.43
Other average first-preference swing	−12.54	−15.35	−10.36

Source: Author's calculation from AEC (2019b).

The demise of the NXT, and the limited appeal of its successor, the Centre Alliance—despite holding on to the seat of Mayo, represented by Rebekha Sharkie—proved advantageous for the major parties. South Australia was the only jurisdiction where Labor (3.8 per cent) and the Liberals (5.7 per cent) both increased their Statewide share of the primary vote (see Table 11.7). And, while neither restored fully its pre-2016 first-preference vote, nor did either lose any of its existing seats.

Tasmania

By Nick Economou

Tasmania accounts for only five of the 151 seats in the House of Representatives, but it is very rare for national election campaigns not to focus on at least two of these seats. This reflects the reality that the two perennial battleground seats of Bass and Braddon, which cover the northeast and northwest of the State, are always marginal and consistently hold out the hope to the major party in Opposition that they can be won.

With the published national opinion polls fuelling expectations of a government-changing election, and given the recent by-election result in Braddon, Labor might have been confident of holding all four of its Tasmanian seats. Whatever Liberal Party strategists thought of the opinion polls, the government's strategy was clear enough: defence of government would require winning at least Braddon from Labor and possibly taking Bass as well. As it turned out, the Liberal strategy in Tasmania was successful. Labor was defeated in both Braddon and Bass. Tasmania was a significant failure for the Labor campaign while the effort put into campaigning in the north by Prime Minister Scott Morrison was rewarded with gains that allowed the government to increase its overall House of Representatives majority.

Contextual factors

In March 2018, a State election was held in which the incumbent Liberal Government was re-elected despite some expectations that Premier Will Hodgman (now retired) might struggle to win a lower house majority. Confusingly, having obtained a swing towards it and having increased its total seat share, Labor also appeared to have performed creditably in this contest. The problem with this, however, was that Labor gains had occurred at the expense of the Greens rather than the Liberals, and— arguably of greater significance—there was a serious differential in Labor's performance in the northern divisions compared with those in the south.

The campaign in Tasmania

By the halfway point of the campaign, monitoring by the Australian Broadcasting Corporation (ABC) of the campaign visits conducted by Morrison and Bill Shorten noted how often Morrison had visited Tasmania and that Braddon was one of the most oft-visited seats in the Prime Minister's campaign travels (Doran et al. 2019). *The Advocate*—the newspaper published in Burnie and read across the Braddon electorate—was even more enlightening on how the major party campaigns were going. The paper noted (presumably with some disapproval) that not only had the Opposition leader been to the southern Tasmanian seats more often than to the north, he had also promised money for southern indulgences of which northerners disapproved, such as a commitment of more federal funding for the Hobart-based Museum of Old and New Art (MONA). And, if that was not bad enough, Shorten also promised to support Tasmania having a team in the Australian Football League (Bailey and Jarvie 2019). In so doing, he aligned himself (perhaps inadvertently) with those who were advocating that the Tasmanian team be based in Hobart—a cardinal error for a leader whose primary objective should have been to curry favour with interests in Launceston, Burnie and Devonport.

Regional results

The Statewide result was a curious mix of contrary swings, the only consistency of which lay in the sharp distinction in voting behaviour between the Tasmanian north (Bass and Braddon) and the south (Franklin and Clark). The north–south divide was also evident in the sprawling division of Lyons, where booths in centres in the north (Deloraine, Longford and Prospect) were won on the two-party-preferred vote by the (disendorsed) Liberal, while the two-party majority for Labor tended to get stronger the closer booths were to Hobart. Labor secured a large share of the Statewide two-party-preferred vote (55.9 per cent, down by 1.4 percentage points) but could win only two (that is, 40 per cent) of the five seats.

The regional swings give a better account of what happened. The two-party-preferred swing to the Liberals in Bass was 5.8 per cent and in Braddon, 4.8 per cent. On the other hand, the swing in Franklin was 1.5 per cent to Labor, making this one of the safest Labor divisions in the country, and in Lyons, the two-party-preferred swing of 1.3 per cent also went to Labor. Clark, meanwhile, firmed for the Independent Andrew Wilkie, with a swing of 4.3 per cent. The significance of these regional variations lay in the transfer of seats. With swings towards them, incumbents in Clark (Wilkie), Franklin and Lyons (both Labor seats) were re-elected. Bass and

Braddon, however, changed, with the Liberal candidates, Brigit Archer and Gavin Pearce, winning their respective seats from Labor incumbents. This was precisely the outcome the Liberals' national strategy had been geared to achieve and, as such, the importance of the Tasmanian result lay in its contribution to the return of the Morrison Government with a majority.

It is difficult to interpret the deeper meaning of the Tasmanian contribution to the 2019 election. At one level, the result conforms to a longstanding pattern in which Labor wins the Statewide two-party vote but does not win all, or many, of the five available seats. Denison/Clark appears to be the preserve of Wilkie, and Tasmania's most notoriously volatile electorates, Bass and Braddon, defied the Statewide result by being won by the Liberal Party, as they have been known to do in the past. Tasmania's regionalism was particularly noticeable in this election. The south of the State continued to be the electoral base for the social-democratic parties, including Labor and the Greens. On this occasion, the north of the State swung to the Liberals and, in the case of the northwest coast, embraced the populism of a candidate such as Jacqui Lambie.

The Australian Capital Territory

By John Warhurst

There were two distinctive aspects to the ACT campaigns. The first were local ACT issues. These included the funding of national institutions, including the National Gallery of Australia, National Library of Australia, National Museum and the Australian War Memorial. In the case of the first three and others, the issue was too little government funding, while in the case of the War Memorial, it was criticism of the overly generous $500 million funding of an expansion plan developed by its Director-General, Dr Brendan Nelson, a former Liberal Opposition leader (Zhou 2019).

Funding of the Australian Public Service and other public service matters are always an issue in the Australian Capital Territory, and this was so again. Labor campaigned on a better deal for the public service, including reducing spending on private consultants. Late in the campaign—controversially, after most pre-poll voting had finished—the government announced cuts of $1.5 billion over four years to the public service to fund its election campaign spending promises (Whyte 2019a).

The second unique aspect was the energetic campaign against conservative Liberal Senator Zed Seselja (Warhurst 2019). He has long been a controversial figure in the Australian Capital Territory among the factionalised Liberal Party and within the Canberra community. He opposed same-sex marriage during the postal survey and abstained from voting on the legislation during 2017. He was also one of the leading young guns supporting Peter Dutton's campaign against Malcolm Turnbull in 2018—both matters way out of character for left-leaning, socially progressive Canberra.

While the two major party senators are almost impossible to shift in Canberra—despite repeated efforts by the Democrats and the Greens, among others—this time the campaign was vociferous. Both the Greens candidate, Penny Kyburz, and Independent Anthony Pesec campaigned hard and they were joined by Unions ACT and Get Up!. Unions ACT ran an allegedly $100,000 Dump Zed campaign (www.dumpzed.org.au [site discontinued]), including leaflets and a polling place presence. Its leaflet linked Seselja, Dutton and Tony Abbott. As voters queued to vote, they were handed empty scratchie cards with the messages 'Under Zed you will get Zilch' and 'Put Zed last. That's where he puts you'. Get Up! distributed how-to-vote cards urging: 'Vote for Climate Change. This time Don't Vote Liberal.' They urged a vote for Kyburz and Pesec because they offered 'very strong support for climate action'. By contrast, Katy Gallagher for Labor was rated a more muted 'Moderate Support for Climate Change' (though the how-to-vote card scarcely distinguished between the three candidates). For his part, Seselja relished the challenge and did not hide behind the Liberal brand. His campaign was personalised as 'Your local candidate for the Senate', using his distinctive brand name 'Zed' on the T-shirts of his many young volunteers.

Regional results

Labor won all three seats easily, but these seats are now more distinguishable in their voting patterns. Labor held its two-party-preferred position in the House of Representatives, despite suffering small negative swings in the southern seat of Bean, where the Independent environmentalist Jamie Christie polled 8.9 per cent and the Greens polled 13.7 per cent (more than 22 per cent in total), and in the northern seat of Fenner. In the central seat of Canberra, new Labor MP Alicia Payne won a two-party-preferred swing of 4 per cent and Tim Hollo (Greens) earned a swing of

4.6 per cent up to 23.7 per cent, making it one of the nation's most Green electorates. In the Senate, Labor and the Liberals split the two seats, but there was a tiny swing against Seselja and a swing towards both the Greens (3.5 per cent, up to 19.4 per cent) and Independent Pesec (5 per cent). This means the anti-Zed campaign was ultimately ineffective, and he won close to a quota in his own right. According to Seselja, that showed that the 'personalised' campaign against him did not work. In reality, he was also protected by the two-seat system, as was always going to be the case.

Canberra remains a 'Labor town' with a strong green tinge (Whyte 2019b). That is also the case at the Territory level. Zed Seselja floats in a sea of red. To some, including former public service commissioner John Lloyd of the Institute of Public Affairs, this pattern is a worrying anomaly with possible implications for the connection between the Australian Public Service and the wider community (Dingwall 2019). The largely conservative ideological character of the ACT Liberals is something of an enigma; moderation might be suggested by the demographics if greater electoral success is desired. Any change in ACT representation in future elections remains highly unlikely.

The Northern Territory
By Will Sanders

At the 2016 federal election, support for the Country Liberals was at a historic low and the two-term Country Liberal Member of the House of Representatives for the Darwin-based seat of Solomon, Natasha Griggs, lost her seat comprehensively with just 34.5 per cent of first-preference votes and 44 per cent of the two-candidate-preferred count. This probably reflected the disarray of the Country Liberal Government in the Northern Territory Legislative Assembly, which had suffered both a change of chief minister and several defections since its election in August 2012 (Smee and Walsh 2016). A month after Griggs's loss, the Country Liberals under Adam Giles lost the August 2016 Legislative Assembly election to Labor under Michael Gunner in a similarly comprehensive fashion.

During the 2019 election campaign, the Northern Territory achieved prominence in the national media just once, when Prime Minister Scott Morrison and Opposition leader Bill Shorten both visited, on Tuesday, 23 April. As well as supporting the Country Liberals' two aspiring women candidates for the House of Representatives and a new woman Senate candidate, Morrison criticised the Gunner Territory Labor Government, which by the end of 2018 was suffering defections over management of its large debt and Budget deficit. Morrison called Gunner's government the 'worst in the country' and argued that 'if you can't manage money, you can't run a country'. The not-so-hidden implication was that poor money management was a problem for Labor, which also extended to Shorten and his federal team. Shorten's task during his Territory visit was the more staid one of supporting two incumbent members of the House of Representatives and a senator seeking re-election. His rhetoric was about 'Territorians looking to the future' and 'taking opportunities', as 'Territorians do'.

When Labor retained its two Northern Territory House of Representatives seats in the 2019 election, this was interpreted by the party faithful in the Territory as a vote of confidence in the Gunner Government and as evidence that Morrison's criticisms of it had misfired (Gibson 2019). While this probably overinterprets the result, the 2016 story above suggests that legislative assembly elections and Commonwealth parliamentary elections in the Territory can interact.

From a larger geographic perspective in 2019, the obvious question is: why was the Northern Territory strong for Labor when Queensland to the east and Western Australia to west were so much more problematic? The political economies of these outlying regions based on resource extraction industries may seem rather similar, but there is something different occurring in the Territory electorally compared with Queensland and Western Australia. One difference is that the Territory, with its much smaller capital city in the north rather than the south, has a larger proportion of public administrators and other white-collar professionals building careers in the jurisdiction but ultimately destined to leave. Gerritsen (2010: 32–33) has called this 'the politics of the expatriates' and notes as a corollary that the 'real Territorians' are the Aboriginal people for whom the Northern Territory is a long-term home. This points to a second big difference from Queensland and Western Australia: the Indigenous proportion of the population in the Northern Territory.

With more than 40 per cent of its population identifying as Aboriginal and/or Torres Strait Islander in the 2016 census, the Northern Territory's second outback seat of Lingiari stands out as the one House of Representatives division in which Indigenous Australians are a high enough proportion of the population to have significant electoral power.

The Country Liberals' 2019 pre-selection in Lingiari of prominent young Warlpiri woman and Alice Springs town councillor Jacinta Price suggested an attempt to attract Aboriginal votes. While her primary vote was 5 per cent higher than her predecessor's in 2016, the Labor vote for the incumbent, Warren Snowdon, was also up 5 per cent. Whereas in 2016 there had been nine candidates in Lingiari (including one prominent Yolngu Independent, who attracted 4.3 per cent of votes), in 2019, there were just six candidates to share the primary vote. While Price was the prominent Indigenous candidate in 2019, her vote was strongest in the regional towns and weaker in the discrete Aboriginal communities. Snowdon, by contrast, won these discrete communities serviced by remote-area mobile polling even more convincingly than in past elections when he had also faced high-profile Aboriginal candidates.

Snowdon's seven-term tenure in Lingiari suggests that the Aboriginality of candidates has made little difference to recent Commonwealth parliamentary elections in the Northern Territory. No doubt, in this one House of Representatives division in which there is such a significant Aboriginal presence, Labor will think hard about an Aboriginal replacement candidate for Snowdon. But in the meantime, Aboriginal voters have not moved in large numbers to support Aboriginal candidates, whether as Independents, for the Country Liberals, for general minor parties or, as in 2013, for Australia's First Nations Political Party.

Since 2010, the AEC has invested significantly in Indigenous electoral participation. In 2019, the AEC produced a table (Table 11.8) as part of its work on enrolment. In the 151 divisions of the House of Representatives grouped in Table 11.8, the two outlying divisions with an 'enrolment rate' compared with the 'estimated enrolment eligible population' in the range 75–80 per cent are Lingiari and Durack, in the Kimberley region of Western Australia. These are also the two divisions with the highest proportions of Indigenous people in their populations. Turnout against enrolment is also a problem in Lingiari, which is the one House of Representatives division in the far-right column of Table 11.9—two categories lower in turnout than any other. Increased enrolment among Aboriginal people in Lingiari could, ironically, decrease turnout further, unless the AEC can also improve Indigenous participation in remote-area mobile polling.

Table 11.8 Enrolment in 151 House of Representatives divisions compared with 'Estimated enrolment eligible population', March 2019

	>98%	>95% <98%	>90% <95%	>85% <90%	>80% <85%	>75% <80%
No. of HoR divisions	54	52	41	1	1	2

Source: Australian Electoral Commission, enrolment statistics.

Table 11.9 Votes cast against enrolment in 151 House of Representatives divisions, July 2019

	>95%	>90% <95%	>85% <90%	>80% <85%	>75% <80%	>70% <75%
No of HoR divisions	1	126	21	2	0	1

Source: Australian Electoral Commission, 2019 Australian federal election results.

Aboriginal electoral power in remote areas of the Northern Territory is real, by virtue of population proportions, and probably explains the different results in the Territory in 2019 compared with remote areas of Queensland and Western Australia. However, enrolment and turnout figures suggest that such Aboriginal electoral power may still have considerable untapped potential.

References

Australian Bureau of Statistics (ABS). 2018. *Australian National Accounts: State Accounts, 2017–18*. Cat. no. 5220.0 Canberra: ABS. www.abs.gov.au/AUS STATS/abs@.nsf/DetailsPage/5220.02017-18?OpenDocument.

Australian Electoral Commission (AEC). 2019a. 'House of Representatives: First preferences by party—Qld'. *Tally Room 2019 Federal Election*. Canberra: AEC. results.aec.gov.au/24310/Website/HouseStateFirstPrefsBy Party-24310-QLD.htm.

Australian Electoral Commission (AEC). 2019b. 'House of Representatives: First preferences by party'. *Tally Room 2019 Federal Election*. Canberra: AEC. results.aec.gov.au/24310/Website/HouseStateFirstPrefsByParty-24310-NAT. htm.

Australian Labor Party (ALP). 2019a. *Labor's Fair Plan for Schools*. Sydney: ALP. www.fairgoforschools.com.au/.

Australian Labor Party (ALP). 2019b. *Nation-Building Infrastructure.* Sydney: ALP. www.alp.org.au/media/1902/nation_building_infrastructure. pdf [page removed].

Bailey, Sue and Emily Jarvie. 2019. 'Week 3 of the 2019 federal election campaign: Analysis'. *The Advocate*, [Burnie], 5 May. www.theadvocate.com.au/story/6106681/candidate-headaches-dog-parties/.

Blaxendale, Rachel and Remy Varga. 2019. 'Marginal motive in transport spending'. *The Australian*, 4 April: 6.

Brown, Greg. 2019. 'Shorten yet to rule out Adani review'. *The Australian*, 23 April: 5.

Chan, Gabrielle. 2019. 'Shorten evokes Whitlam the hero, but is it really going to be his time?'. *The Guardian*, 16 May.

Charlton, Peter. 1983. *State of Mind: Why Queensland is Different.* Sydney: Methuen-Haynes.

Commins, Patrick. 2019. 'Per capita recession looms again'. *Sydney Morning Herald*, 4 March: 23.

Dingwall, Doug. 2019. 'Agencies should consider relocating jobs'. *The Canberra Times*, 4 June.

Doran, Matthew, Andrew Kesper and Emma Machan. 2019. 'Halfway to the election, where have the leaders been?'. *ABC News*, 1 May. www.abc.net.au/news/2019-05-01/federal-election-campaign-heatmap-shows-where-leaders-visiting/11059550.

Fiorina, Morris. 1981. *Retrospective Voting in American Elections.* New Haven, CT: Yale University Press.

Gailberger, Jade. 2019a. 'Boothby battle begins'. *The Advertiser*, [Adelaide], 9 April: 10.

Gailberger, Jade. 2019b. 'Labor makes waves in Bight'. *The Advertiser*, [Adelaide], 9 April: 6.

Gerritsen, Rolf. ed. 2010. *North Australian Political Economy: Issues and Agendas.* Darwin: Charles Darwin University Press.

Gibson, Jano. 2019. 'Northern Territory Labor optimistic of 2020 re-election after federal election results'. *ABC News*, 20 May. www.abc.net.au/news/2019-05-20/election-results-give-nt-labor-optimism-for-re-election-in-2020/11131530.

Hanrahan, Catherine. 2019. 'Vote Compass finds voters are split on economy and environment as most important issue'. *ABC News*, 17 April. www.abc.net.au/news/2019-04-17/vote-compass-election-most-important-issues/11003192.

Hewett, Jennifer. 2019. 'A highly taxing campaign for voters'. *Australian Financial Review*, 15 April: 2.

Hondros, Nathan, Hamish Hastie and Hannah Barry. 2019. 'WA budget inches back into surplus but debt will have to wait a while'. *WAtoday*, 9 May. www.watoday.com.au/national/western-australia/wa-budget-inches-back-into-surplus-but-debt-will-have-to-wait-a-while-20190509-p51lq5.html.

Killoran, Matthew. 2019. 'Backing for coal despite activists'. *The Courier-Mail*, [Brisbane], 20 April: 17.

Killoran, Matthew and Annika Smethurst. 2019. 'Big tax win for Morrison'. *The Courier-Mail*, [Brisbane], 12 May: 11.

Laschon, Eliza. 2018. 'The GST overhaul has been given the green light: Here's what it all means for WA'. *ABC News*, 14 November. www.abc.net.au/news/2018-11-14/gst-explainer-how-will-wa-spend-its-windfall/10493500.

Lewis, R. 2019. 'Labor leaders building bridges in the west'. *The Australian*, 16 May: 9.

Liberal Party of Australia. 2019a. *Election Policies*. Canberra: Liberal Party of Australia. www.liberal.org.au/our-policies.

Liberal Party of Australia. 2019b. *Our Plan for Western Sydney*. Canberra: Liberal Party of Australia. www.liberal.org.au/our-plan-western-sydney.

McKay, Jack. 2019. 'Coal shoulder a sign of the times'. *The Courier-Mail*, [Brisbane], 24 April: 12.

McQueen, Humphrey. 1979. 'States of the Nation: Queensland—A State of Mind'. *Meanjin* 38: 41–51.

Marszalek, Jessica. 2017. 'Greens take it to Trad'. *The Courier-Mail*, [Brisbane], 26 November: 7.

Martinez i Coma, Ferran and Rodney Smith. 2018. 'The States and Territories'. In *Double Disillusion: The 2016 Australian Federal Election*, edited by Anika Gauja, Peter Chen, Jennifer Curtin and Juliet Pietsch, 211–34. Canberra: ANU Press. doi.org/10.22459/DD.04.2018.09.

Murphy, Denis. 1978. 'Queensland's Image and Australian Nationalism'. *Australian Quarterly* 50: 77–91.

New South Wales (NSW). 2018. *Budget Statement 2018–2019*. Budget Paper No. 1. Circulated by The Hon. Dominic Perrottet MP, Treasurer, and Minister for Industrial Relations. Sydney: NSW Government. www.budget.nsw.gov.au/sites/default/files/budget-2018-06/Budget_Paper_1-Budget_Statement_UDPATED_2.pdf.

Queensland Government Statistician's Office (QGSO). 2019. *Employment Growth and Unemployment, Queensland and Australia, 1978–79 to 2017–18*. Brisbane: Queensland Treasury.

Scarr, Lanai. 2019a. 'Federal election 2019: Scott Morrison would call Perth home if he didn't live in Sydney'. *West Australian*, [Perth], 26 April. www.thewest.com.au/politics/federal-election-2019/federal-election-2019-scott-morrison-would-call-perth-home-if-he-didnt-live-in-sydney-ng-b881179309z.

Scarr, Lanai. 2019b. 'The west could be the key in the fight for power'. *West Australian*, [Perth], 13 May. www.thewest.com.au/opinion/lanai-scarr/lanai-scarr-the-west-could-be-key-in-fight-for-power-ng-b881196453z.

Scarr, Lanai and Annabel Hennessy. 2019. 'Federal election 2019: Negative gearing changes may hit Labor heartland'. *West Australian*, [Perth], 8 May. www.thewest.com.au/politics/federal-election-2019/federal-election-2019-negative-gearing-changes-may-hit-labor-heartland-ng-b881184514z.

Smee, Ben and Christopher Walsh. 2016. *Crocs in the Cabinet: Northern Territory Politics—An Instruction Manual on How Not to Run a Government*. Sydney: Hachette Australia.

Viellaris, Renee. 2019. 'A little ray of sunshine'. *The Courier-Mail*, [Brisbane], 18 May: 6.

Warhurst, John. 2019. 'Canberra and the Zed phenomenon'. *The Canberra Times*, 23 May.

Whyte, Sally. 2019a. 'Coalition's $1.5b cut from public service'. *The Canberra Times*, 17 May.

Whyte, Sally. 2019b. 'Election 2019: How successful were the effort of Independents and the Greens in Canberra?'. *The Canberra Times*, 19 May.

Williams, Paul D. 2009. 'Leaders and Political Culture: The Development of the Queensland Premiership, 1859–2009'. *Queensland Review* 16(1): 15–34.

Williams, Paul D. 2011. 'How Did They Do It? Explaining Queensland Labor's Second Electoral Hegemony'. *Queensland Review* 18(2): 112–33.

Williams, Paul D. 2018a. 'Back from the Brink: Labor's Re-Election at the 2017 Queensland State Election'. *Queensland Review* 25(1): 6–26.

Williams, Paul D. 2018b. 'One, Two or Many Queenslands? Disaggregating the Regional Vote at the 2017 Queensland State Election'. *Australasian Parliamentary Review* 33(2): 57–79.

Wills, Daniel. 2019a. 'To the victor, the spoils in road funding splash'. *The Advertiser*, [Adelaide], 3 April: 6.

Wills, Daniel. 2019b. 'Why arithmetic does not add up for South Aussies'. *The Advertiser*, [Adelaide], 11 May: 44.

Worthington, Brett. 2019. 'Federal election 2019: Leaders channel Whitlam as they make their final pitches to voters'. *ABC News*, 17 May. www.abc.net.au/news/2019-05-16/federal-election-day-35-shorten-morrison-whitlam-rwanda/11119682.

Zhou, N. 2019. 'War Memorial expansion's opponents say $500 million better spent on veterans'. *The Guardian*, 23 March.

12

VOTER BEHAVIOUR

Shaun Ratcliff, Jill Sheppard and Juliet Pietsch

On Saturday, 18 May 2019, the incumbent Liberal–National Coalition parties surprised most observers by winning a majority of seats in the House of Representatives. Although the win was narrow—the conservative parties won 77 seats in the 151-seat chamber—this gave them a majority in the lower house of the national parliament. Using new data from the Cooperative Australian Election Survey, this chapter addresses and empirically evaluates some of the narratives about voting behaviour that emerged out of this shock election result, including claims about economic interest, age and ethnicity.

Following this unexpected outcome, one of the narratives that developed around the result was that Prime Minister Scott Morrison's suburban ordinariness provided him and the Coalition parties he led with an advantage over the parties of the left. The left-of-centre Labor Party had, in some accounts, been portrayed as representing inner-city elites, allowing the Liberal–National Coalition parties to win the support of struggling workers employed in manufacturing and retail (see Wright et al. 2019). This included claims that the Labor Party's negative gearing policies—and other plans to tax 'aspirational voters'—actually hurt the very voters they were meant to help.

Related to this, the major parties' strategies in 2019 appeared designed to segment the electorate by age: Labor's housing affordability policy potentially disadvantaged older voters to the benefit of the young, while the Coalition defended the rights of older voters to enjoy the benefits of superannuation and property-related tax minimisation policies. On the surface, these strategies appear sound. Older voters make up a large (and generally Coalition-voting) segment of the electorate.

Another narrative was that the 'ethnic' vote helped the Coalition win the election, stopping Labor 'in its tracks' (Jakubowicz and Ho 2019). In particular, it was asserted that the Australian Marriage Law Postal Survey run by the Australian Bureau of Statistics (ABS) in September 2017 activated the socially conservative politics of certain groups of voters, especially within the Chinese community, with 'ethno-religious prejudices around sexuality and gay culture' having 'a devastating impact on the ALP vote where they were activated' (Jakubowicz and Ho 2019). During this opinion survey regarding the legalisation of same-sex marriage, the Labor Party largely supported the 'yes' case. Conversely, the Coalition was more ambivalent, with some high-profile supporters in its ranks and a large number of opponents. When the parliament subsequently voted to change the *Marriage Act*, almost all Labor parliamentarians voted in support, while several high-profile Coalition members voted against or abstained. It has been argued that this process helped the Coalition lock in the support of socially conservative ethnic groups.

We test these ideas in this chapter. Did the Coalition win working-class voters, or 'battlers', and is there evidence that the Labor Party's tax policies (in this instance, negative gearing) helped drive these shifts? Was this also associated with a large age-related electoral cleavage? Is there evidence of an 'ethnic vote' and was this associated with opposition to same-sex marriage?

We examine these questions using the Cooperative Australian Election Survey (Ratcliff and Jackman 2019). This comprised a sample of 10,316 respondents stratified by age, gender and State collected through the YouGov online panel between 18 April and 12 May 2019. These data were weighted by age, gender, education, language spoken at home and State.

Using these data, we find that older, higher-income voters who owned their own homes continued to support the Coalition at higher rates, whereas lower-income renters and younger voters supported Labor. Support for negative gearing was more concentrated and opposition diffuse. This suggests that Labor's policies on housing affordability and taxation may have been an electoral weakness, rather than a strength. However, this was not for the reasons claimed in the popular narrative.

There is also very little evidence for the assertion that ethnic minorities favoured the Coalition, that they thought the rights of same-sex couples had gone too far or that their attitudes towards this issue drove them towards the Coalition in greater numbers.

Vote by age

Very rarely in Australian electoral politics has either major party made explicit appeals to voters based on their generation or age cohort. This changed in 2019. Both the Labor Party and the Coalition engaged in strategies that incorporated policies that overtly appealed to voters belonging to different age or generational groups. This may not have been intentional (other groups may have been the targets), but regardless, the outcome was the same.

The Labor Party's dual-pronged housing affordability policy—comprising a commitment to reducing franking credit dividends for some self-funded retirees and a cut to negative gearing offsets for property investors— would have disadvantaged (wealthier) older voters and benefitted younger (less affluent) individuals (Kehoe 2019). Negative gearing essentially allows the unrestricted use of tax losses from investment properties to be offset as tax deductions from most other sources of income. Conversely, the Coalition defended the rights of older (income- and asset-rich) voters to enjoy the benefits of existing tax minimisation policies available through superannuation and property investment (Millane 2019).

On paper, these clashing approaches were sound. Older voters have traditionally supported the Coalition in greater numbers. As the population ages, this group increasingly makes up much of its electoral base. The parties of the left (particularly the Greens) have performed better among younger voters for decades, with Labor doing better with those aged under 65 than over and appearing content to lose the support of some older voters in 2019. Labor's shadow treasurer Chris Bowen told voters that 'if you don't like our policies, don't vote for us' (Kehoe and Cranston 2019).

Labor may have been willing to adopt this strategy due to the perception that it had a (potentially temporary) electoral advantage from a surge in the enrolment of young people during the 2017 marriage law postal survey (Betigeri 2019). However, this narrative may not be entirely accurate.

It may be intuitive that young Australians were energised by an issue particularly salient to them and would enrol and vote. Indeed, enrolment among young Australians (aged 18 to 25) increased from 73 per cent in 2011 to 85 per cent in 2018, reversing a previous decline (AEC 2019). However, it is more likely that increased enrolments prior to the 2019 election were due to the AEC's policy of direct enrolment (ANAO 2016). In 2019, approximately two-thirds of all electoral enrolment in Australia occurred through direct updates of the roll by the AEC.

While this difference may seem technical in nature, it is substantively important. Previously unenrolled voters who were mobilised to enrol so they could have a say in the marriage law postal survey have, by definition, at least a minor interest in one contemporary policy issue. Previously unenrolled voters added to the electoral roll do not necessarily have any passing interest in politics and there is no reason for us to assume that they would turn out to vote, given they did not actively enrol themselves. In that sense, stories of 'declining youth turnout' are better characterised as the continuation of an existing trend rather than any new phenomenon. In other words, similar raw numbers of Australians are voting, but the pool of enrolled voters is growing (through direct enrolments).

Individual behaviour in 2019: Same old, same old

If anything, the parties' segmentation of the electorate by age or generational cohort in 2019 reinforced existing patterns. Many young voters abstained, and those who voted tended to support Labor and the Greens. Despite pre-election narratives suggesting young voters would play a disproportionately important role in the outcome, they were unable to remove the Coalition Government.

As a baseline, we can reasonably assume that these intergenerational patterns have become a relatively fundamental feature of contemporary Australian politics. Based on both the Australian Election Study and now the Cooperative Australian Election Survey data, there are clear trends and cross-sectional data. As can be seen in Figure 12.1, a clear pattern concerning age and partisan choice remained at the 2019 election. Young voters preferred Labor over the Coalition, with the Greens only a small way behind the major centre-right parties.

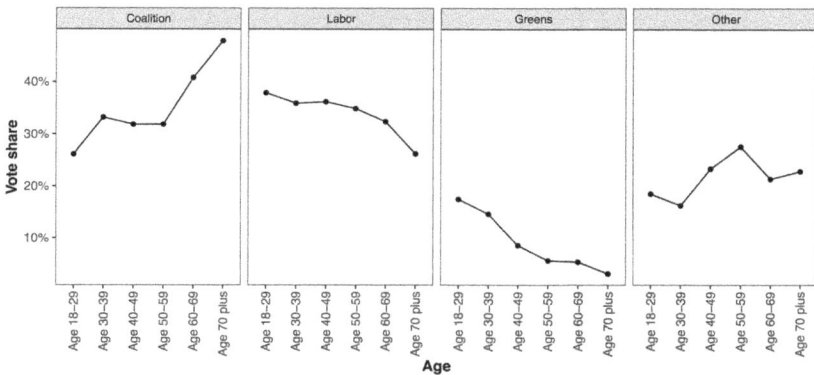

Figure 12.1 First-preference vote intention for the House of Representatives, by age

Source: Ratcliff and Jackman (2019).

Moreover, young voters were the most likely to not enrol or abstain from voting, either risking a fine for non-attendance or avoiding enrolment in the first place (as shown in Figure 12.2).[1]

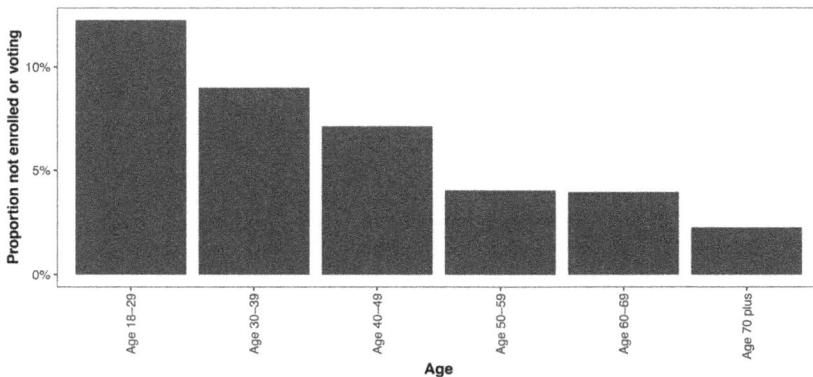

Figure 12.2 Non-voting for the House of Representatives, by age

Note: Non-voting denotes adult Australian citizens who either have not enrolled to vote or did not intend to cast a valid vote.

Source: Ratcliff and Jackman (2019).

---

1   Of course, since being enrolled in an online survey panel and being willing to complete a survey about politics are likely correlated with the act of enrolling and voting, there are limitations to what we can learn from these data about the act of abstaining.

The framing of particularly salient issues in the 2019 campaign—tax policies, housing affordability and wage and wealth inequality—may have been designed to appeal to younger voters, driving them towards the Labor Party and away from the Coalition (and perhaps the Greens). This does not appear to have gone according to plan.

The expectation that Labor's housing policy—which included reducing the tax breaks available to landlords and therefore their incentive to bid real estate prices higher—would appeal to younger votes may have been reasonable. Younger voters are less likely to own their own home and more likely to rent than older voters. However, although these younger voters were less likely to agree that landlords should be able to use losses from rental properties as a deduction on income tax through negative gearing (Figure 12.3), they were not more likely to disagree. Rather, they were more likely to not hold an opinion on this issue.

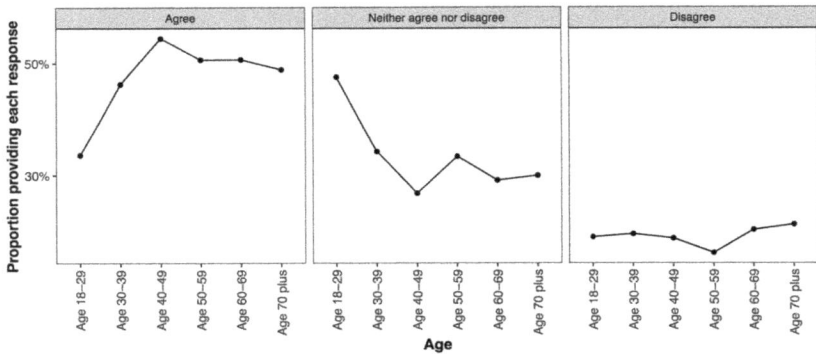

Figure 12.3 Support for the use of negative gearing for investment properties, by age

Note: The question asked was: 'Please say whether you strongly agree, agree, disagree or strongly disagree with each of these statements. Landlords should be able to use losses from rental properties as a deduction on income tax (through negative gearing).'

Source: Ratcliff and Jackman (2019).

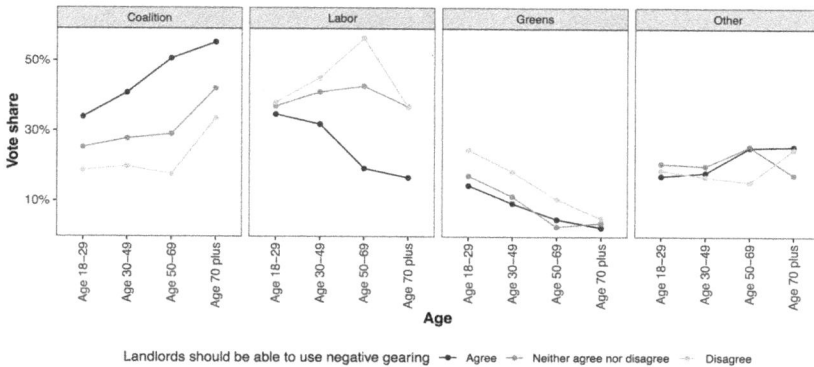

Figure 12.4 First-preference vote intention for the House of Representatives, by support of the use of negative gearing for investment properties and age
Source: Ratcliff and Jackman (2019).

As a result, this issue did not necessarily drive these voters towards the Labor Party. As Figure 12.4 highlights, the relationship between attitudes towards negative gearing and voting intention was strongest for voters aged between 50 and 69. Younger voters, aged between 18 and 29, were much less likely to vote based on their attitudes towards negative gearing. Although we cannot prove the direction of causality, this may suggest that opposition to negative gearing was diffuse and Labor's policy on this issue did little to benefit the party during the campaign.

Economic voting in 2019

Our finding that attitudes towards negative gearing had only a limited association with voting intentions among the young may suggest that the explanation of the result adopted by some in the media—that traditional voting patterns based on economic cleavages have broken down—has some validity. These claims are similar to the 'death of class' thesis, in which it was asserted that (now irrelevant) economic cleavages were a part of specific historical processes linked to the Industrial Revolution (Clark et al. 1993; Pakulski and Waters 1997). As the major political issues of the Industrial Revolution were resolved, ideologies and issues related to economic class became less important. According to these arguments, demand for significant (economic) policy difference disappeared. Instead, class consciousness and economic cleavages have been replaced with social and post-materialist politics (see also Inglehart 1977, 1990, 1997, 2008).

Many of these claims, however, are based on confusion between aggregate movements in voting choice and the behaviour of individuals (see, for instance, Atkins 2019; Crowe 2019; Wright et al. 2019). These writers find that electorates with lower than average incomes, lower levels of education and greater numbers of renters moved towards the Coalition. Besides linking (often small) swings with overall levels of support, they are also guilty of ecological fallacies.

Although the type of occupation an individual has can play an important role in their economic interests and political preferences, this is not necessarily the only (or even most important) driver of politicised economic cleavages. A meaningful analysis of economic interests (or economic class) is driven not by the colour of a voter's collar alone, but also by their access to resources and their relationship with capital (a simplification of the arguments put forward by Braverman 1974; Wright 2000: 25).

Using this more nuanced understanding of economic interests combined with our data, we undertake a deeper analysis of economic voting at the 2019 election. We start by operationalising this concept of economic interests through the examination of voting intention as a function of proximity to capital and access to resources. For this exercise, we consider a voter who owns their own business or a private trust as being closer to the interests of capital and a voter with a higher household income as having greater resources. The results indicate that the commentary on the Coalition's status as the party of the battler has been mistaken.

While the Coalition received some of its highest support from those earning $208,000 or more who own a business or a trust (approximately 60 per cent of the voters who gave the Liberal–National parties their first preference in 2019), the picture was very different among those who could be better described as working class (see Figure 12.5). Associated with, but not necessarily caused by, Labor's policy on housing affordability and taxation, the Coalition also did well among high-income homeowners, while Labor did better with low-income renters (see Figure 12.6). Although, as with age, Labor's advantage with lower-income renters and workers was smaller than the Coalition's lead among higher-income and capital-owning voters.

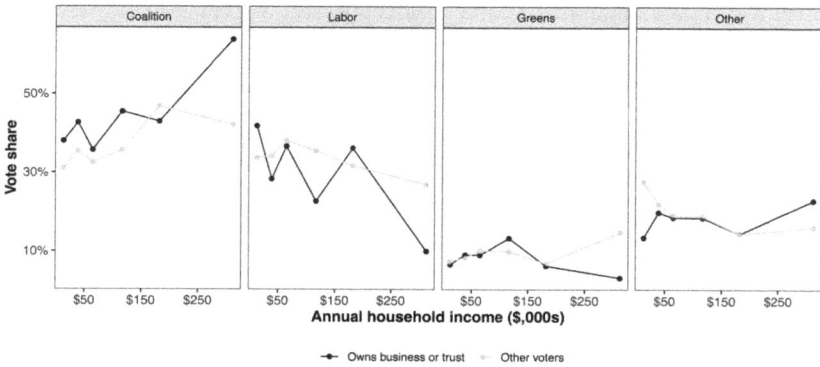

Figure 12.5 Party support by business or trust ownership and household income

Source: Ratcliff and Jackman (2019).

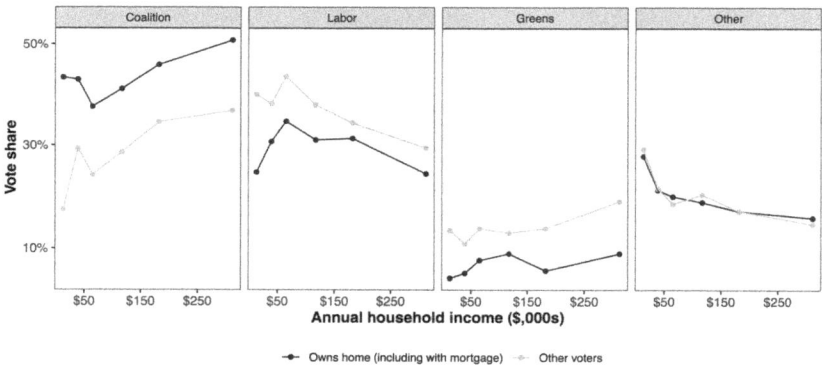

Figure 12.6 First-preference vote intention for the House of Representatives, by home ownership and household income

Source: Ratcliff and Jackman (2019).

Of course, some blue-collar workers voted for the Coalition. However, if we adopt a meaningful definition of the working class—voters who work in blue-collar jobs or sales and services, with lower to middle incomes and who are employees—we find they did not actually provide the Coalition with significant support. Approximately 25 per cent of those with average to lower earnings (with household incomes below $78,000 per annum) supported the Liberal and National parties with their first-preference votes. Conversely, about half of those with the lowest incomes (less than $26,000 per annum) voted Labor. The self-employed in blue-collar and sales and service occupations, with incomes above $208,000 per annum, were the ones who overwhelmingly voted for the Coalition. Contrary to many of the claims made since the election, higher-income voters were the ones who swung away from Labor, defecting to the Coalition in greater numbers than those with lower household incomes (see Figures 12.7 and 12.8).

As we might expect, based on self-interest, voters who owned their own homes (including those with a mortgage) and those with high household incomes were more likely to support the use of negative gearing by landlords (Figure 12.9). These voters were also much more likely to vote for the Coalition (Figure 12.10). However, as discussed above, support for negative gearing was more concentrated, while opposition was diffuse. While those who benefited were more likely to support the Coalition, those who would not benefit—namely, lower-income voters who did not own their own homes—were more likely to not hold an opinion. As with younger voters, their partisan choice appears to have been less associated with their attitudes towards negative gearing. The only high-income group that voted strongly for Labor was that of high-income voters who opposed the use of negative gearing for investment properties.

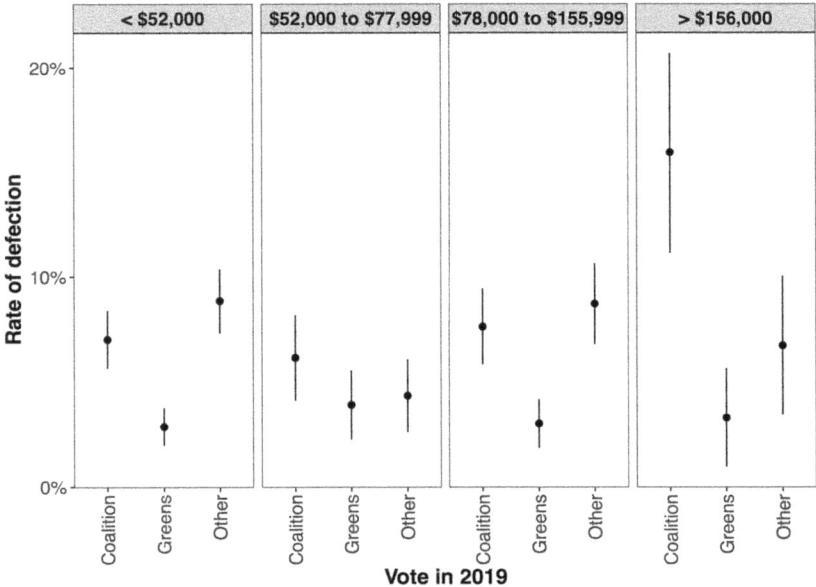

Figure 12.7 First-preference defections from Labor for the House of Representatives, by household income

Source: Ratcliff and Jackman (2019).

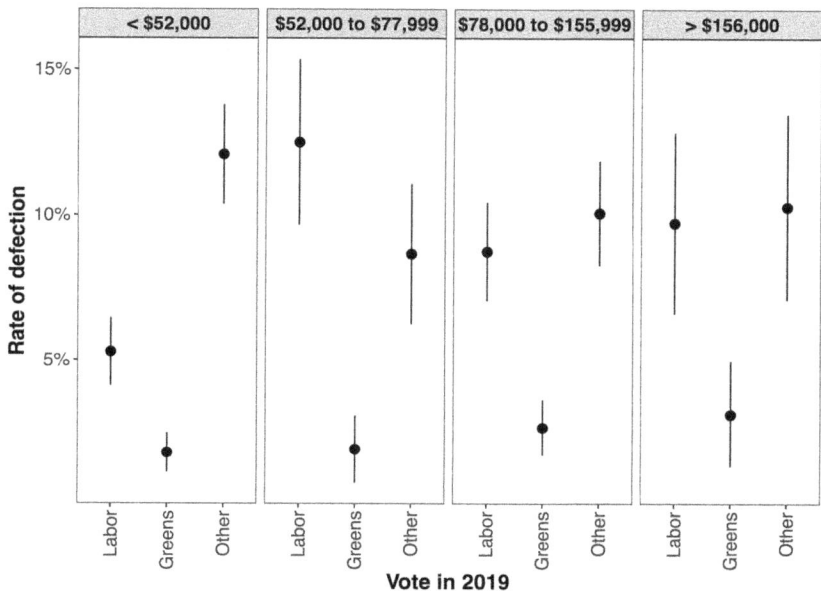

Figure 12.8 First-preference defections from the Coalition for the House of Representatives, by household income

Source: Ratcliff and Jackman (2019).

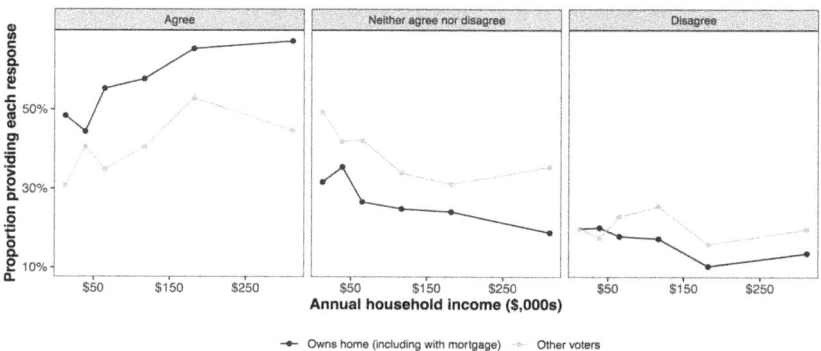

Figure 12.9 Support for the use of negative gearing for investment properties, by home ownership and household income

Note: The question asked was: 'Please say whether you strongly agree, agree, disagree or strongly disagree with each of these statements. Landlords should be able to use losses from rental properties as a deduction on income tax (through negative gearing).'

Source: Ratcliff and Jackman (2019).

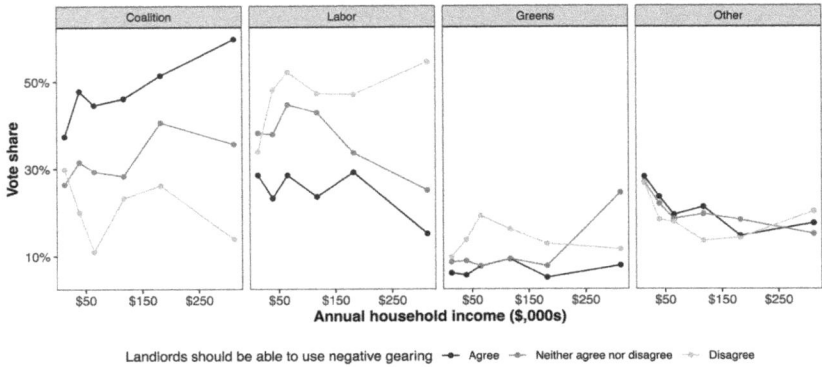

Figure 12.10 Vote intention by support for the use of negative gearing for investment properties and household income
Source: Ratcliff and Jackman (2019).

Vote by ancestry

A final narrative surrounding the election result asserted that the Coalition won with the support of the 'ethnic' vote. Specifically, one claim was that the same-sex marriage plebiscite activated the socially conservative politics of certain groups of voters, especially those from the Chinese community (Jakubowicz and Ho 2019). Is there any evidence that Chinese voters are more conservative on gay rights? Or that the Chinese vote swung away from the Labor Party and influenced the election outcome?

Changing patterns in and attitudes towards immigration

Interest in the possible political influence of the ethnic vote is not new. It attracted a great deal of scholarly attention in the 1980s, when multiculturalism was at its peak. During this period, it was well established that the Labor Party had the edge over the Coalition among Australia's ethnic population (Pietsch 2018), although there was variation across different groups (Pietsch 2017b). This was particularly the case for Australia's new migrant populations from Asia.[2] Part of the interest in the

---

2   In part due to the Hawke Labor Government's actions following the Tiananmen Square massacre in 1989, when it extended temporary permits for Chinese Nationals in Australia and granted permanent visas to 42,000 Chinese temporary visitors (see Pietsch 2018).

ethnic vote is due to the changing nature of immigration to Australia. During the later years of the 20th century, it became more multicultural, temporary and skills-based, focused on workers and students.[3]

These changes in the nature of the immigration system ignited a public debate on population pressures, housing and job security during the 2019 NSW State election, which was held only months before the federal election. This issue became highly salient during the State campaign, with a video released showing NSW Labor Party Leader Michael Daley saying: 'Our children will flee [Sydney] and who will they be replaced with … they are being replaced by young people from typically Asia with PhDs' (Pietsch 2019). Federal Labor immediately went into damage control, concerned about the upcoming federal election and a number of marginal seats with high populations of Asian voters. Revealing the high degree of sensitivity in some of Labor's key migrant-heavy seats about perceptions of racism, Daley later offered his resignation so as not to hurt the federal election campaign.

The 2019 election and the Chinese vote

During the federal election campaign, there was a great deal of concern about how both of the major parties were being perceived among Asian migrants in key marginal seats. This was particularly evident in the middle-suburban Melbourne seat of Chisholm, where it was claimed that East Asian voters made up more than 30 per cent of the population and would be decisive in the outcome for that electorate. In particular, it was pointed out that approximately 20 per cent of Chisholm residents spoke Chinese (Pietsch 2017a). Both the major parties recruited Chinese candidates to

---

3   In the 1950s, almost half of all new migrants arriving in Australia came from the United Kingdom. This declined to 18 per cent by 2016. Over the same period, immigration from the People's Republic of China shifted from a very small proportion of arrivals to Australia to one of the largest (Simon-Davies 2018). By 2016, 3.2 per cent of adults in Australia (including just over 1.6 per cent of citizens) were born in China, and more than 5.7 per cent had Chinese ancestry (including more than 3.6 per cent of citizens) (ABS 2016). In 2017, only 32.5 per cent of the total visas allocated were for permanent residency (Simon-Davies 2018) and many of these applications for permanent visas came from former international students. In recent years, the government reformed the visa system to narrow the list of occupations eligible for permanent visas, adjusted the points test used to evaluate applications, with a stronger emphasis on higher education and English-language ability, and made changes to temporary migration, restricting the type of occupations for which temporary visa applicants could apply (Boucher and Davidson 2019).

appeal to the 'ethnic' voter. The candidate for the Labor Party was Jennifer Yang from Taiwan and the Liberal Party candidate was Gladys Liu from Hong Kong.

At first glance, the claims that the ethnic vote (particularly the Chinese population) swung to the Coalition and helped it to hold marginal seats, such as Chisholm, seems reasonable. Liberal candidate Gladys Liu narrowly won the seat with an active campaign against the Safe Schools program, which was introduced into Victorian schools by the State Government[4] to address the issue of bullying of lesbian, gay, bisexual, transgender, queer and intersex (LGBTQI) students. According to Liu:

> The Chinese believe same-sex [marriage] is against normal practice [and] … Chinese people come to Australia because they want good … things for the next generation, not to be destroyed— they use the word destroyed—[by] same-sex, transgender, inter-gender. All this rubbish. To them, they are just ridiculous rubbish. (Burton-Bradley 2019)

Comments made by Liu in 2016 also surfaced during the campaign, in which she described LGBTQI issues as 'ridiculous rubbish' (Burton-Bradley 2019).

There was also concern that the Liberal campaign displayed Chinese-language signs at polling booths with the appearance of official AEC notices, telling voters that the 'correct' way to vote was to put a number 1 next to the Liberal candidate. These signs were the subject of a High Court challenge (see Chapter 3, this volume). A similar campaign was observed on WeChat, a Chinese-language social media platform, providing how-to-vote instructions that recommended support for Liu (see Karp 2019). There was some concern that this signage would take advantage of language (and other) barriers and divert Chinese-speaking Australians towards the Coalition (Pietsch 2018).

Testing these claims

Combined, these claims assert that the Coalition benefited from the Chinese vote, which was more socially conservative than the rest of the electorate, open to manipulation due to language barriers and strategically located in marginal electorates (including Chisholm). We question these assertions.

---

4   Initially, with some federal funding.

Some of these election narratives regarded the Chinese vote as critical in key seats such as Chisholm in Melbourne and Barton in Sydney (Jakubowicz and Ho 2019). While the Chinese vote is large in these electorates and a few others, it makes up a smaller proportion of the electorate than many of these claims suggest. Most observers mistake the total Chinese population for the citizen population. While more than one-quarter of Chisholm's adult population is ethnically Chinese (self-identifying as having Chinese ancestry), most are not Australian citizens and could not vote in the federal election. Similarly, while nearly one-quarter of Chisholm residents aged over 18 reported speaking a Chinese language at home, most of these Chinese speakers were not Australian citizens. Overall, 14 per cent of Chisholm's adult citizens had Chinese ancestry and just over 11 per cent spoke a Chinese language at home (ABS 2016). This makes the Chinese component somewhat less dominant in these areas than is sometimes asserted. Additionally, regardless of the size of the Chinese vote in Chisholm and similar electorates, there is little evidence Chinese social conservatism (if it exists) was decisive in any way. The first-preference and two-party-preferred swings against the Coalition were actually larger in Chisholm than the Victorian average, suggesting that any appeal to Chinese social conservatism or tricks designed to take advantage of language barriers provided little benefit to the Liberal candidate.

There are also doubts about whether Chinese Australians are actually more socially conservative than other voters, and whether they shifted to the Coalition in 2019. We test this by examining voting intention by respondents' ancestry and attitudes towards same-sex marriage (Figures 12.11 and 12.12). We find that, generally speaking, there is little difference in the attitudes towards same-sex rights by ancestry and that Chinese voters (in our sample, at least) are actually less likely than other voters to say same-sex rights have gone too far.

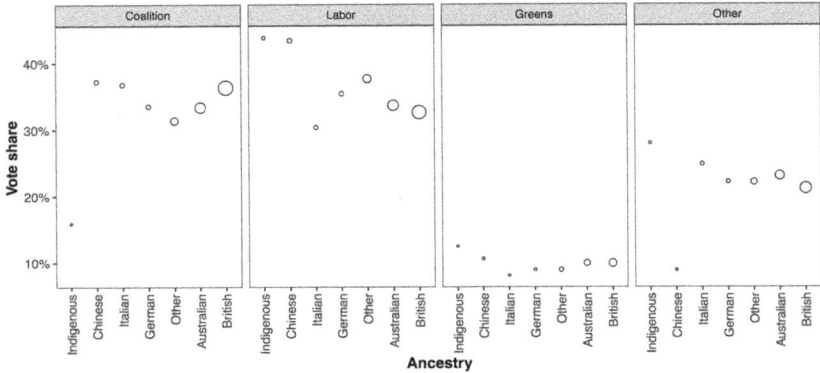

Figure 12.11 First-preference vote intention for the House of Representatives, by ancestry

Note: Points are scaled by the number of weighted respondents identifying with each ancestry category. Respondents were able to select two ancestry categories.

Source: Data from Ratcliff and Jackman (2019).

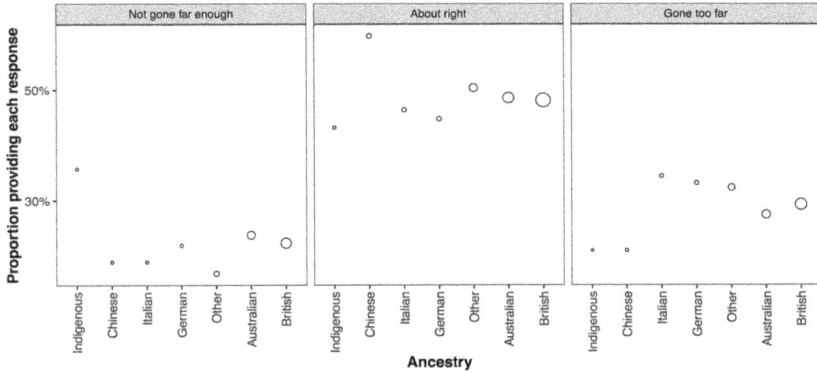

Figure 12.12 Belief that rights for same-sex couples have gone too far, by ancestry

Notes: The question asked was: 'The statements below indicate some of the changes that have been happening in Australia over the years. For each one, please say whether you think the change has gone too far, not gone far enough, or is it about right. The rights of same-sex couples.' Points are scaled by the number of weighted respondents identifying with each ancestry category. Respondents were able to select two ancestry categories.

Source: Ratcliff and Jackman (2019).

We also examined the rate of defection of voters with Chinese ancestry and other voters from the Labor Party and Coalition between 2016 and 2019. Shown in Figures 12.13 and 12.14, these indicate that Chinese Australians did not shift their party support from the Labor Party to the Coalition at a greater rate than other voters. The Coalition may have been slightly more successful holding on to Chinese-ancestry voters, but not to the extent that it would likely have made a major difference to the election result.

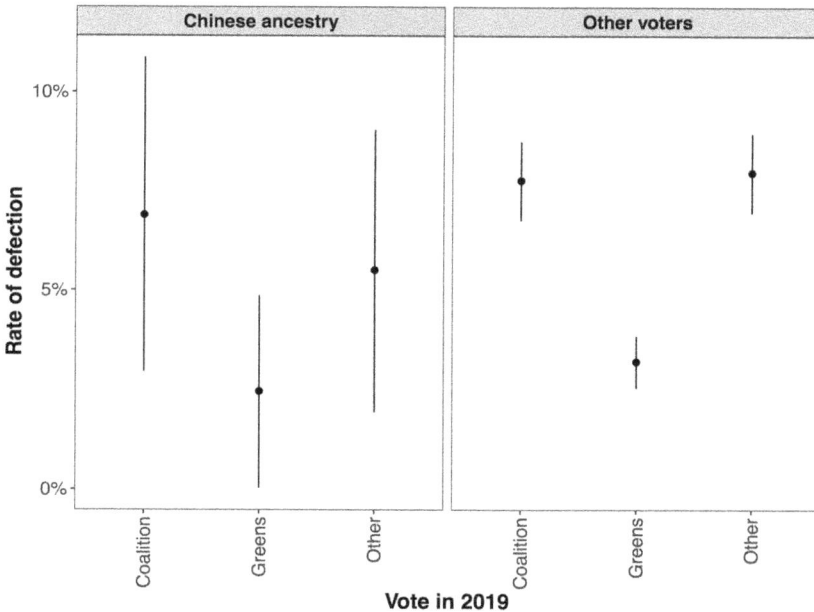

Figure 12.13 First-preference defections from Labor for the House of Representatives, by Chinese ancestry

Source: Ratcliff and Jackman (2019).

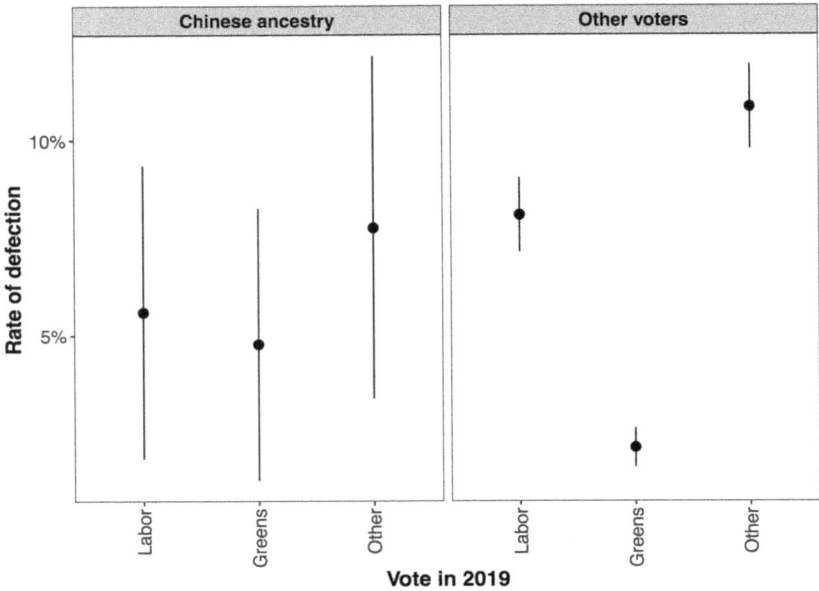

Figure 12.14 First-preference defections from the Coalition for the House of Representatives, by Chinese ancestry

Source: Ratcliff and Jackman (2019).

Discussion and conclusion

The 2019 Australian election was framed around significant policy differences, with real winners and losers. As a result, narratives developed around the (generally unexpected) outcome. It was claimed the centre-left Labor Party had become the party of the elites and its negative gearing policies had reduced its support among the very voters they were meant to help, who instead voted for the Liberal–National Coalition. It was also asserted that the 'ethnic' vote helped the Coalition win the election, with the 2017 same-sex marriage postal survey activating the socially conservative politics of certain groups of voters, and in particular the Chinese community.

We find there is little evidence to support these narratives.

Chinese Australians do not appear to have favoured or swung towards the Coalition. There is little evidence that they thought the rights of same-sex couples had gone too far or that attitudes about this issue drove voters towards the parties of the centre-right. We also find that the traditional economic cleavages remain intact. However, we also find an equally powerful counternarrative to these—one that is supported by the data. Labor made the most explicit pitch to younger, generally lower-income renters—or at least, against older, more affluent voters—of any major party in recent Australian history. It was also expected to win. It did not.

One possible reason is that support for negative gearing is more concentrated, particularly among those likely to benefit from it: the older, the affluent and those who own real estate. Conversely, opposition is limited and diffuse. Those less likely to benefit are generally more likely to not hold an opinion than oppose the policy. Arguably, this limited any electoral benefits Labor may have been able to obtain from its policy in this space.

As the electorate continues to age, the strategy adopted by Labor will probably struggle to attract sufficient numbers of voters in a sufficient number of electorates to win a majority in the House of Representatives. This is not to say that the Labor Party is incapable of forming government in Australia, either now or in the future. However, it may suggest that the dividends earned by electoral strategies that explicitly target younger voters over older ones may decline over time. Moreover, the most salient issues among the population generally—economic management, health, education and the environment—increasingly involve intergenerational trade-offs. An issue such as climate change may be viewed as a form of zero-sum calculation for many voters. For every younger person whose future welfare may be enhanced by actions to reduce the potential effects of climate change, the return from an older voter's superannuation may be jeopardised. The policy reality of this calculation is largely irrelevant. Perceptions are potentially more important. Current and future governments in Australia face the challenge of convincing older generations that they will not be bearing the costs of long-term policies addressing Australia's structural policy challenges.

References

Atkins, Dennis. 2019. 'Coalition cashes in on votes from the poor and little educated voters in the regions'. *The Courier-Mail*, [Brisbane], 11 June. www.courier mail.com.au/news/opinion/coalition-cashes-in-on-votes-from-the-poor-and-little-educated-voters-in-the-regions/news-story/3cec0fb6dacba91b42d4b5 db772e0864.

Australian Bureau of Statistics (ABS). 2016. *Australian Census*. [Findings based on the use of ABS TableBuilder data]. Canberra: ABS.

Australian Electoral Commission (AEC). 2019. *Enrolment Activity by State and Enrolment Type: January 2019*. Canberra: AEC. www.aec.gov.au/Enrolling_ to_vote/Enrolment_stats/type/2019/02.htm.

Australian National Audit Office (ANAO). 2016. *Third Follow-up Audit into the Australian Electoral Commission's Preparation for and Conduct of Federal Elections*. Auditor-General Report No. 6 of 2015–16. Canberra: ANAO. www.anao.gov.au/work/performance-audit/third-follow-audit-australian-electoral-commissions-preparation-and-conduct.

Betigeri, Aarti. 2019. 'Young, energised, ready to vote, and maybe decide two elections'. *The Interpreter*, 16 May. Sydney: The Lowy Institute. www.lowy institute.org/the-interpreter/young-energised-ready-vote-and-maybe-decide-two-elections.

Boucher, Anna and Amy Davidson. 2019. *The Evolution of the Australian System for Selecting Economic Migrants*. Washington, DC: Transatlantic Council on Migration, Migration Policy Institute.

Braverman, Harry. 1974. 'Labor and Monopoly Capital: The Degradation of Work in the Twentieth Century'. *Monthly Review* 26(3)(July–August). doi.org/ 10.14452/MR-026-03-1974-07_1.

Burton-Bradley, Robert. 2019. 'Liberal Chisholm candidate Gladys Liu caught disparaging LGBTI issues, blames Chinese community'. *ABC News*, 23 May. www.abc.net.au/news/2019-04-15/chisholm-candidates-comments-on-same-sex-marriage-released/11004596.

Clark, Terry Nichols, Seymour Martin Lipset and Michael Rempel. 1993. 'The Declining Political Significance of Social Class'. *International Sociology* 8: 293–316.

Crowe, David. 2019. 'Labor failed to understand the "aspirational" voter'. *Sydney Morning Herald*, 30 May. www.smh.com.au/federal-election-2019/labor-failed-to-understand-the-aspirational-voter-20190530-p51sqq.html.

Inglehart, Ronald. 1977. *The Silent Revolution: Changing Values and Political Styles Among Western Publics*. Princeton, NJ: Princeton University Press.

Inglehart, Ronald. 1990. *Culture Shift in Advanced Industrial Society*. Princeton, NJ: Princeton University Press. doi.org/10.1515/9780691186740-003.

Inglehart, Ronald. 1997. *Modernization and Postmodernization*. Princeton, NJ: Princeton University Press.

Inglehart, Ronald. 2008. 'Changing Values Among Western Publics from 1970 to 2006'. *West European Politics* 31(1–2): 130–46.

Jakubowicz, Andrew and Christina Ho. 2019. 'Was there an "ethnic vote" in the 2019 election and did it make a difference?'. *The Conversation*, 4 June. theconversation.com/was-there-an-ethnic-vote-in-the-2019-election-and-did-it-make-a-difference-117911.

Karp, Paul. 2019. 'Labor mulls legal challenge over misleading how-to-vote instructions on WeChat'. *The Guardian*, 28 May. www.theguardian.com/australia-news/2019/may/28/labor-mulls-legal-challenge-over-misleading-election-signs-in-chisholm.

Kehoe, John. 2019. 'Labor channels Gen X, Y discontent'. *Australian Financial Review*, 17 April. www.afr.com/news/policy/tax/labor-channels-gen-x-y-discontent-20190417-p51evi.

Kehoe, John and Matthew Cranston. 2019. 'Chris Bowen fights for his political career'. *Australian Financial Review*, 21 May. www.afr.com/news/politics/national/chris-bowen-fights-for-his-political-career-20190521-p51pii.

Millane, Emily. 2019. 'The newest election split isn't left versus right, it's young versus old—and it's hardening'. *The Conversation*, 30 April. theconversation.com/the-newest-election-faultline-isnt-left-versus-right-its-young-versus-old-and-its-hardening-116079.

Pakulski, Jan and Malcolm Waters. 1997. 'The Death of Class'. *Capital & Class* 21(2): 192–93. doi.org/10.1177/030981689706200114.

Pietsch, Juliet. 2017a. 'Explaining the Political Under-Representation of Asian Australians: Geographical Concentration and Voting Patterns'. *Political Science* 69(2): 161–74. doi.org/10.1080/00323187.2017.1345283.

Pietsch, Juliet. 2017b. 'Trends in Migrant and Ethnic Minority Voting in Australia: Findings from the Australian Election Study'. *Ethnic and Racial Studies* 40(14): 2463–80. doi.org/10.1080/01419870.2016.1250937.

Pietsch, Juliet. 2018. *Race, Ethnicity and the Participation Gap: Understanding Australia's Political Complexion*. Toronto: University of Toronto Press. doi.org/10.3138/9781487519544.

Pietsch, Juliet. 2019. 'Our guest writes about how we talk about race in challenging times'. *University News*, [University of Western Australia], 27 March. www.news.uwa.edu.au/2019032711302/uwa-ppi/our-guest-writes-about-how-we-talk-about-race-challenging-times.

Ratcliff, Shaun and Simon Jackman. 2019. *Cooperative Australian Election Survey*. Sydney: University of Sydney.

Simon-Davies, Joanne. 2018. *Population and Migration Statistics in Australia*. Parliamentary Library Research Paper 2018–19, 7 December. Canberra: Parliament of Australia. www.aph.gov.au/About_Parliament/Parliamentary_Departments/Parliamentary_Library/pubs/rp/rp1819/Quick_Guides/PopulationStatistics.

Wright, Erik Olin. 2000. *Class Counts: Comparative Studies in Class Analysis*. Cambridge: Cambridge University Press. doi.org/10.1017/CBO9780511488917.

Wright, Shane, Noel Towell and Megan Gorrey. 2019. 'The left–right identity fault line cracks through the quinoa curtain'. *Sydney Morning Herald*, 21 May. www.smh.com.au/federal-election-2019/the-left-right-identity-fault-line-cracks-through-the-quinoa-curtain-20190520-p51p9o.html?.

PART 3.
ACTORS

13

THE AUSTRALIAN LABOR PARTY

Rob Manwaring

The Australian Labor Party was widely predicted to win the 2019 federal election, and against these expectations it fell short. This chapter offers an outline of some of the decisive factors in Labor's campaign that shaped its unexpected loss. Immediately following the election defeat, there was a plethora of commentary that sought to offer explanations for Labor's poor electoral performance. Post election, Labor's own review confirmed many of the common explanations for the defeat (ALP 2019). This chapter seeks to distil this wider commentary and make some evaluative judgements about the range of factors posited for the poor result. As the editors argue in the opening chapter of this volume, the result can be seen as 'overdetermined', with a plethora of possible factors to account for the result.

The chapter is organised in the following way. First, the analytical approach of the chapter is briefly outlined—a comparative 'hybrid' approach. Second, Labor's result is located in the wider debates about the crisis of European social democracy. Third, the chapter gives a brief description of the key features of Labor's campaign. Fourth—and the core of the chapter—the key factors that shaped Labor's campaign performance are outlined.

Ideas, institutions and individuals

In the study of labour and social-democratic politics, a range of analytical approaches is available (see Randall 2003). The hybrid approach adopted here follows the work of British political scientist Tim Bale (for example, Bale 2010). The chapter examines the performance of Labor through three key themes: individuals, ideas and institutions. In brief, the theme of 'individuals' examines issues of agency, the role of key actors and, crucially, a focus on leadership factors. The theme of ideas explores the impact of the role of ideology and related policy issues in explaining Labor's defeat. The institutional theme explores the wider structural factors that contributed to Labor's defeat, and this includes Labor's campaign, but also wider factors such as the turbulence in the Australian party system. Overall, these three themes are interconnected and interdependent. Agents and actors offer ideas and policies, which are shaped by the institutional and structural context.

The crisis of social democracy

Before focusing on Labor's campaign, it is useful to contextualise Labor's defeat in the wider crisis of social democracy (Bailey et al. 2016; Keating and McCrone 2013; Manwaring and Kennedy 2018). While the Australian 2019 election result was a surprise, against the backdrop of the wider decline of the electoral fortunes of the family of social-democratic and labour parties, it is probably less surprising. Much like its European counterparts, Labor's structural vote, if gauged by its first preferences, appears to be in decline (see Figure 13.1). In 1983, Labor won nearly 50 per cent of the primary vote; in 2019, it was down to 33 per cent. Labor has not won an election outright since Kevin Rudd's 2007 win. It is notable that Labor's past three election results are among the lowest first-preference tallies it has received since the 1980s. The ALP's 2010 national review outlined and acknowledged many of the features of the structural decline of the party, especially declining union density, declining party membership and a decline in supporters' identification with the party (Manwaring 2011).

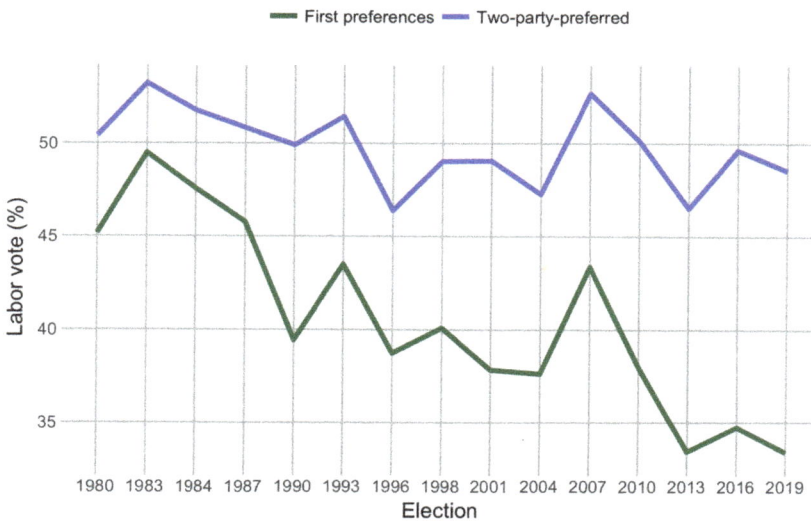

Figure 13.1 ALP first preferences, 1980–2019
Source: Compiled by author.

A comparative perspective only reaffirms this ongoing structural problem. In Figure 13.2, Labor's vote share is compared with a range of key sister centre-left parties, and this suggests a much wider issue for Labor than just the specific problems that shaped its 2019 performance. Ultimately, the centre-left parties face a wider structural change in the family of party systems and an erosion of their support base. They are struggling to win elections. In 2019, the main traditional centre-left parties were out of office in a range of countries, including the United Kingdom, France, Germany and Italy. While there are clear outliers and positive cases (Portugal, Denmark and New Zealand, for example), there remain ongoing debates about how the centre-left might revitalise its mission (Keating and McCrone 2013). The result of the 2019 Australian election, with Labor's electoral woes, can offer insights into the wider debates about the crisis of social democracy.

Carol Johnson, in her insightful chapter on ideology in this volume, argues that Labor pursued a relatively traditional social-democratic strategy. While agreeing with this judgement, I would emphasise that Australian Labor in 2019 offered a 'technocratic' form of social democracy. By technocratic, following Rundle (2019), we can suggest that Labor's agenda, while egalitarian, was focused more on specific policy fixes, mechanisms and instruments than on offering a coherent vision of a more egalitarian Australia.[1] Labor's technocratic approach seemed to distance itself from the everyday concerns of the wider public. Despite the breadth of Labor's policy agenda—and like many of its European sister parties—it is facing similar structural problems in galvanising its support base.

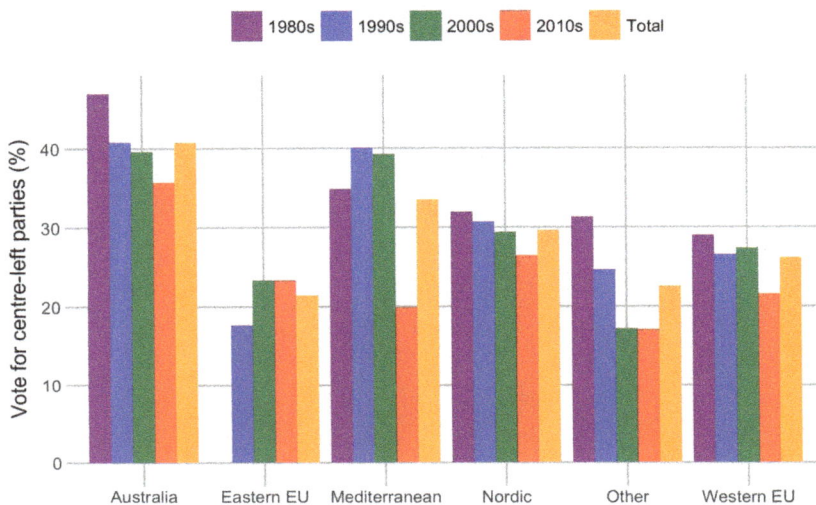

Figure 13.2 Centre-left parties' share of the vote

Source: Manifesto Project Dataset (version 2019b): doi.org/10.25522/manifesto.mpds.2019b.

Labor's campaign

Labor's campaign had four key features: it was the result of a long-term strategy, it was policy rich, it reflected positional differences and it strongly emphasised distributional outcomes.

Labor's campaign was a two-election campaign and, ultimately, its roots, key messages and policy approaches were entrenched from the 2013 election loss and Bill Shorten's time as leader. At the 2016 election, Labor's campaign strategy was policy-rich and made a virtue of a relatively strong

1   In this chapter, the term 'technocratic' social democracy is used to broadly describe Labor's agenda. It is technocratic in two main senses. First, following Rundle (2019), Labor's primary concern was focused on specific policy fixes (for example, the franking credit tax concessions) to fill a diffuse, ill-defined 'vision' of social democracy. In contrast, a more coherent form of social democracy has, arguably, a clearer definition of its core mission, and its policy approaches stem from this. Second, it was technocratic in that Labor was either unwilling or unable to redeploy more 'traditional' policy instruments (such as a more expansive welfare state) and, as a result, it had to rely on and find more specific indirect tax policy instruments.

front bench. As Stephen Mills outlines in his chapter in this volume, Labor offered a 'challenger' campaign in 2019 and again sought to make a virtue of the strong, unified front bench. Labor's policy focus was a deliberate attempt to remove attention from Shorten's leadership limitations and public unpopularity. In 2016, Labor set out its '100 popular policies'. The foundations for the 2019 campaign were laid from 2013. Given the better than expected results at the 2016 election, this was seen as a solid strategy.

Labor offered a 'big target' strategy, in that it sought to win office by giving salience to key policy issues that showed clear positional space between itself and the Coalition. Moreover, as detailed in Figure 13.3, Labor set out many more policies (69 listed) than the Coalition (42).[2] Across the range of 22 issues covered in Figure 13.3, it is striking that in only three areas (business, small to medium enterprises and defence) did the Coalition have 'more' prominent policies than Labor. Labor's was an ambitious, wide-ranging policy agenda, which, judging by the election result, was perceived as too ambitious, unworkable or reckless.

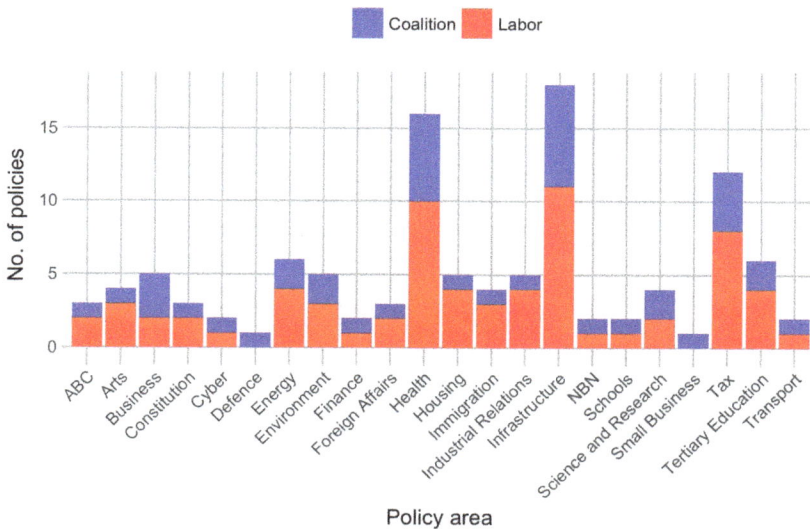

Figure 13.3 Key policy offerings of major parties, 2019 federal election
Source: Donegan and Jeyaratnam (2019).

2   Data taken from *The Conversation*'s overview of key policy issues for each of the two main parties (Donegan and Jeyaratnam 2019). Note this is not a comprehensive overview of all the major parties' policies, but it does give a useful proxy indicator of the number of headline policy issues presented by each party.

Labor's key campaign slogan was its message of a 'Fair go for Australia'. As a slogan, it lacked flair or innovation, but it did largely reflect the distributional impact of Labor's agenda. In trying to understand the impact of election campaign effects, we can distinguish between the impact of valency and positional types of election issues (Brady and Johnston 2006: 8). Valency issues reflect shared ends but parties offering different routes to the same ends. Positional issues are those for which parties offer quite different policy choices for voters. There is some evidence that, unlike countries such as the United Kingdom (Brexit aside), in Australian election campaigns valency issues have not been a striking feature (see McAllister et al. 2015). Labor's 2016 and 2019 campaigns strongly reflect a campaign shaped by a strong focus on policy *positional* differences.

While Labor has often campaigned on the theme of equality or fairness, what was markedly different in its 2019 'fair go' campaign was a much stronger focus on tackling economic inequality by targeting high-income earners and big business—the 'big end of town'. Yet, rather than seek to reduce economic and social inequality through 'traditional' social-democratic 'tax and spend' approaches (such as a more expansive welfare state), it used more 'technocratic' measures, especially through hitherto rather little-known tax concessions. There were three main themes to Labor's tax policy campaign, centring on income tax, housing and tax concessions:

- Tax relief for low and middle-income earners (Labor pledged to match the Coalition's tax relief rebate of $1,080 for those earning less than $48,000 and offered tax relief worth up to $350 for low-income workers earning up to $37,000).

- Abolition of negative gearing for investors buying existing houses from January 2020 and halving of capital gains tax discount for investment properties.

- Ending of cash rebates for excess franking credits, preventing self-funded retirees receiving tax refunds (creating an estimated revenue of $10.7 billion over four years).

Labor's strategy was clear. First, the tax cuts for low to medium-income earners were to neutralise criticism that Labor was anti–tax cuts, and to highlight the Coalition's far more regressive, and long-term, staged tax plan. Second, the focus on tax concessions framed them as an outdated 'gift' for high-income earners and the revenue created would enable Labor to underwrite its ambitious spending plans. This technocratic approach meant that Labor could avoid having to reform more traditional taxation mechanisms such as income tax or social insurance increases or reheating the debates about the GST. Third, the appeal to reform housing tax concessions was part of a bid to tackle housing affordability and access issues. Labor sought to temper anxiety about its ambitious tax reforms by promising a larger surplus than that promised by the Coalition (Chan 2019).

The second part of Labor's campaign was a series of ambitious spending pledges, which included:

- $2.3 billion Medicare cancer plan and $2.4 billion dental-care plan for older people
- additional $3.3 billion to public schools over three years
- commitment to introduce a 'living wage', pegged to the national minimum wage
- new $5 billion fund to modernise electricity transmission infrastructure
- reverse penalty rate cuts for retail and hospitality workers
- pay increase for childcare workers.

Overall, Labor's campaign was pitched around core themes of significant tax changes to increase government revenue, linked to a clear redistributive agenda, across a range of areas.

To some extent, this was an uneventful campaign for Labor, in that there were relatively few gaffes, unexpected events or specific missteps that proved decisive. As Brady and Johnston (2006) note, election campaigns are not limited to the usual short four–five-week campaign prior to the election date (see also Chapter 2, this volume). Labor's campaign in 2019 needs to be understood as part of a two-election strategy, with the core of its policy agenda built into the foundations of the run-up to the 2016 campaign. Labor hoped it could reassure voters about its ambitious, policy-rich agenda by releasing many of the key flagship proposals early. A key event in Labor's 2019 campaign was the 2018 ALP national conference. Here, as explored below, a number of key damaging policy issues, especially immigration, were 'neutralised' in a bid to demonstrate electoral capacity (Norman and Belot 2018).

The short campaign reflected key tensions in Labor's strategy. On the one hand, it wanted to appeal with an ambitious, wideranging policy agenda, yet on the other, it was forced to be defensive and temper its ambition by downplaying any potential negative economic impacts. The overall claim made here about Labor's campaign is that, arguably, very few *specific* events had decisive electoral effects on the results; rather, a wider range of factors might better explain the election result and, crucially, Labor's loss.

Individuals

In this section, we consider the key factor of agency and, specifically, the role of leadership factors that proved decisive in the election loss. A prevailing narrative both throughout and after the election result was that Labor's campaign was held back by having Shorten as leader (Cameron and McAllister 2019; Murphy 2019; Powell 2019). The Liberal campaign was negative and its 'Bill we can't afford' slogan neatly captured specific anxieties about Labor and Shorten's ability to govern or secure wider electoral support. Yet, polling data and AES data on leadership might suggest that, while this was a factor, it was only one of a number. First, despite claims about Morrison's more 'presidential' campaign, the impact of personalisation and individual leadership on electoral outcomes seems mixed. Intriguingly, despite the high churn of Australians prime ministers over recent years, since 2004, AES data suggest there has been a steady decline in voters citing the party leader as a key consideration in their voting decision (Cameron and McAllister 2016: 24). At the 2004 election, 'party leader' was cited by 19 per cent of those polled, but by only 9 per cent at the 2016 election. Yet, there is no doubt that Shorten was never able to cut through and achieve much in the way of widespread popularity and it is noteworthy that he was more unpopular than Tony Abbott in 2013 (Cameron and McAllister 2019). Labor's effort to counter this was by presenting a strong front bench, although, as Stephen Mills notes (in Chapter 23, this volume), this had at best a limited impact.

Late in the campaign, in what was clearly crass overreach, Sydney's *Daily Telegraph* launched a scathing attack on Shorten for what it claimed was his misrepresentation of his background and his upbringing by his mother. An emotional Shorten hit back at the media and, among the political commentariat, this appeared to help soften his image and 'humanise' him. However, this incident arguably had no impact on improving his public image, as Shorten was consistently deemed an unpopular leader in the polls (Martin 2019). In terms of public persona, Shorten certainly fell well short of veteran party leader and legend Bob Hawke, who passed away at the end of the campaign, but also striking is the difference with Jacinda Ardern in New Zealand, where leadership effects clearly played a part in turning around the electoral fortunes of New Zealand Labour.

We can note other individuals and actors involved in shaping Labor's campaign, although their overall impact was seemingly negligible. One key moment in the campaign was at Labor's official launch, which saw together for the first time Hawke, Paul Keating and, critically, Kevin Rudd and Julia Gillard. It was a specific effort to show party unity and to contrast with the more recent leadership instability that characterised Morrison's rise to power. In sum, we can note that Shorten's lack of appeal may have helped fuel misgivings among some about a potential Labor government. Yet, in and of itself, it offers just a partial explanation.

Ideas

Labor's loss is arguably rooted in the tensions, dilemmas and limitations posed by its ideational and policy agenda. A useful framework with which to understand the dilemmas and trade-offs in political and policy ideas is provided by Jenny Stewart's (2009) work on policy values. Stewart distinguishes between different types of values, two of the main types of which are 'outcome' and 'design' values (Stewart 2009: 27–28). Outcome values reflect the desired end point and design values reflect the institutional choices made to implement these values. Stewart's key insight is that values often entail 'shadow' values that are sometimes 'sacrificed' (in her example, 'greenness' can come at the expense of economic growth) (Stewart 2009: 27). For the purposes of this chapter, the central point is that it was not just the breadth of Labor's ideological and policy agenda, but also the inherent value conflicts and trade-offs, that ultimately hampered its electoral performance. Here we can identify four key policy and ideational trade-offs in Labor's agenda:

1. vision versus policy specificity
2. outputs versus outcomes (tax versus spend)
3. environmental issues versus economic growth
4. inequality versus efficiency.

As outlined above, Labor offered one of the most policy-rich agendas in its recent electoral history. It offered a broad canvas, with key flagship issues in areas including environmental and climate policy, health, energy and tax policy. One upshot was that Labor was unable to sufficiently control the discussion of its policy agenda—an insight shared by a number of contributors to this volume and indeed by the ALP in its post-election review (ALP 2019). Initially, Shorten's focus was on the election as a 'referendum on wages', but during the short campaign it quickly moved on to other issues—for example, threatening that it would be the 'climate change election' (Aly 2019; Robinson 2019). The 'fair go' proved an inadequate organising theme to give coherence to the new agenda. As political scientist Stuart Ball (2005) notes, to win government, an Opposition needs a 'new agenda'; and, while Labor clearly had this, it proved insufficiently coherent. In sum, diversity came at the expense of focus.

One criticism levelled at Labor was that it lacked an overarching, credible narrative or 'vision' (Rundle 2019). Labor was forced to spend a significant part of the campaign explaining its policy agenda, rather than outlining its future aspirations for the country. Perhaps a telling moment in the campaign that captured Labor's dilemma was during the second televised leaders' debate when Morrison was happy to concede time to Shorten with the quip, 'Bill has more taxes to explain'. Touché. One insightful comparison has been made with Ed Miliband's ill-fated election campaign in 2015 in the United Kingdom (Chiu 2019). Miliband was often hamstrung by launching numerous policies and then losing valuable political capital by having to explain them (Bale 2015). Labor had some similar struggles. On announcing the pay increase for childcare workers—a seemingly popular policy—Labor was forced to explain why this sector was singled out for special treatment. Tellingly, the Liberals were not penalised for having no such plans. Likewise, in one clear moment of electoral jitters, Labor quickly decided to adopt the Coalition's housing policy to offer a guarantee for first-time homebuyers. In brief, Labor's focus on policy detail, with numerous policy and spending offerings, came at the cost of explaining its core mission.

A second, ultimately damaging, policy trade-off that Labor did not manage to resolve was the balance between policy outputs and outcomes. The difficulty here is to have clear linkages between the mechanisms and instruments that will be employed in government and the tangible public goods that will be delivered as a result. The net effect was that Labor had to devote disproportionate time to explaining its tax policy (outputs) at the expense of describing the potential benefits of the changes (outcomes). In a revealing interview after the election result, Labor Deputy Leader Tanya Plibersek acknowledged this as a factor, especially with what she saw as a credible infrastructure plan for Queensland (ABC 2019). The upshot is that Labor appeared to suffer electorally from having a weak link between its key policy mechanisms (especially the fears raised about its tax agenda) and the speed, tangibility and credibility of the eventual outcomes.

This fed into a further policy trade-off between the environment/ climate policy and economic growth. It seemed a shrewd tactical move by Labor to coopt the Coalition's National Energy Guarantee (NEG), buttressed with a strong commitment to a renewable energy target of 50 per cent by 2030. Adopting the NEG was a way to neutralise previous damaging debates about introducing a carbon pricing mechanism. Yet, Labor lacked credibility here, in part because of its ambivalence over the Adani coalmine, which became something of a lightning rod for wider uncertainty about Labor's ability to balance environmental and economic concerns (Aly 2019).

Finally, we can note a policy dilemma that proved damaging to Labor's campaign: the trade-off between equality and efficiency. This was compounded by Labor not explaining its flagship policies clearly enough. For example, Labor's tax policy was targeted at the 'top end of town'. The eventual election result suggested that—most strikingly in Queensland— it was unclear who was meant by the 'top end of town'. Here, Labor was seemingly prioritising reducing economic inequality rather than stimulating economic and employment growth (and market efficiency). This focus on tackling (in)equality over efficiency was most keenly felt by relatively well-paid workers in the resources sector who feared job insecurity from both the end of the mining boom and the debates about the future of energy in the country. Likewise, Labor's 'franking' credits policy was convincingly relabelled a 'retiree' tax, in part because it was not fully clear which groups might be adversely affected. It was another policy that required further explanation. The more fundamental problem with the franking credits policy was that Labor was perceived to be targeting the most affluent groups at the expense of offering a nuanced policy agenda that enabled broader economic growth and market efficiency. It is worth contrasting the ALP's approach to tackling inequality with that of New Labour in the United Kingdom. New Labour targeted its rhetoric and policy at uplifting the most economically vulnerable groups rather than having direct confrontation with the wealthiest groups. In contrast, the ALP explicitly targeted a suite of policies at 'the top end of town', which gave license to the scare campaign that it would introduce a 'death tax'.

Overall, we might make some tentative evaluations of Labor's policy and ideological agenda. Following Brady and Johnston (2006: 8), we can differentiate between two key areas of effective campaigning: *persuasion* and *priming*. In terms of persuasion, Labor was damaged by the scare campaign about its tax plans. It is striking that not only the Liberals, but also the UAP, the Centre Alliance and others explicitly targeted Labor on its supposed 'retiree tax'. The election result suggests Labor could not satisfactorily resolve a number of the policy trade-offs outlined above. As a result, Labor was not persuasive enough on its policy agenda. Second, Brady and Johnston (2006: 8) note the role of priming, in which 'campaigns can shape public opinion by making certain issues salient to voters'. Labor had problems with *priming* the public on its policy agenda. The breadth of its agenda meant it proved difficult to sufficiently hold key swing voters on its core campaign issues—for example, wage stagnation.

It is worth noting that, while Labor lost, against expectations, it lost only narrowly. The close and unexpected result can obscure the significant amount of work Labor undertook to build its ideational and policy agenda. Critically, at its 2018 national conference, it had neutralised the issue of immigration—much to the chagrin of refugee advocacy groups. This might not have had any negative impact for Labor, but it certainly gave them no positive uplift. Similarly, the vexed issue of increasing the Newstart allowance was 'parked' by Labor by its promise of a review. It was striking, too, that seemingly controversial social policies, such as the progressive and well overdue policy announcement about access to abortion services, did not have any significant public backlash. Interestingly, this issue reflects Labor's ongoing shift to expand its concept of equality (Johnson, Chapter 5, this volume).

In sum, Labor's ability to persuade and prime on its ideological commitments and policy was curtailed, due in part to some of the difficult policy trade-offs interwoven in its agenda. Labor did not lose the battle of ideas, not least because the Coalition offered so few in reply; rather it was punished due to some of the policy tensions inherent in its offerings. However, none of these was fully apparent until the polling booths closed.

Institutions

Institutional factors encompass both the role of key *institutions* in shaping electoral outcomes and what is more accurately described as *structural* factors, such as the changing shape of Australia's party system. Institutional and structural factors clearly had an impact on Labor's performance.

The Labor machine seemingly ran a campaign beset by various difficulties (Williams 2019). Immediately after the election, a number of anonymous Labor sources pointed out that Noah Carroll, who led Labor's campaign, had made some strategic mistakes. A key finding from Labor's own post-election review was the party's failure to establish a formal campaign committee (ALP 2019: 9). Moreover, the decision to base the campaign headquarters in Western Sydney proved a mistake (Uhlmann 2019). Labor's internal polling also, apparently, was far from accurate (indeed, much like the national polls), which may have created inaccurate feedback loops for campaign headquarters. Labor's polling may have underestimated Shorten's unpopularity. While Labor raised funds and mobilised volunteers and the like, its strategic message failed to cut through in the right marginal seats. Again, much of this may have been apparent only after the poor result for Labor.

A second institutional factor that some critics pointed to was the role of Chris Bowen as shadow treasurer. Much was made of his quip that 'people can always choose to not vote for us' in his defence of the franking credits policy. However, according to some anonymous Labor sources, it was his institutional role as treasurer that may have proved damaging. Arguably, a key role as (shadow) treasurer is to have the thankless task of saying 'no' to shadow Cabinet colleagues in their ambitious spending claims. In part, the argument is that Bowen was insufficiently resilient in reining in Labor's spending pledges. This, of course, remains speculative, and the impact is hard to measure.

We might also note other institutional factors, perhaps including the lacklustre campaign run by the ACTU (see Chapter 20, this volume; also Karp 2019). At certain elections, union campaigns have helped Labor—notably, the WorkChoices campaign of 2007, but also at the State level, with union mobilisation assisting Daniel Andrews in Victoria, for example. The ACTU's 'Change the rules' campaign, while worthy in aiming at systemic change, was seen as misconceived and, crucially, lacking public cut-through. Labor may not have been hindered by the campaign, but it seemed to have no positive impact on the result. We might also add here that the impact of factional stability within the party, with the ALP clearly learning the lessons of the Rudd–Gillard years, was neutral, rather than positive.

Finally, we can note other institutional factors—not least the issue of campaign spending. Labor's campaign can only be seen in the wider context of the campaigns of other parties, and especially their different funding levels. Critically, Clive Palmer's UAP spent significantly more than Labor, with an estimated $55 million outspending of Labor's $13–15 million (Koslowski 2019). The negative UAP advertisements had little direct electoral benefit to Palmer's party, but they helped bolster the Liberals in an effective scare campaign. These institutional factors link with Shorten's post-election critique of the 'vested interests' that Labor faces. Indeed, Labor has always faced systemic pressures within a capitalist market economy (for example, Johnson 2019).

Finally, we can point to wider structural changes, especially in Australia's party system, having a clear impact—less as an explanatory factor to describe Labor's loss in 2019, and more in placing tougher structural constraints on Labor's ability to manoeuvre. Two related factors play out here. First, as noted elsewhere, Australia's party system is shifting and, again, we see record numbers of voters turning away from the major parties. The rise of the minor parties and the role of Independents are significant for the major parties, but this also means that elections are now far more seat-by-seat in focus, and Labor cannot rely on the same residual support. If we link this to the wider issue of the crisis of social democracy, this raises key issues for Labor and its future relations with the Greens, and the extent to which it must countenance future regular coalition-building (see Holloway et al. 2018). Labor appears to be in structural decline and this is linked to declining union density and declining party membership.

Conclusion

Against expectation, polling and wider predictions, Labor lost the 2019 election. A plethora of articles in the immediate aftermath, many insightful, provides clues as to what proved decisive in Labor's loss. The approach outlined here emphasises the range of institutional, ideational and individual factors that shaped the loss. The combination of an unpopular leader, an effective scare campaign targeting the policy tensions in Labor's ambitious agenda, linked to some wider institutional problems, meant that, while the overall result was close, Labor fell far short of its hopes. The Australian Labor Party is, then, another case of the ongoing travails of the centre-left, although compared with its Dutch, German, French or even UK counterparts, it has a firmer base on which to rebuild.

References

Aly, Waleed. 2019. 'What happened to the climate change election?'. *Sydney Morning Herald*, 23 May. www.smh.com.au/federal-election-2019/what-happened-to-the-climate-change-election-20190522-p51q4m.html.

Australian Broadcasting Corporation (ABC). 2019. 'Post-election special'. *Insiders*, [ABC TV], 19 May. www.abc.net.au/insiders/sunday-19-may-post-election-special/11128206.

Australian Labor Party (ALP). 2019. *Review of Labor's 2019 Federal Election Campaign*. Canberra: ALP. alp.org.au/media/2043/alp-campaign-review-2019.pdf.

Bailey, David, Jean-Michel de Waele, Fabien Escalona and Mathieu Vieira. eds. 2016. *European Social Democracy during the Global Economic Crisis: Renovation or Resignation?* Manchester: Manchester University Press.

Bale, Tim. 2010. *The Conservative Party: From Thatcher to Cameron*. Cambridge: Polity Press.

Bale, Tim. 2015. *Five Year Mission: The Labour Party Under Ed Miliband*. Oxford: Oxford University Press.

Ball, Stuart. 2005. 'Factors in opposition performance: The Conservative experience since 1867'. In *Recovering Power: The Conservative Party in Opposition since 1867*, edited by Stuart Ball and Anthony Seldon, 1–27. Basingstoke, UK: Palgrave Macmillan. doi.org/10.1057/9780230522411_1.

Brady, Henry and Richard Johnston. 2006. *Capturing Campaign Effects*. Ann Arbor, MI: University of Michigan Press.

Cameron, Sarah and Ian McAllister. 2016. *Trends in Australian Political Opinion: Results from the Australian Election Study 1987–2016*. Canberra: School of Politics and International Relations, The Australian National University. legacy.ada.edu.au/ADAData/AES/Trends%20in%20Australian%20Political%20Opinion%201987-2016.pdf.

Cameron, Sarah and Ian McAllister, 2019. 'Labor's election loss was not a surprise if you take historical trends into account'. *The Conversation*, 20 May. theconversation.com/labors-election-loss-was-not-a-surprise-if-you-take-historical-trends-into-account-117399.

Chan, Gabrielle. 2019. 'Labor costings reveal budget surplus of $217bn by 2022–23'. *The Guardian*, 10 May. www.theguardian.com/australia-news/2019/may/10/labor-costings-reveal-budget-surplus-of-217bn-by-2022-23.

Chiu, Osmond. 2019. 'Australian Labor's Miliband moment'. *Tribune*, [London], 19 May. tribunemag.co.uk/2019/05/australian-labors-miliband-moment.

Donegan, Andrew and Emil Jeyaratnam. 2019. 'Compare the pair: Key policy offerings from Labor and the Coalition in the 2019 federal election'. *The Conversation,* 14 May. theconversation.com/compare-the-pair-key-policy-offerings-from-labor-and-the-coalition-in-the-2019-federal-election-116898.

Holloway, Josh, Narelle Miragliotta and Rob Manwaring. 2018. 'Issue Competition between Green and Social Democratic Parties in Majoritarian Settings: The Case of Australia'. *Australian Journal of Political Science* 54(1): 18–36. doi.org/10.1080/10361146.2018.1529228.

Johnson, Carol. 2019. *Social Democracy and the Crisis of Equality: Australian Social Democracy in a Changing World*. Singapore: Springer Singapore. doi.org/10.1007/978-981-13-6299-6.

Karp, Paul. 2019. '"Vanity project": Critics round on ACTU's $25m campaign after Labor's election loss'. *The Guardian*, 21 May.

Keating, Michael and David McCrone. eds. 2013. *The Crisis of Social Democracy in Europe*. Edinburgh: Edinburgh University Press. doi.org/10.3366/edinburgh/9780748665822.001.0001.

Koslowski, Paul. 2019. '"At least $50 million": Clive Palmer to spend more than Liberals and Labor in huge election binge'. *Sydney Morning Herald*, 17 January. www.smh.com.au/politics/federal/at-least-50-million-clive-palmer-to-spend-more-than-liberals-and-labor-in-huge-election-binge-20190117-p50rvi.html.

McAllister, Ian, Jill Sheppard and Clive Bean. 2015. 'Valence and Spatial Explanations for Voting in the 2013 Australian Election'. *Australian Journal of Political Science* 50(2): 330–46. doi.org/10.1080/10361146.2015.1005005.

Manwaring, Rob. 2011. 'The paradox at the heart of Labor's review'. *Inside Story*, 1 March. insidestory.org.au/the-paradox-at-the-heart-of-labors-review/.

Manwaring, Rob and Paul Kennedy. eds. 2018. *Why the Left Loses: The Decline of the Centre-Left in Comparative Perspective*. Bristol: Policy Press. doi.org/10.1332/policypress/9781447332664.001.0001.

Martin, Sarah. 2019. 'Bill Shorten fights tears as he pays tribute to mother after Daily Telegraph's "rubbish" attack'. *The Guardian*, 8 May. www.theguardian.com/australia-news/2019/may/08/bill-shorten-fights-back-tears-as-he-defends-mother-against-daily-telegraphs-rubbish-attack.

Murphy, Katherine. 2019. 'Labor's path to victory is open—but have voters made peace with Bill Shorten?'. *The Guardian*, 11 April. www.theguardian.com/australia-news/2019/apr/11/labors-path-to-victory-is-open-but-have-voters-made-peace-with-bill-shorten.

Norman, Jane and Henry Belot. 2018. 'Bill Shorten outlines plan for government at Labor's national conference after protest ambush'. *ABC News*, 16 December. www.abc.net.au/news/2018-12-16/bill-shorten-outlines-plan-for-government-after-protest-ambush/10624786.

Powell, Mark. 2019. 'Ten reasons Labor lost the unlosable election'. *Spectator Australia*, 19 May. www.spectator.com.au/2019/05/ten-reasons-labor-lost-the-unlosable-election/.

Randall, Nick. 2003. 'Interpreting Labour's ideological trajectory'. In *Interpreting the Labour Party: Approaches to Labour Politics and History*, edited by John Callaghan, Steve Fielding and Steve Ludlam, 8–22. Manchester: Manchester University Press.

Robinson, Geoffrey. 2019. 'Labor's election defeat reveals its continued inability to convince people it can make their lives better'. *The Conversation*, 20 May. theconversation.com/labors-election-defeat-reveals-its-continued-inability-to-convince-people-it-can-make-their-lives-better-117082.

Rundle, Guy. 2019. 'Labor's focus on "big ticket" rather than "big picture" is a problem'. *Crikey*, 1 May. www.crikey.com.au/2019/05/01/big-picture-not-big-ticket-labor/.

Stewart, Jenny. 2009. *Public Policy Values*. Basingstoke, UK: Palgrave Macmillan. doi.org/10.1057/9780230240759.

Uhlmann, Chris. 2019. 'A brutally effective campaign ruthlessly exploited Labor's mistakes'. *Sydney Morning Herald*, 21 May.

Williams, Pamela. 2019. 'Knives out as wounded ALP looks for who's to blame'. *Australian Financial Review*, 23 May.

14

THE LIBERAL PARTY

Nicholas Barry

The Liberal Party entered the 2019 election campaign in a similar position to 2016. Its previous three years in office had been characterised by internal instability, ideological conflicts, policy stagnation and, ultimately, a change in leadership, with Scott Morrison replacing Malcom Turnbull as prime minister. Such instability normally suggests a government heading to electoral defeat and this was reflected in polling that consistently showed Labor leading the two-party-preferred vote, albeit by a relatively small margin. As a result, many political commentators were surprised on election night when the Coalition was returned to office, with the Prime Minister himself declaring he had 'always believed in miracles'.

This chapter analyses the Liberal campaign in 2019 and explores its broader implications for the Liberal Party's ideological and organisational direction. After a brief summary of voting patterns, the first section analyses the key features of the party's campaign strategy, comparing it with the 2016 campaign. It argues that, although both campaigns were light on policy detail, the 2019 campaign was more negative in its orientation, made greater use of online campaigning and was more in keeping with traditional Liberal campaign themes. The second section focuses on party organisation. It argues that there was a significant shift in the lead-up to the campaign as sitting Liberal MPs publicly criticised the underrepresentation of women within the party and called for the introduction of quotas. It seems unlikely, however, that major reform will occur in this area in the foreseeable future given the hostility to quotas and feminism within powerful sections of the party. This section also examines disputes over the preselection process in New South Wales in the lead-up to the 2019 campaign, arguing that it illustrates how difficult it is to democratise internal party processes. The third section of the chapter focuses on party ideology. Although some thought the Liberals would lose safe seats to moderate Independents in 2019, this occurred only in the seat of Warringah. Instead, the likely effect of the election was to reinforce the conservative ascendancy within the Liberal Party.

The 2019 campaign

Although the election result was widely described as a disaster for Labor, in terms of seat share, the overall picture throughout the country was one of relative stability. The Liberals gained four seats and the LNP gained two. Three of the Liberal gains and the two LNP gains were from Labor. The Liberals also won a seat previously held by an Independent. It was a similar story in terms of the Liberal Party's primary vote. According to the AEC, the party's share of the primary vote declined by around 2 per cent in Victoria and Western Australia, while there was a small increase of around 0.5 per cent in Queensland. The largest gain was in South Australia, where the Liberals achieved a 5.5 per cent increase as a result of the 16.9 per cent decline in the Centre Alliance vote. As discussed elsewhere in this volume, the capacity of the Liberals to retain and win marginal seats in Queensland and Tasmania was crucial to the outcome of the election, and it is likely this was partly a result of a significant increase in support for right-wing populist parties.

One of the major similarities between the 2016 and 2019 Liberal campaigns was the absence of major policy announcements. Turnbull's 2016 campaign focused strongly on corporate tax cuts that were set out in the 2016 federal Budget, and it featured few other major policies (Barry 2018: 278). Similarly, tax cuts announced in the 2019 federal Budget—handed down shortly before Morrison called the election—were key to the Morrison campaign. However, the 2019 Budget focused on income tax cuts, including a cash rebate of $1,080–$1,215 for workers earning $50,000–$90,000, targeting a group that received little from the 2016 Budget (Murphy 2019a). It also entailed a medium-term flattening of the income tax system, so those with yearly incomes of $45,000–$200,000 will pay a marginal tax rate of 30 per cent from 2024 (Karp 2019a), and $100 billion of infrastructure spending over the next 10 years, focusing particularly on transport (Chan 2019). The large corporate tax cuts the government had previously supported were put aside (see Chapter 5, this volume).

One of the major internal criticisms of the 2016 Liberal campaign was that it was not negative enough (see Barry 2018: 280). In contrast, attacks on the trustworthiness of Opposition leader Bill Shorten and Labor's record on economic management were central to the 2019 campaign, and a major focus of Liberal campaign advertising. Labor's relatively detailed set of policy announcements, particularly its policies on negative gearing and dividend imputation, were particular targets for criticism. Multiple advertisements used the slogan 'Labor: It's the Bill Australia can't afford' (Liberal Party of Australia 2019a, 2019b), while others described Shorten as 'the greatest risk to Australia's economy in a generation' (Liberal Party of Australia 2019b). Mills (Chapter 23, this volume) suggests that aspects of the Liberal campaign in fact went beyond a merely negative campaign and became, instead, a scare campaign using misleading language such as 'retiree tax'. Liberal advertising also falsely claimed that Labor was planning to reintroduce a 'death tax'—a claim that was widely shared through social media (Murphy et al. 2019).

Another major difference between the 2016 and 2019 elections was the Liberal Party's capacity to engage in more effective online campaigning. One of the major criticisms of the 2016 campaign was that the party was lagging well behind Labor in this area (for example, Meers 2016; Barry 2018). However, this changed in 2019, with the Liberals running a more organised and sophisticated social media campaign. Reports suggest there were significantly higher levels of engagement with the Liberal Party's Facebook page and Scott Morrison's Instagram account than with Labor's Facebook page and Shorten's Instagram account (Bourke 2019). The videos posted on the Liberal Facebook site also received a much higher number of views than Labor's. There were 17,630,800 views of Liberal Facebook videos, while Labor Facebook videos were viewed only 5,940,500 times (Carson and Zion, Chapter 22, this volume; Knaus 2019).

The rise of online campaigning also led to concerns about the integrity of the campaign. The Liberal Party benefited from Facebook posts that falsely claimed Labor was planning to introduce an inheritance tax, although the posts were unauthorised and the Liberals denied they were responsible for them (Wroe 2019). Similarly, Liberal supporters used WeChat to target campaign messages at the Chinese community, spreading false information about Labor policies, with claims that Labor would increase the intake of refugees to 320,000 in 10 years and that 'this group of refugees will surpass Australia's entire Chinese immigrant population, and there will be more in the coming years and taxpayers will have to pay for it' (Zong, cited in Karp 2019b). Another message falsely claimed that Labor would extend the Safe Schools program to all schools around Australia and that the aim of the program was 'to teach students same sex sexual intercourse' and 'that the following vocabulary cannot be used: dad, mum, older brother, younger brother, older sister, younger sister, uncle, aunt, boy, girl, pregnant, and other gendered words' (Tomazin and Zhuang 2019). Although there is no indication the Liberal Party was officially involved in this campaign, the Liberal candidate (and now Member) for Chisholm, Gladys Liu, ran a similar campaign against Safe Schools on WeChat in 2016 when she chaired the Victorian Liberal Party's communities engagement committee (Hendrie 2016; Zhuang and Tomazin 2019).

Another notable feature of the 2019 campaign was the emergence of Advance Australia, a conservative response to left-wing activist organisation GetUp!. According to its website, Advance Australia 'is not a political party or aligned to any political organisation', but it is led by Gerard Benedet, who was previously a Liberal staffer (Seo 2019). Two of the four major campaign issues listed on its website were targeted at Labor policies (on dividend imputation and emissions reduction). Its two other areas of focus were also issues that were major concerns of the Liberal Party's conservative wing—preventing Australia Day being shifted from 26 January and changing Section 18C of the *Racial Discrimination Act*—while four of the five MPs it targeted for support during the 2019 campaign were conservative Liberals (Koslowski 2019). The emergence of this organisation is potentially significant because one of the Liberal Party's longstanding concerns—repeated in the aftermath of the 2016 campaign—was its weak capacity for on-the-ground campaigning (Brett 2003; Barry 2018), and the emergence of Advance Australia potentially helps address this deficit. Although the organisation was ultimately unsuccessful in one of its chief aims—to help Tony Abbott retain his seat of Warringah (Koslowski 2019)—Advance Australia reportedly attracted 32,000 members in its first six months and $1.2 million in donations (Seo 2019). Its website also lists a number of wealthy backers on its advisory council, including Maurice Newman and Sam Kennard, so it is not impossible that it could become a significant campaign presence in the future. However, it is too early to reach any firm conclusions about what, if any, impact it will have in the long term.

Although the Liberal campaign in 2019 departed in significant ways from its 2016 campaign, it is also important to note that some of the key themes were in keeping with a much longer Liberal tradition. In her work on the Liberal Party, Judith Brett (1992, 2003) has identified a continuous strand running through the rhetoric of the party and its prewar non-Labor predecessors. The rhetorical strategy is to identify the Labor Party with class war and sectional interests, while positioning the Liberal Party as the party that is about the national interest and/or the interests of hardworking 'mainstream' Australia. Brett has argued that, in the postwar period, the foremost Liberal exponents of this approach were Robert Menzies, with his emphasis on the 'Forgotten People', and more recently, John Howard, who was 'able to adapt the language and thinking carried in his party's political traditions to the circumstances of his political present' (Brett 2003: 184).

Although Morrison did not exhibit Menzies's or Howard's creative use of language, he did draw on themes that were in line with this longstanding Liberal tradition. In fact, the speech he gave at the Liberal Party campaign launch had striking similarities with the kind of language Menzies, Howard and others had used. Morrison emphasised that the Liberal Party stood for aspiration and the 'promise of Australia' in contrast to Labor's 'politics of envy'. His speech was filled with references to the importance of the family, the home and hard work, framed around Morrison's own family and experiences:

> Mum is a woman of great and practical faith, quietly and patiently loving us, always. Life is about what you contribute, not what you accumulate. That's what mum and dad have taught me. It's about serving others, because in life, it's people that matter.
>
> My family story is not uncommon in our country. Australians quietly going about their lives with simple, decent, honest aspirations. Get an education. Get a job. Start a business. Take responsibility for yourself, support others. Work hard. Deal with whatever challenges come your way. Meet someone amazing. I did, there she is, Jenny. Create a life and a family together. Work even harder to support them and give them the choices and hopefully, an even better life than the one that you have. Save for your retirement and your future. Strive, wherever possible, to be making a contribution rather than taking one. Leaving a legacy. (Morrison 2019)

There are parallels here with Menzies's 'Forgotten People' speech. Alongside the emphasis on the family (and, by implication, the home), there is a clear emphasis on moral values, reflecting the longstanding Liberal belief that 'the middle-class ... is not just an economic class but a moral category whose members are defined by their political values, social attitudes and moral qualities as much as by their social and economic position' (Brett 1992: 41). This is reflected in the emphasis on contributing and not accumulating, saving for the future (cf. Brett 1992: 59–60) and leaving a better life for one's children. It is also a (presumably deliberate) attempt to distance the Liberals from Turnbull's emphasis on Australia as 'a nation that is agile, that is innovative, that is creative' (Turnbull and Bishop 2015), which has connotations of entrepreneurial activity and constant change in a digital economy.

In his victory speech on election night, Morrison emphasised that his election win was for the 'quiet Australians'. Although this was probably an attempt to draw a line between his prime ministership and the perceived rancour and leadership instability that had characterised Australian politics since 2007 (Murphy 2019b), there was an obvious similarity to Menzies's phrase 'the Forgotten People'. Thus, the 2019 campaign represented a return to some longstanding themes of Liberal campaigns in Australia, which was perhaps a reflection of Labor's renewed engagement with traditional issues of class and material inequality.

Party organisation and the 2019 election

The 2019 election also drew attention to a number of organisational issues confronting the Liberal Party. In particular, one of the marked features of the lead-up to the 2019 campaign was greater public discussion of the underrepresentation of women in the party. This issue had attracted some attention in the 2016 campaign because the number of women Liberal MPs was the lowest it had been since 1993 (Norman 2018a; see also Barry 2018: 285). However, at that time, few sitting federal MPs were prepared to comment publicly on the issue. In the lead-up to the 2019 election, this changed, with Liberal senators Jane Hume and Linda Reynolds and MPs Melissa Price and Julia Banks publicly drawing attention to the problem (Norman 2018a).

The push for change gained further impetus following the leadership spill that resulted in Turnbull being replaced as prime minister. Many political commentators thought Morrison was less qualified for the job than foreign minister Julie Bishop, who was an experienced and popular politician, and they drew links between this and the Liberal Party's underrepresentation of women. Moreover, a number of women within the Liberal Party, including Senator Lucy Gichuhi and Julia Banks, publicly alleged that supporters of leadership candidate Peter Dutton had engaged in forms of bullying and intimidation during the leadership dispute (Yaxley 2018). Minister for Women Kelly O'Dwyer supported these claims, commenting that 'it is clear to me that people were subjected to threats and intimidation and bullying' (Norman 2018b).

One of the Liberal Party's leading internal critics, Julia Banks, the Member for Chisholm, decided to quit the Liberals following the leadership change and sit as an Independent. In her speech to the parliament announcing this decision, Banks stated:

> Equal representation of men and women in this parliament is an urgent imperative which will create a culture change. There's the blinkered rejection of quotas and support of the merit myth, but this is more than a numbers game. Across both major parties, the level of regard and respect for women in politics is years behind the business world. There is also a clear need for an independent whistleblower system, as found in many workplaces, to enable reporting of misconduct of those in power without fear of reprisal or retribution. Often when good women call out or are subjected to bad behaviour, the reprisals, backlash and commentary portray them as the bad ones: the liar, the troublemaker, the emotionally unstable or weak, or someone who should be silenced. (Banks, in Commonwealth Parliament of Australia 2018)

In this way, Banks drew attention to the effect of the culture and behaviour within the parliament on female underrepresentation, while calling for the introduction of quotas to bring about more equal representation. Liberal frontbencher Sussan Ley also suggested this was a reform that should be considered (Murphy 2018). This is particularly notable as Ley became Minister for the Environment following the election, which means that, for the first time in recent memory, there is a sitting federal Liberal frontbencher who has seriously raised the prospect of introducing quotas.

There is substantial evidence that quotas are an effective way of addressing a gender imbalance in the representation of MPs (Baird and Bold 2019). However, the idea of affirmative action underlying quotas sits uneasily with Liberal Party ideology, as affirmative action reflects an acknowledgement that structural inequalities have played a role in generating the underrepresentation of women. Acknowledging this fact sits uneasily with both neoliberalism, with its emphasis on individuals competing in an unfettered free market, and conservatism, which is hostile to feminism and opposed to forms of intervention that challenge existing hierarchies. It is perhaps unsurprising that other parties on the right around the world tend to have a problem with the representation of women. For example, after the May 2019 elections for the European Parliament, all parties on the left and centre-left had at least 40 per cent female representation (Politico 2019). In contrast, most parties on the right and centre-right had female representation rates of less than 30 per cent (the exception was the Europe of Freedom and Direct Democracy group, which had 40.48 per cent). Given the broader ideological context, and the fact Morrison has explicitly rejected calls for quotas (SBS 2018), it is hard to imagine any significant action on this issue occurring in the next three years. Nonetheless, recent events suggest influential women within the Liberal Party are becoming increasingly concerned about underrepresentation and are prepared to publicly call for reform.

Another ongoing organisational issue for the Liberal Party relates to preselection. Over the past 10 years, the party has faced criticism, particularly in its NSW division, for a lack of democracy in the preselection process (Staley 2008: 23; Reith 2011: 23; Barry 2018: 161, 163–64). In the wake of the 2016 election, there was a strong push to adopt proper membership plebiscites for preselections in the NSW division, as recommended by a 2014 review led by former prime minister John Howard (Nicholls 2014). This culminated in the 'Warringah motion', which proposed the adoption of a 'one-vote, one-member approach' to membership involvement in preselections (McNally 2018). This motion was initiated by the Warringah branch of the party and backed by former prime minister and member for Warringah Tony Abbott (Chan 2017). The motion was passed with the support of 61 per cent of delegates attending the NSW Liberal Futures convention, which was a special convention held in 2017 to discuss preselection reforms (Knaus and Chan 2017). However, it was subsequently rejected at the annual general meeting of the NSW division in 2018, which instead endorsed the 'Bennelong motion', which was a 'watered-down' alternative that gave party members the ability to preselect candidates while leaving 'around 10 per cent of the preselection vote' with the party hierarchy (McNally 2018).

This shows how difficult it is to achieve internal party organisational reform, particularly if the reforms in question involve a 'democratising' of internal party processes. The problem is that it is difficult to achieve reform without winning agreement from those wielding power within the party under the existing structures. Because existing powerbrokers generally benefit from preserving the status quo, they are likely to be reluctant to embrace reform (see Coghlan and Denton 2012; Gauja 2012, 2017; Miragliotta 2013; Barry 2015, 2018). This is partly reflected in the fate of the Warringah motion, which was largely being pushed by the party's right faction (which was likely to increase its power if preselection processes were democratised) and opposed by the moderate and centre-right factions, which currently wield most power within the NSW division (Nicholls 2017).[1] Nonetheless, the reform that occurred—even in its watered-down form—still had some significance, even if did not go as far as advocates of the Warringah motion desired. In the wake of the Bennelong motion being passed, Abbott, for example, stated: 'The Liberal Party is still too much of an insiders' club, but it's much less of an insiders' club than it was' (cited in McNally 2018). Ultimately, the reform contributed to the defeat of Senator Jim Molan at the 2019 election. Molan, who was actually a supporter of party democratisation, ended up being preselected for the unwinnable fourth position on the Coalition's NSW Senate ticket (Hunter and Loussikian 2018).

A final twist in the recent history of Liberal Party preselection reform in New South Wales was Scott Morrison's intervention to convince the State executive to cancel preselection votes in four seats so the sitting members were automatically re-endorsed (see Gauja and Taflaga, Chapter 4, this volume; Tillett 2018). The primary aim was to save conservative MP Craig Kelly, who was reportedly in danger of being dumped as the Liberal candidate for Hughes. Morrison's intervention was clearly against the spirit of party democratisation and it further illustrates how difficult it is to achieve meaningful reform. Even when watered-down measures such

---

1   As is often the case with internal party debates over organisational reform, there were other issues at play. In particular, the push for reform became entangled in the acrimony associated with the leadership dispute between Tony Abbott and Malcolm Turnbull (Chan 2017), while there were also concerns over potential branch-stacking (Nicholls 2017).

as the Bennelong motion are adopted, there will always be a temptation for State executive intervention to cancel preselections or overturn decisions made at the local level, particularly when the authority of the parliamentary leader is at stake.

Party ideology

The 2019 election result also has important implications for the ideological direction of the Liberal Party and its place in the party system. The major points of disagreement within the Liberals are not over economic policy, where there is support for a broadly neoliberal approach, but over social and environmental issues.[2] When Turnbull took the party leadership from Abbott in the lead-up to the 2016 campaign, some believed this would mean a change in the ideological direction of the party as Turnbull had more progressive views on social and environmental issues than Abbott and many other Liberal MPs. However, from the outset of his prime ministership, Turnbull was constrained by internal forces within the Coalition. To win the leadership and become prime minister, he made agreements with conservative Liberal MPs and the Nationals to retain Abbott's proposed plebiscite on same-sex marriage, rather than have a vote on the issue in parliament (Hartcher 2019b). Ultimately, the catalyst for the end of his prime ministership was climate change policy, which also ended his time as Opposition leader in 2009. Turnbull's energy policy, the NEG, aimed to bring about a 26 per cent cut in carbon emissions by 2030 (Knaus 2018). Although a majority of the party room supported the policy, Abbott and a number of other conservative MPs threatened to cross the floor on the Bill. As a result, Turnbull dropped the reduction target from the NEG; however, this was not enough to save him from being deposed as prime minister following a leadership challenge led by conservative MPs.

---

2   There is not space in this chapter for a detailed account of what is meant by the terms 'conservative' and 'progressive'. However, in brief, a conservative in this context refers to an MP who wants to preserve cultural traditions (or, more accurately, their perception of a particular set of cultural traditions) against the demands of those who are pushing for 'progressive' reforms. The 'progressives' are generally aiming for social reforms that improve the status of disadvantaged and oppressed minorities and environmental reforms aimed at reducing carbon emissions and promoting environmental sustainability. In recent times, core issues of division within the Liberal Party (and beyond) have occurred over issues such as marriage equality, the *Racial Discrimination Act* and climate change, which have pitted conservative MPs against 'moderate' MPs who are somewhat more progressive on social and environmental issues.

The constraints Turnbull faced as Liberal leader and the fact he was replaced with the more ideologically conservative Morrison clearly illustrated the ascendancy of conservative forces within the Liberal Party on social and environmental issues. In light of this, some commentators (for example, Hartcher 2019a) thought this might give Independent candidates more of a chance to win some blue-ribbon Liberal seats where voters were economically conservative but more progressive on social and environmental issues. The Wentworth by-election, triggered by Turnbull's resignation from parliament, reinforced this belief, with former Australian Medical Association president Kerryn Phelps winning the safe Liberal seat as an Independent, running on a campaign that emphasised the importance of action on climate change. With a number of high-profile socially progressive but economically conservative Independents running in similar seats around the country—including Zali Steggall in Warringah, Oliver Yates in Kooyong and ex-Liberal MP Julia Banks in Flinders—and the loss of Indi to Cathy McGowan in 2013 and Mayo to NXT candidate Rebekha Sharkie in 2016 (Hartcher 2019a), it seemed possible that the Liberal Party was facing the defection of more moderate voters who were alienated by the conservative direction of the party, particularly on environmental issues.[3]

The election did not, however, ultimately result in an influx of progressive Independents in safe Liberal seats. Steggall won the seat of Warringah from Abbott, who experienced a 12.64 per cent decline in his first-preference vote, and there were significant results in the formerly safe Liberal seats of Indi (where Independent candidate Helen Haines replaced the retiring McGowan) and Mayo (where Sharkie was returned, now for the Centre Alliance). However, sizeable swings in other seats did not result in victory for progressive Independent candidates. For example, an 8.24 per cent decline in the Liberals' first-preference vote in Kooyong did not result in victory for Yates, while Phelps was defeated by Dave Sharma in Wentworth, despite a 14.82 per cent fall in the Liberal first-preference vote (compared with the 2016 election). Overall, the results of the 2019 election do not demonstrate an imminent threat to the Liberal Party from progressive Independents in blue-ribbon seats. However, the rise of high-profile challengers, the fall in the Liberal first-preference vote in some of

---

3   Although she was not as strongly supportive of action on climate change as some of the other Independents, Louise Stewart in Curtin could possibly be added to this list, as could the Greens candidate in Kooyong, Julian Burnside—a high-profile barrister and campaigner for a more humanitarian approach to refugee policy.

these seats, the loss of Warringah and the likelihood that climate change will become an increasingly salient issue in future campaigns do suggest there is potential for change in the near future.

Because the Liberals went to the 2019 election with relatively few major policy commitments, it is unclear what their policy agenda for the next three years will be beyond the income tax cuts and transport spending announced in the 2019 Budget. However, there are a number of reasons to think the party is likely to move further to the right. Having deposed the Liberal Party's most high-profile moderate, Malcolm Turnbull, as party leader and won an unexpected election victory under Morrison, conservative forces within the Liberal Party are likely to have been emboldened to pursue a conservative agenda. Adding to this is the retirement of other high-profile moderates such as Julie Bishop, Julia Banks and Kelly O'Dwyer. Combined with the importance of PHON and UAP preferences in deciding the election in key marginal seats, it seems likely that conservative forces will be in the ascendant.

Early indications seem to bear this out. There had been be a renewed push by some within the Liberal Party to amend Section 18C of the *Racial Discrimination Act* to remove the reference to speech that offends. This was one of the major issues on the agenda during the Abbott Government's first term, and it was also part of the election manifesto of the IPA that was sent to Coalition MPs in the lead-up to the 2019 election (Bennett, Chapter 21, this volume; Crowe 2019). On the issue of climate change, the collapse of the NEG left Australia in an unstable position on energy policy. Given this uncertainty has attracted the ire of business groups—which are one of the core Liberal constituencies—the Morrison Government is likely to face pressure to act on this issue. However, balanced against this is the political strength of the fossil fuel industry, opposition to major cuts in carbon emissions from conservative Liberal MPs, the fact climate change policy played a key role in the demise of three of Australia's past four prime ministers and Morrison's past support for coal.

Conclusion

Despite the internal instability and policy stagnation of its second term in office, the Coalition Government was returned for a third term on the back of a highly negative small-target strategy that made Labor's tax policies and leadership the main focus. The Liberal Party significantly improved its digital campaigning in 2019, but its attacks on Labor drew on longstanding themes in its own campaign history. Although there were some signs that 2019 might mark a shift in attitudes on the underrepresentation of women within the party and the start of a process of ideological fragmentation, ultimately, no significant change occurred in either direction. Considering the authority Prime Minister Scott Morrison is likely to wield within the party on the back of an election victory that was perceived to be a 'miracle', the ideological and organisational status quo seems likely to persist for at least another three years.

References

Baird, Julia and Sam Bold. 2019. 'Conservative parties around the world have a problem—and women are losing patience'. *ABC News*, 8 February. www.abc.net.au/news/2019-02-07/women-in-parliament-labor-liberal/10783234.

Barry, Nicholas. 2015. 'Party reviews and organisational reform'. In *Contemporary Australian Political Party Organisation*, edited by Narelle Miragliotta, Anika Gauja and Rodney Smith, 154–68. Melbourne: Monash University Press.

Barry, Nicholas. 2018. 'The Liberal campaign'. In *Double Disillusion: The 2016 Australian Federal Election*, edited by Anika Gauja, Peter Chen, Jennifer Curtin and Juliet Pietsch, 277–96. Canberra: ANU Press. doi.org/10.22459/dd.04.2018.12.

Bourke, Latika. 2019. 'How the Liberals beat Labor at its own game'. *Sydney Morning Herald*, 26 May. www.smh.com.au/federal-election-2019/how-the-liberals-beat-labor-at-its-own-game-20190523-p51qki.html.

Brett, Judith. 1992. *Robert Menzies' Forgotten People*. Sydney: Sun Australia.

Brett, Judith. 2003. *Australian Liberals and the Moral Middle Class*. Melbourne: Cambridge University Press. doi.org/10.1017/CBO9780511481642.

Chan, Gabrielle. 2017. 'Liberals warned party will split if NSW preselection reforms rejected'. *The Guardian*, 17 July. www.theguardian.com/australia-news/2017/jul/17/liberals-warned-party-will-split-if-nsw-preselection-reforms-rejected.

Chan, Gabrielle. 2019. 'Roads, rails and car parks get $100bn infrastructure spend in Australian budget—but over a decade'. *The Guardian*, 2 April. www.theguardian.com/australia-news/2019/apr/02/australia-federal-budget-2019-infrastructure-frydenberg-treasurer-budget.

Coghlan, Jo and Scott Denton. 2012. 'Reviewing Labor's Internal Reviews 1966–2010: Looking Forwards, Looking Backwards'. *Melbourne Journal of Politics* 35: 19–38.

Commonwealth Parliament of Australia [*Hansard*]. 2018. *House of Representatives Parliamentary Debates, Official Hansard*, 27 November, p. 11571.

Crowe, David. 2019. 'Coalition MPs urged to sell the ABC and support a flat tax in IPA call'. *Sydney Morning Herald*, 16 April. www.smh.com.au/federal-election-2019/coalition-mps-urged-to-sell-the-abc-and-support-a-flat-tax-in-ipa-call-20190416-p51enu.html.

Gauja, Anika. 2012. 'The "Push" for Primaries: What Drives Party Organisational Reform in Australia and the United Kingdom?'. *Australian Journal of Political Science* 47(4): 641–58. doi.org/10.1080/10361146.2012.731490.

Gauja, Anika. 2017. *Party Reform: The Causes, Challenges and Consequences of Organisational Change*. Oxford: Oxford University Press. doi.org/10.1093/acprof:oso/9780198717164.001.0001.

Hartcher, Peter. 2019a. 'How conservatives stole the Liberal Party'. *Sydney Morning Herald*, 2 February. www.smh.com.au/national/how-conservatives-stole-the-liberal-party-20190201-p50v6i.html.

Hartcher, Peter. 2019b. '"He sold everything he believed in": The price Turnbull paid to become prime minister'. *Sydney Morning Herald*, 28 March. www.smh.com.au/politics/federal/he-sold-everything-he-believed-in-the-price-turnbull-paid-to-become-prime-minister-20190321-p516ad.html.

Hendrie, Doug. 2016. 'How a Chinese-language social media campaign hurt Labor's chances'. *The Guardian*, 9 July. www.theguardian.com/australia-news/2016/jul/09/how-a-chinese-language-social-media-campaign-hurt-labors-election-chances.

Hunter, Fergus and Kylar Loussikian. 2018. 'Surprise Liberal pre-selection result spells end of Jim Molan's Senate career'. *Sydney Morning Herald*, 24 November. www.smh.com.au/politics/federal/surprise-liberal-preselection-result-spells-end-of-jim-molan-s-senate-career-20181124-p50i3t.html.

Karp, Paul. 2019a. 'Coalition budget woos low and middle-income earners with $19.5bn tax cuts'. *The Guardian*, 2 April. www.theguardian.com/australia-news/2019/apr/02/coalition-federal-budget-2019-woos-low-and-middle-income-earners-with-195bn-tax-cuts-in-budget.

Karp, Paul. 2019b. 'Penny Wong blasts "malicious" WeChat campaign spreading fake news about Labor'. *The Guardian*, 7 May. www.theguardian.com/australia-news/2019/may/07/penny-wong-blasts-malicious-wechat-campaign-spreading-fake-news-about-labor.

Knaus, Christopher. 2018. 'Australian PM dumps key climate policy to stave off leadership revolt'. *The Guardian*, 20 August. www.theguardian.com/australia-news/2018/aug/20/australian-pm-dumps-key-climate-policy-to-stave-off-leadership-revolt.

Knaus, Christopher. 2019. 'Liberal Party also beat Labor on Facebook in 2019 Australian federal election'. *The Guardian*, 4 June. www.theguardian.com/australia-news/2019/jun/04/liberal-party-also-beat-labor-on-facebook-in-2019-australian-federal-election.

Knaus, Christopher and Gabrielle Chan. 2017. 'Tony Abbott–backed motion for NSW Liberal preselections wins party support'. *The Guardian*, 23 July. www.theguardian.com/australia-news/2017/jul/23/tony-abbott-backed-motion-for-nsw-liberal-preselections-wins-party-support.

Koslowski, Max. 2019. 'Advance Australia, the conservative GetUp!, comes to Tony Abbott's rescue'. *Sydney Morning Herald*, 13 March. www.smh.com.au/politics/federal/advance-australia-the-conservative-getup-comes-to-tony-abbott-s-rescue-20190312-p513ht.html.

Liberal Party of Australia. 2019a. 'The Bill Australia Can't Afford'. *YouTube*, 15 April. www.youtube.com/watch?v=i5saOqqjTs0.

Liberal Party of Australia. 2019b. 'The Bill Australia Can't Afford'. *YouTube*, 22 April. www.youtube.com/watch?v=F_1a1KoYi-U.

McNally, Lucy. 2018. 'Tony Abbott's Warringah motion for more conservative control in NSW Liberals fails to pass'. *ABC News*, 11 February. www.abc.net.au/news/2018-02-10/warringah-motion-fails-to-pass/9419172.

Meers, Daniel. 2016. 'Angry Tasmanian Senator Eric Abetz takes aim at Coalition election campaign'. *Mercury*, [Hobart], 15 July. www.news.com.au/national/federal-election/angry-tasmanian-senator-ericabetz-takes-aim-at-coalition-election-campaign/news-story/4c3982ff4f91c125a83b3e326a38474e.

Miragliotta, Narelle. 2013. 'Explaining the (Lack of) Use of Radical Candidate Selection Methods by Australia's Major Parties'. *Australian Journal of Politics and History* 59(1): 113–26. doi.org/10.1111/ajph.12007.

Morrison, Scott. 2019. 'Coalition campaign launch, [Speech], 12 May'. Canberra: Liberal Party of Australia. www.liberal.org.au/latest-news/2019/05/12/coalition-campaign-launch.

Murphy, Katharine. 2018. 'Liberal Party should consider quotas for female MPs, Sussan Ley says'. *The Guardian*, 6 September. www.theguardian.com/australia-news/2018/sep/06/liberal-party-should-consider-quotas-for-female-mps-sussan-ley-says.

Murphy, Katharine. 2019a. 'Budget 2019: Scott Morrison breaks with past budget catastrophes in bid to save his skin'. *The Guardian*, 2 April. www.theguardian.com/australia-news/2019/apr/02/australia-federal-budget-2019-scott-morrison-election-josh-frydenberg-coalition-labor.

Murphy, Katharine. 2019b. 'Scott Morrison won the unwinnable election. Now the hard part begins'. *The Guardian*, 22 May. www.theguardian.com/australia-news/2019/may/22/scott-morrison-won-the-unwinnable-election-now-the-hard-part-begins.

Murphy, Katharine, Christopher Knaus and Nick Evershed. 2019. '"It felt like a big tide": How the death tax lie infected Australia's election campaign'. *The Guardian*, 8 June. www.theguardian.com/australia-news/2019/jun/08/it-felt-like-a-big-tide-how-the-death-tax-lie-infected-australias-election-campaign.

Nicholls, Sean. 2014. 'Former prime minister John Howard backs democratic reform of NSW Liberal Party'. *Sydney Morning Herald*, 23 July. www.smh.com.au/national/nsw/former-prime-minister-john-howard-backs-democratic-reform-of-nsw-liberal-party-20140723-zvyvk.html.

Nicholls, Sean. 2017. 'More than $13,000 spent on member registrations in bid to "buy" the Liberal Party'. *Sydney Morning Herald*, 20 July. www.smh.com.au/national/nsw/more-than-13000-spent-on-member-registrations-in-bid-to-buy-the-liberal-party-20170720-gxf9jz.html.

Norman, Jane. 2018a. 'Liberals' lack of female representation is costing them votes, so senior women are speaking out'. *ABC News*, 27 February. www.abc.net.au/news/2017-11-27/liberal-party-lack-of-women-costing-votes/9175150.

Norman, Jane. 2018b. 'Peter Dutton's backers refused to leave Liberal Party members' offices, demanded they reveal votes during spill'. *ABC News*, 7 September. www.abc.net.au/news/2018-09-07/nasty-tactics-dutton-backers-liberal-spill-revealed/10212110.

Politico. 2019. 'The European Parliament's gender gap'. *Politico*, 20 April. www.politico.eu/interactive/share-of-women-meps-by-political-group-and-country/.

Reith, Peter. 2011. *Review of the 2010 Federal Election*. Canberra: Parliament of Australia. parlinfo.aph.gov.au/parlInfo/search/display/display.w3p;query=Id%3A%22library%2Fpartypol%2F934846%22.

Seo, Bo. 2019. 'GetUp and Advance Australia go head-to-head'. *Australian Financial Review*, 23 April. www.afr.com/news/politics/national/getup-and-advance-australia-go-head-to-head-20190418-p51fb3.

Special Broadcasting Service (SBS). 2018. 'Morrison rejects gender quotas to boost female numbers'. *SBS News*, 11 September. www.sbs.com.au/news/morrison-rejects-gender-quotas-to-boost-female-numbers.

Staley, Tony. 2008. *Review of the 2007 Federal Election Campaign & Review of the Liberal Party Federal Constitution*. Canberra: Liberal Party of Australia.

Tillett, Andrew. 2018. 'Scott Morrison's ugly win shuts down Malcolm Turnbull support for dumping Craig Kelly'. *Australian Financial Review*, 3 December. www.afr.com/news/politics/scott-morrisons-ugly-win-shuts-down-malcolm-turnbull-support-for-dumping-craig-kelly-20181203-h18nxt.

Tomazin, Farrah and Yan Zhuang. 2019. 'Safe Schools scare campaign targets Chinese-Australian voters'. *Sydney Morning Herald*, 27 April. www.smh.com.au/federal-election-2019/safe-schools-scare-campaign-targets-chinese-australian-voters-20190427-p51hrk.html.

Turnbull, Malcolm and Julie Bishop. 2015. 'Vote on the Liberal Party leadership, Press conference, Parliament House, Canberra, 15 September'. [Transcript]. www.malcolmturnbull.com.au/media/transcript-vote-on-the-liberal-party-leadership.

Wroe, David. 2019. 'Labor demands Facebook remove "fake news" posts about false death tax plans'. *Sydney Morning Herald*, 19 April. www.smh.com.au/federal-election-2019/labor-demands-facebook-remove-fake-news-posts-about-false-death-tax-plans-20190419-p51fpk.html.

Yaxley, Louise. 2018. 'Liberal Party grappling with how to boost number of women in federal parliament'. *ABC News*, 11 September. www.abc.net.au/news/2018-09-11/liberal-women-quotas/10230298.

Zhuang, Yan and Farrah Tomazin. 2019. 'Labor asks questions of WeChat over doctored accounts, "fake news"'. *Sydney Morning Herald*, 6 May. www.smh.com.au/national/labor-asks-questions-of-wechat-over-doctored-accounts-fake-news-20190506-p51kkj.html.

15

THE NATIONAL PARTY OF AUSTRALIA

Geoff Cockfield

By early 2019, the Nationals looked set to lose ground in the forthcoming election. There were the usual problems of shrinking rurality in electorates along the eastern mainland coast and impending competition from minor parties, Independents and, in some regions, the Liberals. The Coalition was lagging in the opinion polls and the Nationals had struggled to articulate positions for—and in some cases develop substantial policies on—some key rural issues such as water allocations, mining developments, migration and the state of the dairy industry. More unusually, the federal Nationals were also in the mainstream news with three federal parliamentary members subject to scrutiny and ridicule for their personal behaviour, an unplanned leadership change, talk of further leadership challenges and pre-election criticisms of Coalition policy by Nationals' candidates.

Yet, in the national election, the Nationals held all their House of Representatives seats and even increased their hold on the most marginal seats. The aim of this chapter is to try to explain this, considering the focuses of the campaign, strategies around preferences and policy issues and what the party represented to rural and regional voters. In summary, the Nationals were able to restore some internal stability prior to the election, concentrate resources and messaging on the seats they held and do advantageous preference deals. The result demonstrated that the Nationals, and perhaps the Coalition more generally, can have a degree of dysfunction and a limited policy agenda and still attract sufficient votes to be in government, provided they seem to represent particular values and positions.

The candidates

The Nationals contested 29 House of Representatives seats—close to the same number as in 2016. Through the Queensland Liberal National Party (LNP), there were seven 'Nationals'[1] candidates running in winnable seats, with six of those successful. The Victorian party also concentrated its efforts, contesting only four seats (for three wins). The Nationals did not run candidates in the Labor-held seats of McEwen (peri-urban), Ballarat and Bendigo (based on regional cities), as they had in 2016.[2] In New South Wales for this election, the State party was slightly more aggressive and competed with the Liberals for the regional seats of Gilmore and Eden-Monaro. The Nationals had not contested Gilmore for 40 years and the party has never held Eden-Monaro. The South Australian Nationals, a party that was revived in the 1960s after being extinguished through a merger in 1932, made a rare foray into the federal sphere, contesting the seat of Barker. The Tasmanian National Party returned to the federal arena for the first time since 1996. The State party was re-established in 2018, with candidates selected for three seats (Bass, Braddon and Lyons) and two others for the Senate for the 2019 election. In Western Australia, following concerted but unsuccessful attempts to re-establish a presence in the federal parliament in 2013 and 2016, the State Nationals scaled back their efforts in 2019, contesting only three seats (Durack, O'Connor and Pearce), covering the wheat belt and the northern and western remote areas.

As in recent elections, in 2019, the most common background of candidates was in small–medium regional businesses, with 25 of the 39 candidates (10 for the Senate) in this category. There were two candidates who could be considered primarily commercial farmers, with only Mark Coulton (Parkes) making it into parliament, though many more candidates had rural backgrounds and interests, including agricultural landholding. Both Nationals Leader Michael McCormack and Deputy Leader Bridget McKenzie are somewhat typical of the modern

---

1   LNP candidates, like those from the Country Liberal Party (CLP), affiliate with one or the other of the federal Coalition parties after an election, though intending allegiances are usually signalled during the campaign.
2   Under Coalition agreements in Victoria and New South Wales, either party may contest any seat where there is no sitting member recontesting. In reality, such contests are restricted to regional and rural electorates.

Nationals, having lived and worked in regional areas but being one or two generations removed from the farm. Despite this, or perhaps because of it, they are both great supporters of farming people and communities.

Less than 20 per cent of the candidates for lower house seats were women, with only two contesting winnable seats (Capricornia and Mallee). Michelle Landry increased her margin in Capricornia, while Anne Webster became the new member for Mallee. Webster was preselected for Mallee after the previous member, the married Andrew Broad, stepped aside after personal exchanges with a woman on an international 'dating' website made the news in early 2019 (Wroe and Crowe 2018). The Nationals continued to use Senate preselections to address their historical gender imbalance. In 2019, six of their 10 Senate candidates were women, with Susan McDonald from Queensland, Perin Davey from New South Wales and Sam McMahon from the Northern Territory elected, so that four of the Nationals' five post-election senators were women. Davey's campaign was somewhat disrupted by attempts to encourage below-the-line voting to elevate the chances of the fourth listed Liberal, Jim Molan. Had the Molan support campaign succeeded, the Nationals would have been without a senator in New South Wales, even though that State party is strongly coalitionist. After the election there were a record seven women in the 21-member federal party room. The Nationals continued with a woman Deputy Leader, Bridget McKenzie, who had followed from former NSW Senator Fiona Nash in that role.

The Nationals were at risk of losing support among rural and regional women because of the Broad story, former leader Barnaby Joyce's marital breakdown and relationship with a staffer (Livingston 2018) and a complaint of inappropriate behaviour against Joyce (Chan 2018). Joyce's situation led to him vacating the party's leadership in early 2018. Efforts to preselect more women were probably influenced by the need to clean up their image, but the Nationals may also have been recognising the importance of women in regional small business, farm businesses and community and industry organisations and more general social change.

Policies and the campaign

The Nationals entered the 2019 election trying to balance a number of politically difficult issues and some of these were addressed through campaign policy statements (see Table 15.1 for a summary of positions). First, while mining developments offer the prospect of regional jobs, there are many rural people opposed to them generally or in the particular. Despite some previous vacillation, the National Party ended the 2019 election campaign as a strong supporter of mining. There were two aspects to this: the Nationals held and continued to hold after the election the resources portfolio, under Senator Matt Canavan (from Queensland), which has a strong development focus; and, second, for many regional areas, especially in Queensland, mining investment is one of the few industries that offers the prospect of additional jobs. Nationals members in central Queensland seats (Capricornia, Herbert, Flynn and Dawson) made a proposed coalmining development by Indian company Adani and the related jobs a central issue (Murphy 2019a). Local campaign advertising highlighted Queensland Labor's and federal Labor's vacillations on support for the development, while candidates even welcomed the confrontations that came from a pre-election anti-Adani protest roadshow led by former Greens leader Bob Brown (Koziol 2019). These candidates and other members of the Queensland LNP staked out a more general pro-coal position, with some even implying just before the election that they would split from the Coalition unless the Cabinet committed to support and even fund a new coal-fired power station in north Queensland. Scott Morrison adroitly defused this with a promise to 'evaluate' the case (Coorey 2019).

Table 15.1 Summary of issues, Nationals campaign positions and Coalition policy positions

Issue	Nationals position	Coalition position
Adani (Carmichael) coalmine proposal	Full support and subsidies where needed	Accelerated approvals prior to the election
New coal-fired power stations	Prioritise a north Queensland facility and subsidise if needed#	Evaluate the feasibility
Murray–Darling Basin (MDB) water allocations	Prioritise agriculture in allocations Establish a national water grid	Extend regional development funding in MDB regions

Issue	Nationals position	Coalition position
Dairy industry	Mandatory code of conduct for processors Market information provision Energy-efficiency grants Grants for farmer cooperatives Australian Competition and Consumer Commission (ACCC) dairy specialist More money for ACCC agriculture unit	Same as Nationals
Migrant labour	Enable working visas for those in agriculture Regional migrant visas Overall reduction in migration	Same as Nationals
Small business	Lower taxes for small and medium-sized enterprises Protection from 'big' business* Marketing support* Women entrepreneur program*	Lower business taxes
Vegan farm protests	Increase penalties for property trespass Enforce restrictions on published farm information	Promised legislation (Foley 2019)

It was not clear whether or not all Nationals supported this.

* No detail, just general undertakings.

Source: Foley (2019); The Nationals (2019a, 2019b).

Second, the Murray–Darling Basin (MDB) Plan, which includes limiting water extractions, was also in the news, with allegations of fraudulent activities around government programs and reports of mass fish deaths (Davies 2019; Hamilton-Smith 2018). The Nationals wanted water policies that recognised 'the continued importance of agriculture' and included the building of more dams and the establishment of a national water grid under a statutory authority (The Nationals 2019a), which would be a major institutional change in Australia's federal system. In response to the fish deaths—and perhaps with the threat of the Shooters, Fishers and Farmers Party (SFFP) in mind[3]—there were a number of promises to support recreational fishing (The Nationals 2019a). On the other hand, the Nationals stayed well away from any flirtation with changes to gun laws in the wake of the mass shootings in Christchurch, New Zealand. Prior to the massacre, some Coalition State governments and individual members, including the Deputy Leader, Bridget McKenzie, had engaged with gun lobbyists and were pushing for the 'easing' of some legislative restrictions on certain types of guns (Patel 2016).

3   The SFFP won two seats from the Nationals in the NSW State election earlier in 2019.

Third, the Nationals have long struggled with what to do for farmers since the deregulation of commodity marketing support systems. The dairy industry was an election issue for the Nationals in 2016 and continuing low prices and drought made it evident that there had been little real policy change or impact since. For the 2019 election, the Nationals again supported a mandatory code of conduct—aimed largely at processors— and a range of other measures trying to influence prices in a market context (Table 15.1) (The Nationals 2019a).

A fourth policy dilemma for the Nationals is migration. They are generally nationalist and socially conservative but migrants and temporary workers are an increasingly important source of labour for agricultural industries and a potential source of more people in rural areas otherwise experiencing depopulation. For this election, the party supported 'multiculturalism', though with an emphasis on 'integration' and a proposal to encourage migrants to move to regional areas, but with the proviso that the focus would 'remain *firmly* on attracting skilled migrants' (The Nationals 2019b, emphasis added).

There were also some fundamental issues for the Nationals in the areas of small business and agriculture. There were general policy aspirations in support of small business (Table 15.1), but the centrepiece, and perhaps major Coalition policy, was tax cuts. For agriculture, there would be continued drought relief and promises about the benefits of forthcoming trade agreements. As with the Adani protests, a series of protests by vegan activists presented the Nationals with an opportunity to bolster their anti-post-materialist credentials, which played well in the regions. The animal welfare activism 'threat' would be addressed through increasing legal penalties (Table 15.1).

The overall approach for the campaign was for sitting members to focus on local concerns and agrarian and small business rhetoric and issues, supported by fearmongering about Labor and the Greens. Party Leader Michael McCormack spent much of his time in his electorate of Riverina, with two to three visits to central Queensland seats and one or two to Lyons and Braddon in Tasmania (Doran et al. 2019). He did not visit Western Australia, South Australia or the NSW north coast seat of Richmond, which was held by Labor but was a former Nationals stronghold. Scott Morrison was also active in visiting central Queensland—somewhat in contrast to the 2016 election, when Malcolm Turnbull's regional visits were limited and nearly always taken in tandem with Barnaby Joyce.

Joyce kept a low national profile during the campaign, focusing on his electorate of New England and the revived threat of Independent Tony Windsor. This suggests, with the exception of the Tasmanian visits, that the focus was overwhelmingly on the winnable seats.

Results

The Nationals held all their House of Representatives seats and retained five senators (AEC 2019). As usual, the proportion of seats exceeded the proportion of votes (Figure 15.1), reflecting the geographical concentration of support and the focus of campaigning on a limited number of electorates. The proportion of House of Representatives seats declined very slightly due to an additional seat (making 151) in the parliament since the previous election. The Senate result was a closer reflection of overall support, with the Nationals ending up with 6.5 per cent of senators—less than the proportion for the Greens.

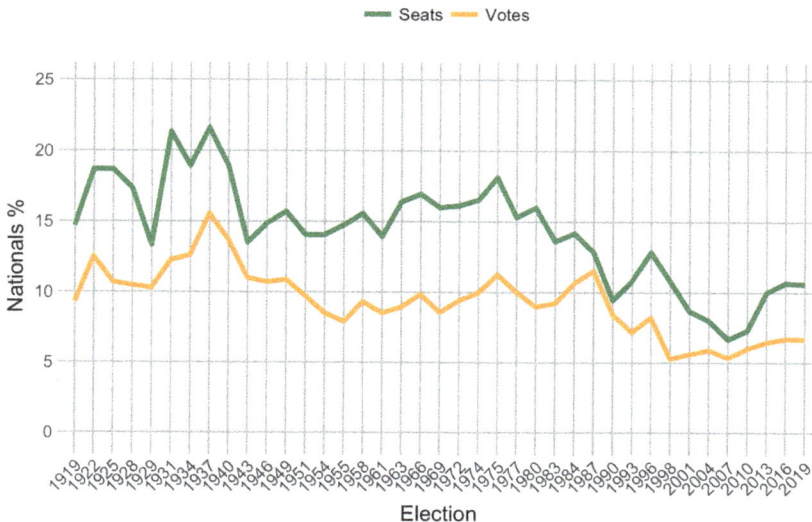

Figure 15.1 Country/National Party share of primary votes and seats for the House of Representatives at national elections

Note: LNP votes are divided between the Liberals and Nationals based on expected party alignment in Canberra, to analyse historical trends.

Sources: Adapted from UWA (various years); AEC (2019).

The Nationals increased both their primary and their two-party-preferred (TPP) vote in nine of the 16 seats they won (AEC 2019). They increased just the primary vote in two seats and just the TPP margins in another two. In line with the overall Queensland result for the Coalition (discussed in Chapter 11, this volume), the Nationals substantially increased the TPP gaps in the previously marginal central Queensland seats of Capricornia, Dawson and Flynn. Most surprising was the result for Dawson, given that sitting member, George Christensen, was yet another National in the media spotlight—in his case for spending substantial periods, including parliamentary business periods, over the previous four years in the Philippines (Wroe 2019).

The Nationals finished the election with no seats with margins of less than 6.5 per cent, with Anne Webster having the narrowest margin, though should she choose to run again, she will not have competition from the Liberals and should increase this with a 'sophomore surge' (first-term incumbency bonus). In New South Wales, the SFFP had little impact on the Nationals' final outcomes, since, of the western NSW seats, the SFFP only contested Calare, for less than 18 per cent of the vote, and in that seat the Nationals increased their TPP vote. Indeed, the flurry of activity of the minor parties, including PHON and the UAP, may have worked in favour of the Nationals. The Coalition arranged a preference deal with the UAP while the Nationals—differing from most of the Liberal preference deals—elevated PHON above Labor. McCormack, in an unusual burst of honesty on preferences, said the party needed to do what it took to win, though he also argued that PHON was closer to the Nationals on values and policies than were Labor or, especially, the Greens (Murphy 2019a). This rapprochement with PHON carried some risk given that, during the previous term of government, there had been attempts by 'alt-right' groups to infiltrate the NSW Nationals, which led to some hasty expulsions (McGowan 2018).

The results did, however, reaffirm that the federal Nationals are confined to the eastern grain, sugar and dairy zones, with parts of the sugar and dairy zones slipping from their grasp over time with peri-urban development. Outside the seats the Nationals already held, attempts at expansion were very unsuccessful. In New South Wales the Nationals received less than 13 per cent of the primary vote in Gilmore and less than 7 per cent in Eden-Monaro, leaving the Liberal Party with significant rural representation in southern New South Wales. In Indi, the Nationals' vote decreased significantly to 9.5 per cent, suggesting that if Independent

Helen Haines, successor to Cathy McGowan, is defeated at a future election, Indi will most likely return to the Liberals. Similarly, the Liberals are the dominant party in rural and remote South Australia, Tasmania and Western Australia. In Western Australia, the Nationals lost ground from the previous election in the three electorates they contested. For the Senate, the WA Nationals' vote share declined, with a quota well below that of PHON and below that for the Help End Marijuana Prohibition (HEMP) Party, as was also the case with the Tasmanian Nationals. For the Tasmanian electorates of Bass and Braddon, neither Nationals candidate received more than 3 per cent of the primary vote. In Lyons, Deanna Hutchinson won almost 16 per cent of the votes, but this was the electorate in which the Liberal candidate was disendorsed just before the election. In Barker (SA), Miles Hannemann won only 2.5 per cent of the vote. Thus, the 'revived' parties made little impression.

The results suggest that the only realistic intermediate prospect for expansion of the Nationals' footprint is Kennedy in Queensland. For the 2019 election, however, Bob Katter increased both his primary and his TPP votes, so regaining this seat for the Nationals looks set to hinge on the health and inclinations of the sitting member and perhaps the intentions of his son, Robbie Katter, who is a member of the Queensland Parliament. While three NSW coastal/rural seats all swung further to the Nationals, to the north in Richmond, the Nationals' primary vote decreased slightly and Labor's Justine Elliot slightly increased her margin, suggesting this seat is no longer in the Nationals' heartland (for an explanation of demographic change in this region, see Cockfield 2009).

Cabinet, Coalition and policy directions

Once again, the Liberal Party needed the Nationals to form government. There have been only three elections since 1922 in which the Liberals (or their predecessor parties) could have governed alone (for a full review, see Botterill and Cockfield 2015). Despite the pre-election dissension from some Queensland parliamentarians (Clarke 2019), the Coalition parties had a reasonably harmonious campaign. The two leaders worked well together, and Scott Morrison was quite popular in regional areas. Post election, all indications are that the Nationals will settle into a collaborative approach under McCormack. There were at least two threats to a collaborative Coalition. First, Joyce remained in the party room and, prior to the election, indicated his interest in a return to the leadership (Crowe 2019). His style—in contrast to recent leaders such as John Anderson, Tim Fischer, Mark Vaile and probably McCormack—was to be more combative and openly independent within the Coalition.

Second, and related to Joyce's leadership ambitions, the Queensland Nationals MPs may be emboldened to engage in further bouts of 'independence', with, for example, some wanting to start debates about enabling nuclear power in Australia (Murphy 2019b), which could be politically risky for the Coalition. This may be part of a more general problem for the Coalition, with an assertive Queensland LNP developing its own agendas, rather than just feeding into the two Coalition parties at the federal level. While the LNP has not yet proved a successful party in terms of longevity in office at the State level, it is the dominant party in Queensland federally, holding more than two-thirds of Queensland's House of Representatives seats after the 2019 election.

Against that, Morrison is likely to have considerable authority within the joint party room, given his central role in the Coalition campaign, and McCormack is likely to favour quiet negotiation over flourishes of independence. Furthermore, the case for Joyce's return to the leadership may have been diminished by the election result. Joyce was not given a post-election ministerial position and did not even retain his role as drought envoy; and other possible leadership contenders, such as David Littleproud (Maranoa), who did become Deputy Leader when McKenzie stepped down in early 2020, were waiting in the wings, so a resurrection might not be a simple matter.

The Nationals have one less member of Cabinet, though they gained an additional outer ministry. Trade—so often in the past a portfolio of the Country (then National) Party—remains with the Liberals, however, the Nationals have water resources, as part of an omnibus portfolio, as well as infrastructure, which is a key area of concern for regional politics. Decentralisation remained a named part of MP for Gippsland Darren Chester's outer-ministry portfolio that also includes regional services and local government. Decentralisation was introduced to a portfolio in Morrison's first ministry and it remains to be seen whether this is more than just a symbolic naming. Efforts at decentralisation have previously been most associated with Labor governments (1945–49 and 1972–75).

Explaining the result

Despite the internal ructions, unfavourable media related to personal behaviour and no great policy initiatives in the previous two terms of government, the Nationals were able to hold their ground. The Nationals and the Coalition more generally were able to establish a reasonable level of discipline just before the campaign proper, the preference deals seemed to work and competition from minor parties, such as the SFFP, was more limited than expected, probably partly due to resource constraints. Morrison was popular in the bush, especially after taking decisive action on recovery after severe floods in northern Queensland early in 2019, and he followed this up by making drought a priority immediately after he assumed the prime ministership (PM&C 2018; Karp 2019). There was pork-barrelling around infrastructure and facilities in target electorates, but this may not have been decisive, given that, in the three most marginal seats of central Queensland, Labor's spending promises far exceeded those of the Nationals (Irvine and Wright 2019).

Perhaps this election suggests more about some general tendencies in national elections in Australia. The Coalition parties can win elections despite some degree of disunity, adverse perceptions of leadership, no great policy reforms and a thin policy agenda. Fearmongering about Labor and 'progressive' politics can work and may work especially well in regional areas. From a survey of attitudes and values, weighted to regional areas and conducted in 2016 by the author and others, there is evidence of the generally assumed social conservatism in the bush. Using some survey items adapted from the work of Shalom Schwartz (Schwartz et al. 2010, 2014), we examined the values of some 1,400 Australians, with 66 per cent of those recruited from regional areas. Factor reductions were used to identify related survey items, which were turned into scales about 'security and patriotism' and 'equality and freedom'—each constructed from three seven-point scale questions. We also asked a series of questions about attitudes towards climate change and these were converted to a scale from four seven-point scale questions. As expected, these constructed factors significantly correlated to voting intention at that time, prior to the 2016 election. Intending Liberal and Nationals voters had the highest scores on 'security and patriotism' and the lowest scores for 'equality and freedom' and 'concern about climate change'.

For this chapter, I re-examined the data by dividing the respondents by electorate types: 'eastern rural' electorates, which included all the Nationals' electorates plus some adjacent ones held by the Liberal Party; 'other regional' electorates; and 'metropolitan' electorates. The average of ratings for 'security and patriotism' from respondents in the eastern rural electorates was higher than those from other areas, while that for 'equality and freedom' was lower. The differences in ratings were not great (see Figure 15.2), but they were statistically significant (p values of 0.023 and 0.05, respectively). While there were no significant differences for 'concern about climate change' by electorate type, there was a difference by State, with Queensland respondents having the lowest average rating. The key point from this is that the background narratives of the Coalition in recent years about nationalism, national security and the threat of Labor's 'equality' agenda may play particularly well in the Nationals' heartland. In addition, concerns about the climate change impacts of additional coalmines might be somewhat smaller in Queensland than in other areas.

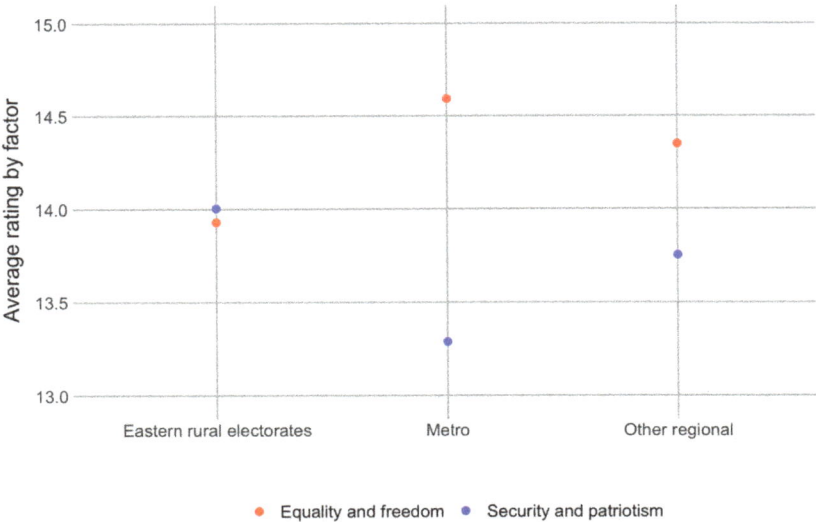

Figure 15.2 Ratings for the factors of 'security and patriotism' and 'equality and freedom'
Source: 2016 survey by Linda Courtenay Botterill, Helen Berry and Geoff Cockfield.

Conclusion

The Nationals saved more than the furniture in the 2019 election, preserving the house they had steadily rebuilt since 2007 (see Figure 15.1). They remain a significant party in that they are usually needed for the non-Labor parties to form government and they continue to hold important portfolios in Cabinet. They are able to project values related to social conservatism, nationalism and community, despite members not always living up to those purported values. Anti-Labor sentiment—a foundational element of the Country Party—has now broadened to encompass the Greens and, most recently, animal welfare activism, so that mobilising against this supposed threat axis is now entrenched in popular discourse and campaigning.

The election result, along with a historical tendency to leadership stability, may keep McCormack in place. On the other hand, there may be further agitation, with Joyce remaining ambitious and some of the Queenslanders feeling both entitled and important. They would, however, do well to think about what strategies have worked for the Country Party/Nationals and that is stable coalitions. Efforts at independence, as in Western Australia, have not really worked in even the medium term, nor has direct competition with the Liberals. And, once a State party is extinguished, it can be hard to revive, though there were mergers and demergers in Queensland prior to the LNP that did not cripple the State Country Party/Nationals. The Nationals are, however, unlikely to be able to deliver substantial benefits to the agricultural sector and rural communities given the constraints of coalition, market deregulation, drought, population movement to major towns and cities and the general difficulties of running small businesses. That may not, however, matter so much provided the Nationals are seen as representing agriculture, small business and some notion of the community values of the 'real' Australia.

References

Australian Electoral Commission (AEC). 2019. *2019 Federal Election Results*. Canberra: AEC. www.aec.gov.au/Elections/Federal_Elections/2019/index.htm.

Botterill, Linda Courtenay and Geoff Cockfield. 2015. 'From "Unstable" to "Stable" Minority Government: Reflections on the Role of the Nationals in Federal Coalition Governments'. *Australian Journal of Politics and History* 61(1): 53–66. doi.org/10.1111/ajph.12086.

Chan, Gabrielle. 2018. 'Barnaby Joyce accuser Catherine Marriott hailed by WA Nationals as she tells of her pain'. *The Guardian*, 1 November. www.the guardian.com/australia-news/2018/nov/01/barnaby-joyce-catherine-marriott-hailed-wa-nationals-as-she-tells-of-pain.

Clarke, Melissa. 2019. 'Coalition senator's reported threat to Environment Minister could spark Adani appeal, lawyers say'. *ABC News*, 9 April. www.abc.net.au/news/2019-04-09/lawyers-eye-coalition-threat-as-grounds-for-adani-appeal/10982834.

Cockfield, Geoff. 2009. 'A rural party in an urban nation'. In *The National Party: Prospects for the Great Survivors*, edited by Linda Courtenay Botterill and Geoff Cockfield, 42–80. Sydney: Allen & Unwin.

Coorey, Phil. 2019. 'PM concedes to Nats, pledges to consider new coal plant in Qld'. *Australian Financial Review*, 26 March. www.afr.com/news/politics/national/pm-pledges-to-consider-a-new-coal-plant-in-queensland-20190326-p517j8.

Crowe, David. 2019. '"I'm the elected deputy prime minister of Australia": Barnaby feels no guilt over challenge to Nationals leader'. *Sydney Morning Herald*, 11 March. www.smh.com.au/politics/federal/i-m-the-elected-deputy-prime-minister-of-australia-barnaby-feels-no-guilt-over-challenge-to-nationals-leader-20190311-p5137j.html.

Davies, Ann. 2019. '"The Darling will die": Scientists say mass fish kill due to over-extraction and drought'. *The Guardian*, 18 February. www.theguardian.com/australia-news/2019/feb/18/the-darling-will-die-scientists-say-mass-fish-kill-due-to-over-extraction-and-drought.

Department of the Prime Minister and Cabinet (PM&C). 2018. *Joint Agency Drought Taskforce*. Canberra: Australian Government. www.pmc.gov.au/domestic-policy/joint-agency-drought-taskforce.

Doran, Matthew, Andrew Kesper and Emma Machan. 2019. 'Where have the leaders been and what does it mean for the election?'. *ABC News*, 18 May. www.abc.net.au/news/2019-05-18/federal-election-campaign-heatmap-shows-sought-after-seats/11124898.

Foley, Mike. 2019. 'Jail time for animal activists under government's new plan'. *The Canberra Times*, 10 April. www.canberratimes.com.au/story/6017816/coalition-pledges-to-lock-up-militant-activists/?cs=14231.

Hamilton-Smith, Lexie. 2018. 'Cotton farm execs accused of $20m fraud over Murray–Darling water funding'. *ABC News*, 28 August [Updated 9 January 2019]. www.abc.net.au/news/2018-08-28/cotton-executives-20-million-fraud-allegation-norman-farming/10172736.

Irvine, Jessica and Shane Wright. 2019. 'See what the Coalition and Labor are promising in your electorate'. *WAToday*, 29 April. www.watoday.com.au/federal-election-2019/see-what-the-coalition-and-labor-are-promising-in-your-electorate-20190422-p51g3z.html.

Karp, Paul. 2019. 'Morrison offers cheap loans to flood-afflicted graziers in north Queensland'. *The Guardian*, 1 March. www.theguardian.com/australia-news/2019/mar/01/morrison-offers-cheap-loans-to-flood-afflicted-graziers-in-north-queensland.

Koziol, Michael. 2019. 'Us versus them: The angry and unpredictable politics of north Queensland'. *Sydney Morning Herald*, 5 May. www.smh.com.au/federal-election-2019/us-versus-them-the-angry-and-unpredictable-politics-of-north-queensland-20190502-p51jf2.html.

Livingston, Angus. 2018. 'Malcolm Turnbull pressures Barnaby Joyce to quit'. *The Land*, 16 February. www.theland.com.au/story/5232061/turnbull-pressures-joyce-to-quit/.

McGowan, Michael. 2018. 'NSW Young Nationals expel and suspend members over far-right links'. *The Guardian*, 15 October. www.theguardian.com/australia-news/2018/oct/15/nsw-young-nationals-expel-and-suspend-members-over-far-right-links.

Murphy, Katherine. 2019a. '"Do what it takes": Nationals leader defends preference deals with One Nation'. *The Guardian*, 30 April. www.theguardian.com/australia-news/2019/apr/30/do-what-it-takes-nationals-leader-defends-preference-deals-with-one-nation.

Murphy, Katherine. 2019b. 'Keith Pitt on nuclear power, self-styled experts and how Canberra crushes free thinking'. *The Guardian*, 12 July. www.theguardian.com/australia-news/2019/jul/12/keith-pitt-on-nuclear-power-self-styled-experts-and-how-canberra-crushes-free-thinking.

Patel, Uma. 2016. 'Adler shotgun: Nationals senator Bridget McKenzie says heavy restrictions are irrational'. *ABC News*, 10 December. www.abc.net.au/news/2016-12-10/bridget-mckenzie-urges-mps-to-vote-against-adler-restrictions/8108810.

Schwartz, Shalom H., Gian Vittoria Caprara and Michele Vecchione. 2010. 'Basic Personal Values, Core Political Values, and Voting: A Longitudinal Analysis'. *Political Psychology* 31(3): 421–52. doi.org/10.1111/j.1467-9221.2010.00764.x.

Schwartz, Shalom H., Gian Vittorio Caprara, Michele Vecchione, Paul Bain, Gabriel Bianchi, Maria Giovanna Caprara, Jan Cieciuch, Hasan Kirmanoglu, Cem Baslevent, Jan-Erik Lönnqvist, Catalin Mamali, Jorge Manzi, Vassilis Pavlopoulos, Tetyana Posnova, Harald Schoen, Jo Silvester, Carmen Tabernero, Claudio Torres, Markku Verkasalo, Eva Vondráková, Christian Welzel and Zbigniew Zaleski. 2014. 'Basic Personal Values Underlie and Give Coherence to Political Values: A Cross National Study in 15 Countries'. *Political Behavior* 36(4): 899–930. doi.org/10.1007/s11109-013-9255-z.

The Nationals. 2019a. *Our plan for a stronger agriculture, fisheries and forestry sector*. Press release, 2 May. Canberra: National Party of Australia.

The Nationals. 2019b. *Our Plan for Population, Migration and Better Cities*. Policy document. Canberra: National Party of Australia.

University of Western Australia (UWA). various years. *Australian Politics and Elections Database*. Perth: University of Western Australia. elections.uwa. edu.au/.

Wroe, David. 2019. '"Member for Manila": MP puts overseas travel before key campaign slogan'. *Sydney Morning Herald*, 18 April. www.smh.com.au/federal-election-2019/member-for-manila-mp-puts-overseas-travel-before-key-campaign-slogan-20190417-p51f59.html.

Wroe, David and David Crowe. 2018. 'Nationals MP Andrew Broad to quit parliament over "sugar daddy" scandal'. *Sydney Morning Herald*, 18 December. www.smh.com.au/politics/federal/nationals-mp-andrew-broad-to-quit-parliament-over-sugar-daddy-scandal-20181218-p50mwx.html.

16

THE AUSTRALIAN GREENS

Stewart Jackson

In May 2019, green parties were surging across Europe in the elections for the European Parliament, reaching their highest vote and representational levels of all time. In contrast, the Australian Greens saw some gains in the vote in the Senate, but only as a partial recovery towards the levels of support they enjoyed in 2010. Climate change, described by former prime minister Kevin Rudd as 'the greatest moral, economic and social challenge of our time', was expected to be a key focus for the election. Yet this did not occur; so, what happened?

First, it must be acknowledged that the Australian Greens (the Greens) did have a better election result than in 2016. The 2019 election brought a renewed focus on the environment, a reduced number of parties on the Senate ballot paper and an opportunity to focus on rebuilding the party's vote and image. The Greens retained their Senate seats in all six States, significantly increasing their vote in South Australia and Queensland. This chapter will explore why the election did not in fact become the climate change election, including some of the dynamics at play within the party, as well as the nature of the Greens' campaign.

Candidates

The Greens fielded candidates in all 151 House of Representatives seats and 35 in the Senate contest. Two of the House of Representatives candidates (in Lalor and Parkes) resigned over social media posts. Across all candidates, the Greens came close to gender parity (50.5 per cent men), and also fielded the only 'sex unspecified' candidate of the election.

In the Senate, the Greens nominated six candidates in New South Wales, Victoria, Queensland and Western Australia, four in South Australia, three in Tasmania and two each in the Northern Territory and the Australian Capital Territory. At this election, the party was also defending six of the nine Senate seats won in 2016. The senators standing for the Greens were not, however, the same team that had been successful in 2016. Two key replacements, one due to Section 44(i) of the Constitution and one to retirement, saw Jordon Steele-John replace Scott Ludlam in Western Australia and Mehreen Faruqi replace Lee Rhiannon in New South Wales. Disability advocate Steele-John took the seat previously held by the popular Ludlam after Ludlam discovered post election that he was in fact a New Zealand citizen, and Rhiannon lost her preselection to Faruqi in what some saw as a changing of the guard in New South Wales (for a fuller discussion of Section 44 issues, see Hobbs et al. 2018). Larissa Waters in Queensland had also fallen foul of Section 44 post election, with her seat initially taken by former Australian Democrat Senator Andrew Bartlett, but Bartlett resigned early to allow Waters to retake her seat, having renounced her previously unknown Canadian citizenship. All six defending senators had won three-year half-terms in 2016, so now had the opportunity to win full six-year terms.

In the House of Representatives, Adam Bandt recontested his seat of Melbourne, local firefighter Jim Casey challenged Anthony Albanese again in Grayndler, while Bartlett took on Liberal MP Trevor Evans in Brisbane. These would be the target seats in Victoria, New South Wales and Queensland, respectively. The Greens in Victoria also had hopes for three further seats: Cooper (formerly Batman), Macnamara (Melbourne Ports) and Wills. The party had come close to taking Batman in the 2016 election, though had faded slightly at the by-election in 2018. With a new candidate in Cooper, former Greens Senate candidate David Risstrom, the party might have been forgiven for thinking its chances were indeed good in that seat. Equally, the former MP for Melbourne Ports, Michael Danby, retired at the election, leaving an open seat, and the Greens, with 2016 candidate Steph Hodgins-May recontesting, might have fancied their chances.

Results

The results show an overall increase in the Greens' Senate vote of just over 1.5 per cent, but the House of Representatives staying fairly stable. When we examine the State-by-State results, we can see the results overall are buoyed by increases in Queensland and South Australia. This is repeated in the House of Representatives. One point to note is that the South Australian result is most likely due to the disappearance from the ballot paper of Nick Xenophon and his NXT ticket, which had polled more than 21 per cent in 2016.

Table 16.1 Preliminary Australian Greens results

State	Senate		House of Representatives	
	Primary	Change	Primary	Change
NSW	8.73	1.32	8.71	−0.24
Vic.	10.62	−0.25	11.89	−1.24
Qld	9.94	3.12	10.32	1.49
WA	11.81	1.48	11.62	−0.44
SA	10.91	5.03	9.61	3.40
Tas.	12.57	1.41	10.12	−0.10
ACT	17.71	1.61	16.85	1.76
NT	10.24	−0.54	10.15	1.06
National	**10.20**	**1.58**	**10.40**	**0.17**

Source: AEC (2019).

As can be seen from Figure 16.1, there was steady growth in votes for the Australian Greens from 1998 to 2010 and the resumption of a slight upward trend from 2016.

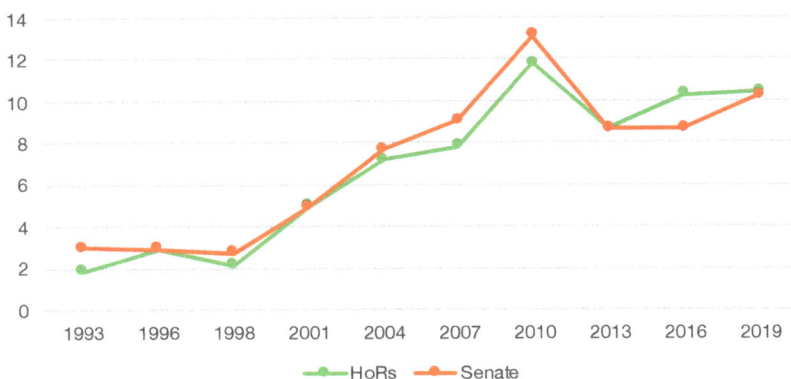

Figure 16.1 House and Senate results for the Australian Greens, 1993–2019

Source: AEC (2019).

We can compare these with results from recent European Parliament elections in which Greens polled particularly strongly: Germany, 20.5 per cent; Belgium, 15.2 per cent; France, 13.5 per cent; Denmark, 13.2 per cent; the United Kingdom, 11.8 per cent; Sweden, 11.5 per cent; Ireland, 11.4 per cent; and the Netherlands, 10.9 per cent. Of the major Western European nations, it was only in Italy that Greens failed. For green parties in the European Parliament, this meant increasing their numbers by almost 50 per cent, from 55 to 74 (European Parliament 2019). In Germany—the new powerhouse of green politics—the Greens appear to be close to replacing the Social Democrats as the main Opposition party. The Australian Greens therefore sit towards the lower end of success when seen in comparison with their European cousins, even while they can claim to be one of the first green parties in the world (Crowley 1996: 532).

What is clear from the results, however, is that the Greens' Senate vote in the three largest States is now lagging behind that in all other States and the Australian Capital Territory. The situation in the House of Representatives is a little more complicated, but the overall impression is that the vote increase the Greens experienced in 2016 (from the low of 2013) has eased. Yet it is also obvious that the explanation is more complicated than that. A closer look at the seats where the Greens polled more than 20 per cent (Table 16.2), which includes those that are current and future potential target seats for the party, shows some interesting developments.

Table 16.2 Divisional Australian Greens results

Seat	Vote	+/–
Melbourne	49.30	4.70
Wills	26.62	–4.29
Macnamara	24.24	0.08
Griffith	23.65	6.67
Canberra	23.31	4.59
Grayndler	22.55	0.31
Brisbane	22.37	2.94
Higgins	22.47	–1.72
Kooyong	21.24	2.65
Cooper	21.14	–15.53
Ryan	20.35	1.59
Richmond	20.32	–0.12

Source: AEC (2019).

One point to note is that, with exception of Richmond, these are all inner urban seats. The trend of Greens doing particularly well in inner urban seats has been documented before (Jackson 2018) but is demonstrated again here. However, it might also be noted that, apart from the seat of Melbourne, the Victorian Greens did not have a successful election. Falls in Wills (–4.3 per cent), Higgins (–1.8 per cent) and, most dramatically, in Cooper (–15.5 per cent), with a status quo result for Macnamara (0.1 per cent), suggest a stagnation of Greens support in Victoria. The result in Kooyong, where high-profile barrister Julian Burnside took on Treasurer Josh Frydenberg—although heralded as a potential boilover— yielded a small primary swing of 2.6 per cent, and a TPP result of 44.3:55.7 (a larger, 7.1 per cent swing). In Melbourne, the increase in the primary vote was 4.7 per cent, though only a 2.8 per cent swing on TPP, with sitting MP Adam Bandt returned easily after the ALP candidate, Luke Creasey, withdrew partway through the campaign after injudicious social media comments by him came to light (Doran and Sweeney 2019). While good overall results in Melbourne and Kooyong were recorded, this was also less than might have been expected.

The problematic results in Victoria mirror in some way the problems the party faced in the 2018 Victorian State election, in which the Greens were expected to win new seats while retaining their upper house seats. However, a bruising (and ultimately unsuccessful) Batman by-election in March 2018, with claims of undermining of the Greens candidate by disgruntled party members and local councillors, left a pall over the campaign. This overshadowed the win for the Greens in the Northcote by-election the previous November. The end result of the election was very mixed, with the Greens retaining two of their previously held seats (Melbourne and Prahran), winning the seat of Brunswick, but losing Northcote to the ALP. The upper house vote was down only slightly but, combined with a preference cartel between minor parties put together by Glenn Druery, the Greens lost four of their five seats (VEC 2018).

In a similar fashion, the NSW branch of the party emerged from a bitter, divisive and damaging previous year, yet recorded a solid rise in their Senate vote, even as the vote for the House of Representatives stagnated. The NSW State election in March, just two months before the federal election, meant keeping the party campaigning through two major elections in the first five months of the year, which it managed in relatively good order.

A year earlier, in May 2018, the 'Eastern Bloc' faction of the party had won the key preselections for the State's upper house (Visentin 2018). This was followed by Rhiannon's departure from the Senate in August 2018 after being defeated by Faruqi. The year was rounded out with the ouster from the party of State MP Jeremy Buckingham, prompting bitter attacks from both within and outside the party, but with the national party refusing to get involved. The beginning of 2019 started with a challenge in the courts to the existing State preselections, but once this was dismissed, the party successfully returned all its sitting MPs up for election, with their three State lower house MPs increasing their margins. Buckingham ran as an Independent but polled only 0.26 per cent, compared with his former party's 9.73 per cent (NSW Electoral Commission 2019). Finally, MLC Justin Field—not up for election until 2022 and a factional ally of Buckingham's—resigned from the party in April 2019, just before the federal election was called. However, for the first time in a number of years, the Greens were able to enter an election reasonably unified, with a popular candidate. The campaign period was therefore one of bringing the success and unity of the State campaign into the federal arena, with Faruqi's election perhaps signalling a change for the better for the NSW party.

A different story again can be seen in the Queensland branch of the party, with an increase in votes across the inner urban seats of Brisbane: Griffith, Ryan, Moreton and Lilley. This followed on from successful 2017 State and 2016 Brisbane City Council elections, in which the Greens won their first assembly seat in their own right and their first Brisbane City councillor—both in single-member districts. The campaign was boosted by the return of Larissa Waters. The Queensland party therefore presented a unified campaign. However, one element not effectively dealt with was Bob Brown's 'Stop Adani caravan', which appeared to galvanise anti-Greens sentiment in some quarters (SBS 2019b). This would indicate that the Greens have not found an appropriate role for their high-profile former leader.

South Australia saw the most dramatic shift in Greens fortunes, although this is also easily ascribable to the lack of the NXT ticket on the ballot. At the same time, the Greens' increase of 4.9 per cent was second only to the Liberal Party in terms of recovery of vote, suggesting that NXT voters in South Australia are now at least partly identifying the Greens' Sarah Hanson-Young as a fair replacement for their aspirations. While not recovering to its 2010 level, the House of Representatives vote for the Greens of 9.61 per cent remains the second-best result in nearly 30 years of the Greens contesting South Australian seats, and a substantial recovery from the 2016 result.

In the other States and Territories, the rises were generally more muted. While the Australian Capital Territory, Tasmania and Western Australia all recorded rises of around 1.5 per cent, this was really more of a status-quo result, and certainly in the case of Western Australia, it did not return the party to the 15.6 per cent heights of the 2014 Senate by-election. In the House of Representatives, the results were again muted, with no opportunities to advance in the inner urban seats of Perth, Canberra or Denison.

Campaign focus

If we are to believe the political rhetoric leading up to polling day, this was the 'climate change election'—as had been claimed for the elections in 2007 and 2010 (Grube 2014). Certainly, this was the point made by a series of polls and commentary in the lead-up to the election, with electors suggesting climate change was a significant issue (Hanrahan 2019;

Kassam 2019; SBS 2019a; Wade 2019a, 2019b). But was this borne out by the election media of the Greens themselves? Greens Leader Richard Di Natale's 'Leader's Address' to the National Press Club on 1 May highlighted that climate change, along with a series of other issues, would be important for the Greens campaign, but was clearly not the sole focus (Di Natale 2019). The Greens might therefore be expected to focus their media specifically on climate change. As we can see from Table 16.3, however, a different picture emerges—of many different issues covered by multiple voices.

Table 16.3 Australian Greens' media releases, 2019 campaign

Candidate	Media releases	Topic
Di Natale	7	Employment (1), Bob Hawke (1), health (1), democracy (1), environment (1), foreign affairs (1), Budget (1)
Bandt	9	Industrial relations (2), environment (6), employment (1), science and technology (1), election campaign (1)
Siewert	22	Employment (2), social security (5), mental health (4), environment (2), election campaign (1), Indigenous affairs (7), housing (1)
Hanson-Young	12	Environment (8), energy (1), Budget (1), communications (1), election campaign (1)
Whish-Wilson	8	Energy (3), environment (3), Budget (2)
Rice	17	Transport (2), environment (6), agriculture (2), LGBTQI issues (2), Budget (3), foreign affairs (2)
McKim	2	Environment (1), election campaign (1)
Waters	8	Environment (2), democracy (1), infrastructure (1), energy (2), election campaign (2)
Steele-John	6	Environment (2), disability (2), election campaign (2)
Faruqi	8	Animal welfare (1), housing (1), child care (2), environment (1), education (1), election campaign (2)

Source: Media releases as listed on Greens' webpage, from 1 April 2019 to 18 May 2019: greensmps.org.au/terms/article-type/media-release.

This needs to be considered in the context of a campaign that appeared to be driven by a particular agenda on the Coalition side—that of the paramount leader (Morrison) battling it out with the challenger (Shorten). The ALP's election material tended to emphasise the group nature of the ALP front bench, but Morrison's relentlessly personalised campaign meant that Shorten was the key focus. In the context of a presidential-style campaign, the State-based and MP-focused campaign of the Greens struggled to cut through.

Taken together, we might consider Norris's (2000, 2004) concept of the 'premodern', 'modern' and 'postmodern' campaigns. The constituency turn for which the ALP had been lauded in Victoria (Mills 2014) remained a core part of the Greens' campaign, especially as they struggled to match the funding to run the kind of successful television advertising associated with 'modern' campaigning. The form of meta-campaigning associated with the postmodern campaign—using the party's social media access as the principal avenue for influencing voters—might then be seen as the key to a new form of Greens campaigning. Indeed, Hanson-Young, with 157,000 Twitter followers (more than Di Natale's 127,000), might be seen as pursuing the archetypal campaign, with some 120 tweets on a variety of issues during the campaign. Yet this form of campaigning can also be viewed as primarily supporting a more localised campaign structure in South Australia (particularly in relation to local issues such as the Murray–Darling river system).

When we follow this through and examine the number of followers and posts on Facebook for the various MPs, we find a shift in focus. For instance, more than half of Hanson-Young's posts on her Facebook page (for which she has 134,000 followers) covered environmental issues (44 of 83). The majority of these posts focused on three particular issues: the Murray–Darling river system, the Great Australian Bight and climate change. Certainly, in terms of the Greens' more outwardly facing campaign, the focus was much more on the environment than on the general set of issues that Hanson-Young normally has carriage of and is known for. The other thing platforms such as Facebook offer is the potential for at least some interaction. Although the site did not record a large number of conversations between Hanson-Young and others, it did have videos, commentary from volunteers and endorsements from high-profile individuals (Hanson-Young highlighted two, from columnist and commentator Jane Caro and former Australian cricketer Jason Gillespie.) As to whether this works, the simple fact of having 134,000 followers suggests some level of penetration. By way of comparison, Hanson-Young featured in only 14 stories in the main South Australian daily, the Adelaide *Advertiser*, with climate change and the Great Australian Bight featuring in seven of those.

Table 16.4 Social media followers of Greens candidates

MPs	Twitter	Facebook	Instagram
Di Natale	125,000	112,000	17,000
Bandt	179,000	125,000	7,000
Siewert	13,000	21,000	1,000
Hanson-Young	157,000	134,000	7,000
Whish-Wilson	17,000	26,000	2,000
Rice	11,000	26,000	2,000
McKim	17,000	38,000	2,000
Waters	64,000	80,000	15,000
Steele-John	10,000	34,000	6,000
Faruqi	21,000	60,000	5,000

Sources: Twitter, Facebook and Instagram.

While the numbers contained in Table 16.4 are just 'viewing figures', they give some idea of the apparent social media preferences of each of the MPs. Hanson-Young is a significant performer on Facebook and Twitter but much less so on Instagram. In at least some respects, this fits with activity shifts and preferences noted in how campaigns use social media (Kreiss et al. 2018). Instagram is clearly favoured, at least to some degree, by Di Natale and Waters, while Bandt is a heavy user of Twitter. By way of comparison, former Greens Senator Scott Ludlam, much noted for both his tech-savviness and his following, still retains 117,000 Twitter followers and tweets regularly on issues of democracy, climate change and energy.

Campaign structure

As with previous Greens campaigns, the core campaign structures were housed within the State branches. The national office, apart from providing extensive research elements, left the running of the individual State campaigns to the State branches (see Kefford 2018). That there were six senators up for election meant there were parallel structures operating (a State-based structure as well as the national parliamentarians and national campaign coordinator). This election was the second without the necessity of preference negotiations around the group voting ticket (GVT), but it remained important to ensure consistency and the distribution of how-to-vote material. The negotiations themselves were then directed to supporting particular candidates and parties, with the result that 82 per cent of Greens preferences favoured the ALP over the Coalition (see Raue, Chapter 9, this volume).

This structuring also meant that the bulk of funding for the campaign was held at the State level. Whether this lack of centralisation worked for or against the party should be the subject of further investigation, as it would appear that, although the individual States still contribute funding to the national body, this is primarily for the maintenance of the national organisation, as opposed to actual campaigning. National campaigning itself still reflects only an equivalent proportion of party funding to the NSW or Victorian campaign budgets. For the more populous States such as New South Wales and Victoria, regular staffing (in New South Wales, approximately10 full-time and part-time staff) is supplemented with four to five campaign-specific staff. In less populous States such as Western Australia, regular staffing numbers double in size.

Conclusion

The Greens would be fairly pleased with the result, given the major party posturing. Morrison's focus on Shorten set up a presidential-style campaign—a recurring feature of Australian elections—that did not allow the Greens the freedom they might otherwise have enjoyed. The party had struggled somewhat with internal issues over the year preceding the election, with resolution being reached only in New South Wales. The lack of resolution clearly dogged the party in Victoria, even as New South Wales seemed to emerge more united, if somewhat battered. The results do, unfortunately, have the capacity to reignite tensions both within and between the State parties. Certainly, both the NSW and the Victorian branches will have troubling fulfilling national funding priorities given their loss of State MPs. Even while returning their sitting senators and State MPs, for the Victorian and NSW parties, the loss of five and two State MPs, respectively, with only a marginal increase in the federal vote means a possible period of financial belt-tightening.

The shift in the vote in Queensland, however, would have to be seen as a high point for the party. The Queensland Greens—once constantly beset by internal division—are now winning seats at all levels of government. The resurgence of the South Australian party, coupled with steady results elsewhere, places the party in a moderately good position going forward. This would appear to indicate that the Greens are not in any immediate danger of following the path of the Australian Democrats.

With a wait until August 2020 for the Northern Territory election (followed in October by both the Australian Capital Territory and Queensland), the party will have an opportunity to consolidate, build more robust internal processes and rebuild membership and funding.

References

Australian Electoral Commission (AEC). 2019. 'House of Representatives: Divisional results'. *Tally Room 2019 Federal Election*. Canberra: AEC. results. aec.gov.au/24310/Website/HouseDefault-24310.htm.

Crowley, Kate. 1996. 'The Tasmanian State Election 1996: Green Power and Hung Parliaments'. *Environmental Politics* 5(3): 530–35. doi.org/10.1080/09644019608414286.

Di Natale, Richard. 2019. '2019 Federal Election: Richard Di Natale at the National Press Club'. *YouTube*, 30 April. www.youtube.com/watch?v=USdJLhO-K2Q.

Doran, Matt and Lucy Sweeney. 2019. 'Federal election 2019: Labor's Melbourne candidate Luke Creasey withdraws after rape jokes, lewd comments emerged'. *ABC News*, 3 May. www.abc.net.au/news/2019-05-03/federal-election-labor-candidate-luke-creasey-withdraws/11076194.

European Parliament. 2019. *2019 European Election Results*. [Online]. www.euro parl.europa.eu/election-results-2019/en.

Grube, Dennis. 2014. 'The gilded cage: Rhetorical path dependency in Australian politics'. In *Studies in Australian Political Rhetoric*, edited by John Uhr and Ryan Walter, 99–118. Canberra: ANU Press. doi.org/10.22459/SAPR.09.2014.05.

Hanrahan, Catherine. 2019. 'Vote Compass finds voters are split on economy and environment as most important issue'. *ABC News*, 17 April. www.abc.net.au/news/2019-04-17/vote-compass-election-most-important-issues/11003192.

Hobbs, Harry, Sangeetha Pillai and George Williams. 2018. 'The Disqualification of Dual Citizens from Parliament: Three Problems and a Solution'. *Alternative Law Journal* 43(2): 73–80. doi.org/10.1177/1037969X18777910.

Jackson, Stewart. 2018. 'The Australian Greens' campaign'. In *Double Disillusion: The 2016 Australian Federal Election*, edited by Anika Gauja, Peter Chen, Jennifer Curtin and Juliet Pietsch, 297–316. Canberra: ANU Press. doi.org/10.22459/DD.04.2018.13.

Kassam, Natasha. 2019. *2019 Lowy Institute poll: Australian attitudes to climate change*. Media release, 8 May. Sydney: Lowy Institute. www.lowyinstitute.org/publications/media-release-2019-lowy-institute-poll-australian-attitudes-climate-change.

Kefford, Glenn. 2018. 'Digital Media, Ground Wars and Party Organisation: Does Stratarchy Explain How Parties Organise Election Campaigns'. *Parliamentary Affairs* 71(3): 656–73. doi.org/10.1093/pa/gsx084.

Kreiss, Daniel, Regina G. Lawrence and Shannon McGregor. 2018. 'In Their Own Words: Political Practitioner Accounts of Candidates, Audiences, Affordances, Genres, and Timing in Strategic Social Media Use'. *Political Communication* 35(1): 8–31. doi.org/10.1080/10584609.2017.1334727.

Mills, Stephen. 2014. 'Rules for radicals comes to Carrum'. *Inside Story*, 5 December. insidestory.org.au/rules-for-radicals-comes-to-carrum.

Norris, Pippa. 2000. *A Virtuous Circle: Political Communications in Postindustrial Societies*. Cambridge: Cambridge University Press. doi.org/10.1017/CBO9780511609343.

Norris, Pippa. 2004. 'The Evolution of Election Campaigns: Eroding Political Engagement?'. Political Communications in the 21st Century Conference, University of Otago, Dunedin, New Zealand, January.

NSW Electoral Commission. 2019. *NSW State Election Results 2019: Saturday, 23 March 2019*. Sydney: NSW Electoral Commission. pastvtr.elections.nsw.gov.au/sg1901/Home.

Special Broadcasting Service (SBS). 2019a. 'More Australians than ever before are worried about climate change, polling finds'. *SBS News*, 17 April. www.sbs.com.au/news/more-australians-than-ever-before-are-worried-about-climate-change-polling-finds.

Special Broadcasting Service (SBS). 2019b. 'Adani issue hurt Labor in Qld: Canavan'. *SBS News*, 19 May. www.sbs.com.au/news/adani-issue-hurt-labor-in-qld-canavan.

Victorian Electoral Commission (VEC). 2018. *State Election 2018 Results*. Victoria: VEC. www.vec.vic.gov.au/Results/State2018/Summary.html.

Visentin, Lisa. 2018. 'Cate Faehrmann and David Shoebridge triumph in Greens preselection'. *Sydney Morning Herald*, 12 May. www.smh.com.au/politics/nsw/cate-faehrmann-and-david-shoebridge-triumphant-in-greens-preselections-20180509-p4ze7e.html.

Wade, Matt. 2019a. 'A record share of Australians say humans cause climate change: Poll'. *Sydney Morning Herald*, 1 April. www.smh.com.au/environment/climate-change/a-record-share-of-australians-say-humans-cause-climate-change-poll-20190328-p518go.html.

Wade, Matt. 2019b. 'Australians more worried about climate change than most other nations: Poll'. *Sydney Morning Herald*, 6 May. www.smh.com.au/national/australians-more-worried-about-climate-change-than-most-other-nations-poll-20190505-p51kb5.html.

17

THE MINOR PARTIES

Glenn Kefford

The 2019 federal election is noteworthy for many reasons. One of the defining stories should be that the ALP and the Liberal–National Coalition have been unable to draw voters back from the minor parties and Independents. Put simply, the long-term trend is away from the major parties. In this election, there was a small nationwide increase in the vote for minor parties and Independents in the House of Representatives, while in the Senate there was a modest decline. The State-level results are more varied. The Coalition lost ground in some places and maintained its vote in others. The ALP vote, in contrast, was demolished in Tasmania and in Queensland. Almost one in three Queenslanders and Tasmanians decided to support a party or candidate in the House other than the ALP or the Coalition. Across the entire country, this was around one in four (see Figure 17.1). In the Senate, Queensland and Tasmania again had the largest non–major party vote. These results are dissected in greater detail in other chapters in this volume, but they suggest that supply-side opportunities remain for parties and candidates expressing anti–major party sentiments. Put simply, the political environment remains fertile for minor party insurgents.

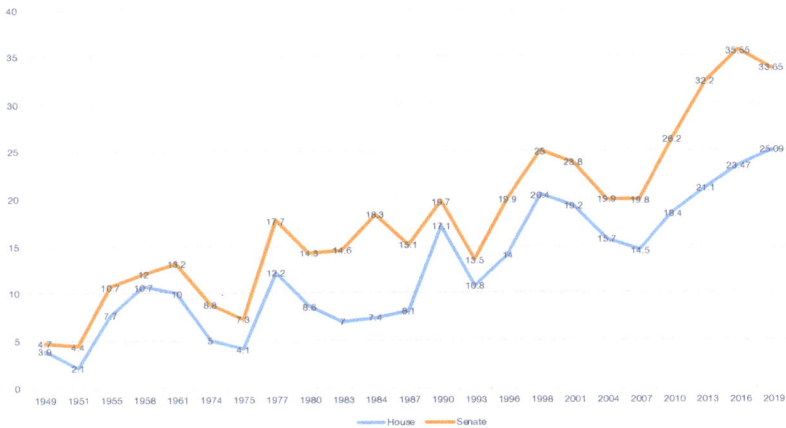

Figure 17.1 First-preference votes for minor parties and Independents

Source: Compiled with data kindly provided by Antony Green and from Australian Electoral Commission (2016 and 2019).

In terms of seat composition, the minor parties have remained unchanged in the House, with Katter's Australian Party (KAP), the Australian Greens (discussed in Chapter 16, this volume) and Centre Alliance (formerly the NXT) holding on to their respective seats. However, it is in the Senate where things have changed dramatically.[1] The government is presented with a streamlined Senate crossbench compared with what it faced after the 2016 election. In total, the Senate crossbench will consist of 15 representatives from the minor parties: nine Greens, two from the Centre Alliance, two from Pauline Hanson's One Nation (PHON), one from the Australian Conservatives and one from the Jacqui Lambie Network (JLN). In contrast, after the 2016 election, the crossbench was 20-strong.

Beyond the results, and a discussion of how important minor party preference flows were to the outcome (see Raue, Chapter 9, this volume), there were two critical stories about the minor parties that emerged from the 2019 election that will be the focus of this chapter. First, while there has been much discussion of the way the major parties and the Greens have used social media for the past decade or more (Gibson and McAllister 2011), this is the first election in which there has been a significant expansion in social media usage by the other minor parties.

---

1   The number and type of minor parties in the Senate are further complicated by the Section 44 disqualifications; some senators who were elected as a result of disqualifications subsequently switched parties or created their own (discussed in Chapter 3, this volume).

At a time when the traditional media landscape is fragmenting, this allows these parties to bypass the talking heads and deliver their messages directly to voters. Second, the re-emergence of Clive Palmer on the national political scene is an important part of the story—most of all for what it says about power and influence in Australian politics. Palmer reportedly spent over $60 million and, while he failed to win a seat and ended up with a meagre share of first preferences, at the very least, he contributed to the framing of the election in the minds of voters. These issues are worthy of further examination and are unpacked below.

The minor parties embrace digital

For a decade or more, there has been increased interest in how various political actors are embracing the digital age (Chen 2013, 2015). Many analyses have suggested that the use of digital media by the non-Greens minor parties has been at a basic level, with rudimentary candidate pages that were lacking in how they engaged their audience (Chen 2012; Kefford 2018). The 2019 contest was different. What this election showed is that the minor parties are, albeit slowly, increasing the sophistication and scale of their social media and digital campaigns.[2] When the social media and digital advertising of the KAP, JLN, PHON, United Australia Party (UAP), Centre Alliance, the Australian Conservatives and Fraser Anning's Conservative National Party (CNP) are analysed, we see evidence of significant investment in the digital space.

Unsurprisingly, Facebook remains the dominant mode for minor parties to interact with voters and the minor parties appear to have been well served by their social media accounts before and during the election campaign. As Esposito (2019) demonstrated, the Facebook pages for Fraser Anning (CNP), Pauline Hanson (PHON) and Malcolm Roberts (PHON) featured 'in the top five performers for the year when it comes to total interactions on the platform'.[3] The reach of and voter engagement with the social media accounts of key minor party actors were also significant during the campaign. As Table 17.1 demonstrates, engagement with the

---

2   For a larger discussion of social media use, see Bruns and Moon (2018). McSwiney (2019) also noted that right-wing minor parties in 2019 were primarily using social media for issue framing.
3   Palmer (discussed more in the section below) had an unusual digital journey after the previous election. His online presence after the 2016 election started to resemble and be influenced by the alt-right (Caccamo 2018), but, as the election drew closer, these influences seemed to diminish and he ran an orthodox digital campaign with social media at the centre.

social media accounts of key minor parties during the official campaign period (11 April–18 May) was comparable with that of the major parties.[4] Pauline Hanson's Facebook page had the most interactions, and this is perhaps unsurprising given it has one of the highest number of followers of any of Australia's political pages. With seven of these posts receiving over 10,000 interactions, and with more than 250,000 followers on the platform, it is likely that each of these posts was viewed by hundreds of thousands of voters. In total, Hanson had 11 of the top 20 posts by engagement numbers and all of the top seven. The UAP, JLN and Anning's pages had the remaining posts in the top 20.

Table 17.1 Top 20 minor party campaign posts on Facebook by number of interactions

Date	Interactions	Party/candidate and link	Content
6 May	30,209	PHON: www.facebook.com/PaulineHansonAu/posts/990539244483721	Anti-ALP
30 April	24,936	PHON: www.facebook.com/PaulineHansonAu/posts/986838414853804	Internal PHON problems and response
1 May	23,705	PHON: www.facebook.com/PaulineHansonAu/posts/987248828146096	Internal PHON problems and response
17 April	22,353	PHON: www.facebook.com/PaulineHansonAu/posts/979164695621176	Anti-Turnbull
8 May	17,587	PHON: www.facebook.com/PaulineHansonAu/posts/991268844410761	Hanson visiting supporter
29 April	17381	PHON: www.facebook.com/PaulineHansonAu/posts/985985544939091	Policy: $15–20 billion on dam-building in north Queensland
16 May	14,360	PHON: www.facebook.com/PaulineHansonAu/posts/996513533886292	Attack on mainstream media

---

4   These data come from Crowdtangle's Google Chrome plugin, which provides data on the social media engagement of various pages. Interactions here are the combined number of reactions, comments and shares of the post. As a point of comparison, the most interactions a post from the main ALP page received during the campaign was around 35,000 and the main Liberal Party page was approximately 37,000. These figures are current for 31 May 2019.

Date	Interactions	Party/candidate and link	Content
14 April	13,798	JLN: www.facebook.com/jacquilambienetwork/posts/1122791707928356 [page discontinued]	Lambie joke and photos
12 May	11,581	Anning: www.facebook.com/senatorfraseranning/posts/707083586374005	Racism/visas for white South African farmers
14 May	10,676	UAP: www.facebook.com/CliveFrederickPalmer/posts/2441739792512210	Anti-Labor/Greens
14 April	10,587	JLN: www.facebook.com/jacquilambienetwork/posts/1122756534598540	Anti–major party
9 May	9,670	Anning: www.facebook.com/senatorfraseranning/posts/705012946581069	Racism/ban on Muslim immigration
13 May	9,509	UAP: www.facebook.com/CliveFrederickPalmer/posts/2440482705971252	Anti-Labor, claim of deals with China
28 April	9,149	Anning: www.facebook.com/senatorfraseranning/posts/699190917163272	Racism/support for white South Africans
16 May	9,002	Anning: www.facebook.com/senatorfraseranning/posts/709512019464495	Anti–major party, anti–mainstream media
30 April	8,688	PHON: www.facebook.com/PaulineHansonAu/posts/986642288206750	Internal PHON problems and response
17 April	8,659	Anning: www.facebook.com/senatorfraseranning/posts/692901687792195	Racism/claim that 'fake refugees' are entering country
2 May	8,114	PHON: www.facebook.com/PaulineHansonAu/posts/987836294754016	Anti-ALP/Shorten
10 May	8,093	PHON: www.facebook.com/PaulineHansonAu/posts/992611410943171	Anti–major parties
7 May	6,931	PHON: www.facebook.com/PaulineHansonAu/posts/991111161093196	Results in NSW election

Note: The Facebook pages of Hanson, Lambie, UAP, Palmer, Anning, the Australian Conservatives, Brian Burston, KAP and the Centre Alliance were all analysed as part of this analysis of social media engagement.

Source: Crowdtangle (see Footnote 6).

In terms of targeting, there is evidence to suggest that the minor parties have started to embrace targeting across various platforms and search engines. On Facebook, evidence of the UAP and PHON using targeted ads during the campaign was identified via the Facebook ad library, as well as through searches of some of the party pages and examination of the ads they were running. Some of the targeting was, however, more than a little unusual. For example, one PHON Senate candidate for New South Wales had targeted 'people over the age of 18 who lived in Victoria', while another targeted ad on Facebook, from the UAP, targeted 'people aged 16 to 38 who live in Australia'.[5] There were also a number of reports of UAP advertising spreading across other areas of digital media, including YouTube and mobile game apps, as well as in Google search results (Bogle 2019; Vitorovich 2019). This is all evidence of the trajectory of minor party campaigning, which is increasingly heading online.

The increased use of social media by the minor parties to connect with voters during the election campaign is unsurprising, but it does present challenges. This is changing the nature of electoral politics and how issues are framed in the minds of voters. Given that increasing numbers of voters are accessing their political information solely from social media, Facebook and other platforms provide opportunities for minor parties to reach vast numbers of voters in an affordable way. The danger, however, is that parties willing to produce misinformation or provocative content seem to do better on the platform and, as a result of the network effects of social media, this information can spread rapidly across the political landscape. This problem is likely to only get worse.

The return of Clive

Clive Palmer's return to the federal political arena was significant, not because he won a swag of Senate seats and a seat in the House—as he did in 2013 with his Palmer United Party (PUP) (Kefford and McDonnell 2016, 2018)—but because of what his 2019 campaign says about power in Australia. An extremely wealthy individual, Palmer has a résumé that, among many other things, includes the rapid disintegration of his previous party as a result of incompetence and infighting, not paying the

---

5   These descriptions are taken from Facebook's advertising information, which provides limited details on the targeting strategy used.

workers of his Queensland Nickel refinery an estimated $7 million in lost wages and benefits (Ferrier 2019) and being an absentee parliamentarian when he was the member for Fairfax between 2013 and 2016 (Evershed 2014). He spent a reported $60 million[6] on a campaign that contributed to how the election was framed in the minds of at least some voters and delivered significant preferences to the government, hurting the ALP along the way.[7]

Given the UAP's eventual nationwide vote was 3.4 per cent in the House and 2.3 per cent in the Senate, voters might be wondering what exactly the point of all this was. Perhaps we will never know. But Palmer's return to the federal political arena raises a variety of questions about our democracy, including how we want elections to be funded, whether we think wealthy individuals should be able to pour this amount of money in and whether we care if the messaging from our parties and candidates for office is completely detached from anything resembling truth or facts. Ultimately, Palmer has burnt through another set of candidates and $60 million dollars with an amateurish, self-interested campaign, and maybe he does not care, but perhaps we should.

The campaign the UAP ran received significant media coverage from the outset. First, in April and May 2018, billboards started to emerge across the country with Palmer's image and the slogan 'Make Australia great'. Then, in January 2019, Palmer began advertising through the mass media. Television advertisements—which were accused of infringing the copyright of a song from the band Twisted Sister—generated plenty of media attention for Palmer and were 'broadcast on the Seven, Nine and Ten networks between 50 and 167 times in the first week of January alone' (Whitbourn 2019).[8] Around this time, hundreds of thousands of text messages were sent out from the UAP claiming that, 'when elected, United Australia Party will ban unsolicited text messages which Labor & Liberal have allowed'. The text message also contained a link to the UAP's

6   See Chapter 3 (this volume) for more on the advertising spend.
7   It should be noted, however, that in no seat in the House did this change the outcome, so the UAP's preferences had no direct effect on who won government. But as Raue (Chapter 9, this volume) demonstrates, around 65 per cent of UAP preferences flowed to the Coalition.
8   One version of the ad focused on the National Broadband Network, stating that $55 billion had been spent on it and it still did not work (Swanston 2019). Another started off with an image of disgraced former Labor Senator Sam Dastyari, with the headline: 'Labor Senator's expenses paid by the Chinese Government.' This was followed by 'No more foreign control' (Whitbourn 2019).

website. Again, this generated substantial media coverage for the party. But what modest gains the party may have made via increasing its name recognition were surely undone by the ill will generated by the tactic.

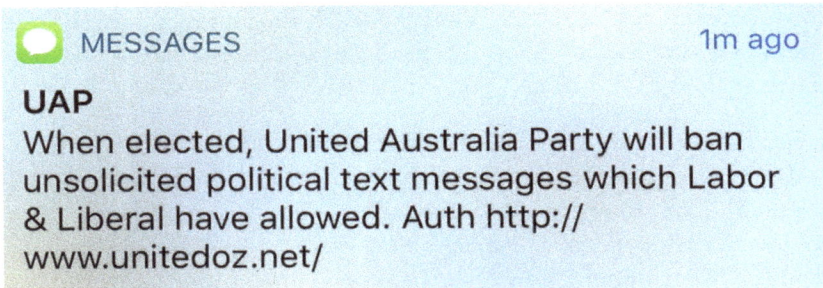

Plate 17.1 Copy of UAP text message sent to voters
Source: Brent Davidson, Twitter account, 16 January 2019.

The contrast with PUP's 2013 campaign was stark. In 2013, when Palmer and his PUP tasted success, they had a set of policies that were generous to everyone and were designed to harvest a protest vote (Kefford and McDonnell 2016), but their messaging was largely an attack on both major parties with their slogan 'Not the Liberal way or the Labor way, but the right way' being emblematic of this (Kefford and McDonnell 2016). In 2019, with at least double the amount of funds injected into the campaign, Palmer and the UAP released, *word for word*, the same national policies as 2013, with one change: there was no need to 'dump the carbon tax' as that had already been achieved (UAP 2019h).[9] Moreover, as opposed to 2013, when the campaign messaging was filled largely with generic, anti–major party rhetoric, in 2019, the messaging from the UAP was completely detached from reality, primarily targeted the ALP and was filled with what can only be described as lies.[10]

One media release and message spread across social media was titled: 'Labor and China's Communist government conspiring against Australia' (UAP 2019e). Another said: 'Bill Shorten will hit us with another trillion

---

9   To describe the policies of PUP and the UAP as lacking in detail would be a very generous assessment. Instead, they published four policies on their website and then a range of policies were floated at points throughout the election campaign. An example of this was a post that said the party would 'increase the age pension by $150 per week' (UAP 2019g). Another was that they would reduce power costs by 50 per cent, once elected (UAP 2019b).

10   To be clear, there were numerous videos, posts and media releases that attacked the major parties together, but there was no advertising that attacked the LNP or Morrison in the way that some of the UAP's advertising did the ALP.

dollars of taxes and costs' (UAP 2019c). A third claimed that Labor's negative gearing policy would allow 'foreign companies to claim tax deductions that Australians will not be able to' (UAP 2019a). Beyond the anti-Labor messaging, Palmer's economic nationalism was exemplified by ads that asked: 'Did you know that a Chinese communist controlled company owns an airport in the Pilbara? Now another Chinese owned company has bought another airport near Perth for just $1' (UAP 2019d). This video has, thus far, been viewed 1.4 million times on Facebook. Another of the UAP's fabrications was that the major parties would not deliver a tax cut until 2024 (UAP 2019f); this was spread across social media widely and promoted via paid advertising. Over and over, the messaging from Palmer and the UAP was not just loose with the truth, it had absolutely no connection with it.

This is all evidence of Palmer's malignant influence in Australian politics. While it could be argued that in 2013 he sought to damage the major parties and have his business interests advanced, his campaign resonated because of increasing dissatisfaction with the major parties and Australian democracy. He was subsequently able to have some input on policy as a result of the numbers he held in a finely balanced Senate. The 2019 campaign was something altogether different. Palmer and his UAP actively spread misinformation and falsehoods across the political landscape, which may sow further seeds of discontent in the Australian body politic.[11] Internationally, Palmer's gigantic personal investment and complete domination of his party are not unparalleled (Kefford and McDonnell 2018), but it is worth considering whether any plutocrat has spent this much money and ended up with as little in return. Perhaps we are fortunate that this is the case.

Conclusion

The 2019 federal election has provided more evidence of the challenges Australian democracy confronts. It is becoming increasingly difficult for the major parties to build a coalition of voters large enough for them to govern across a country where the interests and preferences of the States and regions are increasingly contradictory. So, while the crossbench

---

11 The scholarship on negative advertising and attack ads has long suggested that negative advertising can weaken political efficacy. See Ansolabehere et al. (1994).

in the Senate has shrunk, the nationwide vote for minor parties and Independents in the Senate has decreased slightly and there are certainly challenges for each of the minor parties, the reality is that voters are not returning to the major parties in any significant way. Voters continue to spray their first preferences across a wide range of minor parties, depending on the State or Territory in which they live and whether they live in the major metropolitan areas or in the regions. There is an opportunity for a fourth force to emerge in Australian federal politics, especially on the right, but thus far none of the party entrepreneurs has had the resources or knowhow to pull this off.

The challenges of institutionalising, outlined in the 2016 election book (Kefford 2018), remain for the minor parties. Indeed, we have seen some of these challenges come to fruition. Since the previous election, Nick Xenophon departed the parliament, the NXT became the Centre Alliance and, notwithstanding Rebekha Sharkie holding on to the seat of Mayo, their vote in the Senate has collapsed. While Katter remains very popular in his stronghold of Kennedy, his party has made little headway at the federal level beyond this seat. Katter, who has held the seat for 26 years, is 74 years old and the question must be asked, how much longer can he continue? The JLN and PHON probably have reason to be most optimistic. Lambie has been returned to the Senate for six years and, given the state of play in Tasmania, there is a significant opportunity for her to be a long-term senator for the State. PHON has overcome crisis after crisis and still managed to increase its Senate vote in Queensland. With two senators, the party is, again, in a critical position given the finely balanced numbers in that chamber, but whether the party can remain united given all the evidence to the contrary remains to be seen.

Australia's minor parties remain critical in many ways. They are vehicles through which frustration at the major parties and the political establishment is channelled. They represent interests that the major parties are perceived to overlook. They often determine what policy passes through the Senate, securing deals along the way for their home States or favoured issues. While there is significant fragmentation on the right— far more than on the left—and these parties appear to be fighting for the same electoral space, the situation is more complex. These parties are pulling voters away, not just from the Coalition, but also from the ALP, suggesting the drivers of de-alignment are multidimensional. The major parties are therefore caught in a bind. They are losing their share of first preferences to minor parties, hence, their need to compete with them. But they also require preferences from these parties—thus, they often need to find ways to cooperate. Australia's institutional architecture, therefore, continues to produce pressure points that challenge the major parties and provide opportunities for the minor parties.

References

Ansolabehere, Stephen, Shanto Iyengar, Adam Simon and Nicholas Valentino. 1994. 'Does Attack Advertising Demobilize the Electorate?'. *American Political Science Review* 88(4): 829–38. doi.org/10.2307/2082710.

Australian Electoral Commission (AEC). 2016. 'First preferences by party'. results. aec.gov.au/20499/Website/HouseStateFirstPrefsByParty-20499-NAT.htm.

Australian Electoral Commission (AEC). 2019. 'First preferences by party'. *Tally Room 2019 Federal Election*. Canberra: AEC. results.aec.gov.au/24310/ Website/HouseStateFirstPrefsByParty-24310-NAT.htm.

Bogle, Ariel. 2019. 'Clive Palmer's ad deluge shows Google and Facebook need to step up transparency, experts say'. *ABC News*, 22 May. www.abc.net.au/news/ science/2019-05-22/clive-palmer-election-advertising-google-facebook-transparency/11133596.

Bruns, Axel and Brenda Moon. 2018. 'Social Media in Australian Federal Elections: Comparing the 2013 and 2016 Campaigns'. *Journalism & Mass Communication Quarterly* 95(2): 425–48. doi.org/10.1177/1077699018766505.

Caccamo, Cameron. 2018. 'Clive Palmer is locked in a battle with the alt-right for control of his own Facebook meme page'. *Junkee*, 1 March. junkee.com/ clive-palmer-facebook-memes/148917.

Chen, Peter John. 2012. 'The new media and the campaign'. In *Julia 2010: The Caretaker Election*, edited by Marian Simms and John Wanna, 65–84. Canberra: ANU Press. doi.org/10.22459/J2010.02.2012.05.

Chen, Peter John. 2013. *Australian Politics in a Digital Age*. Canberra: ANU Press. doi.org/10.26530/oapen_459921.

Chen, Peter John. 2015. 'New media in the electoral context: The new normal'. In *Abbott's Gambit: The 2013 Australian Federal Election*, edited by Carol Johnson and John Wanna, with Hsu-Ann Lee, 81–94. Canberra: ANU Press. doi.org/10.22459/ag.01.2015.05.

Esposito, Brad. 2019. 'Australia's far-right is winning Facebook this year'. *Pedestrian*, 2 April. www.pedestrian.tv/news/australia-far-right-facebook/.

Evershed, Nick. 2014. 'Clive Palmer has attended only 7.7% of votes in parliament'. *The Guardian*, 16 September. www.theguardian.com/news/datablog/2014/sep/16/clive-palmer-has-attended-only-77-of-votes-in-parliament.

Ferrier, Tracey. 2019. 'Palmer promises QN workers' cash from Tuesday'. *Brisbane Times*, 29 April. www.brisbanetimes.com.au/national/queensland/palmer-promises-qn-workers-cash-from-tuesday-20190429-p51i6m.html.

Gibson, Rachel and Ian McAllister. 2011. 'Do Online Election Campaigns Win Votes? The 2007 Australian "YouTube" Election'. *Political Communication* 28(2): 227–44. doi.org/10.1080/10584609.2011.568042.

Kefford, Glenn. 2018. 'The minor parties' campaigns'. In *Double Disillusion: The 2016 Australian Federal Election*, edited by Anika Gauja, Peter Chen, Jennifer Curtin and Juliet Pietsch, 335–57. Canberra: ANU Press. doi.org/10.22459/dd.04.2018.15.

Kefford, Glenn and Duncan McDonnell. 2016. 'Ballots and Billions: Clive Palmer's Personal Party'. *Australian Journal of Political Science* 51(2): 183–97. doi.org/10.1080/10361146.2015.1133800.

Kefford, Glenn and Duncan McDonnell. 2018. 'Inside the Personal Party: Leader-Owners, Light Organizations and Limited Lifespans'. *The British Journal of Politics and International Relations* 20(2): 37–94. doi.org/10.1177/1369148117750819.

McSwiney, J. 2019. 'Social networks and digital organisation: Far right parties at the 2019 Australian federal election'. Australian Political Studies Association Annual Conference, Adelaide, 22–25 September.

Swanston, Tim. 2019. 'Clive Palmer dismisses condemnation from band Twisted Sister over political ad's song use'. *ABC News*, 2 January. www.abc.net.au/news/2019-01-02/clive-palmer-twisted-sister-song-use-legal-action-threat/10680234.

United Australia Party (UAP). 2019a. 'Negative gearing'. Advertisement on Facebook, 17 April. Brisbane: UAP. www.facebook.com/UnitedAusParty/videos/1511252845677034/.

United Australia Party (UAP). 2019b. 'Power costs'. Advertisement on Facebook, 20 April. Brisbane: UAP. www.facebook.com/UnitedAusParty/videos/803993329986888/.

United Australia Party (UAP). 2019c. 'Tell Shifty he's dreamin''. Advertisement on Facebook, 16 April. Brisbane: UAP. www.facebook.com/UnitedAusParty/videos/2150526838398767/?v=2150526838398767.

United Australia Party (UAP). 2019d. 'Protect & defend Australia with United Australia'. Advertisement on Facebook, 29 April. Brisbane: UAP. www.facebook.com/UnitedAusParty/videos/637172920077666/.

United Australia Party (UAP). 2019e. *Labor and China's Communist Government conspiring against Australia*. Media release, 6 May. Brisbane: UAP. www.united australiaparty.org.au/labor-and-chinas-communist-government-conspiring-against-australia/.

United Australia Party (UAP). 2019f. 'No tax cuts till 2024'. Advertisement on Facebook, 10 May. Brisbane: UAP. www.facebook.com/UnitedAusParty/photos/a.353343041461681/2056629854466316/?type=3&theater.

United Australia Party (UAP). 2019g. 'Pensions'. Advertisement on Facebook, 15 May. Brisbane: UAP. www.facebook.com/UnitedAusParty/photos/a.3533 43041461681/2057791651016803/?type=3&theater.

United Australia Party (UAP). 2019h. *United Australia Party National Policy*. Brisbane: UAP. www.unitedaustraliaparty.org.au/national_policy/.

Vitorovich, Lily. 2019. 'Palmer's UAP leads multi-million-dollar cash splash'. *The Australian*, 9 May. www.theaustralian.com.au/inquirer/palmers-uap-leads-multimilliondollar-cash-splash/news-story/bfe4ca4399a40e3449d4b93c3a0520f0.

Whitbourn, Michaela. 2019. 'Palmer "flagrantly infringed" copyright in Twisted Sister song'. *Sydney Morning Herald*, 12 February. www.smh.com.au/entertainment/music/palmer-flagrantly-infringed-copyright-in-twisted-sister-song-20190212-p50x7u.html.

18

THE INDEPENDENTS

Jennifer Curtin and Jill Sheppard

The impact of Independents on the fortunes of Liberal–National Coalition governments is often overshadowed by a focus on the minor parties' presence and power in the Senate. This ignores the fact that Independents have been a fixture in the lower house since 1996 and, at various times over this period, either Labor or the Coalition have needed their support to govern. Most recently, this was the case for newly anointed Prime Minister Scott Morrison. Following the election of Independent Kerryn Phelps to Malcolm Turnbull's former seat of Wentworth in October 2018, Morrison's government no longer held a majority. In November that year, on the day after Phelps was sworn in, Liberal MP Julia Banks quit the Liberal Party to sit as an Independent. Although both Phelps and Banks stated their preference to see the government run its full term, these Independents and others proved themselves thorns in the Coalition's side. In November 2018, Cathy McGowan introduced a Bill to establish a national integrity commission with wideranging powers to address perceived corruption and, in December, Phelps introduced the Medevac Bill, the aim of which was to bring asylum seekers detained offshore to Australia for medical treatment. Meanwhile, Banks's presence on the crossbench was a constant reminder of the allegedly toxic culture of the Liberal Party.

These incumbent Independents, and other aspiring Independent candidates, were a highly visible part of the 2019 campaign landscape for a number of reasons. First, alongside the traditional local constituency battles for votes, nationally, a number of Independents banded together to champion issues of government integrity, the politics of water and climate change.[1] Second, there was a small but noisily expressed public disillusionment with the Liberal Party—in part as a response to the nature of Turnbull's dismissal, but also in reaction to allegations of sexism and cronyism and resistance to addressing issues of climate change and coalmining. Thus, in addition to seeing Independents in the Coalition's rural and regional heartlands, the possibility of Independent representation extended to the leafy Liberal suburbs of the major cities. Finally, the 2019 election was to be the year of Independent women. It remains rare to see women elected as Independents in Australia, yet in 2019, the percentage of Independent women candidates increased significantly (up from 12.9 per cent in 2016 to 23.2 per cent). This chapter examines each of these dimensions of the Independents' campaigns and then reviews the results and implications for the future of Independents. For, although history was made when Independent candidate Helen Haines replaced Cathy McGowan as the member for Indi, it is not yet evident that the winning strategies employed in rural and provincial electorates will translate into ongoing success for urban liberal Independents.

The campaigns: A focus on both local and national

Independents have proved critical to government stability in recent years and their increasing presence can be credited to a combination of factors: a preferential electoral system, single-member districts, the presence of compulsory voting and general disenchantment with the major political parties, particularly among those who live in safe rural and regional seats. Although the election of growing numbers of Independents is not unique to Australia, elsewhere Independents tend to succeed in systems with open party lists and low electoral thresholds (Brancatti 2008).

Nonetheless, international and Australian scholarship points to one common feature associated with successful Independents: the need to be a 'local notable'. This normally requires candidates to be known for

---

1   Peter Andren was also known for his progressive stance on asylum seekers and parliamentary integrity as the MP for Calare, and Independents have worked together before—for example, in setting up the Independent Candidate's Advisory Network (to encourage others to stand as Independents). However, Andren, Tony Windsor and others chose not to form a 'group' to advance substantive policy issues (Costar and Curtin 2004: 21–23).

something before standing as an Independent—as local councillors or mayors, sports stars or media personalities (Costar and Curtin 2004). However, the election of McGowan in the Victorian seat of Indi in the 2013 federal election represented something both traditional and new. Her win was traditional in the sense that it reinforced a three-decades-long, low-level trend whereby a geographical concentration of voters eschewed major party loyalties in favour of local candidates.

This has been particularly evident in rural and regional electorates when the Coalition is in government. Alongside this, were several new dimensions. McGowan's campaign approach, which harnessed communities of support around the electorate, promoted both visibility and voice for the voters of Indi. Her base was far more diverse and inclusive than the discontent tapped 20 years earlier by Pauline Hanson's One Nation. McGowan spoke to young and old from across the political spectrum, many of whom had eschewed tribal party politics and were searching for a different kind of local representative (Curtin and Costar 2015; Curtin 2018).

Another particular feature of the 2019 election was that Independent candidates were better resourced and ostensibly cooperated more closely than in previous years (Grattan and Seaborn 2019). Whereas successful Independents in recent decades have had experience either as party-endorsed legislators or within party institutions, the current cohort of Independent candidates and MPs is markedly different. Instead, they are attracting support from less partisan sources. Two specific but related circumstances appear to have led to this phenomenon: the first is the decline in support for and trust in the major political parties, which has led directly to community-based organisational support for candidates such as Haines; and the second is frustration among many voters over the dearth of progressive climate change policies among those same parties (see, for example, Kassam 2019).

The first form of support, with Voices for Indi as the exemplar, has been covered widely (Curtin and Costar 2015; Grattan and Seaborn 2019; Hendriks 2017). The second is less well understood. A broad coalition of climate change activists—including tech entrepreneur Mike Cannon-Brookes, Australian billionaire's son Simon Holmes à Court and former prime minister Malcolm Turnbull's son, Alex—privately funded environmentally progressive Independents. Some of these funds were channelled through Climate 200 Pty Ltd, an organisation that was registered in April 2019 and which donated $40,000 to Julia Banks,

$35,000 to Helen Haines, $37,000 to Rob Oakeshott, $47,500 to Kerryn Phelps, $145,000 to Oliver Yates and $50,000 to Independent Senate candidate Anthony Pesec (AEC 2019a). By contrast, Zali Steggall's campaign was funded by a range of wealthy individuals and was claimed to be the most well-resourced of any Independent campaign in Australian history, with a $1.1 million war chest (Chambers and Caisley 2019; Maley 2019). This kind of organisation among Independent candidates—based both locally on shared concerns and nationally on specific issue domains—is certainly unprecedented in Australian politics.

Once elected, the 'creative' deliberative approach McGowan practised with the support of Voices for Indi gave her constituents an opportunity to participate in the practice of representation, demystifying federal politics in the process and creating 'respectful, authentic, skilled citizen politicians' (Haines 2019a; Hendriks 2017). Then, in November 2018, Voices for Indi invited around 550 registered campaign volunteers to a January 2019 meeting in the town of Benalla to determine a 'succession process' in advance of McGowan's anticipated retirement prior to the 2019 election (Chan 2018b). Although unprecedented, this approach was deemed necessary for a number of reasons: to 'Keep Indi Independent', to continue to build on McGowan's legacy of 'doing politics differently' and to ensure the campaign infrastructure created to support McGowan remained intact (Koslowski 2019a).

A meeting of around 200 volunteers endorsed Haines as the preferred candidate in mid-January and she began establishing her credentials as a worthy successor to McGowan. She spoke of the importance of valuing inclusion, diversity, listening and 'recognising the power within communities' by building on 'our little movement started in 2013, and what Cathy McGowan championed in office', to 'pass it on to the next community representative who will come after' (Haines 2019a).

Haines's policy positions were informed by conversations with citizens and her own experience in public health. She took an openly pro-choice stance on euthanasia and abortion and supported more funding for health care, education, aged care, the ABC and sharing regional grants across Australia, rather than privileging Coalition-held seats (Haines 2019b; Somerville and Johnson 2019). Haines opposed the Adani coalmine—differentiating herself from both the Liberal and the National candidates—and was a strong advocate for clean energy and climate change mitigation. In so doing, she invoked the progressive tendencies of some farmers who also recognised the need for new policies on energy and water (Haines 2019b).

Voices for Indi provided dynamic and coherent support for the new candidate, marshalling the well-known 'orange army' of 1,600–1,700 volunteers (spread across Indi's numerous small rural towns and the City of Wodonga). In the end, this amounted to roughly one volunteer for every 20 first-preference votes Haines received. Given the 21-day pre-polling period, this level of 'humanpower' proved critical (Koslowski 2019c). The ground campaign once again had a 'traditional' pre-cartel party feel, with face-to-face conversations, handmade paraphernalia sold at school fetes and music festivals and the requisite colour-coordinated bumper stickers and T-shirts. Haines also used ubiquitous new platforms—in particular, Facebook and Twitter. However, these only supplemented her highly visible presence around the electorate—often accompanied by the still-popular McGowan, thus helping voters to see that a transition from one Independent to another was both simple and natural. This double act was also apparent online, with McGowan's 20,000-plus followers on Twitter regularly reminded of her support for Haines. Their campaign activities were sufficiently successful to attract the attention of Advance Australia (Martin 2019).

The Voices for Indi movement proved contagious in 2019, with a community group called Voices of Warringah (VOW) created to support an alternative candidate to Tony Abbott, who local activists argued had refused to engage with liberals on issues such as climate change and same-sex marriage. These Warringah-based activists formed a committee and interviewed candidates, eventually selecting former Olympian Zali Steggall. 'Kitchen table conversations', pioneered in Indi, were hosted, social media accounts activated and volunteers mobilised.

GetUp! was also prominent in the campaign to oust Abbott, as were at least four other grassroots groups (Davies 2019). Dowse (2019a) recalls there being more than 700 people present at a GetUp! meeting in December 2018, well in advance of Steggall confirming her candidacy. The collective raison d'être of these activists was to unseat Abbott and get climate change on to the Liberals' policy agenda. In a sense, these two issues amounted to a single-issue campaign for Steggall; moderate Liberals were angry at Abbott's determined denial that renewable energy and climate mitigation strategies were necessary let alone desirable (Dowse 2019a). This was probably most visible at the Vote Tony Out rally, which attracted an estimated 1,000 protesters and featured former State-level Independent MPs, both of whom endorsed Steggall (Dowse 2019b).

Steggall's campaign also attracted considerable attention from conservative campaigning organisation Advance Australia (see Chapter 21, this volume). Advance Australia released a crude video (later removed) and large billboards linking Steggall to Labor Leader Bill Shorten. These were strategically located on at least one of several main roads through the electorate (and on roaming trucks). Meanwhile, Steggall incurred the wrath of shock jocks on radio station 2GB and talkback listeners who argued her supporters were playing the worst kind of dirty politics by linking Abbott and then-convicted Catholic Cardinal George Pell on posters.

Steggall took lessons on campaigning as an Independent from both McGowan and Phelps. Similar to Haines, who was surrounded by orange in Indi, and Phelps by supporters in purple, Warringah was awash with volunteers wearing aqua-coloured T-shirts. It was estimated that Steggall had marshalled over 1,000 supporters on the ground (Dowse 2019a), along with a well-positioned office up the road from Abbott's, a strong social media presence and an experienced team of fundraisers and tacticians.

Steggall also shared with Phelps and Banks the expertise of Damien Hodgkinson, whose experience in community campaigning helped win Phelps the by-election in Wentworth.[2] Hodgkinson's company, DEM Asia, was reported to be working with eight Independent candidates in setting up campaign infrastructure on the ground, including donor and volunteer databases and advertising, and administering postal vote ballot systems (Middleton 2019). The candidates maintained this was not an Independents' alliance, but rather a means by which to counterbalance the significant resources and knowledge available to the major party candidates (Tingle 2019). It was alleged that the Liberals were sufficiently concerned by Steggall's prospects that the party was spending as much as $2 million in the electorate. In Wentworth, voters were also targeted with an onslaught of Liberal-funded mail-outs and robocalls in the final week of the campaign (Witt 2019).

---

2 Hodgkinson was assisted by Anthony Reed and communications specialist Darrin Barnett, a former media adviser to Julia Gillard (Middleton 2019).

There were differences, however, between the campaigns of Steggall and Phelps, on the one hand, and Haines on the other. Steggall and Phelps were running against high-profile Liberal candidates in blue-ribbon urban electorates and their target demographic was disaffected moderate liberals concerned with the Liberal Party's position on climate change. While refugees and some local issues were raised, the campaign messaging concentrated primarily on climate and did not engage in the anti-establishment narrative often associated with non-party candidates. The *Sydney Morning Herald*'s SmartVote tool indicated that Haines, Yates, Steggall and Phelps all held more progressive stances than both the Liberals and Labor on environmental protection and law and order (including the treatment of asylum seekers). However, Steggall and Phelps differed in that they were closer to the Liberals on the economy and were openly opposed to Labor's tax package (Koslowski 2019b).

But 2019 also looked different to previous elections in two other ways. First, a number of Independents expanded their messaging in an effort to force a collective focus on national issues beyond the obvious one of climate change. The focus on national issues was driven in part by a newer breed of Independents—what some have termed the 'sensible centre'—made up of progressive urban Liberals (Denniss 2018). Fifteen Independent candidates ran a video across social media platforms that asked voters to 'rethink the role of Independents', from being political disruptors (thereby distancing themselves from some of the minor parties) to being a 'force for constructive debate' (Tingle 2019).

Prior to this, 12 Independent candidates had jointly called for immediate action on the allegations of misuse of public funds relating to the 2017 purchase of water rights by the federal government from Eastern Australia Irrigation, which was dubbed 'Watergate'. The signatories demanded the government adopt a comprehensive national integrity commission (Crowe 2019). These initiatives followed the parliamentary work of Independent MPs—notably, McGowan and Phelps—who successfully leveraged the balance of power held by the Independents and minor parties to push for change to the medical evacuation regime for asylum seekers on Manus Island and Nauru and to highlight the need for a federal integrity commission to address political corruption. Phelps noted that, during the campaign, the Independents would look to 'cooperate and share resources' and take a stand on issues of national importance, but reassured voters that this would not undermine their autonomy or their freedom to disagree with one another (Tingle 2019).

The second distinct feature of 2019 was the gender factor. In October 2018, Phelps had issued a call to arms to other women Independents to run for public office (Davies 2018). By March 2019, a number of high-profile women had put themselves forward as Independent candidates, including Louise Stewart in Julie Bishop's former seat of Curtin, Western Australia; Steggall; Alice Thompson in the seat of MacKellar; and Banks in the seat of Flinders. Media outlets around the country were documenting the 'rise of impressive female independent candidates' (Karvelas 2019).

The emergence of strong female independents who were economically conservative but radical on issues such as climate change was seen as a challenge to the Coalition. These women 'invaders' were said to be a consequence of the Coalition being internally split on environmental policy as well as the resistance of both the Liberal Party and the Nationals to selecting, promoting and fostering a culture inclusive of women (Clark 2019; Kenny 2019). Voters were reminded that Steggall, Phelps and Banks were economically conservative, socially progressive women who would normally fit easily within a centre-right party, but who had chosen to run as outsiders (Karvelas 2019). The fallout from the Liberal leadership battle, and its impact on Julie Bishop, remained a constant undercurrent as a result.

Three Sydney-based women lawyers had established 'WomenVote' in advance of the federal election and—like the now 40-year-old strategy of the Women's Electoral Lobby—scored parties on five policies of importance to women. They also used a bright-pink bus to travel to key electorates to canvass women voters' views and ask questions of candidates. They began their campaign in Wentworth and then travelled to Warringah, highlighting that women Independents were standing up for women (Smith 2019). Other women's groups also profiled women Independents. *Women's Agenda* provided a range of information about the candidates on its website, while 'Connecting Women' organised a panel discussion on gender equality in the electorate of Warringah (Dowse 2019b).

Women were also involved in organisation on the ground; four of the five VOW executive members were women and its secretary, Kathryn Ridge, had run as an Independent at the 2017 NSW by-election after former premier Mike Baird retired (Chan 2018a). Images of Phelps's purple-clad volunteers regularly featured groups of women, and photos of McGowan and Haines campaigning together were an implicit reminder that for too long Independent politics had been dominated by men. Haines said politics and the people of Indi needed intelligent rural women as representatives (Priestley 2019). It is difficult to assess the impact of women who helped run the campaigns of the women Independents, but in the case of Indi, Wentworth and Warringah, we do know that all three were explicitly committed to positive rather than negative narratives. The day after the election, a collage displayed in Warringah included the words 'Love Wins' (Dowse 2019c).

The results

In 2019, fewer Independent candidates stood for the House of Representatives than in 2016 (95 compared with 108), but the number elected increased by one, to three.[3] The share of the vote Independents received increased to 3.37 per cent (up from 2.8 per cent), although this figure masks a wide variation across States. Independents in South Australia, Western Australia and Queensland attracted less than 1.5 per cent compared with between 3.5 and 5 per cent in New South Wales, Victoria, the Australian Capital Territory and the Northern Territory, and 13 per cent in Tasmania (the last boosted by Andrew Wilkie's success).

Two incumbent Independents ran in 2019: Andrew Wilkie in the renamed and redistributed Tasmanian seat of Clark and Phelps in Wentworth. As indicated in Table 18.1, Wilkie extended his already tight hold on the sparsely populated seat to the south of Hobart, winning sufficient primary votes to be elected outright and increasing his overall margin to 72 per cent. In a sense, Clark is different to the 'usual' regional Independent seat in that the contest was between Wilkie and Labor, rather than a Coalition party candidate.

Phelps, however, was unsuccessful. Second-time Liberal candidate Dave Sharma won Wentworth despite Phelps increasing her primary vote by 3 per cent. Commentators argued that the anger over Turnbull's demise had dissipated, which, in combination with the polls predicting a Labor win and the scare campaign equating voting Independent with support for Labor, undermined Phelps's chances.

---

3   The drop in the number of Independent candidates may have been a result of the doubling of the deposit required of candidates (see Chapter 3, this volume). Reforms to the Senate electoral system in 2016 also reduced the chances of Independents' success. Nonetheless, 57 Independents nominated for Senate election. Of these, Anthony Pesec was the highest-profile candidate. A climate change and renewable energy activist, he campaigned as a progressive alternative to ACT incumbent Liberal Zed Seselja. Pesec received 12,604 votes—just less than 5 per cent of the vote (but almost 80,000 votes short of being elected).

Table 18.1 Results for selected Independents, 2016 and 2019

Candidate	Primary vote		Percentage change	TPP		Percentage change
	2016	**2019**		**2016**	**2019**	
Andrew Wilkie (Clark, formerly Denison, Tas.)	44.07	50.05	6.02	67.78	72.12	4.35
Rob Oakeshott (Cowper, NSW)	26.29	24.49	−1.80	45.44	43.21	−2.23
Kevin Mack (Farrar, NSW)		20.49			39.06	
Zali Steggall (Warringah, NSW)		43.46			57.24	
Kerryn Phelps (Wentworth, NSW)	29.19 (by-election 2018)	32.43	2.53	51.12	48.69	−2.43
Alice Thompson (MacKellar, NSW))		12.99			Placed 3rd	
Julia Banks (Flinders, Vic.)		13.79			Placed 3rd	
Helen Haines (Indi, Vic.)	34.76 (McGowan)	32.35	−2.41	54.83	51.39	−3.44
Oliver Yates (Kooyong, Vic.)		8.98			Placed 4th	
Louise Stewart (Curtin, WA)		7.75			Placed 4th	

Sources: Compiled by the authors from AEC (2019b); and Curtin (2018).

Wilkie was joined by two new Independents, Haines and Steggall, representing two quite different seats (urban and rural), and both making history: Steggall because the seat of Warringah had always been held by the Liberal Party and Haines because, for the first time federally, one Independent succeeded another. Haines's campaign, like McGowan's in 2016, was challenging in that she was subject to a three-cornered contest, meaning an exchange of preferences between the Liberals and Nationals. It took 25 days to declare the result, with Haines unable to retain McGowan's level of support. The seat of Indi is now one of Australia's most marginal electorates. Steggall, on the other hand, received a healthy 43 per cent primary vote, which translated into a fairly safe margin of 7 per cent.

Of the remaining high-profile candidates, only Rob Oakeshott came close to the 25 per cent primary vote considered the required minimum to have a chance of winning. The Liberal Party's Sussan Ley held her seat of Farrer on primary votes (50.7 per cent), although Kevin Mack secured 39 per cent of the two-party preferred—a swing against Ley of 7 per cent. Oliver Yates was prolific on social media but failed to reach double figures in Kooyong. He was seeking to unseat Treasurer Josh Frydenberg but the presence of a high-profile Greens candidate, Julian Burnside, complicated the choice for voters concerned about the environment (Burnside won 16 per cent of the primary vote). Julia Banks and Alice Thompson both received more than 12 per cent but failed to draw sufficient votes away from either the Liberal or the Labor candidates.

The cases of Indi, Clark and Warringah reinforce the argument that Independents will often succeed when voters believe political parties have failed to address both local and national interests. These successes are also a reminder that compulsory preferential voting in single-member districts aids the cause of Independents, because disillusioned constituents are compelled to vote and Labor and the Coalition are more likely to direct preferences to Independents than to each other. Thus, when an Independent candidate wins 25 per cent of the primary vote, they have a strong chance of garnering sufficient preferences to reach the required 50 per cent plus one. In most cases, this makes the seat 'marginal' (the contemporary exception is Wilkie).

In the case of rural and regional electorates, this marginal status can result in additional government largesse when the Coalition is in power, reinforcing the power of Independents. However, the example of Phelps suggests the same does not apply to the new urban liberal Independent. For, despite emulating the Indi model, Phelps, Banks, Yates, Steggall and others like them may be perceived as single-issue (climate change) protest candidates, attracting those only momentarily disaffected with their natural party of choice. Whether Steggall can marshal a permanent base of support for the 'sensible centre' remains to be seen.

References

Australian Electoral Commission (AEC). 2019a. *AEC Transparency Register*. Canberra: AEC. transparency.aec.gov.au/.

Australian Electoral Commission (AEC). 2019b. *2019 Federal Election*. Canberra: AEC. www.aec.gov.au/Elections/Federal_Elections/2019/index.htm.

Brancatti, Dawn. 2008. 'Winning Alone: The Electoral Fate of Independent Candidates Worldwide'. *Journal of Politics* 70(3): 648–62. doi.org/10.1017/S0022381608080675.

Chambers, Geoff and Olivia Caisley. 2019. 'Federal election independent candidates backed by Climate 200 funding vehicle'. *The Australian*, 5 November. www.theaustralian.com.au/nation/politics/federal-election-independent-candidates-backed-by-climate-200-funding-vehicle/news-story/1a4c635f0bee627b2a8f97f007491090.

Chan, Gabrielle. 2018a. 'Tony Abbott faces campaign using tactics that defeated Mirabella in Indi'. *The Guardian*, 6 October. www.theguardian.com/australia-news/2018/oct/06/tony-abbott-faces-campaign-using-tactics-that-defeated-mirabella-in-indi.

Chan, Gabrielle. 2018b. 'Cathy McGowan succession process launched by Indi community group'. *The Guardian*, 30 November. www.theguardian.com/australia-news/2018/nov/30/cathy-mcgowan-succession-process-launched-by-indi-community-group.

Clark, Andrew. 2019. 'Independent invaders could decide election'. *Australian Financial Review*, 3 May. www.afr.com/news/politics/national/blue-ribbon-battles-independent-invaders-could-decide-election-20190503-p51jp5.

Costar, Brian and Jennifer Curtin. 2004. *Rebels with a Cause: Independents in Australian Politics*. Sydney: UNSW Press.

Crowe, David. 2019. 'The "price of power": Key independents list their conditions for support in next parliament'. *Sydney Morning Herald*, 1 May. www.smh.com.au/federal-election-2019/the-price-of-power-key-independents-list-their-conditions-for-support-in-next-parliament-20190430-p51iqe.html.

Curtin, Jennifer. 2018. 'Independents return and the "almost" hung parliament'. In *Double Disillusion: The 2016 Australian Federal Election*, edited by Anika Gauja, Peter Chen, Jennifer Curtin and Juliet Pietsch, 359–80. Canberra: ANU Press. doi.org/10.22459/DD.04.2018.16.

Curtin, Jennifer and Brian Costar. 2015. 'The contest for rural representation: The celebrated contest over Indi and the fate of independents'. In *Abbott's Gambit: The 2013 Australian Federal Election*, edited by Carol Johnson and John Wanna, with Hsu-Ann Lee, 275–91. Canberra: ANU Press. doi.org/10.22459/AG.01.2015.16.

Davies, Anne. 2018. 'Kerryn Phelps and her purple army shake up politics-as-usual in Wentworth stunner'. *The Guardian*, 20 October. www.theguardian.com/australia-news/2018/oct/20/kerryn-phelps-and-her-purple-army-shake-up-politics-as-usual-in-wentworth-stunner.

Davies, Anne. 2019. '"And this is Mosman!": Genteel Warringah rocked by election rancour'. *The Guardian*, 16 May. www.theguardian.com/australia-news/2019/may/16/genteel-warringah-rocked-election-rancour-abbott-steggall.

Denniss, Richard. 2018. 'Progressive ideas are becoming the new "sensible centre" of Australian politics'. *The Guardian*, 28 November. www.theguardian.com/commentisfree/2018/nov/28/progressive-ideas-are-becoming-the-new-sensible-centre-of-australian-politics.

Dowse, Sara. 2019a. 'Warringah rises up'. *Inside Story*, 24 April. insidestory.org.au/warringah-rises-up/.

Dowse, Sara. 2019b. 'Something's afoot in Warringah'. *Inside Story*, 7 May. insidestory.org.au/somethings-afoot-in-warringah/.

Dowse, Sara. 2019c. 'Warringah's win'. *Inside Story*, 20 May. insidestory.org.au/warringahs-win/.

Grattan, Michelle and Jane Seaborn. 2019. 'The Independents: The cases of Warringah and Wentworth'. In *From Turnbull to Morrison: Understanding the Trust Divide*, edited by Mark Evans, Michelle Grattan and Brendan McCaffrie, 281–94. Melbourne: Melbourne University Publishing.

Haines, Helen. 2019a. *Helen Haines' Bio*. Wangaratta, Vic.: Voices for Indi. voicesforindi.com/candidate-identification-process/more-about-helen-haines/.

Haines, Helen. 2019b. *Helen Haines launches campaign for Indi*. 7 April. www.helenhaines.org/campaign_launch [page discontinued].

Hendriks, Carolyn M. 2017. 'Citizen-Led Democratic Reform: Innovations in Indi'. *Australian Journal of Political Science* 52(4): 481–99. doi.org/10.1080/10361146.2017.1374345.

Karvelas, Patricia. 2019. 'Women are pushing to the front of the queue in 2019 Australian politics'. *ABC News*, 30 January. www.abc.net.au/news/2019-01-30/zali-steggall-tony-abbott-kelly-odwyer-australian-politics-women/10761552.

Kassam, Natasha. 2019. *Lowy Institute Poll 2019*. Sydney: Lowy Institute. www.lowyinstitute.org/publications/lowy-institute-poll-2019.

Kenny, Mark. 2019. 'Liberals lose yet another high-profile woman, yet still no action on gender'. *The Conversation*, 21 January. theconversation.com/liberals-lose-yet-another-high-profile-woman-yet-still-no-action-on-gender-110158.

Koslowski, Max. 2019a. 'Cathy McGowan, trailblazing independent MP, to quit politics at the election'. *Sydney Morning Herald*, 14 January. www.smh.com.au/politics/federal/cathy-mcgowan-trailblazing-independent-mp-to-quit-politics-at-the-election-20190114-p50r6v.html.

Koslowski, Max. 2019b. 'Are independents really from the "sensible centre"? Smartvote Australia asked 50 of them'. *Sydney Morning Herald*, 7 May. www.smh.com.au/federal-election-2019/are-independents-really-from-the-sensible-centre-smartvote-australia-asked-50-of-them-20190507-p51kr2.html.

Koslowski, Max. 2019c. '"A school fete on steroids": How the first ever independent handover triumphed'. *Sydney Morning Herald*, 20 May. www.smh.com.au/federal-election-2019/a-school-fete-on-steroids-how-the-first-ever-independent-handover-triumphed-20190520-p51p6y.html.

Maley, Jacqueline. 2019. 'Steggall's campaign was powered by a $1.1 million donations war chest'. *Sydney Morning Herald*, 4 November. www.smh.com.au/politics/federal/steggall-s-campaign-was-powered-by-a-1-1-million-donations-war-chest-20191101-p536nh.html.

Martin, Lisa. 2019. 'Independent's day? The orange army and its battle for Indi'. *The Guardian*, 23 April. www.theguardian.com/australia-news/2019/apr/23/independents-day-the-orange-army-and-its-battle-for-indi.

Middleton, Karen. 2019. 'The campaigner behind Phelps, Banks and Steggall'. *The Saturday Paper*, No. 242, 2–8 March. www.thesaturdaypaper.com.au/news/politics/2019/03/02/the-campaigner-behind-phelps-banks-and-steggall/15514452007567.

Priestley, Angela. 2019. '"I have strength in my hands": Midwife Helen Haines to take on major parties, replacing Cathy McGowan'. *Women's Agenda*, 13 January. womensagenda.com.au/latest/i-have-strength-in-my-hands-midwife-helen-haines-to-taking-on-major-parties-replacing-cathy-mcgowan/.

Smith, Alexandra. 2019. 'Wentworth candidates board the big pink bus'. *Sydney Morning Herald*, 1 May. www.smh.com.au/federal-election-2019/wentworth-candidates-board-the-big-pink-bus-20190501-p51j2q.html.

Somerville, Erin and Sian Johnson. 2019. 'Independent MP accuses federal government of politicising regional grants'. *ABC News*, 6 March. www.abc.net.au/news/2019-03-06/mcgowan-lodges-official-complaint-over-grant-announcements/10876004.

Tingle, Laura. 2019. 'Federal election 2019: Independents band together to take on political parties'. *ABC News*, 7 May. www.abc.net.au/news/2019-05-07/independents-advert-takes-on-political-parties-laura-tingle/11084804.

Witt, Merrill. 2019. 'Independents' success offers silver lining'. *CityHub*, [Sydney], 22 May. www.altmedia.net.au/independents-success-offers-silver-lining/139639.

19

BUSINESS

John Wanna

For the first time in many federal elections, business did not play a major or prominent role in the 2019 campaign. Business groups had been comparatively active in many previous federal elections, in 2004, 2007, 2013 and 2016, asserting their values and priorities while combatting government policies they resented—notably, the mining rental resource tax in May 2010. In 2010, business remained on the sidelines, seemingly perplexed over the sudden 'leadership coup' against Kevin Rudd, while generally positive towards the fiscal stimulus that Labor had engineered to combat the Global Financial Crisis.

In 2019—again, following much leadership turmoil, this time in the Coalition Government—business once more largely opted to leave the election result up to the voters and not run a vigorous campaign to influence the outcome. Somewhat paradoxically, the Opposition Labor leadership later blamed big business and sections of the corporate media for their election loss.

Nevertheless, business did try to change the tenor of debate away from short-term and local considerations to longer-term positive and proactive agendas. Mostly, business stressed the need for stability and certainty in governance, a clear sense of direction and confidence-building for the economy. It repeatedly called for further economic and structural reform, fewer impediments to business and for the next government to push ahead with much needed reforms including on climate change. Business Council of Australia (BCA) Chief Executive Officer (CEO) Jennifer Westacott said:

> For the last few elections, it has been a race to the bottom to take things off the agenda and limit options and choices … a blame game and an anti-business agenda and anti-growth agenda are not going to solve the issues that Australia confronts. (Quoted in Uren 2019)

Perhaps what was less expected was that business stressed the need for cooperation for better outcomes overall and implicitly criticised the heightening of the politics of envy in the 'class war' against the 'top end of town'.

Business also wanted a clear winner, not a hung parliament, giving the next government a clear mandate (see Garvey and Gluyas 2019). A less rabble-like Senate was also preferred, with many executives hoping for a smaller crossbench of 'maverick' senators. Sections of business had generally been pleased with the Coalition's Budget for 2019–20 (which promised a surplus of $7 billion and economic growth rates of 2.75 per cent, later reduced to 2.5 per cent), which was delivered in the final sitting days of parliament and on the eve of the election being called, but they were sceptical about whether such an economic plan on its own could turn things around.

'Meek and mild' so 'business hardly played a role'

Business groups and senior CEOs widely expected a Labor victory, especially after more than 50 consecutive Newspolls showed Labor holding a commanding lead in the two-party-preferred vote. The National Retail Association (2019), for instance, informed its members to expect a Labor win because 'Labor has led in every major opinion poll for the past two and a half years and is still the favourite'. In many ways, business lapsed into a fatalistic 'groupthink' and became resigned to the polls and the fact that a change of government was imminent. It also appeared to believe what the polls were saying, and it is worth recalling that a Newspoll in mid-March 2019 had the Labor Party ahead by a margin of 54–46 per cent—an eight-point lead eight weeks out from the election. In such circumstances, business apparently adopted a series of tactical strategies: battening down while awaiting Labor's victory, not antagonising Labor in the lead-up to the campaign proper and not running advertisements attacking Labor or boosting the Coalition. Many CEOs also began overtly currying favour with Labor leaders, hoping to prosper or retain influence under their rule. Interestingly (and as discussed in Chapter 11, this volume), the re-election of a Liberal–National Government in New South Wales under Gladys Berejiklian was not seen by either business or the media as a harbinger of better prospects for the Coalition, even though its regional focus certainly was a fillip to Scott Morrison.

Business commentators reported that 'big business was bracing for Bill Shorten and bracing for more class war' (Fullerton 2019), and that it may regret not having a fuller strategy or may revert to behind-the-scenes lobbying (Uren 2019). Conservative columnists such as Chris Kenny (2019) noted once the election was over:

> Big business hardly played a role. In fact, many on the Coalition side have long been frustrated about the way corporate Australia had become meek and mild on major economic debates, seemingly to align itself with a prospective Labor government in Canberra.

Columnists in the business pages of News Corp newspapers claimed: 'Some people close to PM [Prime Minister] Scott Morrison had grumbled … about the business lobby's poor contribution during the campaign' (Glasgow and Lacy 2019d). Glasgow and Lacy (2019c) reported:

> It is the view of many in Team Morrison that the BCA was missing in action during the election campaign … [and] the BCA's board … like most of corporate Australia had been bracing for life in Bill Shorten's Australia.

At one political panel event held for business in the final week of the campaign, only one businessman, Alastair Kinloch from AMP Limited (Glasgow and Lacy 2019b: 17), said he felt the tide had turned and that the Coalition could scrape back in; the other people present were apparently incredulous.

As a former economist with the Australian Chamber of Commerce and Industry (ACCI), Greg Evans (2019), wrote in the aftermath of the election:

> Today the business sector is not a policy influencer and is mostly missing in action. A centrepiece of the government's third term agenda is to deliver income tax cuts to middle Australia, yet business provided no impetus for this. There was always a strong economic case to return bracket creep to individuals, especially

when other factors were weighing on wages growth. Surprisingly, this was overlooked by industry. Instead, business had a one-dimensional tax approach and, after failing to secure company tax reductions, had nothing left to say … the business voice was virtually silent. It did not contribute a reform agenda or highlight and oppose those policies detrimental to its interests and to the economy.

It must be said that many business commentators were uniformly hostile to Labor's proposed policies, but not many actively endorsed the Coalition, perhaps seeing it as the least-worst alternative. These included Robert Gottliebsen, Terry McCrann, Chris Kenny, Allan Wood, Don Stammer, Matthew Cranston and Michael Stutchbury. *The Australian*'s David Uren and the *Australian Financial Review*'s Phillip Coorey, Jennifer Hewett and Adele Ferguson were notable exceptions to this apparent hostility. Moreover, many conservative economic columnists regularly attacked Labor's tax plans, including Henry Ergas, Jonathan Pincus, Tony Shepherd, Judith Sloane, Niki Savva, Adam Creighton and Nick Cater. Many of these journalists and commentators had close personal connections to the Coalition or larger business associations.

The semi-retired financial journalist (and *Sky News* commentator) Alan Wood wrote a rabid weekly column in *The Weekend Australian* throughout the lead-up to the election, predicting the 'end of Australia' if Labor won. In an article entitled 'Labor lays out 165 steps to economic destruction', Wood (2019) ventured:

> Before the campaign started, I noted that Bill Shorten and Chris Bowen had made it official and public: they had formalised a two-stage strategy to destroy Australia. That was far too gentle; back then we were yet to know the half of it. If you want to be afraid, really afraid, go to the Labor Party's policies website. All the promises are listed, one by one, and linked to the semi-specific policy detail. As of Friday night, one week out from the election, they added to 165. Just let that number sink in. I doubt that we've ever seen anything remotely, *remotely*, approaching that sort of promised utterly pervasive government intrusion into our lives both in broad societal but very directly in individual terms.

He then went on to castigate as many of Labor's policies as he could squeeze into his 1,200-word column, before ending with: 'A Shorten–Bowen government won't just change the country, it will destroy it.'

Thus, many sectors of business remained relatively silent; business was, in effect, 'sitting out' the election. It was also reticent to be seen as a very active player because Bill Shorten was making the 'big end of town' and 'fat-cat employers' a major part of his campaign rhetoric. Shorten's comment about business leaders being sent to the 'naughty corner' if he won may have further discouraged some business leaders from speaking out on issues about which they normally would have in the course of events.

Others called for a more collaborative approach—for instance, the CEO of the Property Council of Australia (PCA), Stephen Conry, said:

> There are too many instances where political leaders or ministers respond to industry groups by saying 'but of course you'd say that, because it's relevant to your industry'. We need more industry groups or industry associations collaborating to argue why both sides of politics should get together [on] issues such as tax reform … business wanted overall tax reform, but this would need bipartisan support. (Quoted in Condon 2019)

This begs the question: *should* business have played a more significant role? Certainly, some leading Coalition ministers thought so, and were later critical of the benign role adopted across the sector (Frydenberg 2019). Other commentators argued that 'business failed to explain their views' in the months leading up to and during the campaign (M. Kenny 2019). But business generally took the view that to take on a more strident profile in the campaign would prove counterproductive, and might only encourage more radical oppositional groups such as the ACTU and GetUp! to spend even more than they were already investing in a Labor win (reputedly $3.2 million by the ACTU and $4.7 million by GetUp!), in addition to the millions coming from individual unions such as the Australian Education Union and the National Tertiary Education Union, which were spending $1.6 million to support school education and universities (see also Scott, Chapter 20, this volume). In addition, the consistency of the opinion polls predicting a comfortable Labor victory possibly also silenced the larger business associations, although some smaller sectional associations were more vociferous.

There was much media speculation that the Coalition would see its election funding from business sources dry up, but in the event, funding seemed to materialise, although the Coalition allocated these funds very prudently towards sandbagging the seats it needed to hold, while targeting a small number of Labor seats as vulnerable in Queensland and Tasmania.

This funding stream may have been motivated by the desire to ensure that the Coalition would remain a viable political force in the event it was consigned to Opposition.

Business association advocacy

Business associations speaking for their members largely focused and spoke out on problems or issues close to their constituencies' interests. Most associations did not address issues across a wide canvas, in contrast with the pattern in recent decades. Some groups produced an explicit policy priorities statement of variable length—for example, the Australian Industry Group (Ai Group) produced a seven-page list, while the National Farmers' Federation (NFF) produced a glossy eight-page agenda (NFF 2018; see also NFF 2019)—but many simply put forward industry-specific or sectoral policies through news releases. The most prominent issues were policies to stimulate economic and regional growth; policies on energy and carbon emissions reduction; pro-coal and anti-coal sentiments, especially over the emblematic Adani coalmine in Queensland; and issues such as the severe drought and water restrictions in rural Australia, banking reform and credit availability and increased funding for cultural industries. Interestingly, many firms talked of Aboriginal engagement, constitutional reconciliation and 'working together' to seek meaningful change and reducing gaps—for example, the accounting firm PricewaterhouseCoopers' (2019) 'Parity' campaign to end 'disparity'. Table 19.1 collates the election priorities for Australia's main business associations.

Table 19.1 Business associations: Summary of key concerns, 2019 federal election

Association	Economy	Labour market & industrial relations	Fiscal, taxation, credit	Climate, energy, environment	Social, community	Technology, digital literacy	Good government
Business Council of Australia	• *Plan for a Stronger Australia* • Accelerate growth • Restore business confidence • Drive competition • Better infrastructure • Stronger regions • Population and migrant increases	• Increase real wages in line with productivity • More agile labour market • Wage safety nets and enterprise-based agreements • Job creation • Skills and training • Retain ABCC[1] and ROC[2]	• Lower tax burden, especially reduce company tax burden • Stronger Budget and return to surplus • Government to impose spending and tax caps • Preserve AAA credit rating • Increase credit availability	• Deal with climate change • Support Paris Agreement • Business needs long-term investment certainty • Integrate energy and climate change policies • Lower energy prices • Remove coal seam gas moratoriums • Limit vehicle and agricultural emissions	• Higher living standards, ameliorate entrenched disadvantage • Newstart is inadequate • Indigenous engagement and constitutional recognition • Better intergovernmental relations on health, mental health and vocational education and training	• Improve digital literacy • Government to review future skills and literacy levels	• Voters want clear directions • Parliament should work constructively • Better services/better value • Remove red tape and regulations

Association	Economy	Labour market & industrial relations	Fiscal, taxation, credit	Climate, energy, environment	Social, community	Technology, digital literacy	Good government
Minerals Council of Australia	• Global competitiveness is essential, structural reforms still needed • Investment and productivity • Trade liberalisation	• Increase skilled and flexible workforce • Workplace safety is crucial • Regional jobs strategy	• Reduce Australia's internationally uncompetitive tax levels • Lower corporate tax • Support mining and coal exports and exploration • Po–uranium • Fuel tax credits • Need for Budget repair	• Sustainable development goals • Reliable energy at least cost • Reduce risks of climate change • Long-term market mechanisms • Support for nuclear power, but also for carbon price and capture • Support for Adani coalmine	• Revitalise regional communities • Respect human rights • Gender equity targets • Partnership with Indigenous organisations	• Support technological innovation • Data-driven industries • New digital skills • Focus on STEMM[5]	• Government to deliver policy certainty for investment • Streamline approval processes
Australian Industry Group	• Clear policy directions (Building on Success) • Reboot policies for prosperity and growth • Promote investment • Lift productivity performance • Business costs too high • Youth unemployment too high	• Need for improved skills, education and training • Greater flexibility in sclerotic industrial relations system • Low wage growth a problem • Wage increases linked to productivity • Focus on job creation and apprenticeships • Fair workplace relations	• Real action on tax reform • Return to Henry Tax Review to reopen debate • Support for government's tax cuts plan • Research and development capabilities • Defence procurement to support opportunities for Australian companies	• Develop credible climate change policy • Durable and well-integrated climate and energy policies • Reduce carbon emissions • Address crisis facing Australia's waste disposal	• Greater social cohesion needed • Broader community prosperity needed	• Digital skills needed • Improve digital literacy • STEMM shortage acute	• Growing public dissatisfaction and distrust with government • Need for national leadership • Avoid poorly conceived and populist proposals

Association	Economy	Labour market & industrial relations	Fiscal, taxation, credit	Climate, energy, environment	Social, community	Technology, digital literacy	Good government
National Farmers' Federation/ AgForce	• Need for national agriculture strategy • Sectoral investment target of $100 billion by 2030 • Export strategies • Northern Australia plan • Extend agricultural starter loans • Develop emerging trade sectors (e.g. horticulture) • Bilateral trade agreements (e.g. with Indonesia) • Encourage regional entrepreneurship	• Agricultural workforce strategy needed • Recruitment program needed to attract youth to work in agriculture • Decentralisation and resettlement • Increase migrant intake/visa workforce • Stop abuse of bonded labour • Caution against wage breakout	• Competitive tax system required • Reduce taxes • Tax geared towards internationally competitive sectors • Provide critical infrastructure • Fuel-tax credits • Supportive regulatory environment • Treatment of farm trusts • 150% tax deductions for farm insurance	• Support NEG • Rewards for emission offsets from emission reduction fund • $1 billion for environmental stewardship fund • Sustain Murray–Darling Basin Plan agenda • The new Federal Environment Protection Authority not to include water compliance • Land clearing issues • Drought management	• Farm safety initiatives • Country road black spots program • Stress on social effects of water buy-back schemes • Mental health in rural and regional Australia	• Improve regional telecommunications • Regional connectivity • Digital literacy important to remote communities	• Government to work cooperatively with industry • Reduce non-tariff barriers in markets • Bipartisan support for Murray–Darling Basin Plan • Animal welfare partnerships

Association	Economy	Labour market & industrial relations	Fiscal, taxation, credit	Climate, energy, environment	Social, community	Technology, digital literacy	Good government
Australian Chamber of Commerce and Industry	• Highlight importance of small business to the economy • Governments to encourage economic growth • Lower inflation needed • Develop tourism infrastructure	• Better workforce relations • Increased flexibility in industrial relations • Investment in skills and employment services • Retain safety net of employment conditions • Enterprise bargaining • Less complex industrial relations regulations	• Restrain public spending and lower debt • Budget surpluses • Lower taxes • Fast-track small to medium enterprise company tax reductions • Facilitate competitiveness • Maintain equity focus • Government action to provide credit and asset write-downs	• Cut energy prices • Need energy reliability • To ensure affordability of energy, include coal and natural gas supplies • Clear policy needed to reduce emissions	• Higher living standards • Mutual obligation necessary in social welfare system • Aboriginal reconciliation • More affordable child care	• Support new technologies for industrial competitiveness	• Parliament to work in national interest, governing for all Australians • Greater collaboration between governments; streamline regulations
National Retail Association	• Stronger growth agenda needed • Focus on economic management • Job creation • Problem of low wage growth • Opposed to 'top end of town' rhetoric as too divisive	• Support for small business job growth • Opposed to reversal of penalty rate cuts	• Support income tax cuts for individuals • Lower interest rates • Stronger Budget • Reduce debt • Support moves to restore trust in banking sector	• Importance of environmental sustainability • Reduce use of plastic • e-waste bans or plans for proper disposal needed	• Policies to promote financial security for women • Encourage disability employment • Increased crime reporting	• Promotion of take-up of new technologies for retail sector	

Association	Economy	Labour market & industrial relations	Fiscal, taxation, credit	Climate, energy, environment	Social, community	Technology, digital literacy	Good government
Australian Banking Association/ Financial Planning Association	• Relax lending policies • Create an incentivised investment fund for business • Opposed to further banking reforms or regulations • Productivity orientation • Improve customer protection policies	• Reduce the complicated regulatory environment • Commit to overhaul of banking staff pay to eliminate bonuses tied to sales volumes	• Support for fair and efficient tax system, but opposed to Labor's franking credit cuts and negative gearing changes and increases in capital gains tax on properties • Opposed to new bipartisan levy of $554–640 million to restore trust in banking		• Pledges to commit assistance for natural disasters to assist recovery measures		
Real estate and building sectors (REIA, MBA, HIA, PCA)[3]	• Promotion of investment • Business-friendly economic policies • Infrastructural investment needed • More investment in housing, offices and community facilities	• Flexible skilled workforce • Up-skilling vocational education programs • Apprenticeships • Higher skilled migrant intake levels • Safety concerns on worksites • Opposed to abolition of ABCC[1] and wants greater accountability for unions on sites	• Opposed to Labor's 'retiree' tax increases • Warned of higher rents • Need for Budget repair • Overhaul tax system • Lower taxes and stamp duty concessions • Opposed to the cumulative GST costs				• Government should eliminate waste in public sector • MBA targeted 10 'building seats', opposing Labor's housing policies

Association	Economy	Labour market & industrial relations	Fiscal, taxation, credit	Climate, energy, environment	Social, community	Technology, digital literacy	Good government
Insurance Council of Australia	• Improve business efficiencies • Invest in nation-building infrastructure • National regulation of building and construction sector	• Regional growth strategies needed to spread job opportunities	• Renew tax reform agenda • Stronger Budget • Banking reform • Remove inefficient and unfair State taxes and levies • Remove duties on insurance products	• Call for environmental sustainability and positive steps towards climate change to reduce incidence of catastrophic weather events			• Government to reduce regulatory burden on business • Better government–industry cooperation
Medical associations (AMA, RACGP, PGA)[4]		• Distribution of medical workforce • Regional disadvantage • Too much reliance on overseas-trained doctors in rural and remote areas	• Lift the 'freeze' on the Medicare rebate to patients and increase bulk-billing incentives to GPs	• National strategy for health and climate change needed • Link environmental sustainability to health care	• Health is the core social issue • Sought a further $1 billion spending on Medicare with prominent full-page ads • More investment across sector • Regional health plans • Aboriginal health issues • Aged care • Full funding of National Disability Insurance Scheme • Pharmaceutical Benefits Scheme under pressure • Support for community pharmacies • Care of refugees	• e-health and telehealth initiatives welcomed • Better access to National Broadband Network for regional Australia	• Improve intergovernmental relations on health delivery

Association	Economy	Labour market & industrial relations	Fiscal, taxation, credit	Climate, energy, environment	Social, community	Technology, digital literacy	Good government
Climate Change Council			• Support Labor's $200 million infrastructure plan to create electric vehicle charging network across Australia	• Clean energy policies needed • Long-term strategies • Lower prices for energy • Zero emissions policy • Mandate for solar • Anti-Adani mine • Great Barrier Reef deterioration an issue	• Support Labor's target of 50% of government vehicles being electric by 2025 and 50 per cent of all vehicle sales to be electric by 2030		• Opposed to 'misleading debates' from politicians on climate change • Rebuild capacities of Climate Change Authority
Shareholders Association, Financial Services Council, Self-Managed Superannuation Fund Association	• Importance of shareholders and the self-managed super fund sector to economy and growth • Promote export of financial services to rest of world • Protection of superannuation investments		• Ran campaign against ALP's 'misleading franking credits proposal' • Urged vote no to ALP's 'retiree taxes' • Increase incentives for savings • Increase concessional and non-concessional caps for super • Lower compliance costs			• More investment in technology and innovation	• Government to provide better regulatory environment

[1] ABCC = Australian Building and Construction Commission

[2] ROG = Registered Organisations Commission

[3] REIA = Real Estate Institute of Australia; MBA = Master Builders Australia; HIA = Housing Industry Association; PCA = Property Council of Australia

[4] AMA = Australian Medical Association; RACGP = Royal Australian College of General Practitioners; PGA = Pharmaceutical Guild of Australia

[5] STEMM = science, technology, engineering, mathematics and medicine

Source: Compiled by the author from business associations' electoral manifestos on their websites 2019.

Business collectively was racked by worry about the nation's economic future, slackening economic growth and global trade wars. It generally thought no major party had an appetite for dealing with the difficult policy issues facing Australia—and it was accusing most politicians of 'kicking the can down the road'. Almost all businesses strongly supported Budget repair measures and pleaded for lower taxation for both companies and individuals. Some issues on which one might have expected business to find a voice were relatively overlooked or ignored, including a crackdown on multinational tax avoidance, lower interest rates and a looming interest rate cut by the Reserve Bank of Australia, immigration levels, asylum seeker issues and the 'Medevac' Bill allowing the relocation of offshore detainees whose medical conditions were thought significant by doctors (discussed in Simms, Chapter 2, this volume). Business in general did not seek to inflame the proposed Indian-owned Adani coalmining project, which was contentiously granted federal environmental approval on the eve of the caretaker period, but still awaited State government approvals (see Williams, Chapter 11, this volume).

Big business and the BCA were quoted as 'sounding the alarm that yet another election will pass without any serious commitment to economic reform' while warning about 'the rise of an anti-business agenda' (Uren 2019). The BCA's Westacott argued that 'the idea that we can go for another 10 to 15 years without [a] major economic downturn is fanciful and naive' (Uren 2019). The BCA highlighted the political shortcomings of the present adversarial approach to politics and the lack of progress on tax reform and developing a sustainable energy policy. The association's priorities were growth policies, increased productivity, increased real wage growth in alignment with productivity and no return to the industry-based award determinations sought by the ACTU (see Scott, Chapter 20, this volume). Like many business groups, the BCA urged consistent action against climate change while calling for removal of the moratorium on coal seam gas production in eastern Australia. This relaxation was also advocated by the Minerals Council of Australia (MCA), which also endorsed nuclear power as a way of guaranteeing reliable energy at competitive prices. The miners supported continued coal production but were largely quiet on Adani until after the election and insisted on greater measures to reduce emissions.

The Ai Group, representing Australian manufacturers, stressed the importance of lifting the levels of skills, training and education in the workforce and 'urged all parties to support' these opportunities, including greater investment in the science, technology, engineering, mathematics and medicine (STEMM) capabilities of the workforce. The Ai Group stressed the need for prosperity and growth along with social cohesion, and it called on the next government to reopen debate on the tax reform agenda and re-examine many of the proposals put forward in the comprehensive but not influential *Australia's Future Tax System* report, known as the Henry Review (Henry et al. 2009). It also argued that climate change and energy policies had to be durable and well integrated to safeguard Australia's economic future.

The NFF and AgForce Queensland were (along with bankers and doctors) the most self-interested in their concerns. They called for a 'national agricultural strategy' and an 'agricultural workforce strategy', better trade access and bilateral agreements and government delivery of greater international competitiveness for the sector. They called for reduced taxes, support for farming families, including agricultural starter loans, and increased temporary migrant intakes. Water management was a huge concern, especially with large parts of the continent in drought. The NFF (2019) did not support 'pausing' the Murray–Darling Basin Plan (as some high-profile Independent candidates were advocating) but called for greater attention to the 'devastating effects on rural communities from the removal of consumptive water'. It also advocated that, if Labor's proposed Federal Environmental Protection Authority (FEPA) were established, water should not be included in its remit, and it was 'not convinced that the inclusion of the compliance arm of the Murray–Darling Basin Authority (MDBA) should be part of a new FEPA'. As in previous elections, the NFF and AgForce had an extensive set of environmental demands, including rewards for emission offsets, carbon farming, drought management, dedicated government funds to support environmental sustainability involving land management and the exclusion of farming from restrictive environmental policies, including restrictions on land clearing. Like other business groups, they advocated a national energy policy.

The ACCI and Small Business Association of Australia advocated tax relief, opposed what they and the Coalition termed Labor's 'retiree taxes' and supported greater flexibility for small businesses, better workplace relations and reduced energy costs. The National Retail Association also advocated tax cuts and lower interest rates, opposed restoring penalty rates and called for a stronger economic growth agenda from government. The Insurance Council of Australia prioritised national infrastructure and business efficiency, regional growth and for government to renew the tax reform agenda. The Australian Medical Association (AMA), the Royal Australian College of General Practitioners (RACGP) and the Pharmaceutical Guild of Australia (PGA) wanted an extra $1 billion spent on Medicare payments to doctors and greater investment across the health sector and community pharmacies, and took out full-page advertisements stressing health as a core issue for government. These health lobbyists insisted on more resources going to their sector but did not publicly endorse one side of politics over another. The AMA also urged better care for asylum seekers and refugees, while the RACGP urged greater attention to primary care in health funding. RACGP advertisements that portrayed sick people complaining 'I can't afford to see a doctor' were rejected publicly by other groups of doctors, who claimed the advertisements were misleading.

A few associations were more political in their messages and seemed to endorse Chris Bowen's off-the-cuff remark to retirees that 'if you don't like our policies, don't vote for us' (paraphrased) (Chapman 2019). Master Builders Australia (MBA) targeted 10 'building seats' where levels of housing construction were highest, claiming house prices would fall and rents rise under Labor, and ran press and TV advertisements opposing Labor's taxation policies. The Self-Managed Superannuation Funds Association warned Labor that 1 million self-managed superannuation funds in Australia were not happy with what they called Chris Bowen's retiree taxes and, along with other retirement income bodies, it claimed the entire debate was 'misleading'. The Australian Banking Association opposed further reforms imposed on the banking sector and especially resented proposed levies on the major banks (a $640 million levy over four years by Labor and a $554 million budgetary measure from the Coalition funded by an industry levy) and attacked the proposed changes to franking credits, negative gearing and capital gains. The various housing associations—for example, the Real Estate Institute of Australia (REIA), the MBA and the Housing Industry Association (HIA)—strongly opposed any increased financial burdens on the fragile housing market, warning of declining rental availability and increased rents, but also put in a demand for reduced stamp duties, despite this being a State government matter. The PCA endorsed estimates that Labor's property taxes would cost the housing and real estate sector $32.4 billion over 10 years (Kelly and Roddan 2019).

Interestingly, increases to the Newstart and youth allowances were advocated by two associations (the BCA and the MCA), but not, as might have been expected, the National Retail Association.

A few CEOs spoke out

Mining tycoon Clive Palmer played the most activist role in the campaign as a leading business identity and through his party, the UAP (see Kefford, Chapter 17, this volume). Other CEOs were vocal only episodically about issues of concern to them in the months leading up to the election, and most eschewed making comments that could be construed as partisan. The most salient issues about which they spoke personally were energy reliability, climate change, emissions reduction, economic growth prospects, the importance of investment certainty, tax cuts and Budget repair.

With the heavy emphasis on the rival tax plans offered by the major parties, some business leaders debated the relative virtues of tax cuts versus interest rate stimulus. The Commonwealth Bank's CEO, Matt Comyn, came down firmly on the side of tax cuts, claiming they 'were the best to stimulate the economy, and stimulate speedily, better than further cuts to interest rates' (Moullakis 2019). Business generally favoured the tax cut proposals of both major parties but believed the Coalition's policies were preferable and more reform oriented. Occasionally, suggestions to increase the GST or broaden its base were made, although builders opposed the cumulative effects of the GST in the housing and building sectors.

Perhaps having a 'bob each way', business leaders did try to make overtures to a potential incoming Labor government, attending political events and holding lavish parties as fundraising ventures and occasions to meet and greet. More than 500 well-wishers and party-goers attended Shorten's post–Budget Reply celebration at the National Convention Centre Canberra, which featured influential CEOs, business association leaders and 'half-billionaires', including business tycoon Marcus Blackmore and many other celebrity guests (Glasgow and Lacy 2019a). A host of private business functions were also designed to court the politicians who business collectively thought would be running the country. Visy boss Anthony Pratt held two of the most lavish parties, first for Morrison (at $10,000 per head) and then for Shorten and his team, on 27 March in his Melbourne mansion, Raheem. Presumably expecting a Labor win, Pratt also attended Labor's election night party (which soon turned into a wake), as did Ian Silk, CEO of AustralianSuper.

The tax pushback from financial advisers

Although the real estate and building associations routinely opposed Labor's policies cutting concessionary payments to landlords and retirees, a prominent group of media-savvy financial advisers was very animated in their hostility to Labor's so-called retiree taxes. These advisers, with access to regular media as well as the more specialist digital investor newsletters and advisory platforms, included Robert Gottliebsen, Terry McCrann, Don Stammer, Tony Shepherd and Chris Kenny. A particularly public stoush took place between Labor's shadow treasurer Chris Bowen and columnist Gottliebsen over the latter's relentless criticisms of Labor's tax proposals (which he called unfair, inequitable, unreasonable, non-consultative, retrospective, and so on) and the former's aggrieved resentment of the persistent attacks. Labor proposed ending the cash reimbursement of company taxes paid on behalf of individuals under the dividend imputation scheme (franking credits) to individuals and other associates who were not required to pay income tax. Gottliebsen forensically attacked Labor's franking credits policy and warned of its likely impact on many retirees and small businesses, who he claimed were 'white hot' over the proposals. He also claimed presciently as early as February 2019 that the issue could result in the Coalition winning the campaign (Gottliebsen 2019).

The Financial Planning Association, which represented 14,000 financial advisers, also campaigned against Labor's proposed changes. Many observers suggested the campaign waged by financial advisers on complicated topics that were relatively abstruse to most voters was one of the reasons for a shift in voting preferences, labelling it an intergenerational struggle over 'tax versus benefits' between cashed-up baby boomers and millennials wanting instantaneous gratification. Some financial journalists argued that Labor's proposed industrial relations policies (the resumption of penalty rates, industrial-based bargaining, government wage subsidies, more union rights at work) would disproportionally affect companies with substantial employee expense ratios (Kirby 2019).

Substantive campaign issues affecting business

Other issues of concern to business that emerged during the campaign were the slowing rate of economic growth and what further structural reforms were necessary to stimulate growth. This debate had many dimensions. There were divisions within the electorate over whether to maintain the status quo or push for more structural reform to deliver international competitiveness. A further salient issue was the extent to which Labor's redistributive policies were desirable versus the smaller-government pitch adopted by the Coalition, with business largely favouring the latter. Towards the end of the campaign, Morrison began warning that now was not the right time to elect Labor and that he wanted 'this election to be a choice about aspiration and continuing to support aspiration or surrender aspiration to government in the form of higher taxation and bigger spending' (Benson 2019). He had earlier stressed to business leaders that 'the Australian economy will be weaker under Labor' (Remeikis 2019). He subsequently argued that elections were usually fought over about 2 per cent of the federal Budget, while this one was being fought over a substantial 6 per cent of budget outlays. While sections of the business community highlighted poor wages growth and a lack of consumer spending as problems for the domestic economy, others saw the big versus smaller government debate as the hip-pocket politics of envy pitting Australians against each other.

Three other divisive issues percolated throughout the campaign: the Adani coalmine, and climate change reform linked to energy and water.

Passionate rifts over the controversial Adani Carmichael coalmine in the Galilee Basin in Queensland saw it become the most talked about economic and environmental policy of the election (see Simms, Chapter 2, and Economou et al., Chapter 11, this volume). Media reports cited much reputational damage to the Queensland mining sector, especially coal, with surveys claiming voters believed miners were motivated only by 'self-interest, power and influence' (Long 2019). Attitudes to the Adani mine reflected the fractured values across the Australian federation, with southern States largely opposed and the northern mining States supportive of the project. The issue also highlighted regional opportunities—contrasting rural areas with limited or declining job prospects with the bigger cities where employment growth was more certain. Adani also placed Labor on the horns of a dilemma: facing a choice between losing environmental (and young) votes in the cities and losing working-class regional voters—and consequently the party placed a moratorium on its MPs speaking out on the mine (Owens 2019). However, the Adani proposal also became an emblematic cause célèbre, and the various hold-ups to its final approval guaranteed that it remained the most controversial mining project in the country. While Adani had been working through the approvals process for nearly nine years, other mining projects were approved close to the election and yet others, such as Palmer's Waratah coal project, were quietly awaiting developmental approval.

Adani was also linked to broader climate change issues and the preparedness of governments to take coordinated and coherent action. Business was strongly in favour of environmental action to reduce emissions, not least to provide clarity for future investment decisions. It should also be noted that many larger businesses were already preparing to report on their climate change mitigation actions under the requirements of Australian Accounting Standards Board financial reporting. Such businesses were therefore accepting of the need to undertake emissions reform and frustrated by the lack of decision-making from the political class. The lack of direction in sustainable energy policy was also an issue, with disappointment at the failure of government to guarantee energy supplies and wield 'big stick' penalties against power companies.

Finally, the nationwide drought and resulting water shortages were a massive problem affecting four states (New South Wales, Victoria, Queensland and South Australia). Many farmers faced close to zero water allocations and many country towns were on drastic water restrictions. The effectiveness and value for money of the Murray–Darling Basin Plan with its $13 billion price tag and associated water buybacks were widely disputed. Much more obvious were the impacts of severe water restrictions on towns, farms, families, livestock and crops. Those affected by the plan were more resigned than hopeful but were critical that further amendments were policy on the run (as with Labor's water policy announced on 6 May, which was opposed by the NSW division of the NFF).

The wash-up: 'There is a God!'— Collective reactions from business

On the first Monday after polling day, business writer Ticky Fullerton (2019) wrote that the collective reaction of business to the unexpected election result was: 'There is a God after all.' The sigh of relief among investors on the same day was manifested in a $33 billion rebound in the stock market. Adani received fast-tracked approvals from the Queensland Government for the remaining groundwater issues within three weeks of the election. The media reported heightened business and consumer confidence, first homebuyers re-entering the housing market, retirees resuming their lust for ocean cruising and spectacular increases in small business loans. The MBA (2019) also reported a 'post-election bounce in housing'. However, there were signs of economic malaise, with the Reserve Bank of Australia confirming in early June that economic growth had fallen to just 1.8 per cent (down from the 3 per cent predicted in December and 2.75 per cent in the April Budget), causing the bank to cut interest rates by 0.25 per cent on 2 June. There was much nervousness about a looming international trade war and increased tariff barrier protectionism.

Many business leaders acknowledged that the Coalition had campaigned virtually alone (especially Scott Morrison, who conducted an almost solo campaign effort), certainly without much business involvement. On the other hand, they also believed they had not been prepared for or consulted on Labor's ambitious array of policies, which Labor's frontbenchers had largely disseminated to interested constituencies rather than consulting with them.

The Treasurer and Deputy Liberal Leader, Josh Frydenberg, addressed a BCA dinner event post election and singled out its CEO Westacott, claiming she was 'a rare voice of business not to vacate the field' (Glasgow and Lacy 2019d). But he later admitted that Alan Joyce, CEO of Qantas, had been courageous for 'taking a stand on the front page of his masthead ... against Labor's industrial relations policy'. A cartoon depicting this Frydenberg event showed business leaders receiving their nametags and a begging bowl before entering the venue to take their seats.

Bill Shorten, in his first address to the reassembled ALP Caucus on 30 May, blamed 'powerful vested interests', 'corporate Leviathans' and a 'financial behemoth' (Palmer) for Labor's loss, as well as sections of the corporate media (principally, News Limited) who he claimed abhorred Labor. Anthony Albanese, Shorten's successor as Labor leader, announced Labor would be reviewing all the policies it took to the election and quickly downplayed the 'class warfare' rhetoric of his predecessor. He promised Labor would be 'pro-business' under his leadership and, in his initial critique of the Shorten-led campaign, he said the party's policy proposals had 'alienated small business-people' (Bramston 2019).

The 2019 federal election results confounded almost everyone. Labor ardently believed it would be the next government and the election was but a final coronation. The Coalition probably believed it would spend time in Opposition—attested by the large number of Coalition politicians opting to retire prior to the election. The Greens thought they would be in some form of coalition with Labor in a power-sharing arrangement or holding the balance of power in the Senate. Palmer and Pauline Hanson thought they would be the future kingmakers in any government formation. The union movement thought—wrongly—it would orchestrate leaders and groups who were expecting a change of government. However, business may come to regret not advocating for a more comprehensive policy agenda or may revert to exerting behind-the-scenes influence to shape policy directions.

References

Benson, Simon. 2019. 'PM's final pitch: It's not time'. *The Australian*, 16 May: 1.

Bramston, Troy. 2019. 'Shorten blames media, "corporate Leviathans" for loss'. *The Australian*, 31 May: 6.

Chapman, Ken. 2019. 'The result: Chris Bowen's "advice" sealed it for this voter'. [Letter to the Editor], *The Age*, [Melbourne], 20 May. www.theage.com.au/national/the-result-chris-bowens-advice-sealed-it-for-this-voter-20190519-h1ekli.html.

Condon, Trudy. 2019. 'Property council chief urges sector co-operation'. *The Australian*, 16 May: 23.

Evans, Greg. 2019. 'Business missing in policy fight'. *The Australian*, 17 June: 12.

Frydenberg, Josh. 2019. 'Impromptu address to the BCA's "Tower of Power" dinner event'. Melbourne, 23 May.

Fullerton, Ticky. 2019. 'Prayers answered but economic risks remain'. *The Australian*, 20 May: 25.

Garvey, Paul and Richard Gluyas. 2019. 'CEO's call for reform: "Chance to end a decade of chaos"'. *The Australian*, 12 April: 19.

Glasgow, Will and Christine Lacy. 2019a. 'Vitamin King Marcus Blackmore's tonic for Bill Shorten'. [Margin Call], *The Australian*, 5 April: 17.

Glasgow, Will and Christine Lacy. 2019b. 'The man who tipped the Coalition'. [Margin Call], *The Australian*, 21 May: 17.

Glasgow, Will and Christine Lacy. 2019c. 'BCA quick to rebuild Coalition ties'. [Margin Call], *The Australian*, 24 May: 17.

Glasgow, Will and Christine Lacy. 2019d. 'BCA lovefest'. [Margin Call], *The Weekend Australian*, 25–26 May: 16.

Gottliebsen, Robert. 2019. 'Small business a poll sleeper as anger builds'. *The Australian*, 20 February: 29.

Henry, Ken, Jeff Harmer, John Piggott, Heather Ridout and Greg Smith. 2009. *Australia's Future Tax System: Report to the Treasurer*. Canberra: Commonwealth of Australia. www.treasury.gov.au/review/the-australias-future-tax-system-review.

Kelly, Joe and Greg Brown. 2019. 'It's not me, it's them, Bill tilts at windmills'. *The Australian*, 31 May: 1, 6.

Kelly, Joe and Michael Roddan. 2019. 'Labor takes fight to PM on economy'. *The Weekend Australian*, 11–12 May: 1, 10.

Kelly, Katrina. 2019. 'Politics of grievance condemns millennials to taxing times'. *The Weekend Australian*, 11–12 May: 22.

Kenny, Chris. 2019. 'Sore loser's last tone-deaf blow'. *The Australian*, 31 May: 6.

Kenny, Mark. 2019. Commentary as panellist. *The Drum*, [ABC TV], 6 June. www.abc.net.au/news/2019-06-06/the-drum-thursday-june-6/11188040.

Kirby, James. 2019. 'The shares likely to be pressured by ALP win'. *The Australian*, 15 February: 26.

Long, Stephen. 2019. 'Queensland mining's reputation is in the pits due to coal according to industry survey'. *ABC News*, 15 May. www.abc.net.au/news/2019-05-15/queensland-mining-reputational-crisis-due-to-coal-survey-finds/11112234.

Master Builders Australia (MBA). 2019. *More evidence of post-election bounce in housing market*. News release, 3 July. Canberra: MBA. www.masterbuilders.com.au/Newsroom/More-Evidence-Of-Post-Election-Bounce-In-Housing-M.

Moullakis, Joyce. 2019. 'CBA chief lays out blueprint to win back trust'. *The Australian*, 29 May: 17, 20.

National Farmers' Federation (NFF). 2018. *2030 Roadmap: Australian Agriculture's Plan for a $100 Billion Industry*. Canberra: NFF.

National Farmers' Federation (NFF). 2019. 'The NFF's federal election priorities'. *2019 Federal Election Campaign*. Canberra: NFF. nff.org.au/media-release/2019-federal-election-campaign/.

National Retail Association. 2019. 'Election 2019: What is [sic] means for businesses and retail'. *Policy and Advocacy News*, 14 May. Brisbane: National Retail Association.

Owens, Jared. 2019. 'Labor MPs silent on union Adani row'. *The Australian*, 19 February: 2.

PricewaterhouseCoopers. 2019. 'Advertisement'. *The Australian*, 17 May: 13.

Remeikis, Amy. 2019. 'Scott Morrison again links Labor with recession after previously ruling it out'. *The Guardian*, 5 March. www.theguardian.com/business/2019/mar/05/scott-morrison-revives-claims-of-recession-under-labor-government.

Savva, Niki. 2019. *Plots and Prayers: Malcolm Turnbull's Demise and Scott Morrison's Ascension*. Melbourne: Scribe Press.

Uren, David. 2019. 'Economic reform urgent, says business council'. *The Australian*, 11 April: 4.

Wood, Alan. 2019. 'Labor lays out 165 steps to economic destruction'. *The Weekend Australian*, 11–12 May: 38.

20

UNIONS

Andrew Scott

Participation by peak trade union bodies and their affiliates in the 2019 federal election continued a tradition established in 2007 of major public political campaigns by unions. In that election, the ACTU campaigned against the Howard Government's unpopular 'WorkChoices' industrial relations laws, which had come into operation in 2006. WorkChoices reduced the employment conditions of millions of workers. The ACTU's campaign against the laws helped elect the Labor Party led by Kevin Rudd to government from Opposition, and the Rudd Government then repealed significant parts of those laws.

At the next election, in 2010, unions played a prominent defensive campaign role that helped to protect the Gillard Labor Government. Australian union peak councils have since given priority to spearheading campaign efforts that seek changes of government from the Liberal–National Coalition to Labor.

Some of these campaigns have had strikingly positive effects, such as in the 2014 Victorian State election. In that campaign, the human faces of ambulance paramedics and firefighters were successfully presented to win support from voters for specific, long-delayed wage rises rewarding the valued work in the community done by those emergency services personnel.

In the 2016 federal election, when Labor nearly dislodged Malcolm Turnbull following Tony Abbott's overthrow as prime minister in 2015, unions were again widely credited for a professional and effective grassroots campaign. That campaign highlighted the need for improved wages of lower-income workers in the outer suburbs and regions. It also urged better provision of public health and education.

Australians' views on union and business power

By 2007, the proportion of Australians regarding unions as having too much power had dropped to little more than one-third—down from more than two-thirds in the early 1990s when the first steps towards enterprise bargaining were taken. After 1993, the proportion of Australians thinking big business had too much power rose above the proportion regarding unions as having too much power for the first time in the past half-century (1969–2019), according to the AES and its predecessor surveys. The proportion of Australians who think big business has too much power has stayed above the proportion who think trade unions have too much power ever since those lines crossed after 1993 (Cameron and McAllister 2016: 84).

Australian unions' efforts to rectify this unfair, long-term imbalance against working people included playing a prominent role in the string of by-election campaigns held during the 45th parliament, in 2017 and 2018. Most of those by-elections resulted from disqualification of parliamentarians ruled technically ineligible for election under Section 44(i) of the Australian Constitution (see Chapters 2 and 3, this volume).

Although none of the by-elections prompted by disqualification resulted in a change of seats from one party to another, one notable change of individual personnel occurred when former ACTU president Ged Kearney, a former nurse, entered the House of Representatives for Labor after the Batman by-election on 17 March 2018. She comfortably defeated the challenge from the Greens, whose vote had steadily risen in that seat in the six previous electoral contests. Kearney reversed the trend against the ALP in Batman because of her contrast with the two preceding male Labor MPs, who were preoccupied with factions and machinery or were out of step with some widespread socially progressive views held in that electorate in Melbourne's northern suburbs.

Examples of union campaign themes in 2019

The Australian Nursing and Midwifery Federation (ANMF) ran advertisements on YouTube in the 2019 national election campaign dramatically presenting the plight of Ruby, one of many patients in aged care facilities suffering from the lack of a legally sanctioned minimum nurse/carer to resident ratio. The ANMF, a union representing members in a feminised industry, argued that 'our parents and grandparents deserve the quality of care that they once gave to us but across Australia people like Ruby are suffering because of chronic understaffing'. It declared that it was time to act to ensure 'our loved ones … have at least a minimum number of nurses and carers on every shift'. The campaign asked voters to enter their postcode on a website to identify their local politician and thus enable a letter to be sent by the union to those MPs who were not supporting better staff-to-patient ratios in aged care facilities.

The Australian Education Union's 'Fair Funding Now' campaign, meanwhile, featured advertising on social media and a fleet of 10 branded vans travelling across Australia to engage with school staff and parents in local communities. That campaign highlighted the much bigger commitments to government school funding given by Labor and the Greens than by the Coalition parties.

The union covering cleaners in the Australian Capital Territory, United Voice, maintained a high profile following a strike by its members employed in the Commonwealth Parliament House in the previous term through its campaign to achieve a pay rise for the workers who 'clean the people's house' but who had received no wage increase for five years (United Voice 2018).

'Change the rules'

The ACTU, in its own television and radio advertisements in the lead-up to the election, featured different individual workers from different industries and age groups speaking about the difficulties of long hours and job insecurity. Those advertisements then declared: 'This is not Australia. Change the Government to Change the Rules.'

A more general 'Change the Rules' campaign had been launched by the ACTU soon after the election of Sally McManus as its secretary (McManus 2017), financed by its now well-established levy on ACTU-affiliated unions for campaigning purposes.

That campaign—to alter the laws set by politicians for employment relationships—had multiple objectives, including to make corporations and wealthy individuals pay a higher share of tax, to give working people more power and to overcome job insecurity associated with a highly casualised workforce. As part of this—and following the scandals revealed by the banking royal commission and the subsequent Hayne report— an emboldened ACTU embarked on a confident national 2019 election campaign in 16 targeted seats, as part of which it also conducted opinion polls (see Chapter 8, this volume).

Table 20.1 ACTU targeted seats

State	Seat	Party holding seat prior to election	Margin by which seat held prior to election (%)
NSW	Banks	LIB	1.44
	Gilmore	LIB	0.73
	Reid	LIB	4.69
	Robertson	LIB	1.14
Vic.	Corangamite	ALP*	0.03
	Dunkley	ALP*	1.03
Qld	Capricornia	LNP	0.63
	Flynn	LNP	1.04
	Forde	LNP	0.63
	Herbert	ALP	0.02
	Leichhardt	LNP	3.95
	Petrie	LNP	1.65
WA	Pearce	LIB	3.63
	Swan	LIB	3.59
SA	Boothby	LIB	2.71
Tas.	Bass	ALP	5.42

* Notionally after redistribution
Source: Karp (2019a).

The results, however, fell well short of those ambitions.

Union overreach in Victoria

Expectations were especially raised in Victoria after the November 2018 landslide re-election of the Andrews State Labor Government, which was widely seen as a reward for that government's proven positive first-term performance in building big public infrastructure and other policy initiatives. There was also a perceived hostility in that progressive State towards the dumping as prime minister of the comparatively small-l liberal Malcolm Turnbull by the forces behind arch-conservative Peter Dutton, which resulted in Scott Morrison's elevation to the prime ministership in August 2018.

The Victorian Trades Hall Council was, however, unable at the federal election to achieve its own ambitious aims to win further seats (beyond the ACTU's own targeted seats) held by the Liberal Party with high margins between 6 and 13 per cent. These included the outer southern Melbourne electorate of Flinders and the eastern Melbourne suburban electorates of Deakin, Menzies, Higgins and Kooyong.

Table 20.2 Victorian unions' additional targeted seats

Seat	Margin held by Liberal Party before election (%)
Flinders	7.01
Deakin	6.44
Menzies	7.81
Higgins	7.38
Kooyong	12.82

Source: Hannan (2019).

While many of the voters in the very affluent seats of Higgins and Kooyong are small-l liberal voters with socially progressive views on issues such as climate change and refugees, they are, above all, economic or market liberals who are not likely to respond positively to trade unions. The average swing to the Labor Party in those five seats was just over 3 per cent and the Liberal Party's hold on all of them was not seriously threatened.[1]

---

1   All references to swings and seat margins in this chapter are in two-party-preferred terms and all data on results are from the AEC website.

The Victorian unions also failed to achieve a Labor win in the less affluent seat of Chisholm in Melbourne's mid-eastern suburbs (which it had held from 1998 to 2016), despite a swing to the ALP there of more than 2 per cent. Nor did the ALP win the outer south-eastern suburban Melbourne seat of La Trobe (which it had held from 2010 to 2013); indeed, there was a swing against it there of more than 1 per cent. There were swings of between 1 and 2 per cent to the ALP in Dunkley and Corangamite, but these electorates had already been rendered notionally Labor by redistributions. They made up two of only three targeted seats in which the ACTU succeeded Australia-wide. Labor does now hold 21 of the 38 federal seats in Victoria but that is likely to be close to the maximum it can expect to win.

Outcomes in the ACTU's targeted seats nationally

The only other ACTU-targeted seat nationally that Labor won was Gilmore in New South Wales. There was a swing to Labor of more than 3 per cent in Gilmore but this was due to the imposition of a controversial Liberal Party candidate, which divided the established local Coalition politicians. Nevertheless, the ALP holds 24 of the 47 federal electorates in New South Wales (and gained a 1.5 per cent swing towards it in the ACTU-targeted seat of Reid in that State).

The ALP also holds all three seats in the Australian Capital Territory and both seats in the Northern Territory. The ACTU campaign lost two electorates that it was aiming for Labor to retain: Bass in Tasmania (with a swing of nearly 6 per cent against Labor) and Herbert in north Queensland (with a swing against Labor of more than 8 per cent).

The ALP's problems in winning a national majority include the fact that it holds only two of the five seats in Tasmania, only five of the 10 seats in South Australia (despite a 1.3 per cent swing towards Labor in the ACTU-targeted seat of Boothby) and only five of 16 in Western Australia (where the only positive for the ACTU at the 2019 election was a swing of nearly 1 per cent to Labor in the targeted seat of Swan). The ALP's biggest problem, however, is that it holds only six of the 30 seats in Queensland.

Jobs versus the environment in Queensland

The ACTU campaign failed to gain any of the five seats it was seeking to win for Labor in Queensland. The worst trend was in the central Queensland seat of Capricornia, where there was a swing of nearly 12 per cent against the ALP in an electorate the party had held from 1998 to 2013. The result was not much better in Flynn, a seat closer to Brisbane, where the swing against Labor was nearly 8 per cent. In Forde, south of Brisbane, the swing against Labor was also nearly 8 per cent, and in Brisbane's outer northern suburbs, the seat of Petrie (which Labor held from 2007 to 2013) swung against Labor by nearly 7 per cent. Forde and Flynn, and the seat of Leichhardt in far north Queensland, which was also unsuccessfully targeted by the ACTU, had all been held by Labor from 2007 to 2010.

How Queensland differed from the rest of Australia in 2019 was the salience of the issue of jobs versus the environment, particularly in the five seats closest to the proposed Adani coalmine (see Chapter 11, this volume). This exposed the need for more effective material economic policies, from both Labor and unions, which connected with workers, families and communities threatened by the phasing out of coal and other declining industries and for a 'just transition' into tangible, adequate and secure new employment in renewable energy or elsewhere, including through substantial investment in quality skills retraining.

Skills and jobs, including the potential for many new jobs such as through further investments in major solar power expansion, needed to be a much bigger Labor policy focus. The plight of workers in central and north Queensland who were feeling insecure about their future employment proved to be a disastrous blind spot for Labor.

Different unions, and different divisions within unions, had put forward conflicting policies on the proposed Adani coalmine, to be located in the electorate of Capricornia. Some in the unions—like some in the ALP—signalled opposition to the mine in line with environment-minded voters in inner Melbourne and Sydney. Others did not rule out support for the mine in accordance, for example, with the position held by the Queensland mining division of the CFMMEU.

This equivocation caused serious losses of votes from Labor in coalmining communities in Queensland and beyond (for example, the Hunter electorate in New South Wales), and there were also large swings against Labor in regional communities worried about job losses more generally (including in the Tasmanian seats of Bass and Braddon). Parallels can be drawn in this respect with Labor's seat losses in Tasmania in the 2004 'forestry' election (see Simms and Warhurst 2005).

Labor's loss of working-class voters

One initial interpretation of aggregate data advanced by the Grattan Institute was that Labor lost votes particularly among people on low incomes with less formal education and who were further from the centre of capital cities (Chivers 2019). The Australian National University's Ben Phillips, meanwhile, found from Australian Bureau of Statistics (ABS) census and AEC data that a particularly strong driver of the two-party-preferred swing to the Coalition at the electorate level was the share of blue-collar workers—an overall correlation of 61 per cent, which was even stronger for Queensland (Phillips 2019).

This, however, is at odds with the interpretation of comprehensive survey data, which emphasises the extent of support still given to Labor compared with the Coalition by voters who work in blue-collar, sales or services jobs, have lower to middle incomes and who are employees (see Chapter 12, this volume). It would be helpful to have such survey data disaggregated by geographic region in sufficiently large numbers to better compare the extent of Labor's loss of working-class voters in Queensland (or in particular regions of Queensland, as discussed in Chapter 11, this volume) with the trends in other States.

It is unlikely that the proportion of unionists voting Labor as their first preference in 2019 rose to as high as the 63 per cent who voted Labor in 2007. The actions by the Coalition Government then had weakened the working conditions of millions of voters, which was a central policy reason for the election of the Labor Party led by Rudd from Opposition to office.

Some media commentators have asserted that working-class people turned away from Labor in 2019 because those workers had suddenly been transformed into capitalists. The voting trend was more likely because many workers were very worried about the risk of job losses.

Insecurity about employment may, ironically, have made many working people in Australia at the 2019 election more likely to stay with the incumbent government (despite its own turnover of leaders) rather than risk the set of miscellaneous but substantial policy changes put forward by Labor, for fear that those might bring further economic uncertainty. This is doubly ironic given that Labor in 2019 had specific policies to move workers currently categorised as 'casual' into more secure permanent work. That policy, however, did not assure those workers who feared total losses of their jobs in particular industries and regions.

Attempts to make the election a 'referendum on wages'

The election was characterised by Shorten and other Labor frontbenchers from March 2019 as a 'referendum on wages', following widespread concern about the longstanding trend of wage stagnation in Australia. Labor promised to gradually increase the minimum wage to turn it into a 'living wage'. The ALP also indicated that it would allow a long-time objective of unions for a return to 'pattern bargaining', or multi-employer bargaining, to replace the reduction of bargaining to the individual enterprise level since the early 1990s, which had so weakened union power and real wages.

Pattern bargaining would only be allowed though for employees in low-wage sectors such as early childhood education and care. This was certainly an appropriate sector on which to focus given that its highly feminised workforce makes it representative of the continuing, serious problem of gender wage inequality in Australia. However, the ALP's announcement of how it would achieve higher wages for early childhood education and care workers was not made until late in the election campaign and it involved large spending, with very complex details. These needed clearer design and more detailed explanation.

Labor also promised to amend legislation to reinstate the full penalty wage rates previously paid on Sundays and public holidays to approximately 700,000 workers in fast food, retail and hospitality outlets, pharmacies, clubs and restaurants. These wage rates were in the process of a phased reduction as a result of a Fair Work Commission decision in February 2017.

The ALP further committed to impose bigger punishments on perpetrators of wage theft, ensure labour hire workers received the same pay as those directly employed, make sure workers in the so-called gig economy were properly paid and toughen measures against sham contracting. The Coalition parties, by contrast, avoided these topics and successfully steered debate on to other issues.

The credibility problem for unions and Labor

Previous Labor governments had established and implemented the very rules that unions and Labor in 2019 said needed to be changed. This created a credibility problem. The Hawke and Keating governments introduced enterprise bargaining, and the Rudd and Gillard governments did not fully roll back the Howard Government's WorkChoices policies. Bill Kelty, who was the ACTU's secretary when enterprise bargaining and steep union membership decline started in Australia, made campaign appearances in 2019. His proclamation at the beginning of an advertisement broadcast by the ALP that 'Shorten is essentially a disciple of Hawke and Keating' did not help Labor overcome that historical credibility problem.

Shorten's well-known previous role as national secretary of the AWU partly helped, but also partly hindered, his campaign in the 2019 federal election. Prominent, potent and lingering criticisms had been made that, as a union official, he was prepared to compromise the interests of workers in favour of employers (Schneiders et al. 2015). Further, he was portrayed as being, in major personality respects, a 'shape-shifter' who tried to simultaneously adopt 'contradictory stances', to put on different masks in an attempt to be all things to all people, which raised serious questions about what he actually stood for (Millar and Schneiders 2015). These traits likely contributed to his consistently poor public opinion poll ratings on the attribute of trustworthiness.

Rupert Murdoch's *The Australian* newspaper reported on 24 April that Shorten had told a coal export terminal worker on Queensland's central coast, in response to that worker's request, that he would consider reducing taxes for workers earning $250,000 or more a year (Brown and Lewis 2019). But very few individuals in those kinds of occupations receive income anything like that. The only occupations in Australia that average above $250,000 taxable annual income are in fact surgeons, anaesthetists, internal medicine specialists and financial dealers (ATO 2019).

Yet Shorten failed to do what Barack Obama had in reply to a strikingly similar challenge from a worker to his plans to tax higher income earners during his successful 2008 US presidential election campaign. Obama rhetorically and confidently asked a large outdoor crowd in a New Hampshire apple orchard: 'How many plumbers do you know that are making a quarter-million dollars a year?'

Sky News Australia then showed on 9 May how Shorten suffered an awkward encounter at a freight company north of Brisbane (Sky News 2019) when two male fluoro-vested workers refused to shake his hand because they did not like him. That media outlet, also Murdoch-owned, might have portrayed those two individual workers as not liking the Labor leader because they were on high incomes and felt his tax policies were an enemy to their aspirations; however, the workers may not have liked Shorten for reasons other than having individual ambitions to become low-taxed, very high-income workers—perhaps because they thought he had been a weak union official or because they felt he did not care enough about Queensland jobs.

Unions after the 2019 election

Unions are collective agents to realise opportunities for working people to get ahead from a foundation of secure employment and decent wages. Unions and Labor need to be clearly and consistently on the same wavelength as most workers in expressing those central priorities. Employment and income security are the most important ingredients in forming the common ground between different left-of-centre constituencies. Economic policies that promote this security in people's lives build scope for the pursuit of more compassionate, outward-looking social and environmental policies.

Following the 2019 election result, unions need to make more widely a persuasive case about the details of exactly which rules they want to change, how such changes can be implemented and the specific short-term and medium-term benefits these changes will bring to the lives of many individual workers.

There will now be further discussion among unions of the relative priorities of grassroots workplace organising vis-a-vis electoral/political campaigns using media including advertising, to resolve tensions between these priorities. Unions spent $6.5 million on advertisements in the 2019 election and $25 million had been spent on the 'Change the Rules' campaign overall up to the aftermath of the election (Karp 2019a, 2019b). This was similar to the amount spent by unions in preceding federal elections and confirmed the advantage for Labor over non-Labor parties of having a strong union base in terms of both people and money. However, the financial resources the unions could muster in 2019 were dwarfed by the unprecedented big-spending advertising intervention in the election by Clive Palmer's corporations (as discussed in Chapters 17 and 19, this volume).

Nearly three-quarters of voters still think big business has too much power, whereas less than half think unions do, according to the latest available data (Cameron and McAllister 2016: 84). The gap between the two views is the highest it has been since 2007, and those data pre-date the scandals uncovered by the banking royal commission. These sentiments suggest there is still a successful electoral basis for more precisely focused, credible campaigning by unions—for more popular and better resonating policies aimed more accurately at the needs of their core constituencies—than was mounted in 2019.

References

Australian Taxation Office (ATO). 2019. *Taxation Statistics 2016–17*. Canberra: Commonwealth of Australia. www.ato.gov.au/About-ATO/Research-and-statistics/In-detail/Taxation-statistics/Taxation-statistics-2016-17/?anchor=Individuals#Chart5.

Brown, Greg and Rosie Lewis. 2019. 'Shorten to "look at" high-earner tax cuts'. *The Australian*, 24 April.

Cameron, Sarah M. and Ian McAllister. 2016. *Trends in Australian Political Opinion: Results from the Australian Election Study 1987–2016*. Canberra: School of Politics and International Relations, The Australian National University.

Chivers, Carmela. 2019. 'Election 2019: The result wasn't the only surprise'. *Grattan Blog*, 4 June. Melbourne: Grattan Institute. blog.grattan.edu.au/author/carmela_chivers/.

Hannan, Ewin. 2019. 'Unions eye seven seats to swing poll'. *The Australian*, 11 April.

Karp, Paul. 2019a. '"Vanity project": Critics round on ACTU's $25m campaign after Labor's election loss'. *The Guardian*, 23 May.

Karp, Paul. 2019b. 'Election review finds unions had wrong slogan for right message'. *The Guardian*, 8 August.

McManus, Sally. 2017. 'Sally McManus: Address to Nexgen 2017, International Convention Centre, Sydney, 27 June'. Melbourne: ACTU. www.actu.org.au/actu-media/speeches-and-opinion/sally-mcmanus-address-to-nexgen-2017.

Millar, Royce and Ben Schneiders. 2015. 'The shape-shifter'. *The Age*, [Melbourne], 20 June.

Phillips, Ben. 2019. 'Electoral swing by share of blue-collar workers'. *ABC News*, 24 May. www.abc.net.au/news/2019-05-24/electoral-swing-by-share-of-blue-collar-workers/11145754.

Schneiders, Ben, Royce Millar and Nick Toscano. 2015. 'Shorten's $1m union bonanza'. *The Age*, [Melbourne], 18 June.

Simms, Marian and John Warhurst. eds. 2005. *Mortgage Nation: The 2004 Australian Election*. Perth: API Network.

Sky News. 2019. 'Workers snub Bill Shorten's handshake'. *Sky News Australia*, 9 May. www.youtube.com/watch?v=8lc7kBHcxW4.

United Voice. 2018. *Uncertain future for Parliament House's hard-working cleaners.* Media release, 15 May. Canberra: United Voice ACT. www.medianet.com.au/releases/160886/.

21

THIRD PARTIES AND THINK TANKS

Ebony Bennett

Though few seats changed hands, the 2019 federal election produced an unexpected result, shocking the Coalition and Labor and the numerous third-party organisations, think tanks, non-governmental organisations (NGOs), charities and activist groups that engaged in the electoral debate.

Third-party organisations and think tanks play important roles in federal elections. While there are numerous organisations that engage with federal election campaigns, this chapter will discuss the scope and effectiveness of the electoral campaigning activities of progressive organisation GetUp! and its conservative counterpart, Advance Australia, in their target electorates—including phone banking, doorknocking, paid advertising and generating free media and fundraising. It will also examine the activities of three think tanks in shaping the public policy debate: the Canberra-based think tank The Australia Institute, and the Melbourne-based Grattan Institute and Institute of Public Affairs (IPA).

GetUp! and Captain GetUp

On election night, Antony Green (2019) tweeted: 'Politics is often about expectations. Tonight's seat numbers are almost exactly the same as in 2016. Then it was worse than expected, this time it is better. And doesn't that change the speeches.'

Similarly, in 2016, GetUp! was widely credited as a formidable campaigning outfit with the power to topple sitting Liberal MPs from office, raising expectations for its 2019 electoral performance that failed to materialise. Though GetUp! was certainly not the only organisation campaigning in seats such as Bass and Dickson in 2016, it was GetUp! that was largely credited with (or blamed for) Andrew Nikolic losing the seat of Bass and the 5.2 per cent swing against Peter Dutton in the Queensland seat of Dickson, and it was therefore seen as a force in the swing against the incumbent Coalition Government.

GetUp! is now well established as a large and influential organisation in Australian politics, sitting alongside Australia's major established political parties in terms of its membership, organising capacity and ability to mobilise people to action. GetUp! (2019a) describes itself as an independent movement with more than a million members, 'working to build a progressive Australia and bring participation back into our democracy'. GetUp! is unique in Australian politics and it is very effective at irritating the conservative side of politics. It advocates for progressive issues its members care about such as climate change, saving the Australian Broadcasting Corporation (ABC), housing affordability and health care. Its campaigning efforts this election did not meet expectations.

In 2019, GetUp! kept the same election strategy as in 2016, targeting conservative politicians it dubbed 'hard-right blockers' to disrupt their influence in politics. Though the GetUp! campaign was a presence in 29 seats, most of its campaigning focused on MPs labelled by GetUp! members as 'hard-right Liberal–National Party blockers' in the seats of Warringah, Flinders, Boothby, Pearce, Menzies, Dickson and Kooyong, who had wrecked progressive policies and stifled public debate on climate change, refugees, multiculturalism, economics and democratic participation.

GetUp! shortlisted its targeted seats by surveying its members, inviting them in January to nominate the 'hard-right MPs they want booted from Parliament', and subsequently announced Dutton and Tony Abbott as the 'country's most loathed politicians' (GetUp! 2019b). In March 2019, GetUp! (2019c) announced Greg Hunt as its next electoral target (though Hunt is not commonly understood to belong to the Coalition's hard right), citing his role as 'the numbers man for Peter Dutton's failed leadership coup' and his 'terrible record on climate change'. GetUp! then expanded its targeted seats from five to seven and aimed to double its volunteers from the 2016 election (3,736). National director Paul Oosting acknowledged it was the organisation's most ambitious approach to date and that GetUp! had set itself a huge task. He was correct.

While GetUp! employed standard election tactics in terms of organising and advertising, with a reported election advertising spend of $4 million, its strategy of targeting hard-right blockers was different to most third-party campaigns, which focus primarily on marginal seats or on specific issue-based campaigns. Seats such as Kooyong and Menzies were considered safe, even blue-ribbon, Liberal seats, but were part of a tranche of Victorian Liberal seats that were possibly 'up for grabs' following Labor's strong victory at the recent State election. That calculation proved to be overly ambitious, but GetUp! was not alone in making it.

Table 21.1 GetUp!'s 2019 campaign, nationally and for Warringah

	2019 National (Warringah)	2016
Volunteers	9,433 (1,865)	3,736
Doorknocks	36,315 (26,630)	
Phone calls	712,039 (157,592)	40,218
Total voter contacts	748,354 (183,222)	

Source: Supplied by GetUp! to the author.

Table 21.2 2019 election outcomes in seats targeted by GetUp!

Target electorate	Outcome
Dickson (Qld)	2.9% swing to LNP; LNP re-elected with 54.6% of TPP
Warringah (NSW)	18.3% swing against LNP; IND defeats LIB with 57.2% of TPP
Flinders (Vic.)	1.4% swing to ALP; LIB re-elected with 55.6% of TPP
Menzies (Vic.)	0.3% swing to ALP; LIB re-elected with 57.5% of TPP
Kooyong (Vic.)	7.1% swing against LNP; LIB re-elected with 55.7% of TPP
Pearce (WA)	3.9% swing to LNP; LIB re-elected with 57.5% of TPP
Boothby (SA)	1.3% swing to ALP; LIB re-elected with 51.4% of TPP

Source: AEC (2019).

While Tony Abbott lost his blue-ribbon seat of Warringah to Independent Zali Steggall, no other hard-right blocker targeted by GetUp! lost their seat, leaving former Nationals leader and Member for New England, Barnaby Joyce (in Sky News Australia 2019), to boast on election night: 'Went for the sucker trap again didn't you? Put all your resources into a seat you weren't going to win, so you burned up all your resources in other seats you could have.'

Oosting acknowledged GetUp! had not achieved what it set out to do, but said its strategy was formed and expectations set in the context of a predicted nationwide swing against the government that also failed to materialise. Oosting later denied claims from targeted Liberal candidates Nicolle Flint and Kevin Andrews that they were harassed and slandered by GetUp! (Ferguson 2019).

GetUp! had radically ramped up its phone-banking capacity compared with the 2016 federal election, while its doorknocking efforts appear to have been concentrated in Warringah. However, evidence suggests the ability of tactics such as doorknocking, phone-banking and advertising mail-outs to persuade voters to switch their vote during general elections is limited (Kalla and Broockman 2018).

The tactics employed in the campaign led to questions about whether targeting blockers gave incumbents an 'underdog' status and accusations that the campaign had alienated voters. Benedict Coyne, the Greens candidate for Dickson, told *The Guardian*:

> At the risk of generalising, there is a sense that Dutton was able to play the victim card, you know, 'GetUp! and all these outsiders are coming here to do this to me', and that certainly speaks to his base to come and defend him whether it's true or not. (McGowan 2019)

Dutton's margin in Dickson shrank from 6.7 to 1.6 per cent in 2016; in 2019, there was a 2.9 per cent swing towards him. GetUp! has credited its volunteers with limiting the swing in Dickson to 2.9 per cent (compared with the 4.3 per cent swing to the Coalition across Queensland in 2019).

Third-party campaigns can have persuasive effects when particular candidates take unusually unpopular positions or positions in conflict with the values of their electorates and where third-party campaigns make a special effort to identify persuadable voters (Hersh and Schaffner 2013). Abbott, although a long-term incumbent member, had positions on climate policy that were out of step with those of his electorate. While

Dutton was the architect of controversial policies as home affairs minister, perhaps his positions were not so far out of step with his electorate of Dickson as those of Abbott with his electorate of Warringah. A clear difference between the successful Warringah campaign and the other seats targeted by GetUp! was the presence of a high-profile and well-respected Independent candidate in Zali Steggall, in addition to a high-profile blocker in Abbott, who was out of touch with his electorate.

Tactics that worked well for GetUp! in 2016 backfired in 2019, although arguably their most prominent mistake occurred in the electorate in which they had their only success. A satirical television ad depicting Abbott as an apathetic surf lifesaver letting someone drown was universally judged a mistake and was withdrawn by GetUp!. A conversation guide for volunteers phone-banking in Treasurer and Deputy Liberal Leader Josh Frydenberg's seat of Kooyong incorrectly instructed them to say that 'Josh Frydenberg was part of the coup that removed Malcolm Turnbull as Prime Minister'. Oosting then made several other errors, including incorrectly describing the Treasurer as the deputy prime minister and then the finance minister, when defending the guide and GetUp! in a live interview on Jon Faine's *ABC Mornings* program (Faine 2019). The interview was described by some in the media as a 'car crash' (Koziol 2019).

The electoral outcomes in GetUp!'s target seats show the limits of its approach; enthusiastic volunteers and money alone are not enough to shift safe seats. International experience suggests GetUp! could have a more meaningful, persuasive impact if it focused its efforts on issue-based campaigns. Third-party campaigns have had success using doorknocking to increase turnout, but Australia's compulsory voting makes this intervention unnecessary (John and Brannan 2008).

GetUp!'s perceived electoral success in 2016 also provoked a substantial backlash. A complaint from Liberal MP Ben Morton sparked an AEC investigation into whether or not GetUp! should be considered an associated entity of a political party. The complaint—one of a number made after the 2016 federal election—was perceived primarily as an attempt to depict GetUp! as a creature of the Labor Party and the Greens, undermining its reputation for independence. The AEC ultimately concluded for the third time that GetUp! was not an associated entity and ruled that the fact an organisation advocates an agenda on one side of the political spectrum does not mean it is 'operating' for the benefit of all registered parties on that side of the spectrum (AAP 2019).

Following several failed attempts to start a 'conservative GetUp!' as a counterweight, Advance Australia was launched in November 2018 to little public fanfare, but with the backing of high-profile businessmen, including storage company director Sam Kennard and former ABC chairman Maurice Newman. Its national director is Gerard Benedet, former chief of staff to former Queensland LNP treasurer Tim Nicholls. It had extraordinary early success; while it reported 27,500 members and raised $395,000 in donations in March (Koslowski 2019), by the next month, it reported 32,000 members and $1.7 million in donations for the election (Van Extel 2019)—about half of GetUp!'s election advertising spend.

Advance Australia targeted many of the same electorates as GetUp!, though there is less information available on its target seats, campaign activities or the engagement of its 32,000 members in efforts such as doorknocking and phone-banking.

Advance Australia's campaigning was prominent in Warringah, but it also campaigned against Greens candidate Julian Burnside in Kooyong, Centre Alliance's Rebekha Sharkie in Mayo and Independents Helen Haines in Indi and Julia Banks in Flinders (see Chapter 18, this volume). Looking at Advance Australia's campaign targets, one could argue it was about as successful as its progressive counterpart, GetUp!—which is to say, not very. Neither Burnside nor Banks was elected, but Abbott's loss in Warringah was the most prominent scalp of the campaign. Sharkie was comfortably re-elected in Mayo, while Haines was elected as successor to popular Independent Cathy McGowan in Indi. It is not clear how Advance Australia spent the $2 million it raised, whether the money was raised primarily from large donors or whether it followed GetUp!'s example of raising millions of dollars from thousands of small donors. If Advance Australia has a broad base of small donors from which its donations came, it would be the most successful attempt to date to create a 'conservative GetUp!'.

Perhaps the most interesting character to come out of the 2019 election was that of 'Captain GetUp'. Benedet said the role of the mascot was to give people 'the facts about the left-wing activists who support "fake" independents' (SBS 2019).

The caped crusader was Advance Australia's most visible contribution to the campaign, but his role in exposing the 'political correctness' of his rival was limited. The caped crusader was widely ridiculed upon his debut and was arguably more effective at promoting GetUp! than undermining it. Captain GetUp also caused problems for the Abbott campaign in Warringah when the person inside the costume was filmed inappropriately gyrating against a poster of Steggall (SBS 2019).

Captain GetUp is still active on Twitter, but only time will tell whether Advance Australia is able to provide the conservative side of politics with the membership, volunteers, fundraising and organising capacity, and issue-based campaigning to rival that which GetUp! provides for progressive politics. GetUp! will certainly be examining how best to deploy its considerable resources and the enthusiasm of its members for greater impact in the future.

Think tanks

Think tanks such as The Australia Institute, the Grattan Institute and the IPA play an influential role in elections by generating ideas that shape the public policy debate and help to popularise certain ideas and policy proposals, and by releasing research reports, engaging with the media, briefing policymakers and engaging with the public via conferences and other events (Stone 1996).

Rather than attempt to define exactly what constitutes a think tank, Stone identifies shared characteristics that distinguish them from other groups: organisational independence, self-determination of research agendas, a strong policy focus, a degree of expertise and a concentration on influencing public debate (James 1998).

The Australia Institute describes itself as 'one of the country's most influential public policy think tanks, conducting research that contributes to a more just, sustainable and peaceful society'; the Grattan Institute describes itself as 'a non-partisan think tank providing independent, rigorous and practical solutions to some of the country's most pressing problems'; while the IPA describes itself as an 'independent, non-profit public policy think tank, dedicated to preserving and strengthening the foundations of economic and political freedom'. Each think tank describes itself as independent, though the media often describes

The Australia Institute as 'progressive', the IPA as 'conservative' and the Grattan Institute as 'centrist'. None of them is affiliated with a political party, unlike the Menzies Research Centre (Liberal Party), the Chifley Research Centre (ALP), the Page Research Centre (the Nationals) or the Green Institute (Australian Greens), each of which is funded in part by a Commonwealth grant-in-aid. These affiliated groups are not examined in this chapter. Other, unaffiliated think tanks such as the Melbourne-based Per Capita were also modelling the impact on families of the competing tax policies on offer in the election but cannot be examined in the confines of this chapter.

While many other organisations seek to influence the public policy debate—including charities and NGOs, trade unions and environmental groups—Abelson (2002: 57–63) asserts that think tanks possess unique attributes that afford them greater opportunity to influence public policy, including their expertise and close ties to policymakers, and calls for a 'holistic' approach to assessing their effectiveness that acknowledges that think tanks 'possess different resources, which, not surprisingly, affect the nature and extent of activities they undertake' and that each will differ in which stage of the policy cycle it prioritises on any given issue: issue articulation, policy formulation and/or policy implementation.

As this book examines the federal election, this chapter will necessarily focus on the effectiveness of the think tanks in issue articulation or 'agenda-setting' and policy formation, not policy implementation. According to Kingdon, 'think tanks may often be unable to influence the final choice made by policymakers, but they can do much to set—and perhaps expand—the limits of respectable debate' (Steelman 2003: 164).

During the 2019 election, The Australia Institute's most effective, but perhaps least visible, contribution to the public policy debate was to shift the economic debate to focus more on revenue. Over the past decade, The Australia Institute has published dozens of research reports on the importance of Australia having a strong revenue base, closing tax loopholes such as negative gearing and the capital gains tax discount, addressing the rising cost to the Budget of superannuation tax concessions and the cost of dividend imputation and franking credit refunds. The overarching purpose of this body of work is to shift the public debate beyond simplistic arguments about debt and deficit towards a more inclusive discussion about the kind of Australia we want to see and how it will be funded.

The Australia Institute was successful in seeing some of its ideas taken up as policy by Labor and other parties and candidates in both the 2016 and the 2019 elections, including achieving cross-party support to establish an independent anticorruption commission, as well as Labor's policy to abolish franking credit refunds for people who pay no tax. This was effectively labelled by the Coalition as 'Labor's tax on retirees' and made a centrepiece of the scare campaign against Labor.

In terms of agenda-setting, arguably the institute was most effective on the issue of a federal independent commission against corruption. Over several years, The Australia Institute released a series of research reports that established the need for a federal anticorruption commission to fill the gaps in Australia's integrity system. It also commissioned polling that showed such a body would attract support from a majority of voters across the political spectrum (Aulby 2017). The Australia Institute established a National Integrity Committee, comprising former judges such as the Hon. Anthony Whealy QC and renowned corruption fighters such as David Ipp QC to design a blueprint for implementation (National Integrity Committee 2017). In January 2018, in a speech to the National Press Club, Opposition leader Bill Shorten announced that Labor would establish such a commission if it were elected and, by December that year, the government announced it would establish a Commonwealth integrity commission, taking the issue from one rejected by both major parties to a bipartisan issue within just a few years. While Labor's policy stayed close to the blueprint set out by the National Integrity Committee at The Australia Institute, the Coalition's model was weaker in several respects (National Integrity Committee 2019).

On the issue of dividend imputation and franking credits—which became central to the 2019 federal election campaign—a majority of Australians have little understanding or are unaware of what franking credits are or how they work (Essential Research 2018a, 2018b).

The Australia Institute's research set out the case for abolishing the cashing out of franking credits for those who pay no tax and during the campaign it attempted to explain Australia's system of dividend imputation and franking credits and to bust economic myths as they appeared in the media and on social media. As a research body with no advertising budget or organising capacity, the institute's efforts were no match for the scare campaign in terms of reach or effectiveness.

The Australia Institute's chief economist, Richard Denniss, compared the success of the 'retiree tax' scare campaign with Labor's efforts to promote its policy to eliminate out-of-pocket costs for cancer care:

> As one of the architects of the idea that ended up becoming Labor's biggest revenue measure—the $11 billion plan (over four years) to abolish tax refunds to people who pay no tax—I can honestly say that I never expected it to wind up at the centre of a national election campaign. Not because I think it's a bad idea—and not because I think political parties should hide their plans the way Abbott hid his plans to slash spending back in 2013—but because I can say with confidence that almost no one knows what an imputation credit is, and everyone knows what cancer is. (Denniss 2019: 27)

The Australia Institute's most visible contribution to the public policy debate in terms of media coverage was its distributional analysis of the Morrison Government's planned income tax cuts package, which conservatively estimated that at least $77 billion of the benefits of tax cuts would go to people earning more than $180,000 per year (Grudnoff 2019).

The $77 billion figure was first put to Minister for Finance Mathias Cormann by David Speers on *Sky News* in the first week of the campaign (Sky News Australia 2019). Cormann rejected the figure but provided no official figures. Several different journalists put the figure repeatedly to different ministers during the course of the election campaign, but no government figures were forthcoming. Labor leapt on the refusal of ministers to answer the question and used the $77 billion as part of its opposition to the tax cuts package throughout the campaign.

Senator Cormann promised in the first week of the campaign that the government would provide its own distributional analysis, but none was forthcoming. These kinds of distributional analyses of income tax cuts are relatively straightforward and form a standard part of the way the federal Budget measures are critiqued each year; it was the dismissive attitude of the government, as well as its refusal to provide its own Treasury numbers, that was unexpected during this campaign.

The Australia Institute also sponsored an open letter in Melbourne's *Age* newspaper on 16 May, signed by 62 climate scientists and other prominent Australians, urging the 46th Parliament to make climate change a top priority (The Australia Institute 2019). Prominent signatories included Nobel Prize winners Professor Peter Doherty and Dr Sue Wareham, former Australian of the Year Professor Fiona Stanley, former Australian chief scientist Professor Penny Sackett and many of Australia's leading scientists from disciplines including climate change, health, economics, energy and finance. Other research areas covered by The Australia Institute in the lead-up to and during the election campaign period included water buybacks in the Murray–Darling Basin Plan and the impacts of climate change.

The IPA's main election contribution was the manifesto *20 Policies to Fix Australia* that it sent to MPs (Roskam and Wild 2019). The manifesto suggested withdrawal from the Paris Agreement, implementation of a flat income tax, legalising nuclear power, abolishing the Renewable Energy Target, ending all subsidies to wind, solar and hydroelectricity generators and privatising the ABC. Many of these were long-term policy objectives the IPA has promoted over several terms of parliament. The IPA characterises the Coalition's repeal of the carbon price in 2014 as one its greatest achievements and a 'victory for mainstream Australians over the political class' (Barro 2019a).

While relatively few of the IPA's issues gained traction during the 2019 federal election campaign—perhaps in part because the Coalition's campaign focused so narrowly on tax cuts—it played an influential role within the Liberal Party in the lead-up to the election and is likely to gain prominence post election during the 46th Parliament.

In previous years, several of the IPA's election demands found favour within the Coalition but met with strong opposition from the public when it came to the policy implementation stage. For example, former prime minister Tony Abbott backed several IPA proposals when he was in Opposition, including its call to scrap Section 18C of the *Racial Discrimination Act* (Crowe 2019)—an issue that remains in the IPA's 2019 manifesto. However, moves to repeal Section 18C were ultimately abandoned by the Abbott Government following a huge community backlash (Griffiths 2014).

In the lead-up to the 2019 federal election, the IPA proved effective at persuading the Liberal Party to adopt its policy of privatising the ABC. This policy found favour with the Young Liberals, which then put forward a motion to the Liberal Party's federal council calling for the Turnbull Government to privatise the ABC except for regional services (Norman 2018). The vote was backed by a large majority, including at least four of the party's top federal officials and at least one federal Liberal MP, according to footage obtained by the *Sydney Morning Herald* (Crowe 2019). Communications minister Mitch Fifield was the only Liberal who spoke against the motion, despite having made six complaints about the ABC in as many months in his role as minister.

This demonstrates the IPA's effectiveness at both agenda-setting—successfully catapulting the issue of privatising the ABC on to the national election campaign agenda—and influencing the policy formulation of the Liberal Party. Ultimately, this policy found little favour in the electorate, as happened with the policy to abolish the cashing out of franking credits. Importantly, despite finding enthusiastic supporters among party members, several ministers went into 'damage control' when news of the vote broke and was met with a strong community backlash. Fearing it would give Labor ammunition to run another 'Mediscare'-style campaign, Treasurer Josh Frydenberg assured voters that the ABC 'is not going to be sold and it can never be sold' (Remeikis 2019).

In September 2018, the Coalition Government announced it would not be replacing the Renewable Energy Target, which expires in 2020, effectively fulfilling one the IPA's key policies (Sydney Morning Herald 2018). Following the federal election, the IPA's call to legalise nuclear power in Australia has been taken up by the Morrison Government. Energy minister Angus Taylor requested a parliamentary inquiry into the use of nuclear energy in Australia, though he said Australia's moratorium on nuclear energy would remain in place (Macmillan 2019). There is no doubt other parts of the IPA's manifesto, such as removing red tape, have also re-entered the national debate post election.

The Grattan Institute released a research report in March 2019 advocating for the introduction of a universal Medicare-style dental health scheme. The report showed that 'about 2 million Australians who required dental care in the past year either didn't get it or delayed getting it because of the cost—and the poor and disadvantaged are most likely to miss out on care' (Duckett et al. 2019: 3).

Little more than a month later, and just a few weeks out from the federal election, Labor announced it would introduce dental subsidies for nearly 3 million pensioners (Barro 2019b). The Grattan Institute's CEO, John Daley, said its scheme was 'clearly the basis for the recent ALP election promise to go down this path', but added that 'policy reform always has many parents'.

The Grattan Institute also joined The Australia Institute in publishing research during the campaign on the income tax cuts package. The Grattan Institute's research estimated, based on the government's own Budget forecasts, that spending cuts of $40 billion by 2030 would be required to meet the government's promises. The research received widespread coverage but was dismissed by the Prime Minister as 'absolute complete rubbish' (Hutchens 2019). This is despite the institute working closely with the government to implement education funding reforms just a few years previously, showing that influence over policy implementation on one issue does not necessarily translate to effective advocacy or influence on other policy fronts.

Conclusion

The 2019 federal election result upended widespread expectations as well as conventional wisdom. Some have argued that the result was a rejection of Labor's progressive policy platform and that low and middle income-earners abandoned Labor, but as explored in Chapter 12 of this volume, there is little evidence to support these narratives, with economic cleavages remaining largely intact.

While third-party organisations such as GetUp! and Advance Australia are unlikely to change their political bent in response to election results, their tactics, target seats and the resources they devote to election campaigning are more likely to change.

It is difficult to measure the effectiveness of think tanks, as they tend to measure success 'by how much influence they have in shaping public opinion and the policy preferences and choices of leaders' (Abelson 2002: 88–89), which is hard to capture via simple metrics such as media mentions. It is even more difficult to unpick the particular influence of think tanks given other groups such as unions and NGOs seek to have similar influence—sometimes on the same issues. Overall, it is also worth considering how the political climate 'can enhance or diminish the profile of some think tanks' (Abelson 2002: 125–26), waxing and waning with the perceived or actual political fortunes of the political parties in the parliament.

However, there is no doubt think tanks did help shape and influence the political debate during the 2019 federal election, whether by helping certain issues gain national prominence (agenda-setting) or by persuading political parties to adopt their policies (policy formulation).

The Coalition's unexpected election win left the Morrison Government with a relatively light policy agenda for the new parliament (Murphy 2019), which think tanks will now seek to fill, shape and direct with their own policy agendas.

References

Abelson, Donald E. 2002. *Do Think Tanks Matter? Assessing the Impact of Public Policy Institutes*. Montreal: McGill–Queen's University Press. doi.org/10.7202/1063734ar.

Aulby, Hannah. 2017. *The Case for a Federal Corruption Watchdog*. Canberra: The Australia Institute.

Australian Associated Press (AAP). 2019. 'Activists GetUp! ruled independent of parties by Electoral Commission'. *SBS News*, 18 February. www.sbs.com.au/news/activists-getup-ruled-independent-of-parties-by-electoral-commission.

Australian Electoral Commission (AEC). 2019. *2019 Federal Election Tally Room*. Canberra: AEC. results.aec.gov.au/24310/Website/HouseDefault-24310.htm.

Barro, Christiane. 2019a. 'The think tanks shaping Australia: The Institute of Public Affairs'. *The New Daily*, 10 June. thenewdaily.com.au/news/national/2019/06/10/institute-of-public-affairs/.

Barro, Christiane. 2019b. 'The think tanks shaping Australia: The Grattan Institute'. *The New Daily*, 12 June. thenewdaily.com.au/news/national/2019/06/12/grattan-institute-think-tank/.

Butler, Josh. 2019. 'Inside GetUp!'s ambitious campaign to crush Dutton and the Liberal right'. *10 Daily*, 6 May. 10daily.com.au/news/politics/a190506xdrlg/inside-GetUp!s-ambitious-campaign-to-crush-dutton-and-the-liberal-right-20190506.

Cockburn, Paige and Sarah Whyte. 2019. 'GetUp! pulls Tony Abbott lifesaver election ad after widespread criticism'. *ABC News*, 24 April. abc.net.au/news/2019-04-24/GetUp!-pulls-tony-abbott-ad-over-climate-change/11041878.

Crowe, David. 2018. 'Footage from Liberal Party meeting reveals who voted to sell the ABC'. *Sydney Morning Herald*, 18 June. smh.com.au/politics/federal/footage-from-liberal-party-meeting-reveals-who-voted-to-sell-the-abc-20180618-p4zm5e.html.

Crowe, David. 2019. 'Coalition MPs urged to sell the ABC and support a flat tax in IPA call'. *Sydney Morning Herald*, 16 April. www.smh.com.au/federal-election-2019/coalition-mps-urged-to-sell-the-abc-and-support-a-flat-tax-in-ipa-call/-20190416-p51enu.html.

Denniss, Richard. 2019. 'The Morrison Election: What We Know Now'. *The Monthly*, June: 20–31. themonthly.com.au/issue/2019/june/15593 97600/richard-denniss/morrison-election-what-we-know-now.

Duckett, Stephen, Matt Cowgill and Hal Swerissen. 2019. *Filling the Gap: A Universal Dental Care Scheme for Australia*. Melbourne: Grattan Institute. grattan.edu.au/report/filling-the-gap/.

Essential Research. 2018a. 'Understanding of franking credits'. *Essential Report*, 27 March. www.essentialvision.com.au/understanding-franking-credits.

Essential Research. 2018b. 'Dividend imputation'. *Essential Report*, 4 December. www.essentialvision.com.au/dividend-imputation.

Faine, Jon. 2019. 'Mornings'. *ABC Radio Melbourne*, 17 April.

Ferguson, Richard. 2019. 'GetUp! chiefs face complaint to parliamentary committee'. *The Australian*, 18 July.

GetUp!. 2016. *Election 2016: People Powered Impact*. Sydney: GetUp Limited. cdn.getup.org.au/2037-Getup-Election-Report-MP-2016_(1).pdf.

GetUp!. 2019a. *Hitting the hard-right with people power!*. Media release, 7 January. Sydney: GetUp Limited. www.getup.org.au/media/releases/2019/01/hitting-the-hard-right-with-people-power/.

GetUp!. 2019b. *Dutton, Abbott country's most loathed politicians*. Media release, 17 January. Sydney: GetUp Limited. www.getup.org.au/media/releases/2019/01/dutton-abbott-country-s-most-loathed/.

GetUp!. 2019c. *Greg Hunt the next GetUp target*. Media release, 14 March. Sydney: GetUp Limited. www.getup.org.au/media/releases/2019/03/greg-hunt-the-next-getup-target/.

GetUp!. 2019d. *Who? What? How?* Sydney: GetUp Limited. www.getup.org.au/about.

Green, Antony. 2019. 'Politics is often about expectations'. Twitter, 18 May. twitter.com/antonygreenabc/status/1129751172116566016.

Gregory, Katherine. 2019. 'Federal election 2019: Tony Abbott says Warringah campaign "pretty personal" in secret recording'. *ABC News*, 12 May. www.abc. net.au/news/2019-05-12/tony-abbott-zali-steggall-getup-advance-australia-in-warringah/11100424.

Griffiths, Emma. 2014. 'Government backtracks on Racial Discrimination Act 18C changes; pushes ahead with tough security laws'. *ABC News*, 6 August. www.abc.net.au/news/2014-08-05/government-backtracks-on-racial-discrimination-act-changes/5650030.

Grudnoff, Matt. 2019. *A Bit Rich: A Government Plan to Make Tax Less Progressive.* Canberra: The Australia Institute.

Hersh, Eitan and Brian Schaffner. 2013. 'Targeted Campaign Appeals and the Value of Ambiguity'. *The Journal of Politics* 75(2): 520–34. doi.org/10.1017/s0022381613000182.

Hutchens, Gareth. 2019. 'Morrison Government tax cuts to come at a cost, analysis shows'. *West Australian*, [Perth], 16 April. www.thewest.com.au/politics/federal-election-2019/morrison-government-tax-cuts-to-come-at-a-cost-analysis-shows-ng-b881171007z.

James, Simon. 1998. 'Diane Stone, Capturing the Political Imagination: Think Tanks and the Political Process'. *Public Administration* 76(2): 408–10. doi.org/10.1111/1467-9299.00108.

John, Peter and Tessa Brannan. 2008. 'How Different Are Telephoning and Canvassing? Results from a "Get out the Vote" Field Experiment in the British 2005 General Election'. *British Journal of Political Science* 38(3): 565–74. doi.org/10.1017/s0007123408000288.

Kalla, Joshua and David Broockman. 2018. 'The Minimal Persuasive Effects of Campaign Contact in General Elections: Evidence from 49 Field Experiments'. *American Political Science Review* 112(1): 148–66. doi.org/10.1017/s0003055417000363.

Koslowski, Max. 2019. 'Meet Gerard Benedet, the man who could save conservatives—or take them down with him'. *Sydney Morning Herald*, 16 March. www.smh.com.au/politics/federal/meet-gerard-benedet-the-man-who-could-save-conservatives-or-take-them-down-with-him-20190315-p514l1.html.

Koziol, Michael. 2019. 'GetUp! boss in car-crash interview over claims Josh Frydenberg was "part of Liberal coup"'. *Sydney Morning Herald*, 17 April. www.smh.com.au/federal-election-2019/GetUp!-boss-in-car-crash-interview-over-claims-josh-frydenberg-was-part-of-liberal-coup-20190417-p51f1h.html.

Livingstone, Angus. 2019. '"Dopey" GetUp wasted resources: Barnaby Joyce'. *Newcastle Herald*, 18 May. www.theherald.com.au/story/6131747/dopey-GetUp-wasted-resources-barnaby-joyce/.

McGowan, Michael. 2019. '"Hindsight is a wonderful thing": How GetUp's election campaign fell flat'. *The Guardian*, 26 May. www.theguardian.com/australia-news/2019/may/26/hindsight-is-a-wonderful-thing-how-getups-election-campaign-fell-flat.

Macmillan, Jade. 2019. 'Nuclear power in Australia to be examined by multi-party parliamentary inquiry'. *ABC News*, 3 August. www.abc.net.au/news/2019-08-03/parliamentary-enquiry-to-examine-nuclear-power-in-australia/11380666.

Murphy, Katharine. 2019. 'GetUp boss under fire for claim Josh Frydenberg was part of Liberal leadership coup'. *The Guardian*, 17 April. www.theguardian.com/australia-news/2019/apr/17/getup-boss-under-fire-for-claim-josh-frydenberg-was-part-of-liberal-leadership-coup.

National Integrity Committee. 2017. *The Principles for Designing a National Integrity Commission*. Canberra: The Australia Institute.

National Integrity Committee. 2019. *Feedback on the Consultation Paper: A Commonwealth Integrity Commission—Proposed Reform*. Canberra: The Australia Institute. www.tai.org.au/content/feedback-consultation-paper-commonwealth-integrity-commission-proposed-reform.

Norman, Jane. 2018. 'Liberal Party members vote to privatise ABC and move Australia's Israel embassy to Jerusalem'. *ABC News*, 16 June. www.abc.net.au/news/2018-06-16/liberal-members-vote-to-privatise-abc-move-embassy-to-jerusalem/9877524.

Remeikis, Amy. 2019. '"Never": Senior Liberals in damage control after party vote to privatise ABC'. *The Guardian*, 17 June. www.theguardian.com/australia-news/2018/jun/17/never-senior-liberals-in-damage-control-after-party-votes-to-privatise-abc.

Roskam, John and Daniel Wild. 2019. *20 Policies to Fix Australia*. Parliamentary Research Brief, 12 April. Melbourne: Institute of Public Affairs. ipa.org.au/wp-content/uploads/2019/04/IPA-Research-20-Policies-to-Fix-Australia.pdf.

Sky News Australia. 2019. 'Election Night Broadcast, 2019'. *Sky News Australia*, 18 May.

Special Broadcasting Service (SBS). 2019. 'Conservative hero Captain GetUp rubs up against Zali Steggall poster'. *SBS News*, 15 April. www.sbs.com.au/news/conservative-hero-captain-getup-rubs-up-against-zali-steggall-poster.

Speers, David. 2019. 'Speers on Sunday'. *Sky News Australia*, 14 April.

Steelman, Aaron. 2003. 'Do Think Tanks Matter? Assessing the Impact of Public Policy Institutes by Donald E. Abelson'. [Book review], *The Cato Journal* 23(1): 163–65.

Stone, Diane. 1996. *Capturing the Political Imagination: Think Tanks and the Policy Process*. London: Frank Cass.

Sydney Morning Herald. 2018. 'Angus Taylor confirms government "won't be replacing" renewable energy target'. *Sydney Morning Herald*, 18 September. www.smh.com.au/politics/federal/angus-taylor-confirms-government-won-t-be-replacing-renewable-energy-target-20180918-p504j1.html.

The Australia Institute. 2019. 'An open letter to the next Parliament of Australia'. *The Age*, [Melbourne], 15 May: 17.

Van Extel, Cathy. 2019. 'Proxy war: The outsiders campaigning for the major parties'. *RN Breakfast*, [ABC Radio], 10 May. abc.net.au/radionational/programs/breakfast/proxy-war-the-outsiders-campaigning-for-the-major-parties/11099892.

Williams, Pamela. 2016. 'Federal election 2016: GetUp! proves force to be reckoned with'. *The Australian*, 9 July. www.theaustralian.com.au/nation/politics/federal-election-2016-getup-proves-force-to-be-reckoned-with/news-story/049de92ad4c625fa510f4e2c9563b813.

Zhou, Naaman. 2019. 'Captain GetUp: Conservative group's satirical superhero debuts to ridicule'. *The Guardian*, 9 April.

PART 4.
MEDIA

22

MEDIA COVERAGE

Andrea Carson and Lawrie Zion

In accounting for the 2019 federal election result, Opposition leader Bill Shorten extended the blame for his loss beyond his political opponents to the media. He told his party room that powerful vested interests had campaigned against Labor through sections of the media itself and had got what they wanted. Like recent fallen Australian political leaders before him—including Tony Abbott, Malcolm Turnbull and Julia Gillard— Shorten felt the media, among others, played a part in his political downfall: 'Obviously, we were up against corporate leviathans, a financial behemoth, spending unprecedented hundreds of millions of dollars advertising, telling lies, spreading fear' (Osborne 2019). No names were mentioned, but likely in Shorten's crosshairs were Rupert Murdoch's daily metropolitan newspapers and pay television station *Sky News Australia*, which repeatedly ran negative stories, panel discussions and headlines describing Shorten as 'The great divider' (Rolfe 2019). But Shorten might also have been referring to a number of radio presenters with whom he declined to do interviews during the campaign, including 3AW's Neil Mitchell in Melbourne and 2GB's Alan Jones in Sydney, both of whom described Shorten as 'toxic' to voters (Osborne 2019). Both are right-of-centre commentators employed by Macquarie Media, in which Nine Entertainment Co. has a dominant share. Nine's newly acquired financial daily, the *Australian Financial Review*, also urged voters to stay with the Coalition in its election-eve editorial.

But how much do Australia's traditional media—comprising newspapers, radio and television—influence an election outcome through their political coverage? It is a vexed question, particularly in the internet age, when media audiences are fragmented across traditional and digital platforms. It is further complicated by a backdrop of economic decline for traditional media outlets with limited resources and shrinking newsrooms. Since the previous election, changes to cross-media ownership laws in 2017 resulted in further consolidation of Australian media. The reforms enabled television network Nine to take over the Fairfax mastheads and end Fairfax's 177-year name association with the Australian media industry. During the campaign, another round of redundancies also saw Perth's only daily newspaper, the *West Australian*, shed 30 journalism jobs. Funding cuts to the national broadcaster, the ABC, since the 2016 election have also seen job losses across the network. News Corp also shed 55 jobs shortly after the election (Watkins and Dyer 2019).

Yet, notwithstanding this turbulence and transition for the established media, party leaders still perceive mainstream media power as a key factor in their political fortunes. Complicating this is a climate of public distrust towards the media, with Australians increasingly concerned about 'fake news' (62 per cent compared with the global average of 55 per cent) and falling levels of trust in the news media (Fisher et al. 2019: 16–17).

Measuring media effects on voter behaviour is notoriously difficult. Researchers have found many factors can influence voters' responses to campaign coverage—such as voters' level of political engagement, with the 'least engaged' more susceptible to political messaging (Albaek et al. 2014); the importance of the issue (Wlezien 2005); the use of negativity in messaging (Carson et al. 2020); and the type of media platform on which the story is conveyed, with television generally considered the most powerful (Lau and Rovner 2009). Given these complexities, this chapter leaves aside attempts to gauge audience perceptions and media effects. Rather, our aim is to assess traditional media's election coverage outputs, focusing first on front-page newspaper stories—the issues editors prioritise over others—then the political content available on radio and television during the 2019 campaign and, last, a brief word about the campaign on social media.

How the press reported the 2019 election campaign

Traditional media remains a worthy area of study. While more and more Australians are migrating to the digital sphere to get their news, the majority of Australians (57 per cent) still use offline sources as their main source of news (Fisher et al. 2019: 13). We examine newspaper and broadcast media because they remain Australia's largest collective employer of journalists and produce more original news stories than alternative sources. As such, they have the capacity to set the news agenda for other media (intermedia effects), including online and social media (Sikanku 2011). For example, Australia's traditional media outlets occupy seven of the top 10 'most read' Australian digital news sites each month (Pash 2019). Collectively, Australia's press duopoly of Nine and News Corp have about 32 million monthly views. Adding in the ABC's websites, this figure swells to 40 million, meaning that 'traditional' media's online audiences account for more than two-thirds (69 per cent) of the views of the top 10 digital news sites each month (Pash 2019).[1]

To assess how Australia's 12 major daily newspapers covered the election, we collected front pages from Monday to Saturday editions during the 37-day campaign.[2] The population was 377 front pages, accounting for absences during Easter and Anzac Day when some outlets did not publish. Front pages and their election stories were the units of analysis because they provide a sense of indicative coverage, rather than complete coverage of the campaign. They offer a snapshot of the stories that editors believe are of high news value, thus earning a place on the premium page of their newspaper, which is designed to attract readers' attention. These stories are replicated online. Thus, tracking page-one stories provides an overview of the election issues that were highlighted to the public during the campaign and were given attention over other topics. Each front page was given a binary code for the presence or absence of election coverage. If present, an election article was coded for its primary topic and sentiment. If there were more than one election story, the dominant story was selected. Sentiment was judged in terms of being negative, positive

---

1   The top 10 news sites were (from one to 10): news.com.au, nine.com.au, *ABC News* websites, smh.com.au, *Daily Mail Australia*, *Yahoo!*, *The Guardian*, Fairfax Digital Regional Network, *The Age* [Melbourne] and the *Daily Telegraph* [Sydney].
2   We exclude Sunday papers as not all mastheads in the study produced a Sunday edition.

or neutral overall for the political party that featured most prominently in the story.[3] The same methodology was used in 2016, thus providing similar data for cautious comparisons.

First—and as found in 2016—federal election campaigns are newsworthy events in Australia. Election stories featured on 69 per cent of eligible front pages (compared with 50 per cent in 2016, which was a longer, eight-week campaign). This finding is consistent with international studies of election coverage (Deacon and Wring 2015: 313). However, there are considerable differences in the frequency of front-page coverage between mastheads and capital cities (see Figure 22.1). While many of the same stories were shared across masthead groups, this occurred across both major newspaper groups but was particularly evident with Nine's papers. A total of 24 of 32 front pages of *The Age* (Melbourne) and the *Sydney Morning Herald* carried the same election story, often using identical headlines.[4] In a nation that has highly concentrated ownership of its press compared with other democracies, this is problematic. Convergence of news stories across the masthead group is a way of adapting to limited resources following journalist redundancies, but it can limit story diversity and give more weight to some election issues than others. Compared with 2016, story convergence had more than doubled in 2019. In 2016, the carriage of the same stories on the front pages of the *Sydney Morning Herald* and *The Age* occurred 11 times (Carson and McNair 2019: 434).

Figure 22.1 shows that Australia's two national newspapers, *The Australian* and the *Australian Financial Review*, along with the capital-city dailies of Melbourne, Sydney and Perth—*The Age*, the *Sydney Morning Herald* and the *West Australian*, respectively—featured election news on their front pages most days. This was not the case with Darwin's irreverent *NT News* or even, somewhat surprisingly, the daily paper of the nation's capital, *The Canberra Times*.

---

3   A random selection of 10 per cent of the story population was recoded by an independent researcher, Dr Andrew Gibbons of the University of Texas, Austin. The intercoder reliability was 80 per cent.
4   The dates for which the same or very similar stories were published on the front pages of *The Age* [Melbourne] and the *Sydney Morning Herald* were: 12, 14, 15, 17, 18, 22, 24, 25, 28, 29 and 30 April; 4, 5, 6, 7, 8, 9, 10, 11, 12, 13, 15 and 17 May and polling day, 18 May.

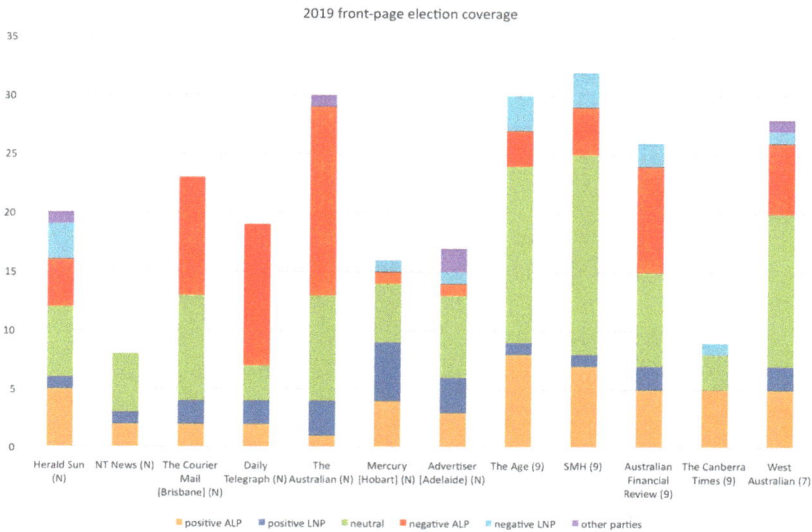

Figure 22.1 2019 election coverage in daily metropolitan Australian newspapers

Notes: No. = 258 election front-page stories; missing data = 12 stories or 2.9% per cent; newspaper owners are in parentheses, 'N' = News Corp, '9' = Nine Entertainment Co. and '7' = Seven West Media.

Source: Authors.

We also find that the amount of front-page election coverage increased across the five-and-a-half-week campaign. This is not surprising because the start of the official campaign was interrupted by the Easter holiday and major media stories such as racehorse Winx winning her last race, the Sri Lankan bombings, the arrival of a British royal baby and France's devastating Notre-Dame Cathedral fire. Also, early voting opened on 29 April, the start of week four of the campaign, suggesting that party messaging intensified to attract maximum media attention to reach voters before casting their ballot sometime during the final weeks (see Figure 22.2).

Tone of coverage

About one-third of election stories were neutral in tone (100 stories, or 38 per cent). However, of the stories that were not neutral in their overall message, more were negative (81 stories) than positive (72 stories)—a feature consistent with US studies (Patterson 2016). Many more front-page stories focused on the ALP (115 stories) than on the Coalition (38 stories), which might be because Labor was expected to win, although stories about the ALP tended to be negative (66 stories) rather than positive (49 stories) overall (see Figure 22.2).

If we simply compare the negative and the positive stories about the two major parties, the disproportionate front-page coverage given to Labor and its leader, Bill Shorten, becomes clearer. Figure 22.3 compares the negative coverage of the major parties from 2016 with that for 2019 as a percentage of the number of front pages assessed for each campaign.[5] In percentage terms, hostility towards Labor was almost unchanged from 2016 to 2019 (18 per cent compared with 17 per cent). In fact, the ALP had proportionally more positive page-one stories in 2019 than in 2016's press coverage (13 per cent compared with 3 per cent), when the party achieved a better electoral result.

The stories focused on Labor covered wideranging issues; however, overwhelmingly, the negative coverage focused on the costs of Labor's policies and tax increases that would follow if elected. Other prominent negative stories for Labor targeted the leadership of Shorten, the party's unclear position on the proposed Adani coalmine in Queensland and its plan to scrap franking credits for self-funded retirees who did not pay tax. More negative headlines about Labor came from the Murdoch stable of newspapers than from Nine, with the exception of Nine's *Australian Financial Review*. Conversely, the negative headlines directed at the Coalition came predominantly from the Nine stable of newspapers. However, overall there were fewer negative front pages about the Coalition and, in the case of the first week, there were no negative front-page stories. The page-one topics that were negative for the Coalition concentrated on inadequate costings or details in its policies on climate change, roads, housing and unemployment, and on being behind in the polls.

The positive stories for both major parties were fewer. For Labor, these included positive responses to policies addressing hospital funding, child care, violence against women, lifting wages for the low paid and Labor's lead in the polls. Positive Labor policy stories were more common in the Nine mastheads than in the Murdoch-owned papers and were often syndicated.

---

5   As 2016 was a longer campaign, the figure is expressed as a proportion of the front pages assessed to make the two election years comparable.

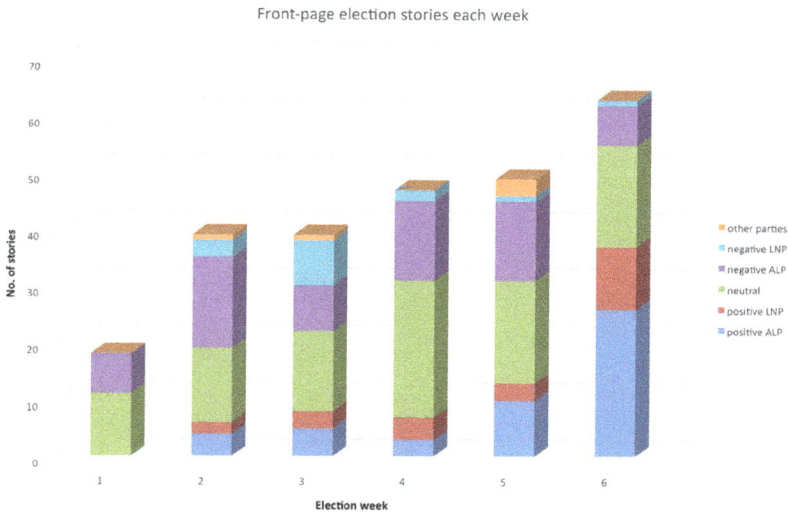

Front-page election stories each week

Figure 22.2 Comparing sentiment of stories about parties and their leaders

Notes: No. = 258 front pages with election stories; no. = 107 non-election front pages (not shown here).

Source: Authors.

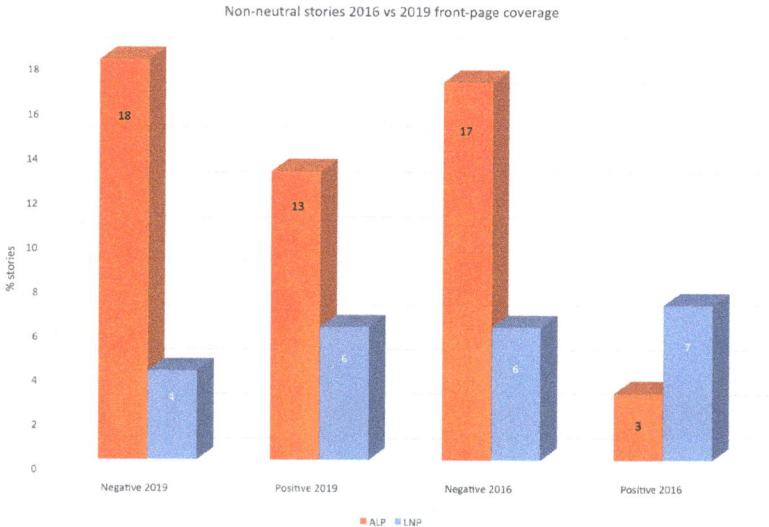

Non-neutral stories 2016 vs 2019 front-page coverage

Figure 22.3 Comparing the proportions of stories in the 2016 and 2019 election campaigns that were not neutral in sentiment

Notes: In 2019, no. = 365, missing data = 12 stories; in 2016, no. = 518, missing data = 10 stories.

Source: Authors.

Stories paying tribute to the legacy of former prime minister Bob Hawke, who died days before the final ballot, also increased the proportion of positive Labor stories. These results contradict a perception that coverage of the Labor Party was more often negative, at least in quantitative terms, in the press during the 2019 election campaign than during the previous election.

The press and issue agenda-setting

Turning further attention to the issues that made it to the front pages of Australia's daily newspapers, topics varied from State to State, yet stories most frequently placed on page one covered policies about taxation, the economy, housing, interest rates and concerns over Labor's proposed tax increases and expenditure if elected to office (see Figure 22.4). These economically focused policy areas are often associated more favourably with the Coalition than with Labor—something known as 'issue ownership' (Konstantinidis 2008). Less common on page one were topics of which Labor typically has issue ownership, such as health, education and workers' pay and conditions. From this perspective, the selection of issues by editors that made front-page headlines collectively fitted the Coalition's framing of the election campaign better than Labor's.

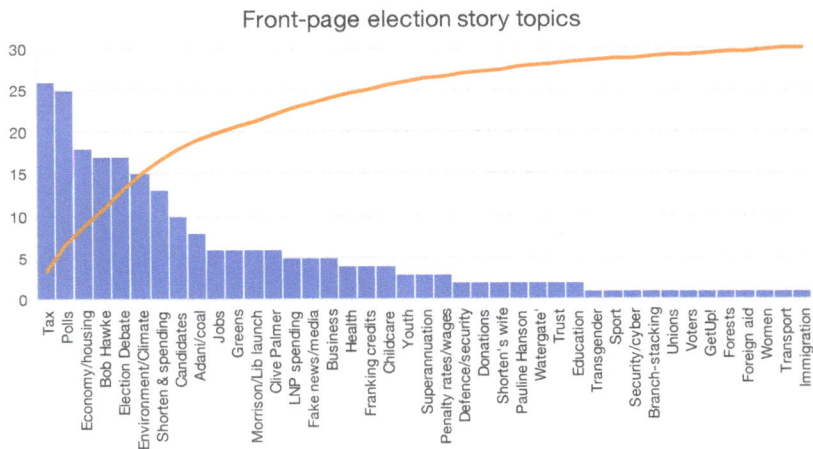

Figure 22.4 Story topics most commonly featured on the front pages of the daily press during the 2019 election campaign

Notes: No. = 39; orange denotes process stories; blue denotes policy-focused topics.

Source: Authors.

The data show that stories about tax and concerns about Labor's spending dominated the front-page coverage in weeks one and two of the campaign, setting up an election narrative. Jobs and penalty rates—issues promoted by Labor—were among the top issues of week three, but this media attention was divided by Clive Palmer's big advertising spend and his role as a possible preference-deal kingmaker. Further, the role of former Nationals leader Barnaby Joyce in signing off on a multimillion-dollar sum of taxpayers' funds as part of a water buyback scheme—dubbed 'Watergate'—also made headlines in the Nine papers and was the subject of a long and much commented on interview with Joyce on the ABC Radio program *RN Drive* on 22 April, in which he denied any wrongdoing in the decision.

The top three election topics that dominated week four's coverage were the first leaders' debate, in Western Australia, which was televised on Channel Seven (12 front-page stories); the environment, including the future of Queensland's controversial Adani coalmine (10 stories); and a number of stories about candidates from both major parties withdrawing after unsavoury content was discovered on their social media sites or caches (four stories). Week five reverted to issues about the economy and related concerns about housing affordability and interest rates. Negative headlines about Labor's plan to scrap franking credits for Australians who did not pay tax, such as self-funded retirees, also featured. The economy again dominated the campaign's final week until Hawke's death overwhelmed the coverage.

Television coverage

While television remains an important source of news, the number of Australians relying on it for election news has declined steadily over time, from 63 per cent in 1969 to 25 per cent in 2016 (Cameron and McAllister 2016: 8). But analysing the reach of any particular medium is complicated by the fact that content is no longer necessarily confined to specific platforms; a little-watched interview segment from a TV program might develop a much larger audience via social media or radio and online platforms provide access to content on demand that are not recorded in ratings results.

These factors notwithstanding, television coverage of the campaign followed a broadly familiar pattern, culminating in election night broadcasts. However, there were some noteworthy features, one of which was the more prominent role played by the free-to-air commercial Network 10 and its coverage of political events through its news–current affairs panel program *The Project*.

Ahead of the announcement of the 18 May election date, the program broadcast an extended and uninterrupted interview in which co-host Waleed Aly challenged Prime Minister Scott Morrison about whether the Liberal Party had a problem with Islamophobia, and pressed him to address a news report from 2011 that said while he was shadow immigration minister, he urged a 2010 Shadow Cabinet meeting 'to capitalise on the electorate's growing concerns about "Muslim immigration", "Muslims in Australia" and the "inability" of Muslim migrants to integrate' (Remeikis 2019).

The 35-minute interview materialised after Morrison threatened to sue Aly following comments the latter made in a broadcast editorial about the mass murder of 50 Muslim worshippers in Christchurch that also referenced the aforementioned 2011 news report. Both that editorial and the subsequent interview with Morrison reflected a more agenda-setting role for the Network 10 program; as Australian TV veteran and Network 10 consultant on news and current affairs Peter Meakin commented, the interview indicated that the show was more than 'a court jester sniggering on the sidelines' (Watkins 2019).

Despite lower ratings in recent years, the program's particular significance within the news media ecology is that its viewers are predominantly in the 18–49-years age bracket, while its competition on Nine, Seven and the ABC have ageing demographics, with many viewers aged over 60. Moreover, its reach is exponentially extended through social media; Aly's emotional and personal editorial in response to the shootings in Christchurch drew 427,000 viewers on TV, but on social media it was seen almost 14 million times via the show's Twitter and Facebook pages alone (Watkins and Dyer 2019).

The Project also led the television coverage of the 'Watergate' affair referenced earlier, featuring reports by independent journalist Michael West and the show's own Hamish McDonald. Yet while described in a program tweet on 5 May as a story 'that just won't go away: the murky, taxpayer-funded water buyback that's raised a lot of questions', it failed to sustain significant traction across the lifespan of the campaign, as the press analysis showed.

As always, TV provided a platform throughout the campaign for contenders to attempt to move beyond standard talking points—though, not surprisingly, these were also amplified ad nauseum—and to land 'gotcha' punches against a number of hapless candidates, most notably, One Nation's Steve Dickson, who resigned in disgrace after *A Current Affair* aired footage filmed by *Al Jazeera* of the Senate candidate 'making derogatory comments and groping a woman in undercover footage filmed in a Washington DC strip club' (Hunter and Crockford 2019).

Meanwhile, one of the most prominent fixtures on the small screen throughout the contest, beginning well before the campaign itself, was UAP founder, Clive Palmer, who eschewed interviews for a saturated advertising blitz, which included as many as 150,000 television ads (McCutcheon 2019). This tactic failed to win him a single seat, but may have helped thwart Labor's ambitions, especially in Queensland.

'Sky News Australia'

With much focus during the campaign on the election coverage of News Corp papers, the performance of the Murdoch-owned *Sky News Australia* was scrutinised elsewhere in the media, and criticised by Labor leaders past and present, especially its 'after dark' line-up, which features mostly right-wing hosts, including Peta Credlin, Andrew Bolt, Chris Kenny, Alan Jones and Paul Murray. Described by some as a 'Foxification' of the pay-TV channel, the line-up has produced an increase in ratings (Lallo 2019). And, while available only as a pay channel in most metropolitan areas, some *Sky News* programming was for the first time during an election campaign available on free-to-air TV in regional areas through the WIN network in Queensland, New South Wales, Victoria, South Australia and Western Australia, and Statewide across Tasmania and the Australian Capital Territory. Of the markets where TV ratings are available, the nightly reach during the election campaign was just over 60,000 nationally, with the largest monitored audiences in New South Wales and Queensland, and more than half of that total audience was aged over 65 (see Figure 22.5).

Sky News audience share on WIN

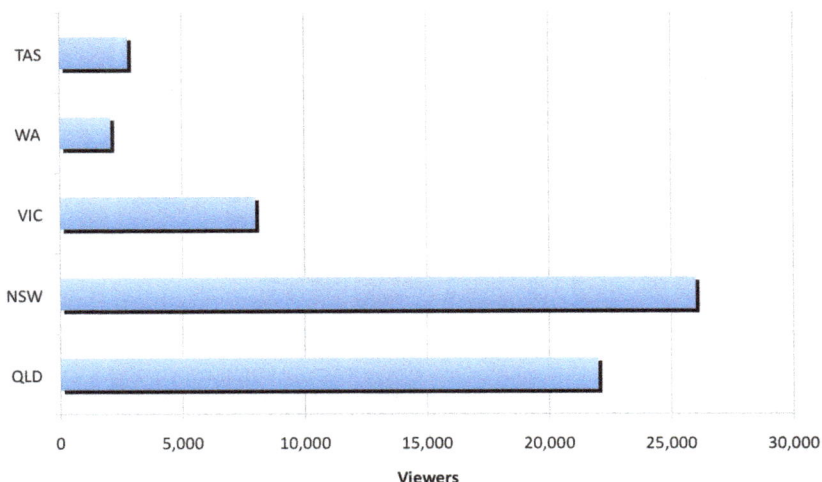

Figure 22.5 Ratings figures for *Sky News* content on free-to-air television during the 2019 election campaign

Note: South Australia and some smaller regional markets were not monitored by Regional Tam and are thus not included in the graph.

Source: Authors, using Regional Tam ratings figures of average evening reach from 21 April to 18 May 2019.

Analysis conducted by *The New Daily* website of *Sky*'s programming over three consecutive nights found that anti-Labor commentary was seven times more likely to appear on the news service than negative rhetoric about the Coalition. PHON received more than twice as many positive comments as negative, 26 to 11, on *Sky*, while the Greens received not one positive comment and 28 negative comments (Stapleton 2019).

So contentious was the coverage that it became the subject of an on-air exchange on *Sky* itself between Murray and morning host Kieran Gilbert, during which Gilbert said to Murray in response to an apparent swipe from the latter: 'You're not a big fan of Bill Shorten's. He could have orchestrated the second coming and you probably wouldn't have been too positive about it. So that's the starting point isn't it?' (Meade 2019).

The possible impact of *Sky News*'s evening coverage on the election outcome needs to be seen in the context of the station's relatively small, albeit growing, share of the overall television audience; with repeat and catch-up viewers factored in, the weekly reach of *Paul Murray Live* averages 275,000 viewers, with *The Bolt Report* nearing 240,000 and *Credlin* on almost 200,000 (Lallo 2019).

Whatever the possible influence of *Sky News*, it is important to distinguish between viewership of the station content itself and the audiences that some of its presenters command through other media formats. For instance, Bolt's blog, published via News Corp daily newspaper sites (outside the paywall), is billed as the nation's most read political blog, while Alan Jones's 2GB radio breakfast program—which has a 17.6 per cent share of the Sydney radio audience—is also syndicated to Brisbane's 4BC (Kelly 2019). Jones, whose political influence has long been debated (Salter 2006; McKenzie-Murray 2018), was highly critical of Labor throughout the campaign and predicted a Coalition victory. And, following the election, in reference to the refusal of Shorten to appear on his program, Jones commented that 'no-one's ever won an election boycotting this program' (Jones 2019).

ABC coverage

ABC TV's campaign coverage included standard programming on its main station and more extensive interviews on its *News 24* channel, many of which were conducted between 4 pm and 6 pm by Patricia Karvelas and replayed during her subsequent 6 pm *RN Drive* program on ABC Radio National. The network's *News Breakfast*, 7 pm news and current affairs program, *7.30*, featured a steady mix of daily commentary, interviews with politicians and profiles of swing seats, with particular focus on the normally safe seat of Warringah, which former prime minister Tony Abbott lost to Independent and former Olympian Zali Steggall. Even the weekly current affairs program *Four Corners*, which did not broadcast election stories during the campaign, featured a special entitled 'Abbott's End', which was broadcast two days after the poll and chronicled the successful campaign that saw him ousted from the seat he had held for 25 years.

Interviews with politicians and election analysis also featured on the weekly Sunday morning program, *Insiders*, and on the Monday night panel program, *Q&A*. Over the course of the campaign, *Q&A* included an episode focused on Queensland, featuring five political candidates, two standard episodes that included a mix of politicians and other panellists and a program on which the sole guest was Bill Shorten. Scott Morrison declined an invitation to appear as the sole guest on the program (McMahon 2019).

Throughout the campaign, the ABC positioned its inhouse psephologist Antony Green as its trump card, featuring him extensively in promotions of its election coverage in acknowledgement of his growing stature over a three-decade career. The national broadcaster also provided ongoing public opinion findings from its own Vote Compass survey,[6] which were a common talking point across its network.

Satirical takes on the election campaign were provided by *The Weekly with Charlie Pickering* and in interstitial sketches from comedians Mark Humphreys and Sammy J. A notable absence from the network's campaign programming in 2019 was the comedy team known as 'The Chaser', whose two-decade relationship with the ABC had included regular election-year programs that were successful in terms of both ratings and awards. The team revealed in late 2018 that the ABC would not be funding them (Moran and Cooper 2018). Also absent from the national broadcaster was the human interest interview-format program *Kitchen Cabinet*, presented by Annabel Crabb, which provided a different kind of engagement with many leading politicians during the 2016 election campaign.

The ABC was briefly an issue in its own right ahead of the 2019 campaign when Prime Minister Morrison eschewed convention by directly appointing Ita Buttrose as new ABC Chair, despite her not having been on the shortlist for the position (Jeffrey and Staff 2019). The appointment of Buttrose followed a period of instability in the corporation following the sacking of former managing director Michelle Guthrie in September 2018, and the subsequent resignation of ABC chair Justin Milne in the wake of allegations of political interference (Meade 2018). Commenting ahead of official confirmation that Buttrose would take up the role, Shorten said that while Buttrose was competent, qualified and 'very respected', the then mooted appointment amounted to 'more political interference' (Koslowski 2019). However, this controversy proved short-lived.

---

6   Andrea Carson is on the academic advisory panel of Vote Compass.

Election debates

Televised debates between leaders have been a staple of Australian campaigns but have arguably become less important over time. Just 21 per cent of Australians reported watching a debate in 2016—down from 71 per cent in 1993 (Cameron and McAllister 2016: 9). Over time, the debates have also come to be seen as an increasingly unreliable predictor of electoral success, with leaders either dodging them or setting conditions on where and when they are held (Carson 2019).

This held true in 2019. While in general (but by no means unanimous) terms Shorten was seen as the better performer across the three debates, neither leader delivered a decisive blow in any of the encounters. The first debate, broadcast on multiple channels of the Seven network, attracted less than 1 million viewers across metropolitan and regional areas—a far cry from the 3.4 million–strong audience that watched the 2010 campaign leaders' debate between Julia Gilliard and Tony Abbott, which was screened on the three free-to-air networks and the ABC (Craig 2012: 112). The second of the 2019 debates, which screened on *Sky*, attracted fewer than 100,000 viewers—less than 40 per cent of the audience for each of two rugby league matches screened on the pay-TV network on the same night (Dyer 2019)—but produced one of the more memorable exchanges between the two leaders, when Shorten described Morrison as 'a classic space invader' after the Prime Minister appeared to physically close in on him on the stage.

The final debate, hosted by the National Press Club and broadcast on ABC TV and *Sky* in prime time, garnered a respectable 882,000 viewers—but was eclipsed by Seven's reality program *House Rules* (975,000 viewers) (Rigby and Kelly 2019).

Election night coverage

For the first time, all networks covered election night to some extent, though in the case of SBS, coverage commenced after 10 pm, by which time it was already evident that the Coalition was likely to be returned to government. In ratings terms, the ABC dominated, attracting an even larger audience share than for the 2016 election, and averaging 1.34 million viewers nationally through the combined audience of its main channel and *News 24*. It was well ahead of Nine (597,000), Seven Network (489,000) and Network 10, whose figure of 170,000 was just 3.6 per cent of the free-to-air audience (Burrowes 2019).

It may not have figured in the ratings, but election coverage also featured on community television stations delivered by The Junction, a network of students involved in a reporting project of journalism schools at more than 20 Australian universities. The world-first election programming was broadcast on Melbourne-based community TV station Channel 31 and relayed to Adelaide and Perth as well as via the Community Broadcasting Association of Australia's network of radio stations.

Political messaging on social media

As noted earlier, this was a campaign fragmented across multiple dimensions: time, with school holidays distracting voters and early voting interrupting campaign messaging for some; geography, with different issues gaining traction in different States, such as the Adani coalmine in Queensland; and media platforms, with political messaging shaped by both traditional and social media logics.

Different media logics present obvious resourcing challenges and costs for political parties, which aim to tailor political messaging to different users of social media sites, whether it be Facebook, Instagram, Twitter, YouTube or Snapchat. According to Facebook analytics (using the tool CrowdTangle), the official pages of the two major political parties and their leaders attracted 2.29 million user interactions during the official campaign. Interactions included shares, comments and reactions such as 'likes'.

Analysis of these data shows that Labor and Bill Shorten were attracting more interactions than the Coalition before and during the first week of the campaign. However, as Figure 22.6 shows, this quickly reversed by the second week, notwithstanding that Morrison had fewer Facebook followers than Shorten at the outset of the campaign (148,000 versus 235,000). One of the reasons for this change was the increased frequency of postings and strategic use of video by Morrison and the Coalition on Facebook.

● Scott Morrison (ScoMo) ● Bill Shorten MP ● Liberal Party of Australia
● Australian Labor Party ● LNP - Liberal National Party

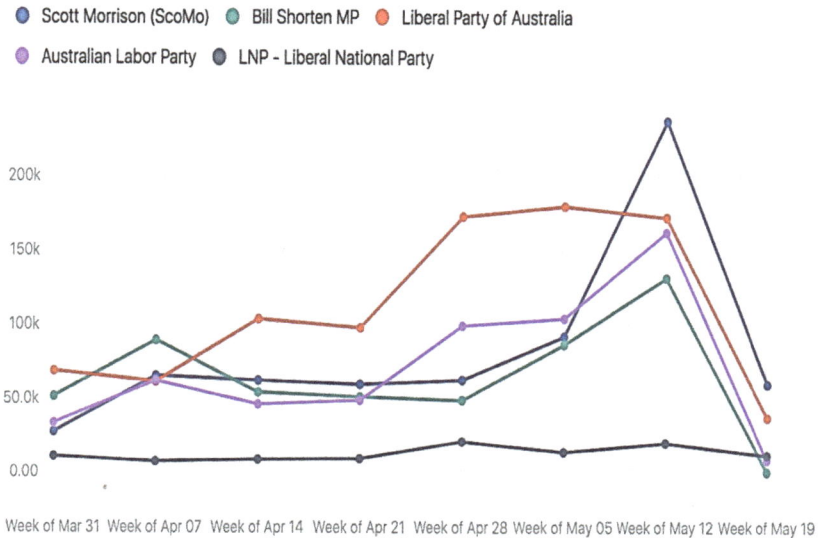

Figure 22.6 The total number of online interactions with the major political parties and their leaders' political communications before and during the 2019 election campaign
Source: Authors, using CrowdTangle data.

An analysis of the types of messages shows that the Liberals' Facebook page posted more content than Labor's (671 versus 435 posts), as was the case with Morrison's page compared with Shorten's (175 versus 165 posts). Morrison's posts were often more personal in nature, including about how Morrison proposed to his wife, Jenny (posted the day after calling the election). The election itself was called by Morrison using a Facebook video post before alerting reporters. In the final week of the campaign, 'ScoMo', as Morrison labels himself on Facebook, posted 30 videos compared with Shorten's 14, garnering 1.4 million views compared with Shorten's 236,000 views. The same pattern occurred between the Liberals' official Facebook page and Labor's. Between the day the election was called and polling day, 173 videos were posted on the Liberals' Facebook page, attracting 7.94 million views compared with Labor's 154 videos, which were viewed 2.77 million times. While these metrics do not include paid online advertising or other social media sites, the Facebook data show that the Liberals reached a larger audience through their strategic online communications during the campaign despite having fewer followers.

Labor was highly critical of some of the online election campaign content—notably, references to the so-called death tax, which appeared following a Seven Network news story on its breakfast program *Sunrise* in July 2018, which, in turn, followed up on a *Daily Telegraph* story speculating about unions wanting to reintroduce an inheritance tax (Holderhead 2018). The Seven Network segment was reposted by Labor's opponents, including Pauline Hanson, along with commentary that Labor would introduce a death tax if elected (Hanson 2018). While the 'death tax' was fake news, it did evolve from mainstream media coverage and was therefore difficult for some viewers to discern as false. As argued elsewhere in this volume, this reinforced a negative campaign message that a vote for Labor meant an increase in taxes.

Conclusion

The political communications of the 2019 campaign were fragmented not just across the traditional media platforms of radio, television and the press, but also across social media sites and paid and free media. They were also interrupted by major news events and holidays such as Easter and Anzac Day. These distractions disrupted news reporting and possibly voters' attention to election news during segments of the campaign. Early voting also saw a record number of Australians (see Chapter 3, this volume) make up their minds before the campaign had concluded. Election coverage also varied between States in story selection and intensity.

This theme of fragmentation brings us back to the plausibility of the claim made by Bill Shorten after the election that the media was implicated in his election defeat, through opponents with deep pockets 'telling lies' and 'spreading fear'.

While it is impossible to refute or defend these claims with precision, the newspaper data presented here show election coverage of Labor was quantitatively no more negative than the press coverage of the 2016 election campaign when Labor won more seats. However, the types of stories that made front-page headlines in 2019 more often amplified issues that the Coalition was promoting in its campaign messaging than those perceived to work more strongly for Labor. The front-page emphasis on tax increases and Labor spending at a time of economic uncertainty for Australians supported the Coalition's campaign narrative. Moreover, the diversity of topics was further compromised by newspaper stablemates syndicating the same page-one stories. The coverage of Labor on *Sky News*'s programming and its free-to-air broadcasting into regional areas via the WIN network (albeit to a small audience) also reinforced negative messages about Labor.

Whether these media choices were an artefact of the agenda-setting effectiveness of the Coalition or of the media itself, they served to complement the key slogan of the Coalition: 'The Bill Australia can't afford.' Further, the Coalition's tactical use of social media, particularly its use of video posts, saw Morrison and his party attract more viewers to their election stories on Facebook than their political opponents. Social media also provided a platform that enabled third parties and other actors, in addition to the Coalition, to spread a fear campaign falsely claiming that Labor would introduce a 'death tax'. While these different media platforms reach different publics, stories about extra taxes and Labor spending—whether true or not—coalesced to serve the Coalition's key message, giving some credence to Shorten's criticism of election coverage.

As noted in the introduction, however, caution is needed in any estimation of the overall impact media coverage has on voters' choices, particularly with record numbers of Australians voting before the campaign concluded. Examining media content provides some indication of what election issues voters may have encountered in the 2019 campaign, but it does not tell us how they responded to them at the ballot box.

References

Albaek, Eeik, Arjen van Dalen, Nael Jebril and Claes H. de Vreese. 2014. *Political Journalism in Comparative Perspective*. New York: Cambridge University Press. doi.org/10.1017/CBO9781139567367.

Burrowes, Tim. 2019. 'ABC wins the election ratings while Ten slumps to 3.6%'. *Mumbrella*, 19 May. mumbrella.com.au/abc-wins-the-election-ratings-while-ten-slumps-to-3-6-580222.

Cameron, Sarah and Ian McAllister. 2016. *Trends in Australian Political Opinion: Results from the Australian Election Study 1987–2016*. Canberra: School of Politics and International Relations, The Australian National University. www.australianelectionstudy.org.

Carson, Andrea. 2019. 'Leaders try to dodge them. Voters aren't watching. So, are debates still relevant?'. *The Conversation,* 3 May. theconversation.com/leaders-try-to-dodge-them-voters-arent-watching-so-are-debates-still-relevant-115456.

Carson, Andrea and Brian McNair. 2019. 'Still the main source: The established media'. In *Double Disillusion: The 2016 Australian Federal Election,* edited by Anika Gauja, Peter Chen, Jennifer Curtin and Juliet Pietsch, 421–51. Canberra: ANU Press. doi.org/10.22459/DD.04.2018.19.

Carson, Andrea, Aaron J. Martin and Shaun Ratcliff. 2020. 'Negative Campaigning, Issue Salience and Vote Choice: Assessing the Effects of the Australian Labor Party's 2016 "Mediscare" Campaign'. *Journal of Elections, Public Opinion and Parties* 30(1): 83–104. doi.org/10.1080/17457289.2018.1563093.

Craig, Geoffrey. 2012. 'Debates, town hall meetings, and media interviews'. In *Julia 2010: The Caretaker Election,* edited by Marian Simms and John Wanna, 111–20. Canberra: ANU Press. doi.org/10.22459/J2010.02.2012.07.

Deacon, David and Dominic Wring. 2015. 'Still life in the old attack dogs: The press'. In *The British General Election of 2015,* edited by Philip Cowley and Dennis Kavanagh, 302–35. Basingstoke, UK: Palgrave Macmillan. doi.org/10.1057/9781137366115_12.

Dyer, Glenn. 2019. 'Second leaders' debate fails to pull in viewers'. *Crikey,* 6 May. www.crikey.com.au/2019/05/06/ratings-leaders-debate-bombs/?utm_source=Insider&utm_medium=email&utm_source=newsletter&ins=VFRTNFVqVUhHQlJzVmJrcGplOXVCUT09.

Dyer, Glenn and Emily Watkins. 2019. 'News Corp cuts 55 jobs, but no mention in its papers'. *Crikey,* 4 June. www.crikey.com.au/2019/06/04/news-corp-cuts-jobs/.

Fisher, Caroline, Sora Park, Jee Young Lee, Glen Fuller and Yoonmo Sang. 2019. *Digital News Report: Australia 2019.* Canberra: News and Media Research Centre, University of Canberra.

Hanson, Pauline. 2018. 'Bill Shorten proposes death tax with union's support', Facebook, 21 July. www.facebook.com/PaulineHansonAu/videos/bill-shorten-proposes-death-tax-with-unions-support/817012815169699/.

Holderhead, Sheradyn. 2018. 'Inheritance tax in union's list of demands for Bill'. *Daily Telegraph,* [Sydney], 20 July. www.dailytelegraph.com.au/news/national/inheritance-tax-on-list-of-union-demands-for-bill-shorten/news-story/fbd72672d54eb4d5796bad80b3b12dff.

Hunter, Fergus and Toby Crockford. 2019. 'Steve Dickson resigns from One Nation after undercover strip club sting'. *Sydney Morning Herald*, 30 April: 5. www.smh.com.au/federal-election-2019/steve-dickson-resigns-from-one-nation-after-undercover-strip-club-sting-20190430-p51ifo.html.

Jeffrey, Yasmin and Staff. 2019. 'Who is new ABC chair Ita Buttrose and how did she get the top job?'. *ABC News*, 28 February. www.abc.net.au/news/2019-02-28/ita-buttrose-abc-chair-announcement-who-is-media-veteran/10855214.

Jones, Alan. 2019. 'Bill's boycott proves fatal, how Alan Jones predicted the election'. *2GB*, 20 May. Sydney: Macquarie Media. www.2gb.com/bills-boycott-proves-fatal-how-alan-jones-predicted-the-election/.

Kelly, Vivienne. 2019. 'Sydney radio ratings: Alan Jones climbs to 17.6% audience share in breakfast'. *Mumbrella*, 4 June. mumbrella.com.au/sydney-radio-ratings-alan-jones-climbs-to-17-6-audience-share-in-breakfast-582606.

Konstantinidis, Ioannis. 2008. 'Who Sets the Agenda? Parties and Media Competing for the Electorate's Main Topic of Political Discussion'. *Journal of Political Marketing* 7(3–4): 323–37. doi.org/10.1080/15377850802008350.

Koslowski, Max. 2019. 'Labor distances itself from the ABC chair process, but has no qualms with the result'. *Sydney Morning Herald*, 25 February. www.smh.com.au/politics/federal/labor-distances-itself-from-the-abc-chair-process-but-has-no-qualms-with-the-result-20190225-p51058.html.

Lallo, Michael. 2019. 'Sky's jump to the right has boosted ratings—but at what cost?'. *Sydney Morning Herald*, 27 May. www.smh.com.au/entertainment/tv-and-radio/sky-s-jump-to-the-right-has-boosted-ratings-but-at-what-cost-20190527-p51rlx.html.

Lau, Richard R. and Ivy Brown Rovner. 2009. 'Negative Campaigning'. *Annual Review of Political Science* 12(1): 285–306. doi.org/10.1146/annurev.polisci.10.071905.101448.

McCutcheon, Peter. 2019. 'Clive Palmer to spend $60 million on election campaign advertising blitz, senator claims'. *ABC News*, 1 May. www.abc.net.au/news/2019-04-29/clive-palmer-sixty-million-dollar-election-advertising-blitz/11053778.

McKenzie-Murray, Martin. 2018. 'The power of Alan Jones'. *The Saturday Paper*, No. 226, 13–19 October. www.thesaturdaypaper.com.au/news/politics/2018/10/13/the-power-alan-jones/15393492006987.

McMahon, Neil. 2019. '"He is wrong": Coalition minister rebukes John Howard in "last-chance" Q&A'. *Sydney Morning Herald*, 14 May. www.smh.com.au/entertainment/tv-and-radio/he-is-wrong-coalition-minister-rebukes-john-howard-in-last-chance-q-and-a-20190514-p51mz2.html.

Meade, Amanda, 2018. 'Chair of Australian public broadcaster quits in meddling row'. *The Guardian*, 27 September. www.theguardian.com/media/2018/sep/27/chair-of-australian-public-broadcaster-abc-resigns-meddling-claims.

Meade, Amanda. 2019. 'Sky News at war as Paul Murray and Kieran Gilbert trade blows: "Let's get into it"'. *The Guardian*, 12 April. www.theguardian.com/media/2019/apr/12/sky-news-at-war-as-paul-murray-and-kieran-gilbert-trade-blows-lets-get-into-it.

Moran, Robert and Nathanael Cooper. 2018. 'The ABC is "in a death spiral": The Chaser launches war on Aunty'. *Sydney Morning Herald*, 20 November. www.smh.com.au/entertainment/tv-and-radio/the-abc-is-in-a-death-spiral-the-chaser-launches-war-on-aunty-20181120-p50h44.html.

Osborne, Paul. 2019. 'Shorten blames loss on "vested interests"'. *The Canberra Times*, 30 May. www.canberratimes.com.au/story/6191965/shorten-blames-loss-on-vested-interests/?cs=14231.

Pash, Chris. 2019. 'Top 10 Australian digital news sites for February'. *Ad News*, 12 March. www.adnews.com.au/news/top-10-australian-digital-news-sites-for-february.

Patterson, Thomas E. 2016. *News Coverage of the 2016 National Conventions: Negative News, Lacking Context*. HKS Working Paper No. 16-051. Cambridge, MA: John F. Kennedy School of Government, Harvard University. doi.org/10.2139/ssrn.2884835.

Remeikis, Amy. 2019. 'Scott Morrison tells Waleed Aly he sought to lower fears on Islam, not exploit them'. *The Guardian*, 21 March. www.theguardian.com/australia-news/2019/mar/21/scott-morrison-tells-waleed-aly.

Rigby, Brittney and Vivienne Kelly. 2019. '600,000 metro viewers watch final leaders' debate on ABC'. *Mumbrella*, 9 May. mumbrella.com.au/600000-metro-viewers-watch-final-leaders-debate-on-abc-578637.

Rolfe, John. 2019. 'The great divider'. *Daily Telegraph*, [Sydney], 15 May: 1.

Salter, David. 2006. 'Who's for Breakfast, Alan Jones?'. *The Monthly*, May. www.themonthly.com.au/monthly-essays-david-salter-whos-breakfast-mr-jones-sydney039s-talkback-titan-and-his-mythical-power.

Sikanku, Etse G. 2011. 'Intermedia Influences among Ghanaian Online and Print News Media: Explicating Salience Transfer of Media Agendas'. *Journal of Black Studies* 42(8): 1320–35. doi.org/10.1177/0021934711417435.

Stapleton, John. 2019. 'Dark side of Sky at night: Analysis of Murdoch TV network reveals extent of anti-Labor comments'. *The New Daily*, 14 May [updated 16 May]. thenewdaily.com.au/news/election-2019/2019/05/14/andrew-bolt-sky-news-labor/.

Watkins, Emily. 2019. 'How The Project started setting the news agenda'. *Crikey*, 28 March. www.crikey.com.au/2019/03/28/how-the-project-started-setting-the-news-agenda/?ins=aGFQd0h3b2hFaU5mU3NqdkZOR295Zz09.

Watkins, Emily and Glenn Dyer. 2019. 'The Project is one of Ten's few winners, but who's watching (and where)?'. *Crikey*, 29 March. www.crikey.com.au/2019/03/29/the-project-is-one-of-tens-few-winners-but-whos-watching-and-where/.

Wlezien, Christopher. 2005. 'On the Salience of Political Issues: The Problem with "Most Important Problem"'. *Electoral Studies* 24(4): 555–79. doi.org/10.1016/j.electstud.2005.01.009.

23

PARTY CAMPAIGN COMMUNICATIONS

Stephen Mills

Election campaign communications—the most visible public manifestation of an electoral contest—paradoxically remain somewhat obscured from academic analysis. This is because the central element of a communications project, its strategic rationale, remains tightly held among the rival elite campaign professionals. We can, however, by working backwards from the observed communications output, infer many of the strategic considerations that went into the design of the campaigns. Applying this method to communications by the two major parties in the 2019 election campaign helps explain the unexpected Coalition victory.[1]

Analysis of Liberal and Labor communications—especially television advertising and direct voter contact—suggests the parties adopted fundamentally different strategic approaches. To draw on international frameworks for the analysis of campaign communications (for example, Trent and Friedenberg 2004), we can say Labor selected a challenger-style, policy-centred communications strategy, incorporating a largely positive and broad-based message of change. The Liberals—content with a narrower electoral victory—opted for a fiercely negative style, contrasting the risk of Labor and the unpopularity of Opposition leader Bill Shorten

---

1   The author expresses his gratitude to representatives of both major party campaigns for their input. All judgements remain the responsibility of the author.

with its own, largely policy-free agenda, emphasising incumbency and leadership. As a result, the campaign was fought over the promises and leadership of the Opposition rather than the record and prospects of the Coalition Government.

It also seems clear that the Liberals executed their strategy with greater consistency and impact than did Labor. Liberal ads carried the message that Prime Minister Scott Morrison had stabilised a divided government and delivered a surplus Budget with imminent tax cuts, while also highlighting the risk posed by Labor to the economy and to families, small businesses and pensioners. Labor's extensive package of spending promises proved unfocused and unwieldy and its key revenue initiatives fatally vulnerable to scaremongering and exaggeration, while its attack on the government misfired.

Strategic approaches

For campaign managers, strategy is defined as the path to electoral success (Mills 2014). Different campaign organisations identify different goals: in the 2019 campaign, the Coalition and the Labor Party adopted office-seeking strategies, contesting every seat in both chambers of parliament and campaigning in every medium to form government; the Greens and Independent candidates pursued seat-winning strategies; activist groups such as GetUp! and the ACTU aimed to defeat certain incumbents; Clive Palmer's big-spending populism aimed to defeat the ALP.

Strategic-level choices are ultimately determined by each party's campaign director, supported by an elite assemblage drawn from the parliamentary wing, federal and State branch head offices and external experts in market research, advertising, digital media and the like. Their choices are driven by collective professional judgement, informed by market research and other data about the relative and changing strengths and weaknesses of the campaign contestants. In 2019, the Liberals' campaign director was the party's federal director, Andrew Hirst; Labor's was its national secretary, Noah Carroll (Williams 2019a; Patrick 2019).

The two teams adopted starkly different strategies. Labor entered the election year with a proven strategy of contrasting the 'cuts and chaos' under a disunited Coalition Government with their own political stability, well-signalled revenue measures and a promised raft of welfare and other initiatives. Labor's expectation—supported by polling and key by-election results—was for potentially substantial electoral gains in Queensland, Victoria and Western Australia. The Liberals were more parsimonious. Never aiming for a big win, they sought to protect all their existing seats and win a targeted handful of Labor and Independent seats. After the tumultuous cycle of leadership change and internal division, this strategy depended on Morrison stabilising the government, silencing internal critics, hiding vulnerable ministers in 'witness protection' (away from media scrutiny) and setting up a favourable 'one on one' leadership contrast of Morrison with Shorten. A pre-election Budget promising a return to surplus and tax cuts would also allow a fierce attack on Labor's supposedly unaffordable policy agenda.

Campaign managers can select from a repertoire of strategic designs, refined in previous electoral contests and adapted to current requirements in ways most likely to persuade target voters (Trent and Friedenberg 2004: 81; Mills 2014: 178–79). Available designs include incumbency or challenger campaigns (Trent and Friedenberg 2004: 80–111), positive or negative campaigns (Nai 2018) and leader-centred or policy-centred campaigns. In their study of campaign communications in the US electoral context, Trent and Friedenberg (2004) provide a checklist of communications typically associated with the challenger and incumbency strategies (Table 23.1). Labor's communications output—its attack on the government, its optimism and moderate tone, its change orientation and Shorten's careful delegation of attack lines to key shadow ministers—represents a good fit with many of the challenger criteria (shown in bold in Table 23.1). The incumbency checklist likewise elucidates several aspects of the Liberals' campaign (also shown in bold).

Table 23.1 Challenger and incumbent communications styles

'Challenger style' (Shorten, ALP)	'Incumbency style' (Morrison, Liberal)
• **Attacking the record of opponents** • **Taking the offensive position on issues** • **Calling for change** • **Emphasising optimism for the future** • **Appearing to represent the philosophical centre of the political party** • **Delegating personal or harsh attacks in an effort to control demagogic rhetoric** • Speaking to traditional values rather than calling for value changes	• **Creating pseudo-events to attract and control media attention** • **Creating special task forces to investigate areas of public concern** • **Appropriating federal funds/grants** • **Emphasising accomplishments** • **Interpreting/intensifying a foreign policy problem** • Making appointments to State and federal jobs/party committees • Consulting or negotiating with world leaders • Manipulating the economy • Endorsements by party and other leaders • Creating and maintaining an 'above the fray' posture

Source: Adapted from Trent and Friedenberg (2004).

Tactical executions: Labor

Within these strategic parameters, party campaign managers need to make tactical decisions about how to execute the strategy and express its narrative. The checklist in Table 23.1 illustrates the linkage between strategic choice and tactical execution: challenger and incumbent strategies find their expression in forms of communication such as attacks, calls for change, interpretations and so on. Likewise, strategic choice gives rise to the campaign's overall message or narrative, which can also be drawn from a repertoire of available options (Bartlett and Rayner 2014; Medvic 2018: 270–72).

Tactical decisions are technical in nature. Specific messages—slogans, TV advertisements, social media posts, news media stories, leader speeches, debate responses and so on—are crafted for execution on digital, electronic, print and interpersonal channels that best link the campaign with its target voters. Thus, tactical executions are visible manifestations of the more covert strategic deliberations. Given the finite financial, human and intellectual resources available to the campaign organisation—based on its size, structure, membership, wealth, political orientation and level of professionalisation—these tactical decisions necessitate trade-offs and strong organisational coordination to deliver with consistency. In fact, both major parties organised themselves in 2019 in broadly similar fashion, with separate teams responsible for news media, electronic advertising and digital media; Labor also had a separate team for direct voter contact (DVC).

The contrasting Labor and Liberal strategic approaches gave rise to strongly contrasting tactical executions. This can be illustrated by considering four 30-second television advertisements, two Labor and two Liberal. Television advertising continues to be the most expensive item in campaign budgets, though its share shrank in 2019 relative to radio and print (Pash 2019). Both parties used it to hammer home their main arguments and to frame themselves and their opponents. Each ad considered here was widely broadcast on TV during the election campaign and also distributed on YouTube.

The first ad, titled 'Scott Morrison—Only for the Top End of Town' (Plate 23.1), served as the vehicle for Labor's negative attack on Morrison's political character and policy record (ALP 2019b). The ad uses black-and-white images of Morrison, Tony Abbott and Peter Dutton to link the Prime Minister with the Liberals' unpopular and divisive right faction. The voiceover opens with ironic praise: correcting an impression that Morrison 'hasn't done very much', it asserts 'he's done plenty'. The audio continues by blaming Morrison for cutting funding for schools and hospitals, supporting cuts to penalty rates and pensions, supporting corporate tax cuts and opposing the banking royal commission. 'When it comes to what matters to working and middle-income Australians', it concludes, 'Morrison is out of touch and only for the top end of town'.

Plate 23.1 ALP 30-second television commercial, 'Scott Morrison—Only for the Top End of Town'

Source: www.youtube.com/watch?v=5baNQ4gSxaU. Reproduced with permission of the ALP.

The second ad, 'Labor: A fair go for Australia' (ALP 2019c), presents Labor's positive policy message built on the central theme of fairness and introduces its senior leadership. Bill Shorten is depicted in a powerful role (office, desk, urban background) opening and closing the ad, and is seen in a 'high-vis' vest in the community. Five senior shadow ministers appear in outdoor settings, summarising policies on health and hospitals, energy prices and climate change, school funding, wages and job creation. Each successive speaker adds to the previous speaker's sentence and the last four repeat the slogan 'for a fair go', demonstrating the unity and rapport of the team and the breadth of the policy package.

Taken together, these ads express the party's strategic intent. What they suggest, however, is that the strategy itself was flawed. As a result, both ads misfired. Considering the negative ad, it seems that Labor, having used the 'top end of town' tag effectively against the previous prime minister, Malcolm Turnbull, who was lampooned as the top-hat-wearing 'Mr Harbourside Mansion', sought to carry forward and apply the same critique to the current Prime Minister. Yet the baseball-cap-wearing dad from 'the Shire' proved to be a different and more elusive target; Labor's strategy had not taken account of the new reality. Likewise, the strategy recycled Labor's previously successful attacks on Liberal cuts to welfare spending, but this also faltered in the wake of the 2019 federal Budget, which had not announced new cuts. Indeed, the 'cuts and chaos' theme Labor had been promoting since before the campaign began[2] was, according to Labor's market research, failing to hurt Morrison (Williams 2019b). On the evidence of this ad, then, Labor's strategy seemed flat-footed—reluctant to shift from attack lines that had damaged Turnbull and unable to identify and target the vulnerabilities of Morrison. Ultimately, with the campaign half-over, Labor did switch its line of attack, pivoting to tarnish Morrison by association with Coalition preference deals with PHON and Clive Palmer. But this proved insufficient in itself and was swamped by Palmer's advertising barrage in the campaign's final weeks.

The positive ad also exposed a deeper communications problem about Labor's impressive range of policy promises. Its strategic intent is clear: roll out the positive benefits of Labor's platform; present a stable and united team, ready to govern; and push back against Shorten's poll-demonstrated

---

2   See, for example, Shorten's video posted on Facebook (Shorten 2019a). Shorten continued the theme in his speech in Burwood, in Sydney, on 14 April: 'After six years of cuts, chaos, of division— friends, it is time for change. It is time, friends, for a stable, united Labor Government' (Shorten 2019c).

unpopularity as leader by emphasising his capable team.[3] But in enumerating the individual policies, it fails to demonstrate (as opposed to assert) how these constitute an overall 'fair go plan' or to prosecute (as opposed to assume) the overall case for expansive policy change. This problem was perceptively foreshadowed by Trent and Friedenberg (2004), who warned that challengers taking the offensive position on issues should probe and question the incumbent but should 'never present concrete solutions for problems'. Yet Labor entered the campaign with a set of detailed policy promises, on both the revenue and the spending sides, and continued to announce new spending commitments during the campaign. Indeed, Labor offered the biggest policy offering of any Opposition party since Liberal Leader John Hewson's *Fightback!* package in 1993. At the end of the 2019 campaign, Labor's website featured no less than 178 separate commitments.

Labor, and Shorten, however, appeared to lack an overarching theme or narrative for these policies. This was not for lack of trying. At a rally at the Revesby Workers Club in Sydney in October 2018, Shorten launched Labor's 'Fair Go Action Plan'. Six months later, delivering his Budget reply speech in the House of Representatives, he declared the election would be a 'referendum on wages' (Shorten 2019b). At a campaign rally in Sydney on 14 April 2019, he declared: 'After six years of cuts, chaos and division, it is time for change.' In his final campaign speech, on 16 May, at a Whitlam-style rally in Blacktown, he declared a Shorten government would take the climate change emergency seriously. But, as with the TV ad, the speeches failed to encapsulate the disparate elements of the platform in a compelling rationale for change. On 28 April, for example, Shorten (2019d) declared it was 'time to draw the threads of the story together, to explain to the Australian people the vision we offer'.[4] But he then listed nine separate 'threads' without providing the story. His Blacktown rally concluded with a stirring peroration that listed

---

3   Likewise, Shorten's travelling party on the campaign bus also saw him surrounded by senior female leaders—Tanya Plibersek, Penny Wong and Kristina Keneally—demonstrating Labor's stronger representation of women and allowing Shorten to delegate attack roles to others. Labor used the same technique in 1980, positioning Opposition leader Bill Hayden in a 'triumvirate' of the more popular NSW Premier Neville Wran and ACTU President Bob Hawke (Weller 1983: 72).
4   The nine threads were jobs, wages, Medicare, education, infrastructure, the NDIS, tax fairness, a better deal for pensioners, help with the cost of living and 'real action on climate change'.

16 separate policies.[5] *Crikey* commentator Guy Rundle was surely right when he observed mid-campaign that Labor's campaign was 'big ticket … not big picture' (Rundle 2019). In the immediate campaign post-mortem, Deputy Labor Leader Tanya Plibersek acknowledged: 'When you've got such a large agenda, it's sometimes hard to explain all of the details to all of the people who benefit' (ABC 2019).

Tactical executions: Liberal

Turning to the Liberal Party's television advertising, we see a simpler, stronger and more impactful form of campaign communication. The first ad, titled 'Labor can't manage money' (Liberal Party of Australia 2019c), uses a violent image—the smashing of a piggy bank and theft of its contents, repeated three times—and colloquial language to frame Labor as the party of financial mismanagement and deficit ('breaking the bank') and of leadership turnover. By contrast, the post-Budget Coalition is the party of surplus ('turning it around'). The ad concludes with a black-and-white image of Shorten and a clever pun that brought together the unpopularity of Shorten with fear of the Opposition's economic policies: 'Labor: The Bill Australia can't afford.'

The second Liberal ad, titled 'Australia can't afford Labor' (Liberal Party of Australia 2019b), features another image of violent destruction: framed family photographs being squeezed and broken in a vice labelled 'Labor' (Plate 23.2). The contrast between the photographs, representing the domestic sphere, and the rusty vice, representing the industrial sphere, has conceptual echoes of Robert Menzies's 'Forgotten People'. The point of the ad is to personalise the hurt of Labor's revenue measures (colloquially, 'put the squeeze on') on Australian families, small businesses and retirees. To substantiate this claim, the ad ruthlessly reduces Labor's complex range of fiscal initiatives to 'taxes': limits on negative gearing concessions become 'housing taxes'; elimination of cash rebates from franking credits becomes a 'retiree tax'; a commitment to carbon emissions targets becomes an 'electricity tax', and so on. While technically flimsy, the argument has

---

5   The text of the Blacktown speech was not posted on Labor's website but was carried in full by *The Guardian* (Remeikis 2019). The 16 reasons were wage rises, Sunday penalty rates, childcare assistance, Closing the Gap, Indigenous constitutional recognition, the NDIS, restoration of school funding, tertiary education access, apprenticeships, dental care, cancer treatment on Medicare, a national integrity commission, having an Australian head of state, infrastructure spending, arts spending and saving the ABC.

rhetorical strength and throws Labor's disparate policies together into a single comprehensible category—something Labor could not do. Invoking the deep-seated popular view about Labor's skills in economic management, the ad closes with the damning conclusion: 'Labor can't manage money. That's why they're coming after yours.' The final few seconds are devoted to the same image of Shorten and the same pun.

Plate 23.2 Liberal Party 30-second television commercial, 'Australia can't afford Labor'

Source: www.youtube.com/watch?v=eWcTKF6G66E. Reproduced with permission of the Liberal Party of Australia.

Characterising Shorten as an unaffordable 'bill' was a masterstroke that became the unifying message for the Liberals' entire campaign. It was widely used on Liberal Party direct mail, along with dark images of Labor's threatened 'taxes', and appeared on the bunting adorning polling stations on election day. In the wake of the election victory, Adelaide ad agency KWP was quick to claim credit for the slogan, as well as 'marketing strategy, strategic messaging, creative execution and production' for the Liberals' federal campaign (Cheik-Hussein 2019).[6]

If simplicity of language, starkness of image and consistency of argument are hallmarks of effective advertising, these ads suggest a Coalition win. But Trent and Friedenberg's analysis also helps to explain their effectiveness. First, they suggest challengers such as Labor face a double hurdle: the need to persuade voters of the need for change, while also

---

6   This treatment is reminiscent of the Coalition's 2004 attack on then Labor Leader Mark Latham as inexperienced; his name was featured with a learner driver's L-plate.

demonstrating that they are capable of bringing it about. Labor may have cleared the first hurdle, but it fell at the second, thanks to Shorten's longstanding unpopularity and the ruthless way this was exploited by the incumbent. At the same time, Trent and Friedenberg (2004: 101) warn challengers that 'the more detailed [they] become in offering solutions, the more material they provide to be attacked themselves'. Labor's policy-rich package indeed offered abundant material for the Coalition's attack. The Coalition's simple, consistent, focused, negative communications proved more effective than the cluttered policy-heavy messages from the Opposition. Morrison, a former Liberal campaign director in New South Wales and tourism advertising executive, proved a capable marketer. By the time of the federal Budget, Labor's spending initiatives had lost much of their original rationale—as a solution to Liberal cuts—and, during the course of the campaign, had been transformed by negative attacks into an extravagant, unaffordable risk.

Liberal attacks were strengthened by the party's active social media campaign (further discussed in Chapters 14 and 22, this volume). The Liberal digital team appears to have been given creative license to post shareable 'boomer memes' on Facebook around *Game of Thrones* episodes (Bourke 2019), and to provide rapid response to campaign events, such as a tweet mocking Bill Shorten's ride on a merry-go-round (Liberal Party of Australia 2019a). The Liberals also produced effective US-style 'snackable' ads (The Halo Group 2019)—for example, a six-second ad that simply used one cycle of the piggy bank being smashed. By contrast, Labor's attack ad could not be similarly cut down; its ironic praise of Morrison might inadvertently impress an inattentive listener who does not wait for the litany of unpopular decisions that follows.

Alessandro Nai defines negative campaigning as 'competing candidates and parties ... attack[ing] their rivals' ideas, policy proposals, past record and character flaws' (Nai 2018: 1). The Coalition's ads certainly fit that definition. Yet in their reductive simplicity, these ads are more than merely negative. They sit firmly in an increasingly acrimonious and tendentious Australian electoral tradition of 'scare campaigns', designed to incite fear through exaggerated claims about opponents' policies. Was labelling the abolition of a cash rebate on franking credits a 'retiree tax' merely robust electoral critique or was it factually inaccurate—a lie? The difficulty of answering that question underlines the challenge facing post-election calls for tighter trade practices–style regulation of misleading and deceptive claims in election campaigns. Yet there is surely a need for a broader critical vocabulary that covers the spectrum of attack, from acceptable negative critique and exaggeration to questionable incivility and misrepresentation and fearmongering and to outright falsehood and lying.

Labor, of course, could have done more to immunise itself against what it must have expected as inevitable attacks on any campaign promise to change revenues or taxes. Yet this seems to have been a strategic blind spot. Its efforts to do this on negative gearing, for example—such as a 15 May Facebook post, 'Attention Property Investors', and a website, www.negativegearing.org.au, to 'explain the facts on negative gearing'— were too little and too late. Some of the attacks, however—notoriously, the shadowy digital scare campaign for a non-existent 'death tax' (Murphy et al. 2019; Koslowski 2019)—were more difficult to deter or refute, as to do so served only to draw attention to the falsehood.

Tactical executions: Direct voter contact (DVC)

While most tactical executions are channelled through some form of mass media, parties and campaign organisations, especially on the progressive side, have over the past decade invested significant effort in a form of unmediated campaigning, DVC. In this form of 'micro-targeting' (Issenberg 2012) or 'personalised political communications' (Nielsen 2012), voters are identified through party databases for individual contact by campaign volunteers, who seek to engage them in persuasive conversations in their homes, either face-to-face or by phone.

The practice was pioneered by the campaigns of Barack Obama in the United States in 2008 and 2012 (McKenna and Han 2014) and has been adopted in Australia by Labor. DVC contributed to Labor wins in Victorian State elections in 2014 and 2018, Queensland State elections in 2015 and 2017, in New South Wales in the 2016 federal election and in the June 2018 'Super Saturday' by-elections—notably, in the seat of Longman. Organisationally, Labor's DVC effort is managed by State branches, with the database, data analysis and organising software principally federal responsibilities.

Table 23.2 Direct voter contact: ALP

	2019	2016
Phone calls	1,100,000	536,497
Doorknocking	1,000,000	1,083,000
Total voter contacts	2,100,000	1,619,497
Numbers of volunteers	25,000+	16,200

Source: Data provided by ALP.

Labor's DVC effort in 2019 was significantly larger than in 2016 (Table 23.2). Labor's federal head office had proclaimed the 2016 campaign would be 'the biggest grassroots effort in Australia's history', with volunteers conducting 'one million conversations' (Erickson 2016). But in 2019, more than 25,000 volunteers organised 10,000 events at which they conducted around 2.1 million voter conversations in more than 15 key seats.

The ACTU, the Greens, online activist group GetUp! and several Independent candidates also invested effort in DVC in previous elections, and all did so again in 2019. The ACTU's experience in fieldwork dates back to its successful 'Your Rights at Work' campaign in 2007. In 2019, the ACTU mounted a substantial fieldwork effort under the banner of its 'Change the Government, Change the Rules' campaign, using predictive modelling based on surveys of 120,000 union members nationwide to identify and target persuadable voters for volunteer conversations (Workplace Express 2019). ACTU volunteers conducted doorknocking and phone banks in 16 target electorates. In a parallel effort, Victorian union organisers targeted seven seats.

Yet, as Table 23.3 shows, these efforts were largely unsuccessful. Of the 10 electorates in which Labor mounted its largest DVC efforts, measured by the raw number of phone calls and doorknocks, only one (Gilmore, ranked 10th) changed hands from Coalition to Labor. Two others (Bass and Braddon) shifted the other way. The ACTU's efforts succeeded in only three electorates, two of which (Dunkley and Corangamite) had already been redistributed to become notionally Labor. The Victorian unionists' effort failed in every seat (Karp 2019a, 2019b).

Table 23.3 Electorates targeted for direct voter contact, 2019

ALP (top 10)	ACTU (by State)	Victorian Trades Hall Council
Pearce (WA) Dickson (Qld) *Bass* (Tas.) Forde (Qld) Bonner (Qld) *Braddon* (Tas.) Reid (NSW) Chisholm (Vic.) Petrie (Qld) Gilmore (NSW)	Qld: Forde, Capricornia, Flynn, Petrie, Leichhardt, *Herbert* NSW: Banks, Gilmore, Reid, Robertson Vic.: Dunkley, Corangamite WA: Swan, Pearce Tas.: *Bass* SA: Boothby	Kooyong, Higgins, Flinders, Menzies, Deakin, La Trobe, Chisholm

Note: Seats underlined won; seats italicised lost.

Source: Column one: Data provided by ALP; Columns two and three: Data provided by Karp (2019b).

GetUp! also substantially lifted its DVC effort compared with 2016 (Vromen 2018) but was successful in only one of its seven targeted seats, Warringah (further discussed in Chapter 21, this volume). The two successful volunteer-based campaigns by Independent candidates—Zali Steggall's in Warringah and Helen Haines's in Indi—are also dealt with elsewhere (see Chapter 18, this volume).

There are several possible explanations for Labor's DVC failures. Organisationally, Labor had lost a key figure with the retirement in February of Victorian Assistant State Secretary Stephen Donnelly. Over seven years, Donnelly had been the driving force in Victoria behind the creation of the 'Community Action Network', which was modelled on his experience as a union organiser and then an Obama volunteer in 2012. Perhaps in part due to his departure, Labor's massive electoral win in the Victorian 2018 State elections did not carry over into the federal results.

A further possible factor may lie in the changing mix of phone calls and doorknocking. US experience suggests a doorknock conversation with a persuadable voter is more effective than a phone call. Yet, as Table 23.2 shows, Labor doorknocking declined relative to phone calls, from two-thirds of the total output in 2016 to less than half in 2019. This may have been driven by the vagaries of the electoral calendars: doorknocking tends to occur on weekends, and the 2016 double-dissolution campaign ran over seven whole weekends, while the 2019 campaign ran over five, one of which was Easter, when most campaigning was suspended. Further, telephones are becoming more congested with political messaging during elections, with marginal-seat voters already anecdotally unhappy with robocalls and robopolls; volunteer-led persuasion calls may be unable to compete for attention.

The most likely explanation, however, is that the electoral effectiveness of DVC is highly dependent on the prevailing political context. When voters are already dissatisfied with a leader or party, DVC conversations will encounter greater barriers. This appears to have been the case with the big but unsuccessful DVC efforts mounted by the British Labour Party's 'Four Million Conversations' campaign on behalf of Ed Miliband in 2015 (LabourList 2015) and by Hillary Clinton's US presidential bid in 2016 (Allen and Parnes 2017). Like Miliband and Clinton, Shorten's campaign struggled to counter negative campaigns and to articulate its agenda persuasively. In these circumstances, the personalised messaging of DVC apparently could not be heard against a louder or more urgent national message.

The Liberals, for whom DVC has never been a major campaign focus, attempted a larger effort in 2019. Labor has its traditions of community and union organising and its energetic volunteer base of Young Labor activists; GetUp! has mobilised its own digitally savvy support base. But with an older membership, the Coalition has typically preferred a more mediated campaign style of advertising, direct mail and social media. Despite possessing a formidable database, Liberal DVC efforts have also been fragmented among State divisions, some of which remain unready to devote resources to the effort. Yet Labor's effective management of its data and volunteers has been noted by conservative campaigners with some envy (Murphy 2016), and Liberals acknowledge the need to compete in some way in every form of campaigning. Previous DVC efforts have seen organised phone banking and flying squads of volunteers arriving in target seats. Among Liberal DVC efforts in 2019, a volunteer phone bank was set up in the Liberal Party's Canberra headquarters, R.G. Menzies House.

In summary, Labor entered the 2019 election campaign with a stable and united leadership, a credible and extensive policy platform, solid polls and great expectations. Its unexpected defeat can be attributed in part to a failure to recalibrate its campaign strategy after the advent of Morrison and the delivery of the pre-campaign federal Budget. Shorten struggled to articulate a vision behind the policy platform and a rationale for change and to prosecute Labor's claim to govern; he never overcame his deep-seated unpopularity. Labor could not overcome the determined negativity of a more strongly motivated incumbent.

These particular shortcomings—serious enough in themselves—point to a more generalised failure of strategy. In previous elections, campaign directors of both major parties have made it their personal and distinctive responsibility to formulate and execute a campaign strategy, defining the path towards electoral success and centrally focusing all the party's resources on achieving that goal. Strong and successful campaign directors have made it their business to harness the party leadership in a joint effort of disciplined coordination (Mills 2014: 179, 258). In 2019, Labor's campaign strategy appears not to have followed that proven path. As noted at the outset of this chapter, strategic failures can only be inferred from tactical communications executions, but in the case of Labor's 2019 campaign, they seem abundantly clear. Indeed, they have been subsequently confirmed by its election campaign post-mortem, which found there was no documented strategy, no body responsible for strategic deliberation and decision, no unifying campaign narrative and no identified pathway to victory (ALP 2019a). While the Liberals have not seen it necessary to publish a similar review of their campaign, one would likely have applauded its documented campaign strategy, its narrow but identified path to victory, its unifying narrative and its leader working in disciplined harness with the party's campaign team.

References

Allen, Jonathan and Amie Parnes. 2017. *Shattered: Inside Hillary Clinton's Doomed Campaign*. New York: Crown. doi.org/10.15446/cp.v13n26.73730.

Australian Broadcasting Corporation (ABC). 2019. 'The deputy party leaders join Insiders'. [Transcript]. *Insiders*, [ABC TV], 19 May. www.abc.net.au/insiders/both-deputy-party-leaders-join-insiders/11128272.

Australian Labor Party (ALP). 2019a. *Review of Labor's 2019 Federal Election Campaign*. Canberra: ALP. alp.org.au/media/2043/alp-campaign-review-2019.pdf.

Australian Labor Party (ALP). 2019b. 'Scott Morrison—Only for the Top End of Town'. *YouTube*, 16 April. Canberra: ALP. www.youtube.com/watch?v=5baNQ4gSxaU.

Australian Labor Party (ALP). 2019c. 'Labor: A Fair Go for Australia'. *You Tube*, 17 May. Canberra: ALP. www.youtube.com/watch?v=1J9j21jnX8w.

Bartlett, David and Jennifer Rayner. 2014. '"This campaign is all about …": Dissecting Australian Campaign Narratives'. *Communication, Politics and Culture* 47(1): 51–78.

Bourke, Latika. 2019. 'How the Liberals beat Labor at its own game'. *Sydney Morning Herald*, 26 May: 51. www.smh.com.au/federal-election-2019/how-the-liberals-beat-labor-at-its-own-game-20190523-p51qki.html.

Cheik-Hussein, Mariam. 2019. 'Adelaide indie KWP claims authorship of "The Bill Australia Can't Afford"'. *Ad News*, 21 May. www.adnews.com.au/news/adelaide-indie-kwp-claims-authorship-of-the-bill-australia-can-t-afford.

Erickson, Paul. 2016. 'A million'. Email to ALP supporters, 21 May.

Issenberg, Sasha. 2012. *The Victory Lab: The Secret Science of Winning Campaigns.* New York: Broadway Books.

Karp, Paul. 2019a. '"Breaking down the myths": Blue-ribbon Liberal seats on unions' long target list'. *The Guardian*, 20 April. www.theguardian.com/australia-news/2019/apr/20/breaking-down-the-myths-blue-ribbon-liberal-seats-on-unions-long-target-list.

Karp, Paul. 2019b. '"Vanity project": Critics round on ACTU's $25m campaign after Labor's election loss'. *The Guardian*, 23 May. www.theguardian.com/australia-news/2019/may/23/vanity-project-critics-round-on-actus-25m-campaign-after-labors-election-loss.

Koslowski, Max. 2019. 'With one click, the Liberals inadvertently unleashed the ultimate scare campaign'. *The Age*, [Melbourne], 1 June. www.theage.com.au/federal-election-2019/with-one-click-the-liberals-inadvertently-unleashed-the-ultimate-election-scare-campaign-20190601-p51tgy.html.

LabourList. 2015. 'Four million conversations in four months: Miliband says Labour will speak to millions before election day'. *LabourList*, 4 January. labourlist.org/2015/01/four-million-conversations-in-four-months-miliband-says-labour-will-speak-to-millions-before-election-day/.

Liberal Party of Australia. 2019a. 'Every time Bill comes around, he's got a new tax'. Twitter, 20 April. Canberra: Liberal Party of Australia. twitter.com/liberalaus/status/1119511272402214915?lang=en.

Liberal Party of Australia. 2019b. 'Australia Can't Afford Labor'. *YouTube*, 4 May. Canberra: Liberal Party of Australia. www.youtube.com/watch?v=eWcTKF6G66E.

Liberal Party of Australia. 2019c. 'Labor Can't Manage Money'. *YouTube*, 4 May. Canberra: Liberal Party of Australia. www.youtube.com/watch?v=SVc2G4A_Gd4.

McKenna, Elizabeth and Hahrie Han. 2014. *Groundbreakers: How Obama's 2.2 Million Volunteers Transformed Campaigning in America*. New York: Oxford University Press. doi.org/10.1093/acprof:oso/9780199394593.003.0001.

Medvic, Stephen K. 2018. *Campaigns and Elections: Players and Processes*. 3rd edn. New York: Routledge. doi.org/10.4324/9781315164274.

Mills, Stephen. 2014. *The Professionals: Strategy, Money and the Rise of the Political Campaigner in Australia*. Melbourne: Black Inc.

Murphy, Katharine. 2016. 'Cory Bernardi and the Liberals are right to be scared of Labor's volunteer army'. *The Guardian*, 6 July. www.theguardian.com/australia-news/2016/jul/06/election-2016-cory-bernardi-liberals-labor-volunteer-army?CMP=share_btn_link.

Murphy, Katharine, Christopher Knaus and Nick Evershed. 2019. '"It felt like a big tide": How the death tax lie infected Australia's election campaign'. *The Guardian*, 8 June. www.theguardian.com/australia-news/2019/jun/08/it-felt-like-a-big-tide-how-the-death-tax-lie-infected-australias-election-campaign.

Nai, Alessandro. 2018. 'Going Negative, Worldwide: Towards a General Understanding of Determinants and Targets of Negative Campaigning'. *Government and Opposition* (26 October): 1–26. doi.org/10.1017/gov.2018.32.

Nielsen, Rasmus Klein. 2012. *Ground Wars: Personalized Communication in American Campaigns*. Princeton, NJ: Princeton University Press. doi.org/10.1080/10584609.2013.749620.

Pash, Chris. 2019. 'The winners from Australia's changing election advertising spend mix'. *Ad News*, 3 June. www.adnews.com.au/news/the-winners-from-australia-s-changing-election-advertising-spend-mix.

Patrick, Aaron. 2019. 'Scott Morrison's fate rests on a new generation of Liberal operators'. *Australian Financial Review*, 28 January. www.afr.com/news/politics/election/scott-morrisons-fate-rests-on-a-new-generation-of-liberal-operators-20190125-h1agum.

Remeikis, Amy. 2019. 'Shorten says Labor will take climate "emergency" seriously—as it happened'. *The Guardian*, 16 May. www.theguardian.com/australia-news/live/2019/may/16/federal-election-2019-shorten-and-morrison-set-to-deliver-final-pitches-to-voters-politics-live?page=with:block-5cdce81f8f088c3e913d727d.

Rundle, Guy. 2019. 'Labor's focus on "big ticket" rather than "big picture" is a problem'. *Crikey*, 1 May. www.crikey.com.au/2019/05/01/big-picture-not-big-ticket-labor/.

Shorten, Bill. 2019a. 'After 5 years of Liberal cuts, chaos and division, it's time we put the fair go back at the heart of our nation'. Facebook, 4 March. www.facebook.com/BillShorten/posts/2187840947919121?comment_id= 2187843821252167&reply_comment_id=2187928787910337&comment_ tracking=%7B%22tn%22%3A%22R%22%7D.

Shorten, Bill. 2019b. '2019 Budget-In-Reply Address, Canberra. 4 April'. www. billshorten.com.au/2019_budget_in_reply_address_canberra_thursday_4_ april_2019.

Shorten, Bill. 2019c. 'Address to 2019 federal election volunteer rally, Sydney, 14 April'. www.billshorten.com.au/address_to_2019_federal_election _volunteer_rally_sydney_sunday_14_april_2019.

Shorten, Bill. 2019d. 'Address to the Victorian Labor federal election volunteer rally, Melbourne, 28 April'. www.billshorten.com.au/address_to_the_victorian_ labor_federal_election_volunteer_rally_melbourne_sunday_28_april_2019.

The Halo Group. 2019. *Snackable Content: Short, Sweet and Extremely Filling*. New York: The Halo Group. www.thehalogroup.com/snackable-content-short-sweet-extremely-filling/.

Trent, Judith S. and Robert V. Friedenberg. 2004. *Political Campaign Communication: Principles and Practices*. Edited by Robert E. Denton Jr and Virginia Tech. 5th edn. Lanham, MD: Rowman & Littlefield.

Vromen, Ariadne. 2018. 'GetUp! in election 2016'. In *Double Disillusion: The 2016 Australian Federal Election*, edited by Anika Gauja, Peter Chen, Jennifer Curtin and Juliet Pietsch, 397–420. Canberra: ANU Press. doi.org/ 10.22459/DD.04.2018.18.

Weller, Patrick. 1983. 'Labor in 1980'. In *Australia at the Polls: The National Elections of 1980 and 1983*, edited by Howard R. Penniman, 55–78. Sydney: George Allen & Unwin.

Williams, Pamela. 2019a. 'Inside the team that lost it for Labor'. *Australian Financial Review*, 21 May. www.afr.com/news/politics/national/inside-the-team-that-lost-it-for-labor-20190520-p51p8x.

Williams, Pamela. 2019b. 'Who's to blame? Knives out for wounded Labor'. *Australian Financial Review*, 23 May. www.afr.com/news/politics/national/ who-s-to-blame-knives-out-for-wounded-labor-20190522-p51py9.

Workplace Express. 2019. 'Conversations with members crucial in Change the Rules election campaign'. *Workplace Express*, 11 April.

24

CARTOONS, MEMES AND VIDEOS

Lucien Leon

Prior to the 2007 federal election, which saw the emergence of web 2.0 technologies in political campaign communication and democratic discourse, political satire was mediated almost exclusively by the media troika of television, newspapers and radio. The increasing hybridisation of media platforms popularised a new form of political satire: the video mash-up. A defining moment of the pre-campaign period in 2007 was when then Prime Minister John Howard launched a new climate policy in an ill-judged and awkward first foray on to YouTube, giving tech-savvy citizen comics an opportunity to lampoon the release with their own satirical videos. This episode amplified a narrative that the incumbent government was out of touch, adding to a palpable mood for change in the electorate (Flew 2008; Williams 2008).

More recently, a newer brand of online visual satire has arrived in the form of image macros. These are culturally familiar images with brief, witty captions superimposed on them and popularly known in their replicated form as 'memes'. It has been widely remarked that memes are the new political cartoons. However, memes are produced by anonymous amateurs and gain legitimacy from repeated online transmission rather than location in legacy media. Their capacity to influence political discourse was first observed in the 2012 US presidential campaign, when 'Big Bird' and 'binders of women' memes proved so damaging to Republican candidate Mitt Romney (Tay 2014; Graeff 2015; Rentschler and Thrift 2015).

In Australia in 2015, 'Choppergate' memes were credited with helping bring down then Speaker of the House of Representatives Bronwyn Bishop (Turton 2015; Purcell 2015). Memes have become part of the fabric of everyday political engagement (Dean 2018) but they also have the potential to be weaponised by political parties and to polarise and misinform the electorate (Renner 2017).

In this chapter, I examine how the satirical mosaic of cartoons, memes and videos circulating throughout the 2019 federal election responded to and illuminated the key themes and events, and to what extent the imagery was a reliable gauge of the public mood heading into the polls. In determining what images among the extensive volume of material should be included in the sample, I have given preference to content with broad public reach. Current newspaper readership and viewing figures validate the inclusion here of cartoons published in the editorial pages of the nation's metropolitan daily newspapers and video content broadcast or streamed on network media platforms. Also included are selected videos from the satirical 'Honest Government Ad' internet video series. Created by film and media company The Juice Media, these videos—which mimic the imagery and prosody of government advertising—have attracted millions of views across Facebook, Twitter, Instagram and YouTube and a dedicated audience of more than 300,000 subscribers.

The memes that featured in the mainstream news media were sourced almost exclusively from a pool of 618 memes mediated by six Facebook groups: ALP Spicy Meme Stash, The Simpsons Against the Liberals, Innovative and Agile Memes, Clive Palmer's Put Australia First, Australian Green Memes for Actually Progressive Teens and Australian Young Greens. These groups have an aggregated subscriber base of over 500,000 people, each of whom is a potential link to additional social networks. The sharing and reposting of these memes, as well as their intermediation with legacy news media, extend the reach of these images from beyond their partisan base to a wider mainstream audience. I have observed that the memes mediated by these groups provide a comprehensive cross-section of the more popular memes proliferating online in discussion forums and feeds on Twitter, Instagram and Snapchat, and on this basis present a viable sample for this analysis. In aligning the satirical responses with the election outcome, the images collectively frame a narrative of voters who were unimpressed with the incumbent government's infighting and lack of a coherent climate policy but not so much as to seriously consider an alternative they did not trust or did not understand.

Heading into the campaign

In addition to offering a choice between two unpalatable options, the campaign straddled the public holiday periods of Easter and Anzac Day and was punctuated by significant newsworthy events. The retirement of a champion racehorse, the first image of a black hole, the Notre-Dame Cathedral fire, terrorist attacks in Sri Lanka, the birth of a royal baby, the Eurovision song contest, the final episodes of *Game of Thrones* and the death of beloved former prime minister Bob Hawke presented satirists with a rich vein of metaphors, but distracted fatigued voters from assessing platform and policy differences between the parties.

The first event to capture the public's imagination was a meme-rich exchange that occurred in the lead-up to the campaign. Tony Abbott's Twitter video documenting his delight at discovering a street library while doorknocking in his Warringah electorate presented a gift to citizen satirists (Plate 24.1). The 20 March video attracted more than 1,000 replies in the first 24 hours, almost all of them mocking Abbott's ignorance of a well-established community initiative (Plate 24.2). The meme responses became the story, reinforcing a perception that Abbott was an out-of-touch conservative standing in an electorate increasingly concerned about the progressive issues of climate change and refugees. It was a free hit for his opponent, Independent Zali Steggall, before the campaign had even begun.

Tony Abbott
@HonTonyAbbott

Follow

It's amazing the things you see and learn when you're door knocking. The Tango Avenue street library is a testament to the strong community we have throughout Warringah.

I've never seen anything like this before

Tango Avenue Street Library

5:12 PM - 20 Mar 2019

Plate 24.1 Tony Abbott, Tango Avenue Street Library
Source: Tony Abbott, Twitter account, 20 March 2019.

Plate 24.2 Various responses to Tango Avenue Street Library, Tony Abbott, Twitter account, 20–21 March 2019

Sources: @MattBasely; @Mason Hell-Cat; @LezBeFranc; @EllieCarless.

A dirty campaign

Two early satirical interventions by activist groups foreshadowed the ugly campaigning that was to be endemic throughout the campaign as a whole. Advance Australia's video featured their mascot suggestively rubbing up against a photoshopped billboard image of Steggall and Bill Shorten (Plate 24.3). Ten days later, activist group GetUp! misfired with its video portraying Tony Abbott as a surf lifesaver refusing to save a drowning swimmer (Plate 24.4). Both videos were retracted after public outcry. Cartoonist Jon Kudelka sums up the efforts of the respective groups with his own satirical intervention (Plate 24.5).

Plate 24.3 Still showing an image sequence from Captain GetUp video, 13 April 2019

Source: www.news.com.au/video/id-5348771529001-6026202939001/captain-getup-accused-of-sexism-with-billboard [video removed].

Plate 24.4 Still showing an image sequence from GetUp! Australia video, 23 April 2019

Source: www.youtube.com/watch?v=3-MKqCGY5bs [video removed].

Plate 24.5 Jon Kudelka, 'Modern campaigning'
Source: *The Australian*, 25 April 2019.

Voter uninterest and pre-polling

When Bill Shorten bit into his democracy sausage on 18 May, he declared that it tasted like 'a mood for change' (Coughlan 2019). Every major opinion poll seemed to confirm this judgement and the bookies were not even at the institutional sizzle; they had paid out punters betting on a Labor victory three days earlier. And yet the supposed mood for change was not borne out by the major parties' seat-by-seat polling, the reporting of journalists 'on the road' or citizen chatter on social media (Koslowski 2019)—all of which indicated that the prevailing flavour was one not of change but of uninterest. Two cartoons, by David Pope and Michael Leunig, bookend the campaign period and sum up the apathy that undermined Shorten's case to voters (Plates 24.6 and 24.7).

Plate 24.6 David Pope, 'Economic inputs of Australia!'
Source: *The Canberra Times*, 12 April 2019.

Plate 24.7 Michael Leunig, 'Short story'
Source: *The Age*, [Melbourne], 15 May 2019.

Plate 24.8 Cartoon by Andrew Dyson

Source: *The Age*, [Melbourne], 27 April 2019.

Plate 24.9 Cartoon by Mark Knight

Source: *Herald Sun*, [Melbourne], 5 May 2019.

Voter uninterest was signalled early and throughout the campaign by an unprecedented number of people casting pre-poll votes. Nearly 5 million people cast an early ballot, with the Coalition doing significantly better than Labor among early voters (see Chapter 9, this volume). Pre-polling attracted attention from cartoonists but was not addressed at all in memes. Andrew Dyson (Plate 24.8) anticipated this dynamic with his portrayal of the lone polling-day voter as a progressive with a vegetarian dog, while Mark Knight (Plate 24.9) commented on the potential ramifications of pre-poll voting on candidate choice by touching on another one of this election's features: the disendorsement of candidates by their party due to compromising social media histories.

The leaders

Bill Shorten and Scott Morrison entered the campaign with substantial baggage. Despite an ambitious and expansive suite of policies, Shorten's wooden public persona compounded residual trust issues over his role in the downfall of two Labor prime ministers. A disastrous intervention by Sydney's *Daily Telegraph* about Shorten's mother afforded him the opportunity for a heartfelt rebuttal that connected with many voters, but its humanising potential was neutralised by the sympathy directed at Morrison after an attempted egging at a Country Women's Association event the same day. David Rowe, in inimitable style, articulates both Shorten's inability to cut through to an uninterested electorate and the fickle nature of public opinion (Plates 24.10 and 24.11). On the incumbent's side, Morrison was an accidental prime minister bereft of a reform agenda and commanding an unpopular and chaotic ministry. The cartoons by Pat Campbell (Plate 24.12) and Cathy Wilcox (Plate 24.13) neatly capture the bunker vibe underscoring Morrison's presidential-style campaign. A high proportion of memes appearing on the main party-affiliated Facebook sites personalised the campaign by focusing on these same perceived weaknesses of the party leaders (Plate 24.14 and 24.15).

Plate 24.10 David Rowe, 'Packing room …'
Source: *Australian Financial Review*, 3 May 2019.

Plate 24.11 David Rowe, 'Hold the front page!'
Source: *Australian Financial Review*, 9 May 2019.

Plate 24.12 Pat Campbell, 'Army of the un-policies'
Source: *The Canberra Times*, 15 April 2019.

Plate 24.13 Cathy Wilcox, 'Team ScoMo'
Source: *Sydney Morning Herald*, 1 May 2019.

literally no one:

Bill:

Plate 24.14 Meme by Innovative and Agile Memes

Source: Facebook, 23 April 2019.

Plate 24.15 Meme by ALP Spicy Meme Stash

Source: Facebook, 5 May 2019.

Two companion videos produced by the ABC's satirical news program *The Weekly with Charlie Pickering* highlighted the challenges each of the leaders faced in elevating their public image. The first video, 'Australian Labor Party Robotics', presents Shorten as 'The Billbot', an automaton whose failed programming initiates maladroit behaviour that fails to convince voters that it is human (Plate 24.16). Many of the awkward actions and utterances satirised in this clip as examples of a malfunctioning robot were also featured in an unembellished montage released by the Liberal Party on the same day as *The Weekly*'s clip. 'Ladies and Gentlemen, Mr Bill Shorten' became the most-watched video produced by a political party, garnering more than 1.1 million views. The reductive characterisation of Shorten's public persona in the two videos leverages the popular perception that he is not authentic, not 'one of us'. In reference to the consistently poor personal approval ratings that plagued Shorten throughout his tenure as Opposition leader, *Sunrise* program host David Koch observed in an interview with Shorten that 'the more people see you, the more they don't like you' (Seven Network 2019).

The second ABC video, 'Rebranding Scott Morrison', presented a fictitious public relations (PR) company's response to the brief of 'turning a terminally unpopular politician into a vote winner' (Plate 24.17). The clip lists all the electoral challenges facing Morrison, from his refusal to support a banking royal commission to the perception that 'the party's got a problem with women'—and frames a PR strategy to mollify them in the minds of voters. Says one half of the PR duo:

The hardest part of this brief was that if ScoMo talks about the past it reminds voters about the spills, but if he talks about the future it could trigger another one. He needs to keep voters hypnotised in the present.

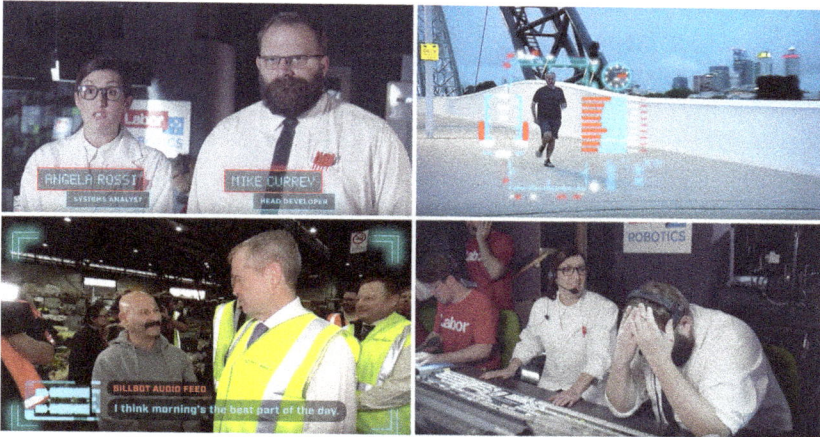

Plate 24.16 Still showing an image sequence from *The Weekly with Charlie Pickering*'s mash-up video 'Australian Labor Party Robotics', 10 May 2019

Source: www.youtube.com/watch?v=ecbDqnsdfVM.

Plate 24.17 Still showing an image sequence from *The Weekly with Charlie Pickering*'s mash-up video 'Rebranding Scott Morrison', 15 May 2019

Source: www.youtube.com/watch?v=5c_UO5PCklY&t=6s.

The premise of the clip, which was viewed nearly 800,000 times on Facebook, cleverly alludes to Morrison's former role in successful marketing campaigns for New Zealand and Australian tourism. Fashioning himself as a folksy, daggy dad and reducing his platform to a lexicon of catchy phrases were deft smoke-and-mirrors manoeuvres that camouflaged ministerial liabilities and paucity of vision.

The climate election

Alongside the respective personal characteristics of the leaders, the climate issue dominated progressive social media (Plates 24.18 and 24.19), but it did not take long for Labor's climate platform—a putative party strength—to be derailed. When the ALP led into the campaign with a proposed target on electric car sales, small business minister Michaelia Cash immediately reframed the initiative as a threat to tradesmen, announcing that the Liberal Party would 'stand by our tradies' and 'save their utes' (ABC 2019a). Kudelka illustrates the implied messaging: that snide, sanctimonious, inner-city progressive types want to run over the livelihoods of honest, hardworking Aussies (Plate 24.20).

Nurse: Sir you've been in a coma since 2013

Me: oh boy I can't wait to see the action the government has taken on climate change

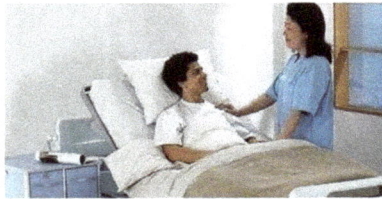

Plate 24.18 Meme by ALP Spicy Meme Stash
Source: Facebook, 19 April 2019.

when the Liberals know that climate change exists but say it's too expensive to do anything about it

Plate 24.19 Meme by Australian Young Greens
Source: Facebook, 2 May 2019.

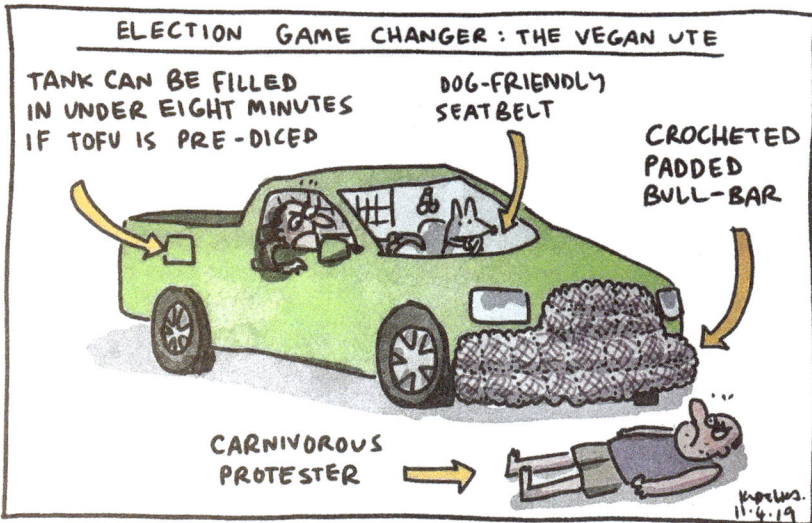

Plate 24.20 Jon Kudelka, 'Election game changer: The vegan ute'
Source: *The Australian*, 11 April 2019.

Variations of this narrative were effectively transferred to every plank of Labor's climate platform—most notably, with respect to the proposed Adani Carmichael coalmine. Labor's ambivalent support of the project offered little reassurance to voters concerned about climate change, on the one hand, or those prioritising jobs in the mining sector on the other.

The 'Adani convoy' galvanised the positions of both sides and left Labor with no clear strategy for securing the Queensland seats needed to win government (see Chapter 11, this volume). At the same time, Labor's decision to support fracking in the Northern Territory's Beetaloo Basin and promise of $1.5 billion towards a gas pipeline development in northern Australia left it open to accusations of inconsistency on greenhouse emissions (ABC 2019c). In his cartoon, Dyson (Plate 24.21) reminds us that Morrison was managing his own balancing act, toning down his support for the Adani mine so as not to alienate climate-conscious Victorian voters. With both leaders having little to say about an issue that was expected to dominate the campaign, David Pope draws on Anzac imagery to depict this curious truce (Plate 24.22).

Plate 24.21 Andrew Dyson, 'Balanced diet'

Source: *The Age*, [Melbourne], 11 April 2019.

Plate 24.22 David Pope, 'The great "climate election" Anzac Day truce …'

Source: *The Canberra Times*, 25 April 2019.

Shorten's inability to provide clear costings on Labor's climate change commitments in a tetchy exchange with journalists on day five of the campaign gifted Morrison the opportunity to paint Labor as economically irresponsible. Coupled with Shorten's gaffe the following day over taxes on superannuation and another gaffe in the second week over tax cuts for people earning more than $250,000 a year, Morrison was able to conflate broad public distrust of Labor's economic management with broad public distrust of Shorten. Mark Knight's cartoon at the start of the Easter weekend summarises Shorten's predicament (Plate 24.23), while meme creators seized on Shorten's interview presentation as being indicative of his policies as a whole (Plate 24.24).

Plate 24.23 Mark Knight, 'Scrutiny'
Source: *Herald Sun*, [Melbourne], 19 April 2019.

Who's the bigger flake?

an actual flake   Bill after 15 seconds in front of cameras

Plate 24.24 Innovative and Agile Memes, 'Who's the bigger flake?'
Source: Facebook, 28 April 2019.

Baby boomers

Morrison presented himself as not just the leader who could deliver job security to 'hardworking Australians'; he was also the leader who could deliver incentives and rewards to workers and protect the entitlements of self-funded retirees and pensioners. In a move telegraphed a year earlier when he was still treasurer, Morrison gathered up Labor's tax policies—including the aforementioned curtailing of superannuation tax concessions, withdrawal of dividend imputation (or 'franking') credits, cessation of negative gearing and winding back of the capital gains tax concession—and neatly repackaged them as a 'retiree tax'. *The Australian*'s Johannes Leak—in characteristically partisan style—shows Shorten winning a debate few people seemed to care about but losing an argument a great many people cared very much about (Plate 24.25). The idea that Shorten was robbing pensioners gained traction (Plate 24.26). By the time someone finally managed to explain in simple terms what franking credits were, voters had stopped listening (Plate 24.27).

Plate 24.25 Cartoon by Johannes Leak
Source: *The Australian*, 6 May 2019.

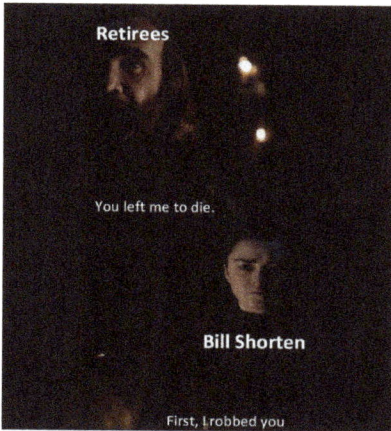

Plate 24.26 Meme by Innovative and Agile Memes
Source: Facebook, 18 May 2019.

Plate 24.27 888 Memes for Oldest Continuously Functioning Trades Hall Teens, 'Franking credits'
Source: Facebook, 9 May 2019.

Preferences

While the question of preferences was of no discernible interest to internet satirists, a suite of 25 cartoons interrogated the spectacle of Clive Palmer's $60 million intervention in the campaign. Brisbane's *The Courier-Mail* unsurprisingly focused on Palmer's failure to pay entitlements to Queensland Nickel workers, while other newspapers looked at how the flow of UAP preferences to Morrison might impact the election result and what concessions might be demanded in return. The Hobart *Mercury*'s Christopher Downes channels Norman Rockwell in a beautifully rendered image showing a nervous Morrison observing Palmer's political track record (Plate 24.28), while Rowe pairs Palmer with the embattled Pauline Hanson in illustrating Morrison's poll-driven compromise (Plate 24.29).

Ultimately, UAP and PHON preferences in Queensland contributed to a 9 per cent swing to the Coalition in the five 'Adani seats' (see Chapter 11, this volume). In the lead-up to polling day, a prescient Mark Knight cartoon employs the metaphor of a topical Australian Football League controversy in describing the impact of Palmer's campaign on Shorten's prime ministerial ambitions (Plate 24.30); while in the aftermath of the election, Pope summarises the irony of a political party leader achieving his policy ambitions despite not having secured a single seat (Plate 24.31).

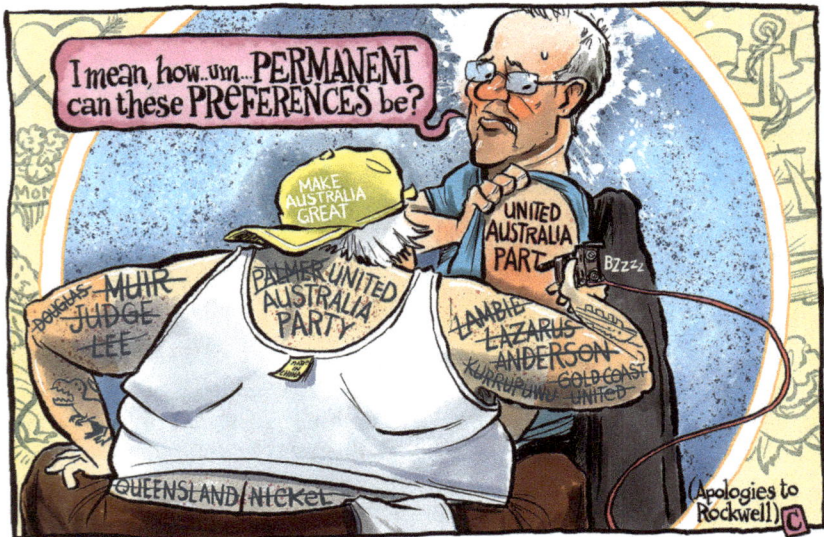

Plate 24.28 Cartoon by Christopher Downes
Source: *Mercury*, [Hobart], 30 April 2019.

Plate 24.29 David Rowe, 'Live poll dancers'

Source: *Australian Financial Review*, 1 May 2019.

Plate 24.30 Cartoon by Mark Knight

Source: *Herald Sun*, [Melbourne], 14 May 2019.

Plate 24.31 Cartoon by David Pope
Source: *The Canberra Times*, 23 May 2019.

The outcome

As seen in preceding chapters, Labor failed to make a compelling case for change. Despite a host of Coalition failures and missteps in government—articulated in excoriating detail in The Juice Media's 'Honest Government Ad: 2019 Election' viral video (Plate 24.32)—Labor was unable to match Morrison's strong messaging (see Chapter 23, this volume). ABC TV video editor Huw Parkinson's take on the election, published on polling day, was conceived at least one week before the result was known—and yet the metaphor he chose to frame the election was, very aptly, the *Back to the Future* movie trilogy (Plate 24.33). While Parkinson had his tongue firmly in his cheek, Scott Morrison was deadly serious when he announced in a debate few cared about that he had 'brought the Budget back to surplus next year' (ABC 2019b).

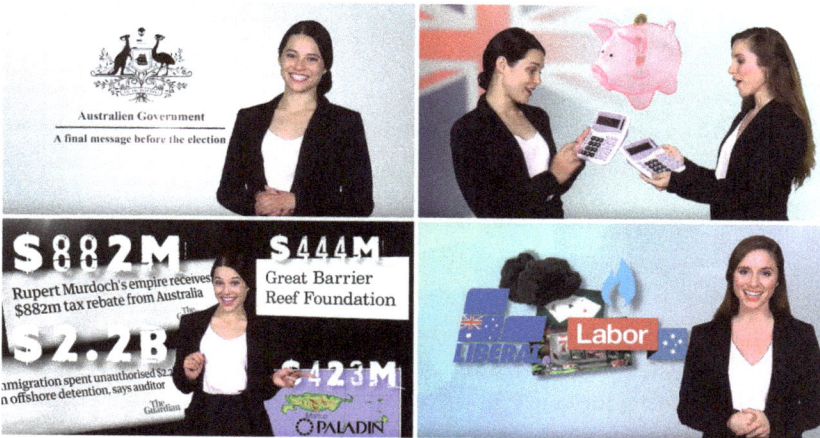

Plate 24.32 Still showing an image sequence from The Juice Media's mash-up video, 'Honest Government Ad: 2019 Election', 6 May 2019

Source: www.youtube.com/watch?v=OJrXl3rBbSA&t=3s.

Plate 24.33 Still showing an image sequence from Huw Parkinson's mash-up video, 'Back to the Polls', 18 May 2019

Source: www.youtube.com/watch?v=cp_Ad0G-X_k.

Conclusion

The above examples demonstrate the various ways in which cartoons, memes and videos responded to the key themes and developments of the federal election. The cartoons—authored by professional satirists and located in immediate textual proximity to the reported news of the moment—covered a broad range of campaign topics and were acutely responsive to events playing out within the 24-hour news cycle. A cross-platform newspaper readership of around 16 million suggests that reports of their demise are an exaggeration—but perhaps only slightly. For example, the audience trend is away from print media and towards online editions where the cartoon does not enjoy the same prominence on the op-ed page. Inevitably, if not already, they will give way to memes and videos as the default satirical images. The memes circulating throughout the campaign were narrower in topical scope than the cartoons and distilled the concerns of the electorate into the issues of taxation, the economy, climate change, Liberal leadership and voter distrust of Bill Shorten. Interestingly, Andrea Carson and Lawrie Zion write in Chapter 22 (this volume) that the front-page stories appearing in Australia's major daily newspapers were—with the notable exception of Liberal leadership—dominated by much the same topics. At their best, memes can be an effective satirical and democratic tool through their participatory modes of production and dissemination. They can promote broad public discourse and scrutiny of political players by mirroring some voter sentiments and highlighting policy positions. The temporal nature of videos makes them more labour-intensive to produce than cartoons and memes, but also affords a more expansive canvas on which to lampoon their targets. The adverse public response to the video satire produced by political lobby groups presents a cautionary note for would-be satirists promoting a partisan agenda.

The increasing prominence of memes in democratic discourse raises some interesting points for discussion that are beyond the scope of this chapter. For example, political players and citizen comics alike now share a common publication and communication platform. The proliferation and weaponisation of memes produced and disseminated by partisan groups, rather than engaged citizens, are blurring the lines between propaganda, advertising and journalism—and may have significant implications for satire specifically and democratic discourse more broadly. In addition, the capacity for memes to reinforce insular online communities (or 'echo chambers') and promulgate misinformation is an emerging field of research that, in light of the 'death tax', has particular relevance to this campaign. Notwithstanding these concerns, when viewed collectively, the visual satire produced and disseminated throughout the campaign not only presented a clear and critical engagement with the events as they transpired, but also provided a reliable gauge of the electoral mood. Consequently, the body of satirical work can reasonably be seen as having succeeded as one of the more dependable predictors of the final result when many of the traditional indicators got it so famously wrong. After a campaign in which the two major parties presented the clearest policy differences in decades, voters decided they were not that interested in either of them. The result seemed to surprise a great many people. Looking over their aggregated contributions to the election campaign, it's difficult to imagine that the satirists were among them.

References

Australian Broadcasting Corporation (ABC). 2019a. *ABC News*, [ABC TV], 8 April.

Australian Broadcasting Corporation (ABC). 2019b. *Australia Debates: Leaders' Debate*, [ABC TV], 24 April.

Australian Broadcasting Corporation (ABC). 2019c. 'Beetaloo Basin gas project emissions could dwarf Adani, experts warn'. *RN Breakfast with Cathy Van Extel*, [ABC Radio], 14 May. www.abc.net.au/radionational/programs/breakfast/beetaloo-basin-gas-project-emissions-would-dwarf-adani/11110200.

Coughlan, Matt. 2019. 'Shorten's mood for change on election day'. *The Canberra Times*, 18 May.

Dean, Jonathan. 2018. 'Sorted for Memes and Gifs: Visual Media and Everyday Politics'. *Political Studies Review* 17(3): 255–66. doi.org/10.1177/1478929918807483.

Flew, Terry. 2008. 'Not Yet the Internet Election: Online Media, Political Commentary and the 2007 Australian Federal Election'. *Media International Australia* 126(1): 5–13. doi.org/10.1177/1329878X0812600103.

Graeff, Erhardt. 2015. 'Binders full of election memes: Participatory culture invades the 2012 U.S. election'. *Civic Media Project*, 10 March. Cambridge, MA: MIT Media Lab. www.media.mit.edu/publications/binders-full-of-election-memes-participatory-culture-invades-the-2012-u-s-election/.

Koslowski, Max. 2019. 'The expert who predicted Trump, Brexit—and Scott Morrison'. *Sydney Morning Herald*, 19 May.

Purcell, Charles. 2015. 'How the power of the meme brought down Bronwyn Bishop'. *The Walkley Foundation*, 4 August. www.walkleys.com/how-the-power-of-the-meme-brought-down-bronwyn-bishop/ [page discontinued].

Renner, Nausicaa. 2017. 'Memes trump articles on Breitbart's Facebook page'. *Columbia Journalism Review*, 30 January. www.cjr.org/tow_center/memes-trump-articles-on-breitbarts-facebook-page.php.

Rentschler, Carrie and Samantha Thrift. 2015. 'Doing Feminism in the Network: Networked Laughter and the "Binders Full of Women" Meme'. *Feminist Theory* 16(3): 329–59. doi.org/10.1177/1464700115604136.

Ross, Sheryl Tuttle. 2002. 'Understanding Propaganda: The Epistemic Merit Model and Its Application to Art'. *The Journal of Aesthetic Education* 36(1): 16–30. doi.org/10.2307/3333623.

Seven Network. 2019. *Sunrise*, [7Plus Television], 5 May.

Tay, Geniesa. 2014. 'Binders full of LOLitics: Political Humour, Internet Memes, and Play in the 2012 US Presidential Election (and Beyond)'. *European Journal of Humour Research* 2(4): 46–73. doi.org/10.7592/EJHR2014.2.4.tay.

Turton, Shaun. 2015. 'How social media destroyed an Australian politician'. *Revolution Digital*, [Blog], 4 August. www.revolutionweb.com.au/social-media/how-social-media-destroyed-an-australian-politician/.

Williams, Paul. 2008. 'The 2007 Australian Federal Election: The Story of Labor's Return from the Electoral Wilderness'. *Australian Journal of Politics and History* 54(1): 104–25. doi.org/10.1111/j.1467-8497.2008.00487.x.